The Black Family
in Slavery and Freedom
1750-1925

Five generations of one family on Smith's plantation, Beaufort, South Carolina

THE BLACK FAMILY IN SLAVERY AND FREEDOM, 1750-1925

HERBERT G. GUTMAN

VINTAGE BOOKS
A Division of Random House
New York

First Vintage Books Edition, September 1977
Copyright © 1976 by Herbert G. Gutman

All rights reserved under International and Pan-American Copyright
Conventions. Published in the United States by Random House, Inc.,
New York, and simultaneously in Canada by Random House of Canada
Limited, Toronto. Originally published by Pantheon Books, a Division
of Random House, Inc., in September 1976.

Library of Congress Cataloging in Publication Data

Gutman, Herbert George, 1928-
The Black family in slavery and freedom, 1750-1925.

Includes bibliographical references and indexes.
1. Afro-American families—History.
2. Afro-Americans—History.
3. Afro-Americans—Social conditions.
I. Title.
[E185.86.G77 1977]   301.42'0973   77-4364
ISBN 0-394-72451-8

Since this page cannot legibly accommodate all acknowledgments,
they can be found on the following two pages.

Photograph on cover shows five generations of one family
on Smith's plantation, Beaufort, South Carolina.
Used by courtesy of the Library of Congress.

Manufactured in the United States of America

Grateful acknowledgment is made to the following for permission to reprint previously published and facsimile material:

The Association for the Study of Afro-American Life and History: Excerpt from "The Freedmen's Bureau and Civil Rights in Maryland" from the *Journal of Negro History*, vol. 37, no. 3 (1957), pp. 221–247: by W. A. Low. Also, excerpts from letters on pp. 523–528 of *The Mind of the Negro as Reflected in Letters During the Crisis*, by C. G. Woodson.

Broadside Press: "Ancestors," by Dudley Randall, from *More to Remember*. Copyright © 1971 by Dudley Randall. "The Idea of Ancestry," by Etheridge Knight, from *Poems from Prison*. Copyright © 1968 by Etheridge Knight.

The Dietz Press, Inc.: Excerpts from letters from *Virginia Silhouettes: Contemporary Letters Concerning Negro Slavery in the State of Virginia*, by Mrs. George P. Coleman.

Duke University Library: Undated fragment of a household list of slaves belonging to Henry Watson, Henry Watson Papers.

Greenwood Press, a division of Williamhouse-Regency, Inc.: Excerpts from vol. 2; vol. 4, pp. 62–65, 290–295; vol. 5, pp. 174–178, 92–94; vol. 6, pp. 72–73; vol. 7, pp. 49–55; vol. 9, pp. 267–270, of *The American Slave: A Composite Autobiography*, edited by George P. Rawick.

Harper & Row Publishers, Inc.: Excerpt from *Bases of the Plantation Society*, by Aubrey C. Land; "What shall I give my children?" from *The World of Gwendolyn Brooks*. Copyright 1949 by Gwendolyn Brooks Blakely.

Holt, Rinehart & Winston, Inc.: Nine lines from "Speech to those who say Comrade" from *Public Speech*, by Archibald MacLeish. Copyright 1936, © 1964 by Archibald MacLeish.

Journal of Social History: Excerpt from a letter, pp. 46–71 of "Privileged Slaves and the Process of Accommodation," by Robert S. Starobin, from *Journal of Social History*, no. 5 (fall 1971). Copyright © 1971 by Peter N. Stearns.

Kent State University Press: Excerpt from "Resistance to Slavery," by George Frederickson and Christopher Lasch, from *Civil War History*, vol. 13, no. 4. Copyright © 1967 by Kent State University Press.

Alfred A. Knopf, Inc.: Excerpts from pp. 59 and 206–213 of *All God's Dangers: The Life of Nate Shaw*, by Theodore Rosengarten. Copyright © 1974 by Theodore Rosengarten; also, four lines of verse from "Bandanna Ballads," by Howard Weeden, and two lines of verse from "Christmas Night in the Quarters," by Irwin Russell, on pages 180–185 of *The New South Creed: A Study in Southern Mythmaking*, by Paul M. Gaston. Copyright © 1970 by Paul M. Gaston.

Little, Brown and Company: Letter from *Life and Labor in the Old South*, by Ulrich B. Phillips.

Louisiana State University, Baton Rouge: Fragment of slave birth register for Stirling Plantation, West Feliciana Parish. Louisiana Department of Archives and Manuscripts.

Macmillan Publishing Co., Inc.: Excerpts from pp. 97 and 99–100 of *The Life and Times of Frederick Douglass*. Introduction Copyright © 1962 by Macmillan Publishing Co., Inc.

MIT Press: Excerpt from essay by Laura Carper in *The Moynihan Report and the Politics of Controversy*, edited by Lee Rainwater and William L. Yancey.

The South Carolina Historical Society: One page of the Good Hope Register, Orangeburg, South Carolina.

UNESCO: Excerpt from the article "Toward an Afro-American History," from *Journal of World History*, vol. 13, no. 2 (1971)

University of Virginia Library: Fragment from John C. Cohoon account book, Cedar Vale Plantation, Nansemond County, Virginia.

Vanderbilt University Press: Excerpt from a letter in *Dear Ones At Home: Letters from Contraband Camps*, edited by Henry Lee Swint, 1966.

Franklin Watt, Inc.: Excerpts from letters on pp. 87–92, 105, 57, 42–57, and 131 of *Blacks in Bondage: Letters of American Slaves*, by Robert S. Starobin.

William and Mary Quarterly: Excerpt from "The Maryland Slave Population, 1658 to 1730," by R. R. Menard, from *William and Mary Quarterly*, 3rd ser., vol. 32 (1975).

Yale University Press: Excerpt from a letter on p. 343 of *A Union Officer in the Reconstruction*, by J. H. Croushore and D. M. Potter. Copyright 1948 by Yale University Press. Excerpts from letters which appear in *The Children of Pride*, by Robert Manson Myers. Yale University Press, 1972.

To
Judith Mara Gutman
for many reasons
and with love

The contempt we have been taught to entertain for the blacks makes us fancy many things that are founded neither in reason nor in experience.

ALEXANDER HAMILTON

. . . The poor man . . . feels himself out of the sight of others, groping in the dark. Mankind takes no notice of him. He rambles and wanders unheeded. In the midst of a crowd, at church, in the market . . . he is in as much obscurity as he would be in a garret or a cellar. He is not disapproved, censured, or reproached; he is only not seen.

JOHN ADAMS

It is a peculiar sensation . . . this sense of always looking at one's self through the eyes of others, of measuring one's soul by the tape of a world that looks on in amused contempt and pity.

W. E. B. DU BOIS (1903)

The brotherhood is not by the blood certainly,
But neither are men brothers by speech—by saying so:
Men are brothers by life lived and are hurt for it. . . .

Brotherhood! No word said can make you brothers!
Brotherhood only the brave earn and by danger or
Harm or by bearing hurt and by no other.

Brotherhood here in the strange world is the rich and
Rarest giving of life and the most valued,
Not to be had for a word or a week's wishing.

ARCHIBALD MACLEISH (1936)

. . . I am invisible, understand, simply because people refuse to see me. Like the bodiless heads you see sometimes in circus sideshows, it is as though I have been surrounded by mirrors of hard, distorted glass. When they approach me they see only my surroundings, themselves, or figments of their imagination—indeed, everything and anything but me. . . .

RALPH ELLISON (1952)

Contents

Charts

ILLUSTRATIONS

Tables

Appendix A

Appendix B

Introduction
and Acknowledgments

This volume—a study of the Afro-American family between 1750 and 1925 as well as of the origins and early development of Afro-American culture—was stimulated by the bitter public and academic controversy surrounding Daniel P. Moynihan's *The Negro Family in America: The Case for National Action* (1965). The post–World War II migration of poor southern blacks to northern cities together with a regularly high level of urban black male unemployment severely strained the adaptive capacities of these men and women. Drawing upon the influential historical studies of such writers as E. Franklin Frazier and Stanley M. Elkins, Moynihan identified these troubles with "the deterioration of the Negro family" and rooted those difficulties in a historical process that had its origins in the enslavement of seventeenth- and eighteenth-century Africans: "It was by destroying the Negro family that white America broke the will of the Negro people." Three centuries of "injustice" had caused "deep-seated structural distortions in the life of the Negro American"; a "tangle of pathology" resulted; the disorganized "black family" was at its "center." Moynihan, it should be emphasized, had not created a fictive history; he reported what was then conventional academic wisdom. His most severe critics shared that historical perspective with him. "The most rudimentary type of family organization," Abram Kardiner and Lionel Ovesey had written years earlier of the slave family, in *The Mark of Oppression: Explorations in the Personality of the American Negro*, "was not permitted to survive, to say nothing of the extensions of the family. The mother-child family, with the father either unknown, absent, or, if present, incapable of wielding influence, was the only type of family that could survive."

The controversy between Moynihan and his critics sparked a preliminary study in 1967–1968, which led to this book. In its origins that early study, a joint effort with Laurence A. Glasco, now teaching at the University of Pittsburgh, tested the historical arguments on which the "Moynihan Report" rested, and whatever value it retains belongs as much to Glasco as to me. Our objective was simple: if enslavement caused the widespread development among Afro-Americans of "a fatherless matrifocal [mother-centered] family" sufficiently strong to be transmitted from generation to generation, thereby affecting the beliefs and behavior of descendants of eighteenth-century African slaves who lived in mid-twentieth-century northern urban ghettos, such a condition should have been even more common among urban Afro-Americans closer in time to slavery. The "tangle of pathology" should have been as severe (if not more severe) in 1850 and 1860 as it was in 1950 and 1960.

Glasco and I studied the Buffalo, New York, black community by examining New York State manuscript census schedules for 1855 and 1875 (which, unlike the 1850, 1860, and 1870 federal manuscript censuses, indicated household relationships) and then for 1905 and 1925. Our major findings are briefly summarized below:

- At all times in this eighty-year period, the Buffalo black community was composed mostly of lower-class blacks: most were day laborers or service workers; very few had skills; hardly any had middle-class status. Until the 1920s, few labored in the city's factories.
- The double-headed kin-related household always was the characteristic Buffalo Afro-American household, ranging from 82 to 92 percent of all households. The double-headed household did not decline in importance over time.

These Buffalo lower-class blacks bore no visible relationship to an alleged "tangle of pathology." The sociologist E. Franklin Frazier argued in his classic *The Negro Family in the United States* (1939) that poor urban blacks lived in communities "from which practically all institutional life had disappeared" and in which families were "losing their internal cohesion." That had not happened to the Buffalo blacks.

Preliminary coauthored papers detailing these and other findings, delivered at the 1968 Wisconsin Conference on the History of American Political and Social Behavior and the 1968 Yale Conference on Nineteenth-Century Cities, were well received, but critics worried about the "typicality" of the Buffalo Afro-Americans. (They are typical, but these were nonetheless legitimate criticisms.) Rather than publish these papers, I decided first to examine southern rural and urban black households in 1880 and data on ex-slave marriages and households in 1865 and 1866 recorded by the Freedmen's Bureau. These findings confirmed the Buffalo study, and a paper incorporating these findings and generally critical of E. Franklin Frazier's *The Negro Family in the United States* was read at the 1969 Association for the Study of Negro Life and History meetings and the 1970 Organization of American Historians meetings, published in *Annales* in 1972 and republished in the *Journal of Interdisciplinary History* in 1975.

After that, the study was enlarged in two ways: First, New York City black households in 1905 and 1925 were examined. In 1925, that meant studying the occupational and household status of the members of 13,924 black households and subfamilies, nearly all in central Harlem. The 1925 findings are detailed in Chapter 10 but summarized below:

- 85 percent of New York City kin-related black households were double-headed.
- Thirty-two of these 13,924 were father-absent households and subfamilies headed by women under thirty and containing three or more children.
- Between 7 and 8 percent of females aged twenty-five to forty-four headed male-absent households and subfamilies. Twenty years earlier, the percentage had been higher (10 percent).
- Three in four males aged forty-five and older were unskilled laborers and service workers, and in that year three in four of the households headed by males forty-five and older were headed by unskilled laborers and service workers.
- Five in six children under the age of six lived with both parents.

These were the same New York City blacks about whom Nathan Glazer and Daniel P. Moynihan had written in *Beyond the Melting Pot: The Negroes, Puerto Ricans, Jews, Italians, and Irish of New York City* (1963): "Migration, uprooting, urbanization always create problems. Even the best organized and best integrated groups suffer under such circumstances. But when the fundamental core of organization, the family, is already weak, the magnitude of these problems may be staggering. The experience of slavery left as its most serious heritage a steady weakness in the Negro family."

Second, at the same time as the study moved forward in time to examine the New York City black population in the first third of this century, it moved backward in time to the years between 1861 and the start of Radical Reconstruction. I was very much concerned that nearly all the findings were based upon quantitative data. I did not then (and do not now) consider myself a "quantitative historian." Such study valuably indicates *regularities* in behavior but explains far less than it describes. I therefore turned to the voluminous Freedmen's Bureau records and to the vast literary record left by other northern and southern whites dealing with southern blacks during and after the Civil War to find evidence that might help explain what the quantitative data described. As measured by the types of households inhabited by most poor southern rural and urban blacks and by poor migrant northern blacks between 1855 and 1925, enslavement had not created among them "a tangle of pathology." The 1861–1868 sources detailed the powerful expression of affective Afro-American familial and kin beliefs and behavior in the wartime and immediate postwar years. Chapters based upon that evidence were read in 1971 and penetratingly criticized by the historians John Hope Franklin and C. Vann Woodward and the anthropologist Sidney W. Mintz. In different ways, each asked the same questions: "Why?" "What are the sources of this behavior and these beliefs?" Evidence of southern black behavior after the general emancipation does not begin to explain what sustained common slave beliefs and behavior.

This study seeks to answer these questions. A small portion of what these colleagues then read is included in this volume. The rest will appear in a subsequent volume devoted to the Afro-American slave and ex-slave between 1861 and 1868. I remain indebted to Franklin, Mintz, and Woodward for "forcing" these questions upon me. Mintz deserves special thanks. Answering them became much less difficult and far more engaging because this learned and humane cultural anthropologist began patiently to re-educate a social historian. My debt to him is clear in the pages that follow. Chapters 1 through 8 were written between 1972 and 1975, and in that time Stanley Engerman also provided valued assistance. Materials uncovered in his own research were generously shared with me and so were his critical abilities.

This study is an examination of the Afro-American family prior to and after the general emancipation, but it is also a study of the cultural beliefs and behavior of a distinctive lower-class population. It examines its adaptive capacities at critical moments in its history. Slavery is viewed as an oppressive circumstance that tested the adaptive capacities of several generations of men and women. To focus on the "family" also means to focus on "culture." Socialization nearly always occurs first in families, and it is through families that historically derived beliefs usually pass from generation to generation. The assumption that slaves could not develop and sustain meaningful domestic and kin arrangements denies them that capacity and often serves to "explain" why so many slaves and their immediate descendants were "disorganized" in their social life and "pathological" in their individual behavior. E. Franklin Frazier summed up this view of lower-class black culture in discussing early twentieth century urban migration:

> The widespread disorganization of family life among Negroes has affected practically every phase of their community life and adjustments to the larger white world. Because of the absence of stability in family life, there is a lack of traditions. Life among a large portion of the urban Negro population is casual, precarious, and fragmentary. It lacks continuity and its roots do not go deeper than the contingencies of daily living. This affects the socialization of the Negro child.

Alexis de Tocqueville put it similarly a century earlier:

> There exists, indeed, a profound and natural antipathy between the institution of marriage and that of slavery. A man does not marry when he cannot exercise marital authority, when his children must be born his equal, irrevocably destined to the wretchedness of their father; when, having no power over their fate, he can neither know the duties, the privileges, the hopes, nor the cares which belong to the paternal relation. It is easy to perceive that every motive which incites the freedman to a lawful union is lost to the slave by the simple fact of his slavery.

Frazier and de Tocqueville did not misperceive the oppressive nature of enslavement but underestimated the adaptive capacities of the enslaved and those born to them and to their children. A Freedmen's Bureau officer who traveled over the South in the summer and fall of 1866 did not make that mistake. "He loves to congregate in families, in groups, in villages," concluded John Alvord of the ex-slave. "This was his habit originally in Africa, and the plantation always had some *social* features which, in a measure, alleviated the negro's bondage. To this they are habituated, and for it they show a fondness." Alvord was an unusual observer. Much of what he noticed escaped the attention of nearly all his contemporaries, northern and southern alike.

A study of a particular process of social and cultural adaptation, this book is divided into two parts. *Part One* (Chapters 1 to 8) examines different aspects of the development of the slave family and enlarged slave kin group.

• *Chapter 1* deals with the slaves and ex-slaves during and just after the Civil War. They were the last generation of slaves. Despite a high rate of earlier involuntary marital breakup, large numbers of slave couples lived in long marriages, and most slaves lived in double-headed households. Chapters 2 to 8 study some of the adaptive social and cultural arrangements within the slave experience that begin to explain what is described in the first chapter.

• *Chapter 2* explores the development of the slave family and slave kin networks on a South Carolina plantation owned by the ancestors of John Foster and Allen Dulles. A slave birth register kept for nearly a century shows that long slave marriages were compatible with distinctive slave sexual practices (particularly childbirth prior to a mother's marriage), that distinctive slave marriage rules (particularly taboos against blood-cousin marriage) existed which allow us to uncover the importance of the slave kinship group, and that slave children often were named for blood kin (particularly fathers, aunts and uncles, and grandparents). The same document also establishes the importance of viewing the slave experience in an enlarged time perspective. It shows how common familial belief and behavior after 1830 had their roots in adaptive slave practices that had begun much earlier.

• *Chapters 3 and 4* reconstruct slave familial domestic arrangements and kin networks in very different settings from the one that existed among the slaves studied in Chapter 2. Virginia, North Carolina, Alabama, and southern and northern Louisiana slaves are studied. External "variables"—such as the age of a plantation and the presence or absence of its owner, a plantation's location, what its slaves grew, and the involuntary breakup of slave families —are examined to see how they affected slave familial and kin life. Patterns similar to those that existed on the South Carolina plantation are found everywhere. Long-lasting slave marriages and families derived their inner strength from a cumulative slave experience with its own standards and rules of conduct. Common slave marital rules and intensive naming for slave blood kin are found on all the plantations, including those which started during the War for Independence. The severe disruptions associated with the transformation of farms into plantations, and especially with the sale and forced migration of slaves from the Upper to the Lower South, spread a common slave culture over the entire South.

• *Chapter 5* explores some of the larger cultural and social meanings suggested by slave naming-practices. The practices are seen as clues to the significance slaves attached to the enlarged kin group. It is also suggested how and why slave kin obligation was transformed into an enlarged slave conception of social obligation which, in turn, served as the underlying social basis of developing slave communities.

• *Chapter 6* considers the slave surname, showing that the retention of owners' surnames over time was a cultural device by which slaves identified with a family of origin as early as the War for Independence. Such behavior reinforced given-name practices, emphasized again the importance of the enlarged kin group, and symbolized separation from an owner over time.

• *Chapter 7* relates these findings to some other (not all) aspects of slave life and behavior (as diverse as flight and marriage ritual), to the inaccurate perceptions of the slave "family" by contemporary northern and southern whites, and finally, to the explicit "models" meant to explain slave behavior in historical studies by E. Franklin Frazier, Kenneth M. Stampp, Stanley M. Elkins, and Eugene D. Genovese.

• *Chapter 8* focuses on certain important but neglected eighteenth-century social and cultural processes affecting Africans and Afro-Americans and essential to an understanding of later developments in the slave family and enlarged kin group.

Part Two (Chapters 9 and 10) shifts from the slaves to the ex-slaves and their descendants in the late nineteenth and early twentieth centuries.

• *Chapter 9* returns to the slaves and ex-slaves studied briefly in Chapter 1 and examines their beliefs between 1861 and 1867 by studying the slave soldier as husband and father, the slave parent as revealed in attitudes toward abusive child apprenticeship, slave sexual beliefs and practices, and slave attitudes toward legal marriage. In this chapter, however, the "slaves" are nearly all ex-slaves. A comparison between ex-slave and southern white marriage "rates" is also made. No differences are found between the two groups.

• *Chapter 10* together with *Appendix A* (which includes data drawn from federal and state manuscript censuses) examines the black household in the rural and urban South in 1880 and 1900 and in New York City in 1905 and 1925. Changes in the composition of the black household over time are described, but they do not indicate that a "breakdown" followed either the initial adaptation to legal freedom or early-twentieth-century northward migration.

• A brief *Afterword* moves us quickly and very tentatively into the present, suggesting some of the larger historical processes (a modern Enclosure Movement and a modern Poor Law) affecting the material and familial condition of poor rural southern blacks migrating to northern urban centers after 1930.

The most important single piece of historical evidence in this book is neither an isolated statistic, a historical "anecdote," a numerical table, nor a chart. It is the photograph that adorns the jacket of this book and serves as its frontispiece. That picture was taken during the Civil War, and I am indebted to Judith Mara Gutman for finding it at the Library of Congress and to Willie Lee Rose for helping to identify it. We know only that these few enslaved Afro-Americans belonged to the planter William Joyner Smith and that the photograph itself was entitled, *"Five generations on Smith's plantation, Beaufort, South Carolina."* Those who study the tables and charts in this book should keep that magnificent photograph before them. The charts and tables tell mostly about men, women, and children like those portrayed in this unusual document. I hope that readers will know the "five generations" better after finishing this book.

This work is much better—not as good as it should be but very much better than it would have been—because of the generous cooperation and assistance of many students and former students, colleagues, friends, and others.

Copying names and numbers from the pages of the various state and federal manuscript censuses summarized in Chapter 10 and the tables that accompany them is a time-consuming and thankless work. I know that from personal experience. I did some of the transcribing and all of the computations (without the assist-. ance of a computer but with the help of Marta Gutman and Nell Gutman). Most of the data-gathering was done by a group of unusually cooperative and intelligent undergraduate and graduate students. Lillian Williams gathered the initial Buffalo data. Those for the southern urban and rural blacks in 1880 were collected by Elizabeth Ewen and Ursula Lingies. Carol Wasserloos collected the 1880 Paterson, New Jersey, data, and Mark Sosower did the same for the 1880 Jones County, Mississippi, whites. Mark Sosower also transcribed demographic and social data about the 1905 New York City blacks, and Sosower together with Leslie Neustadt and Richard Mendales collected information on the 1905 New York City Jews and Italians and 1925 New York City blacks. Karen Kearns worked through the 1900 federal manuscript censuses. I am greatly in debt to these people, and to the State University of New York at Buffalo, the University of Rochester, the City College Alumni Fund, and the University of Chicago Department of History for supplying the funds that made this work possible. The funds supplied by the University of Chicago deserve brief explanation. Colleagues there were supervising research on Afro-American migration to northern cities and shared some research monies with me to permit me to study the 1905 and 1925 New York State manuscript censuses. I am much indebted to John Hope Franklin, Richard C. Wade, and William Cohen for that unusual generosity.

A semester off with full pay granted by the University of Rochester together with a Social Science Research Council Faculty Research Fellowship permitted me to spend an uninterrupted year (1970–1971) working on this study. In the final stages of the research, three graduate students helped with the research: Jonathan Scott Ware, Karen Kearns, and Leslie Rowland.

Cooperation from other people working in Afro-American history made accessible otherwise obscure data they had gathered. Stanley Engerman first called my attention to the invaluable Good Hope birth register discussed in Chapter 2 and supplied me with it and similar registers gathered in his own work. That data allowed me to begin re-examining slave family and kinship arrangements. Several graduate students and former graduate students working in Afro-American history shared some of their findings: Edward Magdol (studying the freedmen and the land question), John O'Brien (studying Richmond, Virginia, blacks between 1865 and 1870), Leslie Rowland (studying Kentucky blacks during and just after the Civil War), and John Strawn (studying Mississippi blacks during and just after the Civil War). Students and former students also shared information drawn from other research: Michael Gordon, Robert Greenberg, Gregory Kealey, Janet Harding McGowan, Douglas V. Shaw, Daniel Walkowitz, and Allis R. Wolfe. Still other people made material available from their own work: Armstead Robinson, Ira Berlin, William Cohen, Frank Freidel, Donald Nieman, Mary Beth Norton, Robert Twombly, Joel Williamson, and Peter H. Wood. Barry Crouch and Allan Kulikoff deserve special thanks. Crouch, who has unrivaled knowledge of the Texas blacks during Reconstruction, shared some of it with me. Kulikoff let me study his manuscript on eighteenth-century Prince George's County, Maryland, and use some of the data there in Chapter 8.

Since this work began, several other studies dealing with the black family during and after slavery have appeared. While not always agreeing with them, I have profited from the works of Robert Abzug, Andrew Billingsley, John Blassingame, Robert W. Fogel and Stanley Engerman, Eugene D. Genovese, Theodore Hershberg and his associates, Peter Kolchin, Paul Lammermeier, Elizabeth H. Pleck, George Rawick, and Crandell Shifflett. All those working in this field also are indebted to the very original unpublished dissertation on the slave family by Bobby Jones ("A Cultural Middle Passage: Slave Marriage and Family in the Antebellum South," University of North Carolina (1965).

The splendid staffs of several major libraries facilitated my research at all times. The staff at the National Archives made its vast resources available, and this would have been a very different study without the cooperation of Lewis Blair, Robert Clarke, and Elaine Everley. A week of intensive research at the North Carolina State Archives in Raleigh benefited greatly from the cooperation of C. R. C. Coker and his fine staff. The Interlibrary Loan staff at the University of Rochester grew tired of me but never complained. And the staff at the Southern Historical Collection, so well housed at the University of North Carolina, made my research there unusually productive. I also had splendid cooperation from the staffs of the City College, Columbia, Cornell, Harvard, and New York Public libraries. In addition, particular libraries in the South filled numerous specific requests, and the individuals who proved so helpful are thanked in the appropriate places in the text.

An early version of this text was typed by Claire Sundeen, and the final version by Edna Friedman, who worked without complaint and with great skill under an unusually tight schedule.

I have learned a great deal from an unpublished paper, "An Anthropological Approach to the Study of Afro-American History"

(1974), by Sidney W. Mintz and Richard Price. They generously permitted me to quote from it in this study. When published, that essay will quickly become a classic statement describing the relations between social history and historical anthropology.

Portions of this manuscript have been critically read by a number of people. I have already indicated how the shape of this work changed after such readings by John Hope Franklin, Sidney W. Mintz, and C. Vann Woodward. The late David Potter and the late Robert Starobin were very helpful when this work first started. My former colleagues at the University of Rochester, Christopher Lasch and Perez Zagorin, encouraged this work by their probing skepticism in frequent conversations. Early versions of some chapters were scrutinized helpfully by John Bracey, David Brion Davis, George Fredrickson, Eugene D. Genovese, Virginia Yans McLaughlin, Daniel Patrick Moynihan, Irving Sanes, Ann Firor Scott, Joan Wallach Scott, Stephan Thernstrom, and E. P. Thompson. The preliminary chapters on the slave family benefited from sharp comments by Leon Fink, Eric Foner, Stanley Elkins, August Meier, William Eric Perkins, and especially John Strawn. Ira Berlin and Stanley Engerman read the full draft of a nearly final version, and a major shift in emphasis followed their detailed criticisms. Berlin also made me aware of an unconscious and very misleading emphasis in the interior analysis of quantitative sources that weakened the over-all analysis and promised to misdirect the attention of other readers. A final draft was generously read and splendidly criticized by Stanley M. Elkins, Leon Fink, Eric Foner, Judith Mara Gutman, Aileen Kraditor, William Eric Perkins, and Harold Woodman. They brought very different sensibilities and perspectives to that draft. All improved it by their scrupulous and honest criticisms. Not all of their criticisms and suggestions could be handled, but this book is far, far better because they read that draft. I hope they too see how their comments improved it. Yet other debts, some indirectly related to this work but all affecting it, deserve mention here: debts to editors like André Schiffrin, copy editors like Jeanne Morton, old teachers like Merle Curti and John Hope Franklin, and old and new friends like Charles B. Forcey and Dorothy and E. P. Thompson. If readers find reason to dispute particular historical formulations and the uses of particular historical evidence, their quarrel is entirely with the book's author. Many readers will doubtless give a different meaning to much of the evidence. That is welcomed, indeed encouraged.

This book belongs to Judith Mara Gutman and Nell Lisa and

Marta Ruth Gutman. Two teen-agers grew into young women while this study grew more and more unmanageable, and in that time Judith Mara Gutman published several books. One of them, *Is America Used Up?*, probed the disappearance of an older America and the creative values associated with that earlier time. It worried with good reason about why so many of our contemporaries accept "the disjointed rubble about them as the most normal thing in the world." I fear that this work served too long as ever-present evidence of such disjointed rubble. If it no longer does, she knows why.

H.G.G.

Nyack, New York
September 30, 1975

PART
ONE

The Birthpangs of a World

—W. E. B. Du Bois

Yes, suh, I'm born in slavery and not 'shamed of it, 'cause I can't help how I'm born.

CHARLEY HUNT (1937)

Prefabricated Negroes are sketched on sheets of paper and superimposed upon the Negro community; then when someone thrusts his head through the pages and yells, "Watch out there, Jack, there's people living under here," they are all shocked and indignant.

RALPH ELLISON (1964)

1

Send Me Some of the Children's Hair

It is difficult to get a clear picture of the family relations of slaves, between the Southern apologist and his picture of cabin life, with idyllic devotion and careless toil, and that of the abolitionist with his tale of family disruption and cruelty, adultery, and illegitimate mulattoes.

W. E. B. DU BOIS (1909)

Can a people . . . live and develop over three hundred years simply by reacting? Are American Negroes simply the creation of white men, or have they at least helped to create themselves out of what they found around them?

RALPH ELLISON (1964)

This is a book about ordinary black men, women, and children mostly before the general emancipation but after that time, too—a study of enslaved Afro-Americans, their children, and their grandchildren, how they adapted to enslavement by developing distinctive domestic arrangements and kin networks that nurtured a new Afro-American culture, and how these, in turn, formed the social basis of developing Afro-American communities, which prepared slaves to deal with legal freedom. This book is also about poor Americans, nonwhites who spent a good portion of their American experience enslaved. It is therefore concerned with a special aspect of American labor history: those men and women who labored first in bondage and then mostly as half-free rural workers. Methods are used and questions are asked that take account of the many unique circumstances associated with enslavement but nevertheless remain appropriate to a study of the development and behavior of all exploited and dependent social classes, slave and free, white and nonwhite. The same approach, for example, will be used to study Afro-Americans before and after slavery, a point emphasized not to argue that slaves and free workers had a similar history but rather to suggest that the same questions can and must be asked of such classes to understand important similarities and differences between them.

.   .   .

This is not a study of well-known Americans but seeks to understand men like Laura Spicer's ex-slave husband and the South Carolina ex-slave Sam Rosemon and women like the early-nineteenth-century slave mother Hannah Grover and the mid-nineteenth-century slave wife and mother Sarah Boon. Only bits and pieces of their individual histories survive, fragmentary clues about who these four people were and what they believed. Our concern is with what sustained and nurtured their beliefs and behavior. Nothing more.

These four persons were not related to one another, and their separate slave lives spanned the full century between the War for Independence and the general emancipation. Each revealed a strong attachment to a family. Hannah Grover, known earlier as Hannah Van Buskerk, wrote her son Cato on June 3, 1805. "I long to see you in my old age," the slave woman began:

> Now my dear son I pray you to come and see your dear old Mother—Or send me twenty dollar and I will come and see you in Philadelphia—And if you cant come to see your old Mother pray send me a letter and tell me where you live what family you have and what you do for a living—I am a poor old servant I long for freedom. . . . I love you Cato   you love your Mother—You are my only son.

A postscript added: "If you have any love for your poor old Mother pray come or send to me My dear son I love you with all my heart." She had not seen Cato since 1785.

Sarah Boon's husband was a free black carpenter, and she lived on her owner's farm near Raleigh, North Carolina. She and her husband had their troubles. Although it pained her to learn of his "bad health" in 1850, she would not accept his denial that he had lived with another woman: "When the subject was broach before you and that worman eather of you mad no reply."

> [L]et it be eather way. My Dear Husband I frealy forgive. I have no doubt that you will find it in the end that I was rite. I wish it to be banished from our memoreys and it neve be thought of again and let us take a new start and join on together as we have binn doing for many years. Miss Marian has given t[o] me great concorlation but before that I was hardly able to creep [sleep?] I hope you will concider my fealings and give me sentiments of your mind in ancer to this letter

She urged him to work nearer to her home; "witch would be a great prise to me than all the money you could make." A "little son" had apparently been sold, and she awaited word about him, promising to tell him when she heard. Her letter ended:

> I wish you to rite me word when you are rite you coming out. I do not thing it is rite to for me for sutch a long absence from me if I cant come to join you. [You] can come to me. we are all well as to health. I feel very loanesome be sertin to answer this letter as soon as you get it. I have nothing more at present, onley I remain your Affectnate Wife untill Death[1]*

Sam Rosemon and Laura Spicer's slave husband also were deeply attached to their families. Like Hannah Grover and Sarah Boon, they had been separated from them. But their letters were written just after the emancipation. Rosemon sought his South Carolina parents, and Spicer, who had remarried, grieved over an earlier forced separation from his slave wife and children. Rosemon had made it to Pittsburgh from South Carolina and sent a letter asking the Greenville, South Carolina, Freedmen's Bureau about his parents Caroline and Robert Rosemon:

> To the freedmen Bureau in Greenville, S.C.
>
> Dear freinds the deep crants of rivous ceprate ous but i hope in God for hours prasous agine and injoying the same injoyment That we did before the war begun and i am tolbile know but much trubbel in mind and i hope my truble Will not Be all Ways this Ways. . . .
>   [I] inquire for Caline then inquire for marther live at Fane Ranson and Harriett that live at doct Gant and if you heir from tham let me know if you Plese soon Writ to Pittsburg Pa to Carpenters No 28
>   Robard Rosemon that lived in Andison Destrect my farther and Carline my mother i remien your refractorate son
>   SAM ROSEMON[2]†

* Notes begin on page 545.
† Sam Rosemon's letter can be "translated" as follows:
To The Greenville, South Carolina, Freedmen's Bureau:
Dear Friends. Although deep rivers separate us, I hope to God that we can enjoy ourselves as we did before the Civil War. I am well but very much troubled. I seek information about my mother Caroline and about Harriet, who lived at Dr. Gants, and about my father Robert Rosemon, who lived in the Anderson district. If you hear from them, please write to me at 28 Carpenter Street, Pittsburgh, Pa. Your stubborn and unmanageable son SAM ROSEMON.

Sometime before the Civil War, Laura Spicer and her children were sold from their husband and father. They considered coming together again after the emancipation, but Spicer had remarried. Letters passed between them. "I read your letters over and over again," Spicer once wrote. "I keep them always in my pocket. If you are married, I don't ever want to see you again." Another letter revealed his turmoil, and he pressed Laura to find a husband:

I would much rather you would get married to some good man, for every time I gits a letter from you it tears me all to pieces. The reason why I have not written you before, in a long time, is because your letters disturbed me so very much. You know I love my children. I treats them good as a Father can treat his children; and I do a good deal of it for you. I am sorry to hear that Lewellyn, my poor little son, have had such bad health. I would come and see you but I know you could not bear it. I want to see and I don't want to see you. I love you just as well as I did the last day I saw you, and it will not do for you and I to meet. I am married, and my wife have two children, and if you and I meets it would make a very dissatisfied family.

Send me some of the children's hair in a separate paper with their names on the paper. Will you please git married, as long as I am married. My dear, you know the Lord knows both of our hearts. You know it never was our wishes to be separated from each other, and it never was our fault. Oh, I can see you so plain, at any-time, I had rather anything to had happened to me most than ever to have been parted from you and the children. As I am, I do not know which I love best, you or Anna. If I was to die, today or tomorrow, I do not think I would die satisfied till you tell me you will try and marry some good, smart man that will take care of you and the children; and do it because you love me; and not because I think more of the wife I have got than I do of you.

The woman is not born that feels as near to me as you do. You feel this day like myself. Tell them they must remember they have a good father and one that cares for them and one that thinks about them every day—My very heart did ache when reading your very kind and interesting letter. Laura I do not think I have change any at all since I saw you last.—I think of you and my children every day of my life.

Laura I do love you the same. My love to you *never* have failed. Laura, truly, I have got another wife, and I am very sorry, that I am. You feels and seems to me as much like my dear loving wife, as you ever did Laura. You know my treatment to a wife and you know how I am about my children. You know I am one man that do love my children. . . .[3]

These few letters are quite unusual historical documents. Some may have been written by an amanuensis. Most adult slaves and former slaves, of course, could not write. But the letters' importance does not rest upon whether they were a common form of slave expression. They were not. What is important is their relationship to the beliefs and behavior of other slaves who left no such historical records. Women like Hannah Grover and men like Laura Spicer's slave husband were not unusual Afro-Americans. Their letters were individual expressions of an adaptive and changing slave culture that had developed in the century preceding the general emancipation.

This study of the Afro-American family reaches back into the eighteenth century and moves forward to the Harlem tenements of 1925, but its chief focus is on the Afro-American family in the decades just before emancipation and in the few years following it. The novelist Albion W. Tourgee wrote in 1888, "Much has been written of the slave and something of the freedman, but thus far no one has been able to weld the new life to the old."[4] The evidence in this study deals mostly with some of the important relationships between these two critical moments in the Afro-American experience. It unfolds a very different story from that found in the pages of E. Franklin Frazier's pioneering study *The Negro Family in the United States* (1939) and in nearly all other standard works on this important subject that rest heavily upon this influential book.

The recovery of records of viable Afro-American families and kin networks during and after slavery makes it possible to begin a long overdue examination of how there developed among black Americans a culture shaped by the special ways in which they adapted first to the harshness of initial enslavement, then to the severe dislocations associated with the physical transfer of hundreds of thousands of Upper South slaves to the Lower South between 1790 and 1860, and later to legal freedom in the rural and urban South and in the urban North prior to 1930. The sociologist T. B. Bottomore reminds us that "the family transmits values which are determined elsewhere; it is an agent, not a principal."[5]

But for it to be an "agent," there must be links between generations of different families. Without them, it is difficult for a culture
to be transmitted over time, and members of developing social
classes cannot adapt to changing external circumstances. That
is so for slaves and nonslaves.

The family condition and familial beliefs of some Virginia,
North Carolina, Mississippi, Louisiana, Tennessee and Kentucky
Afro-Americans between 1863 and 1866—*the last slave generation*
—are examined first. Who these ex-slaves were and the types
of families they lived in between 1863 and 1866 pose questions
about who they had been in the half century preceding the
general emancipation and who they would become in the half
century following it. Evidence about them in 1865 provides
important clues to who their slave grandparents had been in
1815 (before the rapid spread of slavery from the Upper to the
Lower South) and who their grandchildren would be in 1915
(at the beginning of the twentieth-century migration of rural
southern blacks to northern cities). The emancipation freed the
slaves not only of their owners but also of the constraints that had
limited their ability to act upon their slave beliefs, and their
behavior during and shortly after the Civil War reveals aspects
of that earlier belief system otherwise difficult for the historian
to discern. Early-twentieth-century historians and social scientists
suggested such continuities, but either their racial beliefs or the
flawed sociohistorical "models" they used to explain lower-class
behavior over time led them to stress "continuities" that had no
relationship at all to the behavior of ordinary ex-slaves.[6]

No one better illustrates this misdirected emphasis than the
sociologist E. Franklin Frazier. Frazier, of course, was not a racist
and vigorously combatted the racial scholarship that dominated
early-twentieth-century historical and social-science writings. But
he underestimated the adaptive capacities of slaves and ex-slaves
and therefore wrote that their families, "at best an accommodation to the slave order, went to pieces in the general breakup of
the plantation system." He had the ex-slave laborer and field hand
in mind when he asked:

What authority was there to take the place of the master's in
regulating sex relations and maintaining the permanency of
marital ties? Where could the Negro father look for sanctions
of his authority in family relations which had scarcely existed
in the past? Were the affectional bonds between mother and

child and the solidarity of feeling and sentiment between man and wife strong enough to withstand the disorganizing effects of freedom? In the absence of family traditions and public opinion, what restraint was there upon individual impulses unleashed in these disordered times? To what extent during slavery had the members of slave families developed common interests and common purposes capable of supporting the more or less loose ties of sympathy between those of the same blood or household?

The "crisis" accompanying emancipation "tended to destroy all traditional ways of thinking." "Promiscuous sexual relations and constant changing of partners became the rule" among "demoralized blacks," and the rest hardly fared better. "When the yoke of slavery was lifted," he wrote, "the drifting masses were left without any restraint upon their vagrant impulses and wild desires. The old intimacy between master and slave, upon which the moral order of the slave regime had rested, was destroyed forever." Frazier's influential writings paradoxically fed the racist scholarship he attacked. Frazier's error was not that he exaggerated the social crisis accompanying emancipation but his belief that the "moral order of the slave regime . . . rested" on "the old intimacy between master and slave."[7] Some slaves experienced such intimacies, but neither the beliefs and behavior of most slaves nor their familial arrangements depended upon so fragile a bond. The familial condition of the typical ex-slave differed greatly from that emphasized by Frazier and so many others. That is illustrated in the pages which follow. Why the typical ex-slave family was composed of a poor husband, his wife, and their children and what that meant are the subject of the rest of Part One of this book.

No slave family was protected in the law, but upon their emancipation most Virginia ex-slave families had two parents, and most older couples had lived together in long-lasting unions. That is made clear in Union Army population censuses of Montgomery (1866), Princess Anne (1866), and York (1865) county blacks and in Freedmen's Bureau 1866 marriage registers for Louisa, Nelson, Rockbridge, and Goochland county blacks, the only such documents found in the Virginia Freedmen's Bureau manuscript records.[8] The three population censuses describe the composition of 1870 black households in which two or more members had either blood or marriage ties, and the four marriage registers record the renewal of 2817 slave marriages.[9]

Although the blacks in these seven counties had experienced slavery in very different ways, the typical Virginia ex-slave family had at its head a male ex-slave who had been either a common laborer or a field hand[10] (Table 6, page 38). Whether these slaves had lived in plantation or farm counties or in counties with few or many slave residents did not matter. Neither did the diverse ways in which the Civil War had affected these places.[11] Despite their many different slave experiences, these blacks shared a common occupational status. They were very poor. A small number of men had artisan skills, mostly carpenters, blacksmiths, and shoemakers, and hardly any had higher status. A few were servants, but in Montgomery, York, Goochland, and Louisa counties between 85 and 91 percent of all occupations were recorded as farmer, farm laborer, and laborer[12] (Table 7, page 39). The three population censuses show that most Montgomery, York, and Princess Anne families, composed mostly of poor ex-slaves, had adapted to and absorbed the shocks of enslavement, war, emancipation, and migration. Relatively few Montgomery blacks—no more than 12 percent—lived as "single" persons.[13] The rest were members of immediate families. Nearly two-thirds of the 1866 Princess Anne blacks had lived in that county fewer than four years. No significant differences existed between long-time residents and migrants. The same percentage in each group lived in families. The York census was sufficiently detailed to reveal that few blacks—less than one in twenty—lived alone, and that the typical household was of modest size. Only 7 of the 997 York households with two or more residents had ten or more persons in it. The largest had fourteen. About one in six had between six and nine residents; more than four in five had between two and five residents.

Equally important, most Montgomery, York, and Princess Anne households with two or more residents had in them either a husband and wife or two parents and their children (Table 1). The more mobile York and Princess Anne blacks had fewer single-parent households than the Montgomery blacks. More significantly, the uniformity in household composition among these ex-slaves in three distinct social settings and the fact that more than three-fourths of the households contained either a father or a husband cast doubt on conventional assertions that slavery had shattered the immediate slave family and made the two-parent household uncommon among poor, rural blacks fresh to legal freedom.

TABLE 1.   COMPOSITION OF BLACK HOUSEHOLDS WITH TWO OR
MORE RESIDENTS, MONTGOMERY, YORK, AND
PRINCESS ANNE COUNTIES, VIRGINIA, 1865–1866

Type of household	Montgomery County	York County	Princess Anne County
Husband-wife	18%	26%	17%
Husband-wife-children	54	53	62
Father-children	5	5	4
Mother-children	23	16	17
Number	498	997	375

Black York, Montgomery, and Princess Anne families also cast
doubt on the common belief that large numbers of slaves and ex-
slaves viewed the single-parent household as a conventional
domestic arrangement. Hardly any young York and Montgomery
women headed such households. Five York women aged fifteen to
nineteen—less than 3 percent of all women in that age group—
lived with a child and without a husband. Two women aged fifteen
to nineteen headed Montgomery County households. Ten times
that many fifteen-to-nineteen-year-old Montgomery women lived
with either a husband or a husband and their children. Women
aged forty and over headed about one-third of male-absent Montgomery households, and just over half of such York households
were headed by women that old. An unknown number of these
women were widows, survivors of conventional two-parent slave
families. The women heading households, and especially the
younger women among them, deserve study. Some probably had
never married. But their household status should not be
exaggerated in importance or confused with the household status
of the typical adult woman (Table 8, page 42).

Proof that many Virginia slaves had enduring marriages is
found in the Goochland, Louisa, Nelson, and Rockbridge county
1866 marriage registers. Virginia law did not require ex-slaves to
renew marital ties: a February 1866 statute simply declared those
then living together as husband and wife. But the Virginia Freedmen's Bureau ordered county Bureau officers to register such
marriages. The blacks in the four counties for which registers
survive lived in diverse settings. Goochland and Louisa, for
example, were important Virginia plantation counties and predominantly black in population[14] (Table 6, page 38). Depending
upon their county of residence, the registrants revealed two im-

portant facts: many had lived in long-lasting marriages, and most registrants were farm laborers and field hands. Nelson and Rockbridge couples reported the length of their marriages but did not give their occupations. Eight Nelson couples had lived together more than half a century. Nearly similar percentages of Rockbridge and Nelson ex-slaves recorded lengthy marriages: slightly more than half in each county had lived together as husband and wife at least ten years, and the percentage living together twenty or more years was about the same for both groups (Table 2). Rockbridge registrants also gave their ages, allowing for an age-specific analysis. Men and women forty and older in 1866 had lived with the same spouse for many years: three in four at least ten years, nearly two in three at least twenty years, and slightly more than one in five at least thirty years. Middle-aged and elderly Rockbridge ex-slaves had not lived in either casual "mating" arrangements or loose sexual alliances.

TABLE 2.   LENGTH OF SLAVE MARRIAGES REGISTERED IN NELSON AND ROCKBRIDGE COUNTIES, VIRGINIA, 1866

Years married	Nelson County	Rockbridge County
Under 10	45%	49%
10–19	24	18
20–29	16	22
30–39	8	7
40+	7	4
Number	616	230
Unknown	4	6

LENGTH OF SLAVE MARRIAGES AND AGES OF MALE AND FEMALE REGISTRANTS, ROCKBRIDGE COUNTY, VIRGINIA, 1866

Years married in 1866	Age of Registrant in 1866					Number
	15–19	20–29	30–39	40–49	50+	
Under 2	50%	9%	9%	5%	1%	30
2–9	50	82	46	24	16	194
10–19	0	9	38	17	9	84
20–29	0	0	7	50	34	102
30+	0	0	0	4	40	50
Number	6	114	113	111	116	460
Age unknown						12

Most of the registrants, moreover, were unskilled laborers and farm hands, not servants and artisans, a fact that contradicts the assertion that double-headed households had existed mostly among "elite" slaves. Much that flaws the study of slaves and ex-slaves flows from this belief: the alleged inadequacy of the slave father and husband, the absence of male "models" for young slave children to emulate, the prevalence of the "Sambo" personality, the insistence that slave marriage usually meant little more than successive polygyny, and the belief that the "matrifocal" household (a "natural" adaptation by most blacks to the "realities" of slavery) prevailed among the mass of illiterate plantation field hands and laborers. These misconceptions accompany another erroneous belief: that when slaves did honor the two-parent household they did so either as a result of the encouragement offered to "favored" slaves by owners or because daily contact between whites and slave servants and artisans (as contrasted to slaves living in the "quarters") permitted these few slaves to "imitate" marriage "models" common among owners and other whites. Implicit in such arguments, none of which rests on significant evidence, is the assumption that such "models" were infrequent among the slaves themselves, an assumption that has encouraged simplified and misleading descriptions of slave socialization and slave culture.

The occupations of Goochland and Louisa male registrants show *who* had lived in double-headed slave families. None of the 719 Goochland and 1229 Louisa registrants had high-status occupations. About 13 percent of the Goochland and 9 percent of the Louisa registrants were either artisans or servants. The rest had unskilled rural occupations. In his influential study, E. Franklin Frazier argued that some slave families acquired "considerable stability" but believed this happened mainly among "the better-situated slaves," "where the father was, for example, a skilled mechanic and had acquired a responsible position in the plantation organization."[15] But the Goochland and Louisa men included very few privileged ex-slaves, and that is their significance. Occupational distributions for all adult Goochland and Louisa males in 1866 do not exist, but if they approximated the distribution for all Montgomery males listed in the 1866 population census, it means that two-parent households were not more common among house servants and artisans ("elite" slaves) than among unskilled field hands and laborers. If they were, a far higher percentage of Goochland and Louisa artisans and house servants should have registered their marriages. The percentage with such occupations who registered marriages, however, closely approximates that found in the distribution of all Montgomery male occupations (Table 7, page 39). Artisans and servants should have registered marriages out of proportion to their place in the population for yet other reasons. Servants had daily contact with white employers, and bureau registration probably was more readily known to them than to field hands and laborers. Artisans had greater mobility than farm laborers; they, too, had an advantaged position in registering marriages. But only a very small percentage of the Goochland and Louisa registrants were servants and artisans. Their scant number is good reason to dismiss as unfounded the assertion that it was mostly the "better-situated slaves" and ex-slaves who lived in two-parent households.

Evidence of long marriages is found in all slave social settings in the decades preceding the Civil War. Young slaves learned about marital and family roles from whites and free blacks, but they also had the opportunity to learn from other slaves, a fact confirmed by the nearly twenty thousand North Carolina ex-slaves in seventeen different counties who registered slave marriages with county clerks and justices of the peace in the spring of 1866 after the North Carolina legislature had ordered the registration of all continuing slave marriages. The law required their registration and the payment of a twenty-five-cent fee by the early fall of 1866. Registration books and copies of the "Negro Cohabitation Certificates" native white officials used in seventeen of the state's eighty-six counties survive.[16] The registrars did not record ages, but the little regularly noted makes these an unusually valuable comparative record. Couples everywhere gave their full names and (except in Pasquotank County) told how long they had lived together as husband and wife. Not one surviving register is from a western Carolina mountain county (a region with relatively few slaves), but the seventeen registers available included two Piedmont counties, one that hugged the South Carolina border, six with access to the Atlantic Ocean (one of which—New Hanover—included Wilmington, the state's major seaport and by far its most important city), and eight coastal-plain counties, all east of Raleigh and all essential to North Carolina's plantation economy. About 30 percent of all North Carolina slaves twenty and older had lived in these seventeen counties in 1860, and 18,904 men and women from these same places registered 9452 marriages in 1866. Drawn from just a few counties, the *registrants* totaled about 14 percent of North Carolina's *entire* 1860 adult slave population.

Nearly similar percentages of slave couples everywhere reported long-lasting marriages (Table 3). About one in four couples had lived together between ten and nineteen years, and slightly more than one in five at least twenty years. Nearly one in ten registrants recorded marriages that had lasted thirty or more years.[17] Insignificant percentage-point differences existed between the counties. Almost the same percentage of Warren and New Hanover registrants, for example, reported marriages of twenty

TABLE 3.　NUMBER OF MARRIAGES REGISTERED AND YEARS MARRIED BY FORMER NORTH CAROLINA SLAVES IN SEVENTEEN COUNTIES, 1866

County	Number of marriages registered, 1866	Number giving years married, 1866	Years married			
			Less than 10	10–19	20+	30+
PIEDMONT						
Orange	931	928	47%	27%	26%	10%
Lincoln	275	235	56	25	19	6
CAPE FEAR						
New Hanover	1392	1358	53	25	22	8
Robeson	583	542	55	27	18	7
ATLANTIC COAST						
Pasquotank	326	not given	n.g.	n.g.	n.g.	n.g.
Washington	221	204	47	28	25	13
Hyde	196	194	46	25	29	9
Beaufort	411	392	58	23	19	8
Currituck	72	69	30	33	37	12
COASTAL-PLAIN PLANTATION						
Warren	1488	1478	51	28	21	7
Johnston	560	557	52	27	21	9
Nash	430	420	52	26	22	10
Edgecombe	996	974	53	26	21	10
Franklin	800	781	52	27	21	9
Richmond	310	188	52	27	21	10
Bertie	297	296	48	27	25	12
Halifax	163	163	42	25	33	13
TOTAL	9452	8778	51	27	22	9

or more years. Warren was the state's premier plantation county, and New Hanover its most heavily urbanized county. The social differences between these two counties direct attention to the most important fact these blacks revealed: settled slave marriage "models" and domestic arrangements existed in all types of slave settings. The uniformities reported described only the length of slave marriages and did not indicate that these registrants had shared similar slave experiences. That is the essential point. How these slaves had lived can be approximated very crudely by examining five different measures of dissimilarity: the degree of urbanization, the sex ratio, the density of the slave population, access to free blacks, and patterns of slave ownership that suggest community and social structure. The widespread diversity in these counties is indicated in Table 9, page 43.[18] We consider only the distribution of slaves in 1860, a measure that allows for a comparison between the North Carolina blacks and *Lower South* slaves in settings where the plantation system and the social structure associated with it were much more common than in North Carolina.

Most North Carolina slaves in 1860 were not a part of the plantation economy, but registrants in the eight plantation counties (Bertie, Edgecombe, Franklin, Halifax, Johnston, Nash, Richmond, and Warren) shared a common slave setting with blacks living on large Lower South and South Carolina plantations.[19] Three in five Edgecombe and Franklin slaves and about three in four Halifax, Bertie, and Warren slaves were owned in units of twenty or more slaves in 1860. Except for the Nash County slaves, at least one in five belonged to units of fifty or more slaves. That percentage rose significantly in Bertie, Halifax, Edgecombe, and Warren counties, important staple-producing tobacco and cotton counties, which were neither stagnant Upper South counties nor settings dominated by small family farms worked by a few slaves. Warren County, for example, grew nearly 19 percent of the 1860 North Carolina tobacco crop. Cotton, however, was the coastal-plain plantation region's major crop, and in 1860 two in every three bales of North Carolina cotton came from there. Not surprisingly, these counties had patterns of slave ownership similar to statewide Alabama, Georgia, Louisiana, Mississippi, and South Carolina patterns of slave ownership (Table 10, page 44). Slave occupations on the coastal-plain tobacco and cotton plantations remain unknown but should not have differed much from those in Montgomery County, Virginia (where

85 percent of men were laborers) and from those in Goochland and Louisa counties, pre-eminent Virginia plantation counties. The typical North Carolina plantation county couple registering a marriage in 1866 almost surely lived in densely black areas and worked the land as field hands or common laborers. Long-lasting marriages had existed among them just as long-lasting slave marriages were found among Mississippi, Louisiana, and Alabama slaves during and right after the Civil War.[20]

The North Carolina registrants also showed that a special relationship did not exist between long slave marriages and the large plantation. Couples living in predominantly farm settings and in the county with North Carolina's largest city registered long marriages in the same proportion as men and women living in predominantly plantation counties. A plantation setting therefore was not a prerequisite for a long slave marriage.

Much in their social experience went unreported when these nearly nineteen thousand ex-slaves registered marriages, but the little they revealed—the length of their marriages—uncovers an aspect of slave life essential to comprehending slave behavior and belief prior to and just after the emancipation. These men and women had not reported that North Carolina slaves lived in "stable" marriages or families. Nor did what they had experienced mean that the forcible breakup of marriages and families had occurred infrequently. (Mostly older children and unmarried young adults were sold, and between 1830 and 1840 the rate of increase in the North Carolina slave population was less than 0.1 percent compared with a 24 percent rate of increase for the southern slave population. This was caused partly by owners' selling teen-age children from their parents who lived in settled slave marriages.) Instead, because the registers showed that settled slave marriages existed in very diverse social circumstances, it meant that young slaves everywhere learned from other slaves about marital and familial obligations and about managing difficult daily social realities. Adult slaves in long marriages were direct "models," making it possible to pass on *slave* conceptions of marital, familial, and kin obligation from generation to generation. The domestic arrangements visibly accessible to young slaves were not just those of shattered slave families and the more secure families of owners, other whites, and free blacks. How married slaves dealt with family life and social existence over time taught them much more than what they could learn from better-advantaged whites or from scattered communities of free blacks.[21]

Although these North Carolina and Virginia ex-slaves revealed that many ordinary Upper South slaves, including plantation field hands, had lived in long marriages, that record told little about how the decisions of slaveowners affected slave marriages. Testimony detailing how frequently sale had disrupted their marriages, however, comes from Mississippi and northern Louisiana ex-slaves. In March 1864, John Eaton, the Superintendent of Contrabands in the Department of the Tennessee and Arkansas, issued a military edict (Special Order 15) instructing Union Army clergy to "solemnize the rite of marriage among Freedmen," give such blacks "neat" marriage certificates, and record these marriages in registration books. Even before this order, northern missionaries had pressed legal marriage upon contraband Mississippi Valley blacks within the Union Army lines.[22] Special Order 15 did not require that married slaves renew their ties before an army clergyman, and those who did so acted voluntarily.[23] Ex-slaves in and near Davis Bend, Vicksburg, and Natchez, Mississippi, registered 4627 marriages.[24] Officiating clergy did not charge fees, but some blacks paid them with rewards such as a silver dime, some postal currency, "half a dime," and a sweet potato (this from a woman who "begged" a chaplain to take "a small token" for what had been done "for her and her family"). The first Vicksburg marriage, which took place on April 10, 1864, at the Presbyterian Church and involved the "reputed [slave] son of a former Governor of Virginia," William Smith, was ridiculed in the local press as "a marriage in high life." Between that date and the early fall, 1456 Vicksburg marriage ceremonies were performed. In one day, a chaplain married 102 couples. A white slave trader married his quadroon concubine, for whom he had allegedly paid three thousand dollars. She had rejected him "because, as she said, she now had become free" and wanted a legal marriage. The trader agreed. A white cleric, "altogether unwilling to assist at mixed marriages," refused to conduct the service but relented after the trader said he had "married her in the sight of God five years ago."[25] Other unusual marriage renewals took place. An old man arrived at a Vicksburg church without his wife, who was "washin' dat day and couldn't be present 'veniently." The oldest registrant in the early Vicksburg days was eighty-eight years old. He had been born in 1776.[26]

The officiating clergy gathered unusual social and demographic data from those registering slave marriages or marrying for the first time. Nearly all reported their age, their color, the color of each of their parents, their earlier slave marriages, the reasons

these marriages had ended, and the length of these earlier
marriages. Most registrants described themselves *and their parents*
as "black." They apparently had a choice or, at least, the
officiating clergy made subtle color distinctions among them, including "black," "brown," "yellow," "coffee," "mulatto," "white,"
and "1/4 white." Each registrant also gave the color of his or
her parents, a designation that could not have been made by
the registrars. The "fractional" designations used to describe
many parents also suggest that the registrants knew a great deal
about their grandparents. Overall, more than three in five said
that both parents were "black."[27] These men and women refute
the suggestion by some historians that slave marriage bore a
special relationship to mixed "blood." Six registrants claimed a
white mother, and about one in twenty-five (3.7 percent) a white
father. Thirty-seven percent, however, admitted to "mixed color,"
so that more than one in three of these more than nine thousand
Lower South slaves traced white ancestry to racial intermixture
that had occurred among their grandparents and great-grandparents, mixing that had mostly taken place in the eighteenth
century. Unless large numbers of the registrants had French or
Spanish grandparents, these white and black grandparents and
great-grandparents had lived in the Upper South.[28]

Among the male registrants, about two in five served in the
Union Army in 1864 and 1865, but these soldiers, together with
the civilian male registrants and the female registrants, had mostly
lived in Adams County and Warren County, Mississippi, and in
Concordia Parish, Louisiana, in 1860.[29] Many had probably
labored on the large cotton plantations in these three places, which
had ninety plantations with at least one hundred slaves each in
1860, one-tenth of all Mississippi and Louisiana plantations that
big. The registrants, moreover, had lived mostly among blacks
and slaves. Although Natchez and Vicksburg were Mississippi's
most important towns, only about one in eight Adams and Warren
slaves had lived in them. Hardly any free blacks had resided in
these three counties before the Civil War. In 1860, two-thirds of
Warren residents were slaves and so were seven in ten Adams
County and nine in ten Concordia Parish residents.[30]

Their ages indicate that these Mississippi and northern
Louisiana registrants combined two, and perhaps three, generations of distinct slave experiences.[31] A high percentage of all
registrants were men and especially women not yet thirty years
old: nearly two in five men and slightly more than half of all
women (Table 4). All these people had been born after 1835

TABLE 4.   BLACK MARRIAGES BY AGE AND SEX REGISTERED IN
           DAVIS BEND, NATCHEZ, AND VICKSBURG,
           MISSISSIPPI, 1864–1865

Age	Male	Female
15–19	1%	10%
20–29	38	47
30–39	22	21
40–49	20	14
50+	19	8
Number	4612	4591
Age unknown	15	36

and therefore had been born at the time of the interregional transfer of Upper South slaves to the Lower South. If they had had contact with Upper South slavery, it was probably as children or from what they had learned from parents and other older blacks. About one in six registrants were at least fifty years old. These men and women had been born before Mississippi entered the Union as a state (1817), and many among them had probably grown up as Upper South and border-state slaves. Some had been born in the eighteenth century. Four men were at least ninety years old, and a woman, separated by force from an earlier husband with whom she had lived for forty-five years, claimed a full century of life. Natchez officials registered the marriage of a one-hundred-year-old husband and his seventy-eight-year-old wife. When Jacob Wiley and Phoebe Tanner registered their marriage in Davis Bend, he was ninety-three and she was eighty. Life experiences that encompassed the spread of slavery and the physical movement of black men and women from the Upper to the Lower South had not convinced these elderly ex-slaves that legal marriage was a privilege belonging only to the owning class and to other whites.

Registrants gave the clergy information about earlier slave marriages (data examined in detail in Chapter 4), and their testimony unfolded a grim record. One in four marriages registered in 1864–1865 involved one or two persons separated by force from a spouse in an earlier marriage.[32] In marriages in which either partner was at least forty years old in 1864–1865, the percentage in which one or both had experienced an earlier marriage broken by force rose to 35 percent (Table 5). Among people that old, seven in ten marriages registered in 1864–1865 included one

TABLE 5. REASONS FOR THE BREAKUP OF EARLIER SLAVE
MARRIAGES GIVEN IN 1864–1865 BY PERSONS
REGISTERING MARRIAGES IN WHICH ONE OR BOTH
PARTNERS WERE AT LEAST FORTY YEARS OLD, DAVIS
BEND, NATCHEZ, AND VICKSBURG, MISSISSIPPI

Number of marriages registered in 1864–1865 in which one or both partners were at least forty years old	*1910*
Couples in 1864–1865 not reporting an earlier terminated marriage	29%
Couples in 1864–1865 reporting an earlier marriage terminated by mutual consent	4
Couples in 1864–1865 reporting an earlier marriage terminated by desertion	5
Couples in 1864–1865 reporting an earlier marriage terminated by force	35
Couples in 1864–1865 reporting an earlier marriage terminated by death	41

NOTE: *These percentages add up to more than 100 percent because in some instances persons registering marriages had more than one earlier marriage.*

or two people who had been married earlier.[33] Nearly as many of these 1864–1865 marriages included a prior marriage broken by force as broken by death, a more severe indictment of the cost slavery had exacted from Afro-Americans than the most telling words of Frederick Douglass, not to mention William Lloyd Garrison and Harriet Beecher Stowe.

The registration of so many slave marriages by these Mississippi and northern Louisiana blacks impressed Union Army officers among them. Thomas Calahan, who commanded black Mississippi troops, said they had "an almost universal anxiety . . . to abide by first connections. Many, both men and women with whom I am acquainted, whose wives or husbands the rebels have driven off, firmly refuse to form new connections, and declare their purpose to keep faith to absent ones." Neither John Eaton nor Joseph Warren, his chief associate, idealized these marriage renewals. "It is not pretended," remarked Eaton, "that all marriages that have taken place were well advised, or will be happy, or faithfully observed. When marriages among whites shall all prove so, without exception, it will be time to look for such a happy state among the blacks." A year after Special Order 15 had been instituted, Warren said, "I will only remark that the ill-natured predictions of many persons have not been fulfilled.

Marriage is not treated as a light matter." A "few" marriages had ended because of the "inconstancy of the partners," but it put Warren "utterly out of patience to hear people . . . say it is folly to marry the blacks, because they will be fickle, and then quote a single case of unfaithfulness . . . in proof of their monstrous proposition. Would they recommend that the colored people herd together like beasts . . . [and] that marriage be abolished among white people because there are some cases of discontent and fickleness among us?" Their behavior convinced Warren to put aside talk of "the incapacity of the race"; "so many" were "able to 'take care of themselves' without guardianship or tutelage." How the ex-slaves responded to Special Order 15 convinced Eaton that their families had been forcibly broken much more frequently than he had believed, but their attachment to their families impressed him: "Many have said, 'They do not feel these things as we do.' This is utterly false. . . . They are a race of peculiarly keen feelings and domestic tendencies, and they have fewer means of withdrawing their minds from their griefs than we have."[34]

The concern of Mississippi and northern Louisiana ex-slaves serving in the Union Army for their families shows that Eaton and these others had not been deceived. Black Vicksburg soldiers "complained bitterly" in early 1864 that their wives had been "taken away from them and sent they knew not to what camp or plantation." Other black troops found four hundred "exceedingly destitute" ex-slaves, some kin among them, near Videlia, Louisiana, and threatened to desert. "We are concluding to leave our regiment," Laura Haviland, a northern relief worker among them, overheard one ex-slave say, "and build something to shelter and house our children." After she and other sympathetic whites promised relief, the threats subsided. But the soldiers stayed a few days to see what would happen. Other ex-slaves, recruited to garrison a post near Milliken's Bend, were sent to Waterproof. Their families had gathered near Milliken's Bend. "The men complained bitterly," said a supervising white, "about the way they have been treated by being taken away from their wives." They would "submit to the necessity of the occasion provided they can feel that their wives are cared for." But according to Thomas Knox, a New York *Herald* correspondent who had leased a wartime Mississippi plantation, "their affection for their wives and children could not be overcome at once." Their complaints at first were "silenced." A few weeks later, a few soldiers quit Waterproof and made their way back to Milliken's Bend. They ended in the guardhouse, but "others followed their example, and for a while the camp was in a disturbed condition." Desertions occurred daily. "All intended to return to the post after making a brief visit to their families," said Knox. "Most . . . would request their comrades to notify their captains that they would only be absent a short time. Two, who succeeded in eluding pursuit, made their appearance one morning as if nothing had happened and assured their officers that others would shortly be back again."[35]

Such concern for their families was most decisively revealed by ex-slave soldiers in and near Natchez in early April 1864, a few weeks after Special Order 15 went into effect. Treasury Department officials had arranged for the leasing of abandoned plantations to northerners, and some Union Army officers tried to force ex-slaves, who had crowded Natchez and a refugee camp nearby, to labor for the lessees. Late in March, the Natchez army surgeon and chief health officer A. W. Kelly, supported by J. W. Tuttle, the city's military commander, announced that "*idle negroes*" posed a "serious danger" to public health and threatened to spread "the most *loathsome* and *malignant* diseases" among Union Army soldiers. After April 1, only ex-slaves employed by "*some responsible white person* in some legitimate business" and living with their employers could remain in Natchez. Ex-slaves could no longer rent premises, and whites employing them needed Kelly's approval. The protests of a few northern schoolteachers and missionaries led by S. G. Wright, who called Kelly "an inhuman monster" and "*a Fiend*," had no effect. Tuttle rejected their formal complaints, threatened them with punitive action, and said they "appear to think that colored men have a great many more rights than white men." Kelly's edict was enforced. "Mothers," said Wright, "came running to us *weeping*, begging us to go & plead their cause." Parents were separated from their children, and husbands and wives from one another. An observer angrily reported:

> There seemed to be no regard shown to the marriage or parental relations. If the husband was employed by a white person and happened to live at his domicile, he might remain, but his wife must leave the city. Or if the wife was so employed, and her husband so laboring for himself, he must be driven from his family. And if the parents were employed, and the children working for the family or themselves, they must leave the place of their birth.

"Scores" of women and children were moved from Natchez and left "shelterless and destitute" across the Mississippi River in Louisiana. The angered and frustrated Wright pleaded with northern associates to press for intervention by the Secretary of War. "What," Wright reported the ex-slaves as asking, "has the [Emancipation] Proclamation really done for us if military officers are to have the power to drive us from our quiet homes into the streets, separate husband wife parents & children &c?"

Ex-slave Mississippi soldiers checked Kelly's abusive edict. "The colored soldier," the missionaries had warned Tuttle, "hearing that his mother or his wife had been driven from her quiet and comfortable home, simply because she supported herself and was not dependent upon some white person, may feel less inclined to hazard his life in the cause of his country now struggling for *its* life." Many evicted and abused women had husbands in army camps near Natchez, and some went to their husbands "for protection." "I heard colored soldiers yesterday in their madness swear desperately that they would have *revenge. And they will*," Wright privately confided to a northern friend. "I tremble as do many of the officers in the colored regiments, when I witness such expressions and conduct of the soldiers," he added, fearing "blood equalling the day of vengeance in the island of Hayti." The ex-slave soldiers acted decisively. The first night after Kelly's edict was enforced, fifteen deserted their regiments. Three days later, other ex-slave soldiers, their exact number unknown, told their commanding officer that "they could no longer endure the trial of seeing their wives and children driven into the streets, and if he would not at once interfere and protect them they should *positively* do it themselves." Their threat was understood, and the officer released some women and children kept by Kelly. A few days later, Kelly's "health ordinance" was modified. "The colored troops here arose," Wright privately enthused, "& even Dr. Kelly caved in. . . ." A few weeks later, Kelly and Tuttle were relieved of their command. "The people all breathe easier," said Wright.[36]

The Natchez ex-slave women were far more fortunate than ex-slave women living in Memphis in the spring of 1866. A few days after the disarming and discharge of Union Army black soldiers in Fort Pickering nearby, Memphis was the scene of a murderous riot. Local whites, the mostly Irish police prominent among them, killed forty-six blacks, wounded at least seventy others, robbed about one hundred ex-slaves, and burned at least ninety black dwellings, including twelve schoolhouses and four churches. Whites also raped at least five ex-slaves and sexually insulted two others, facts revealed by the testimony these women and other witnesses, including a few whites, gave to a congressional committee. What gives such testimony its importance is not merely the pain and insult experienced by these women. It is rather the willingness of recent slaves to expose their suffering in public so soon after the Civil War's end.

Four of the seven women, including two of those raped, were unmarried. Asked if she was married, the washerwoman Elvira Walker said, "A man boards with me; he is not my husband; he sleeps in the same room." She was alone the night rioters robbed her room. One "put his hands into my bosom," she told the congressional investigators. "I tried to stop him, and he knocked down my hands with his pistol." A second woman, unidentified in the testimony, boarded with Mary Grady, an Irishwoman who kept a grocery and liquor place ("a little shebang") that hostile whites called "a nigger resort" and a "nigger ball-room." Rioters robbed her place and destroyed groceries. The Irishwoman told what followed:

> They went into the back room where my little girl and a black woman were in bed, and asked if there were any arms in there. The black woman said there were not. They then felt of her and wanted to get into bed with her. She told them they would have to kill her before they got into bed with her. Then they wanted my little girl, nine or ten years old, to kiss them. She said no, she would not kiss anybody. Then they tried to feel of her. My husband then called to three or four discharged Union soldiers . . . sleeping in the back part of the house, to get up and come down quickly, that they were doing Mary mighty wrong. The boys got out of bed, and the party, hearing them, left.

No one interceded to assist Frances Thompson and Lucy Smith. The two lived together. A Maryland slave by birth, Thompson, the older of the two, was crippled by a cancer in her foot and walked with crutches. She labored as a washerwoman. A Memphis native, Lucy Smith was seventeen years old. Seven men, including two police officers, broke into their place, demanded and were fed supper, robbed Frances Thompson of one hundred dollars and four "nice" dresses, took another two hundred dollars the older woman was keeping for a friend, and raped both women. The older of the two testified:

When they had eaten supper, they said they wanted some woman to sleep with. I said we were not that sort of woman, and they must go. They said "that didn't make a damned bit of difference." One of them then laid hold of me and hit me on the side of my face, and holding my throat, choked me. Lucy tried to get out of the window, when one of them knocked her down and choked her. They drew their pistols and said they would shoot us and fire the house if we did not let them have their way with us. All seven of them violated us two. Four of them had to do with me, and the rest with Lucy. . . .

Lucy Smith differed slightly in telling what had happened: "After the first man had connexion with me, another got hold of me and tried to violate me, but I was so bad he did not. He gave me a lick with his fist and said I was so damned near dead he would not have anything to do with me. . . . I bled from what the first man done to me. . . . I was injured right smart." Black physicians later attended the two women. Lucy Smith was in bed for two weeks, and the older woman "lay for three days with a hot, burning fever."

Three married women also were raped. Rebecca Ann Bloom was married to the barber Peter Bloom; Lucy Tibbs's husband labored on a steamboat; and Harriet Armour's husband was a discharged Union Army soldier. Only Bloom was with his wife. Tibbs worked on a boat, and Armour was at an army fort. Lucy Tibbs, then four months pregnant and the mother of two young children, was about twenty-four and had come to Memphis from Arkansas at the war's start. "They done a very bad act," she testified. "I had just to give up to them. They said they would kill me if I did not. They put me on the bed, and the other men were plundering the house while this man carried on." Harriet Armour's McMinnville owner had brought her to Memphis before the war, and she married there. Two whites, one named Dunn, came to her place seeking arms, and she told what followed:

What did they do in your room? Mr. Dunn had to do with me twice, and the other gentleman once. And then Mr. Dunn tried to make me suck him. I cried. He asked me what I was crying about, and tried to make me suck it. . . . They just told me I had to do it. They barred the door, and I knew I could not help myself. . . .

Did I understand you that you did not try to prevent them

from doing these things to you? No, sir; I did not know what to do. I was there alone, was weak and sick, and I thought I would rather let them do it than be hurt or punished. . . .

Did they both have revolvers? I do not know; Dunn had. He had his revolver, and he just as much as said I must do it, and I thought I had better give up freely; I did not like to do it, but I thought it would be best for me. . . .

Were there only two men in the room? Only two; but Mr. Dunn had had to do with me twice and the other man, once, which was the same as three.

What kind of a looking man is Dunn? He is a young-looking man. He would be a very nice man, but I do not call him nice now.

Is he an Irishman? No, sir; I think they were both Americans. I never saw him before or since.

Neighbors, including the Georgia-born white Molly Hayes, the black grocer Henry Porter, and the ex-slave Cynthia Townsend, who had purchased her freedom during the war and had known Harriet Armour before her marriage ("she is a very nice woman"), corroborated her sordid story. "She has sometimes been a little deranged since then," said Townsend. "Her husband left her for it. When he came out of the fort, and found out what had been done, he said he would have nothing to do with her any more." The third woman's husband was with her, but his presence could not prevent her rape. "They took me into the other room," said the barber Peter Bloom, "and I heard them trying to ravish my wife, she refusing them." A rioter, Rebecca Bloom testified, "wanted to know if I had anything to do with white men. I said no. He had a knife in his hand, and said he would kill me if I did not let him do as he wanted to. I refused. He said, 'By God, you must,' and then got into bed with me, and violated my person, by having connexion with me, he still holding the knife." A neighbor, who also testified, said that Rebecca Bloom "was kind of bashful about it afterward, but she told us what they did. . . ."

The Memphis rioters had their way for many reasons, including the unwillingness of Union Army officers to let black soldiers nearby protect their families. Two days before the riot, the soldiers had been disarmed. Some kept revolvers, but none had heavier weapons. After the riot began, white soldiers guarded stacked weapons. A white army captain, who later told the congressional committee that he "sympathized with the colored people and . . . was sorry that the men could not get arms . . . to defend their wives and children," said that on the first night of the rioting "many of the colored soldiers wanted their arms." "I heard them say we must have our arms," testified Thomas J. Durnin, and "some twelve or fifteen" rushed the building where the arms were stored. "I gave the order to fire," Durnin remembered. "The men had their bayonets fixed, but the colored soldiers retreated at the first fire." The ex-slaves, Durnin said, "regretted that they had returned their arms" and were "very much excited and begging to have their arms that they might defend the women and children." Despite an order to keep the men in the fort, about one hundred apparently unarmed soldiers "all broke out at once" the first night. The next day, the Memphis mayor, advised by an army officer that if the men got an idea of the disorders nearby "it would be impossible to keep them in," promised the black ex-soldiers that their homes would not be burned and their families protected. An officer reminded the assembled blacks that they "had no arms." The soldiers spoke out, saying they had heard whites "were burning the houses and murdering their wives and children, and that they wanted to go out to protect them." White officers claimed the mayor's assurances calmed the men, but a roll call that day revealed that two hundred men were absent from the fort. Their behavior awaits detailed study of the Memphis riot. We have only the testimony of Tony Cherry, a young discharged soldier who shelled corn on the Mississippi levee and who told the congressional committee that some blacks fired at the white rioters, using "old shot guns they got out of the houses."[37]

Far less dramatic testimony by eight Louisville women in 1863, all but one or perhaps two of them born slaves, revealed yet other dimensions of slave family life at the time of the emancipation. What these women and their husbands took for granted about their marital and parental obligations is what makes their testimony so very important. Charlotte and Lavinia Bell were still slaves. Mrs. Joseph Brady had been born free, but her husband had purchased himself and his first wife. After he purchased himself, Mrs. Dabney Page's husband purchased his wife and their children. Freed in 1846, Elizabeth Thompson lived with her slave husband. They had five children. "My husband," she said, "helps me some by his extra work. His old master hires him out for $7.00 a week, and requires $2.50 a week from him. I have a little boy, eight years old, who makes me $1.50 a week, tobacco stripping, and I have a daughter, thirteen years old, and she makes me $1.25 a week." Lydia Reed and her four children had been purchased by their husband and father for $2100, money Reed had won "by a lottery ticket." Reed earned six dollars a week at the "printing business," and his wife nursed "sick ladies." Mrs. L. Strawthor had purchased her freedom:

> I reckon it is about fifteen or sixteen years since I bought myself. I paid $800 for myself and two children. This house belongs to me, but the ground is leased. I pay $51 a year for the ground. . . . I had a husband when I got my freedom. . . . I didn't help him much except with a little money I had before I was free; and then we went to work and bought the children. It is five years since I had any help from my husband. He is down South somewhere, I suppose, if he is not dead.

"I had to work mighty hard to get this far ahead," she explained.

The other Louisville women detailed the difficulties poor urban slaves and ex-slaves encountered in sustaining immediate families and keeping them together in matter-of-fact language. Asked how long she had been free, Charlotte Burris answered:

> I don't know exactly how long I have been free; about eight or nine years I reckon. My husband bought me. My people moved away and didn't want to take me, and they let him have me. He didn't pay a great deal, but it was as much as I was worth. My mistress said she favored me because I was afflicted. My husband didn't pay more than $25 for me. We have been getting along tolerably well since. My husband is as badly afflicted as I am, but still he does tolerably smart. He doesn't get no great things for wages. He has no regular work, only jobs. White washing season he does tolerably well. I was hired out just as long as I was able to be hired, and then they let my husband buy me.

QUESTION: How old are you?

ANSWER: That is what has grieved me a good deal. I can't tell my age to save my life. You know when children are separated from their parents early, they don't know how old they are.

QUESTION: When you were hired out, how much did they allow you out of it?

ANSWER: Not one cent. . . . After my husband hired me, we had to give $50 a year. I am obliged to do washing yet, sick or well. How else should I earn my living? We have never been dependent; we have never been troublesome to anybody. If it is little, we have enough and are satisfied with what we have.

Slave women, like Charlotte, who did not have husbands reported even greater difficulties. She hired out:

> I have two boys. I pay a dollar a week to him [her owner], and support myself and children, and pay my house rent. I have been hiring myself for over fifteen years. . . . My master doesn't supply me with anything—not even a little medicine— no more than if I didn't belong to him. Each of my children pays him $2.00 a week. They work in tobacconist shops. I support them.

If her thirteen- and seventeen-year-old sons each earned more than two dollars a week, she kept the balance. But if they earned less, she had to "make it good" to her owner, who expected payment every Saturday night. "I have not had good health," said Charlotte. "Sometimes I am ailing but I always keep up enough to try to make my wages. I have only one room and pay three dollars a month for it. I live by washing." Although the slaves Lavinia Bell and her husband lived apart from two of their children, they had a deep concern for them. The Bell woman explained:

> I have been hiring myself eleven years. The white people got two of my children over eleven years old. I have to clothe these two children now. I haven't had a chance to see the other two children for four months. The last time I saw my little girl I hadn't seen her for two months, and I saved a piece of clothing I took off her. (*Upon being requested to show it, she left the room and returned with a small bundle of filthy rags which she said she took from the back of her child, as her chemise.*) I couldn't help crying when I saw it. I pay them $72 a year for myself, and clothe myself, and pay my house rent and doctor's bill, and as soon as my children grow up they take them. That one (*pointing to a bright little boy about nine or ten years old*) is about big enough to go. I washed my little girl, when I saw her, and young master had whipped the child so you couldn't lay your hand anywhere along her back where he hadn't cut the blood out of her. And instead of giving the girl a basin of water, and letting her go to a room and wash herself, they made the children go down to a pond, and wash themselves, just like beasts. My husband is a cook in a hotel. He is hired for $300 a year. His folks never give him anything but a five dollar note once or twice a year.

"All I make," she said, "is by washing and ironing."[38]

A vast amount of other data show that Afro-Americans emerged from slavery with far more than shattered family experiences. What these data disclose about *who* the ex-slaves were in 1865 is reason to re-examine how these men and women behaved after 1865. But the same evidence does not hint at *how* and *why* their condition had come to pass. No more misleading inference could be drawn from these data than to argue that they show that slaves lived in stable families. The typical Virginia ex-slave family in 1865, for example, had two parents in it, but many of the early marriages broken by force that were reported by elderly Mississippi and northern Louisiana slaves in 1864 and 1865 had been broken years before in Upper South states like Virginia. Poor ex-slaves living in Virginia and North Carolina in 1865 had brothers and sisters as well as aunts and uncles and cousins in that year who lived in Mississippi and northern Louisiana.

Understanding how these ex-slaves in 1865 had retained a strong family identification in the Lower as well as in the Upper South requires modification of the prevalent "models" of slave socialization and behavior that characterize much of the writing of slave history. Such "models" usually greatly minimize and sometimes entirely ignore the adaptive capacities of African slaves and several generations of Afro-American slaves. How slaves learned and whom they learned from always affected what they believed and therefore how they behaved and the choices they made. External constraints affected slave behavior, too, so that slave behavior and slave belief were not always congruent.* A vast and diverse scholarly literature, however, seeks to explain slave beliefs and behavior by studying little more than *what* enslavement *did to* Afro-Americans. Such study sparks frequent disputes about whether slaves were "well" or "badly" treated, a recurrent exercise in historical demonology. U. B. Phillips, the generation of historians he so profoundly influenced, and nearly all his most severe critics studied mostly what enslavement did to Afro-Americans. Their answers varied. Racists like Phillips found in bondage institutional arrangements meant to "civilize" Africans. Critics, including such able scholars as Frazier, Kenneth M. Stampp, and Stanley M. Elkins, sharply rejected the racial assumptions of Phillips and his

* For a discussion of the relationships between belief and behavior, see pages 268–270 and 365–366.

followers but focused on the same question. A detailed and often useful monographic literature on nineteenth-century slavery, moreover, nearly always explains variations in slave behavior as responses to *external stimuli* such as location (e.g., the Upper or the Lower South), the size and function of a productive unit (e.g., a farm or a plantation), and the attitudes of slaveowners (e.g., "cruel" or "humane" and "capitalist" or "paternalist"). Such differences are very important in explaining variations in slave belief and behavior, but implicit or explicit reductionist biases affect this influential conceptualization of the slave experience. Early-twentieth-century scholars nearly all believed that slaves could learn only from their owners so that slave culture, a source of slave belief and behavior, was at best "imitative." Later-twentieth-century historians and social scientists substitute behavioral "models" for this crude belief but still often contend that slave belief and behavior involved little more than responses to master-sponsored external stimuli.[39]

How enslavement and the decisions of owners affected Africans and their Afro-American descendants needs careful study, but to examine only that is not to study Afro-American belief and behavior. Variations in owner behavior matter greatly, nearly always defining the external limits of slave behavior. But the study of slave "treatment," in itself invaluable, is not the same as the study of the development of a viable slave culture with its own standards of correct behavior, what the anthropologist Sidney W. Mintz describes as "the repertory of socially-learned and inculcated resources of the enslaved."[40] Inadequate study of how there developed among Afro-American slaves what Mintz calls "historically-derived values, behavior patterns, and practices" obscures and even distorts the meaning of accurately observed slave behavior. A single example drawn from the 1865–1866 Virginia population censuses and marriage registers illustrates this point. This evidence shows that most Virginia slaves lived in two-parent households and that many slave marriages were long-lasting. Three questions, among others, need to be asked to assess its meaning. Are the particular data accurate? If so, why did most slaves live in such households and why did many slave marriages last so long? And finally, what do such regularities in slave behavior disclose about slave beliefs? Answers to the second and third questions cannot be inferred from observed behavior. They result, in part, from the historian's conceptualization of slave society and of the social processes that shaped everyday slave behavior. To assume that slave behavior was primarily a function of slave "treatment" promises different explanations than the assumption that slave belief had its origins within a cumulative slave experience. If most owners, for example, forced their slaves to live with spouses, the length of slave marriages and the composition of slave households would disclose nothing about slave beliefs. But if most owners did not require that slave husbands and wives remain together, the length of slave marriages is extremely important evidence about slave culture and the norms it upheld.

Yet another corrective perspective is needed so that reasons ex-slaves retained such strong family ties are properly understood. It also has to do with socialization. Most studies of slave behavior are *static* in conception and in execution. Slave behavior is examined at a particular moment in time, not over a lengthy time. That perspective makes it nearly impossible to examine how slaves responded to changes in their external circumstance and how one generation of slaves learned from slaves in earlier generations. Mintz points out that slavery "gave rise to special conditions of cultural change," compelling the slaves "to fashion new life-styles in the face of tremendous repression."[41] Study of that process requires an enlarged time perspective. The slaves and ex-slaves described in this chapter—those living in diverse Virginia, North Carolina, Mississippi, northern Louisiana, Tennessee, and Kentucky settings—were not "slaves." *They were the last generation of slaves.*

Philip D. Curtin's very important study *The Atlantic Slave Trade: A Census* (1969) reinforces the need to study slave behavior in an enlarged time perspective. Curtin estimates the number of Africans imported into the United States at slightly less than half a million. By the emancipation, the Afro-American population had increased to more than nine times the number imported, a rapid natural increase that started in the first half of the eighteenth century and continued throughout the period of enslavement. Such population growth contrasted sharply with that of other New World slave populations and, as C. Vann Woodward writes, remains "a neglected historical experience," one that "has gone virtually unnoticed or has been taken for granted by historians of the United States." Curtin's study, moreover, demonstrates that of the fewer than half million Africans brought to the North American continent, nearly half (about 46 percent) came between 1741 and 1780 and about another 25 percent between 1781 and the abolition of the legal slave trade in 1808.[42]

A period of between eighty and one hundred twenty years

separated nearly half of the enslaved Africans brought to the North American mainland from their Afro-American slave descendants at the moment of the general emancipation. Only a few slave generations connect these two moments in time. But a social process of "creolization" (the transformation of the African into the Afro-American) was already well under way by the time the federal Constitution was adopted and before the invention of the cotton gin. Culture formation among the slaves, which began before the War for Independence and well before the plantation system spread from the Upper to the Lower South, blended together African and Anglo-American cultural beliefs and social practices, mediated through the harsh institution of enslavement. Most slaves involved in the spread of the plantation system and of the developing Afro-American culture over the entire South in the six decades prior to the Civil War were the children and the grandchildren of that adaptive eighteenth-century slave culture, a culture neither African nor American but genuinely Afro-American. We have examined briefly decisions made between 1864 and 1866 by about forty thousand different adult ex-slaves, men and women who were still together in families and who registered slave marriages at the end of this process.

The choices they made between 1864 and 1866 can only be assessed by examining how an adaptive culture had developed among them and their forebears in the century and a half preceding the emancipation. That is so because slave belief and behavior at the emancipation were the consequence of a recurrent interaction between accumulating slave historical experiences (culture) as transmitted over time through an adaptive slave-family and kinship system and the changing slave society in which the slaves lived.[43] Radical external changes regularly tested the adaptive capacities of several different slave generations. There was first the adaptation associated with initial enslavement, then the adaptation associated with the spread of plantation slavery from the Upper to the Lower South (1815 to 1860), and finally the adaptation associated with the Civil War and emancipation. How the slaves dealt with these changes in external circumstance—and with other changes which they could not affect such as the development of a farm into a plantation, the sale of a child, and the death or sale of a spouse—depended at all times upon the accumulated experiences and beliefs of the slave men and women who had lived before them. The ex-slave Virginia field hands who remained in families after 1865, the elderly Virginia and North

Carolina husbands and wives who registered long-lasting slave marriages, the Mississippi ex-slave soldier husbands and fathers who acted decisively to protect their families, the Memphis ex-slave women who exposed to the public their sexual abuse, and the poor Louisville slaves and ex-slaves who managed to keep their families together were the children and grandchildren of slaves like Samuel Johnston and Lucinda and Abream Scriven and Maria Perkins.

Johnston and Lucinda were born as eighteenth-century Virginia slaves. Upon his manumission in 1810, Johnston was allowed to remain in Warrenton, and in the next five years he raised sufficient cash to purchase his wife Patty, his daughter Lucy, and his son Samuel. He petitioned the Virginia legislature for their freedom in 1815. For reasons unknown to us, the legislature refused to manumit his children. Johnston filed petitions again in 1820, 1822, 1823, 1824, 1826, 1828, 1835, and 1837.[44] At her death, Lucinda's owner freed her slaves. A Virginia law required manumitted slaves to leave the state unless allowed to remain by the legislature. All but Lucinda left for Tennessee. Like Johnston, she also petitioned the legislature, explaining that her husband was William Roe's slave and that the "benefits and privileges to be derived from freedom could not induce her to be separated" from him. Lucinda feared being sold by the Overseers of the Poor, a sale that might "remove her to a place remote from the residence of her husband." "To guard against such a heart rending circumstance," the 1815 petition read, "she would prefer, and hereby gives her consent, to become a slave to the owner of her husband."[45]

Abream Scriven and Maria Perkins belonged to a later slave generation than Lucinda and Samuel Johnston. Each was separated from a spouse and blood kin—children in both instances and parents as well in the case of Scriven—by sale. Maria Perkins, who lived in Charlottesville, Virginia, sought help from her slave husband, Richard Perkins, in 1852:

Dear Husband I write you a letter to let you know my distress my master has sold albert to a trader on Monday court day and the other child is for sale also and I want you to let [me] hear from you very soon before next cort if you can I don't know when I don't want you to wait till Christmas I want you to tell dr Hamelton and your master if either will buy me they can attend to it know and then I can go afterwards I don't want a trader to get me they asked me if I had got any person to buy me and I told them no they took

me to the court houste too   they never put me up   a man
buy the name of brady bought albert and is gone I don't know
where   they say he lives in Scottesville   my things is in several
places some is in staunton and if I should be sold I don't
know what will become of them   I don't expect to meet with
the luck to get that way till I am quite heartsick   nothing
more
    I am and ever will be your kind wife[46]

Scriven, who belonged to the Georgia planter and clergyman
Charles C. Jones, wrote his wife in 1858:

Dinah Jones
My Dear wife I take the pleasure of writing you these few
[lines] with much regret to inform you that I am Sold to a
man by the name of Peterson atreader and Stays in new
orleans. I am here yct But I expect to go before long but when
I get there I will write and let you know where I am. My Dear
I want to Send you Some things but I donot know who to
Send them By but I will thry to get them to you and my children. Give my love to my father & mother and tell them good
Bye for me. and if we Shall not meet in this world I hope to
meet in heaven. My Dear wife for you and my Children my
pen cannot Express the griffe I feel to be parted from you all

"I remain," the Savannah black ended his letter, "your truly husband until Death   Abream Scriven."[47]
    Men and women like Samuel Johnston, Lucinda, Abream
Scriven, and Maria Perkins were not unusual slaves in their
beliefs and attachments. The behavior of several generations of
slaves listed in plantation slave birth registers over the entire
South makes that clear by showing how common Afro-American
beliefs and behavior developed in quite different slave communities. We shall see that the developing Afro-American culture
had at its core common adaptive slave domestic arrangements and
kin networks and that enlarged slave communities emerged over
time out of these adaptive kin arrangements. Maria Perkins,
Abream Scriven, and these others do not appear again in these
pages. Adam, Eveline, Patty, Captain, Fanny, Jacob, and Yellow
Mary, among others listed in slave birth registers, take their place.
But they were just as obscure as Maria Perkins and Abream
Scriven. They are quite typical of what R. H. Tawney calls "the
ambiguous mass," ordinary men and women to be "seen and
probed from different angles." What Tawney says of the Eliza-

bethan folk was true of them, albeit in special ways: "Something amusing or tragic has occurred at every corner; sweat, in the famous phrase, not to mention blood and tears, is thick on it. There are worse points of departure for history . . . than the visible realities to which such associations cling."[48]

TABLE 6. DEMOGRAPHIC AND SOCIAL DATA ON VIRGINIA COUNTIES, 1860

	Mont-gomery	York	Princess Anne	Rock-bridge	Nelson	Gooch-land	Louisa
Slave population 1860	2219	1925	3186	3985	6238	6139	10,194
County slave 1860	21%	39%	41%	23%	48%	58%	61%
County free black 1860	1%	14%	1%	2%	1%	7%	2%
Sex ratio, adult slaves 20+, 1860 (F = 100)	114.3	103.6	105.3	137.0	105.0	122.0	116.4
Sex ratio, adult blacks 20+, 1865–1866 (F = 100)	92.6	93.3*					
1860 slave population by units of ownership							
Less than 5	15%	11%	20%	15%	9%	9%	5%
5–19	53	47	63	59	33	41	37
20–49	23	22	17	15	34	19	44
50+	9	20	0	11	24	31	14

*The over-all York County sex ratio masked significant differences by age. The population included many more women than men under forty, and many more men than women over forty. As a result, the sex ratios differed greatly by age group: 64.8 (20–39) and 135.0 (40+).

TABLE 7. OCCUPATIONS OF ALL ADULT MALES, TWENTY AND OLDER, VIRGINIA, 1865–1866

I. Montgomery County Population Census, 1866

Age	Farmer	Laborer	Servant	Artisan*	Other	Total	Unknown
20–29	156	24	21	12	0	213	3
30–39	100	5	4	11	0	120	1
40–49	70	2	3	6	0	81	0
50+	81	5	10	11	0	107	2
TOTAL	407	36	38	40	0	521	6

* The artisans included fifteen blacksmiths, nine carpenters, six shoemakers, three wagoners, two barbers, two millers, a tobacco roller, a bricklayer, and a cabinetmaker.

II. York County Population Census, 1865

Age	Farmer	Oysterman	Farmer-oysterman	Laborer*	Servant	Artisan†	Other‡
20–29	58	59	9	31	1	6	12
30–39	47	63	17	45	2	22	14
40–49	76	49	14	68	0	24	10
50+	105	28	12	89	2	25	4
TOTAL	286	199	52	233	5	77	40

Age	Total	Unknown
20–29	176	42
30–39	210	31

TABLE 7. (Continued)

Age	Farmer	Unknown
40–49	241	37
50+	265	69
TOTAL	892	179

* Includes eight woodcutters and twenty teamsters and carters.
† Includes twenty-two carpenters, twenty shoemakers, seventeen sawyers, six blacksmiths, two bakers, wheelwrights, barbers, engineers, and boatbuilders, a cooper, and a miller.
‡ Includes twenty-two soldiers and sailors and five other government employees, four storekeepers, three grocers, two saloonkeepers, two clerks, a physician, and a schoolteacher.

III. Goochland County Marriage Register, 1866

Age*	Farmer	Farm laborer	Laborer†	Servant	Artisan‡	Coal miner	Total	Illegible unknown
20–29	19	94	7	1	9	5	135	3
30–39	32	127	9	5	17	8	198	1
40–49	30	99	10	1	13	6	159	6
50+	56	134	9	3	21	4	227	1
TOTAL	137	454	35	10	60	23	719	11

* Ten males aged fifteen to nineteen also registered marriages. Two did not give occupations, six were coal miners, and the others a farmer and a farm laborer.
† Includes ten boatmen, nine gardeners, six ditchers, and three hostlers.
‡ Includes twenty-eight blacksmiths, twenty-one carpenters, two shoemakers, two engineers, two stonecutters, a tinsmith, a brickmaker, a tanner, a gold miner, and a mechanic.

IV. Louisa County Marriage Register, 1866

Age*	Farmer	Laborer	Servant/waiter	Artisan†	Total	Unknown
20–29	221	33	1	33	288	0
30–39	247	43	2	27	319	0
40–49	231	33	0	28	292	1
50+	272	35	2	26	335	1
TOTAL	971	144	5	114	1234	2

* One male, a farmer, who was not yet twenty years old registered a marriage. Two men, one in his forties and the other older, failed to list occupations. Included among these 1232 men were 34 fathers who were either widowed or separated from their wives. All but one (a laborer) were farmers.

† Includes thirty-two blacksmiths, twenty-three shoemakers, twenty carpenters, ten founders, six sawyers, six bricklayers, three miners, five millers, and four tobacconists.

V. Summary Table by Percentage

Occupational status	Occupations of all males 20+ in population censuses		Occupations of all males 20+ registering marriages	
	Montgomery	York	Goochland	Louisa
Farmer, farm laborer, and other laborer	85%	86%	87%	91%
Servant	7	1	1	.4
Artisan	8	9	8	8.6
Coal miner	—	—	4	0
High occupational status	0	4	0	—
NUMBER	521	892	719	1229

TABLE 8.   MALE-ABSENT HOUSEHOLDS IN MONTGOMERY AND
YORK COUNTIES, VIRGINIA, 1865 AND 1866

I. Age Distribution of Heads of Male-Absent Households

Age of mother	Montgomery County	York County
20–29	38%	24%
30–39	30	23
40–49	18	30
50+	14	23
NUMBER	111	145

II. Heads of Male-Absent Households as a Percentage of Female Age-Specific Groups

Age of mother	Montgomery County Percent heading households	York County Percent heading households
20–29	18%	8%
30–39	23	11
40–49	25	19
50+	17	15
all	16	12
ALL WOMEN	702	1162

III. Percentage of Adult Women in Age-Specific Groups as Contrasted to Percentage of Heads of Male-Absent Households in Age-Specific Groups

Age of mother	Montgomery County Percentage of all women 20+	Montgomery County Percentage of all female heads	York County Percentage of all women 20+	York County Percentage of all female heads
20–29	43	38	36	24
30–39	25	30	25	23
40–49	15	18	20	30
50–59	17	14	19	23

TABLE 9. INDICES OF SIMILARITY AND DISSIMILARITY AMONG NORTH CAROLINA SLAVES, 1860

| | *1860* Total county population | | *1860* Slave sex ratio* F = 100 | | *1860* Minimum slave marriages | *1860* Maximum free black marriages | *1860* Slaves in units | | | | |
	SLAVE	FREE BLACK	ADULTS 20-39	ADULTS 20+			LESS THAN 5	5-9	10-19	20+	50+
PIEDMONT											
Orange	30%	3%	95.3	97.0	730	119	15%	7%	36%	42%	20%
Lincoln	35	1	103.7	106.7	155	13	16	6	41	37	18
CAPE FEAR											
New Hanover	46	4	106.7	98.9	970	134	7	6	35	52	15
Robeson	33	9	101.3	97.0	391	281	12	27	26	35	3
ATLANTIC COAST											
Pasquotank	33	17	130.5	123.6	n.g.	316	12	25	16	47	14
Washington	39	5	118.9	99.1	152	69	7	17	25	51	27
Hyde	36	3	115.4	150.7	150	69	9	23	20	48	15
Beaufort	39	5	119.6	112.8	229	167	8	25	26	41	21
Currituck	34	3	120.8	128.2	60	37	15	21	27	37	5
COASTAL-PLAIN PLANTATION											
Warren	66	3	108.8	107.8	1103	94	3	3	16	78	43
Johnston	31	1	97.5	100.9	507	42	10	9	26	55	24
Nash	40	6	95.6	91.1	320	128	9	17	30	44	14
Edgecombe	48	2	112.8	113.2	732	74	5	9	21	65	33
Franklin	50	4	100.0	102.8	574	112	7	11	21	61	29
Richmond	49	3	106.9	102.5	141	72	8	10	27	55	22
Bertie	57	2	98.7	110.7	228	61	5	6	14	75	12
Halifax	58	13	101.8	102.5	135	492	5	9	13	73	40
STATE	33%	3%					11%	13%	25%	51%	24%

* The free black sex ratio differed greatly from the slave sex ratio. In counties with two hundred or more free blacks (Orange, New Hanover, Robeson, Pasquotank, Beaufort, Nash, Franklin, and Halifax), more male than female free blacks existed only in Orange County. For the age group twenty to thirty-nine, the free black sex ratio was 65.0 in New Hanover and ranged from 81.1 to 88.9 in the other counties. White sex ratios also differed. Except for New Hanover and Hyde, females aged twenty and older outnumbered white males, and the sex ratio in these other counties ranged from 86.3 to 96.3.

TABLE 10.　DISTRIBUTION OF SLAVES BY UNITS OF OWNERSHIP IN NORTH CAROLINA COUNTIES AND IN ALABAMA, LOUISIANA, SOUTH CAROLINA, MISSISSIPPI, AND GEORGIA, 1860

County	Slaves in units of 20 or more	Slaves in units of 50 or more
Warren	78%	43%
Bertie	76	41
Halifax	73	40
Edgecombe	64	33
Franklin	61	29
State		
Alabama	76	45
Louisiana	72	51
South Carolina	69	42
Mississippi	64	52
Georgia	57	24

2

Because She Was My Cousin

They are thought low of by their companions unless they get a husband before the child is born and if they cannot the shame grows until they do get a husband.
HARRY McMILLAN, *a former slave* (1863)

Sally's in de garden siftin' sand,
And all she want is a honey man.
De reason why I wouldn't marry,
Because she was my cousin.
SLAVE WORKSONG (n.d.)

They said we had no souls, that we were animals; but you North folk knew we were first cousins, and so you came down and burst the bonds of wickedness. We are first cousins, aren't we? Didn't Adam and Eve have two sons?
UNIDENTIFIED SAVANNAH BLACK WOMAN (late 1865)

A single South Carolina slave birth register, which makes clear the extent of familial and kin networks among Afro-American slaves and shows that their development depended primarily upon the adaptive capacities of several closely related slave generations, is reason to put aside mimetic theories of Afro-American slave culture and to describe instead how common slave sexual, marital, familial, and social choices were shaped by a neglected cumulative slave experience. In this small South Carolina slave community, most children lived with two parents, and most adults lived in long-lasting marriages. Children were frequently given the names of blood kin from outside the immediate family, and the rules that shaped slave marriage were very different from the rules that existed among the largest resident South Carolina plantation owners. Our interest is in how these common practices developed among the slaves and in what in their experiences sustained them, because that is the only way to begin to comprehend the familial arrangements and moral and social beliefs found among ex-slaves in 1864, 1865, and 1866 and described in Chapter 1.

The social and cultural practices of the slaves living on the

South Carolina Good Hope plantation do not require that much
be known about their owner. Slaves on other large plantations
with very different owners and very different experiences, who are
studied in Chapters 3 and 4, behaved similarly to the Good Hope
slaves. These Santee River cotton-plantation slaves, furthermore,
were not supervised by a resident owner. Their owner, Joseph
Heatly Dulles, the son of an immigrant British hardware merchant who had sided with the British during the War of Independence, was born in 1795, grew up in Charleston, graduated
from Yale, and spent nearly his entire adult life in Philadelphia.
The owner of a plantation about sixty miles northeast of Charleston, Dulles died in Philadelphia, aged eighty-one. He was a direct
forebear of John Foster and Allen Dulles, corporate lawyers and
appointed public servants who figured prominently in reshaping
mid-twentieth-century American society.[1]

How a cumulative slave experience affected the beliefs and
behavior of the Good Hope slaves is learned from a plantation
birth register, which regularly recorded four demographic items
about each newborn slave child: its date of birth, its given name,
and the given names, when known, of both parents.[2] Most plantation whites who recorded slave births rarely listed a father's name,
a social and business convention that rested upon the belief that
because a slave child's status followed that of its mother, the
father's name did not have to be recorded. Because it listed most
fathers' names, and also because of its relative completeness and
the length of time it covered, the Good Hope birth register is an
unusual historical document. The first recorded birth occurred
in Africa in 1760 and the last ninety-seven years later, three years
before Abraham Lincoln's election to the presidency. Listing the
names of at least six blacks born in eighteenth-century Africa and
twelve others not yet ten years old when the Civil War started, the
birth register included more than two hundred slave men, women,
and children and covered nearly the entire formative Afro-
American experience: birth in Africa, enslavement, South Carolina
plantation slavery, the development of an adaptive slave culture,
emancipation, and finally life as legally free men and women.

In 1857, when the last recorded slave birth occurred, 175 men,
women, and children made up the Good Hope slave community
and nearly all were linked together by blood and marital ties
that reached back into the eighteenth century. Children up to the
age of ten were about one-third of the community, and about
10 percent of the slaves were men and women at least fifty years

old. One hundred fifty-four children had been born between 1820 and 1857. About one in five died, mostly before their first birthday. None of the rest lived alone. Eleven had matured and married; the others lived either with one parent or, more commonly, with both parents (Table 11). Twenty-eight immediate families made up this slave community. A widowed parent headed two families; three others contained childless couples; the rest each had in them a mother, a father, and their children. All but a few husbands and wives were close to each other in age. Eleven slaves, ten of them at least fifty years old, lived alone.

Kin networks linked slaves born in different generations, slaves listed as members of separate immediate families, and slaves living alone. A few examples illustrate the intensity of these ties:

• In 1857, Patty, Captain, and Flora lived alone. Patty, born a mainland North American slave before her future owner's father Joseph Dulles left Ireland to become a Charleston merchant and an American slaveowner, was the oldest Good Hope slave and died in that year. Three generations of blood descendants survived her. An African by birth, the widower Captain was surrounded by married children and grandchildren. In 1857, his oldest grandson, Charles, was twenty-one and his youngest, Zekiel, a year old. The widowed Flora lived in the same community as her married sons Dick and Mike, their wives, four grandchildren, six married half brothers and half sisters, and twenty nephews and nieces.

• By 1857, Prince and Elsy, husband and wife for thirty years, had three married daughters (a fourth daughter had died in infancy), seven grandchildren, and twenty-nine nieces and nephews. Prince was Patty's son, and his younger married sister Clarinda and brother Primus lived in the community with their spouses and children.

• Phoebe and Cuffee headed single-parent households. It had not always been so. Cuffee and Gadsey had been husband and wife for at least twenty-three years. She had apparently died. Cuffee did not remarry. In 1857, he lived with two grown sons; his other children had married, and at least ten grandchildren and a great-grandchild lived in the community. Probably widowed, Phoebe was still living with five of her nine children. Jack had been the father of the first four; Tom the father of the rest. Phoebe's oldest daughter was married and had the same given name as Phoebe's mother.

TABLE 11. IMMEDIATE SLAVE FAMILIES ON THE GOOD HOPE PLANTATION, ORANGEBURG, SOUTH CAROLINA, 1857

Husband or father	Age	Wife or mother	Age	Minimal years living together as husband and wife	Children in household		
					Number	Oldest	Youngest
Prince	54	Elsy	51	29	0	0	0
Gabriel	47	Bridget	52	33	0	0	0
Mallio	n.g.	Melia	n.g.	n.g.	0	0	0
Ness	58	Molly	42	23	9	23	1
Abram	56	Clarinda	51	33	8	25	7
Dave	48	Sarah	29	4	4	9	2
Burge	47	Rose	50	21	5	28	8
Cato	47	Patty	52	25	8	26	8
Sambo	46	Lena	n.g.	2	2	6	2
March	46	Candace	n.g.	9	4	16	6
Primus	44	India	39	21	10	21	1
Bill	42	Sophy	24	1	1	1	—
July	38	Nancy	33	15	6	15	1
Jake	37	Duck	42	9	7	17	3
John	n.g.	Beck	37	16	6	13	3
Sumpter	n.g.	Sarah	37	15	11	19	2
Joshua	35	Esther	29	9	3	8	3
Ephraim	33	Harriet	37	12	1	12	—
Lewis	33	Fanny	28	13	5	9	1
Dick	31	Rachel	20	3	1	1	—
James	31	Sophia	25	6	2	5	3

Male	Age	Female	Age				
Joe	30	Susannah	32	11	5	11	2
Major	29	Lettice	24	3	2	9 (?)	1
Mike	29	Hannah	25	7	2	7	1
Adnor	27	Eliza	n.g.	4	2	4	1
Geoffrey	n.g.	Daphne	26	4	1	4 (?)	—
None		Phoebe	48	—	5	21	10
Cuffee	42	None		—	2	21	19

"Single" slaves

Male	Age	Female	Age
Carolina	82	Patty	83
Captain	71	Flora	53
Hector	64	Affy	73
Simmons	71	Mary	39
Titus	65		
Major	53		

• Two young and as yet unmarried mothers lived with their families of origin. The twenty-one-year-old Betty and her two-year-old daughter Leah lived with Betty's father, Burge, and his second wife, Rose. Betty had been named for her paternal grandmother. The seventeen-year-old Gadsey and her two-year-old daughter, Betsey, lived with Gadsey's mother, Duck, and her husband, Jake. Gadsey was not Jake's daughter; she had been born when Duck was living with Wilson.

Similar familial and kin connections existed among plantation slaves over the entire South in the 1840s and the 1850s. And the slaves living in the Good Hope community were typical in other ways of plantation blacks. The age at which a woman had a first child, the size of completed families, and the length of marriages in the Good Hope slave community hardly differed in other plantation communities.

• Good Hope slave women bore a first child at an early age. The ages of twenty-three women whose first children were born between 1824 and 1856 are known: they had a first child at a median age of 19.6 years. The average age differed insignificantly. Three were not yet sixteen, and fourteen were between seventeen and twenty. Two each were aged twenty-one, twenty-two, and twenty-four.* Adequate data on the age of southern white women at the birth of a first child are as yet unavailable; hence the similarities between slave and free white women remain unknown. But these South Carolina slave mothers were far younger at the birth of a first child than European women at that time. Peter Laslett finds that the average age at which seventeenth- and eighteenth-century Englishwomen married was twenty-four, and Pierre Goubert fixes the average age of eighteenth-century Frenchwomen at the birth of a first child at between twenty-six and twenty-seven. The only estimate available to us relating free American women to slaves—that of Moncure D. Conway, a Virginia slaveholder who became an antislavery critic—compared southern slave and free white women in the early 1860s and concluded that "the period of maternity is hastened, the average youth of negro mothers being nearly three years earlier than that of the free race."[3]

• Good Hope children grew up in large families. Among those born between 1800 and 1849, only one in seven had fewer than three siblings, and slightly more than half had seven or more

---

* The median age of fathers at the birth of a first child was older than that of mothers. The ages of nineteen out of twenty-four are known: their median age was twenty-three. Only two were under twenty, and one of them was fourteen.

siblings. Family size increased over time. Twenty-three women had a first child between 1820 and 1849, and not all had completed their families by 1857. About four in five had at least four children; ten women had at least seven children.

• Good Hope children also knew their parents well because most married couples lived in long-lasting unions. The ages of twenty-three of the twenty-six fathers living with their wives or their wives and children in 1857 are known. Among those aged twenty-five to thirty-four, the typical marriage in 1857 had lasted at least seven years, and for men aged thirty-five to forty-four at least thirteen years. July, for example, was thirty-eight years old in 1857, and he and Nancy had been married for at least sixteen years. Six of the nine men forty-five and older had lived with the same wife for at least twenty years. Sambo was not typical of these older men; born in 1811, he was not listed in the birth register as a father until his forty-fourth year, when he and Lena had a child. Lena's first husband, William, had died of fever in 1851 and left her with their infant son, William. The boy's paternal great-grandfather had been a slave named William. Sambo and Lena named their first-born daughter for Sambo's older sister Nancy. Unlike Sambo, other elderly men had nearly all lived in long marriages, lasting on the average at least twenty-four years. Gabriel and Abram each had lived with their wives at least thirty-four years.*

* South Carolina did not require former slaves to register their marriages and reveal how long they had lived together as husband and wife. But we can speculate about what the Good Hope slaves would have reported if it had. In 1857, twenty-two Good Hope couples had lived in marriages ranging from four to thirty-four years, and to these older unions are added new ones formed by slaves unmarried in 1857. About twenty such marriages would have occurred between 1857 and 1866. In registering marriages in 1866, the former Good Hope slaves would have reported lengthy slave marriages in nearly similar proportions to those actually registered by former Virginia and North Carolina slaves. About one in four would have been married between ten and nineteen years and the same percentage for twenty or more years. Such similarities suggest far more than that the Virginia and North Carolina registrants had good memories and had not falsified the length of their earlier marriages. They would also indicate that slaves did not have to share spatial and temporal experiences with the Good Hope slaves in order to carry long marriages into freedom. A contrast between the Rockbridge County registrants and the Good Hope slaves illustrates this point. Only nine Rockbridge whites in 1860 owned thirty or more slaves; one owned between fifty and sixty-nine. About 12 percent of Rockbridge slaves lived on such places. Three in four belonged to whites owning fewer than twenty slaves. Rockbridge blacks therefore could not have shared a common historical experience with the Good Hope slaves. In 1866, one hundred thirty Rockbridge males aged forty and older registered slave marriages. Seven in ten had lived with a wife for at least twenty years. Fourteen Good Hope men of the same age would have registered marriages in 1866, twelve of whom had lived with a slave wife at least twenty years. Long slave marriages did not depend upon the presence of supportive kin networks on a single large plantation. Such kin networks existed among the Good Hope slaves. They could not have existed among most Rockbridge County slaves.

The community that the Good Hope slaves lived in by 1857 casts fresh light on slave, not owner, belief and behavior. The Good Hope absentee owners did not break up slave marriages, but in itself that does not explain Good Hope slave belief and behavior, because other slaves in less fortunate plantation settings behaved similarly. Examination of the full birth register indicates why the slaves themselves—denied the security of legal marriages and subjected to the severe external pressures associated with ownership—sustained lasting marriages and the slave social beliefs and practices associated with them. The North Carolina Supreme Court Justice who wrote in 1853 that "our law requires no solemnity or form in regard to the marriage of slaves, and whether they 'take up' with each other by express permission of their owners, or from a mere impulse of nature, in obedience to the command 'multiply and replenish the earth,' cannot, in the contemplation of the law, make any sort of difference" spoke a legal truth. But the judge, like most nineteenth-century Americans, confused law and culture and therefore had no understanding of why slaves who married outside the law often lived together for many years. That fact and much else are learned about Afro-American slaves by reorganizing the birth register, which listed slave births in chronological order, into separate families grouped in generations that are fixed by the date of a first child's birth in each family[4] (Table 12).

TABLE 12.   GOOD HOPE PLANTATION SLAVE FAMILIES AND
            GENERATIONS, ORANGEBURG, SOUTH CAROLINA,
            1760–1857

First Birth Before 1800

Date	Name of mother	Name of father	Name of child
	BORN "DOWN COUNTRY"		
1775	?	?	Carolina
	BORN IN AFRICA		
1760	?	?	?
1780	?	?	Cyrus
1781	?	?	Lewy
1786	?	?	Captain
1792	?	?	Titus
1797	?	?	Flora

TABLE 12. *(Continued)*

Date	Name of mother	Name of father	Name of child
	PROBABLY BORN ON GOOD HOPE "PLANTATION"		
1. 1764	Rose	Charles	?
2. 1774	Clarinda	J——	Patty
3. 1783	——	——	Hagar
4. 1784	Flora	Sambo	Affy
1797	same	same	Isaac
5. 1786	Elsie	Dick	Simmons
6. 1793	Bess	Hector	Hector
7. 1799	Violet	"On Canal"	Ness
1801	same	Major	Abram
8. ?	Titia	Duke	?
9. 1797	Dolly	Cato	?
1805	same	same	Bridget

First Birth Between 1800 and 1819

Date	Name of mother	Name of father	Name of child
1. 1803	Patty	Primus	Prince
1806	same	same	Clarinda
1813	same	same	Primus
2. 1804	Hannah	Sharper	Major
1805	same	same	Patty
1815	same	same	Molly
3. 1804	Affy	"On Cargo"	Flora
1808	same	July	Nancy
1811	same	Jacob	Sambo
1819	same	July	July
1822	same	same	Joshua
1825	same	same	Susannah
1828	same	same	Mary
4. 1806	Sarah	Stepheny	Elsy
1809	same	same	Phoebe
?	same	John	?
?	same	same	?
5. 1807	Fanny	"Chance R"	Rose
1810	same	Billy	Gabriel

TABLE 12.   (*Continued*)

Date	Name of mother	Name of father	Name of child
6. 1809	Lydia	Cesar	Dave
1813	same	same	Marlbro
1819	same	same	Linda
1820	same	Scipio	?
?	same	same	?
?	same	same	?
7. 1810	Betty	Jacob (Jake?)	Burge
?	same	same	Melice
1819	same	same	Sarah
8. 1810	Teresa	Jacob	Cato
9. 1811	Jenny	Captain	March
1818	same	same	India [Indice]
1819	same	same	Harriet
10. 1815	Amelia	Hector	William
1820	same	same	Jake
11. 1815	Gadsey	Cuffee	Duck
?	same	same	?
?	same	same	?
1829	same	same	(?) *
1831	same	same	Daphne
1833	same	same	Lettice
1836	same	same	?
1838	same	same	Doctor

First Birth Between 1820 and 1839

Date	Name of mother	Name of father	Name of child
1. 1820	Rose	Ness	Beck
1824	same	Adnor	Ephraim
1827	same	same	Joe
1829	same	same	Fanny
1830	same	same	Adnor
2. 1824	Clarinda	Abram	Nancy
1826	same	same	James
1828	same	same	Major
1832	same	same	Cilena
1834	same	same	Ellissa
1836	same	same	Renty
1839	same	same	(Twins died)

* (   ): death noted in register.

TABLE 12.   (*Continued*)

Date	Name of mother	Name of father	Name of child
1841	same	same	Francis
1843	same	same	(Girl)
1844	same	same	Robert
1846	same	same	Amos
1848	same	same	George
1851	same	same	Jesse
3. 1824	Bridget	Gabriel	Lewis
1828	same	same	(William)
4. 1826	Flora	John	Dick
1828	same	same	Mike
5. 1828	Elsy	Prince	Esther
1832	same	same	Sophy
1834	same	same	Statira
1837	same	same	Rachel
6. 1829	Nancy	Tony (?)	Aaron
1836	same	Burge	Betty
1839	same	same	Lavinia
1841	same	same	(Nathan)
1844	same	same	(?)
1845	same	same	(Girl)
1849	same	same	Claudia
1853	same	same	(?)
7. 1828	Phocbc	Jack	Sarah
1833	same	same	?
1836	same	same	Jack
1838	same	same	(Stephney)
1840	same	Tom	Adam
1842	same	same	Eve
1845	same	same	Mark
1847	same	same	Miley
1850	same	same	(?)
8. 1831	Patty	Cato	Ellison
1833	same	same	Sophia
1834	same	same	Cyrus
1836	same	same	Linda
1838	same	same	Teresa
1840	same	same	Moses
1842	same	same	Nelly
1844	same	same	Myers (or Moses)
1846	same	same	Mary
1849	same	same	Henry

TABLE 12. (*Continued*)

Date	Name of mother	Name of father	Name of child
9. 1832	Molly	Johnson	Hannah
1834	same	Ness	Ellen
1838	same	same	Paul
1840	same	same	June
1841	same	same	Emma
1843	same	same	(Richard)
1845	same	same	Luke
1846	same	same	(?)
1847	same	same	Titus
1850	same	same	Lawrence
1851	same	same	Ann
1853	same	same	Boston
1855	same	same	(Girl)
1856	same	same	Friendly
10. 1835	Harriet	Cyrus	(Richard)
1845	same	Ephraim	Matthew
1850	same	same	(Rose)
1851	same	same	(Malinda)
11. 1836	India [Indice]	Primus	Charles
1838	same	same	Israel
1840	same	same	Washington
1842	same	same	(Boy)
1843	same	same	Shadrach
1845	same	same	Jemima
1847	same	same	(Jenny)
1848	same	same	Maria
1850	same	same	Diana
1852	same	same	Roxanna
1854	same	same	Patience
1856	same	same	Zekiel
12. 1837	Duck	Wilson	(Henry)
1840	same	same	Gadsey
1843	same	not listed†	Peter
1845	same	not listed	(Boy)
1848	same	Jake	Miriam
1850	same	same	Georgianna
1854	same	same	Abel
13. 1838	Sarah	Buck	Edmund
1839	same	Ishmael	Louisa
1840	same	same	Eliza
1842	same	Sumpter	Limus

† In the manuscript birth register, where a father was "unknown" the space for his name was left blank.

TABLE 12.   *(Continued)*

Date	Name of mother	Name of father	Name of child
1844	same	same	Shepherd
1846	same	same	Timothy
1848	same	same	Anny
1849	same	same	Christian
1851	same	same	Junius
1853	same	same	Sylvia
1855	same	same	Jonas

First Birth Between 1840 and 1857

Date	Name of mother	Name of father	Name of child
1. 1841	Candace	not listed	Lydia
1844	same	not listed	Minty
1848	same	March	Daniel
1851	same	same	Clarissa
1854	same	same	(Celia)
2. 1841	Beck	John	(Benjamin)
1843	same	same	(Boy)
1844	same	same	Jane
1846	same	same	Violet
1848	same	same	Stephan
1850	same	same	Jasper
1852	same	same	Rina
1854	same	same	Richard
1856	same	same	(Boy)
1857	same	same	Reid
3. 1842	Nancy	July	Abby
1844	same	same	Adeline
1846	same	same	Thomas
1848	same	same	Samuel
1851	same	same	Laura
1854	same	same	(Elijah)
1856	same	same	Sabb
4. 1844	Fanny	Lewis	(Simon)
1845	same	same	(Boy)
1846	same	same	(?)
1848	same	same	Elisha
1850	same	same	Gabriel
1852	same	same	Benjamin
1854	same	same	Bridget
1856	same	same	Phillis
5. 1846	Susannah	Joe	Isaac
1848	same	same	Andrew

TABLE 12. (*Continued*)

Date	Name of mother	Name of father	Name of child
1850	same	same	Ellen
1853	same	same	Ruth
1855	same	same	Jenny
6. 1848	Lettice	not listed	Asbury
1854	same	Major	Derrill
1856	same	same	Rosanna
7. 1848	Little Sarah	not listed	Caleb
1850	same	not listed	Chance
1853	same	Dave	Edward
1855	same	same	Linda
8. 1848	Esther	Joshua	(Girl)
1849	same	same	Elizabeth
1852	same	same	Juliann
1854	same	same	Nathan
9. 1850	Hannah	Mike	Jenkins
1856	same	same	Julia
10. 1851	Lena	(William)	William
1855	same	Sambo	Nancy
1857	same	same	Meta
11. 1851	Sophia	James	(Margaret)
1852	same	same	Alick
1854	same	same	Ritta
12. 1851	Mary	Adnor	(Stillborn)
1853	Eliza	same	Amanda
1856	same	same	Friday
13. 1853	Daphne	Geoffrey	Lucy
1855	same	same	Mary Ann
14. 1854	Rachel	Dick	Boy
1856	same	same	Rebecca
15. 1855	Gadsey	not listed	Betsey
16. 1856	Betty	not listed	Leah
17. 1856	Sophy	Bill	Girl

A few men and far more women had children by more than one slave mate, but between 1800 and 1857 most Good Hope adults settled into permanent unions and most children grew up in such families. That much is clear even though the birth register

is incomplete in two ways.* Despite these gaps, the names of both
parents were recorded for slightly more than two hundred children
born between 1800 and 1857. Forty-one separate families started:
eleven between 1800 and 1819, thirteen between 1820 and 1839,
and seventeen between 1840 and 1857. All newborn children in
three of five families had recorded, next to their names, the same
mother and father. Not including the unlisted fathers, forty-one
women and forty-nine men had one or more children. Seventy-
three of these ninety had all their children by a single mate.
Among the men, three fathers had children by more than one
woman, one relationship suggesting possible polygamous ties.
Jacob, who had children by three different women in 1810 and
1811, was not typical.† Ness and Adnor typified those men who
had children by more than a single woman. Beck was born to
Ness and Rose in 1820. His second child, Ellen, was born in 1832
to Molly. After that, Molly and Ness had twelve more children.
Adnor and Mary had a stillborn child in 1851; two years later,
Adnor became the father of the first of two children by Eliza. In
addition to Jacob, Ness, and Adnor, the names of forty-six other
slave fathers are known. Twelve had children by one woman each
and were never otherwise mentioned in the birth register. Eight
of them fathered a single child each. Jack and Cesar were among
the remaining four. Jack was Phoebe's first husband; they had
four children. She then had another husband. Lydia and Cesar

---

* A small portion is mutilated, so that the names of about a dozen children
born in the earlier generations are unknown. More important, nine births between
1843 and 1855 are listed with the spaces for the fathers' names left blank. Those
who kept the birth register could not—or did not want to—learn the names of
these fathers. That happened on other plantations, too. Sometimes, a woman had
a child by an unnamed father and later settled in with the man for whom this first
child had been named. He was probably the child's father. Other possible fathers
included a married or unmarried resident slave, a white owner, a white employee
such as overseer, and a nonresident slave or free male.

† Among the nearly six hundred former slaves residing in South Carolina and
Texas in the 1930s, three remembered polygamous marital ties. Jake Terriell and
Harry Quarls each claimed more than one wife upon emancipation. Terriell had
two, and Quarls three. Lewis Jones insisted that Fred Tate had purchased his father
as "de breedin' nigger" and that several Tate slave women had children by him.
After emancipation, he settled with Jones's mother. Among the nearly 175 ex-slaves
interviewed in North Carolina, one—the former Wake County slave Andrew Boone
—had a similar recollection: "My father had several children 'cause he had several
women besides mother. Mollic and Lila Lassiter, two sisters, were also his women.
Dese women was given to him, an' no udder man wus allowed to have anything
to do wid 'em. . . . Mother died an' father married Maria Edwards after de surrender. He did not live wid any of his other slave wives dat I knows of." Boone and
his parents, incidentally, had belonged to a clergyman. (*American Slave, Texas
Narratives,* IV, i, 62–65, ii, 237–40, V, iii, 222–23, iv, 78–79; *South Carolina Narratives,* II, i, 337–47, ii, 203–8; *North Carolina Narratives,* XIV, i, 135–37.)

had three children; after that, Lydia had three children by Scipio. The names of Jack, Cesar, and the other ten men did not reappear in the birth register. Their subsequent status is unknown; they may have died or been sold, but they may have remained at Good Hope. Not one was again listed as a slave father.

Even though far more women than men had children by different mates, neither "licentiousness" nor indiscriminate mating characterized Good Hope slave behavior. Most women settled permanently with a husband. About one in three mothers had children by different fathers. Not counting two women who each had a child in 1855 by fathers unnamed in the register, fifteen women had children by more than one man each. Ten (perhaps as many as twelve) of them, however, had children by just two men each. Three of the ten were like Phoebe and had two or more children by a male whose name appeared in the register just that time, suggesting that these women entered into second unions following either the death or the sale of a first husband. The other seven followed a different but more significant pattern. Each had a single child, often a few years before the birth of a second child, and had a second and subsequent children by another mate. Lena did that after her husband William died of fever. So did Rose. Ness had a single child by Rose before marrying Molly to have thirteen children. Rose, in turn, settled in with Adnor, and they then had four children. Eight other women conformed to this pattern. Tony was the father of Nancy's first child; then she and Burge had seven children. Lettice's first child had a father whose name is unknown; after that, she and Major had three children. A handful of women had children by more than two fathers. Affy had seven children by three men, but July was the father of the last four. Sarah had a child by Buck, two by Ishmael, and then eight by Sumpter. The other three women—Duck, Candace, and Little Sarah—each had two children in succession by men unnamed in the register. But these women later married, and in 1857 Duck and Jake, Candace and March, and Little Sarah and Dave lived together as husband and wife.

How these fifteen women behaved over the full family cycle—and the fact that nearly two in three women had all their children by a single mate—indicate the presence of little understood slave sexual, courting, and marital norms. Prenuptial intercourse was common among them but hardly evidence of indiscriminate mating. Most women had all their children by one father. It cannot be learned from the Good Hope register whether pregnancy or actual birth occurred before or after a woman began living in a settled marriage, but birth registers and an incomplete marriage list kept by a North Carolina tobacco planter show that some marriages followed the birth of a child.* A small but significant number of Good Hope women had children by a known father and nearly always later settled into a permanent marriage with another man and had several children by him. A few women had children by unnamed fathers. They, too, later settled in with husbands.

We are not yet finished with the South Carolina Good Hope slaves and will return later in this chapter to see what in their experiences sustained the behavior so far observed among them. But the presence of prenuptial intercourse among them first deserves close examination. Two reasons, among others, dictate that detour. Prenuptial intercourse was common among other slaves, too, and no aspect of slave behavior has been more greatly misunderstood than slave sexual mores and practices. "Many of the plantations," the historian John Blassingame writes as late as 1973, "were so large that it was impossible for masters to supervise both the labor and the sex lives of their slaves. Sexual morality, often imperfectly taught (or violated by whites with impunity), drifted through a heavy veil of ignorance to the quarters. Consequently, for a majority of slaves, sex was a natural urge frequently fulfilled by casual liaisons." The misunderstanding on which such analysis rests is not a new one. Prenuptial intercourse among slaves was noticed and misunderstood by most non-slave contemporaries, too. Such behavior had been relatively common in the society in which the parents and grandparents of mid-nineteenth-century observers of the slaves had lived but was later harshly censured by a shifting moral code. Many mid-nineteenth-century observers believed that prenuptial intercourse

---

* Plantation records rarely record the date of slave marriages, but the North Carolina Pettigrews did so for three women: Patience (January 1847), Amy (November 1848), and Maria (November 1848). Each of these marriages can be matched to the date of birth of a first child. Maria was seventeen when she married Gabriel; her first child was born nearly three years later. But Patience and Amy each had a child prior to the listing of their marriages. The birth register listed the father's name. He was the man each woman later married. Matilda was born to Amy and Glasgow in July 1848; the parents married later that year. Patience and Dick Buck married in 1847, two years after their Charlotte had been born. This evidence is found in the Pettigrew plantation birth lists and slave lists, volumes 13, 22, 25, 29, and 43, Pettigrew Manuscripts, Southern Historical Collection, University of North Carolina.

was evidence of the absence of sexual standards and even indicated "savage," or "natural," behavior. Pro- and antislavery biases and mid-nineteenth-century Victorian beliefs, such as the belief that marriage and hence the "family" required positive legal and contractual sanction to be "real," that "sex" had to be subordinated absolutely to marriage, and that sexual "restraint" (the "ideal of chastity") had to be imposed upon all inferior and dependent classes and races distorted the perceptions of most observers. Articulate defenders of slavery like T. R. R. Cobb, James Henry Hammond, Chancellor Harper, William Grayson, and Robert Toombs considered prenuptial intercourse among slaves justification for racial and class domination. Cobb blamed it on the "natural lewdness of the negro." The *Southern Literary Messenger* said whites had found Africans "*naked* savage[s], prone to the unrestrained indulgence of sensual appetite," and that enslavement slowly "awakened" a "sense of shame" among them. Toombs and others discovered that "fewer children are born out of wedlock among slaves than in the capitals of the two most civilized countries of Europe—Austria and France." According to Hammond, an 1842 parliamentary report proved that among Britain's factory population "illicit sexual intercourse . . . seems to prevail universally in an early period of life." Grayson admitted that young female slaves were "loose in their conduct" but hardly different from "hired laborers." Sexual restraint, Harper explained, was "painful," involved a "constant effort to struggle against the strongest impulses," and depended upon a "refined and intellectual nature." The "great mass of mankind" could only "supply . . . their natural and physical wants." A "large . . . proportion" of slave women, said Harper, "set little value on chastity"; "a woman's having been a mother is very seldom indeed an objection to her being made a wife."[5]

The fullest record of northern observation of slave sexual behavior is found among the witnesses, mostly whites familiar with the South Carolina Sea Island blacks, before the American Freedmen's Inquiry Commission in 1863, a record that emphasized the absence of slave sexual norms and confused prenuptial intercourse with "licentiousness."[6] The Commission entirely ignored, perhaps even consciously suppressed, this testimony in its published reports. A few witnesses, like General Rufus Saxton's aide-de-camp E. W. Hooper, said the slaves "appreciate [chastity] . . .thoroughly." But most agreed with Saxton, the Sea Island military commander, that "the [slave] system . . . destroyed that feeling," that masters "never inculcated it," and that women were "paid . . . a premium to breed as fast as possible." Saxton said women bore children at a "very young age," "often [at] fourteen." Henry Judd believed prenuptial intercourse "universal." "Before marriage," said James Redpath, who spent the early war years with Kansas slaves, there was "no such thing" as chastity. Richard Hinton, who had been with the Missouri slaves, "never heard of one" fifteen- or sixteen-year-old slave girl who had not "copulated with somebody." The most important testimony came from two former slaves; both described widespread prenuptial intercourse. Then about forty years old, Harry McMillan had been born in Georgia but grown up a Beaufort, South Carolina, slave. Asked if "colored women have a great deal of sexual passion" and "all go out with men," McMillan replied, "Yes, sir, there is a great idea of that. I do not think you will find four out of a hundred that do not; they begin at fifteen or sixteen." The well-known Robert Smalls was even more explicit:

QUESTION: Have not colored women a good deal of sexual passion?

ANSWER: Yes, sir.

QUESTION: Are they not carried away by their passions to have intercourse with men?

ANSWER: Yes, sir, but very few lawful married women are carried away if their husbands take care of them.

QUESTION: How is it with young women?

ANSWER: They are very wild and run around a good deal.

Asked "what proportion" had "sexual intercourse before marriage," Smalls answered, "The majority do, but they do not consider this intercourse an evil thing. . . ."[7]

That many slaves distinguished between prenuptial intercourse and "licentiousness" and believed prenuptial intercourse and pregnancy compatible with settled marriage escaped the notice of all but a few observers. A visit to the Sea Islands in 1863 convinced the Yankee journalist Charles Nordhoff that "indiscriminate intercourse" did not exist among slave women "to any great extent." Young women, however, were "not eminently chaste." Angered by a British journalist who condemned black plantation women for not being "vestal virgins," Mary Chesnut confided in her Civil War diary that Virginia and South Carolina slave women "have a chance here that women have nowhere else. They can redeem themselves—the 'impropers' can. They can marry decently, and nothing is remembered against these colored ladies." A Yazoo, Mississippi, owner explained to Frederick Olmsted: "They don't very often get married for good . . . without trying each other out, as they say, for two or three weeks, to see how they are going to like each other." (Eighty years later, an ex-slave called such behavior "a make-out.") Harriet Beecher Stowe learned from a southern white correspondent that after a South Carolina woman's husband was sold to Florida she had to take a new spouse and agreed to what appears to have been a trial marriage, explaining later that "we lib along two year—he watchin my ways and I watchin his ways."[8]

Despite their cultural-bound moralism, observers like Chesnut, the Yazoo owner, and Nordhoff were describing aspects of the sexual and social behavior disclosed by the Good Hope slaves, who demonstrated that prenuptial intercourse and settled marriage were compatible. Their behavior, which distinguished their norms from the prevalent Victorian ones, closely resembled practices found in many other premodern cultures. In 1833, for example, the British physician Peter Gaskell said that "sexual intercourse was almost universal prior to marriage in the [English] agricultural districts," but that "it existed only between parties where a tacit understanding had all the weight of obligation—and that was that marriage be the result." "The moral, customary, and legal rules of most human communities," Bronislaw Malinowski observed a century later, ". . . dissociate the two sides of procreation, that is sex and parenthood." In these cultures, marriage did not mean the "licensing of sexual intercourse but rather the licensing of parenthood." Prenuptial intercourse often served as "a method of arranging marriage by trial and error." Malinowski illustrated such practices by referring to the German peasant "trial night," observing that such courting practices occurred commonly in many premodern cultures and were not "licentious." "The same view," he wrote, "is taken by the savage Melanesian, by the West African, by the Bantu, and by the North American Indian." (He could have added the Good Hope and many other Afro-American slaves to his list.) Their behavior also demonstrated that "sexual repression is as rigid and definite as sexual license is clear and proscriptive" in all cultures, and that "regulated forms of nonconjugal intercourse" were not "subversive of marriage." It will be seen in Chapter 10 that the 1880 and 1900 federal manuscript censuses revealed the persistence among southern blacks of prenuptial intercourse, the birth of a child prior to a marriage, and bridal pregnancy. These same sources, however, also show that relatively few young black mothers headed single-parent households. That was also so among the Good Hope slaves. All women who became mothers before 1855, including those who had children by more than one man and even those whose first children had "unknown" fathers, spent most of their adult lives in settled unions, behavior which suggests that many slaves viewed prenuptial intercourse as a prelude to a settled marriage. If a permanent marriage had not been the expected norm, there should have been many more unmarried mothers under the age of thirty among the Good Hope slaves (and later among mothers listed in the pages of the 1880 and 1900 federal manuscript censuses).[9]

The acceptance of a slave norm that placed great emphasis upon a settled union and the belief that prenuptial pregnancy should be followed by marriage did not mean, of course, that all slaves behaved accordingly. "Sometimes," one old ex-slave recalled, "they would slip there and sleep with the woman and wouldn't marry them at all." Another ex-slave said, "Some of them had children for them what wasn't married to you. No, they would do nothing; they were glad of it. They would be glad to have them little bastards; brag about it." Competing values existed among the slaves, as among their owners and other peoples. In describing his 1828 marriage, the former North Carolina slave Lunsford Lane made it plain that he wanted no part of bridal pregnancy: "When we had been married nine months and one day, we were blessed with a son." Charles Nordhoff met an unhappily married Sea Islander in 1863 who had lived secretly with a younger woman for more than a year. She was about to bear his child, and he was "extremely anxious to marry her before the child is born." The man's slave wife consented to the separation. A plantation white noted in his 1854 diary: "The girl Martha, the wife of Willis, is delivered of a Daughter this morning—she has been married only two months. Her mother says 'she makes quick work of it' and seems distressed. I comfort her, by telling her such things often happen with the first born, but never afterwards." The young woman's mother worried more about her daughter's behavior than did the young woman's owner. But the owner also revealed that slave marriage "often" followed pregnancy. Mary Kindred, a former Texas slave, remembered a "l'il song" her grandmother had sung:

> One mornin' in May,
> I spies a beautiful dandy,
> A-rakin' way of de hay.
> I asks her to marry.
> She say, scornful, "No!"
> But befo' six months roll by
> Her apron strings wouldn't tie.
> She wrote me a letter,
> She marry me then,
> I say, no, no, my gal, not I.

Another ex-slave said, "When I was a girl if you walked with a girl who had a baby we would be cut all to pieces. We wouldn't be allowed to speak to her."[10]

Despite the fact that some slaves everywhere rejected the dominant norm, marriage followed most prenuptial slave pregnancies. "If you fooled up a girl with a arm full of you," said an elderly male ex-slave, "you had to take care of her." Men who refused to marry such women may even have repudiated common norms and thereby won such women communal favor or special concern, an attitude that very much troubled Yankee missionaries and teachers among the wartime Sea Islanders. "It was held no shame for a girl to bear a child under any circumstances," said the journalist Nordhoff, and it dismayed Austa French to find that unmarried mothers were not ostracized. "There is no great gulf between them and the poor, as there is with the voluntary fallen," complained French. Such beliefs so upset one Island Yankee superintendent that he distributed a "very simple" outfit of clothing to the mothers of newborn children but only if they were married. Older women approached the teacher Elizabeth Botume "many times" to ask support for young unmarried mothers, behavior which conformed to their belief system. They once sought help for "poor sick Cumber," an unmarried woman who had suffered much in childbirth and was "bad off." They gave "united testimony," said Botume, aware that "we would have nothing to do with one like her." Botume sent a bundle of clothing, explaining that "their readiness to help the poor erring girl made me ashamed." Time and again, Botume heard the "touching appeals of these poor, ignorant, tender-hearted women for their down-fallen sisters." She finally rejected the plea of the old nurse Aunt Judy, hoping to make "this case an example." Aunt Judy heard Botume out and replied very slowly in a manner that splendidly illustrates what Eric Wolf calls the "ritual pantomime of dependence": "That's so, ma'am. You knows best. You *mus'* be right, fur you'na kin read the Bible, an' so you mus' know best. But I has to go now to the gal, poor creeter! Them wimmins is waitin' on me. . . ." Botume understood herself as well as she understood Aunt Judy, admitting that "her thanks and praise were really humiliating." She gave in, once more sending clothing and groceries. "All day," Botume remembered, "her words were in my mind. 'You *mus'* know best.' What did I know, that I should sit in judgment?" (Botume was unjust to herself. She had the rare capacity among those who had contact with slaves before and after their emancipation to learn from them— even about herself.)[11]

Fidelity was expected from slave men and women after marriage. "If a woman loses her husband," Robert Smalls told the American Freedmen's Inquiry Commission in 1863, "she mourns for him and will not marry for a year and a half unless she is driven to it by want and must have somebody to help her." Aggressive slave husbands guarded their wives. Henry Gladney said his South Carolina father ("Bill de Giant") "didn't 'low other slave men to look at my mammy." A North Carolina Supreme Court Justice observed in 1853 that "as a general rule" slaves "respect the exclusive rights of fellow-slaves who are married." Violence, even murder, sometimes followed suspected or actual infidelity. Tackett killed Daniel in 1819 or 1820, following a dispute over Daniel's North Carolina free black wife, Lotty. When Samuel and Mima, the parents of five children, quarreled and split up, another slave moved in with Mima. Samuel killed him. Years later, John, another North Carolina slave, murdered Shipman, with whom John's wife Flora had allegedly engaged in "adulterous intercourse." Just before the Civil War, Alfred killed the Mississippi overseer Coleman after learning that Coleman "had forced [his wife] to submit to sexual intercourse with him." The Georgia slave Samuel Adams left his wife after she bore a mulatto child, and the Texas slave Harry Pope ended his marriage to Sarah Lucy because she had "a child by another negro." Edward Pierce, who superintended the Yankee Sea Island missionary enterprise, had an urgent call from the black Cato, whose son-in-law Alex had driven Cato's daughter from their cabin. The couple had been married eight or nine years, and Alex believed that Rose's newborn child was not his own. He broke up her bedstead, threw it out of doors, "bundled up all her things [and] . . . threatened to kill the first man who interfered with him in 'his own house.' " Other Sea Islanders complained when Yankee soldiers and civilians tried to "seduce their wives" or when their wives revealed "unfaithfulness" by "going with officers and soldiers." The Yankee magistrate and plantation superintendent Elbridge Gerry Dudley had a visit from a mulatto woman and her "full-blooded black" husband. "Both [were] smart people," recollected Dudley. "She complained that he treated her badly, not with violence, however, and wanted to know what she should do." Her husband's first wife and three children had been sold from him, and he and a second wife had ended voluntarily an unsatisfactory marriage. His third wife had her first child by him before a white physician married the couple. Now, the husband complained, she "went out with some clerks in the Provost Marshal's office." (Dudley later learned that the man's allegations were accurate and advised the woman to "go and live with her mother.") Fidelity was also expected of married men. A Sea Islander caused a stir by taking a new wife, and when the couple came forward to marry in a missionary church, his mother rose and protested, "I take Becca (the second wife) in dis han' and carry her to punishment, an' Sarah in dis han' an' carry her to Christ." Decades later, Zora Hurston described conjuration beliefs and practices among Florida blacks meant to restrain men from engaging in extramarital intercourse. A practice by one woman supposedly prevented her husband from having an erection while with other women. "Tings we lub," a South Carolina slave woman said, "we don't like anybody else hab 'em. . . . What I hide behind de curtain now, I can't hide behind de curtain when I stand before God—de whole world know it den." Mary Chesnut summed up these beliefs. "Negro women are married," said Chesnut, "and after marriage behave as well as other people." "Bad men," she went on, "are hated here as elsewhere."[12]

An adultery trial involving only ex-slaves living in Wytheville, a tiny south-central Virginia town, in early 1866 vividly illustrated slave marital norms. Flora and Joseph Hogan had been married as slaves by the black clergyman Jackson Green, lived together for six years, and had two children. Hogan left his wife in late 1864. They were still slaves. He later explained to a Freedmen's Bureau court:

> I lived [with] her without separation until about one year ago Christmas last. I then left her because she had another man living with her. I saw his things in her room and afterwards

saw them in bed together. I was looking through a window glass from outside of the house and saw them by the light of a lamp which was burning. I afterwards attempted to make up with her but she refused to do so, and left the room and went into another room and sat up all night with another man named David. I never had Connection with her after I proved [*sic*] saw her infidelity.

Hogan then broke up their household furnishings, explaining, "I saw them in bed before I broke up those things." Three black neighbors—Susan, Pharaoh, and Daniel—supported Hogan's allegation. Susan, who had known the couple since their marriage, said that because Flora and David were "staying in the same room together" she "had every reason to suppose they were sleeping together." "They lived peaceably six years together," testified Pharaoh. "I know David stayed in the room before Joseph left her. I never saw him in bed with her but supposed that he slept with her. . . ." Daniel had seen Hogan strike his wife the night he left her, said David and Flora shared a room but that he had never seen them in bed together, and added that "it was the general opinion of people that he left her because she was not true to him." Flora Hogan and David also testified. Neither denied sexual intimacy. Both, however, insisted that Hogan quit his wife before they slept together. Flora Hogan complained that her husband had mistreated her:

> He was always drunk and I never liked him. He treated me very bad whipped me when I was sick in bed. . . . I never stayed with any man before Joseph left. He took away everything and said he was going to get another wife. He destroyed everything in the house. After he left I took up with David and have had one child by him. The child dies in November was three months [old].

David, who said he had lived on the same farm with Flora Percilla before her marriage to Hogan, said:

> [I] never slept with her before. Have been staying with her more than a year. She has had one child since I stayed with her. I never stayed with her before he left her. He broke up everything and left as he said for good. I then thought I would take her. I believe the last child was mine.

The court ruled in favor of Joseph Hogan, but the testimony was far more important than the judgment. Flora Hogan and David admitted they slept together but only after her husband had left her. The witnesses shared beliefs about proper marital behavior.[13]

Group pressures often enforced dominant slave marital norms. For at least a quarter century prior to the Civil War, the Beaufort Baptist Church, most if not all of its members South Carolina slaves, punished people guilty of adultery and fornication. To commit adultery meant suspension from the church for three months. An affirmative vote by church members resulted in readmission. Second offenders were put out for six months. The role played by a black clergyman in a Camden, South Carolina, plantation church strongly impressed Mary Chesnut. After spending an afternoon in his church in October 1861, she wrote scornfully of his sermon: "Those who stole before, steal on, in spite of sobs and shouts on Sunday. Those who drink, drink when they can get it." But "for any open, detected sin they are turned out of church." The slave preacher "requires them to keep the Commandments. If they are not married—and show they ought to be— out of church they go. If the married mothers are not true to their vows, and it is made plain to him by their conduct, he has them up before the church." She believed the slaves were "devoted to their church membership"; the church was "a keen police court." The slave Harry McMillan put it differently to the American Freedmen's Inquiry Commission in 1863 when asked if some slave women had children prior to marriage. "Yes, sir," he replied, "but they are thought low of among their companions unless they get a husband before the child is born and if they cannot the shame grows until they do get a husband." Also emphasizing communal sanctions was the former Darien, Georgia, slave Priscilla McCullough. She described adaptations of West African practices. "I heard many times," she recollected, "bout how in Africa when a girl dohn act jis lak day should, dey drum uh out uh town. . . . In Africa dey gits punished. Sometimes wen dey bad, dey put um on duh banjo. Dat was in dis country. . . . When dey play dat night, dey sing bout dat girl and dey tell all bout uh. Das puttin on duh banjo. Den ebrybody know an dat girl she bettuh change."[14]

It is even possible that slave church initiation served as a social device to redefine the changing social and sexual status of maturing women. That was suggested by Robert Smalls and the Yankee schoolteacher Laura M. Towne to the American Freedmen's Inquiry Commission. Smalls explained that church *initiation*—not mere membership—transformed the sexual behavior of young unmarried black women, publicly bridging the difficult transition from prenuptial sexual freedom to marital fidelity:

> QUESTION: What proportion of the colored girls join the Church?
>
> ANSWER: Most all girls join the Church. Generally between fifteen and sixteen years of age. They go through a certain probation and are admitted as members. No matter how bad a girl may have been as soon as she joins the Church she is made respectable.
>
> QUESTION: Does joining the Church make a difference in her behavior?
>
> ANSWER: Yes, sir, the change is very great—as great as between sun shine and a hail storm. She stops all this promiscuous intercourse with men. The rules of the Church are very strict about it.

The *process* by which they achieved full church membership (what Smalls called "a certain probation") impressed upon young and unmarried women a changed communal expectation as to their sexual behavior. Without connecting it directly to that function, Towne detailed a syncretic Afro-Christian church initiation among coastal South Carolina plantation blacks that apparently applied only to "a young girl" (or "young woman"):

> Their church government is most exact and rigid. Those who know about the examination of candidates for membership in Christian Churches say that among them there is nothing like such a strict examination before admission as obtains here. They have *secret religious societies* and *all their religious ways are peculiar.* When a young girl or young woman begins to have *the desire for a change of heart* she ties an old white handkerchief round her head and wears the poorest and dirtiest clothes she can procure. She must not be seen to [illegible] nor to look up and sometimes she goes into the fields and stays which is called *"being in the bush,"* or "seeking for pray." Then, after being in this state *three months* and attending prayer meetings three times a week, besides Sunday evenings for all that. There the candidate is examined by the *elder* who generally belongs to the society. After he has examined [her] and is satisfied that she is thoroughly in earnest

she is admitted as a member of the society, when after under-going another probation, she is admitted as a candidate for baptism. Then the elders of the church examine the candidate on doctrinal points, subjecting her to a searching inquiry on theological questions. If the result is satisfactory, the candidate is admitted to full membership. [Italics added.]

"Then," the teacher concluded, such women "dress in white and deck themselves with the gayest clothes they can get." Towne and Smalls indicated one way in which the slaves managed the difficult transition to adulthood and from prenuptial sexual freedom to postmarital fidelity.[15]

Church rules also imposed a submissive role upon married slave women. Billy, an old black driver much esteemed among the Sea Islanders, lost their respect during the Civil War because of his second marriage. His dying wife called in the teacher Elizabeth Botume and the black woman Hagar. She addressed Botume:

> I want you to stan' witness fur me. I ain't got long for to stay here, you see. I is goin' shortly, an' I can't lef' poor Billy here all alone. He can't fend fur hisself nohow, an' he can't live alone. So I axes suster Hagar to come here and tuck my place, an' min' Billy, an' the house, an' the dumb creetures fur me. I gives Billy to she. Ef you tell 'em they will know it's all right. An' do please, Missis, put this down in handwriting, so they shall not be toxicated about [it], an' [made] contemptuous by the people, when I is gone.

Her husband Billy stood nearby and nodded his approval. "That's so. You is right," he said. "I am confident," Botume later wrote, that "the sick woman considered this a marriage ceremony honorable and legitimate." But the Island "church people" refused to "sanction the marriage of this old couple." Their black clergyman denied them a church wedding. "They appealed to me again and again to help them out of this trouble," said the white teacher. They even searched out Hagar's first husband. He had deserted her years before but when found agreed to 'affix his mark" to "a bill of renunciation." That did not impress the church elders. Botume finally appealed without success to the black clergyman. "Does it not say [in the Bible]," a church elder asked Botume, " 'Wives submit yourselves to your husbands'?" Botume found it "useless to talk with such a man." Billy and Hagar never married in a church but "lived together, and Hagar took good care of the old man, as she promised to do." The elderly couple, however, was "cut off from the church, which was a great grief to the old man."

After Frances Butler Leigh (Fanny Kemble's daughter) returned to the Georgia Sea Islands to manage her dead father's postwar plantation properties, she noticed that "the negroes had their own ideas of morality, and they held to them very strictly; they did not consider it wrong for a girl to have a child before she married, but afterwards were very strict upon anything like infidelity on her part." Moreover, "the good old law of female submission to the husband's will on all points held good." Once she saw a black woman who had been dropped from the church and was "sitting on the church steps, rocking herself backwards and forwards in great distress." On asking why, Leigh learned "she refused to obey her husband in a small matter." Leigh intervened in her behalf. Church readmission followed but only after the offending woman made "a public apology before the whole congregation."[16]

Folk beliefs, including popular riddles and language, supplemented church rituals, defining the distinctive statuses of slave men and women. A South Carolina Sea Island riddle began, "A rose in de gyaa'den [garden] an' a rose outside. What one you take?" The expected, or conventional, answer revealed much: "Rose in de gyaa'den is married gal, rose outside unmarried gal." "Kin lady," an Alabama black riddle began, "is you a towel dat has been spun, or a towel dat has been woven?" A single woman replied "spun." Put together by her parents, she was still available as a mate. She had not yet been "woven" into an intimate relationship with a husband. "I saw three ships on the water, one fullrigged, one half-rigged, and one with no rigging at all. Which would you rather be?" asked a man of a woman. The first meant married, the second "engaged," and the third unattached. Special words described the status of children born prior to or outside of settled unions. Charles Johnson learned from rural Alabama blacks in the 1920s and early 1930s that such children were "stolen children" or "children by the way." And the elderly South Carolina ex-slave Isaiah Jeffries described himself "as an outside child. . . . Mother had three outside children, and we each had different fathers." When interviewed in the late 1960s, the rural Alabama black Ned Cobb ["Nate Shaw"], then in his early eighties, used similar language. "My daddy had an outside chap by one of Aunt Eva's daughters," said Cobb. "Aunt Eva had this

daughter before her and Uncle Bob married." Cobb's father later
married twice. "Never did know my daddy to boast about his outside children in front of his wives," said Ned Cobb. "He'd drop
his head when they'd begin to shove them acts on him, he'd drop
his head. My dear lovin' mother never . . . have a young-un by a
outside man; it never come up against TJ's ["Nate Shaw's" half
brother] mother to have a young-un by a outside man." The
phrase "outside child" as used by Jeffries and Cobb to distinguish
"illegitimate" and "legitimate" children depended upon a clear
social definition of marriage. Lower-class Trinidad blacks in the
1960s used the same phrase ("outside child") to mean "a child
had by someone other than the person one is living with or
married to," and contemporary single western Nigerian women
living in irregular unions with men are called "outside wives."
Such language in such different social settings tells that quite
different cultures (one West African, another Afro-Caribbean,
and a third Afro-American) used similar words to make distinctions between children born in and outside of settled unions.[17]

"Nate Shaw" was not unusual; these slave patterns of courtship,
sexual behavior, and mating continued into the early decades of
the twentieth century. T. J. Woofter reported such behavior in
Black Yeomanry: Life on St. Helena's Island (1930), as did
Charles S. Johnson in *Shadow of the Plantation* (1934). Some
young Sea Islanders followed the "customs prevailing in the
country," but a significant percentage of births prior to marriage
regularly occurred. Woofter attributed them to inadequate knowledge of contraceptive methods but added significantly that "many
of these couples marry afterwards so that the problem is not so
great as the figures might indicate." "Sexual irregularity," he
added, "after marriage is . . . not noticeable. The social pressure
toward sex morality is applied by the church. Offenders are
regularly turned out after a session with the deacons. They may
get back in, however, after a due course of repentance." Johnson
found similar behavior among rural Alabama blacks but explained
it somewhat differently. "The girl does not lose status, perceptibly,
nor are her chances for marrying seriously threatened," said
Johnson of a woman who had one or more children prior to
marriage. "There is, in a sense, no such thing as illegitimacy."
Although sex "appears to be a thing apart from marriage," Johnson observed that there were "limits to the sexual freedom
tolerated" and that "violators" of these limits were "treated with
unmistakable group disapproval." The community was severe

on the man who violated local usages by refusing to assume "responsibility" and "universally condemned" the "deliberate philandering of young men who 'make follments' on young girls." The beliefs and behavior Woofter and Johnson described had been common among the slave grandparents and great-grandparents of these South Carolina and Alabama Afro-Americans.[18]

Before returning to study further the South Carolina Good Hope slaves, we need to focus more closely on the relationship between childbirth prior to marriage among slaves and the expectations of slaveowners built into the dynamic of Anglo-American enslavement. Prenuptial intercourse and bridal pregnancy usually followed by settled marriage are not peculiar to slave populations but are also to be found in diverse "premodern" populations; the decline of these phenomena is often associated with the early stages of "modernization."[19] That decline, however, did not occur among Afro-American slaves and their immediate descendants, a fact made clear in the 1880 and 1900 manuscript federal census schedules and in later studies by scholars like Woofter and Johnson. Much remains to be studied before these continuities are understood. The sexual, courting, and mating practices of African slaves and their *early* (eighteenth-century) Afro-American descendants, for example, have been little studied, so it is hard to describe how enslavement affected such early practices. Nevertheless, much indirect evidence suggests a close relationship between the relatively early age of slave women at the birth of a first child, prenuptial intercourse, slave attachments to a family of origin and to enlarged slave kin networks, and the economic needs of slaveowners.

Enslavement required more than that human chattel produce commodities: it also required—especially after the abolition of the overseas slave trade—that the slave labor force reproduce itself. Few realized this better than the slaveowners themselves. But it could hardly have been unknown to the slaves that the essential value of adult women rested on their capacity to reproduce the labor force. The system put a high premium on females who began early to bear children, inside or outside of marriage. That premium, however, was measured differently by the slaves and by their owners. The owner viewed the birth of a slave child primarily as an economic fact, but the slave viewed the same event primarily as a social and familial fact. Demonstrated early (and then high) fertility greatly increased a married or unmarried

woman's value to her owner and therefore diminished the likelihood of her sale. We know this because most slave females who were
sold were sold prior to their twenty-fifth birthday, and it was far less
likely that any owner would sell a fecund than a barren woman.
It hardly mattered whether the child was born prior to or after a
slave marriage. But the birth of such a child, from the slave's perspective, had much more to do with the social and familial beliefs
and needs of slave men and women bound together in affective kin
groups. It not-only diminished the probability of the physical
separation of its mother from her family of origin but also made a
marriage, and the future of a new slave family, much more secure.
Two people contemplating marriage surely knew that they might
be sold from one another. Doubtless they realized that if they had
children early, their owners would have both economic and
ethical reasons to allow them to remain together.

   Slaveowners' economic calculations regularly mixed the production of wealth with the reproduction of labor, and efficient
owners measured both in their entrepreneurial calculations. The
former Georgia planter John C. Reed declared that "the greatest
profit of all was what the master thought of and talked of all the
day long—the natural increase of his slaves as he called it." Reed
believed that "slave rearing" was the South's "leading industry"
and that its profit lay "in keeping slaves healthy and rapidly
multiplying." That Reed did not exaggerate is shown by the
metaphors planters often used. Howell Cobb, the Secretary of the
Treasury and president of the Georgia Cotton Planters' Association, said that slave women multiplied "like rabbits," and the
American Cotton Planter described a slave girl who could "breed
like a cat." Owner indifference to the fecundity of their women
would have been economic insanity, especially in view of the
steady increase in the price of slaves. Cobb and Thomas Dew
figured that an owner's labor force doubled through natural increase every fifteen years. Special care afforded to mothers (not
necessarily to "families") was therefore perfectly rational. "Well
treated and cared for, and moderately worked," said the American
Cotton Planter, "their natural increase becomes a source of great
profit to their owner. Whatever therefore tends to promote their
health and render them prolific is worthy of his [the owner's]
attention." The Alabama planter John A. Calhoun explained
that "over-work produces premature old age, bodily deformity
and debility of constitution, and checks the increase of females."
Large crops might result, but new slaves then had to be bought at

"high prices." Success came to "those who 'make haste slow' and will not 'kill the goose to obtain the golden egg.' " "Reckless propagation," said Fanny Kemble, meant "less work and more food." A Virginia woman's uncle regularly gave a small pig to the mother of a newborn child. James Hammond of South Carolina gave each mother a muslin or calico frock—when her infant was thirteen months old. According to the historian William D. Postell, "all the rules of plantation management clearly stated that pregnant women were to be particularly cared for. . . ." On the Prudhomme plantation in Louisiana such women worked in the general yard. The rice planter P. C. Weston pronounced that "women with six children alive at any one time are allowed all Saturday to themselves." Accused by his Georgia employer John B. Lamar of abusing the slaves, the overseer Stancil Barwick denied that he had caused "the wimmin loosing children." "Treaty," he explained, "lost one it is true. I never heard of her being in that way until she lost it. She was at the house all the time. I never made her do any work at all." Louisine had worked in the fields while pregnant and miscarried in her fifth month. Barwick claimed "she was workt as she please . . ." and called his account "a true statement of case . . . pon my word of honner. . . ."

Planters sometimes even explicitly ignored the completed family in their businesslike calculations. The frequent reports of over-seers on the Mississippi plantations of absentee owner James K. Polk always mentioned the birth of a new slave child but never a slave marriage. When the Yankee reporter Thomas W. Knox arrived in the Mississippi Valley in 1863, he found a "model" plantation business ledger published in New Orleans, which included blank spaces for "supplies . . . lists of births and deaths . . . time and amount of shipments of cotton, and for all the ordinary business of a plantation." There were "no blanks for marriages." The anonymous author of " 'Profits of Farming'—Facts and Figures" explained in the *Southern Cultivator* in 1858 that he would not own "any gang of negroes where there was no increase." "[N]egro population," he boasted, "increases more rapidly than whites." He could "name a dozen Planters . . . worth $200,000 to $2,000,000 . . . who began with a few negroes and a small parcel of land," but wrote of his own success instead:

I own a woman who cost me $400 when a girl, in 1827. Admit she made me nothing—only worth her victuals and clothing. She now has three children, worth over $3000 and have been field hands say three years; in that time making enough to pay their expenses before they were half hands, and then I have the profit of all half hands. She has only three boys and a girl out of a dozen; yet, with all her bad management, she has paid me ten per cent. interest, for her work was to be an average good, and I would not this night touch $700 for her. Her oldest boy is worth $1250 cash, and I can get it.

That same year and in the same journal another writer boasted that "our negro property increase at the rate of three per cent per annum . . . a gain which is compounding from year to year." These two authors never described their slave assets ("a few negroes" and "our negro property") in familial terms. Nor did they ever mention the value of adult slave men as either husband or father. The need to reproduce the labor force caused many such owners to view the slave woman primarily as a mother and not as a wife or even as a field laborer. Few owners therefore frowned upon "fornication" and, more important, childbirth prior to (and sometimes outside of) marriage.

Scant evidence shows that owners discouraged prenuptial intercourse among their slaves; in fact, only a single such instance has been found. The aged former planter John Witherspoon DuBose recollected that when his family and their slaves left their Darlington, South Carolina, plantation in 1850 for Marengo County, Alabama, some additional slaves joined them. They were "presents to my mother from her father" and included "half a dozen buxom wenches" and "under the wagon cover . . . a bastard pickaninny of each wench." DuBose's grandfather "had passed a sentence of banishment upon Mittie & Amelia & the others for producing pickaninnies outside of the plantation rule." (DuBose also said that during the trek to Alabama each woman "capture[d] a sturdy buck and all had firmly pledged their hearts and hands in marriage as soon as the new home should be reached." He found their courting practices "very amusing and spectacular." DuBose apparently did not remember that marriage following the birth of a child had been a common slave practice.) DuBose's recollection is very unusual. Chancellor Harper, for example, tolerated what DuBose's grandfather forbade. To Harper it was "just" that free society proclaimed "the unmarried woman who becomes a mother . . . an outcast from society," "cut off from the hope of useful and profitable employment and driven by necessity to further vice." But the unmarried slave mother was "not a less useful member of society than before." "She has not impaired her means of support, not materially lowered her character, or lowered her station in society; she has done no great injury to herself, or any other human being. Her offspring is not a burden but an acquisition to her owner." Harper did not advocate "fornication," but his attitude helps to explain why prenuptial intercourse—so common among diverse "premodern" populations—survived much longer among the slaves and their immediate descendants than among the descendants of eighteenth-century New England Puritans and indentured southern white servants.

Reproducing the slave labor force required only the simple *biological* dyad "mother and child." The *social* dyads "husband and wife" and "father and child" were not essential. Neither was the completed nuclear family. But many owners, who did little to discourage prenuptial intercourse among their slaves, nevertheless encouraged the formation of completed slave families. Some did so for moral reasons, and others did so for economic reasons that had much more to do with the production of commercial crops and the performance of other unskilled and skilled tasks than with the reproduction of the labor force. Slave women mostly counted in the calculations of their owners as mothers, and slave men counted mostly as laborers. Although the reproduction of the labor force did not require the existence of completed slave families, maintenance of labor discipline did. Only those slaves who lived in affective familial groupings (and especially the greatly prized slave husband and father) could respond to indirect and direct incentives that exploited their familial bonds. Monetary rewards based on family labor (such as the slave garden plot) and incentive payments for "extra" work balanced the threat of the sale of relatives and especially of grown children. A husband and father might work harder to get extra rations for his children, to earn cash to purchase a luxury item for his wife, or to prevent his children from being sold.

Ideologues among the slaveowners mixed Christian obligation and economic reality in emphasizing the utility of "family government" among the slaves. The Baptist cleric Holland McTyeire urged owners to encourage slave marriages and to divide slaves "into families." It paid to "gratify the *home feeling* of the servant."

Local as well as family associations, thus cast about him, are strong yet pleasing cords binding him to his master. His welfare is so involved in the order of things that he would not for any consideration have it disturbed. He is made happier and safer; put beyond discontent, or temptations to rebellion and abduction; for he gains nothing in comparison with what he loses. His comforts cannot be removed with him, and he will stay with them.

A cotton plantation overseer near Natchez made the same point differently. Those runaway men who outwitted the dogs, he told Frederick Olmsted, "almost always kept in the neighborhood, because they did not like to go where they could not sometimes get back and see their families. . . . [T]hey would come round their quarters to see their families and to get food, and as soon as he knew it, he would find their tracks and put the dogs on again. . . ."[20]

Pressures within the slave system encouraged early childbirth among slave women, but patterns of sexual behavior among slaves, particularly women, disclose that slaves made difficult choices, often beyond the master's influence. "Old Buford," said an elderly Tennessee ex-slave, "his darkies had chillun by him, and mammy wouldn't do it; and I've seen him take a paddle with holes in it and beat her." "Some of them," another Tennessee woman remembered, "thought it was an honor to have the marsa, but I didn't want no white foolin' with me." The worst whipping John Finnelly recollected from his slave childhood "was give to Clarinda; she hit massa with de hoe 'cause he try to 'fere with her and she try stop him." In an 1865 Georgia divorce trial, the ex-slave Louisa supported her old owner's complaint that the white woman's husband had slept with slave women. She had resisted his advances: once she slept with the white children; another time, she "nailed up the windows of her house." When he got into her room once, she "blew up the light to keep him off her, and he would blow it out." The white persisted and even offered her "two dollars to feel her titties." Occasional reports in southern medical journals and elsewhere described how slave women made yet other choices involving abortive and contraceptive practices.* Among Good Hope women

* The Hancock County, Georgia, physician E. M. Pendleton reported in 1849 that among his patients "abortion and miscarriage" occurred much more frequently among slave than free white women. The cause was either "slave labor" ("exposure, violent exercise, &c.") or, "as the planters believe, [that] the blacks are possessed of a secret by which they destroy the fetus at an early stage of gestation." "All country practitioners," he added, "are aware of the frequent complaints of planters"

who had a first child by one man and later settled into an enduring relationship with a second man, sometimes several years passed before the birth of a second child. It is hard to believe that during that time they practiced sexual abstinence. Nancy, for example, had a first child by Tony in 1829. A second child, the first of seven fathered by Burge over a seventeen-year period, was born to her in 1836. Lettice's first child was born in 1848 by a man whose name is unknown, and she gave birth to the first of two children by Major six years later. The recollections by elderly

---

about the "unnatural tendency in the African female to destroy her offspring." "Whole families of women," he went on, "fail to have any children." The same doctor mentioned "several domestic remedies calculated to produce this effect" but was unsure that slave women knew of them. A much more detailed report of similar practices came from the Murfreesboro, Tennessee, physician John T. Morgan in a paper read before the Rutherford County Medical Society in May 1860. Morgan told that some slave women tried "to effect an abortion or to derange menstruation" by "medicine," "violent exercise," and "external and internal manipulation." Another physician had dealt with a slave woman who stuffed "a roll of rags about two or three inches long and as hard as a stick" into her vagina, but Morgan found it "a very rare thing for negroes to resort to mechanical means to effect an abortion, probably less than white women, on account of their ignorance." Instead, "the remedies mostly used by the negroes to procure abortion" were "the infusion or decoction of tansy, rue, roots and seed of the cotton plant, pennyroyal, cedar gum, and camphor, either in gum or spirits." These are medically questionable as successful emmenagogues; it was their use, not their value, that reveals most about the Tennessee slave women. "Old women" found rue "more effectual than tansy to procure abortion." But rue was not widely cultivated. Single tansy was "more generally known" as an abortifacient and was "being commonly cultivated in our gardens." Cotton plant roots, moreover, were "habitually and effectively resorted to by the slaves of the South for producing abortion." "They think," said Morgan, "it acts in this way without injury to the general health." He himself had not known of a case involving a brew made of cotton root but said another Tennessee doctor had found it "a most excellent emmenagogue in his practice—more so than any remedy he has ever tried." Morgan doubted the effectiveness of camphor as a stimulant to miscarriage but explained:

> From the extent it is employed it must effect something. It is employed extensively as a preventive of conception; . . . they take it just before or after menstruation, in quantities sufficient to produce a little nervousness for two or three days; when it has effect they consider themselves safe. . . . A good many women who are not fruitful after the first birth, use camphor freely, and I have frequently detected its use in this way by the effect of secretions.

A Nashville medical journal summarized the discussion that Morgan's paper provoked among its auditors. One doctor blamed barrenness on "the want of attention and care of negro women" and "the exposure to which they are subject as field hands." Another blamed the slaves. He told of an owner who had kept between four and six slave women of "the proper age to breed" for twenty-five years and that "only two children had been born on the place at full term." The white sold a suspect couple but that did not end "the frequent abortions." Neither did the purchase of new slaves. "Every [new] conception was aborted by the fourth month." The slaves finally admitted that they took "medicine," and showed their owner "the weed which was their favorite remedy." That same physician learned from an-

ex-slaves suggest yet other choices made by slave adults. A few—
nearly all women and nearly always interviewed by blacks—said
their parents withheld sexual information from them as young
teen-agers. Some learned about menstruation after the fact.
("When it first come on," remembered an elderly woman, "I ran
to the branch trying to make it stop. . . . But it didn't bother me.
I was trying to stop it for I didn't know whether I was going to
get a killing for it or not. I didn't know what it was.") Others
said they were "most grown befo' we knowed a thing 'bout man

---

other owner about an "old negro woman" who supplied "the remedy" to his slaves
and had been "instrumental in all . . . the abortions on his place."

In the 1870s, the Bostonian George Stetson attributed the alleged decline in
the southern black population to "the root of the cotton plant," "known to all
negro women as a powerful emmenagogue, . . . everywhere obtainable . . . [and]
extensively used." Half a century later, Newbell Niles Puckett talked with three
southern blacks who described medicinal and magical efforts to prevent conception
or to induce abortion, including swallowing gunpowder mixed with sweet milk or
just "nine bird-shot," drinking separate mixtures of "black haw roots" and bluestone with "red shank" roots followed by the juice of dog-fennel root, and a tea-
spoonful of turpentine each morning for nine consecutive days. A vaginal douche
made from a tea brewed from cockleburr roots mixed with bluestone was intended
to induce menstruation and wash out the fetus. Abortive devices also included a
yarn string saturated with turpentine and worn around the waist for nine days.
Other magical methods included the woman's keeping a copper coin or brass pin
under her tongue during coitus, holding "perfectly motionless during coitus," and
turning on her left side immediately "after the act." Even later than Puckett, the
sociologist Hylan Lewis learned from elderly North Carolina blacks about such
birth control devices as "a brew from an unknown root gotten from the woods, a
brew from the roots of a cotton plant, and a brew from green coffee." The published edition of the Frank Brown Collection of North Carolina Folklore indicates
that North Carolina whites as well as blacks believed that pregnancy could be
"arrested by a strong tea made by boiling cotton roots," and that among Ozark
whites "cotton roots mixed with tansy," pennyroyal, turpentine, and camomile
and cedarberry tea were believed to induce abortion. Certain Pennsylvania and
Illinois whites also believed that camphor and turpentine affected respectively
pregnancy and conception. Much remains to be learned about such beliefs and
practices among Afro-American slaves and emancipated blacks, but even this scattered evidence suggests that they were widespread among rural southern whites
and even some rural northern whites, as well as among slaves.

Nothing much is yet known about the presence of nineteenth-century birth-
control devices among the slaves or their owners and other southern whites. Hints
that some whites and even blacks used such devices are found in the testimony of
Richard Hinton and James Redpath before the American Freedmen's Inquiry
Commission in 1863. Both men were northern abolitionists and hardly objective
witnesses. Neither offered direct evidence. Hinton testified that a slave was ordered
by his dead owner's wife "to sleep with her, and he did regularly." "He said,"
Hinton added, that the widow "procured some of these French articles that are
used to prevent the consequences of sexual intercourse." Redpath believed that
sexual relations were more common between white women and black men than
most contemporaries realized. One example he cited involved a "prominent" white
Mobile woman who gave birth to a mulatto child soon after her marriage. According to Redpath, the woman and her mulatto servant regularly had intercourse,
including on her wedding day. "She had taken no precaution on that occasion," he
said.21

and woman." Some children learned from their mothers that babies were born in "hollow logs" (or that "Aunt Sarah brought the babies"). Adult reproductive functions became known to some only upon marriage. A few described a modified trundle bed that hid parental lovemaking from them, and the South Carolina ex-slave Jacob Stroyer detailed efforts to maintain privacy and even to keep grown siblings apart. Cabins "were built so as to contain two families," and Stroyer remembered how the slaves coped with overcrowding:

> Some had partitions, while others had none. When there were not partitions each family would fit up his own part as he could, sometimes they got old boards and nailed them up, stuffing the cracks with old rags; when they could not get boards they hung up old clothes. When the family increased, the children all slept together, both boys and girls, until either got married, then a part of another cabin was assigned to the one that was married, but the rest would have to remain with their mother and father as they did when children unless they could get with some of their relatives or friends who had small families. . . . [T]he young men slept in the apartment known as the kitchen and the young women slept in the room with their mother and father.

Such decisions reveal the presence of sociosexual standards that affected the choices made by slaves.[22]

It was not always possible to maintain these standards, but slaves fully understood when they were broken. The language slave women used in conversations with Austa French in 1862 to describe involuntary sexual intercourse—words such as "mean" and phrases such as "take away my shame"—makes that clear. "Some drivers an' oberseers," one South Carolina woman told French, "make girls mean to save lick, an' dey mustn't eben look sorry but glad. Some can bear it, some can't, so get mo' task and mo' lick." An overseer, another Sea Islander said, had tried to "raise me wid a pole high as 'at cornhouse, wid clothes over [my] head, fo' take away my shame, so I be mean." Decades later, elderly ex-slaves had vivid recollections of similar happenings. Ben Horry recalled that a black overseer on a South Carolina rice plantation beat his mother after she rejected his sexual advances. Horry also remembered that Susan, a "house woman . . . had three white children. Not WANT 'em. HAB 'em. Woman over-power!" Anna Baker's slave mother resisted a black overseer, too. She fled a Tuscaloosa, Alabama, plantation, "hired out to some dat warnt rich 'nough to have no slave o' dey own," and returned after the Civil War to claim her children. The former Spartanburg, South Carolina, slave Gus Feaster remembered watching from the woods as his mother and "ole Lady Lucy Price" resisted the advances of a white overseer. After "he tuck off his whip and some other garments," they "grab him by his goatee and further down and hist him over in the middle of dem blackberry bushes." Some elderly women told of being forced against their will to cohabit with a slave "husband." Blind and over ninety when interviewed, Rose Williams still hated her former owner and the slave "husband" imposed upon her. She and her parents had been sold from one Texan to another. Her new owner, Hall Hawkins, had kept her family together and did not "force 'em to work too hard," but she never forgave him for forcing upon her a "husband":

> Dere am one thing Massa Hawkins does to me what I can't shunt from my mind. I knows he don't do it for meanness, but I allus holds it 'gainst him. What he done am force me to live with dat nigger, Rufus, 'gainst my wants.
>
> After I been at he place 'bout a year, de massa come to me and say, "You gwine live with Rufus in dat cabin over yonder. Go fix it for livin'." I's 'bout sixteen year old and has no larnin', and I's jus' igno'mus chile. I's thought dat him mean for me to tend de cabin for Rufus and some other niggers. Well, dat am start de pestigation for me.
>
> I's took charge of de cabin after work am done and fixes supper. Now, I don't like dat Rufus, 'cause he a bully. He am big and 'cause he so, he think everybody do what him say. We'uns has supper, den I goes here and dere talkin', till I's ready for sleep and den I gits in de bunk. After I's in, dat nigger come and crawl in de bunk with me 'fore I knows it. I says, "What you means, you fool nigger?" He say for me to hush de mouth. "Dis my bunk, too," he say.
>
> "You's teched in de head. Git out," I's told him, and I puts de feet 'gainst him and give him a shove and out he go on de floor 'fore he knew what I's doin'. Dat nigger jump up and he mad. He look like de wild bear. He starts for de bunk and I jumps quick for de poker. It am 'bout three feet long and when he comes at me I lets him have it over de head. Did dat nigger stop in he tracks? I's say he did. He looks at me steady for a minute and you's could tell he thinkin' hard. Den he go and set on de bench and say, "Jus' wait. You thinks it am smart, but you's am foolish in de head. Dey's gwine larn you somethin'."

"Hush you big mouth and stay 'way from dis nigger, dat all I wants," I say, and jus' sets and hold dat poker in de hand. He jus' sets, lookin' like de bull. Dere we'uns sets and sets for 'bout an hour and den he go out and I bars de door.

De nex' day I goes to de missy and tells her what Rufus wants and missy say dat am de massa's wishes. She say, "Yous am de portly gal and Rufus am de portly man. De massa wants yu-uns fer to bring forth portly chillen."

I's thinkin' 'bout what de missy say, but say to myse'f, "I's not gwine live with dat Rufus." Dat night when he come in de cabin, I grabs de poker and sits on de bench and says, "Git 'way from me, nigger, 'fore I busts yous brains out and stomp on dem." He say nothin' and git out.

De nex' day de massa call me and tell me, "Woman, I's pay big money for you and I's done dat for de cause I wants yous to raise me chillens. I's put yous to live with Rufus for dat purpose. Now, if you doesn't want whippin' at de stake, yous do what I wants."

I thinks 'bout massa buyin' me offen de block and savin' me from bein' sep'rated from my folks and 'bout bein' whipped at de stake. Dere it am. What am I's to do? So I 'cides to do as de massa wish and so I yields.

When we'uns am given freedom, Massa Hawkins tells us we can stay and work for wages or share crop de land. Some stays and some goes. My folks and me stays. We works de land on shares for three years, den moved to other land near by. I stays with my folks till they dies.

Although she had two children by him, Rose Williams quit her "husband." "I never marries," she explained, " 'cause one 'sperience am 'nough for this nigger. After what I done for de massa, I's never wants no truck with any man. De lawd forgive dis cullud woman, but he have to 'scuse me and look for some others for to 'plenish de earth." Another ex-slave, her daughter, then pregnant, had made a different decision. "I used to have one [baby] every Christmas," she explained to the Yankee schoolteacher Lucy Chase, "but when I had six, I put a stop to it, and had only one every other year." "I think they have too many children here," she said of the refugee Virginia slave women in 1863, adding wryly that "the business better kind uh dry up till things is more settled."[23]

Such evidence shows that slaves made limited but highly significant choices affecting their social and sexual being. On this matter, as on others, the Good Hope plantation slaves can tell us much. Duck, Candace, Lettice, and Little Sarah each had children by unnamed fathers in the 1840s and early 1850s. All still lived on the plantation in 1857. That meant that sale—a punishment all owners could use—had not been used to force these pregnant women either to take husbands or even to name the fathers of newborn children. These few women may have been punished in other ways; we do not know. But the choice they made must have been available to all Good Hope women, nearly all of whom named the fathers of their first-born children and regularly settled into permanent unions with them.

Slaves like the typical Good Hope wife and mother chose particular alternatives more regularly than others, choices shaped by slave norms transmitted from one slave generation to another. That is learned by linking together the separate generations of Good Hope immediate families listed in Table 12 and then examining the marital and blood ties that developed among them (Chart 1). We can see how it became possible for the slaves of one generation to absorb changing experiences and pass their meaning on to the next so that cumulative experiences rooted in generational slave familial connections became the primary—not the only—source of an adaptive Afro-American culture. Chart 1, which includes all marriages between 1800 and 1857 and lists all children born in these years, shows the existence over more than half a century of well-defined immediate families bound together by increasingly complex blood and marital ties. The names of thirty-two of forty-two children born in families that started in the 1800–1819 generation are known. Twenty-six of them married and later became parents. Sambo, Daphne, and Phoebe married spouses who had not been born Good Hope slaves. Seven others (Susannah, Mary, Harriet, Dave, Joshua, July, and Lettice) married the grandchildren of those "starting" families. Susannah, Mary, and Harriet, for example, married the grandsons of Fanny and Chance (Joe, Adnor, and Ephraim). The other sixteen men and women married people like themselves, the children of the 1800–1819 generation. The twenty-six men and women born in immediate families that started between 1800 and 1819 became the core of the Good Hope slave community that developed in the half century preceding the general emancipation. Within their new immediate families, they became the parents of two-thirds of the children born between 1800 and 1857. Nearly all of the remaining children were their grandchildren.

Most Good Hope marriages lasted for many years, and parents

Chart 1. Family and Kinship Structure, Good Hope Plantation Slaves, South Carolina, 1774–1857

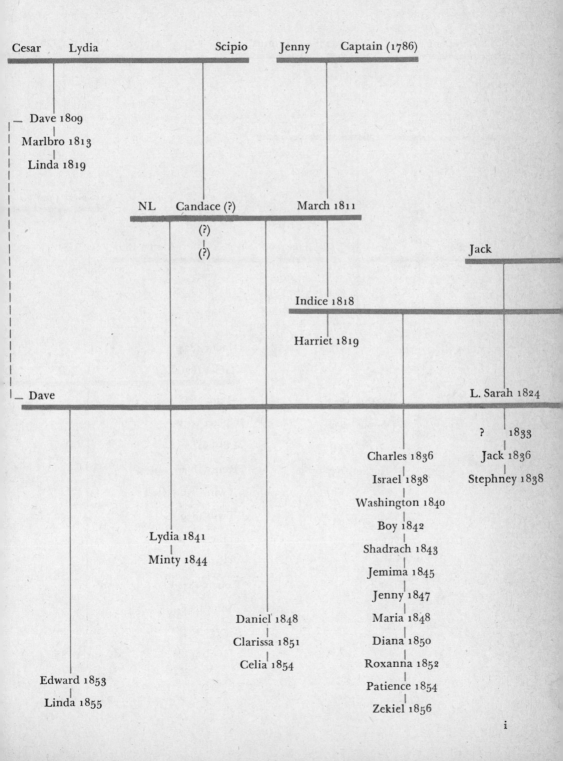

i

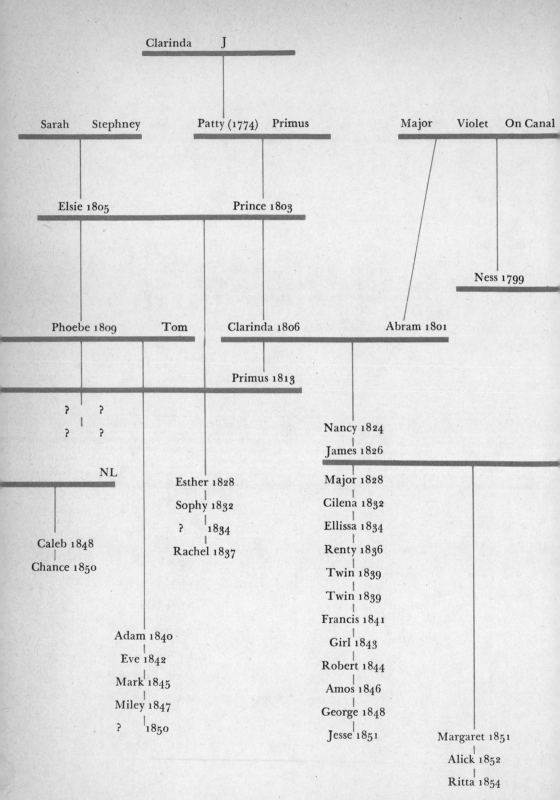

Clarinda   J

Sarah   Stephney   Patty (1774)   Primus   Major   Violet   On Canal

Elsie 1805   Prince 1803

Ness 1799

Phoebe 1809   Tom   Clarinda 1806   Abram 1801

Primus 1813

?   ?

?   ?

Nancy 1824

James 1826

NL

Esther 1828   Major 1828

Sophy 1832   Cilena 1832

?   1834   Ellissa 1834

Caleb 1848   Rachel 1837   Renty 1836

Chance 1850   Twin 1839

Twin 1839

Francis 1841

Girl 1843

Adam 1840   Robert 1844

Eve 1842   Amos 1846

Mark 1845   George 1848

Miley 1847

?   1850   Jesse 1851   Margaret 1851

Alick 1852

Ritta 1854

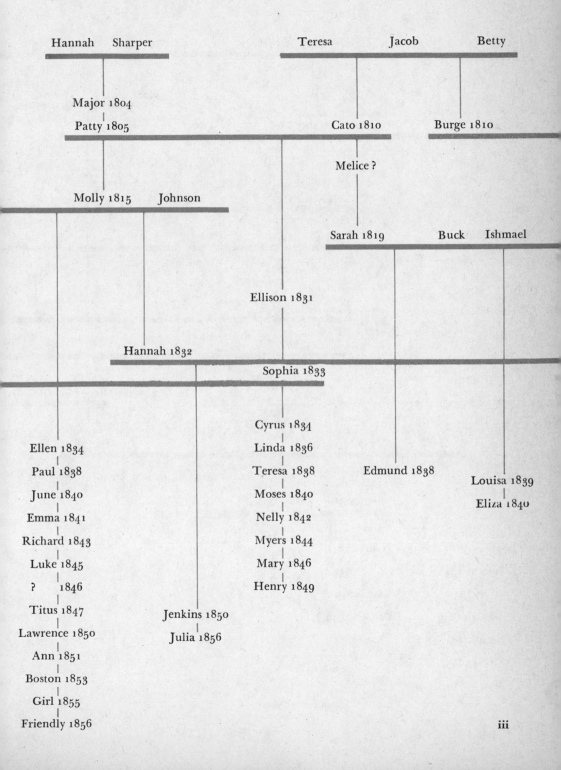

Hannah   Sharper

Teresa   Jacob   Betty

Major 1804
Patty 1805

Cato 1810

Burge 1810

Melice ?

Molly 1815   Johnson

Sarah 1819   Buck   Ishmael

Ellison 1831

Hannah 1832

Sophia 1833

Cyrus 1834
Linda 1836
Teresa 1838
Moses 1840
Nelly 1842
Myers 1844
Mary 1846
Henry 1849

Edmund 1838

Louisa 1839
Eliza 1840

Ellen 1834
Paul 1838
June 1840
Emma 1841
Richard 1843
Luke 1845
?   1846
Titus 1847
Lawrence 1850
Ann 1851
Boston 1853
Girl 1855
Friendly 1856

Jenkins 1850
Julia 1856

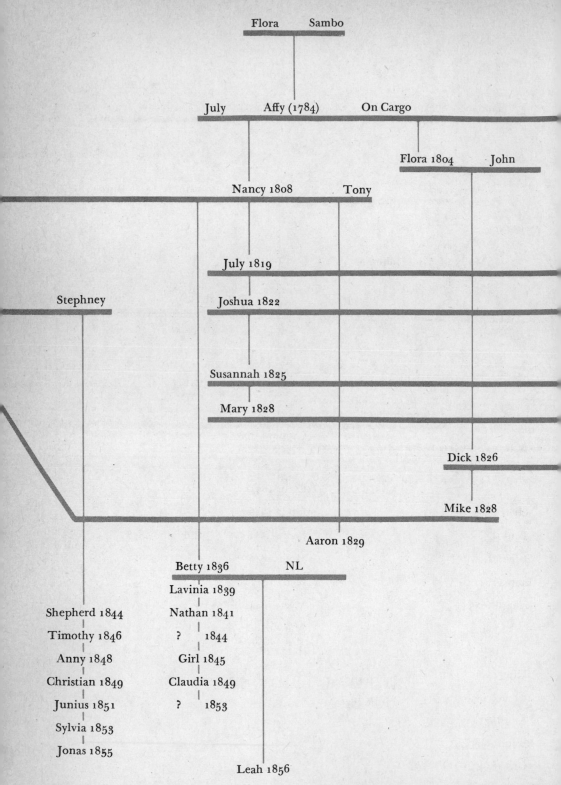

Flora   Sambo

July   Affy (1784)   On Cargo

Flora 1804   John

Nancy 1808   Tony

July 1819

Stephney

Joshua 1822

Susannah 1825

Mary 1828

Dick 1826

Mike 1828

Aaron 1829

Betty 1836   NL

Lavinia 1839

Shepherd 1844   Nathan 1841

Timothy 1846   ?   1844

Anny 1848   Girl 1845

Christian 1849   Claudia 1849

Junius 1851   ?   1853

Sylvia 1853

Jonas 1855

Leah 1856

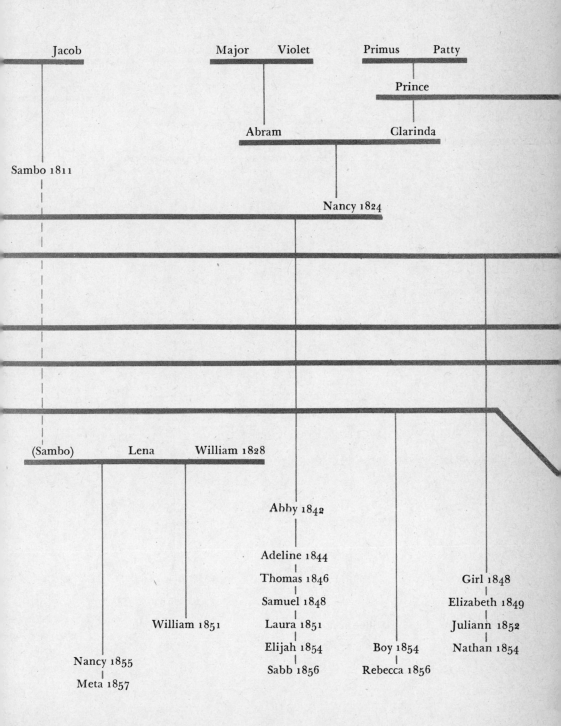

Jacob

Major   Violet

Primus   Patty

Prince

Abram   Clarinda

Sambo 1811

Nancy 1824

(Sambo)   Lena   William 1828

Abby 1842

Adeline 1844

Thomas 1846

Samuel 1848

William 1851   Laura 1851

Elijah 1854

Nancy 1855   Sabb 1856

Meta 1857

Girl 1848

Elizabeth 1849

Juliann 1852

Boy 1854   Nathan 1854

Rebecca 1856

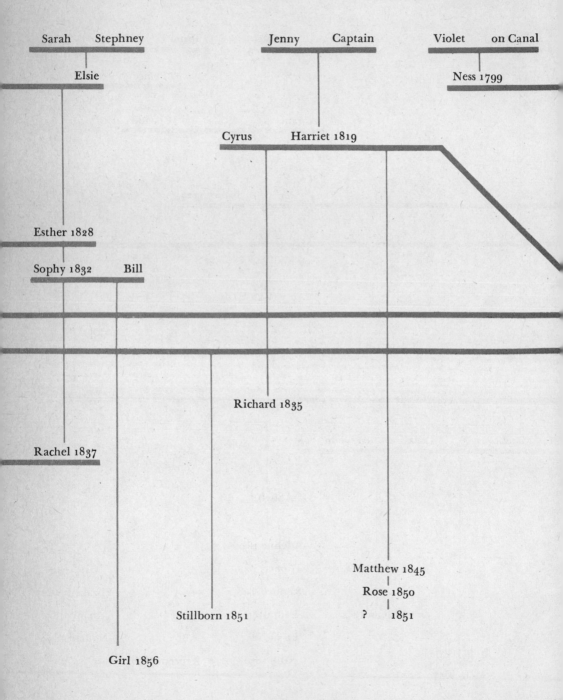

Sarah   Stephney

Elsie

Jenny   Captain

Violet   on Canal

Ness 1799

Cyrus   Harriet 1819

Esther 1828

Sophy 1832   Bill

Richard 1835

Rachel 1837

Matthew 1845

Rose 1850

Stillborn 1851

?   1851

Girl 1856

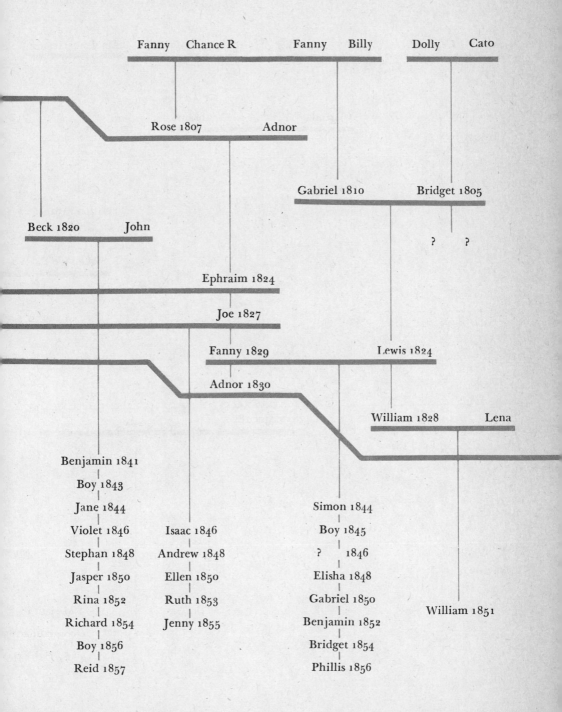

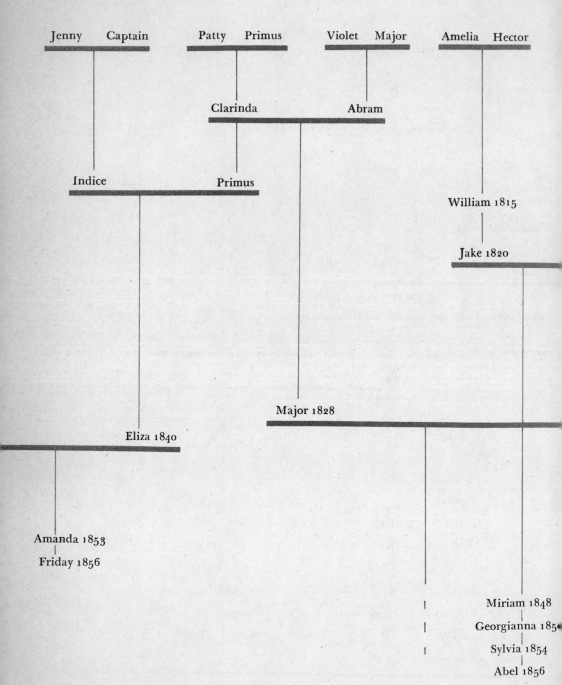

Jenny   Captain   Patty   Primus   Violet   Major   Amelia   Hector

Clarinda   Abram

Indice   Primus

William 1815

Jake 1820

Major 1828

Eliza 1840

Amanda 1853

Friday 1856

Miriam 1848

Georgianna 185

Sylvia 1854

Abel 1856

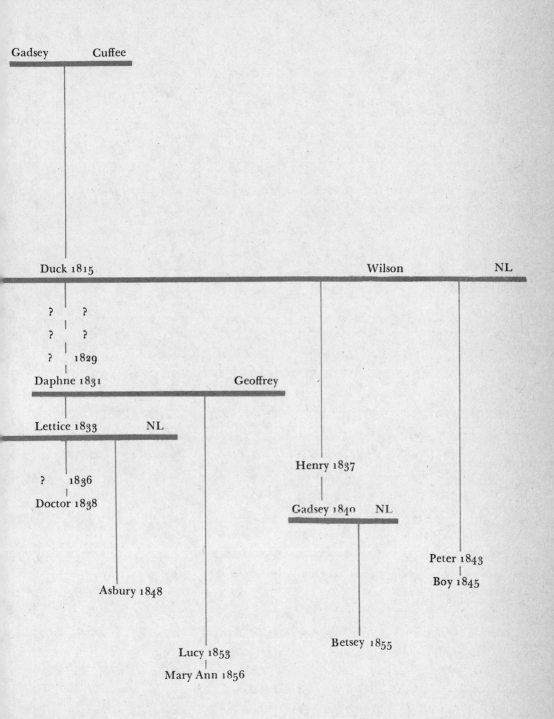

Gadsey   Cuffee

Duck 1815   Wilson   NL

       ?   ?
       ?   ?
       ?   1829
Daphne 1831   Geoffrey

Lettice 1833   NL

       ?   1836
Doctor 1838   Henry 1837

                                                    Gadsey 1840   NL

                                                                                Peter 1843
                                                                                Boy 1845
             Asbury 1848

        Lucy 1853   Betsey 1855
      Mary Ann 1856

Register of Good Hope

Year of Birth	No	Date of Birth		Name	Mother	Father	Time of death	Age
117 living 1847	147	May	17	Jenny	India	Primus	1847 Aug	3 mo.
	148	Oct	22	Miley	Phebe	Tom		
3 Births 120 2 deaths 118	149	Nov	5	Titus	Molly	Ness		
1848	150	Jany	1	Elisha	Fanny	Lewis		1
	151	Feby	9	Anny	Sarah	Sumter		
	152	June	20	Maria	India	Primus		
	153	July	1	Asbury	Lettice			
	154	July	4	Stephen	Beck	John		
	155	Aug.	7	Caleb	L. Sarah			
	156	Nov	7	George	Clarinda	Abram		
	157	"	14	Daniel	Candace	March		
	158	"	16	Miriam	Duck	Jake		
	159	"	27	Samuel	Nanny	July		
	160	"	30	Will	Esther	Joshua	1848 Dec 10	10 d.
12 Births 130 1 death 139	161	Dec	31	Andrew	Susanna			
1849	162	Aug	10	Henry	Patty	Cato		
	163	Aug	18	Claudia	Amey	Burge		
	164	Nov	21	Elizabeth	Esther	Joshua		
4 Births 2 deaths 31	165	Nov	28	Christian	Sarah	Sumter		
1850	166	Jany	3	Jenkins	Hannah	Mike		
	167	Feby	7	Lawrence	Molly	Ness		
	168	Feby	18	Matthew	Phebe	Tom	1851 Jany 23	11 mo.
	169	April	23	Diana	India	Primus		
	170	May	16	Jaspar	Beck	John		
	171	July	15	Chance	L. Sarah			
	172	Aug	2	Gabriel	Fanny	Lewis		
	173	Nov	8	Peter	Harriet	Ephraim	1851 March 19	4 mo.
	174	Nov	29	Georgiana	Duck	Jake		
10 Births no deaths 141	175	Dec	6	Ellen	Susanna	Joe		
1851	176	Jany	17	Margaret	Sophia	James	1851 Mch 12	2 mo.
	177	May	11	Ann	Molly	Ness		
	178	April	27	Jesse	Clarinda	Abram		
	179	June	12	Junius	Sarah	Sumter		
	180	Aug	26	William	Lena	William		

Page from Slave Birth Register, Good Hope Plantation, Orangeburg, South Carolina, 1760–1857

and children in these settled immediate families also increasingly became a part of expanding kin networks. Affinal and consanguinal ties bound together this small group, involving several generations (the first including some native Africans and the last many young slaves who lived through the Civil War and Reconstruction and themselves probably became the parents of twentieth-century Afro-Americans). Slave children born in the 1840s or the 1850s grew up in a slave community made up of interrelated but well-defined immediate families. Such ties rooted them in a shared Afro-American past and helped define the identity of particular men, women, and children, allowing slave children to absorb values from parents, grandparents, other adult kin, and adult non-kin. They were not socialized simply by an owner or an overseer; the choices they later made as adults were shaped by socializing experiences rooted within the developing slave community itself.

The development of intra- and intergenerational ties is illustrated by examining three elderly blacks in 1857—Patty, Affy, and Captain—and those descended from them. In 1857, Captain and Affy were in their early seventies, and Patty died that year, aged eighty-three. Captain was a native African; his parents are unknown. Affy's parents were Flora and Sambo, and Patty's were Clarinda and J_____. Patty's daughter Clarinda, named for a grandmother probably born in the 1740s or the 1750s, married Abram, and they had their first child in 1824 and their thirteenth in 1851. Some of Clarinda and Abram's children also married and had children by 1857. Together with Affy and Captain, Clarinda helped form three of the twelve families that started between 1800 and 1819. By 1857, these three elderly blacks had seen eighty-two grandchildren and twenty-four great-grandchildren born on the Good Hope plantation. (Some double-counting is involved in these numbers.*) About two in five children born between 1800 and 1857 had blood ties to these three persons. Nearly one in four of their grandchildren and great-grandchildren had died by 1857, but some of the twenty-seven born in the 1850s and still alive in 1857 probably lived into the early twentieth century and retained

---

* Three of Patty's granddaughters (Esther, Rachel, and Nancy) married Affy's sons Joshua and July and Affy's grandson Dick. Captain's daughter India married Patty's son Primus. These unions between generations cause some double-counting. But taking them into account, we are still left with seventy-eight *different* grandchildren and great-grandchildren born to the children and grandchildren of Patty, Captain, and Affy.

some awareness of a grandparent, not to mention slave parents, siblings, aunts and uncles, and cousins.

Their explicit awareness of kin ties is disclosed by the way in which the Good Hope slaves selected marital partners and by the names given to many newborn children. A few Good Hope slaves took spouses sold into the plantation or living off of it; most married into the twelve families that had started between 1800 and 1819. By the 1840s and 1850s, most young adult slaves had many blood relatives on the plantation. But only one marriage between 1800 and 1857 involved slaves with close blood ties; Fanny and Lewis had the same grandmother but different grandfathers. Not another union brought together a husband and wife as close to one another as first cousins. Exogamous beliefs existed among the Good Hope slaves, restraints upon marriage fixed by kinship ties. Kinship beliefs are necessary for marital exogamy to exist, and where rules of exogamy exist, as Malinowski points out, "it is clear that repression acts with at least as great force as with us." The slaves' toleration of prenuptial intercourse, therefore, did not imply indiscriminate mating.[24]*

The strength and pervasiveness of slave exogamous beliefs is indicated by their persistence over time on the Good Hope, by their presence among other plantation slaves as will be seen in Chapters 4 and 5, and by yet other evidence. In 1828, Mississippi blacks, their number unknown but most if not all of them probably slaves, posed the following question to a local Baptist Association: "Is it gospel for a Baptist Church to hold members in fellowship who have married relations nearer than Cousins?" It remains unclear whether they were concerned about the practices of fellow-slaves or white church members, but it is their concern over the relationship between church membership and marital rules that is important. A secular work song recollected by the ex-slave Allen Parker is entirely unambiguous in its meaning:

> Sally's in de garden siftin' sand,
> And all she want is a honey man.
> De reason why I wouldn't marry,
> Because she was my cousin.
>
> O, row de boat ashore, hey, hey,
> Sally's in de garden siftin' sand.

* We cannot tell from the available evidence whether the taboo against cousin marriage also applied to prenuptial intercourse.

Neither Parker nor the unknown Mississippi blacks were Good Hope slaves, and that is what makes this evidence so important. In the 1930s, the aged Phillis Thomas, who had been a slave child in Texas, recollected yet another song that emphasized exogamous slave mores:

> Herodias go down to de river one day,
> Want to know what John Baptist have to say.
> John spoke de words at de risk of he life,
> Not lawful to marry you brudder's wife.

Two children of slave parents who had ended up in Arkansas—Lizzie Johnson and Cora Horton—told federal interviewers similar stories about how sale had inadvertently resulted in marriages that violated the primary incest taboo shared by slaves and nonslaves. Lizzie Johnson's Holly Springs, Mississippi, parents had known a man who "married a woman after freedom and found out she was his mother." He had been sold from her when an infant. "They quit," Johnson said, "and he married ag'in. He had a scar on his thigh she recollected. The scar was right there when he was grown. That brought up more talk and they traced him up to be her own boy." Cora Horton's slave parents had come to Arkansas from Georgia via Tennessee, and she heard a similar story from her grandmother. "I don't think these people were held accountable for that, do you?" she asked the interviewer. Cora Horton's people and those of these other women grew up far from the South Carolina Good Hope plantation. Taboos rooted in exogamous beliefs had traveled with slaves in the forced migration that carried hundreds of thousands of blacks from the Upper to the Lower South.[25]

Although rules defining the choice of marital partners existed among slaves and their owners, the Good Hope slaves had not copied the first-cousin marriage taboo from their owners. That is proved by the simple fact that no such taboo existed among the South Carolina planters. Drawing from the 1860 federal manuscript census, Chalmers Gaston Davidson has sketched a collective portrait of the 440 South Carolina men and women (all but forty born in that state) who owned at least one hundred slaves. "They were most amazingly interwed," concludes Davidson, "the marriages of cousins being almost the rule rather than the exception. . . . Nor was this a sectional phenomenon. The Gists of up-country Union, the Mobleys of Fairfield, the Ellerbes of

Chesterfield, and the Westons and Adamses of Lower Richland were altogether as inbred by 1860 as were the Fripps of St. Helena's Parish, the Jenkins-Townsend-Seabrook clan of Edisto Island, or the Maners, Roberts, and Lawtons of St. Peters. The separate septs of Allston, Heyward, and Porcher apparently expected and were expected to marry only within their circle of blood or bond." Intensive endogamy—blood-cousin marriage actually increased in importance over time—also existed among eighteenth-century Prince George's County, Maryland, slaveowning whites, a pattern uncovered by Allen Kulikoff. Slaveowners there were marrying close blood kin at the height of the African slave trade to the mainland North American colonies, a finding showing that marital rules among slaves and their owners had independent histories. But marriage and kinship among eighteenth- and early-nineteenth-century southern whites need far more study before it can be argued that exogamous rules among the slaves either had their roots in an adaptive Afro-American culture or drew directly upon antecedent West African beliefs and practices.* Such study may show, for example, that owners who married blood cousins vio-

---

* Marital rules remain little studied. But Bernard Farber has found evidence of marriage between close blood kin in late eighteenth-century Salem, Massachusetts, where "first-cousin marriage . . . facilitated the creation of alliances and partnerships in business and politics." Farber finds similar ties among Salem artisans and their wives. Endogamy in a developing economy that did not yet know the private corporation as a legal device for accumulating and consolidating wealth may have been a cultural practice shared by aspiring and established Yankee merchants and Carolina cavaliers. Our understanding of the importance of family and kinship ("the world of cousinship") in ordering antebellum southern white society is vastly enlarged in Bertram Wyatt-Brown's brilliant essay, "The Ideal Typology and Antebellum Southern History: A Testing of a New Approach," *Societas,* V (Winter 1975), 1–29.

It is also possible that endogamous marriages occurred among relatively privileged antebellum free Negroes. According to E. H. Fitchett, the tiny free colored Charleston elite was a "class-conscious group" whose "behavior was a replica of that class in white society which they aspired to be like." The St. Phillip's Church marriage book showed "a considerable number of marriages among families who were either business partners or who were identified with the same social and fraternal organizations." "Usage and expectation" meant that mate selection was "made from in-group members." Fitchett did not indicate whether such marriages involved blood kin. John Blassingame's study of postbellum New Orleans blacks describes "a great deal of intermarriage" among "upper-class Negroes." But he does not discuss kin marriage. It may yet turn out that the small but significant amounts of real and personal wealth accumulated by these free black elites encouraged marital alliances more like those of white planters than those of black slaves.

See Bernard Farber, "Family and Community Structure: Salem in 1800," in Michael Gordon, ed., *The American Family in Socio-Historical Perspective* (1973), 100–110; E. H. Fitchett, "The Traditions of the Free Negro in Charleston, South Carolina," *Journal of Negro History,* XXV (1940), 139–42; John Blassingame, *Black New Orleans, 1860–1880* (1973), 161–62.

lated a taboo enforced by other whites so that slaves and non-slavowning whites shared common marital rules. That would mean that slaves did not differ from "whites" but that whites differed among themselves. Evidence of this kind, however, would not be proof that early slave generations had "copied" common non-slave marital rules. In West Africa, marriage between "relatives of legally established affiliation" was "forbidden as incestuous," and descent lines were traced in part to "ensure that no common affiliation" stood "in the way" of marriage. A detailed study of mid-twentieth-century African marriage patterns furthermore shows that "individual choice is limited by prohibitions against marriage with related persons, the extent of which varies from tribe to tribe but is nearly always much wider than in the western world." But little is yet known about eighteenth-century African marital practices. When studied, they, too, promise to reveal the presence of diverse but effective marital rules. The sources of the marital taboos among the Good Hope and other slaves, of course, cannot be inferred from twentieth-century evidence. But their origin counts for far less than the fact that they existed with no legal sanction and no known "white" models and were just as active in the 1850s as in earlier decades.[26]

Exogamous rules reveal much more than the cultural boundaries for selecting marital partners. "The rule of exogamy," the anthropologist A. R. Radcliffe-Brown points out, "is a way of giving institutional recognition to the bond of kinship" and serves as "part of the machinery for establishing and maintaining a wide-ranging kinship system." "A system of kinship and marriage," Radcliffe-Brown also writes, "can be looked at as an arrangement which enables people to live together and co-operate with one another in an orderly social life." It "links persons together by convergence of interest and sentiment and . . . controls and limits those conflicts that are always possible as a result of divergence of sentiment or interest." Particularly observant contemporaries noticed such enlarged Afro-American slave kin groups. "It was months before I learned their family relations," said the teacher Elizabeth Botume of the South Carolina Sea Island slaves. "The terms 'bubber' for brother and 'titty' for sister, with 'nanna' for mother and 'mother' for grandmother, and 'father' for all the leaders in church and society, were so generally used I was forced to believe that they all belonged to one immense family." Among the same slaves "the common name for relative is parent," observed

Laura M. Towne; "they use this word for the whole family even
to cousins." "Parents," Robert Smalls agreed, "mean relations in
general; the same that they mean when they say 'family.' " (That
"parents mean relations in general" may be a clue to the socialization of slave children in enlarged kin groups, a subject that
deserves detailed study.)[27]

Smalls, Towne, and a few others described ties between kin
in different immediate families. "The country people," said Smalls,
"regard their relations more than the city people; they often walk
fifteen miles on a Saturday night to see a cousin." Towne agreed:
"Their affection extends to the whole family. If a cousin is in
want, they admit the claim." Other observers of the wartime
Sea Islanders noticed binding ties between members of different
immediate families. Such observations filled the illuminating diary
of the black Philadelphia schoolteacher Charlotte Forten. An
unidentified plantation superintendent, who, together with four
other whites, lived among blacks on one of the islands, reported
that following a threatened Confederate invasion the whites tried
to "force the men of color to leave their families." But the men
refused, put "the old people and children in little canoes," and
paddled the canoes to places that concealed them. Another time,
a young Parris Island man took a St. Helena's Island wife. "The
two really loved each other," the journalist Nordhoff learned
from John Zacchos, a Greek and a former Cincinnati teacher who
labored as the Parris Island Superintendent of Freedmen. But
the woman remained attached to her family of origin and was
pulled in opposite directions. "They were married in regular
form," said Nordhoff, "but after living some weeks with her
husband the girl returned one day to her father's house and there
remained." Her parents encouraged her to stay with them. A
"number of young fellows" accompanied her husband by boat to
St. Helena's Island and helped spirit the young wife away. A
"bloody" quarrel threatened. Zacchos intervened, heard arguments on both sides, explained that the woman had willingly
married her husband and still loved him, said her parents had "no
more claim on their daughter," and ordered that the couple "live
together." Zacchos followed conventional rules, but the husband
saw that his solution pained his wife and therefore left the final
decision with her. Nordhoff summarized her words: "I your
wife, Sam; I love you; I love my fader and mudder, too; in de
spring and in harvest, when de hard work is in de field, I come
live wid you; when no hard work to do in de field, den I go home

and you come live wid me." "Public opinion," said Nordhoff, "sustained the girl." Her husband accepted the proposal; hers was a "reasonable" arrangement.[28]

Such observations by contemporaries were unusual, partly because of distorted beliefs about the slaves and partly because the slaves hid many of their beliefs from whites. The Georgia slaveholder Charles C. Jones, who believed that slaves had "little *family government*" because most slave "parents are not qualified," admitted that whites "live and die in the midst of negroes and know comparatively little of their real character" because they were "one thing before whites, and another before their own color. Deception toward the former is characteristic of them, whether bond or free. . . . It is a habit—a long established custom, which descends from generation to generation." When Robert Smalls was asked whether "the masters know any thing of their secret life," the ex-slave replied in 1863, "No, sir, one life they show their masters and another they don't show."[29]

Slave exogamy as contrasted to planter endogamy is one reason to put aside mimetic theories of Afro-American culture, and so are the naming practices of slaves. Good Hope blacks named children for members of an immediate family and especially for members of enlarged blood-kin groups, and that happened elsewhere, too[30] (Table 13). The parents of three adults belonging to families that started between 1800 and 1819—the Good Hope slaves closest in time to initial enslavement—are known, and in each either children or grandchildren carried the name of either a father or a grandparent. Enslavement had radically altered the lives of these eighteenth- and nineteenth-century Africans and Afro-Americans and made it impossible for them to recreate the kin groups central to all West African societies. But slavery had not obliterated familial and social memory. In adapting domestic arrangements to enslavement in a distant land, the Good Hope blacks had not surrendered attachments to, and identifications with, immediate and even "distant" kin. Naming practices linked generations of blood kin. The larger social and cultural meaning of these and yet other naming practices is examined in later chapters; it is sufficient here to illustrate how some worked.

Hector, born in 1793, was given his father's name. Affy's first son and first daughter carried the names of Affy's parents, Flora and Sambo. Her second son had the same name as Affy's permanent spouse, July, a West African day name. (Children also may have

TABLE 13.   NAMING PRACTICES AMONG THE GOOD HOPE
PLANTATION SLAVES, ORANGEBURG, SOUTH
CAROLINA, 1793–1855

Date of birth	Name of newborn child	Names of parents	Relation of newborn child to person with same name
1793	Hector	Bess–Hector	Father
1804	Flora	Affy–On Cargo	Mother's mother
1806	Clarinda	Patty–Primus	Mother's mother
1811	Sambo	Affy–Jacob	Mother's father
1813	Primus	Patty–Primus	Father
1819	July	Affy–July	Father
1824	Sarah	Phoebe–Jack	Mother's mother
1828	Major	Clarinda–Abram	Father's father
1828	William	Bridget–Gabriel	Father's father
1829	Fanny	Rose–Adnor	Mother's mother
1830	Adnor	Rose–Adnor	Father
1832	Hannah	Molly–Johnson	Mother's mother
1836	Jack	Phoebe–Jack	Father
1836	Betty	Nancy–Burge	Father's mother
1838	Teresa	Patty–Cato	Father's mother
1838	Stephney	Phoebe–Jack	Mother's father
1840	Gadsey	Duck–Wilson	Mother's mother
1841	Lydia	Candace	Mother's mother
1846	Violet	Beck–John	Mother's father's mother
1847	Jenny	India–Primus	Mother's mother
1849	Elizabeth	Esther–Joshua	Father's sister's daughter
1850	Gabriel	Fanny–Lewis	Father's father
1850	Rose	Harriet–Ephraim	Father's mother
1851	William	Lena–William	Father; father's father's father
1852	Benjamin	Fanny–Lewis	Mother's half sister's son (dead)
1854	Bridget	Fanny–Lewis	Father's mother
1854	Nathan	Esther–Joshua	Father's sister's son (dead)
1855	Linda	Little Sarah–Dave	Father's sister (dead)
1855	Nancy	Lena–Sambo	Father's half sister (dead)

been named for the native Africans Cyrus and Titus, born
respectively in 1780 and 1792. Mutilations in the birth register
make it impossible to connect these two men to the families and
kin groupings in Chart 1. But Patty and Cato named a son
Cyrus in 1834, and Molly, Patty's half sister, and Ness named
a son Titus in 1847.) Captain's daughter India and her husband
Primus had their seventh child in 1847 and named her for Jenny,

Captain's dead wife. Clarinda and Abram named their second son for Abram's father, Major, and Beck and John named a daughter after Beck's grandmother, Violet. Gadsey, born in 1840, also had her grandmother's name. Two of Fanny and Lewis's children (Gabriel and Bridget) had the same names as their father's parents. Phoebe and Jack had four children; the name of one is unknown; a second was called Jack; and the other two were named Sarah and Stephney, after Phoebe's parents. Rose and Adnor had four children between 1824 and 1830; they named their first daughter Fanny after Rose's mother, a son Adnor, and a second son Ephraim, who, in turn, named his first daughter for her grandmother Rose. Overall, in two of three families that started between 1820 and 1849 (and not all of these families were completed by 1857), at least one child was named after a father or an eighteenth-century grandparent. Such naming practices reveal an attachment to a familial "line" and suggest the symbolic renewal in birth of intimate familial experiences identified with a parent or grandparent.

By 1857 the Good Hope slaves were far more than the victims of nearly a century of enslavement. That is made clear by their behavior and especially by the ways in which they retained a social identity rooted in their own cultural traditions and beliefs. The historian of American slave society Ulrich B. Phillips misjudged the slaves profoundly in his influential works. He summed up his most glaring error in a single sentence. "With 'hazy pasts and reckless futures,'" said Phillips of the plantation slaves, "they lived in each moment as it flew." Phillips did no more than paraphrase a popular mid-nineteenth-century belief that an enslaved and racially despised class could not affect its own history and make choices unrelated to the beliefs and practices of an owning class. The South Carolina ex-slave Pen Eubanks put it well in 1937. "I is got memory, but I ain't got no larning; dat I is proud of, kaise I is seed folks wid larning dat never knowed nothing worth speaking about." Eubanks was born in 1854, the same year Fanny and Lewis of Good Hope named their newborn South Carolina slave child for her paternal grandmother Bridget.[31]

The length of their marriages, their exogamous beliefs, and their naming practices are not what is most importantly revealed by the Good Hope slaves. Such behavior and the beliefs on which it rested direct attention to the need for an enlarged time perspective to understand Afro-American slaves prior to and just after the general emancipation. A nearly complete slave birth register has allowed us to examine a small slave community and its development in a time perspective usually unattainable by social historians studying lower-class populations, slave or free, black or white. "If we stop history at a given point," E. P. Thompson points out, "then there are no classes but simply a multitude of individuals with a multitude of experiences. But if we watch these men over an adequate period of social change, we observe patterns in their relationships, their ideas, and their institutions. Class is defined by men as they live their own history, and, in the end, that is its only definition."[32] Concepts such as culture and adaptation—essential to the study of all lower-class populations—require the same enlarged time perspective advanced by Thompson. By examining such groups just at a fixed moment in time, the historian overlooks much that is essential to understanding and explaining their beliefs and behavior.

To illustrate the point let us assume that the Good Hope plantation whites started listing slave births *in 1830, not in 1760*; and that for each baby born between 1830 and 1857, the same information that appears in the complete birth register was recorded. The document is thus not inaccurate but incomplete. Chart 2 reconstructs the slave families on the basis of the data in this fictitious partial register. It shows thirty distinct families, fourteen of them composed of parents and their unmarried children. In seven other families, children had married and started "second-generation" families. The partial register repeats information that is in the complete register: at least five children were born into each of thirteen families; the percentage of slaves bearing children by just a single spouse was the same; a few women had children by unnamed fathers; most slave couples had lived together for many years.

But fixed by so narrow a boundary of time—about thirty years—even so detailed a historical document as Chart 2 fails to reveal a single familial connection rooted in consanguinal and affinal ties that had started prior to 1830. The partial register therefore hides much of what the slaves living between 1830 and 1857 and even later in time had, in fact, experienced and felt. It omits the period when separate families had meshed together into a developing slave community. The full register reveals the development over time of kin networks within a generation and between generations. But one can only infer from the partial register that most Good Hope slaves lived in isolated "nuclear" households, unconnected by blood or marriage to other "nuclear" households. It obscures the fact that first cousins did not marry. It reveals that three sons had their fathers' names, but it does not even hint that a child had the name of a grandparent. Much else remains hidden. It does not disclose, for example, that Duck was the daughter of Gadsey and Cuffee, that Patty and Molly were sisters, that Sophy's grandmother lived there, and that Rachel had two aunts and two uncles among the slaves. Marriages recorded in this partial register fail to connect any two families, and most children listed have kin ties only to their families of origin. The partial register entirely obscures the integrative kin ties formed prior to and sustained after 1830. Chart 2 therefore is a pseudo-historical document. It "shows" that the Good Hope blacks adapted to enslavement by living in conventional "nuclear" families and reinforces the defective view of slave culture as either imitative or derivative in origin. The full register, on the other hand, begins to explain how the interior slave experience over time sustained the expressions of family solidarity revealed by ex-slaves over the entire South between 1864 and 1867 and described in Chapter 1.

The many inadequacies in the partial birth register direct attention to the most severe shortcoming in the vast historiography of American slavery. The study of slave behavior, including the slave family, which begins in 1830 (or even in 1815) starts by ignoring the historical roots (a developing and changing slave culture) of such behavior after 1830. Almost without exception, the most influential studies of the American slave hold the "time factor" constant. Implicit or explicit static, or synchronic, "models" are used to explain slave behavior. That is why so much of this literature must emphasize the ways in which decisions by owners shaped slave belief and behavior. E. Franklin Frazier and Kenneth M. Stampp start their studies of the slave too late in time.[33] Ulrich B. Phillips held the "racial factor" constant over time. Eugene D. Genovese's dialectics remain frozen in time. The sociological model of Stanley M. Elkins and the cliometric model of Robert W. Fogel and Stanley Engerman give no attention to historical time. Static models prevent the slaves from accumulating historical experiences and adapting to changing external circumstances in light of those earlier experiences. The near-total absence of diachronic studies explains why no historical work yet written shows how and why a slave living in the 1850s on the eve of his or her emancipation differed from, or shared values with, his or her grandparents who had lived in the 1790s in the aftermath of their enslavement.

Such an enlarged time perspective explains, for example, Frederick Douglass's early childhood in ways that make him less exceptional than he is usually assumed to have been. Born in 1817, he grew up on Maryland's Eastern Shore in Talbot County. He never knew who his father was. "My only recollections of my own mother," he said, "are of a few hasty visits made in the night on foot, after the tasks were over." But the kin network that surrounded him compensated for these disadvantages. It reached laterally to the children of his mother's sisters; he often played with these cousins. And it reached backward in time to his mother's parents, Isaac and Betsey Bailey ("considered old settlers in the neighborhood"), and especially to "grandmother Betsey," a nurse and gardener, a fishnet maker, and a fisherwoman. Douglass was separated from her and hired out when not yet ten years old. By the time he was in his late twenties he had escaped enslavement and written the *Narrative of the Life of Frederick Douglass*. He included an indelible portrait of his grandmother and declared that more than "any one thing" her mistreatment had caused his "unutterable loathing of slaveholders."

> She had served my old master faithfully from youth to old age. She had been the source of all his wealth; she had peopled his plantation with slaves; she had become a great-grandmother in his service. She had rocked him in his infancy, attended him in his childhood, served him through life, and at his death wiped from his icy brow the cold deathsweat, and closed his eyes forever. She was nevertheless a slave—a slave for life—a slave in the hands of strangers, and in their hands she saw her children, her grandchildren, and her great-grandchildren, divided like so many sheep and then without being gratified with the small privilege of a single word as to their own destiny. And to cap the climax of their base ingratitude, my grandmother, who was now very old, having outlived my old master and all his children, having seen the beginning and end of them, her present owner—his grandson—finding that she was of but little value, that her frame was already racked with the pains of old age and that complete helplessness was fast stealing over her once active limbs, took her to the woods, built

her a little hut with a mud chimney and then gave her the *bounteous* privilege of there supporting herself in utter loneliness—thus virtually turning her out to die. If my poor, dear old grandmother now lives, she lives to remember and mourn over the loss of children, the loss of grandchildren, and the loss of great-grandchildren.

. . . The unconscious children who once sang and danced in her presence are gone. She gropes her way, in the darkness of age, for a drink of water. Instead of the voices of her children, she hears by day the moans of the dove, and by night the screams of the hideous owl. All is gloom. The grave is at the door, and now, weighed down by the pains and aches of old age, when the head inclines to the feet, when the beginning and ending of human existence meet, and helpless infancy and painful old age combine together, at this time for the exercise of that tenderness and affection which children only can bestow on a declining parent—my poor old grandmother, the devoted mother of twelve children, is left all alone, in yonder little hut before a few dim cinders.[34]

Douglass and his grandmother experienced a loneliness that was not shared by Patty and Captain and their grandchildren on the South Carolina Good Hope plantation. But they would have understood the kin network that so shaped Douglass's feelings and beliefs. Although Douglass certainly wished to arouse northern consciences, his description of slave life truthfully depicted the sensibilities of enslaved Afro-Americans rooted in the adaptive domestic arrangements and kin networks that had developed among them in the eighteenth and nineteenth centuries. That is known in the late twentieth century because an ancestor of John Foster Dulles, then living in Philadelphia, ordered that careful records be kept of slave births and deaths. Not in a Bible, to be sure, but in a business ledger.

Enslavement denied Africans and their many Afro-American descendants essential choices available to much better-situated eighteenth- and nineteenth-century Americans. An elderly ex-slave put it well in the 1930s. "White folks," he observed, "do as they please, and the darkies do as they can." He did not mean that enslavement entirely "made over" its victims. He meant that it narrowed the choices slaves could make. And as an ex-slave put it just after the general emancipation, "If a man got to crost de ribber and he can't git a boat, he take a log." A South Carolina Sea Island shoemaker, who had lost an arm fighting with the Union Army but still labored at his craft, said it just as well: "I'se lost an arm but it hasn't gone out of my brains."[35]

3

Take Root There or Nowhere: I

Pleas tell my daughter Clairissa and Nancy a heap how a doo for me Pheaby and Cash and Cashes son James . . . . Give our Love to Cashes Brother Porter and his wife Patience. Victoria gives her Love to her Cousin Beck and Miley.

PHEOBIA AND CASH TO MR. DELIONS (1857)

If . . . a young negro girl meets a coloured man, they curtsey and bow to each other a half a dozen times, and then comes a series of giggles and shakings of the hand, interspersed with questions about uncle Johnson, cousin Jackson, and twenty other darkies of their acquaintance, whose history and welfare seems to afford to both a vast amount of merriment.

ALFRED PAIRPONT (1857)

The most important fact about the Afro-Americans living in the Good Hope slave community in the 1850s is that communities in which slaves had mores and values similar to those of the Good Hope blacks existed over the entire South and had developed among Afro-Americans who experienced enslavement differently from the Good Hope men and women. In this chapter and the one which follows, five plantation communities and their development are studied. All differed in one or more ways from the Good Hope plantation, but the domestic arrangements and kin networks that emerged among their slave residents had much in common with those found in the Good Hope slave community. The differences examined are those usually emphasized by historians to explain variations in slave behavior. They include location, type of ownership, size, and the age of a slave community ("time"). Slave communities are studied in Virginia, North Carolina, Alabama, and Louisiana, places where slaves grew either cotton, tobacco, or sugar. Some had resident owners; others were absentee-owned. Some had the same life span as the Good Hope community; others started either much later or much earlier in time. How sale and purchase as well as gift-transfer affected slave domestic arrangements and kin networks also will be examined.

These and other "external variables" tested the cultural beliefs and practices of slaves differently, but similar domestic arrangements, kin networks, sexual behavior, marital rules, and naming practices existed in all six communities, beliefs sufficiently supported by the developing slave culture to reveal themselves in diverse plantation settings. Slaves differed in other ways from each other and learned from others than themselves, but the fact that slaves everywhere made such similar choices and lived in communities shaped by common mores directs attention to the cultural and social determinants of such behavior within the slave experience and indicates that we are studying how a developing social class took shape as slaves everywhere adapted to the harsh circumstances associated with more than a full century of enslavement.

This chapter and the next one focus on slaves who either spent their full lives on plantations or belonged to men who became plantation owners. Little is yet known about the domestic arrangements and kin networks as well as the communities that developed among slaves living on farms and in towns and cities.[1] Study of such slaves promises to show how these surrounding circumstances tested their adaptive capacities in different ways from those slaves living in plantation settings.[2] But the opportunity to develop expanding kin networks existed among slaves living on farms and small plantations as well as in towns and cities. That is suggested by the fact that the percentage of North Carolina ex-slaves reporting long slave marriages in 1866 was the same in farm and urban settings as in plantation settings (Chapter 1). Some "stability" in family life—and the length of slave marriages is a clue to the presence of such "stability"—was essential to the development of expanded kin networks.

E. Franklin Frazier and most other students of the slave family have argued that "normal" familial arrangements existed among most slaves living on farms or small plantations, and their writings concern mostly large-plantation slaves.[3] Among such slaves, sexual, familial, and social disorganization and "pathology" allegedly thrived. By examining developing slave communities in very diverse plantation settings, that controversial literature is tested at its most relevant point. Moreover, by examining plantation slaves, the appropriateness of a bicultural model of slave socialization is assessed. It was in communities like the one on the Good Hope plantation that slaves lived most distantly from direct supervision by owning whites. Everyday contact with owners had

to be less frequent than on smaller plantations and on farms. It
is the behavior of such slaves that casts doubt on hypotheses that
attribute slave belief and behavior primarily to the decisive influence of the owning class. The size of the plantations is what
matters, not whether their owners viewed themselves as "capitalists" or "paternalists." Their size left a social "space" between
the slaves and their owners but did not create a social vacuum
among the slaves. Communities developed in that social space
everywhere, and in them slaves made common choices rooted in
a cumulative slave experience.

Phoebe and Cash were two such slaves. They lived on one of
three Georgia rice plantations owned by Charles C. Jones. Phoebe
was both a seamstress and a field hand. Cash labored only as a field
hand. They married in 1851. Both had been married earlier and
had had children by these previous marriages. They also had grandchildren. Cash's frequent troubles with the slave foreman Cato
ended in 1857 with the sale of Cash, Phoebe, and some of their
children. A trader took them to New Orleans, and before their
resale they sent a letter to a "Mr. Delions" filled with concern for
the many kin they had been separated from by Jones's decision.
"Pleas tell my daughter Clairissa and Nancy a heap how a doo
for me Pleaby and Cash and Cashes son James We left Savannah
the first of Jany we are now in New Orleans. Please tell them that
their sister Jane died the first of Feby we did not know what was
the matter with her." The letter continued:

> . . . pleas answer this Letter for Clairssa and Let me know
> all that has hapend since i left. Please tell them that the Chil-
> dren were all sick with the measles but they are all well now.
> Clairssa your affectionate Mother and Father sends a heap of
> Love to you and your husband and my Grand Children Phebea.
> Mag. & Cloe. John. Judy. Sue. My aunt Aufy sinena and
> Minton and Little Plaska. Charles Nega. Fillis and all of their
> Children. Cash. Prime. Laffatte. Rick Tonia [sends their love]
> to you all. Give our Love to Cashes Brother Porter and his wife
> Patience. Victoria gives her Love to her Cousin Beck and
> Miley
>
> I have no more to say untill i get a home. I remain your
> affectionate Mother and Father.
>
> PHEOBIA and CASH
>
> P.S.
> Please give my love to Judys Husband Plaska and also Cashs
> love. . . .

A similar "list" could have been drawn up by slaves living in the 1850s on the South Carolina Good Hope plantation, the Louisiana Stirling plantation, the Virginia Cedar Vale plantation, the Louisiana Carlisle plantation, the Alabama Watson plantation, and the North Carolina Bennehan-Cameron plantation. Slaves living in these plantation communities shared common beliefs about family and kin with Phoebe and Cash.[4]

The slaves owned by Lewis Stirling, who are studied first, were like the Good Hope slaves because a slave community developed among them over a relatively long period of time and because few apparently were sold. But important differences also distinguished this community from the Good Hope community. The Good Hope slaves lived in South Carolina, grew cotton, and had an absentee owner. The Stirling slaves lived in Louisiana, grew sugar, and had a resident owner. Three separate birth registers listing the names of 337 children born to seventy-nine slave mothers between 1807 and 1865 on this West Feliciana sugar plantation allow for a direct comparison to the Good Hope blacks.[5] Lewis Stirling inherited real and personal wealth from his father, an eighteenth-century British immigrant who had moved with his North Carolina wife in 1784 to West Feliciana and received Spanish government land grants there. In 1860, the Stirling slaves planted, cut, ground, and processed sugar cane, and their owner hired in additional slaves (some belonging to his wife's family) to supplement their labor. That year, Stirling fixed the value of his real property at $75,000 and his personal property at $226,000. His slaves produced 450 hogsheads of cane sugar, 47,000 gallons of molasses, and 6500 bushels of Indian corn. Thirty separate dwellings housed 138 slaves on this "semi-industrial" plantation.[6]

That the Stirling slave community developed very similarly to the Good Hope slave community is learned by reorganizing the Stirling registers in the same way that the Good Hope register was reorganized. Table 14 includes all children born into the Stirling community, and Chart 3 accounts for sixty-eight of the seventy-nine mothers and 311 of the 337 newborn children. The recurrence of the male names Joe and George in different families of the same generation makes a complete linkage impossible, but that single deficiency does not distort over-all patterns of slave behavior.[7] Some women headed households over the full family cycle that differed from the typical double-headed slave household,

TABLE 14. STIRLING PLANTATION SLAVE FAMILIES AND
GENERATIONS, WEST FELICIANA PARISH,
LOUISIANA, 1807–1865

Generation with First Child Born Between 1807 and 1819

No.	Year	Mother	Father	Child	Date of death
1.*	1807	Fortune	Major	George	1863
2.	1808	Big Judy	Leven	Joe	1842
	1810	same	same	Erwin	1857
	1814	same	same	Linder (Linda)	
	1816	same	same	Eveline	1878
	1820	same	same	Leven	1857
	1821	same	same	Caroline	1821
	1822	same	same	Mary	1852
	1825	same	same	Maretta	1861
	1829	same	same	Henrietta	
3.*	1809	Nelly	not listed	Sam	1863
4.	1810	Sucky	Julius	Sidney	1851
	1813	same	same	Wilson	
	1816	same	same	Marinda	
	1818	same	not listed	Mariah	
	1820	same	not listed	Wesley	
	1823	same	not listed	Baptiste†	
	1827	same	not listed	stillborn	1827
5.	1811	Delia	Ben	Little Joe	
	1815	same	same	Little Ben	
	1817	same	same	Sam	
	1821	same	same	Martin	1821
	1824	same	same	Hester	
6.*	1811	Maddy	Tuckety	Ellen	
	1813	same	same	Bill	
7.	1811	Ginny	Sampson	Clarice	
	1817	same	same	Sampson	
	1819	same	same	Rachel	
	1822	same	same	Monday	
8.	1812	Little Judy	Yanko	Hannah	
	1815	same	same	Liddy	
	1820	same	same	Peter	1843
	1822	same	same	Boy	1822
	1823	same	same	Harriet	1858
	1827	same	same	Washington	
	1830	same	same	Major	1830
	1831	same	same	Jack	

* Not included in Chart 3.
† Marked "a molato."

TABLE 14. (*Continued*)

No.	Year	Mother	Father	Child	Date of death
9.	1813	Miuscuita	Chaney	Sucky	
	1815	same	same	Liddy	
	1817	same	same	Nanny	
	1821	same	same	Sambo	
	1825	same	same	Calab	1830
10.	1813	Sylvia‡	Billy‡	Terise‡	
	1815	same	same	Solomon‡	
	1817	same	same	Dolly‡	
	1819	same	same	Harry‡	
	1822	same	same	Nan‡	
	1824	same	same	Martin	
	1826	same	same	Magdalan	
	1829	same	same	Celeste	
	1831	same	same	Billy	
	1834	same	same	John s.b.	1834
11.	1813	Pendar	Wally	Fortune	
	1816	same	same	Nan	
	1818	same	same	Patsey	
	1823	same	same	Caroline	
12.*	1814	Cutyjob	?	Delia	
	1823	same	not listed	Boy s.b.	1823
13.*	1814	Delia	Charles	Juliana	
	1817	same	same	Charles	
14.	1814	Sarah	not listed	Delily	1877
	1818	same	not listed	Nelly	
	1824	same	not listed	Fanny	1863
	1826	same	Barika	Adam	1892
	1828	same	same	Josephine	1830
	1829	same	same	Rose	1915
15.	1814	Amie	George	Louisa	
	1816	same	same	Jack	1825
16.	1815	Amy	Surry	Jim	
	1817	same	same	Nan	
	1818	same	same	Surry	1820
	1822	same	same	Henny	1822
	1823	same	same	Philip	
	1826	same	same	Prince	
	1828	same	same	Jacob	
	1831	same	same	Frank	
17.	1817	Charlotte	Barlett	Allan	
	1825	same	same	John Anderson	1862

* Not included in Chart 3.
† Marked "a molato."
‡ Purchased as a family.

TABLE 14.   (*Continued*)

No.	Year	Mother	Father	Child	Date of death
18.*	1818	Charity	not listed	Sam (or Joe)	
19.*	1818	Ellen‡	Sambo‡	Dublin‡	
	1821	same	same	Chester‡	
	1823	same	same	Thomas‡	
	1825	same	same	Susan	
	1830	same	same	Ginny	
20.	1819	Belle‡	not listed	George‡	1865
	1822	same	not listed	Sophy‡	
	1825	same	Harry	Alford	
	1828	same	same	Lucinda	1847
	1832	same	same	Louisa	

* Not included in Chart 3.
‡ Purchased as a family.

> NOTE: *This is an incomplete listing of children born in this generation (1807–1819). One of the registers includes the note dated April 23, 1820: "Besides those listed above which are all now living there has been born and died since 1807 up to this date of Delia—3, Jude—4, Linder—1, Amye (African)—1, Delia (African)—1, Miuscuita—3, Cutyjob—3, Sucky—1, Sarah—1, L. Jude—1, Rachel —1, Tuckety—2, Sylvia—1, Charity—1—making 24." The dates of birth and death were not listed. Neither were the names of fathers. It is not probable that any of these dead children are included in the above listing. Miuscuita, for example, was listed in the register as the mother of three daughters born before 1820. All were alive after that date so that the three children listed in this note were additional children born to this woman.*

Generation with First Child Born Between 1820 and 1839

No.	Year	Mother	Father	Child	Date of death
1.*	1820	Patience	not listed	William	
	1822	same	Berum	Angelina	1822
	1823	same	not listed	Jack	
	1825	same	Berum	Marsolee	
	1827	same	same	Sarah	
	1828	same	same	Lucy	
2.	1828	Big Hannah	Yellow Joe	Margaret	
	1832	same	same	Rosabella	
	1834	same	same	Joe	
	1836	same	same	Henry	1842
	1840	same	same	Peter	1842
	1842	same	same	Josephine	
	1845	same	not listed	Kitty	
	1848	same	not listed	Aggy	

TABLE 14.   (*Continued*)

No.	Year	Mother	Father	Child	Date of death
3.	1829	Clarice	not listed	Celia	
	1830	same	not listed	Levi	
	1835	same	John	Willis	1835
	1836	same	same	Ginny	
4.	1829	Terise	not listed	Clarinda	1851
	1831	same	Ben	Diana	
5.	1829	Yel. Liddy	Luke	Francoise	1856
	1835	same	same	Charlotte	1863
	1837	same	same	Hannah	1852
	1840	same	same	Celia	1856
6.*	1830	Ellen	not listed	Emily	
	1834	same	not listed	Arena	
7.	1833	Yel. Louisa	not listed	Nanette	
	1836	same	not listed	William	
	1838	same	not listed	Joseph†	
8.	1833	Dolly	Sidney	Julius Caesar	
9.	1833	Linder (a)	not listed§	Cecele	
	1834	same	not listed§	Primus	1864
	1836	same	Long George	George	
	1838	same	same	Lewis	1840
	1840	same	same	David	
	1842	same	same	Roseale	1847
	1844	same	same	Luke	
	1845	same	same	Ann	
	1847	same	same	Jim	
	1849	same	same	Wilson	
	1851	same	same	Martha	
	1855	same	same	Roseale	
10.	1833	Nelson	Clarinda	Spencer	
	1835	same	same	Affy	
	1838	same	same	Amanda	1847
	1838	same	same	Jane	
	1843	same	same	Rinah	1847
	1845	same	same	Beck	1847
	1846	same	same	Dave	1851
	1848	same	same	Moses	1863
	1848	same	same	Terris	1863
	1851	same	same	Fanny	
	1853	same	same	Abraham	1863
	1853	same	same	Jacob	

* Not included in Chart 3.
† Marked "a molato."
§ On one of the registers Long George is listed as the father of Cecele and Primus.

Table 14. (*Continued*)

No.	Year	Mother	Father	Child	Date of death
	1856	same	same	Georgianna	
	1858	same	same	Martha	1860
	1859	same	same	Marshall	1860
11.	1834	Pendar's Nan	Lit. Ben	Eli	1834
	1835	same	same	Lucy	
	1839	same	same	Ben	1839?
12.	1834	Eveline	Wilson	Mariah	1916
	1836	same	same	Sarah	
	1839	same	same	Serella	
	1841	same	same	Amy	
	1842	same	same	Baptiste	
	1844	same	same	Joe	
	1846	same	same	Betsey	
	1848	same	same	Allace	
	1850	same	same	Affy	
	1853	same	same	Willis	1864
	1855	same	same	Sidney	1865
	1857	same	same	Erwin	1863
	1860	same	same	Sucky	1863
13.	1835	Chaney Liddy	not listed**	Josiah	1835
	1838	same	Jim	Charles	
14.	1835	Lt. Sucky	Peterson	Richard	1835
	1837	same	same	Eliza	1857
	1840	same	same	Liddy	1840
15.	1835	Big Nan	Fort. George	————	1835
	1837	same	not listed	Amy	
	1840	same	not listed	Abby	
	1843	same	not listed	Philip	
16.	1835	Delily	House George	Jack	1916
	1837	same	not listed	Sally	1837
	1839	same	Big Ben	Joe	
	1841	same	same	Delia	
	1843	same	same	Wiley	
	1845	same	same	Wimmy	1845
	1847	same	same	Stephen	
	1849	same	same	Henrietta Ben	1917
	1851	same	not listed	Richard	
17.	1836	Rachel	not listed	Polly	
	1839	same	not listed	Clarice	
18.	1836	Fortune	Joe	Boy	1836
	1837	same	same	Perrinder	1837
	1840	same	Josiah	Charlotte	

** It is marked in on one of the registers: "Wilson is the father."

TABLE 14.   (*Continued*)

No.	Year	Mother	Father	Child	Date of death
19.	1836	Mary	not listed	Yellow Clara	1863
	1841	same	not listed	Leven	1863
	1845	same	not listed	Margaret	
	1846	same	not listed	Anthony	1846
	1848	same	not listed	Paris	1856
	1850	same	not listed	———	1850
20.	1836	Nelly	not listed	Isabella	1917
	1839	same	not listed	Barika	1861
	1841	same	not listed	Lucy	1863
	1843	same	not listed	Edmond	1917
	1845	same	Erwin	Mary	1847
	1848	same	same	Riley	
	1850	same	same	Charles	1855
	1852	same	same	Sarah	
	1854	same	same	John W.	1863
21.	1837	Marinda	Allen	Lige	
	1839	same	same	Phelby	
22.	1839	Sylvia's Nan	not listed	Anderson	

Generation with First Child Born Between 1840 and 1865

No.	Year	Mother	Father	Child	Date of death
1.	1842	Nanny	not listed	Robert	
	1846	same	not listed	Caroline	
	1851	same	not listed	Chaney	
	1854	same	not listed	Ellender	1858
2.	1843	Harriet	not listed	Judy	
	1846	same	Sam Brown	Hester	1848
	1848	same	same	Kipana	
	1850	same	same	Ben	
	1853	same	same	Hannah	1853
	1856	same	same	Martin	
3.	1844	Margaret	not listed	Harriet	
	1847	same	not listed	Henry	
	1850	same	Adam	Peter	
	1852	same	same	Ruffin	
	1855	same	same	Rosabella	1856
	1857	same	same	Thomas	
	1860	same	same	Rosabella	
	1861	same	same	Marian	1862
	1863	same	same	Charlotte	
4.	1844	Maretta	not listed	Amy	1863
	1846	same	not listed	Polly	1847

TABLE 14. *(Continued)*

No.	Year	Mother	Father	Child	Date of death
	1848	same	not listed	Adam	
	1850	same	not listed	Eveline	
	1852	same	not listed	Dan	
	1854	same	not listed	Ginny	
	1857	same	not listed	Leven	
	1860	same	not listed	Linda	
	1862	same	not listed	George	
5.	1844	Frocene	not listed	Primus	
	1847	same	not listed	———	
	1849	same	Sambo	Bob	
	1852	same	same	San Hammon	
	1854	same	same	Jane (?)	
	1856	same	same	York	
	1859	same	same	Isabella	
	1861	same	not listed?	Moses	
	1864	same	Sambo	Catrine	
6.	1846	Sophy	not listed	Sampson	
	1851	same	Sam Jackson	Bella	
	1854	same	same	Monday	1857
	1859	same	same	Couper	
7.	1846	Lucinda	not listed	———	1846
8.	1846	Henrietta	not listed	Antoinette	
	1848	same	not listed	Anthony	
	1850	same	not listed	Ada	
	1852	same	not listed	Albert	1856
	1854	same	not listed	Cary	1856
	1857	same	not listed	Albert	
	1858	same	not listed	Adele	1862
	1862	same	not listed	Nelson	1863
9.	1846	Fanny	not listed	Caleb	
	1849	same	not listed	Peterson	
	1851	same	Anderson	Abya	
	1856	same	same	——— s.b.	1856
10.	1848	Rose	not listed	Catrine	
	1857	same	not listed	Cynthia	1863
	1861	same	not listed	Julia (?)	1863
11.	1850	Rosabella	not listed	Celia	
	1852	same	Alford	Harry	1864
	1855	same	same	Joe	1856
	1858	same	same	Stirling	
	1861	same	same	Walter	1863
	1863	same	same	Cora	
12.	1851	Louisa	Washington	Lucinda	
	1854	same	same	Alford	
	1861	same	same	Talbot	

TABLE 14. *(Continued)*

No.	Year	Mother	Father	Child	Date of death
13.	1852	Francoise	not listed	Rachel	1852
	1855	same	Monday	Levi	1855
14.	1852	Affy	not listed	Amanda	
	1854	same	Jack White	Lad	
	1856	same	same	Hannah	1863
	1859	same	same	Evans	1861
	1861	same	same	Marshall	1861
	1863	same	same	Nancy	1863
	1864	same	same	Hannah	
	1864	same	same	Evans	
15.	1852	Charlotte	not listed	John Butler	1858
	1856	same	not listed	Mary	
	1857	same	not listed	Celia	1863
	1859	same	not listed	Cora	1859
	1860	same	not listed	Paris	
	1862	same	not listed	Nancy	1862
16.	1853	Isabella	not listed	Alexander	
	1856	same	not listed	Charles	
	1859	same	Joseph	Philander	
	1861	same	same	Linda	
	1862	same	same	Nelson	
	1864	same	same	Lucy	
17.	1854	Jane	not listed	Dave	1854
	1858	same	not listed	Rinah	
18.	1856	Cecele	not listed	Virgil	
	1858	same	not listed	Cary	
	1860	same	not listed	Voltaire	
	1863	same	not listed	Linda	
19.	1856	Phelby	Leven	Julius	
	1856	same	same	Bartlett	
	1859	same	Joe T.	Delphy	1862
	1861	same	same	Marinda	1863
	1864	same	same	Lige	
20.	1856	Sarah	not listed	Ned	
	1858	same	not listed	Edith	1863
	1861	same	not listed	Miles	
	1864	same	not listed	Clara	
21.	1857	Esther	not listed	Richard	1857
	1859	same	not listed	Ellen	
	1861	same	not listed	Cementi (?)	1861
	1863	same	Monday	Ginny	1863
	1865	same	same	Clarice	
22.	1857	Mariah	Spencer	Judy	

TABLE 14. *(Continued)*

No.	Year	Mother	Father	Child	Date of death
23.*	1857	Lucy	not listed	Allen	
	1860	same	not listed	Anderson	
24.	1857	Eliza	not listed	Peterson	
25.	1858	Nanette	not listed	William	
	1862	same	not listed	George	
26.	1858	Serella	not listed	Wesley	1859
	1861	same	not listed	Wesley	1862
27.	1859	Kitty	not listed	Fillmore	
	1862	same	Lit. George	Johnson	
28.*	1859	Maria	not listed	Liss	
	1862	same	not listed	Hilary	
29.	1861	Antoinette	not listed	Dudley	
	1863	same	Primus	Duncan	1863
	1865	same	same	Duncan	
30.	1861	Amy	not listed	Hall	1863
31.	1861	Josephine	not listed	Rachel	
	1863	same	not listed	Joe	1863
	1864	same	Wiley	Violet	
32.	1862	Harriet	not listed	Beverley	1863
	1864	same	not listed	Serella	
33.	1862	Clara	not listed	Abram	1863
34.	1863	Betsey	Joe Clay	Delily	
35.	1863	Judy	Lewis	Joshua	
36.*	1864	Ann	not listed	Matilda	
37.	1865	Lit. Margaret	not listed	Kate	

* Not included in Chart 3.

but other familial and social practices within the Stirling slave community were like those within the Good Hope slave community. Its residents practiced exogamy. Children were frequently named for blood kin outside the immediate family. Slaves living in geographically distant places, working different types of plantations, and having different daily relations with an owner shared important common beliefs.

Like the Good Hope slaves, the Stirling slaves lived in a community in which inter- and intragenerational kin networks connecting distinct immediate families developed over time. That some children were born prior to the War of 1812 means that the plantation's original slaves had been settled there prior to the rapid expansion of the plantation system from the Upper to the Lower South. The parents of children born in the 1807–1819 generation were the children of eighteenth-century Africans and Afro-Americans. A few—marked in the registers as "Amye (African)" and "Delia (African)"—were native Africans. The names of other "first-generation" parents—the women Miuscuita and Cutyjob and the men Sambo and Barika—suggest that other native Africans or the grown children of native Africans were among the Stirling slave community's early residents. Some also may have had West Indian origins. Like the Good Hope slaves, the Stirling slaves manifest a distinctive Afro-American culture developing over a surprisingly short time. Born in 1829, Barika's daughter Rose died aged eighty-six in 1915. Her mother Sarah was born late in the eighteenth century, and her father was born just before or after the Louisiana Purchase. Her oldest sister Delily was born during the War of 1812. When Rose died, Woodrow Wilson was president and industries stimulated by another war were attracting rural southern blacks to northern cities.

Early twentieth-century descendants of the Stirling and Good Hope slaves had Louisiana and South Carolina forebears who had lived among slaves sharing common beliefs. Brief though the time period covered by the Stirling registers was, it was long enough to show that exogamous beliefs existed among the Stirling slaves. Marriages occurred among some cousins related by affinal (or marital) ties, but blood first cousins did not marry.[8] The median age (18.7) of forty-nine women at the birth of a first child was slightly but not significantly lower than among the Good Hope women. Prenuptial intercourse was common, but for most women the birth of one or more children prior to marriage did not preclude their marrying later. Between 1807 and 1855, fifty-nine women bore one or more children, twenty-three in unions involving just a single known male and twenty in unions preceded by the birth of one or more children by unnamed fathers.

Nelson and Clarinda, parents of fifteen children born between 1833 and 1859, illustrate the dominant pattern. Sarah, her daughters, and her granddaughters illustrate the subordinate pattern. Delily, Nelly, and Fanny were born to Sarah by unnamed fathers between 1814 and 1824, and then Sarah had three more children by Barika. Nelly had four children by unnamed fathers, and then five more by Erwin. Fanny and Delily were like their mother, as was Nelly's daughter Isabella, who had two children by unnamed fathers before settling into a conventional family with Joseph and

Note: The number in parentheses indicates how many
children were born in each marriage.

Families with Unmarried Children

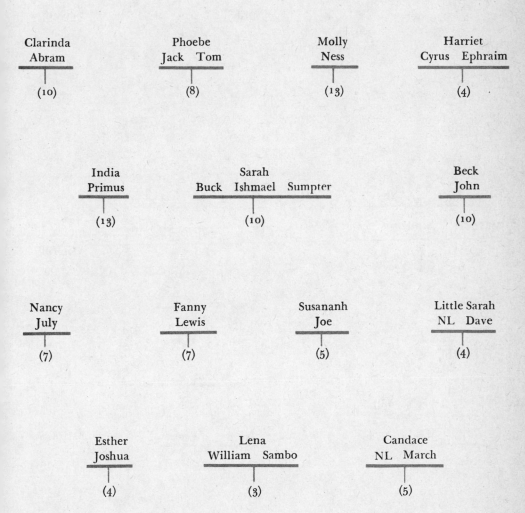

Clarinda Abram	Phoebe Jack Tom	Molly Ness	Harriet Cyrus Ephraim
(10)	(8)	(13)	(4)

India Primus	Sarah Buck Ishmael Sumpter	Beck John
(13)	(10)	(10)

Nancy July	Fanny Lewis	Susananh Joe	Little Sarah NL Dave
(7)	(7)	(5)	(4)

Esther Joshua	Lena William Sambo	Candace NL March
(4)	(3)	(5)

Families with Married Children

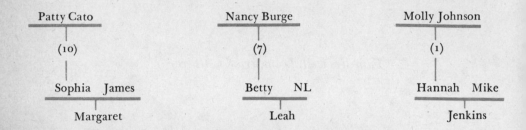

Patty Cato
(10)
Sophia ― James
Margaret

Nancy Burge
(7)
Betty ― NL
Leah

Molly Johnson
(1)
Hannah ― Mike
Jenkins

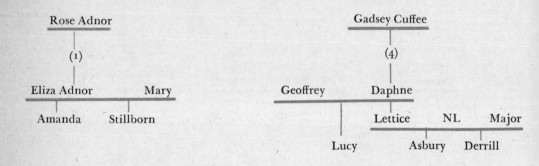

Rose Adnor
(1)
Eliza Adnor ― Mary
Amanda   Stillborn

Gadsey Cuffee
(4)
Geoffrey ― Daphne
Lucy   Lettice ― NL ― Major
Asbury   Derrill

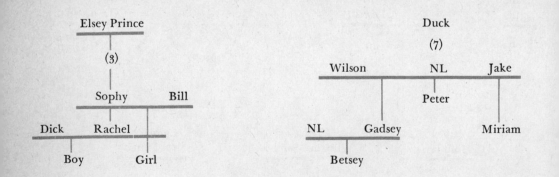

Elsey Prince
(3)
Sophy ― Bill
Dick Rachel
Boy   Girl

Duck
(7)
Wilson ― NL ― Jake
Peter
NL ― Gadsey   Miriam
Betsey

CHART 3. FAMILY AND KINSHIP STRUCTURE, STIRLING PLANTATION SLAVES, LOUISIANA 1807–1865

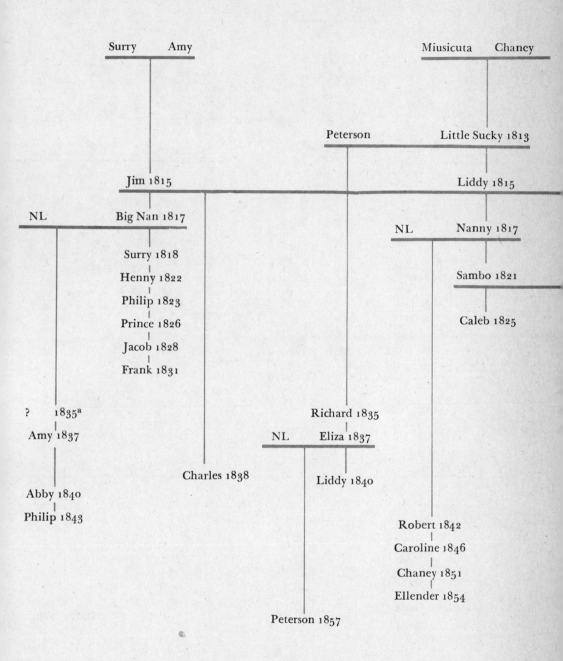

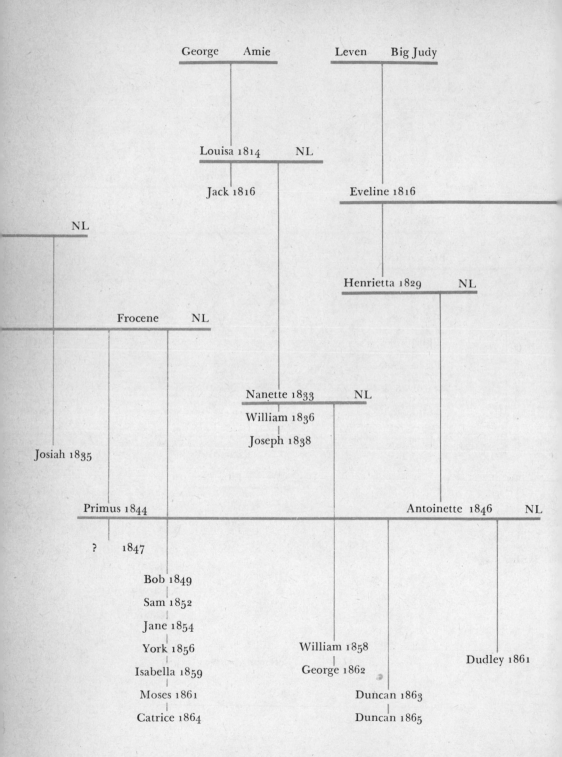

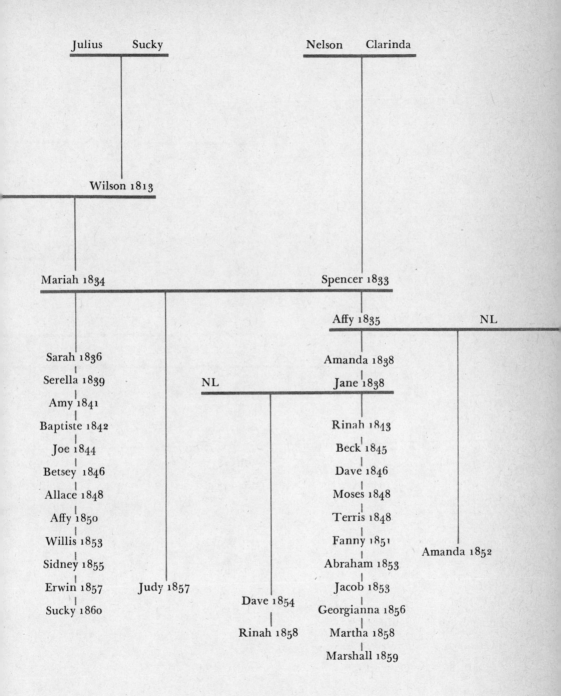

Julius   Sucky

Nelson   Clarinda

Wilson 1813

Mariah 1834

Spencer 1833

Affy 1835   NL

Sarah 1836

Amanda 1838

Serella 1839   NL

Jane 1838

Amy 1841

Baptiste 1842

Rinah 1843

Joe 1844

Beck 1845

Betsey 1846

Dave 1846

Allace 1848

Moses 1848

Affy 1850

Terris 1848

Willis 1853

Fanny 1851

Sidney 1855

Abraham 1853   Amanda 1852

Erwin 1857

Judy 1857

Jacob 1853

Sucky 1860

Dave 1854

Georgianna 1856

Rinah 1858

Martha 1858

Marshall 1859

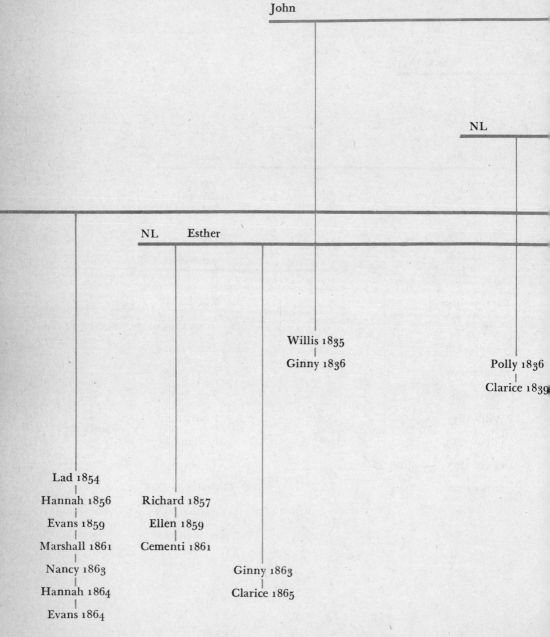

John

NL

NL   Esther

Willis 1835
Ginny 1836

Polly 1836
Clarice 1839

Lad 1854
Hannah 1856   Richard 1857
Evans 1859   Ellen 1859
Marshall 1861   Cementi 1861
Nancy 1863
Hannah 1864   Ginny 1863
Evans 1864   Clarice 1865

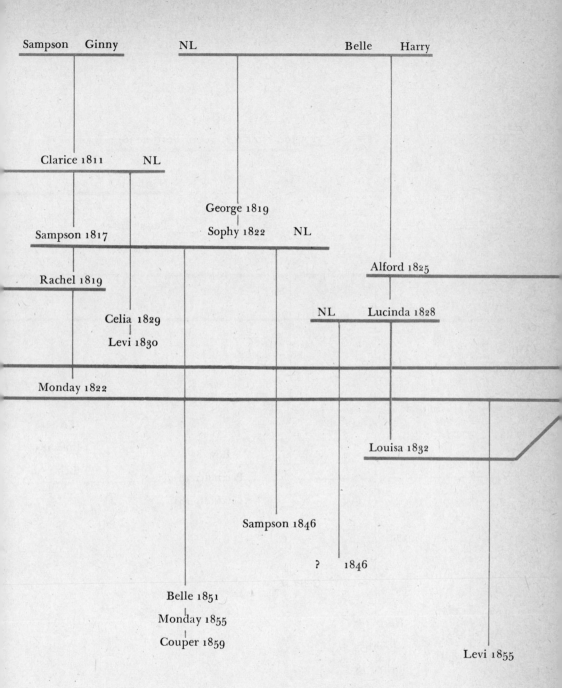

Sampson   Ginny   NL   Belle   Harry

Clarice 1811   NL

George 1819

Sophy 1822   NL

Sampson 1817

Alford 1825

Rachel 1819

NL   Lucinda 1828

Celia 1829

Levi 1830

Monday 1822

Louisa 1832

Sampson 1846

?   1846

Belle 1851

Monday 1855

Couper 1859

Levi 1855

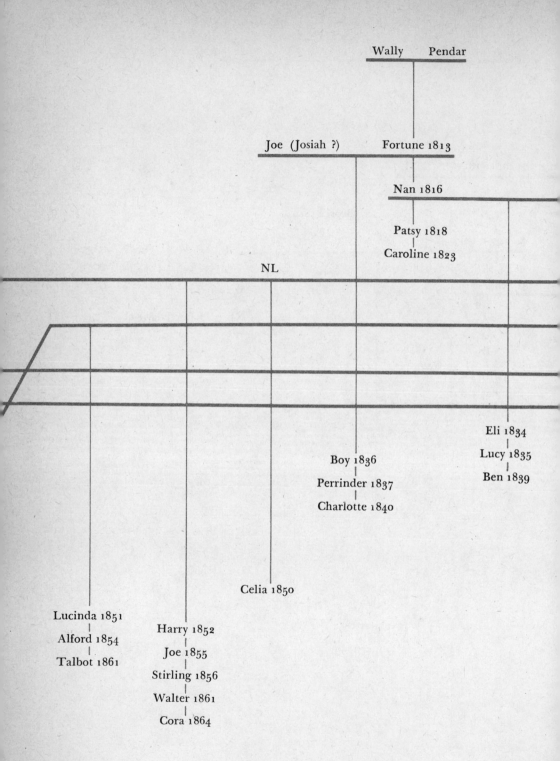

Wally   Pendar

Joe (Josiah ?)   Fortune 1813

Nan 1816

Patsy 1818

Caroline 1823

NL

Eli 1834

Lucy 1835

Boy 1836

Ben 1839

Perrinder 1837

Charlotte 1840

Celia 1850

Lucinda 1851

Alford 1854   Harry 1852

Talbot 1861   Joe 1855

Stirling 1856

Walter 1861

Cora 1864

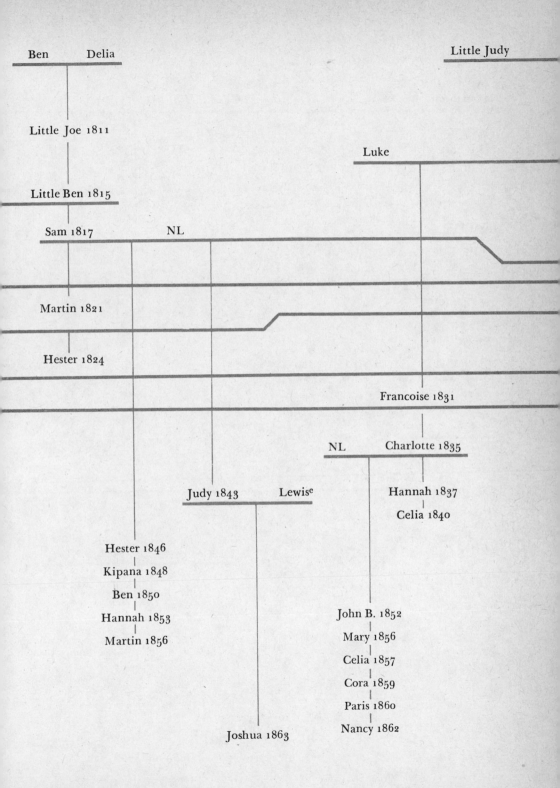

Ben   Delia   Little Judy

Little Joe 1811

                                                      Luke

Little Ben 1815

Sam 1817   NL

Martin 1821

Hester 1824

                                                      Francoise 1831

                                          NL   Charlotte 1835

Judy 1843   Lewis[c]   Hannah 1837
                                                      Celia 1840

            Hester 1846
            Kipana 1848
            Ben 1850
            Hannah 1853   John B. 1852
            Martin 1856   Mary 1856
                                          Celia 1857
                                          Cora 1859
                                          Paris 1860
                        Joshua 1863   Nancy 1862

[b] *Son of Big Ben and Delia.*
[c] *Son of Long George and Linder.*

ix

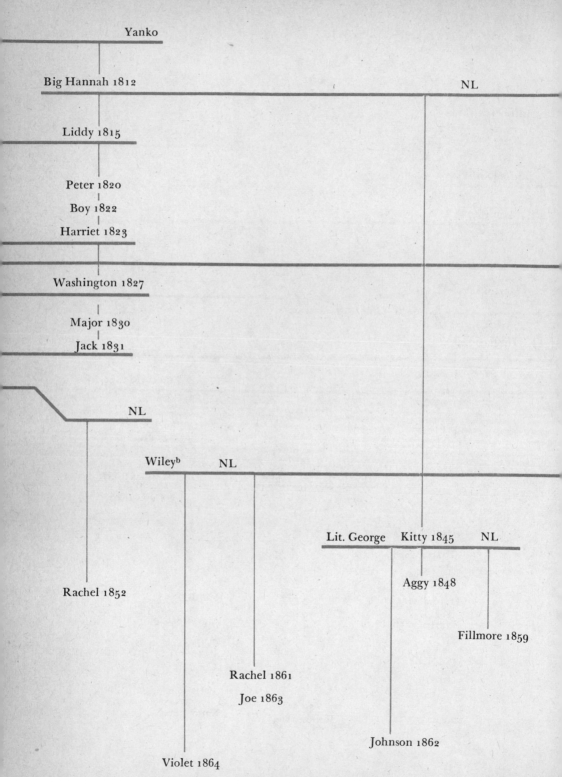

Yanko

Big Hannah 1812   NL

Liddy 1815

Peter 1820

Boy 1822

Harriet 1823

Washington 1827

Major 1830

Jack 1831

NL

Wiley[b]   NL

Lit. George   Kitty 1845   NL

Rachel 1852

Aggy 1848

Fillmore 1859

Rachel 1861

Joe 1863

Johnson 1862

Violet 1864

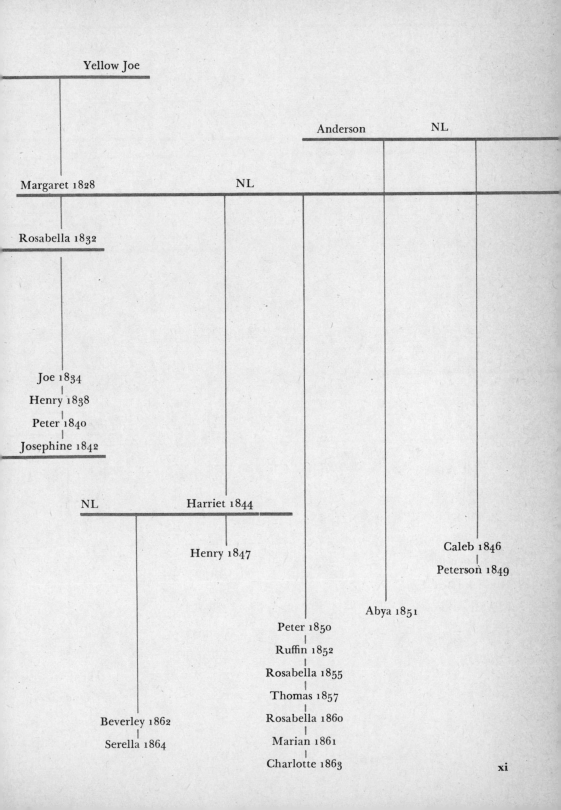

Yellow Joe

Anderson   NL

Margaret 1828   NL

Rosabella 1832

Joe 1834

Henry 1838

Peter 1840

Josephine 1842

NL   Harriet 1844

Henry 1847

Caleb 1846

Peterson 1849

Abya 1851

Peter 1850

Ruffin 1852

Rosabella 1855

Thomas 1857

Beverley 1862   Rosabella 1860

Serella 1864   Marian 1861

Charlotte 1863

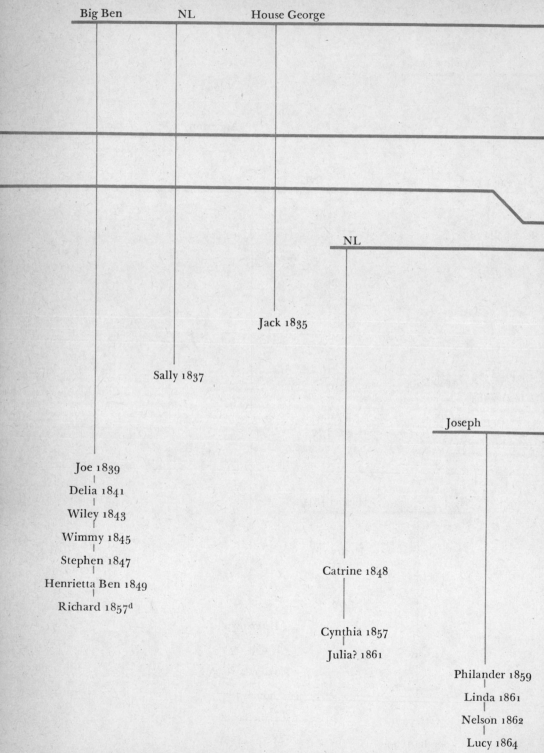

Big Ben   NL   House George

NL

Jack 1835

Sally 1837

Joseph

Joe 1839
Delia 1841
Wiley 1843
Wimmy 1845
Stephen 1847
Henrietta Ben 1849
Richard 1857[d]

Catrine 1848

Cynthia 1857
Julia? 1861

Philander 1859
Linda 1861
Nelson 1862
Lucy 1864

[d] *No father listed for Richard.*

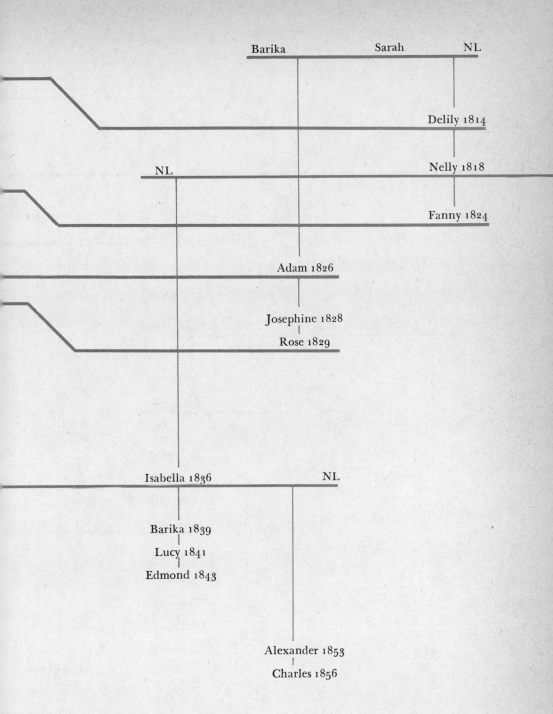

Barika   Sarah   NL

Delily 1814

Nelly 1818

NL

Fanny 1824

Adam 1826

Josephine 1828

Rose 1829

Isabella 1836   NL

Barika 1839

Lucy 1841

Edmond 1843

Alexander 1853

Charles 1856

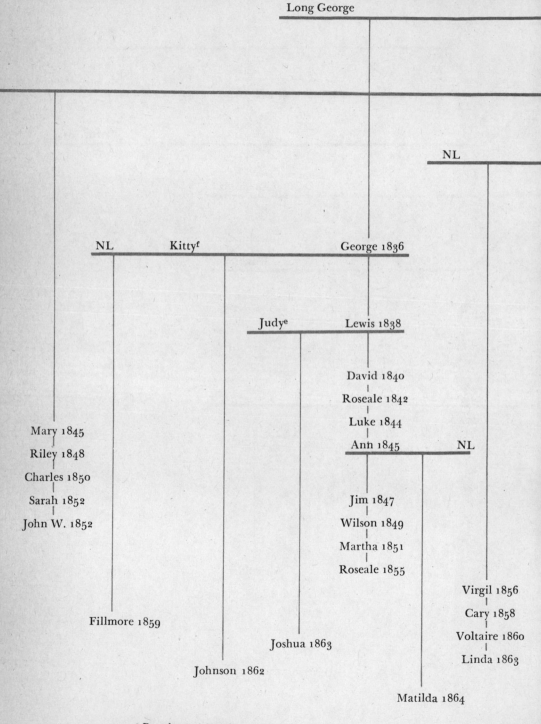

Long George

NL

NL   Kitty^f   George 1836

Judy^e   Lewis 1838

David 1840

Roseale 1842

Luke 1844

Mary 1845   Ann 1845   NL

Riley 1848

Charles 1850

Sarah 1852   Jim 1847

John W. 1852   Wilson 1849

Martha 1851

Roseale 1855

Virgil 1856

Cary 1858

Fillmore 1859   Voltaire 1860

Linda 1863

Joshua 1863

Johnson 1862

Matilda 1864

xiv   ^e Daughter of Harriet and Sam.
^f Daughter of Big Hannah.

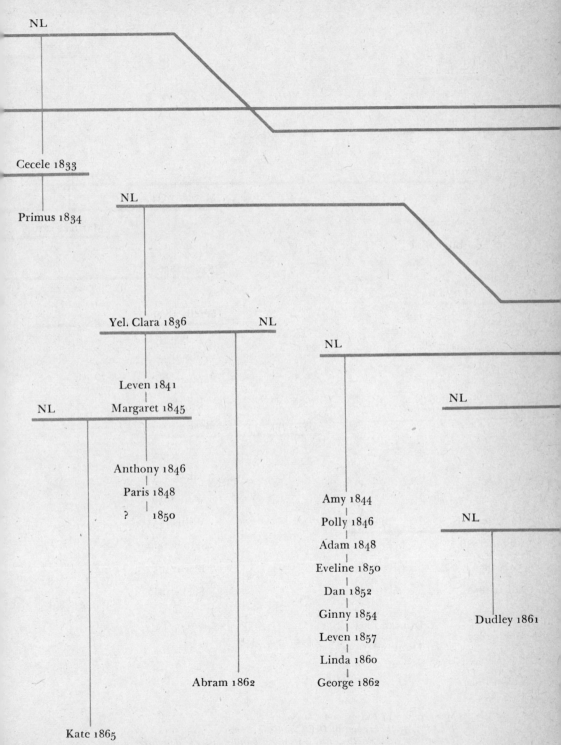

NL

Cecele 1833

Primus 1834

NL

Yel. Clara 1836   NL

NL

Leven 1841

NL   Margaret 1845

Anthony 1846

Paris 1848

?   1850

Amy 1844

Polly 1846   NL

Adam 1848

Eveline 1850

Dan 1852

Ginny 1854

Leven 1857   Dudley 1861

Linda 1860

Abram 1862   George 1862

Kate 1865

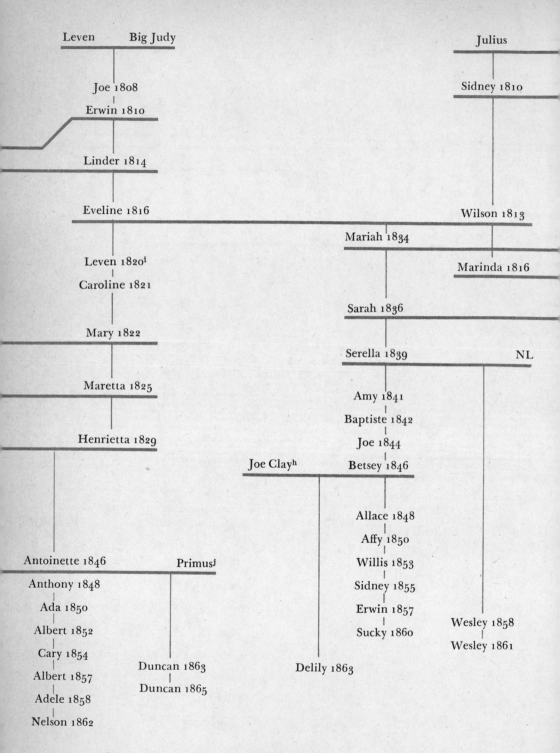

Leven   Big Judy   Julius

Joe 1808   Sidney 1810

Erwin 1810

Linder 1814

Eveline 1816   Wilson 1813

Mariah 1834

Leven 1820[i]   Marinda 1816

Caroline 1821

Sarah 1836

Mary 1822

Serella 1839   NL

Maretta 1825

Amy 1841

Baptiste 1842

Henrietta 1829   Joe 1844

Joe Clay[h]   Betsey 1846

Allace 1848

Affy 1850

Antoinette 1846   Primus[j]   Willis 1853

Anthony 1848   Sidney 1855

Ada 1850   Erwin 1857

Albert 1852   Sucky 1860   Wesley 1858

Cary 1854   Wesley 1861

Albert 1857   Duncan 1863

Adele 1858   Duncan 1865   Delily 1863

Nelson 1862

[g] *Spencer: son of Nelson and Clarinda.*
[h] *Joe Clay: probably son of Delily and Big Ben.*
[i] *Leven married Phelby, his sister's husband's sister's daughter, a niece by marriage.*
[j] *Primus: son of Frocene and unnamed father.*

xvi

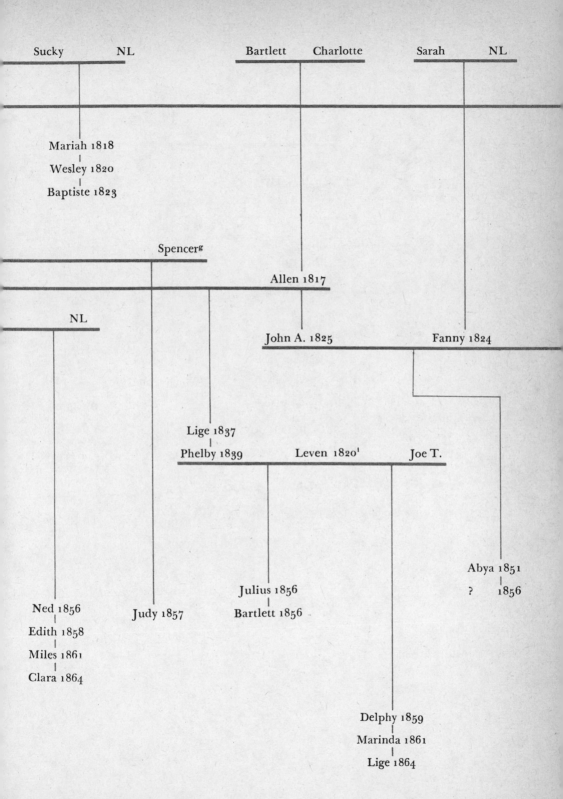

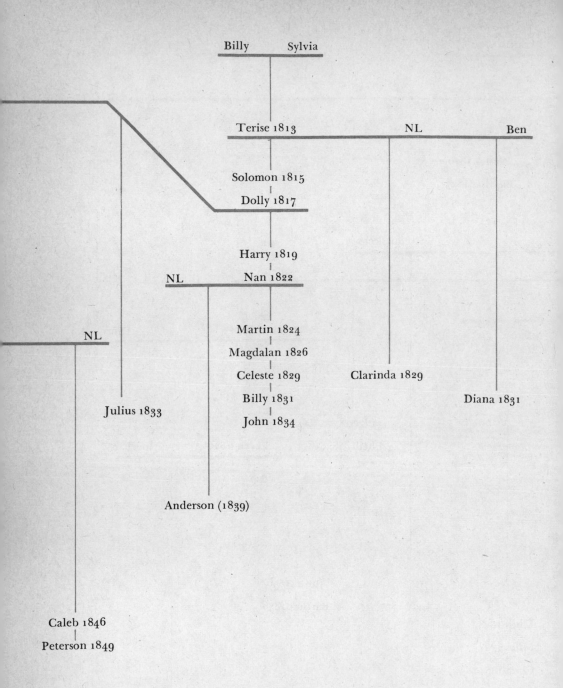

Billy   Sylvia

Terise 1813   NL   Ben

Solomon 1815

Dolly 1817

Harry 1819

NL   Nan 1822

Martin 1824

Magdalan 1826

NL   Celeste 1829   Clarinda 1829

Billy 1831   Diana 1831

Julius 1833   John 1834

Anderson (1839)

Caleb 1846

Peterson 1849

35 Henrietta Daughter of Lucia & B. Judy was born Jan.y 14th 1829

36 Rose Daughter of Barica & Sarah born Dec.r 29th 1829

37 Franswaine Daughter of Liddy & Luke born August 7th 1831, Died March 24th /56

38 Jack Son of L Judy & James born Sept.r 4th 1831

39 Rosabell Daughter of Hannah & Y Joe born 10th of April 1832

40 Louisa Daughter of Bella & Harry born 15th of April 1832

41 Cicile Daughter of Linden & Long George born the 17th of Jan.y 1833

42 Spencer Son of Clarinda & Nelson Born Feb.y 1833

43 Nannette Daughter of Louisa (Yellow) born August 1st 1833

44 Julius Cæsar Son of Dolly & Sidney was born Dec.r 24th 1833

45 Primus Son of Linden and Long George born August 21st 1834

46 Joe Son of Big Hann & Joe born Nov. 24th 18

47 Mariah Daughter of Eve & Wilson born Nov. 10th 18

48 Charlotte Daughter of Liddy & Luke born Feb 24th 1835

49 Affy Daughter of Clara & Nelson was born Ma 25th 1835

50 Jack Son of Delily & Hann George born July 1835

51 William Son of Louis (Yellow) born Jan.y 1st 18

52 Sarah Daughter of Eve & Wilson born June 22d 1

53 Isabell Daughter of Nil born August 9th 1836

54 George Son of Linden Long George born Dec.r 9th 18

55 Lige Son of Marind & Allen born Feb.y 4th 1

56 Hannah Daughter of Liddy & Luke born April 3d 1837. Died Dec 19

57 Eliza Daughter of Sucke & Paterson born June 13 1837

Pages from Slave Birth Register, Stirling Plantation, West Feliciana Parish, Louisiana, 1807–1865

113 Catrine Daughter of Rose was born August 19th 1849

114 Bob Son of Frozene & Sambo was born August 30th 1849

115 Eveline Daughter of Marietta was born Feby. 11th 1850

116 Charles Son of Nelly and Erwin was born March 10th 1850 Died 29th of July 1855

117 Peter Son of Margaret & Adam was born May 10th 1850

Edward Son of Ellen (belonging to Lewis) was born July 7th 1850

118 ada Daughter of Henrietta was born Septr. 16th 1850

Mary had a Dead Child born 25th octr. 1850

119 Affy Daughter of Eveline & Wilson was born octo 26th 1850

120 Ben Son of Harriett Sam Brown was born Novr. 15th 1850

121 Leelia Daughter of Rosabell (Yellow) was born Decr. 8th 1850

122 Richard Son of (D Niles was born March 28, 1851

123 Martha Daughter of Lindu & Long George was born July 8th 185

124 Bella Daughter of Sophy & Sam Jackson was born August 22. 185

125 Chaney Son of Nann was born Septr 3. 185

126 Fanny Daughter of Clarinda & Nilson was born Sept 4th 185

127 Abby Daughter of Anderson Fanny was born Sept. 13th 1857

Pages from Slave Birth Register, Stirling Plantation, West Feliciana Parish, Louisiana, 1807–1865

then becoming the mother of four more children. Far more children were born prior to settled unions among the Stirling than among the Good Hope slaves. Although important, that difference partly may reflect inadequate information accessible to those recording slave births. (Sophy's son Sampson, for example, was begotten by an unnamed father in 1846, and six years later Francoise's daughter Rachel also had an unnamed father. Sam, who married Sophy in 1851, was probably the father of Sophy's earlier child. Sam's father was Sampson. A son Monday also was born to this couple and had the same name as his father's brother. Francoise and Monday had a child named Levi in 1855. After Francoise died, Monday married Esther, and their two daughters were named after Monday's mother Ginny and Monday's oldest sister Clarice, whose dead son had been named Levi. Monday also had an older sister Rachel. He probably was the unnamed father of Francoise's first child.) Like most Good Hope children, most Stirling slave children grew up in large families. The median family starting between 1807 and 1855 had between four and five children, but twenty-two women had at least six children each, and four had between ten and fifteen.[9] Most children growing up in conventional families therefore had several siblings. Nearly nine of ten grew up in households in which a mother had four or more children, and just over half in households with at least seven other children. An important difference over time, however, distinguishing the Good Hope from the Stirling communities, was that first-generation Good Hope slave families were much smaller than those of later generations. In contrast, half of the twenty Stirling women who started slave families between 1807 and 1819 had five or more children. Little Judy and Amy each had eight, Big Judy had nine, and Sylvia had ten.

Although three-fourths of the Stirling women bearing children prior to 1856 formed conventional two-parent households over the full family cycle and four in five children grew up in such households, a significant number of Stirling women headed single-parent households.[10] That was the most important difference between the Stirling and Good Hope slave communities. Nearly one in five children born in families that started before 1855 grew up in households headed by women who had all their children by unnamed fathers. The sisters Yellow Mary, Henrietta, and Maretta had six, eight, and nine children respectively under these circumstances between 1836 and 1862. Between 1807 and 1855, fifty-five children were born to fifteen women by unnamed men;

slightly more than half were the children of Charlotte and these three sisters.[11] Eight of the fifteen had one or two children over the full family cycle. Here was the male-absent slave household that E. Franklin Frazier and so many others contend was the common plantation family, "the maternal family," which Frazier called "in its purest and most primitive manifestation, a natural family group similar to . . . the original or earliest form of the human group." Their presence convinced the historian Kenneth Stampp that "the typical slave family was matriarchal in form." Together with many others, Frazier and Stampp confuse a statistically significant fact—the presence of some male-absent slave households—with the characteristic, or typical, domestic arrangement, an error that wrenches the male-absent household from its *slave* cultural context.[12]

The sisters Yellow Mary, Henrietta, and Maretta and their immediate kin illustrate the relationship between the single-parent household and the larger slave community. They were the daughters of Big Judy and Leven, and had six brothers and sisters. Their sister Caroline died as an infant. Two older brothers— Erwin and Leven—settled into conventional families. After Nelly had four children by unnamed fathers, she and Erwin married and had five more children. Two sisters—Eveline and Linder (Linda)—also married. Linder's first two children were born prior to a settled union. After that, she and Long George became the parents of ten sons and daughters. Eveline married Wilson, and that couple had thirteen children. Erwin, Leven, Linder, and Eveline established households similar to their parents' household. But their sisters Yellow Mary, Maretta, and Henrietta bore children in a different domestic arrangement. Henrietta favored a domestic arrangement different from her parents and several brothers and sisters, but Henrietta's daughter Antoinette lived in the more conventional household. She had a first child by an unnamed father when she was fifteen. After that, Antoinette married Primus. The domestic arrangement revealed by Henrietta was accessible to all Stirling slave women. Most, including her mother, her two sisters, and her daughters, entered into the more conventional domestic arrangement. That fact must be kept in mind in assessing the significance of the male-absent slave household. It was important among the Stirling slaves, but it was far from common.

Atypical in the Stirling community and unknown in the Good Hope community, the single-parent household over the full family cycle nevertheless occurred among the Stirling slaves frequently enough to deserve additional comment. Much of it remains speculative, because nothing in the available evidence allows us to describe the particular circumstances that gave rise to this domestic arrangement. It is unclear whether women formed such households by design or default. All that is known is that fathers' names were never recorded in listing a child born to these women. There is no way to tell whether the mothers—especially the eight with four or more children—had all their children by a single unnamed male or by several different men. It is possible, for example, that some, if not all, of these women had spouses belonging to different owners, and that fact caused the person keeping the register to list just the mother's name. But the large number of children in several of these households together with the fact that not one of these women was sold also suggests that some women may have "freely" established a domestic arrangement different from the two-parent household. Far from revealing the legitimacy of the single-parent household, such behavior may have represented deviation from the community's norm. In no culture is a norm invariably observed.[13]

Women who bore all their children by unnamed fathers, however, were not shunned by their families of origin. In the families in which women had four or more children by unnamed fathers, at least one child in each was named for a member of the mother's family of origin. Two in five of all children born to these women had the name of a blood relative. A son born to Yellow Mary was called Leven, the name of Yellow Mary's father and older brother. Yellow Mary's sister Maretta also named a son Leven, and two of her daughters were named for Yellow Mary and Maretta's older sisters Linder and Eveline. The first son born to Nanette had his maternal uncle William's name, and Nanette's second son was named for his maternal great-grandfather, George. Yet other evidence shows that women who had children outside of marriage were not rejected by their slave parents—for instance, a Union Army register of runaway slaves admitted to Camp Barker, near Alexandria, Virginia, between June 1862 and October 1863, which recorded the marital status of the runaways. George and Corinda Johnson arrived with eight children, including their twenty-two-year-old daughter Matilda, an unmarried mother with two children of her own. Sam and Suka Lomax had seven children with them, including their eighteen-year-old daughter Aleasy and their twenty-year-old daughter Maria. Both daughters were unmarried and each had an infant daughter with her. In a single month, 402 slave women arrived in Camp Barker with either their husbands, their husbands and children, or their children. About 9 percent of these women described themselves as "single," including mothers like Matilda Johnson and Aleasy and Maria Lomax. Many, like them, were young mothers who had not yet married. A few, like the Stirling women Yellow Mary and Maretta, were older women. The thirty-five-year-old Nancy Lemas arrived with her fifteen-year-old daughter Beverley. The thirty-eight-year-old Caroline Toliver brought her three children, ranging in age from three to fourteen, with her. Their grandmother, the eighty-year-old widow Sarah Toliver, accompanied them. Nancy Lemas and Caroline Toliver told Union Army registrars they were "single" women, a fact that indicates that some slave women felt no shame in bearing all their children outside of marriage.[14]

Women who had several children by unnamed men were an important part of the Stirling slave community (far more important than in any other slave community examined in this study), but their relative significance changed over time. Few such families started before 1840. It therefore is doubtful that this arrangement had a direct link to earlier West African domestic arrangements, in which a mother and her children might form a matricentric cell within the framework of an enlarged polygynous family. If such domestic arrangements had been directly related to earlier West African patterns, they should have thrived among first (1807–1819) and second (1820–1839) generation Stirling slaves. Yet of 183 children born prior to 1839, nine in ten grew up in conventional domestic arrangements. An important change— its causes as yet unknown—occurred after 1839; after that date far more women had all their children by unnamed fathers. Nevertheless, the two-parent household was the characteristic arrangement at all times, though declining in importance. Few more mistaken beliefs existed among slaveowners than that enslavement "civilized" Africans and their descendants by forcing upon them (or making accessible to them) the Christian monogamic ideal. Their owner had allowed Stirling slaves to make their own choices. Four in five slaves born into families starting between 1807 and 1855 grew up in conventional double-headed households.

Most Stirling slave children grew up in two-parent households and large numbers of them, including children living in single-parent households, had the names of blood relatives, a fact which indicates once more that Upper and Lower South slaves shared basic beliefs. Two in five of the 232 children born between 1830 and 1865 had the names of kinsmen and kinswomen (Table 15).

TABLE 15. NAMING PRACTICES AMONG THE STIRLING
PLANTATION SLAVES, WEST FELICIANA PARISH,
LOUISIANA, 1807–1865

Date of birth	Name of newborn child	Names of parents	Relation of newborn child to person with same name
1808	Leven	Big Judy–Leven	Father
1814	Charles	Delia–Charles	Father
1815	Ben	Delia–Ben	Father
1818	Surry	Amy–Surry	Father
1819	Sampson	Ginny–Sampson	Father
1831	Billy	Sylvia–Billy	Father
1831	Jack	Little Judy–Yanko	Father
1833	Julius	Dolly–Sidney	Father's father
1834	Mariah	Eveline–Wilson	Father's half sister
1834	Joe	Big Hannah–Yellow Joe	Father
1836	George	Linder–Long George	Father
1836	Ginny	Clarice–John	Mother's mother
1837	Amy	Big Nan	Mother's mother
1837	Hannah	Liddy–Luke	Mother's sister
1839	Ben	Nan–Ben	Father; father's father
1839	Clarice	Rachel	Mother's sister
1839	Barika	Nelly	Mother's husband (stepfather)
1840	Liddy	Little Sucky–Peterson	Mother's sister
1841	Leven	Yellow Mary	Mother's father
1842	Josephine	Big Hannah–Yellow Joe	Father
1842	Baptiste	Eveline–Wilson	Father's half brother
1843	Mary	Nelly–Erwin	Father's sister
1843	Judy	Harriet	Mother's mother
1843	Philip	Big Nan	Mother's brother
1844	Harriet	Margaret	Mother's sister
1844	Amy	Maretta	Mother's sister's daughter
1844	Joe	Eveline–Wilson	Mother's brother (dead)
1846	Antoinette	Henrietta	Mother's sister's son (dead)
1846	Sampson	Sophy	Father; father's father
1846	Hester	Harriet–Sam	Father's sister
1847	Henry	Margaret	Mother's brother (dead)
1848	Anthony	Henrietta	Mother's sister's son (dead)
1848	Adam	Maretta	Mother's brother's wife's half brother
1849	Wilson	Long George–Linder	Mother's sister's husband

TABLE 15.   (*Continued*)

Date of birth	Name of newborn child	Names of parents	Relation of newborn child to person with same name
1849	Henrietta's Ben	Delily–Big Ben	Father
1849	Robert	Frocene–Sambo	Father's sister's son
1850	Affy	Eveline–Wilson	Sister's husband's sister
1850	Ben	Harriet–Sam	Father's father; father's brother
1850	Peter	Margaret–Adam	Mother's brother (dead)
1850	Eveline	Maretta	Mother's sister
1851	Chaney	Nanny	Mother's father
1851	Belle	Sophy–Sampson	Mother's mother
1851	Lucinda	Louisa–Washington	Mother's sister (dead)
1852	Harry	Rosabella–Alford	Father's father
1852	Sam	Frocene–Sambo	Father
1852	Amanda	Affy	Mother's sister (dead)
1852	Sarah	Nelly–Erwin	Mother's mother
1853	Hannah	Harriet–Sam	Mother's sister
1853	Monday	Sophy–Sampson	Father's brother
1853	Alford	Louisa–Washington	Mother's brother
1854	Dave	Jane	Mother's brother (dead)
1855	Roseale	Linder–Long George	Dead sibling
1855	Sidney	Eveline–Wilson	Father's brother (dead)
1855	Levi	Francoise–Monday	Father's sister's son (dead)
1855	Joe	Rosabella–Alford	Mother's father; mother's brother
1855	Rosabella	Margaret–Adam	Mother's sister
1856	Martin	Sam–Harriet	Father's brother (dead)
1856	Hannah	Affy–Jack	Father's sister
1856	Charles	Isabella	Mother's half brother
1856	Julius	Phelby–Leven	Mother's mother's father
1856	Bartlett	Phelby–Leven	Mother's father's father
1857	Judy	Mariah–Spencer	Mother's mother's mother
1857	Leven	Maretta	Mother's father; mother's brother (dead)
1857	Albert	Henrietta	Dead sibling
1857	Erwin	Eveline–Wilson	Mother's brother (dead)
1857	Celia	Charlotte	Mother's sister (dead)
1857	Peterson	Eliza	Mother's father
1858	William	Nanette	Mother's brother
1858	Rinah	Jane	Mother's sister (dead)
1858	Wesley	Serella	Mother's father's half brother

TABLE 15. (*Continued*)

Date of birth	Name of newborn child	Names of parents	Relation of newborn child to person with same name
1858	Cary	Cecele	Mother's sister's daughter (dead)
1859	Marshall	Affy–Jack	Mother's brother (dead)
1860	Rosabella	Margaret–Adam	Dead sibling
1860	Sucky	Eveline–Wilson	Father's mother
1860	Linda	Maretta	Mother's sister
1861	Linda	Isabella–Joseph	Sister's mother's stepfather's sister
1861	Marinda	Phelby–Joe T.	Mother's mother
1861	Wesley	Serella	Dead sibling
1862	George	Maretta	Mother's sister's husband
1862	George	Nanette	Mother's mother's father
1862	Nelson	Isabella–Joseph	Mother's mother
1862	Nelson	Henrietta	Mother's sister's daughter's husband's father
1863	Linda	Cecele	Mother's mother
1863	Joe	Josephine	Mother's father (dead); mother's brother
1863	Nancy	Affy–Jack	Father's sister's daughter's daughter (dead)
1863	Ginny	Esther–Monday	Father's mother
1863	Charlotte	Margaret–Adam	Mother's brother's wife's sister's daughter (dead)
1863	Delily	Betsey–Joe Clay	Father's mother (?)
1863	Cora	Rosabella–Alford	Father's wife's sister's daughter's daughter
1864	Lige	Phelby–Joe T.	Mother's brother
1864	Lucy	Isabella–Joseph	Mother's sister (dead)
1864	Hannah	Affy–Sam	Dead sibling
1864	Evans	Affy–Sam	Dead sibling
1864	Clara	Sarah	Mother's sister's daughter (dead)
1865	Clarice	Esther–Monday	Father's sister
1865	Duncan	Antoinette–Primus	Dead sibling

Here, as elsewhere, that percentage is a minimal percentage. We do not know, for example, whether a child with an unnamed father had the name of that man or his kinsmen and kinswomen. Nor does that percentage include some children whose parents had been sold into the Stirling community and who possibly were

named for a parent's blood relatives.* Most children with kin
names had those of blood relatives. Not one of the twenty-nine
Good Hope slave children with kin names had the name of an
affinal relative. Only nine of the ninety-six Stirling children
named for kin had the name of an affinal relative. Finally, and
most important, the proportion of Stirling children named for kin
increased over time, from 30 percent between 1830 and 1849 to
nearly 50 percent between 1850 and 1865. The passage of time—
a period marked by deepening enslavement and further detachment from West African roots—had been accompanied by a
strengthening of kin identification in the Stirling slave community.

The Stirling slaves Adam and Eveline illustrate some of the
kin networks that developed on this Louisiana sugar plantation
and that were the underpinning of the slave community in 1865.
Eveline was the fourth child born to Big Judy and Leven, and
Adam, the son of Sarah and Barika, also was his mother's fourth
child. At the Civil War's end, Adam was thirty-nine and Eveline
forty-nine. The two were related by an affinal tie. Eveline's sister-
in-law was Adam's half sister. Countless blood ties enmeshed
Adam and Eveline. Adam's infant sister Josephine had died in
1830, but he grew up with another sister, Rose, and with three
half-sisters—Delily, Nelly, and Fanny. Fanny died in 1863. The
date of Nelly's death is unknown, but Delily lived until 1877
and Rose until 1915. Adam married Margaret and had ties to
her family of origin. The first daughter born to Big Hannah and
Yellow Joe, Margaret also was the granddaughter of Little Judy
and Yanko. Big Hannah had eight brothers and sisters, and
Margaret had seven male and female siblings. Margaret and
Adam settled into a permanent union in 1850. Before that, she
had two children by unnamed fathers: Harriet and Henry, named
for a maternal aunt and uncle. Adam and Margaret had seven
children of their own. Peter, their first son, had been named for a
dead maternal uncle, and their first daughter Rosabella for a
maternal aunt. When the young Rosabella died, Adam and

* Frocene was not born a Stirling slave. She appeared in the register first as
the mother of two children born in 1844 and 1847 by unnamed fathers. After that,
she and the Stirling-born Sambo had seven children. Their first two children bore
the names of a paternal uncle (Bob) and their father (Sam). Jane, York, and
Moses were born to Frocene and Sambo later. Years before, when the Stirling
whites had *hired* the couple *York* and *Nelly*, they recorded the names of children
born to them after 1834: Ginny, *Moses*, and *Jane*. In naming three of their children
York, Moses, and Jane, Sambo and Frocene suggest that Frocene was probably
York and Nelly's daughter. Her separation from a family of origin had not severed
her attachment to close blood kin.

Eveline named yet another daughter Rosabella. Adam had two step-grandchildren by 1865 and other kin in the Stirling community. He was an uncle to thirty-five children born to his sisters and half sisters and to his wife's sisters and brothers. Five other children were Adam's grandnephews and grandnieces. Eveline counted even more kin in 1865 than Adam. The third of nine children born to Big Judy and Leven, she married Wilson in 1834 and formed connections to Wilson's sister and brother as well as his half sister and two half brothers. Eveline was an aunt to forty-five children and great-aunt to fifteen more children by 1865. She and Wilson had thirteen children and eight grandchildren born to their daughters Mariah, Sarah, Serella, and Betsey. Seven of Eveline and Wilson's children and five of their grandchildren carried kin names. Two sons, Joe and Erwin, were named for Eveline's brothers and two others, Sidney and Baptiste, for Wilson's brother and half brother. A daughter Mariah had the name of Wilson's half sister, and another daughter had the name of Eveline's son-in-law Spencer's sister Affy. Eveline and Wilson had their thirteenth child—the girl Sucky—in 1860 and named her for her paternal grandmother. A grandson Wesley (born to Eveline's daughter Serella by an unnamed father) was named for his paternal half uncle, and a granddaughter (born to Eveline's daughter Sarah by an unnamed father) was named for her dead maternal aunt's dead daughter Yellow Clara. Another of Eveline's daughters, Betsey, had her first child in 1863. Betsey was married to Joe, and their child was named for its paternal grandmother. A fourth daughter, Mariah, married Spencer, and their first child was called Judy, named for her mother's mother's mother.

When compared, the Stirling and Good Hope slaves show important similarities in their beliefs. A far more significant test of the depth and breadth of the slave cultural beliefs illustrated first by the Good Hope blacks, however, results from a comparison between the Good Hope slaves and those owned by the Virginian John Cowper Cohoon, Jr. The Stirling and Good Hope slave communities had different economic functions and different types of owners. Both communities, however, had developed over a relatively long period of time. Neither community was disrupted by frequent sale. By slave standards, these were two relatively settled slave communities. The similarities in their behavior may have resulted from this fact, making both the Good Hope and Stirling slaves atypical.

The Virginia slaves belonging first to John Cohoon and then

to Cohoon and his sons shared none of these advantages. Cohoon kept birth and death lists as well as sale, purchase, and gift records from the time he started to farm in 1811 or 1813 to his death in 1863, by which time his Cedar Vale plantation, with forty-seven slaves, was one of the largest in Nansemond County. In 1860, only ten of Nansemond's 619 slaveowners held forty or more slaves.[15] Cohoon's records indicate that he put together his initial labor force with slaves who came to him from his father, by marriage, and through purchase. These records permit examination of the relative importance of slaves and their owners in shaping viable and affective slave familial and kin groups. The Cohoon slaves experienced much more disruption than either the Good Hope or the Stirling slaves. Thus, if by 1863 Cohoon's slaves were a genuine community, with kin networks similar to those discerned among the Good Hope and Stirling slaves, they must have created them themselves in the course of the previous half century.

That Cohoon's slaves created such a community is indicated in Tables 16 and 17 and in Chart 4. Similarities existed on all important measures between the Cedar Vale slaves and the Good Hope and Stirling slaves. Two in three women were between seventeen and nineteen at the birth of a first child. None was younger. Seven in eleven marriages prior to 1850 lasted at least thirteen years, three of them at least fifteen years, and another three at least twenty-three years. Fewer children were born before their parents' marriages than in the other two communities. Before 1850, only Betsey had a large number of children by one or more unnamed men. Nearly nine in ten children grew up in conventional households. Exogamy ruled. In naming children for blood kin, the Cohoon slaves conformed to the pattern already discerned. Of the fifty-one children born to the children and grandchildren of Fanny and Jacob and Margaret and Tom between 1840 and 1862, nearly two in five had the names of consanguinal kin.[16]

That all happened even though sale, gift-transfer to Cohoon's sons, and especially death disrupted most Cohoon slave families. Two-thirds of the children for whom evidence is available died before reaching adulthood. By 1862, for example, all six of Nancy and Edmond's children had died, as had Betsey and five of her six children. Harriet and Henry had the largest family, but six of their fourteen children had died by 1852. Cohoon sold Amy (born in 1833), Lucy (born in 1824), and Isaac (born in 1835). Isaac went in 1862 for "attempting to become a Yankee." The dates of the other sales (one for "bad conduct") are unknown. Kin remem-

TABLE 16. COHOON PLANTATION SLAVE FAMILIES AND GENERATIONS, NANSEMOND COUNTY, VIRGINIA, 1811–1863

Generation with First Child Born Between 1811 and 1819

No.	Year	Mother	Father	Child	Status by 1863
1.	1811	Fanny	Jacob	Henry	
	1816	same	same	Mary	dead
	1818	same	same	Charles	
	1824	same	same	Lucy	sold
	1828	same	same	Rachel	
	1831	same	same	Margaret	
	1833	same	same	Jefferson	dead (1852)
	1835	same	same	Matilda	
2.	1815	Margaret	Tom	Tom	
	1817	same	same	Lewis	
	1819	same	same	Jack	
	1821	same	same	Robert	dead
	1822	same	same	Lizzie	
	1824	same	same	Huldah Sr.	given to son William
	1827	same	same	Adeline	given to son Willis
	1831	same	same	Bristol	dead
	1833	same	same	Amy	sold
	1838	same	same	Sylvia	dead
3.	1817	Nancy	Edmond	Betsey	dead (1855)
	1822	same	same	Emaline	dead (1853)
	1824	same	same	Edmond	dead
	1826	same	same	William	dead
	1829	same	same	Martha	dead
	1834	same	same	Dianah	dead

Generation with First Child Born Between 1820 and 1839

No.	Year	Mother	Father	Child	Status by 1863
1.	1823	Jenny	Bob	Philip	
	1825	same	same	Huldah Jr.	
	1828	same	same	Edward	dead
	1830	same	same	Elijah	given to son Willis
2.	1826	Chloe	not listed	Davy	
	1829	same	not listed	Jackson	given to son William
3.	1829	Celia	not listed	Eliza	
	1831	same	not listed	Ellick	
	1835	same	not listed	Isaac	sold
	1838	same	Jack Beeman	Nancy	given to son William
	1840	same	same	Frank	given to son Thomas
	1844	same	same	Cornelius	dead
	1845	same	same	Luke	

Table 16. (Continued)

No.	Year	Mother	Father	Child	Status in 1863
	1849	same	same	Jacob	
	1851	same	same	John	
4.	1836	Mary	Bob	Fanny	dead
	1837	same	same	Jacob	dead
5.	1836	Farley	not listed	William A.	given to son Willis
	1840	same	not listed	Sarah Elizabeth	given to son Willis
	1844	same	Dick Pitts	Emily	given to son Willis
	1846	same	same	Christiana	dead
	1848	same	same	Thomas	given to son Willis
	1850	same	same	Moses	given to son Willis
6.	1836	Betsey	not listed	Adeline	dead
	1838	same	not listed	Easter	dead
	1840	same	not listed	William	given to son William
	1842	same	not listed	Judith	dead
	1843	same	not listed	Sam	dead
	1854	same	not listed	Bob	dead (1856)
7.	1837	Harriet	Henry	Mariah	dead
	1838	same	same	Washington	dead
	1840	same	same	Richard Taylor	
	1841	same	same	Jacob	dead
	1843	same	same	Lucy	dead
	1844	same	same	Fanny	
	1846	same	same	Indiana	
	1848	same	same	Easter	dead (1858)
	1849	same	same	Henry	
	1852	same	same	Wilson	
	185?	same	same	Josiah	
	1857	same	same	Missouri	
	1859	same	same	Jeruzha	
	1861	same	same	unnamed	dead (1861)

Generation with First Child Born Between 1840 and 1863

No.	Year	Mother	Father	Child	Status in 1863
1.	1841	Lizzie	Isaac Holmes	Mariah	given to son Willis
	1844	same	same	Josephine	dead
	1846	same	same	Catherine	dead
	1849	same	same	Amy	
	1851	same	same	Washington	dead
	1853	same	same	Mary Ann	
	1856	same	same	unnamed	dead (1857)
	1858	same	same	unnamed	dead (1858)
	1859	same	same	unnamed	dead (1859)
	1860	same	same	unnamed	dead (1860)
	1861	same	same	Robert	dead (1863)

T<small>ABLE</small> 16. *(Continued)*

No.	Year	Mother	Father	Child	Status in *1863*
2.	1842	Huldah Jr.	Lit. Bob	Miles	
	1845	same	same	Jenny	
	1847	same	same	Samuel	
	1850	same	same	Edward	
	1853	same	same	Sarah Ann	dead (1855)
	1855	same	same	Elijah	
	1857	same	same	Adeline	dead (1863)
	1859	same	same	Sylvia	dead (1863)
3.	1846	Huldah Sr.	Lewis Orton	Lucy Ann	given to son William
	1850	same	same	Lewis	dead
	1851	same	same	Nathaniel	given to son William
	1853	same	same	Mary Virginia	given to son William
4.	18—	Eliza	not listed	Octavia	
	1850	same	not listed	Henrietta	dead (1863)
	185–	same	not listed	Miles Washington	
	1858	same	Henry A.	Andrew Jackson	
	1859	same	same	Samuel William	belongs to son Willis
5.	1850	Rachel	David	Charles Edward	
	1854	same	same	Mary Frances	
	1857	same	same	Alice Amelia	
	1859	same	same	Josephine	
	1860	same	same	Anna Mariah	
	1862	same	same	Thomas	
6.	1850	Margaret	Max	Christopher	dead
	1854	same	same	Lucretia	dead (1855)
	1855	same	same	Florence	
	1857	same	same	Margaret Louisa	
	1858	same	same	———	
	1861	same	same	Georgianna	
7.	1852	Matilda	not listed	Washington	
	1854	same	not listed	Lucy Ann	
	1862	same	John Sanders	John Jefferson	
8.	1853	Emaline	not listed	William	dead (1854)
9.	1857	Nancy	not listed	unnamed	dead (1857)
10.	1859	Mariah	not listed	Isaac	belongs to son Willis
	1862	same	not listed	Nathaniel	belongs to son Willis
11.	1862	Jenny	not listed	Emaline	

TABLE 17.   NAMING PRACTICES AMONG THE CEDAR VALE
PLANTATION SLAVES, NANSEMOND COUNTY,
VIRGINIA, 1811–1863

Date of birth	Name of newborn child	Names of parents	Relation of newborn child to person with same name
1815	Tom	Margaret–Tom	Father
1824	Edmond	Nancy–Edmond	Father
1836	Fanny	Mary–Bob	Mother's mother
1837	Jacob	Mary–Bob	Mother's father
1840	William	Betsey	Mother's brother
1841	Jacob	Harriet–Henry	Father's father
1843	Lucy	Harriet–Henry	Father's sister
1844	Fanny	Harriet–Henry	Father's mother
1845	Jenny	Huldah, Jr.–Little Bob	Mother's mother
1849	Henry	Harriet–Henry	Father
1849	Amy	Lizzie–Isaac Hodges	Mother's sister
1850	Edward	Huldah, Jr.–Little Bob	Mother's brother
1850	Charles	Rachel–David	Mother's brother
1852	Washington	Matilda	Mother's brother's son
1854	Mary	Rachel–David	Mother's sister
1854	William	Emaline	Mother's brother
1854	Lucy Ann	Matilda	Mother's sister
1855	Elijah	Huldah, Jr.–Little Bob	Mother's brother
1857	Adeline	Huldah, Jr.–Little Bob	Father's sister
1857	Margaret	Margaret–Max	Mother
1859	Sylvia	Huldah, Jr.–Little Bob	Father's sister
1859	Isaac	Mariah	Mother's father
1861	Robert	Lizzie–Issac Hodges	Mother's brother
1861	Nathaniel	Mariah	Mother's mother's sister's son
1862	John Jefferson	Matilda–John	Father (and mother's brother)

bered the two women after their sale: Lucy's brother Henry and sister Matilda each named a daughter after her; Lizzie and Isaac Holmes had a daughter Amy, named for Lizzie's younger sister. (The practice of naming a child for a sibling sold away also occurred elsewhere. William Campbell moved from Kentucky to Missouri sometime in the early 1830s and took with him all but one member of a large family, selling the boy Millar to a cousin, who later resold him into the Lower South. Some years later, Millar's sister Malinda—fourteen years old when the separation occurred—named her first-born son for him.)[17] Cohoon sold few slaves but gave many as gifts to his sons. Sixteen Cedar Vale–born slaves, along with Farley, whom he had earlier purchased, went to them. At least one child in ten of thirteen families that started prior to 1850 was either sold or given to the owner's sons.

Cohoon's records are of far greater importance in examining the slave family and enlarged kin group, as well as other aspects of slave belief and behavior, than those left by the owners of the Good Hope and Stirling slaves. Most significantly, they allow us to see how the several generations of Cohoon slaves underwent *a cycle of family destruction, construction, and dispersal that lasted more than half a century,* affected slaves born before and after its start, and was dictated by Cohoon's changing economic circumstances. The same records also make it clear why the behavior of owners toward their slaves requires precisely the same enlarged time perspective as that essential to understanding slave belief and behavior. Owners regularly interacted with their slaves. It is important to study the consequences of such interactions. They describe particular moments in a developing relationship. But it is even more important to examine the behavior of owners over time (say, in 1825 and 1855) in order to assess continuities and discontinuities in the relationship between slaves and their owners.

The *first phase* in the cycle that shaped the Cohoon slave community involved family destruction. Marriage and purchases allowed Cohoon to put together an initial labor force. Cohoon's father gave him one slave named Scotland, and he acquired eight more in 1813 when he married Mary Louisa Everett. Cohoon purchased the rest—at least twenty-eight men, women, and children—from no fewer than *twelve different owners and estates.* The initial labor force and its origins are indicated in Table 18, and the names of those who later married are printed in italics. The early purchases included some women (such as Fanny, Jenny, Chloe, and Farley) with young children and many single adult men and women. Cohoon never bought either a completed slave family or a young married couple. His purchases undoubtedly caused the separation of men, women, and children from immediate families and from families of origin. (When Cohoon and Mary Everett married, some of her slaves were probably separated from immediate kin.) The economic consequences of Cohoon's marriage and slave purchases are indicated in Chart 5. Two of the thirteen slave families that started before 1850 involved men and women *born* Cedar Vale slaves.* The other families had as parents men and women acquired either by

* Huldah, Sr., and Little Bob, and Betsey, all of whose children had unnamed fathers.

TABLE 18.   ACQUISITION OF SLAVES BY JOHN C. COHOON, CEDAR
VALE PLANTATION, NANSEMOND COUNTY, VIRGINIA,
DATES UNKNOWN

Name of former owner	*Name of slave*
1. John C. Cohoon, Sr. (father)	Scotland
2. Mary Louisa Everett (wife)	Simon, Parish, Bristol, Charlotte, Harrison, *Margaret,** *Nancy,** Jim
3. John or Jesse Holland Estate	*Jacob,* Anthony, Africa, *Chloe* and son Davy
4. Jesse Carr	Rachel, Jackson (son of Chloe)
5. John Bevans	Rose,† *Jenny* and children,** Philip, *Huldah* and Edward
6. Harry Carter	*Celia*§
7. Sampson Whitlock Estate	*Fanny* and two children‡
8. George Godwin	*Tom*
9. John Hargroves	Joe
10. James Holladay	Daniel
11. Minton	*Celia*§
12. Culpepper	Harriet**
13. Hoodkey (?)	Bob
14. Frustee (?) Estate	*Farley* and son William A.,** Sally, Cynthia
15. Unknown	Miles, Sr., Jesse

* It is possible that Margaret (Miles and "two unnamed babies") and Nancy (Lucy, Mariah, and Sam) had given birth to children before becoming part of the Cedar Vale and that their children lived on the Cedar Vale place.

† It is possible that Rose also brought children (Tom, Celia, Martha, and Baby) with her to the Cohoon place.

‡ The registers are confused on how many children Fanny had before her sale. It is possible she had as many as six (Mariah, Jacob, Laura, Celia, Davy, and Easter).

§ The Celia purchased from Minton rather than the Celia purchased from Harry Carter may have been the mother of the several children born to a woman of that name on the Cedar Vale plantation.

** Cohoon bought most of these slaves in the years following his marriage, but Jenny and Harriet came sometime around 1830, and Farley came between 1835 and 1840.

marriage† or by purchase.‡ Three slaves married the children of slaves who had not belonged to Cohoon prior to 1813.§ Cohoon also allowed others in this group,** along with children born to this group,†† to marry Edmond, Dick Pitts, Jack Beeman, Isaac Holmes, and Lewis Orton, all of whom belonged to whites nearby.[18]

† Margaret and Nancy.

‡ Jacob, Chloe, Jenny, Celia, Fanny, Tom, Harriet, Bob, Huldah, Jr., and Farley.

§ Huldah, Jr., Harriet, and Bob.

** Celia, Farley, and Nancy.

†† Lizzie and Huldah, Sr.

Chart 4. Family and Kinship Structure, John C. Cohoon's Cedar Vale Plantation, Nansemond County, Virginia, 1811–1863

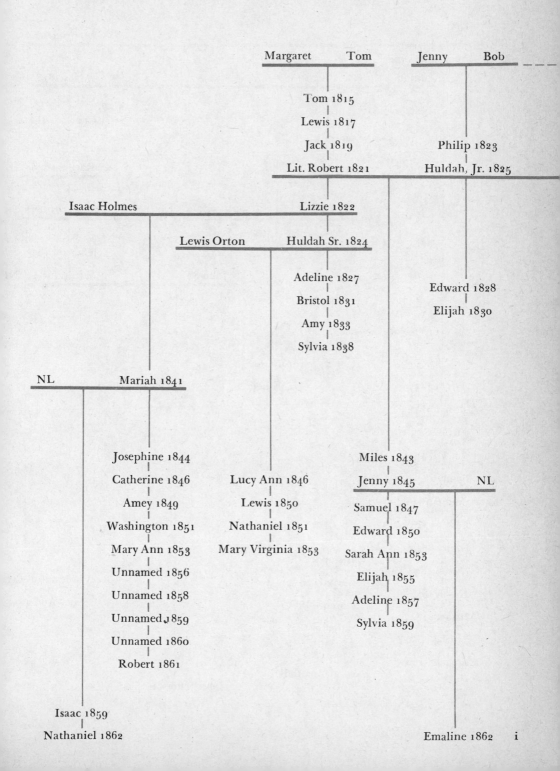

Margaret   Tom   Jenny   Bob – – – –

Tom 1815

Lewis 1817

Jack 1819   Philip 1823

Lit. Robert 1821   Huldah, Jr. 1825

Isaac Holmes   Lizzie 1822

Lewis Orton   Huldah Sr. 1824

Adeline 1827

Bristol 1831   Edward 1828

Amy 1833   Elijah 1830

Sylvia 1838

NL   Mariah 1841

Josephine 1844   Miles 1843

Catherine 1846   Lucy Ann 1846   Jenny 1845   NL

Amey 1849   Lewis 1850   Samuel 1847

Washington 1851   Nathaniel 1851   Edward 1850

Mary Ann 1853   Mary Virginia 1853   Sarah Ann 1853

Unnamed 1856   Elijah 1855

Unnamed 1858   Adeline 1857

Unnamed 1859   Sylvia 1859

Unnamed 1860

Robert 1861

Isaac 1859

Nathaniel 1862   Emaline 1862   i

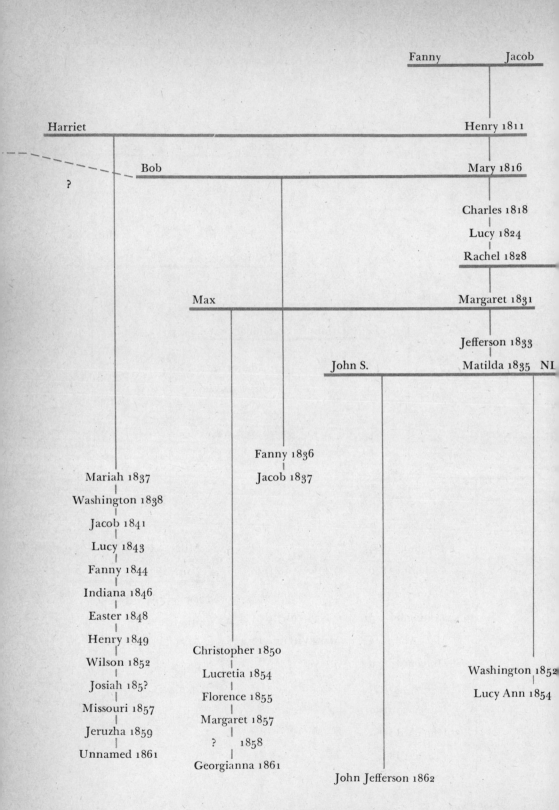

Fanny   Jacob

Harriet   Henry 1811

        Bob   Mary 1816

                                                                  Charles 1818
?
                                                                   Lucy 1824

                                                                  Rachel 1828

        Max   Margaret 1831

                                                                 Jefferson 1833

                              John S.   Matilda 1835   NI

                           Fanny 1836
                           Jacob 1837

    Mariah 1837

Washington 1838

    Jacob 1841

    Lucy 1843

    Fanny 1844

  Indiana 1846

   Easter 1848

   Henry 1849
                        Christopher 1850
  Wilson 1852
                         Lucretia 1854   Washington 1852
   Josiah 185?
                         Florence 1855   Lucy Ann 1854
 Missouri 1857
                         Margaret 1857
 Jeruzha 1859
                           ?   1858
Unnamed 1861
                        Georgianna 1861

                                                  John Jefferson 1862

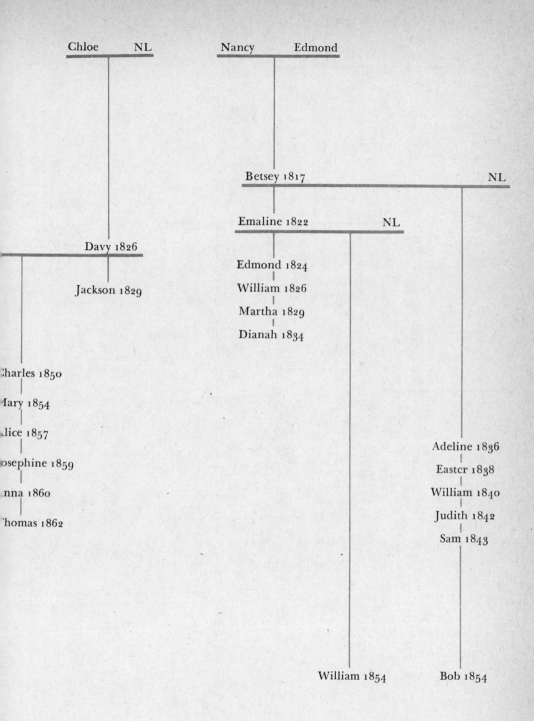

Chloe   NL   Nancy   Edmond

Betsey 1817   NL

Emaline 1822   NL

Davy 1826

Edmond 1824

Jackson 1829

William 1826

Martha 1829

Dianah 1834

Charles 1850

Mary 1854

Alice 1857

osephine 1859

nna 1860

Thomas 1862

Adeline 1836

Easter 1838

William 1840

Judith 1842

Sam 1843

William 1854   Bob 1854

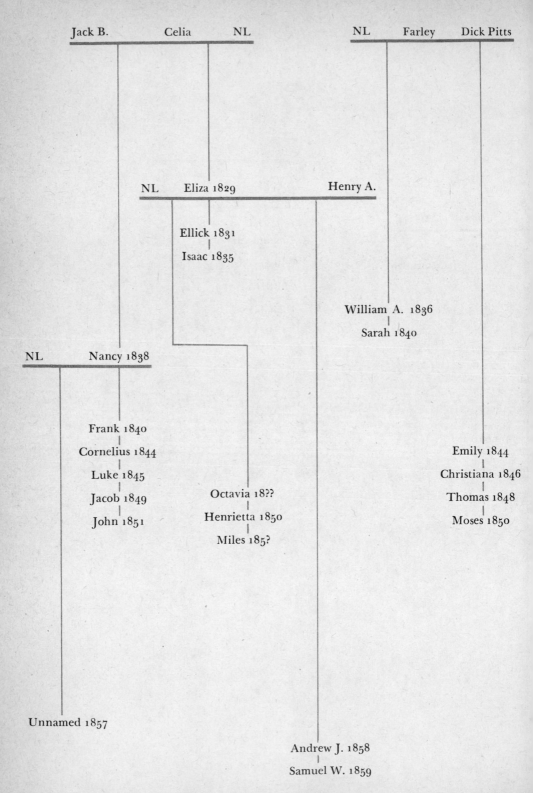

Jack B.   Celia   NL   NL   Farley   Dick Pitts

NL   Eliza 1829   Henry A.

Ellick 1831
Isaac 1835

William A. 1836
Sarah 1840

NL   Nancy 1838

Frank 1840
Cornelius 1844
Luke 1845   Octavia 18??
Jacob 1849   Henrietta 1850
John 1851   Miles 185?

Emily 1844
Christiana 1846
Thomas 1848
Moses 1850

Unnamed 1857

Andrew J. 1858
Samuel W. 1859

Names &c. continued

Daniel	(Part of Jas. Holladay ad'mr _____	(Dead)	60
Jacob	Born my property (_____ child)	(Dead)	61
Easter	ditto do do (_____)	Dead	62
Nancy	ditto do do (Celia's Child)	Given to Wm Jno	63
Sylvia	ditto do do (Margaret's child)	(Dead)	64
Washington	ditto do do (Harriet's Child)	(Dead)	65
Richard Taylor	ditto do do (ditto ditto)		66
William	ditto do do (Betsy's ditto)	Given to Wm Jno.	67
Sarah Elizabeth	ditto do do (Tarley's ditto)	Born to Willis	68
Frank	ditto do do (Celia's ditto)	Given to Thomas	69
Mariah	ditto do do (Lizzy's ditto)	Given to Willis	70
Jacob	ditto do do (Harriet's ditto)		71
Judith	ditto do do (Betsy's ditto)	(Dead)	72
Lucy	ditto do do (Henry & Harriet's ditto)	Dead	73
Miles	ditto do do (Little Bob & Huldah Jr. ditto)		74
Sam	ditto do do (Betsy's child)	(Dead)	75
Emily (or Milly)	ditto do do (Tarley's ditto)	Given to Willis	76
Cornelius	ditto do do (Celia's ditto)	died 29th Jany 1853	77
James Henry	ditto do do (Harriet's ditto)		78
Josephine	ditto do do (Lizzy's ditto)	Dead	79
Jenny	ditto do do (Little Bob & Huldah's)		80
Fanny	ditto do do (Henry & Harriet's)		81
Luke	ditto do do (Celia's Child)		82
Christiana	ditto do do (Tarley's ditto)	Dead	83
Catharine	ditto do do (Lizzy's ditto)	Dead	84
Indiana	ditto do do (Harriet's ditto)		85
Lucy Ann	ditto do do (Huldah Senr. do)	Given to Wm Jno	86
Samuel	ditto do do (Huldah Junr. ditto)		87
Tom	do do do (Tarley's ditto)	Given to Willis	88
Easter	do do do (Henry & Harriet's)	dead	89

*Fragment of Slave Birth Register, John C. Cohoon's Cedar Vale
Plantation, Nansemond County, Virginia, 1811 (1813)–1863*

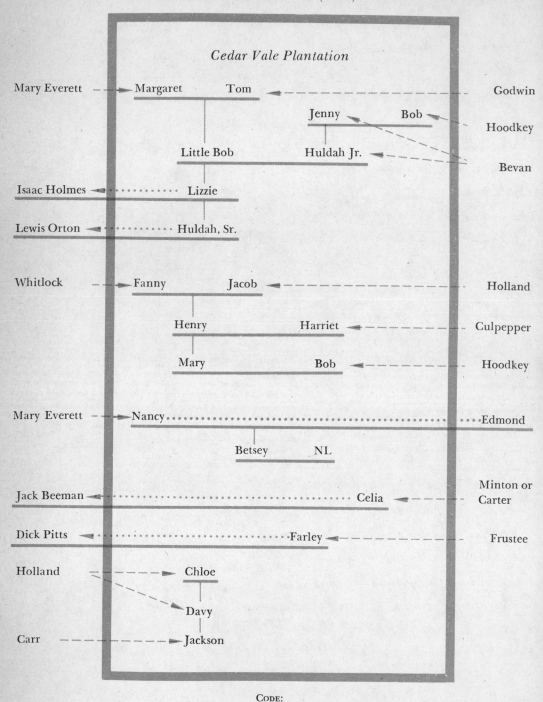

CHART 5. ORIGINS OF SLAVE PARENTS TO CHILDREN BORN ON
JOHN C. COHOON'S CEDAR VALE PLANTATION, NANSEMOND
COUNTY, VIRGINIA, 1811 (1813)–1863

Cedar Vale Plantation

Mary Everett — — → Margaret   Tom ← — — — — Godwin

                          Jenny ← — — Bob ← — Hoodkey

        Little Bob   Huldah Jr. ← — — — — Bevan

Isaac Holmes ← · · · · · · Lizzie

Lewis Orton ← · · · · · · Huldah, Sr.

Whitlock — — → Fanny   Jacob ← — — — — — Holland

        Henry   Harriet ← — — — — Culpepper

        Mary   Bob ← — — — — Hoodkey

Mary Everett — — → Nancy · · · · · · · · · · · · · · Edmond

        Betsey   NL

Jack Beeman ← · · · · · · · · · · · · · · Celia ← — — Minton or
                                                      Carter

Dick Pitts ← — — — — — — Farley ← — — — Frustee

Holland — — → Chloe

        Davy

Carr — — — — → Jackson

CODE:

——————— Husband and wife.
— — — — Sale into Cohoon plantation.
· · · · · · · · · Marriage to male off Cohoon plantation.

vi

Settled immediate families and expanding kin networks developed over time, but their emergence was part of a far more important social process that had begun with the involuntary destruction of an earlier generation of families. To suggest that Cohoon—either as plantation capitalist or as plantation patriarch—"sponsored" the formation of "stable" slave families would be to misinterpret the behavior of men like him. Cohoon became a successful planter by breaking up one generation of slave families, recruiting a labor force thereby, and then encouraging its natural reproduction. These were complementary decisions at different moments in his career, choices dictated primarily by changing economic circumstances and by the desire of a farmer to become a planter.

Many of the decisions Cohoon made affected the shape of the slave kin networks that developed, but the most important was his allowing some women to marry men belonging to different owners. Evidence is lacking, but the adult men Cohoon owned probably had wives and children belonging to other owners. Several considerations probably prompted Cohoon to let women marry off his place. Children born to his slave women whose husbands belonged to others were Cohoon property. Such permissive arrangements increased his assets. The large Nelson County, Virginia, planter Thomas Jefferson Massie explained to his father why owners like Cohoon let slaves marry men with other owners: "Old Amy without a husband would scarcely have been the 'goose which laid the golden egg' had she been denied a husband 'from home,' seeing her master had none at home for her." Denying such marriages "might do for one who holds a 100 or so [slaves]; but the small fry (and 99 of every 100 are small fry) class of owners can't think of it." Nearly all males born Cohoon slaves between 1815 and 1824, moreover, had blood ties to women born in those same years; hence by 1840 Cohoon owned few men eligible— *by slave standards*—to marry Cohoon women and then begin reproducing his labor force and increasing his wealth. That was because slave exogamous beliefs shaped the way in which slaves selected spouses. Such beliefs therefore directly or indirectly encouraged "broad" slave marriages. Marriages off the plantation and the fact that Cohoon never broke up an entire family and never separated a husband and wife by sale "stabilized" the plantation community. Enduring marriages resulted, involving men, women, and children belonging to Cohoon and whites nearby and allowing Cohoon to fulfill the ideal ("the universal" disposition) that spurred slave purchase ("the first use for savings") among whites anxious to improve their social and economic position. "The negro purchased is the last possession to be parted with," said *DeBow's Review*. "If a woman, her children become heirlooms, and make the nucleus of an estate. . . . A plantation of fifty or sixty persons has been established from the descendants of a single female in the course of the lifetime of the original purchasers." Such a woman lived on Thomas R. R. Cobb's father's plantation. She "could call together more than one hundred of her lineal descendants," and the younger Cobb remembered seeing "this old negro dance at the wedding of her great granddaughter." Fanny (purchased from the Whitlock estate) and Margaret (who came to Cohoon when he married) were like this older Cobb woman. Seventy-three blood descendants owned by Cohoon and his sons at one time or another were their children, grandchildren, and great-grandchildren.[19]

Although Cohoon made *different* decisions after 1835 from those that characterized his rise to planter status, they affected the same group of slaves. Slaves whose lives had been disrupted by Cohoon's early purchases and his marriage were later permitted to live in settled families. A farmer who had broken up slave families to create a large agricultural enterprise *became* a planter who allowed slave families to "stabilize" in order to nourish and enlarge that enterprise. Cohoon purchased Fanny and her two children from one estate and Jacob, later her husband, from another estate sometime before 1815, detaching them from daily contact with their immediate families. The same man mourned the sixty-eight-year-old Fanny's death in 1857: "She was a good and faithful servant, leaving many children and grandchildren to mourn her loss." Cohoon wrote that near her name in a death register. He failed to mention that her daughter Lucy, whom he had sold, probably knew nothing of her mother's death. One other slave merited that kind of notice from Cohoon in the death lists. Big Bob died in 1853, and Cohoon wrote by his name, "a valuable servant."

Despite the violent and painful means by which Cohoon had gathered his labor force, his slaves had constructed a community, by the 1850s and early 1860s, that was similar to the South Carolina Good Hope and Louisiana Stirling communities. The process of family fragmentation to which their parents and grandparents had been subjected between 1815 and 1835 distinguished the Cohoon slaves from these South Carolina and Louisiana slaves.

That is why the similarities in behavior among the Cedar Vale, Good Hope, and Stirling slaves are so significant in examining the adaptive behavior of the slaves and in assessing the importance of slave beliefs. Nothing is known about the Good Hope and Stirling slaves before their names appeared in obscure birth registers, but the early Cedar Vale slaves who became the parents of two generations of Cohoon blacks had been scrambled together forcibly from diverse owners by a young Virginian's desire to become a planter. Most were the children of Afro-Americans and the descendants of men and women wrenched much earlier from West African familial and kin groups. Afro-American slaves were the initial victims of Cohoon's enterprise, and his over-all strategy worked well. At his death, he owned forty-seven slaves; his sons owned another eighteen. Measured by standards common to the slaveholding class, Cohoon, whose father had given him one slave, had done quite well. But measured by the standards common to the slave culture, the Cohoon slaves and those belonging to his sons also had done well. Those measures, of course, differ in their historical meaning.

That culture was not merely a plantation culture. It was a slave culture. The behavior of the Cohoon slaves requires us to make that essential distinction. Historians frequently distinguish between the condition of plantation and farm slaves, an important one for many analytic purposes. The behavior of the Cohoon slaves, however, suggests that the distinction is inappropriate in discussing slave marital and sexual beliefs. Only the last generation of Cohoon slaves were born plantation slaves. It is improbable that the detached individuals brought together by Cohoon's purchases at about the time of the War of 1812 had come from large plantations. Most probably came from smaller agricultural units. But even if some had been born plantation slaves, Cohoon's place—the setting in which their community and its closely related families emerged—*became* a fairly large Upper South plantation over the next twenty or thirty years, a development that transformed their slave status. All who became adults in the 1830s and the 1840s also became large-plantation slaves. Their response to that transformation had its roots among slaves who had not been born large-plantation slaves and who carried into developing large plantations important slave beliefs unrelated in origin to large-plantation social experiences.

In 1863, the Cohoon slaves lived on a large plantation. Plantation slaves descended from nonplantation slaves lived in an exogamous slave community characterized by extended kin networks, long marriages, and naming patterns rooted in consanguinal and affinal connections. Before 1830, some may have retained distant but affective connections with kin from whom they had been detached by an owner's marriage and his slave purchases, but extended kin networks did not exist within the developing Cohoon slave community. They emerged after that date. In 1830, as illustrated in Chart 6, five families and a number of single slaves lived together on the developing plantation, but marital ties did not connect these families. The first such tie occurred in 1836 when the widower Bob married Fanny and Jacob's daughter Mary. Their two children, who died in infancy, were named Fanny and Jacob. The next such marriage occurred in 1843 when Huldah, Jr., and Margaret and Tom's son Little Bob married. Five of their eight children were named for blood kin. By slave standards, the Cedar Vale blacks could not have started from a more disadvantaged social and familial circumstance. And yet by the Civil War, men, women, and children whose parents and grandparents had been detached from their kin shared common kin networks and marital and family practices with slaves whose parents and grandparents had lived in more settled plantation communities. The kin networks that developed among the Cedar Vale slaves after 1835 meant that by the late 1850s these slaves lived in a more cohesive social setting than had existed between 1815 and 1830. But these networks, so important in binding the slaves to one another, developed later in time than among the Good Hope and Stirling slaves.

Detached from their late-eighteenth- and early-nineteenth-century Afro-American immediate families, the Cohoon slaves reconstituted themselves in a community characterized by conventional Afro-American families and kin networks. Evidence of their adaptive capacities, their behavior indicates the important influence of slave beliefs learned from eighteenth-century parents and other older kin. Although the Cohoon slaves remained Upper South slaves, the process of family destruction followed by the creation of settled families and the development of kin networks that took place among them occurred time and again over the entire South when aggressive and profit-hungry young owners started careers by purchasing either individuals cut off from immediate families or whole families cut off from developing kin networks. That is what gives the Cedar Vale slaves so much importance. In the decades following the great expansion of the plantation economy to the Lower South and just preceding the

CHART 6. SLAVE FAMILIES OWNED BY JOHN C. COHOON, CEDAR VALE PLANTATION, NANSEMOND COUNTY, VIRGINIA, 1830

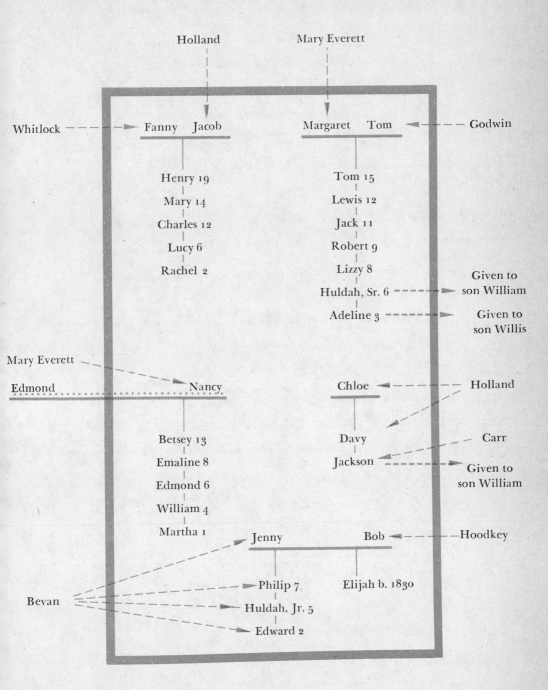

Holland   Mary Everett

Whitlock ----→ Fanny   Jacob   Margaret   Tom ←---- Godwin

Henry 19   Tom 15
Mary 14   Lewis 12
Charles 12   Jack 11
Lucy 6   Robert 9
Rachel 2   Lizzy 8
                  Huldah, Sr. 6 ----→ Given to son William
                  Adeline 3 ----→ Given to son Willis

Mary Everett ---
Edmond ·········· Nancy   Chloe ←---- Holland

Betsey 13   Davy ←---- Carr
Emaline 8   Jackson
Edmond 6   ----→ Given to son William
William 4
Martha 1   Jenny   Bob ←---- Hoodkey

Bevan   Philip 7   Elijah b. 1830
               Huldah, Jr. 5
               Edward 2

CODE:
—————————— Husband and wife.
- - - - - - - Sold into plantation or owned by wife.
· · · · · · · · Marriage to male off plantation.
- - - - - - - Gift to son.

i

1849 Names & Number of Negroes, birth &c. pg 119

        Number brt from page 119 ———— 91

Henry ——— (Henry & Harriet's child) ———— 92

Lewis ———— (Lewis & Huldah child) Dead ———— 93

Moses ———— (Dick Pett & Tabisey child given to Willis ———— 94

Charles Edward (Rachel's child ———— 95

Edward ——— (Little Bob & Little Huldah child) ———— 96

Christopher or Kitt (Margaret's child) Dead ———— 97

John (Eliza do) ———— 98

Washington (Lizzy's do) ———— Dead ———— 99

Nathaniel (Huldah Senr. do) ———— 100

Wilson (Henry & Harriet's do) ———— 101

Washington (Matilda do) ————

Sarah Ann (Robert & Huldah's do) ——— Dead ———— 103

Octavia (Eliza's child) ———— 104

Mary Ann Lizzy's child ———— 705

Mary Virginia (Huldah's child) given to wm John ———— 106

Lucy Ann (Matilda's child) ———— 107

Robert or Bob (Betsey's do (died Augt 1856) ———— 108

Mary Frances / foley Rachel's do ———— 107

William (Emaline do (died 9th June 1854 ———— 110

Josiah (Henry & Harriet child ———— 111

Lucretia Max & Margaret do dead ———— 112

Henrietta Eliza. child ———— 113

Elijah ——— (Little Bob & Little Huldah child) ——— 114

Florence (Max & Margaret's child) ——— 115

Miles Washington Eliza's child) ———— 116

Unnamed (Lizzy's child & died 25th July 1857 ———— 117

Alice Amelia (Rachel's child)

John C. Cohoon's Cedar Vale Plantation, Nansemond County,
Virginia, Fragment of Slave Birth Register, 1811–1863

emancipation, new kin networks like those on the Cedar Vale plantation emerged among plantation slaves—themselves often descended from slaves who had been farm slaves—over the entire South. Two such late developing slave communities—one in northern Louisiana and the other in Alabama—will shortly be examined. By 1865, enough time had passed for these slaves to reveal social and cultural beliefs similar to those held by slaves living in the Good Hope, Stirling, and Cedar Vale communities.[20]

We have not yet finished examining the cycle of family destruction, construction, and dispersal that involved the Cohoon slaves. Sale and gift-transfer as well as cross-owner ("broad") marriage characterized a third stage of the cycle by expanding slave kin networks beyond the boundaries fixed by ownership and therefore made slaves less dependent upon ties to an individual owner. Cross-owner marriages permitted Cohoon to reproduce his labor force, and gift-transfers to his sons (a common practice as yet inadequately studied)[21] allowed them to begin the cycle so successfully managed by their father. Cohoon's economic and familial interests dictated such decisions, which, in turn, had unintended, little-noticed, and profoundly important social consequences among the slaves.

Kin networks broke out of the boundaries fixed by ownership and thereby connected men, women, and children of similar and different slave generations who belonged to different owners. That is seen best in 1863, at the moment of John Cohoon's death, by examining the slaves belonging earlier in time to Cohoon and *some* of the important blood and marital ties that related them to one another. Kin networks had developed from an initial core of Cohoon slaves, but in 1863, men, women, and children were owned by Cohoon and *at least thirteen other whites*. Blood or marital connections bound together people living on at least fourteen estates, but this estimate ignores possible off-plantation marriages by the men Cohoon and his sons owned as well as the possible marriages of Lucy and Amy, who had been sold. If these others also had married slaves belonging to yet different owners, the enlarged kin networks would have involved *twenty-four owners* (Chart 7). Non-Cohoon slaves like John Saunders, Lewis Orton, and Isaac Holmes, who were married to Cohoon slaves, moreover, extended the networks even further, although we cannot trace those ties. Charts 7 and 8 show the inadequacy of examining slave marriage and kinship by studying only the slaves belonging to a single owner At his death in 1863, Cohoon himself owned one completed family, that headed by Rachel and David. The widower Henry lived with seven children. Five men lived "alone," and six women headed seemingly single-parent families. Huldah, Jr., was widowed, but the other five had husbands off the plantation. Lizzie, Matilda, Margaret, Eliza, and probably Celia and their children were separated by ownership and some physical distance from their husbands and fathers. So were Farley and Huldah, Sr., and their children, who belonged to Cohoon's son William. These immediate slave families were two-parent families, but the Cohoon households had only one resident parent in them. Close ties bound together these separated families. Mariah and her two sons, for example, belonged to Cohoon's second son Willis. The fathers of these boys are unknown. Mariah's mother belonged to John Cohoon in 1863, and her father Isaac Holmes had another owner. Matilda and her three children also belonged to the older Cohoon. Her youngest son, John Jefferson, was named for his father, John Saunders, who had a different owner, and his dead maternal uncle Jefferson. Lewis Orton was married to Huldah, Sr., and they also lived apart. The couple's first son, who had died as an infant, had had his father's name. Mariah's oldest son was named for his grandfather Isaac. Her infant son Nathaniel had the same name as his grandmother's sister's son. Mariah's father had a different owner from his wife and children, but he must have regularly visited with them.

Such visits between kin with separate owners—and especially husbands and fathers separated from their wives and children—regularly dot the historical record documenting slave behavior. Ethan Allen Andrews learned that drunken young white men chastised an Upper South slave husband whom they found in bed with his wife and without a pass. A Louisiana cotton plantation overseer remarked that "Jourdan, Simon, and Lewis goes to see their wives," and years after the Civil War Robert Q. Mallard remembered that Liberty County, Georgia, men traveled with passes on weekends to their families. "Saturday night," said Mal-

NOTE: Chart 7 (pages i–viii) indicates some of the blood and marital ties binding the slave men, women, and children who belonged to John C. Cohoon and his sons in 1863. The thick lines in each chart mark the boundaries of ownership. Pages i–iii record husband-wife, possible husband-wife, and parent-child ties. Pages iv–v indicate husband-wife, parent-child, and brother-sister ties. Pages vi–vii show husband-wife, parent-child, and brother-in-law–sister-in-law ties. Page viii shows grandparent-grandchild ties. The full range of blood and marital ties among these slaves can be approximated by imagining that these four charts were superimposed upon one another.

CHART 7. FAMILY AND KIN CONNECTIONS AND SLAVE OWNERSHIP INVOLVING SLAVES ORIGINALLY OWNED BY JOHN C. COHOON, CEDAR VALE PLANTATION, NANSEMOND COUNTY, VIRGINIA, 1863

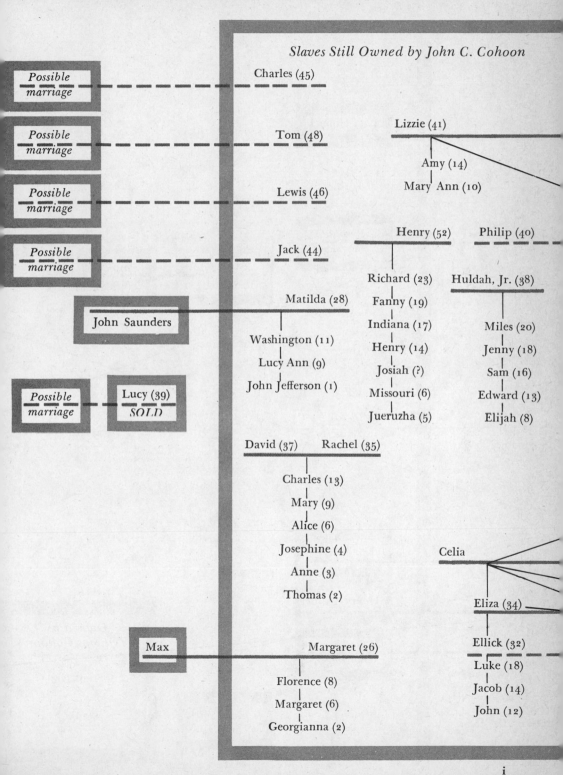

Slaves Still Owned by John C. Cohoon

Charles (45)

Possible marriage

Lizzie (41)

Tom (48)

Possible marriage

Amy (14)
Mary Ann (10)

Lewis (46)

Possible marriage

Henry (52)   Philip (40)

Jack (44)

Possible marriage

Richard (23)   Huldah, Jr. (38)

Matilda (28)

Fanny (19)

John Saunders

Indiana (17)   Miles (20)

Washington (11)   Henry (14)   Jenny (18)

Lucy Ann (9)   Josiah (?)   Sam (16)

John Jefferson (1)   Missouri (6)   Edward (13)

Lucy (39)
SOLD

Possible marriage

Jueruzha (5)   Elijah (8)

David (37)   Rachel (35)

Charles (13)

Mary (9)

Alice (6)

Josephine (4)   Celia

Anne (3)

Thomas (2)   Eliza (34)

Max   Margaret (26)   Ellick (32)

Luke (18)

Florence (8)   Jacob (14)

Margaret (6)   John (12)

Georgianna (2)

i

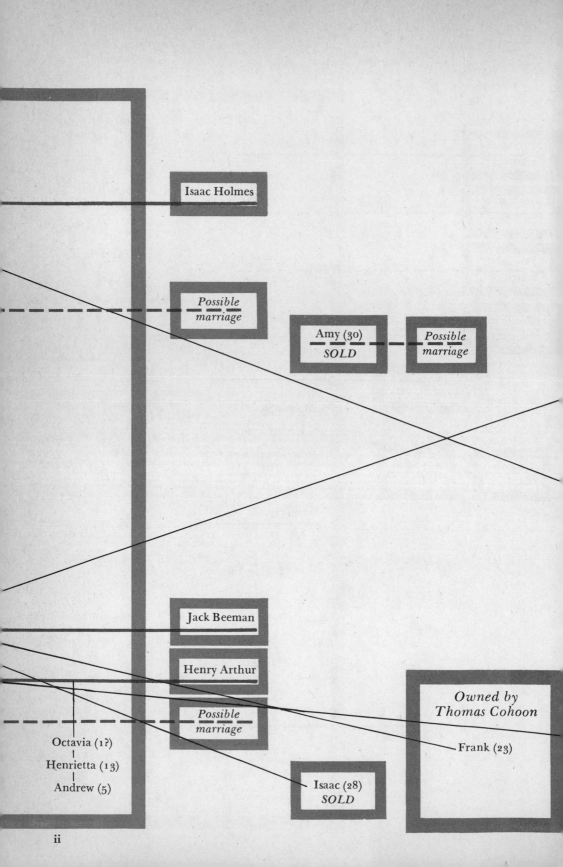

Isaac Holmes

Possible marriage

Amy (30)
SOLD

Possible marriage

Jack Beeman

Henry Arthur

Possible marriage

Octavia (1?)
|
Henrietta (13)
|
Andrew (5)

Owned by Thomas Cohoon

Frank (23)

Isaac (28)
SOLD

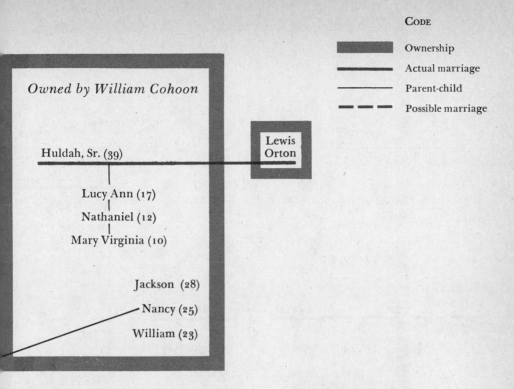

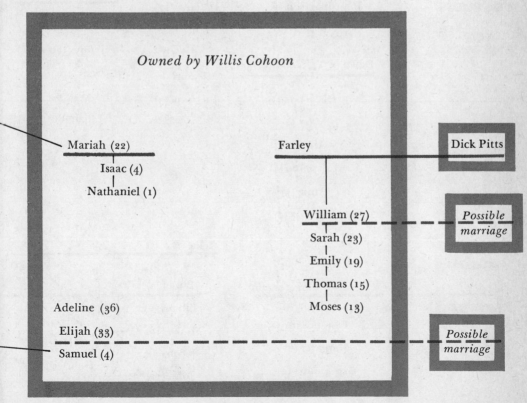

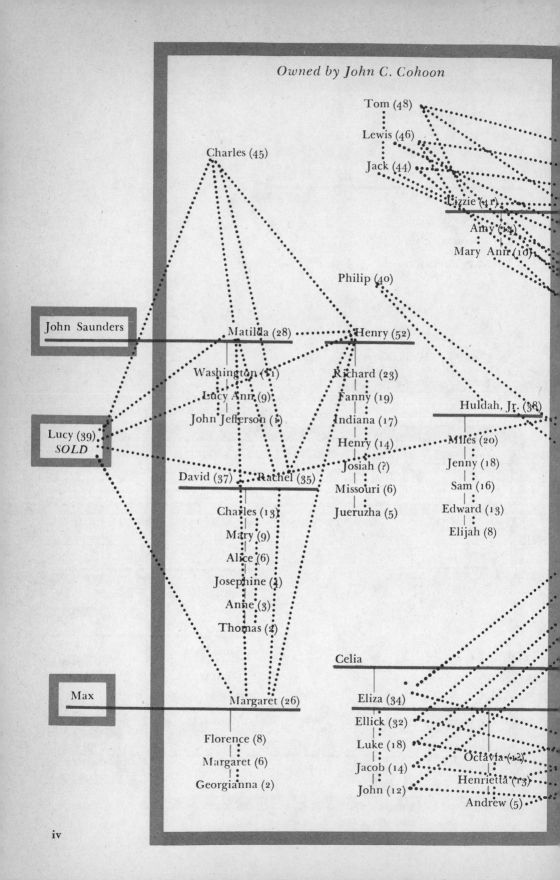

Owned by John C. Cohoon

Tom (48)
Lewis (46)
Jack (44)
Lizzie (41)
Amy (12)
Mary Ann (10)

Charles (45)

Philip (40)

John Saunders

Matilda (28)   Henry (52)

Washington (11)   Richard (23)
Lucy Ann (9)   Fanny (19)   Huldah, Jr. (38)
John Jefferson (1)   Indiana (17)
                      Henry (14)   Miles (20)
Lucy (39)   Josiah (?)   Jenny (18)
SOLD
David (37)   Rachel (35)   Missouri (6) Sam (16)
                           Jueruzha (5) Edward (13)
Charles (13)   Elijah (8)
Mary (9)
Alice (6)
Josephine (4)
Anne (3)
Thomas (2)
                      Celia

Max   Eliza (34)
Margaret (26)
                      Ellick (32)
Florence (8)   Luke (18)   Octavia (12)
Margaret (6)   Jacob (14)   Henrietta (13)
Georgianna (2)   John (12)   Andrew (5)

iv

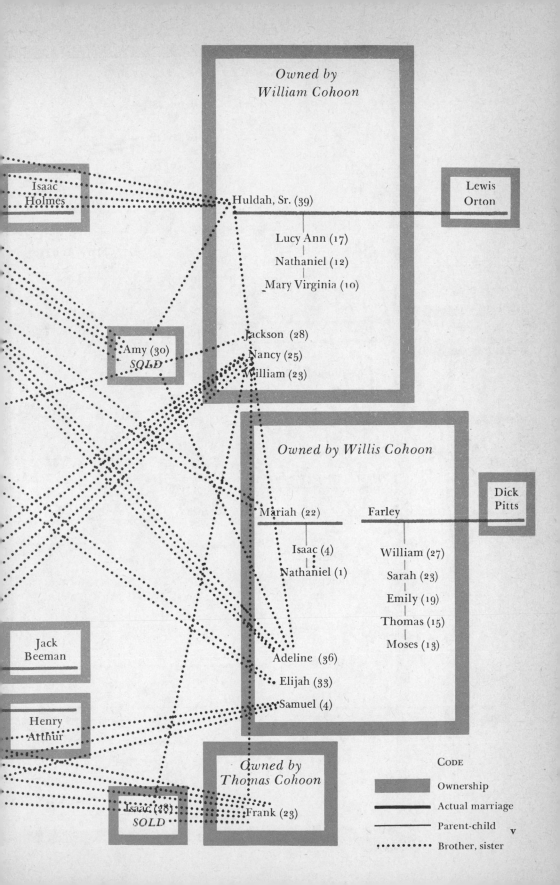

Owned by
William Cohoon

Isaac
Holmes

Lewis
Orton

Huldah, Sr. (39)

Lucy Ann (17)

Nathaniel (12)

Mary Virginia (10)

Jackson (28)

Amy (30)
SOLD

Nancy (25)

William (23)

Owned by *Willis Cohoon*

Dick
Pitts

Mariah (22)   Farley

Isaac (4)

William (27)

Nathaniel (1)

Sarah (23)

Emily (19)

Thomas (15)

Moses (13)

Jack
Beeman

Adeline (36)

Elijah (33)

Henry
Arthur

Samuel (4)

Owned by
Thomas Cohoon

CODE

Ownership

Actual marriage

Parent-child

Isaac (38)
SOLD

Frank (23)

Brother, sister

v

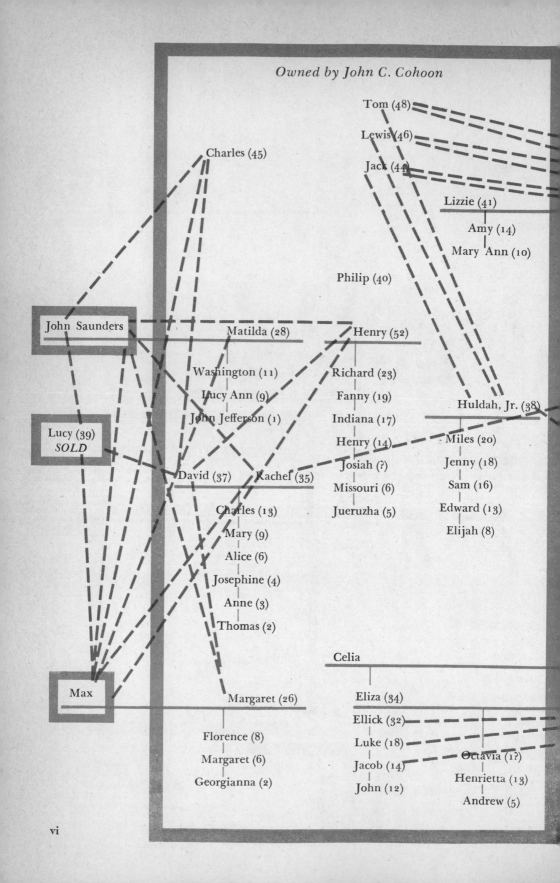

Owned by John C. Cohoon

Tom (48)

Lewis (46)

Jack (44)

Charles (45)

Lizzie (41)

Amy (14)

Mary Ann (10)

Philip (40)

John Saunders

Matilda (28)

Henry (52)

Washington (11)

Richard (23)

Lucy Ann (9)

Fanny (19)

Huldah, Jr. (38)

John Jefferson (1)

Indiana (17)

Lucy (39)
SOLD

Henry (14)

Miles (20)

David (37)

Rachel (35)

Josiah (?)

Jenny (18)

Missouri (6)

Sam (16)

Charles (13)

Jueruzha (5)

Edward (13)

Mary (9)

Elijah (8)

Alice (6)

Josephine (4)

Anne (3)

Thomas (2)

Celia

Max

Eliza (34)

Margaret (26)

Ellick (32)

Luke (18)

Florence (8)

Jacob (14)

Octavia (1?)

Margaret (6)

John (12)

Henrietta (13)

Georgianna (2)

Andrew (5)

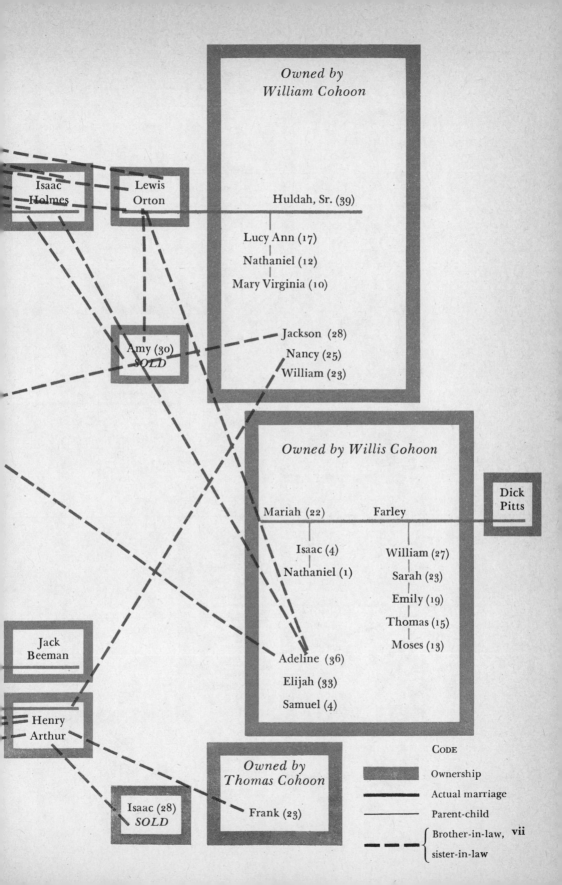

Owned by
William Cohoon

Isaac Holmes

Lewis Orton

Huldah, Sr. (39)

Lucy Ann (17)

Nathaniel (12)

Mary Virginia (10)

Jackson (28)

Nancy (25)

William (23)

Amy (30)
SOLD

Owned by Willis Cohoon

Dick Pitts

Mariah (22)   Farley

Isaac (4)   William (27)

Nathaniel (1)   Sarah (23)

                   Emily (19)

                   Thomas (15)

                   Moses (13)

Jack Beeman

Adeline (36)

Elijah (33)

Samuel (4)

Henry
Arthur

Owned by
Thomas Cohoon

Isaac (28)
SOLD   Frank (23)

CODE

▮▮▮ Ownership

━━━ Actual marriage

─── Parent-child

╏ Brother-in-law, **vii**
╏ sister-in-law

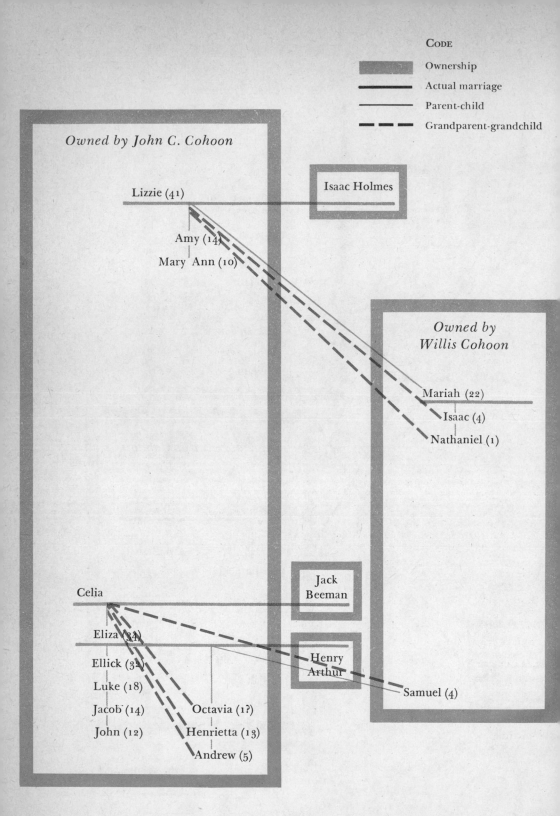

CODE

Ownership

Actual marriage

Parent-child

Grandparent-grandchild

Owned by John C. Cohoon

Lizzie (41)

Isaac Holmes

Amy (14)

Mary Ann (10)

Owned by Willis Cohoon

Mariah (22)

Isaac (4)

Nathaniel (1)

Jack Beeman

Celia

Eliza (34)

Henry Arthur

Ellick (32)

Luke (18)

Samuel (4)

Jacob (14)

Octavia (1?)

John (12)

Henrietta (13)

Andrew (5)

Chart 8.   Slaves Owned by John C. Cohoon at Time of Death, Virginia, 1863

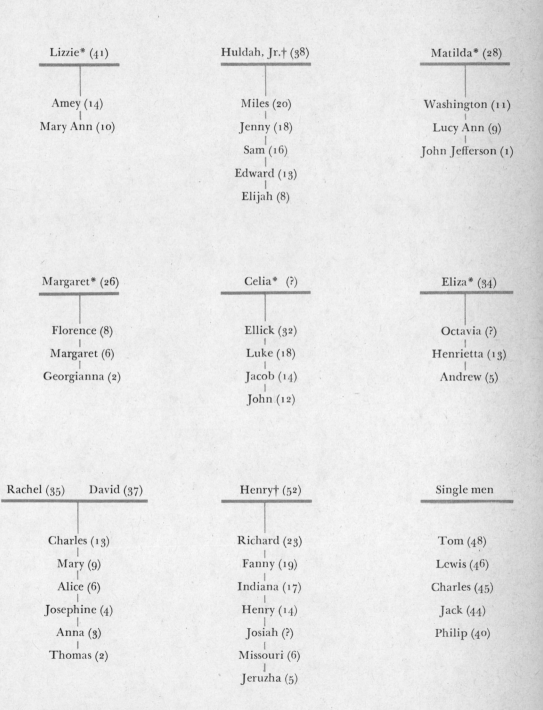

Lizzie* (41)

Amey (14)
Mary Ann (10)

Huldah, Jr.† (38)

Miles (20)
Jenny (18)
Sam (16)
Edward (13)
Elijah (8)

Matilda* (28)

Washington (11)
Lucy Ann (9)
John Jefferson (1)

Margaret* (26)

Florence (8)
Margaret (6)
Georgianna (2)

Celia* (?)

Ellick (32)
Luke (18)
Jacob (14)
John (12)

Eliza* (34)

Octavia (?)
Henrietta (13)
Andrew (5)

Rachel (35)   David (37)

Charles (13)
Mary (9)
Alice (6)
Josephine (4)
Anna (3)
Thomas (2)

Henry† (52)

Richard (23)
Fanny (19)
Indiana (17)
Henry (14)
Josiah (?)
Missouri (6)
Jeruzha (5)

Single men

Tom (48)
Lewis (46)
Charles (45)
Jack (44)
Philip (40)

Husband lives off plantation.
†*Widowed.*

ix

lard, "the roads were, in consequence, filled with men on their way to the 'wife house,' each pedestrian or horseman bearing in his bag his soiled clothes and all the good things he could collect during the week for the delectation of the household." Not all owners, of course, encouraged "broad" marriages and subsequent familial contacts. The Nelson County, Virginia, planter William Massie paid Willis a twenty-dollar bribe to induce him to give up his "broad wife" and take the resident Nancy. But elderly ex-slaves everywhere vividly recollected visits from fathers with different owners. More than a dozen former Fairfield County, South Carolina, children described such visits. "My pappy," said one, ". . . had to git a pass to come to see mammy. He slipped in and out 'nough times to have four children." "My pa," explained Millie Barber, ". . . come sometimes widout de pass. Patrollers catch him way up de chimney hidin' one night; they stripped him right befo' mammy and gave him thirty-nine lashes, wid her cryin' and a hollerin' louder than he." "A man dat has a wife off de place," admitted Caleb Craig, "see little peace or happiness. He could see de wife once a week, on a pass, and jealousy kep him 'stracted de balance of de week, if he love her very much."[22]

Marriages between slaves belonging to different owners posed many difficulties for parents and their children, but such connections also had unintended positive social consequences. Historians describing such marriages often emphasize that the distance created more powerful affective bonds between the mother and her children than between the father and his children. A father who visited his family once, or perhaps twice, a week had a less powerful presence than a resident parent. But such marriages also strengthened extended consanguinal ties. In the father's absence, other kin—maternal parents and the mother's sisters and brothers—probably played significant roles in the daily lives of a mother and her children. Away from their immediate families much of the time, fathers, in turn, probably retained ties to their families of origin, taking meals and even possibly living with married or unmarried brothers and sisters and with one or both parents.

Marriage off the plantation, gift-transfer, and even short-distance sale were responses to the changing economic needs of owners but over time increasingly linked otherwise distinctive immediate slave families and kin groups and reinforced the expansive social and cultural potential explicit in exogamous slave beliefs and practices. Exogamous beliefs meant that marriage partners (and hence wider kin associations) often were recruited from other owners and places nearby, a social process that did not merely emanate outward from a single plantation community but flowed in opposite directions from one unit of ownership to another. Exogamy, by ramifying kin networks throughout a region, served as an extremely effective cultural agency for the diffusion and exchange of slave social beliefs that had no direct connection to marital taboos. Gift-transfer together with short-distance sale, paradoxically, fed this socially expansive thrust. A slave sold or hired to a planter or farmer nearby, given as a gift to an owner's son or daughter, or allowed to marry a mate belonging to a different owner retained kin ties to a family of origin and to the kin groups associated with it. But the same slave could also form new kin ties that supplemented the older ones. Gift-transfer and especially sale had harsh economic origins and cut slaves and their families deeply and painfully, but enlarged slave-kin networks spread over physical space, and enlarged slave communities took shape over the entire South. Communication networks were built upon these enlarged kin networks and undercut the dependence of slaves upon those who owned them.

The process that the Cohoon slaves underwent in the half century preceding their emancipation indicates how owners' decisions helped shape the connections of *different* generations of slave families over time and is sketched in Table 19:

TABLE 19. A MODEL OF THE CYCLE OF SLAVE FAMILY AND KIN NETWORK DESTRUCTION, CONSTRUCTION, AND DISPERSAL

Activity of planter	Phase one	Phase two	Phase three
Age of owner	Young adult	Middle-aged	Elderly or dead
Major objective	Construction of initial labor force	Stabilization and reproduction of labor force	Dispersal of labor force
Devices used	Gift, marriage, and purchase	Natural reproduction and cross-owner marriage	Gift, sale, and estate division
Effect on slaves	Destruction of earlier familial and kin networks	Development of settled families and emergence of new kin networks	Breakup of families formed in phase two and dispersal of kin networks
Stability of slave family	Low	High	Low

Not all planters, of course, followed this pattern; neither did all slaves. Bankruptcy, for example, could end the process at an early moment in time. But nearly all slaves separated by gift, inheritance, or sale in Phase One were detached from developing families and kin networks. An illustration of how the process operated to establish another rising planter is revealed in the birth record kept by a member of the Alabama Torbert plantation family. The Torbert record does not list the names of either mothers or fathers. It gives slave dates of birth and tells whether the slaves were born on the plantation, purchased, or received as gifts. Of the sixty-three slaves born between 1805 and 1865, twenty-four were born before 1846. Only *two* of the twenty-four—Amanda (born in 1843) and Clarinda (born in 1845)—were born on the Torbert plantation. These dates are clues to the process of family formation among these slaves. Nine slaves purchased between 1820 and 1845 for prices ranging from $750 to $1350 were probably young men and women. The rest (thirteen slaves) were gifts from I. Torbert, C. Torbert, J. Torbert, and C. Walker. Some may have come in families; the record does not say. All three slaves born before 1820 came as gifts. Gifts and purchases nearly equaled each other for slaves born between 1820 and 1845. After 1845, Torbert received one slave as a gift and did not purchase any additional slaves. The parents of all but one of the thirty-nine slaves born between 1846 and 1865 were Torbert slaves, the children of parents separated from their families of origin either by sale or by gift transfer.[23]

Emancipation, instead of dissolving the expanding Torbert and Cedar Vale slave kin networks, freed these relationships from external restraints. How that happened among the Cedar Vale slaves can be illustrated by a study of Isaac Holmes's and Lewis Orton's incorporation into the Cedar Vale kin network and by speculating about how that affected their subsequent behavior. Nothing is known about these two men's ties to their families of origin, but when Orton married Huldah, Sr., and Holmes took Lizzie as his wife, they married two of Margaret and Tom's several children and acquired affinal links to Margaret and Tom's other living children and grandchildren, including the widowed Huldah, Jr., married for many years to Margaret and Tom's son Little Bob. Holmes and Orton lived apart from their immediate families. Eight of the eleven children born to Holmes and Lizzie died. Amy and Mary Ann lived with their mother on John Cohoon's place. Mariah, the third surviving child, and her two sons belonged to Willis Cohoon. Orton and Huldah, Sr., had lost a son, and she and her three surviving children belonged to William Cohoon. Huldah, Jr., lived on Cohoon's place; her husband and three of their children had died. Two of her dead daughters had been named for their father's sisters Adeline and Sylvia. Huldah, Jr.'s brother Philip and five of her surviving children also lived on John Cohoon's place. Her daughter Jenny carried the name of her dead maternal grandmother, and her son Edward had his dead maternal uncle's name. Another son, Elijah, owned by Willis Orton, was named after another maternal uncle. At the war's end, Holmes and Orton, along with Max, Dick Pitts, Jack Beeman, Henry Arthur, and John Saunders, probably gathered together their wives and children from their separate owners. Holmes probably paid special attention to his daughter Mariah and her two young children. And it also is probable that Elijah and Philip, and possibly even Holmes and Orton, did the same for the widowed Huldah, Jr., and her five fatherless children.

Nothing, of course, is actually known about how these particular men behaved upon their emancipation, but they should not have differed from the men whose behavior was revealed in an 1866 Freedmen's Bureau, Princess Anne County, Virginia, population register.[24] Princess Anne County, which bordered the Dismal Swamp, was not a plantation county in 1860. Two in five residents then were blacks. The 1866 census recorded black property ownership, literacy (ability to read), and color. About one in ten of 813 adults owned some property. The census taker estimated its value: two-thirds of eighty persons owned less than $100 of property (half of these less than $50), and twenty-six had property valued at between $100 and $299 (five between $200 and $299). Not too much should be inferred from this evidence about their over-all social condition: 94 percent had been slaves prior to 1863; 98.5 percent could not read; and 98 percent described themselves as "black." A significant number lived in families that had been reconstituted after 1863. The census taker listed the last owner of nearly every ex-slave, that owner's 1863 residence, and the antebellum status of all 1866 black residents. Nearly two in three 1866 black residents had moved to Princess Anne County starting in 1863. A scattering of the 1135 migrants had come from distant places, such as Maryland, Knoxville, Augusta, the District of Columbia, and even Brazos, Texas. But 97 percent had moved there from Virginia and North Carolina counties nearby, including Nansemond County. Few had moved more than one hundred

miles, and most had traveled a far shorter distance. Despite their
geographical mobility, fewer than one in ten lived apart from an
immediate family, and most others lived in double-headed households. That had not been so in 1863. Of the 379 1866 families,
all members had been slaves in 356 of them, and in nearly half of
these 356 families all family members had belonged to the same
owner in 1863, most probably sharing the same slave household.
Those families, whose members had belonged to the same owner
and which included single-parent families, had kept together in
the transition to legal freedom. Three in four of these families
were migrant families from outside the country. These migrant
families remained together as regularly as resident Prince Anne
families.

What of the others—those members of immediate families
who had come together from separate owners? More than half of
the households listed in 1866 included husbands and wives as well
as parents and children who had lived with different owners in
1863 (Table 20). Their composition in 1866 explains why so much
geographical mobility accompanied the emancipation. Families
separated by ownership, like those owned by Cohoon and his
sons, were coming together. Not a single male-absent 1866 household included persons belonging to different owners in 1863; but

TABLE 20. ANTEBELLUM LEGAL STATUS AND OWNERSHIP OF
MEMBERS OF BLACK FAMILIES RESIDING IN PRINCESS
ANNE COUNTY, VIRGINIA, 1866

Type of household in 1866	Number of households	All household members in 1866 having the same owner in 1863	Some or all household members in 1866 having different owners in 1863
Husband-wife	56	36%	64%
Husband-wife-children	222	33	67
Father-children	13	31	69
Mother-children	61	100	0
Unknown	4	100	0
Number of households	356*	163	193

* The census listed 379 households. Eleven had only free black members in
1863, and another twelve had as members some antebellum free blacks and some
ex-slaves.

of 291 households with a resident husband or father in 1866, two-thirds had come together from separate owners, a pattern found among both migrant and local families. Some families had come together from more than two owners (not all children had lived with their mothers or belonged to the same owner), but in most instances the wife and child had one owner and the husband (or father) had another owner. It remains unknown how many households were reconstituted and how many were new families. Most probably were reconstituted. Only a few 1866 households had just a father and his children. Not one of these fathers had lived with his children prior to 1863. That these few fathers gathered their children from separate owners is good reason to believe that men like them renewed direct ties with children *and* with their wives. Not all ex-slave fathers did that, and for many reasons. Some of the 1866 male-absent households never had a resident male parent. Others probably earlier had included fathers who then abandoned their families. Yet other fathers had either died or been sold great distances (perhaps remarrying) and had not returned.

Not a single ex-slave mother living with her children had gathered them from separate owners, but men in large numbers had done so. These slave families—like the typical family owned by Cohoon in 1863—had not shared a physical dwelling. But since most migrants after 1863 had traveled relatively short distances, it is probable that physical separation had not removed these fathers so far from their slave wives and children that they lost all contact with them. In an 1866 speech to ex-slaves who had come together to protest their removal from confiscated lands near Yorktown, Virginia, Bayley Wyatt indicated what encouraged such men: "You all 'members de home house and de wife house, how de wife house was often eight or ten miles from de home house, and we would go there Saturday night expectin' to see de wife we had left." (Children in most such slave marriages remained with the mother, who had principal responsibility for their day-to-day rearing, but in calling the father's residence the "home house" Wyatt assigned it a priority in status.) Men who had traveled these distances as slaves had compelling reason to bring their families together as free men. "Their wives and families perhaps resided on some distant plantation," said the Memphis *Argus* in 1865, in explaining why so many men quit old owners, "and they sought to bring the scattered members of a family together." The Maryland judge Hugh Lennox Bond reported from that state: "In the large slaveholding counties, there was an exchange of masters. Husbands joined their wives on neighboring farms, and wives their husbands and children" Standardized obligations did not depend upon cohabitation.[25]

Some ex-slaves listed in the 1866 Princess Anne census had lived in Nansemond County prior to 1863 and may even have known the slaves belonging to John Cohoon and his sons or have been married to their slaves. They may even have been related to them, some through common forebears among whom the initial Cohoon slaves had lived prior to 1815. That remains unknown. But they shared with them a common history. In 1865 Cohoon's slaves lived in closely related but often separately owned immediate families that assisted them in the difficult transition to legal freedom. Little of the credit for this fact belongs to the individual who had first put together so diverse a group of slaves. The many choices made by John Cohoon between 1810 and 1863 mostly posed problems for the slaves he either purchased or saw born to his estate. And the many choices that Cohoon's slaves made were efforts to solve those problems, choices shaped by the beliefs bred in the culture of the slaves but confined and constricted by the society dominated by their owners until 1865.

4

Take Root There or Nowhere: II

. . . i put my trust in the lord to halp me I long to hear
from you all i ritten to hear from yo all Mr. Belekow i
hop you will not for me you no et was not my falt that
I am hear. . . .

i long to hear from my famaly how the ar geten along
you will ples to let me no how the ar geten along. . . .
for god sake let me hear from you all my wife and chil-
dren are not out of my mine nor night

> THOMAS DUCKET, *a slave sold from the District of*
> *Columbia to a Louisiana sugar plantation in 1850, to*
> *a sympathetic District of Columbia white*

. . . you will please to tell my Sister Clary not to Let my
poor children Suffer. . . . Remember me to Sucky &
Humphrey and there family. . . . I should be glad to no
what sort of a life Clary leads. . . . be pleased to inform
me how my little daughter Judith is & if she is now
injoying health. . . . old Granny Judy goes a bout & that
is all. She has life & that is all. Tell Hannah her Sister
is married to Mr. Thornley's Tom. . . .

> GOOLEY, *Virginia, 1807, to her*
> *former owner, living in Kentucky*

We have examined the slave family, slave kin networks, slave
marital rules, slave naming practices, and the development of slave
communities in two settings very different from the one in which
South Carolina's Good Hope slaves lived. Uniformities in slave
behavior have been observed. Other circumstances which slaves
could not influence are examined next: sale from the Upper to
the Lower South and the date when a developing slave community first took shape.

Few more significant social and economic processes affecting
developing slave communities and the slaves' family life and kin
relations had a greater importance between 1815 and 1860 than
the involuntary movement and uprooting of several hundred
thousand Upper South men, women, and children, which accompanied the shift in slave-based export agricultural production from

the Upper to the Lower South. The slaves so far studied escaped that experience. The Good Hope and Stirling slaves showed how Afro-American culture developed *over time* in relatively settled slave communities, and the Cedar Vale slaves showed how similar developments occurred in a relatively unstable local setting. We examine next how that same culture *moved in space* and study the behavior of men and women cut off from immediate Upper South families and developing kin networks by either long-distance sale or migration with an owner. The typical individual involved in this massive forced migration was a single person between fifteen and twenty-nine years of age. Some such persons entered into settled slave communities like the one that developed on the Stirling plantation. But very large numbers were purchased by men who started new enterprises. Two such men were the Mississippi cotton planter Stephen Duncan and the Alabama cotton planter Henry Watson, and it is their slaves who reveal that the slave beliefs and practices found in relatively settled slave communities traveled with the men and women who labored on the developing plantations of the Lower South.

That happened in spite of the disruption of familial and kin ties associated with the interregional shift in the slave population between 1790 and 1860 and especially in the three decades preceding the Civil War. Just how severely interregional migration and attendant sale affected the slave family remains unknown for two reasons. Local sale itself has been little studied, and the records kept of slave transfers in interregional markets such as New Orleans contain too little information to show the effects of sale on either the slave family or slave marriage.[1] Only a single study of sale out of a given area exists, and, despite its importance, it fails to relate such sales to the slave families there.[2] The most careful estimates of sale, moreover, remain useless in the absence of an understanding of the slave family and its development. A single document, however, allows us to begin to examine sale and the breakup of slave marriages and families in ways hitherto unavailable to students of slavery. The behavior of the Duncan and Watson slaves is greatly illuminated by what was recorded in 1864–1865 Davis Bend, Natchez, and Vicksburg, Mississippi, marriage registration books kept by the Union Army clergy, who conducted 4627 marriage ceremonies involving Mississippi and northern Louisiana ex-slaves. The registration of these marriages has been briefly discussed in Chapter 1. Our interest here is in what more than nine thousand ex-slaves revealed about slave marriages, the reasons for their termination, and the length of terminated marriages.[3] All of the ex-slaves who had been married more than once answered questions about these earlier unions.

How and why slave culture traveled from the Upper to the Lower South, and why slaves were able to deal with the suffering associated with the forcible breakup of Upper South families and kin networks is revealed in their answers. That can be learned even though this information has important limitations. It failed to tell how often children born in earlier marriages had been separated from their parents and other kin, and therefore described only the involuntary breakup of *marriages, not families.*[4] If their testimony was typical (and it is the fullest now available), sale disrupted far more slave marriages than proslavery advocates cared to admit. That is seen by examining what *individuals* reported about their prior marital experiences. Just over two in five individual registrants—3846 men and women—had lived with a spouse in an earlier union. Slightly more than half of those at least forty years old in 1864–1865 had been voluntarily or involuntarily separated from a spouse (Table 21). Not all reported marriages ended by the voluntary decisions made either by owners or themselves. Death accounted for a significant percentage of terminated marriages.[5] Nevertheless a high percentage of all blacks twenty years and older—nearly one in six of the registrants—had been separated from a spouse by force. Among men and women aged thirty and older, nearly one in four men and one in five women had suffered such a separation. Even among younger registrants, many of whom married for the first time in 1864–1865, forcible separations were important. About one in ten men and women born between 1835 and 1845 had experienced a forcible separation by 1864, a percentage sufficiently high to indicate that in the pre–Civil War decades the peculiar institution retained its grimmest quality, the breakup of marriages and the damage thereby inflicted on husbands and wives, parents and children.

Because most registrants had not experienced the forcible breakup of an earlier marriage, it might be argued that slavery was much less harsh than its most severe critics had insisted. Such an inference, however, confuses statistical aggregates with social realities. What percentage of slave *marriages*—5 percent, 25 percent, 33 percent, 50 percent, or 66 percent—had to be ended by force or sale to make slaves understand owners' power? Ten percent would have been more than adequate. The breakup of a marriage had a "geometric" impact upon the slaves involved. It

TABLE 21. CAUSES FOR THE END OF PREVIOUS SLAVE MARRIAGES REPORTED BY BLACKS REGISTERING MARRIAGES BY AGE AND SEX, MISSISSIPPI, 1864–1865

Males

Age at time of registration	Number registering	Cause for termination of earlier marriage					Total percentage reporting earlier marriages
		DEATH	FORCE	DESERTION	CONSENT	OTHER	
15–19	34	0%	0%	0%	0.0%	0.0%	0%
20–29	1770	8	10	1	2.0	0.2	22
30–39	1017	15	23	2	3.0	0.5	44
40–49	914	23	25	3	2.0	1.0	54
50+	877	27	24	2	1.5	2.0	58
TOTAL NUMBER	4578*	16% / 749	19% / 864	2% / 86	2.0% / 97	1.0% / 37	40% / 1833

Females

Age	Number	DEATH	FORCE	DESERTION	CONSENT	OTHER	Total percentage
15–19	452	5%	2%	1%	0.4%	0.0%	9%
20–29	2169	22	12	2	2.0	0.3	38
30–39	979	28	20	1	2.5	2.0	53
40–49	642	30	20	2.5	2.0	2.0	54
50+	349	27	22	1	2.0	1.0	54
TOTAL NUMBER	4139*	25% / 1046	16% / 652	2% / 78	2% / 82	0.5% / 22	45% / 1880

* Does not include men and women aged fifteen to nineteen at time of registration. In addition to these, twenty-two men and sixty-one women of different ages reported an earlier union but did not give a reason for its termination.

directly affected a particular husband and wife, their children, their parents, and other kin nearby. It also was known to slave neighbors and to those who came to know the partners after the union's dissolution. Such awareness spread over space following sale, but, when children were involved, it also moved forward in time. From the perspective of the slave, the Virginia ex-slave Cornelius Garner put the problem well: "Boys git to cuttin' up on Sundays an' 'sturbin' Marsa and Missus an' dey comp'y. Finally ole Marsa come clumpin' down to de quarters. Pick out de fam'ly dat got de mos' chillun an' say, 'Fo' God, nigger, I'm goin' to sell all dem chillun o' your'n lessen you keep 'em quiet.' Dat threat was worsen prospects of a lickin'. Ev'body sho' keep quiet arter dat." The threat made by Garner's owner did not require the frequent breakup of slave families or marriages to make it effective. Another ex-slave remembered the "geometric" effect of sale. Susan Hamilton detailed how the breakup of a Charleston marriage shattered two slave families: "One mornin' a couple married an' de next mornin' de boss sell de wife. De gal ma got out in de street an' cursed de white woman fur all she could find." The mother ended up in the Charleston workhouse, and Hamilton remembered her saying, "Dat damn pale-faced bastard sell my daughter who jus' married las' night." Two families had been broken by this sale.[6]

The registrants revealed even more than that force had terminated so many earlier marriages. Unless many registrants lied about multiple separations (some probably did), most claiming earlier marriages had had *one* such marriage. A scattering—about thirty men and women—had been married twice and gave varied reasons for the end of these earlier unions, such as "force and death" and "death and death." Three persons each had been separated from three earlier spouses, and a single elderly man had been cut adrift four times (twice each by death and force). Death and force explained nine in ten earlier terminated marriages. Other reasons also were given. A handful listed "adultery," "abuse," "quarreling," "war," and "rebels." A small and therefore very significant number—two percent each—said "desertion" and "mutual consent" (or divorce). Some blacks surely hid the reasons for voluntary marital breakups from the officiating Yankee clergy, but even if the actual number were several times greater than the percentage reported it was still significant. We shall see why in examining the Duncan cotton-plantation slaves.

Because the ex-slaves reported the number of children born in earlier marriages, their testimony allows us to examine whether the presence of children had deterred owners from separating husbands and wives. Slightly more than half who had known earlier marriages had children in these unions.[7] A higher percentage of men whose marriages had produced children (48 percent) reported a forcible breakup compared to men who had childless marriages (45 percent). Married women with children (34 percent) and without children (34 percent) reported exactly the same percentage of forcible separations from husbands. Among all registrants aged twenty and older, including those married for the first time in 1864–1865, nearly one in ten had experienced the forcible breakup of a childbearing marriage. Among men and women at least fifty years old in 1864–1865, between one in six and one in seven registrants had a similar earlier experience. "Breeding" young slaves for the market was not an issue in these breakups. These were adults, not children, being separated by sale. Even if financial reverses, the payment of debts, and estate divisions had caused most of these separations, it is clear that the presence of slave children had not prevented hard-pressed owners from separating their parents. These percentages, moreover, tell only about husbands and wives separated by force. If the number of children sold from individual families also was known, the percentage of slave families, not slave marriages, broken by the sale of any members would greatly increase. Most sales were of young slaves, not adult marital partners, and their number remains unknown. Even without knowing how many of the children of these Mississippi registrants had been sold, we can see enough about the separation of slave spouses from one another to make it hard to quarrel with the Virginia woman who met her former husband at the Norfolk Ropewalk in 1863. Both had remarried following a forced separation, and she told a northern teacher, " 'Twas like a stroke of death to me. We threw ourselves into each other's arms and cried. . . . White folks got a heap to answer for the way they've done to colored folks! So much they wouldn't never *pray* it away!"[8]

So far what these ex-slaves reported confirmed the classic indictment of slavery by its slave and abolitionist critics. But that was not the only import of their testimony. In reporting the length of terminated slave marriages, they also described why many Upper South slaves retained strong family beliefs when sold or moved (as individuals or in family groups and with or without owners) to the Lower South. Among the registrants, 1842 men and 1911 women indicated the length of their earlier marriages (Table 22). They did not tell *when* these marriages had ended. But more than

TABLE 22. LENGTH OF ALL TERMINATED SLAVE MARRIAGES, MISSISSIPPI, 1864–1865

	Males				Females				Males and females			
		LENGTH OF SLAVE UNION IN YEARS				LENGTH OF SLAVE UNION IN YEARS				LENGTH OF SLAVE UNION IN YEARS		
AGE	NUMBER	UNDER 5	5–14	15+	NUMBER	UNDER 5	5–14	15+	NUMBER	UNDER 5	5–14	15+
20–29	390	79%	21%	0%	841	69%	31%	0%	1231	72%	28%	0%
30–39	450	51	48	1	520	44	50	6	970	47	49	4
40–49	498	34	53	13	357	28	52	20	855	32	52	16
50+	504	27	47	26	193	29	47	24	697	28	47	25
TOTAL	1842	46%	43%	11%	1911	50%	42%	8%	3753	48.4%	42.3%	9.3%

LENGTH OF ALL SLAVE MARRIAGES TERMINATED BY FORCE, MISSISSIPPI, 1864–1865

	Males				Females				Males and females			
		LENGTH OF SLAVE UNION IN YEARS										
AGE	NUMBER	UNDER 5	5–14	15+	NUMBER	UNDER 5	5–14	15+	NUMBER	UNDER 5	5–14	15+
20–29	182	82%	18%	0%	247	75%	25%	0%	429	78%	22%	0%
30–39	241	56	43	1	197	53	45	2	438	55	44	1
40–49	220	36	54	10	128	36	54	10	348	36	54	10
50+	222	31	49	20	77	42	45	13	299	33	49	18
TOTAL	865	50%	42%	8%	649	57%	39%	4%	1514	53%	40.5%	6.5%

half of those at least twenty years old and reporting a terminated marriage in 1864–1865 had lived with a spouse for at least five years. Just over one in four men and women aged twenty to twenty-nine had been married between five and fourteen years.[9] The percentage reporting earlier marriages lasting that long and longer was nearly twice as high among people in their thirties and increased sharply among older men and women, rising to just over two in three for those in their forties and to just over seven in ten for those at least fifty years old. Among men and women forty years and older, one in five had lived in an earlier marriage lasting fifteen or more years. An even higher percentage of those fifty years and older had lived in long marriages: one in four between ten and nineteen years, and another 17 percent at least twenty years. Settled slave marriages—not "casual" matings—had been terminated, two in five of them by force.

Much that appears inexplicable in Table 22 can be clarified by examining once more the South Carolina Good Hope plantation community. Owners had not ended Good Hope slave marriages, but let us assume that financial distress caused the sale of all Good Hope slaves in 1830.* Chart 9 reconstructs Good Hope immediate families and kin networks in 1830. The complex 1857 kin networks studied in Chapter 2 did not yet exist. Third-generation (1820–1839) families had just started. If the seven married couples in 1830 (all except Ness and Rose) were sold as families to rising Mississippi planters and remained together through the Civil War, these adults would all have been in their late fifties. Had they renewed a marriage in 1864, none would have reported a broken earlier marriage. All would have reported long slave marriages, and all could have described the severing of other kin ties, mostly separation from families of origin (older parents and adult siblings). But if sale had separated these men

---

* Economic difficulties and other reasons caused the breakup of plantation communities elsewhere. A single deed of sale describing some of the familial connections of twenty-five slaves sold from the Sea Island Greenwood plantation reads like the reconstructed Good Hope birth register:

Sambo & Jennie his wife and their children Ned Tyrah Rynah Pilot Grace
Penny and her sons Isaac & Jack
Island George & Rynah his wife
William & Nancy his sister and her child Bess
Honor Elizabeths maid
Charles his wife Hagar and their son Allen
Robert & his wife Caty and their children Peter Dubbee and Caty's sister
Dinah & her child
Bess brought back to stay with her Grand Mother Lucy

The listing appears in Johnson, *Social History of the Sea Islands* (1930), 135–36.

and women from one another and each remarried, all would
have reported youthful unions lasting between two and seven
years. Such brief marital experiences did not mean that these
slaves and their unmarried siblings had grown up detached from
kin. All but a few brought with them to Mississippi beliefs learned
from parents and grandparents whose behavior had been shaped
during the late-eighteenth- and early-nineteenth-century adaptation by Africans and their early descendants to enslavement in
South Carolina and other Upper South colonies and states.

Let us shift the moment in time from 1830 to 1850 and assume
that in 1850 all Good Hope adults who had had children starting
in 1820 were sold separately to Mississippi, later remarried, and
renewed their second marriages in 1864. All then would have lived
with a second mate less than fifteen years. The ages of thirty-three
and the years they had been married prior to 1850 are known.
Thirty at least forty years old in 1864 would have reported an
earlier marriage. Three had two earlier marriages. Seven had been
married less than six years, and the other twenty would have
divided evenly in reporting marriages of between six and fifteen
years or sixteen and more years. Such hypothetical evidence
supplements other details obscured in the 1864–1865 registers. In
Mississippi, these South Carolina blacks probably would have
married once. That is so because hardly any of the actual registrants reported more than a single earlier marriage. If the Good
Hope slaves were sold to places like the Stirling plantation, their
South Carolina marital experiences would have been reinforced
by the Stirling slaves whose domestic arrangements and kin networks conformed to those from which sale had detached the Good
Hope slaves. Remarriage could not fully compensate for the vivid
memories and feelings associated with forced separation from a
spouse and from other blood kin, but behavior *after* sale and
separation depended partly upon what slaves had experienced
and learned in earlier marriages, families, and enlarged kin groups.
South Carolina and Louisiana and Mississippi slave cultures were
not that different.

The breakup of marriages by force caused deep personal and
social pain, suffering that no statistic can convert into a "mean" or
"median" average. Although long marriages were relatively less
frequent among persons separated by force than by death, it
nevertheless remains an important fact that couples separated by
force also had lived in settled marriages (Table 22). One in five
in their twenties separated by force had lived with a spouse

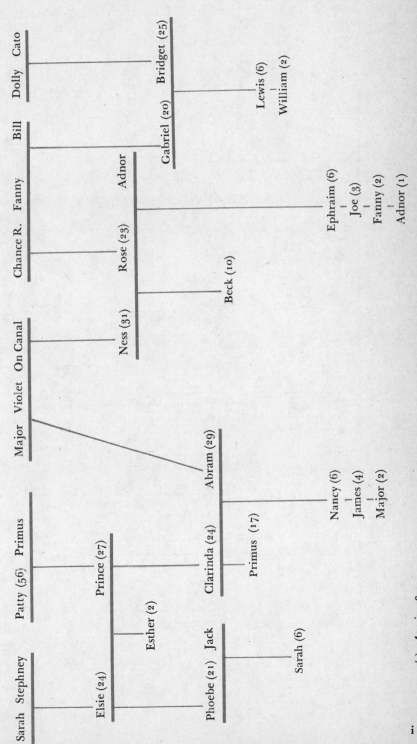

CHART 9. FAMILIAL ARRANGEMENTS AND KIN RELATIONSHIPS,
GOOD HOPE PLANTATION, SOUTH CAROLINA, 1830

( ) : *Age in 1830.*

i

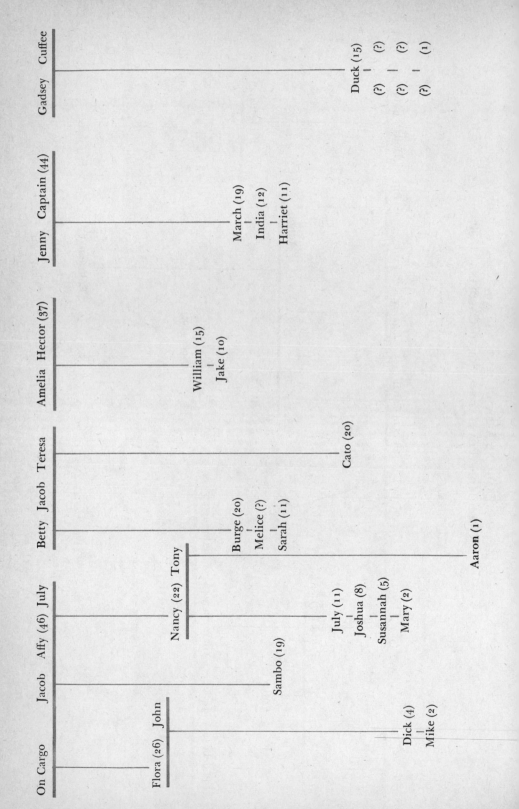

ii

between five and fourteen years. Among those forty and older, about one in three had lived together less than five years, half between five and fourteen years, and the rest (about one in seven) fifteen or more years. Husbands and wives, many of them parents, and not "breeders" and "studs" had been separated by force. Elderly ex-slaves remembered fathers sold into the Lower South or purchased in the Upper South. Adeline Grey was a young child when her South Carolina father was sold or moved to Texas. After the war, he did not return. "You see," his daughter said, "he had chillun out dere, too." Before his death, her Texas father, who then owned three horses, "want one of them to be sent to us chillun here; but no arrangements had been made to get it to us." Virginia Bell's Louisiana parents had both been born in Virginia. Her father was much older than her mother and had "a wife and five children back in Virginia." Sale to Louisiana broke up that family. "Then," Bell said, "he and my mother started a family out here. I don't know what became of his family back in Virginny, 'cause when we was freed he stayed with us." Grey and Bell had fathers who had known settled marriages prior to their separation. The length of many of the marriages reported by the older Mississippi and northern Louisiana registrants furthermore indicates that adverse circumstances and estate divisions probably had caused many involuntary breakups among them. That means that *all* slave marriages were insecure. No slave could predict when an owner would die and how his estate would be divided. No slave could affect the vicissitudes of the business cycle. And no slave could shape an owner's decision to reallocate his investments in human or other capital. That is why slave marriages—however long they lasted—cannot be characterized as stable. And that is why slave parents everywhere had good reasons to socialize their children to prepare for either the possible breakup of their marriages or sale from an immediate family.[10]

The suffering induced by such separations had to be more acute for persons living in relatively long marriages than for men and women who spent a short time together as husband and wife. They had had sufficient *time* to build affective adult relationships. To end such settled marriages by force and for reasons that had nothing to do with the interior quality of a marriage did not mean that these men and women had learned that marriage and kin relations were "dysfunctional" among slaves. Such decisions taught slaves about the arbitrary power owners could—and did—exercise over slave families.

The length of these marriages broken by force had additional significance. Many of these marriages had been sufficiently long-lasting to allow parents to nurture children and to acquaint them with values and mores they had learned from their parents, older kin, and other older non-kin. That is important because of the moment in time when most of these marriages were broken by force. In 1860, nearly all adult Mississippi slaves had been either forced migrants to that state or first-generation Mississippi-born slaves. Only 32,814 slaves had lived in that state in 1820. The number doubled in the next decade and increased from 65,659 to 195,211 between 1830 and 1840. By 1860, the number of slaves in Mississippi was 436,631. Slaves were moved so rapidly and in such large numbers from the Upper to the Lower South between 1820 and 1860 that too little time had passed for them to abandon cultural norms common among Upper South slaves. Younger slaves made up the bulk of this migration. An eighteen-year-old slave sold to Mississippi in 1835 and whose parents had been separated by death or force when he or she was a twelve-year-old had known his or her parents well prior to sale.

Antislavery critics had many good reasons to complain that as a social system slavery weakened the slave household. That is made clear by these Mississippi ex-slaves. And its importance is reinforced by the similar testimony given by Arkansas ex-slaves in marriage registers.[11] But these facts do not mean that slaves accepted such impositions as "normal" and absorbed into their consciousness no more than the deep social and psychic trauma produced by the sale of a spouse or a young or grown child. Instead, supporting institutions developed within slave communities to sustain persons in the grief of separation and to perpetuate the cultural affinity among them for distinctive slave domestic and kin arrangements. Such an adaptation to the reality of actual or potential involuntary separation had to be made if over-all values were to survive. That adaptation took many forms but expressed itself in social arrangements between slaves living in separate households—that is, within the larger slave community. Fictive kinsmen were probably very important after sale and separation. On a Louisiana plantation, Solomon Northup befriended some South Carolina slaves. The elderly Abram, who was his "cabinmate for years," Northup said, "regarded us with a kind of parental feeling, always counseling us with remarkable gravity and deliberation."[12] It is doubtful, moreover, that slaves condemned other slaves who made unusual adjustments to forced separations. Instead, they probably incorporated such behavior into their larger value system.

Two elderly South Carolina ex-slaves remembered such arrangements. Emma Jeter's father lived on a different farm from her mother and could only visit his family twice a year, "laying-by time and Christmas." "Paw got him another wife at Miss Sarah's," his daughter said in explaining why she had "five half-sisters and one half-brother." Emanuel Elmore's father married twice. Dorcas Cooper, Elmore's mother, was his first wife, but he later married "a girl named Jenny." Dorcas Cooper learned she had been sold and fled her owner and family to hide in the woods. Jenny moved in with Elmore's father and cared "so well for her children that she [Dorcas Cooper] liked her." Jenny, Elmore added, continued living "in the same house with pa till my mother died. Pa and Jenny kept us till we got big and went off to ourselves." Jenny "was good to everybody and never fought and went on like ma did. Ma liked her and would not let anybody say anything against her. . . . Jenny never had any children. She was not old when she died, but just a settled woman. We felt worse over her death than we did over ma's, because she was so good to us." Neither Emma Jeter nor Emanuel Elmore condemned such unusual marital arrangements. The very fact that commitment to the two-parent household survived enslavement with the strength it did strongly suggests that the slaves dealt with family disruption in social ways that were consistent with their larger belief system. Otherwise the breakup of marriages in large numbers would have destroyed the values that in fact survived.[13]

The slaves owned by the Mississippi planter Stephen Duncan and the Alabama planter Henry Watson indicate in their behavior that the values associated with slave family life in settled and developing slave communities survived the shift in the slave economy from the Upper to the Lower South. Stephen Duncan's slaves lived on the Carlisle plantation in Concordia Parish, Louisiana. In 1860, 90 percent of Concordia's residents were slaves. The remaining population was composed mostly of white overseers and their families. Like the South Carolina Good Hope slaves and most other Concordia Parish slaves, the Carlisle slave community developed without a resident owner. Stephen Duncan, a Pennsylvanian by birth, had settled in nearby Natchez in 1808. Then a twenty-one-year-old physician, he later married into two local rising plantation families. By the early 1830s, Duncan owned several Mississippi cotton plantations and one, quite possibly the Carlisle plantation, in northern Louisiana. A banker as well as a planter, Duncan invested in railroad stocks and in northern and southern state and municipal bonds. He regularly visited the North and purchased an elegant New York City residence in the 1850s. On the eve of the Civil War, Duncan owned six cotton and two sugar plantations and just over one thousand slaves (twenty-three of them house servants in his Greek revival mansion near Natchez).[14]

Nothing is known about the Carlisle slave community before 1850, but three slave household lists (1851, 1856, and 1861) show how the Carlisle slaves shared similar beliefs with the Good Hope, Stirling, and Cedar Vale slaves.[15] Among the fifty-three men and women at least twenty years old in 1851, a few had been born before 1810 or after 1829. The typical adult slave was a twenty-nine-year-old. Their age distribution in 1851 suggests that most adult Carlisle slaves had either grown up as Upper South slaves or were the children of Upper South slaves moved to northern Louisiana in families or sold there as individuals during the great expansion in Mississippi and northern Louisiana cotton production after 1820. In 1851, Carlisle slaves lived in twenty-eight separate households, the typical household containing between four and five residents. Persons related by blood or marriage (about five in six of the slaves) lived in twenty-one of these households. Three of the remaining seven failed to reappear in subsequent household lists, and the other four each had a single resident. All but one of the twenty-one households contained a completed immediate family; a mother and her children lived in the other one. In one household, a father and his son lived with a completed family.

Many of the cultural practices discerned among the Good Hope, Stirling, and Cedar Vale slaves are found among the Carlisle slaves. Between 1851 and 1861, husbands and wives remained together in fourteen of the twenty households. In two others, the husband-father died, and their widows did not remarry. Chart 10 illustrates common behavior in the Carlisle slave community. Willis and Milly remained married; their family increased in size. When Mingo died, he and Melissa had three children, and their son Big Andrew had married. Still widowed in 1861, Melissa lived with two children and had a grandson. Edmund and Sukey remained together. Phoebe, their daughter, had a child by an unnamed father by 1856 and by 1861 had married Jefferson. Four other women in 1856, usually not yet twenty years old, also had children by unnamed males after 1851. Three of the four lived with a husband named in the 1861 record in a union producing other children. The fourth had her first child in 1861. In the ten-year period, at least a dozen new marriages occurred, involving slaves who had either grown up on the plantation or in a few instances (such as Big Andrew's wife Malvina) been purchased as young adults. Chart 11, which shows some of the marriages involving grown children (such as Merida and Lavinia) from five of the twenty-one 1851 families, indicates how marriage enlarged kin ties between immediate families. But because of the short time period for which evidence exists, the connections indicated are very incomplete. So are the slave naming practices. Household lists that span just a single decade cannot reveal whether children had kin names drawn from outside the immediate family. But in six of the twenty 1851 families with a father at least thirty years old, a son—Little Nat, Little Isaac, Little Jim, Charles G., Little Will, and Little Osborne—had his father's given name.

The naming of a son for his slave father and the decision to marry after having a child by an unnamed father show that the Carlisle slaves could make choices, as does the decision some Carlisle slaves made to end incompatible marriages. Four marriages broke up in the Carlisle slave community between 1851 and 1861. Their dissolution together with the subsequent remarriage by some of the people involved is indicated in Chart 12. Zack married Betsey, whose ex-husband Anthony married Amanda, who had become a Carlisle slave after 1851. Betsey's two sons remained with their mother, but Simon stayed with his father Zack. Zack's ex-wife Sally lived alone in 1856 and in 1861. After Rachel and Davis separated sometime between 1856 and 1861, she lived alone. Two of their older children, Lorenzo and Angelina, married. Angelina settled in with Bob, who had lived with his son in 1851. Davis left Rachel for the young Isabella, who already had a child by an unnamed male in 1856. Five years later, Davis and Isabella had two children of their own, and Nancy, Davis's daughter by Rachel, lived with her father and her young stepmother. In yet another marital shift, Charles and Ellen separated. Each lived alone for a time. But in 1861, Ellen lived with William, Nat and Little Hariett's son, and Charles with Minerva, new to the Carlisle plantation in 1856 and that year the mother of a child by an unnamed father. Five years later, these new marriages all had produced children.

These few marital changes show that the Carlisle plantation managers did not force slave couples to remain together as husband and wife. Because their earlier marriages had produced children, it cannot be argued that these couples had been separated forcibly for failing to increase Stephen Duncan's assets. Duncan's plantation managers probably permitted the slaves to marry and separate at will. That some slaves did so means that similar options probably were available to all Carlisle slaves. Direct or indirect pressures from overseers do not explain what kept together most Carlisle slave marriages. The mores regulating these marriages had their roots within the developing Carlisle slave community and in the beliefs older Carlisle slaves had learned from their parents in other places.

The order and discipline that the Carlisle whites thought essential to their interest did not require settled slave marriages. That is seen on other plantations, too. Zephaniah Kingsley, an early nineteenth-century Florida planter, said he "never interfered in their connubial or domestic affairs, but let them regulate those after their own manner." Another planter told a traveler in the 1820s that he did not meddle with his slaves "in any way further than is necessary for the good of his interests. They may have two or three wives as long as they do not quarrel." Frederick Olmsted encountered the same indifference on a lower Mississippi plantation. Learning that some slave women bore a first child at age sixteen and even at age fourteen, Olmsted probed further:

> . . . [W]hen I asked: "Do you try to discourage this?" the overseer answered: "No, not unless they quarrel." "They get jealous and quarrel among themselves sometimes about it," the manager explained, "or come to the overseer and complain, and he has them punished." "Give all the hands a damned good hiding," said the overseer. "You punish them for adultery, then, but not for fornication?" "Yes," answered the manager, but "No," insisted the overseer, "we punish them for quarreling; if they don't quarrel I don't mind anything about it, but if it makes a muss, I give all four of 'em a warning."

Olmsted incorrectly inferred that slave women were "almost common property." But it is clear that quarreling—not sexual behavior or mating practices—provoked the whites' intervention. They did not interfere so long as the order essential to effective plantation operations was maintained. This policy was stated explicitly by the large Campbell County, Virginia, tobacco planter

CHART 10. FAMILY FORMATION AMONG CARLISLE PLANTATION SLAVES, CONCORDIA PARISH, LOUISIANA, 1851–1861

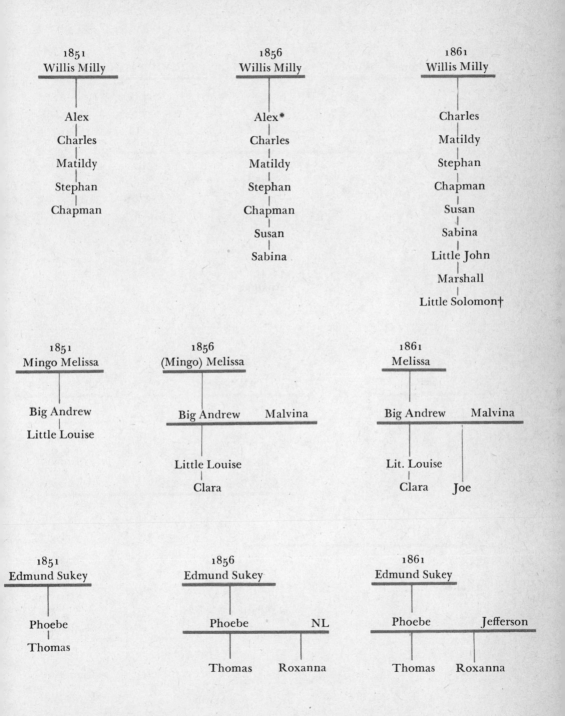

1851
Willis Milly

Alex
Charles
Matildy
Stephan
Chapman

1856
Willis Milly

Alex*
Charles
Matildy
Stephan
Chapman
Susan
Sabina

1861
Willis Milly

Charles
Matildy
Stephan
Chapman
Susan
Sabina
Little John
Marshall
Little Solomon†

1851
Mingo Melissa

Big Andrew
Little Louise

1856
(Mingo) Melissa

Big Andrew   Malvina

Little Louise
Clara

1861
Melissa

Big Andrew   Malvina

Lit. Louise
Clara   Joe

1851
Edmund Sukey

Phoebe
Thomas

1856
Edmund Sukey

Phoebe   NL

Thomas   Roxanna

1861
Edmund Sukey

Phoebe   Jefferson

Thomas   Roxanna

* Alex, aged twenty-five, was sold in 1861.
† Little Solomon was the son of Henry and Little Maria and lived with them in 1851 and 1856. He was born in 1849. This is the only instance found where a child moved into a household with blacks other than his parents.

i

Chart 11. Partial Slave Kin Networks, Carlisle Plantation, Concordia Parish, Louisiana, 1851–1861

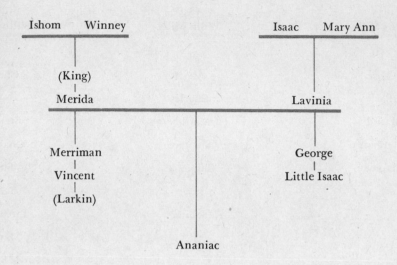

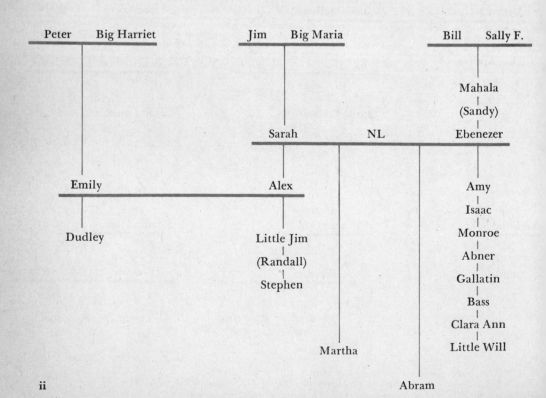

Chart 12. Marital Shifts, Carlisle Plantation, Concordia Parish, Louisiana, 1851–1861

1851   1856   1861

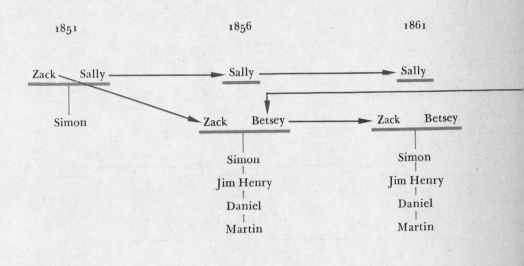

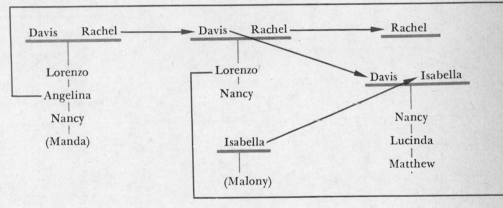

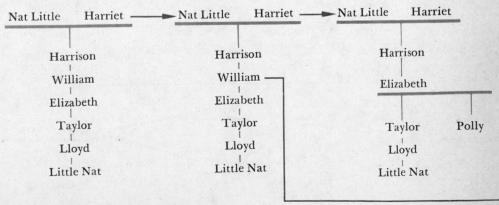

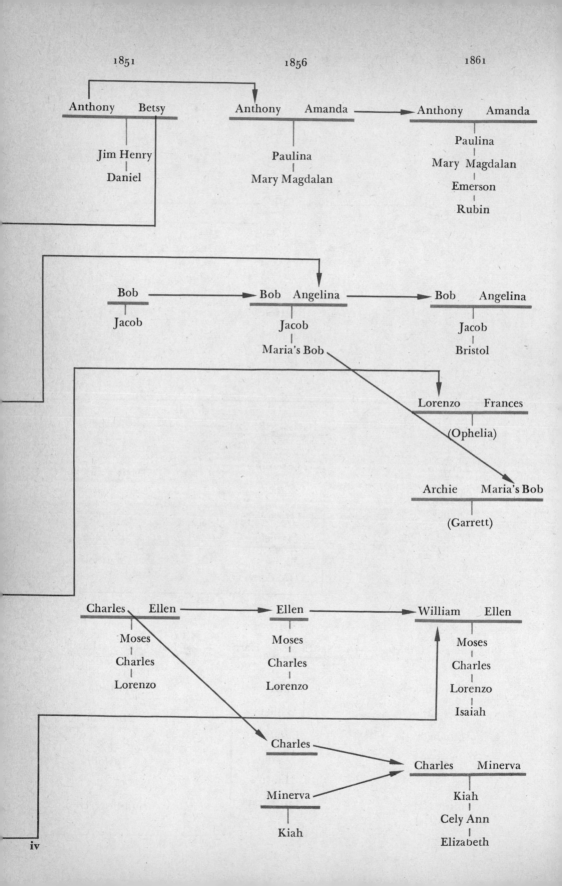

1851   1856   1861

Anthony Betsy   Anthony Amanda   Anthony Amanda

Jim Henry   Paulina   Paulina
Daniel   Mary Magdalan   Mary Magdalan
                             Emerson
                             Rubin

Bob   Bob Angelina   Bob Angelina

Jacob   Jacob   Jacob
         Maria's Bob   Bristol

Lorenzo Frances

(Ophelia)

Archie Maria's Bob

(Garrett)

Charles Ellen   Ellen   William Ellen

Moses   Moses   Moses
Charles   Charles   Charles
Lorenzo   Lorenzo   Lorenzo
                            Isaiah

Charles

Charles Minerva

Minerva   Kiah
                      Cely Ann
Kiah   Elizabeth

and iron manufacturer David Ross. "'Tis well known," he explained in 1812, "that I demand moderate labour from the servants . . . [and] have in great measure left them free only under such control as was most congenial to their happiness. Young people might connect themselves in marriage to their own liking, with consent of their parents who were the best judges. . . ."[16]

Other owners tried to impose standards but gave up in disgust because slave beliefs proved intractable. "As to their habits of amalgamation and intercourse," a Mississippi planter admitted in *DeBow's Review* in 1851, "I know no means whereby to regulate them. I attempted to for many years by preaching virtue and decency, encouraging marriages, and by punishing, with some severity, departures from marital obligations, but it was all in vain." "A Small Farmer" told of similar frustrations: "I have tried faithfully to break up immorality. I have not known an oath to be given for a long time. I know of no quarreling, no calling harsh names, and but little stealing. 'Habits of amalgamation' I cannot stop; I can check it, but only in name." The Georgia planter Charles C. Jones, who believed that plantation management included "the settlement of family troubles," reported that "some owners become disgusted and wearied out, and finally leave the people to their own way," and others believed that "the less the interference on the part of the master the better." The choices slaves made in such settings revealed much more about their own mores than about the mores of those who had power over them. That is why these few Carlisle slave divorces are so important. The decision to remain with a spouse or to dissolve a slave marriage was made by the Carlisle slaves themselves. Most remained together.[17]

That happened elsewhere, too. Among the 9254 Mississippi and northern Louisiana ex-slaves (including a good number of Concordia Parish residents, some of Duncan's ex-slaves, perhaps, among them) who either married in law or renewed slave marriages, a very small number—3.7 percent—reported an earlier marriage that had ended voluntarily, terminated either by "desertion" or by "mutual consent." Neither age nor sex affected the percentage reporting breakups (Table 21). The Carlisle plantation slaves were not the only Afro-American slaves who could choose to end an incompatible marriage.

Henry Watson's Alabama slaves shared much in common with the Carlisle slaves. They also grew cotton and lived in a densely black plantation county. In 1860, Greene County was one of four

Alabama counties with more than twenty thousand slaves. But unlike the Carlisle slaves, the Watson slaves had a resident owner. Henry Watson was not a native southerner. Born in Connecticut, he went South in 1831 as a tutor, settling in 1834 in Greensboro, then a small Alabama village. The region surrounding it had been freshly settled by Virginians and Carolinians, many of whom brought Upper South slaves with them. His white neighbors impressed the Yankee teacher, who found among them "some of the nobility of the old states, the Randolph family, the Taylors, and the Bollings—first rate & intelligent men."[18] Watson emulated them and became a cotton planter. About eighty Greene County whites owned one hundred or more slaves in 1860. Watson had already owned fifty-one in 1843, and despite about a 35 percent infant-mortality rate their number increased—partly through purchase—to one hundred fourteen men, women, and children in 1861. The Yankee planter kept annual slave household lists that included the name and age of each person, the immediate family to which he or she belonged, the name of each newborn child along with its date of birth and its mother's name, and the dates of deaths and sales, lists which permit us to examine how a new slave community developed in a single generation.[19]

Although they had been uprooted from earlier familial and kin groupings, the Watson slaves lived in a community organized around completed slave families. Table 23 shows that hardly any changes in household composition occurred between 1843 and 1861. Households increased in size but remained nuclear in composition. Although the number of families with children doubled, the percentage of children living with a single parent declined sharply. Most children grew up in large families and with parents who lived in settled marriages. In families that started prior to 1850, nine in ten children lived with a mother who had seven or more children. Six women each had between ten and twelve children. (The median age of Watson slave mothers at the birth of a first child hardly differed from Good Hope mothers.) Eleven of sixteen married men at least thirty years old in 1860 had lived with the same woman at least ten years. (Claiborne and Keziah, for example, had been man and wife at least twenty-three years, and Jacob and Peggy at least eighteen years.) Four of the remaining five had shorter marriages because a first wife had either died or been sold. Bill was forty-three years old when his wife Celia died in childbirth; they had lived together at least ten years. Violet was twenty-eight at her death in 1853, and at

TABLE 23.   SLAVES AND THEIR AGES BY TYPE OF HOUSEHOLD, HENRY WATSON PLANTATION, ALABAMA, 1843 AND 1861

1843

HUSBAND, WIFE, CHILDREN

Name	Age	Name	Age
Jacob	25	Robin	22
Peggy	23	Betsey	20
Calvin	1	Jerry	2
Harry C.	43	Claiborne	39
Letty	30	Keziah	28
Mila	8	Major	10
Margaret	4	Sylvia	5
Pheribee	3	Iveson	3
Mary Ann	1	Wesley	1
		Tom	1/12
Bill	46		
Celia	36		
Lucinda	10		
William	8		

1861

HUSBAND, WIFE, CHILDREN

Name	Age	Name	Age
John	44	Jacob	43
Rachel	36	Peggy	41
Lewis	14	Calvin	19
Cornelius	11	Frank	12
Pamela Ann	9	John G.	8
Lloyd	6	Louisa	6
Hannah	3		
Apollonia	1		
Robin	40	Bill	64
Betsey	38	Sally Ann	31
Jerry	20	Martha	14
Jim Henry	16	Aaron	12
Susan	10	Wiley	5
		Joshua T.	2
		Hannibal	6/12
Wm. White	30	Nathan	40
Lucinda	28	Tabitha	38
Charity	12	Isaiah	15
Enoch	6	William A.	6
Nelly	3	Uriah	4
Elisha	9/12	Prinville	3
		Albert	21
		Nelson	19
Abdengo	25	Major	27
Charlotte	21	Margaret	22
Gabriel	1	Washington	1
Claiborne	57	Pleasant	36
Keziah	46	Caroline J.	31
Sylvia	23	Lizzy	15
Joanna	2	Creed	6
Iveson	21	Joe B.	4
Wesley	19	Emily	3
Malinda	13	Barbara	1
Claiborne	9		
Anthony	31	Harry McA.	47
Milly	26	Mary	34
Matilda	6	Amanda	17
Israel	4	Henry W.	13
Abram	2	Lewis	10
Daniel	1	William O.	8
		Ananias	7

TABLE 23.   (*Continued*)

	1843			*1861*	
			HUSBAND, WIFE, CHILDREN		
			Nelson	31	Spencer	41
			Mary Ann	18	Lucy Ann	30
			Richard	12	Victoria	8
			Jenny	1	Alexander	6
					Benjamin	2

1843		1861	
		HUSBAND, WIFE, CHILDREN	
		Nelson 31	Spencer 41
		Mary Ann 18	Lucy Ann 30
		Richard 12	Victoria 8
		Jenny 1	Alexander 6
			Benjamin 2
		Wm. Rowe 33	Sam 38
		Frances 32	Fanny 39
		Silas 5	Allen 9
		Harriet 3	Sam 8
		Marshall 1	Becky 6
			Llewyelen 3
			Sandy 6/12
HUSBAND, WIFE		**HUSBAND, WIFE**	
Cyrus 23		Aaron 70	
Caroline 22		Phillis 70	
Spencer 23		Cyrus 41	
Eveline 24		Caroline 40	
Harry McA. 29		Charles 33	
Violet 18		Sarah 40	
MOTHER, CHILDREN		**MOTHER, CHILDREN**	
Cassy 24		Letty 48	
Jim 4		{ Pheribee 21	
Martha 2		{ Davy 6/12	
		Eliza 15	
Sarah 23		Gibson 11	
Molly Ann 3/12		Reuben 7	
Fanny 23			
Charlotte 3			
Sam 1			
FATHER, CHILDREN		**FATHER, CHILDREN**	
Nathan 22		George 34	
Albert 3		Granville 14	
Nelson 2		Lavinia 9	
UNRELATED HOUSEHOLD			
Francis 14			
Nancy 13			
John Henry 11			
Abdengo 7			
SINGLE PERSONS		**SINGLE PERSONS**	
John 26	Cupid 24	Frank 71	
George 16	Ellen 36	Jim 22	
Rachel 18	Sally Ann 14	John Henry 29	

that time she and Harry McA. had been married at least the same number of years. Harry C. was not included in the 1861 listing. He had died in 1851, and at that time he and Letty had been married at least sixteen years. George was thirty-four in 1861. His wife Anna Maria had either died or been sold sometime in the 1850s, and George lived with his fourteen-year-old son Granville and eight-year-old daughter Lavinia.

The ways in which the Watson slaves conformed to behavior common in other slave communities can be briefly illustrated. Twenty-one different men became fathers of children, two in three by a single woman each. Six of the remaining seven remarried after their wives had either died (four) or been sold (two). Only Henry (sold in 1857) was listed as having had children by different women living in the community. Pleasant and Harry McA. were more typical than Henry. Pleasant and his wife Patience, both born in 1825, had two children in 1845 and 1847. After Patience died, Pleasant married Caroline Jones, who had given birth to three children by unnamed fathers between 1849 and 1851. Pleasant and Caroline Jones became the parents of seven more children. Born in 1814, Harry McA. and his first wife Violet had five children between 1843 and 1852. A few years after her death, Harry McA. married Mary, who, like Caroline Jones, had been the mother of three children by unnamed fathers. Harry McA. and Mary had the first of two children in 1859. Prenuptial intercourse and birth prior to marriage occurred often among the Watson slaves. Fifteen of twenty-nine women each had all her children by the same man. The others had one or more children by unnamed men. Letty had a child by an unnamed father after her husband Henry C. died. She and Henry C. had been the parents of six children. Lucy Ann had a first child by an unnamed father and a second child by Henry, and then settled in with Spencer to bear five more children. Three women (Eliza, Pheribee, and Sylvia) had children and had not yet married at the time Watson stopped keeping records. But by 1860, the other nine women—Caroline Jones, Fanny, Frances, Lucinda, Mary, Mary Ann, Mila, Nancy, and Sarah—had all settled into permanent unions. Fanny illustrated the pattern. She had the first of her three children by unnamed fathers in 1840, and two others in 1842 and 1845. After that nine children were born to Fanny and Sam.

Some young Watson mothers with children by unnamed fathers remained with their families of origin, a fact which indicates that having a child prior to marriage did not cut a daughter off from her family of origin. That was seen among the Stirling slaves, where so many children born to unmarried mothers were named for members of the mother's family. In the Watson community, moreover, the birth of a child did not automatically mean the setting up of a new household. In 1860, for example, Sylvia and her two-year-old daughter Joanna lived with her parents Claiborne and Keziah, and Pheribee and her six-month-old son Davy lived with Pheribee's widowed mother, Letty, and her brothers and sisters. If Pheribee and Sylvia later married, they and their husbands would have established separate households just as Letty and Harry's daughter Mila did. Mila had two children by unnamed fathers and remained with her parents. She then had a child by Henry, and she and Henry set up a separate household. In 1860, Major and Margaret together with their year-old son Washington lived in a separate household. Until then, both had lived with their families of origin. Construction of a separate physical dwelling probably identified a new immediate slave family, but owners, not slaves, were the ones who made such decisions. The building of a new residence required the owner's approval, which must have been contingent on his economic circumstances. An owner pressed for cash or reluctant to part with materials for other reasons would have forced newly-weds to remain apart for a time—each with a family of origin.

By the time of the general emancipation, the Watson slave community had begun to resemble that on the other plantations studied. Its initial members had incorporated slaves purchased after 1843 into the developing family and kin networks. But by the early 1860s, third-generation Watson slave families had hardly started. Nine existed in 1865, and only two had more than four children each. Enlarged kin networks, however, had developed in the two decades prior to the Civil War, and some of the blood and marital ties binding members of this new community are indicated in Chart 13. Bill and Sally Ann's daughter Martha, for example, had married Robin and Betsey's son Jerry. By the Civil War's end, the sixty-nine-year-old Bill had seen twelve children born to his daughters Martha and Lucinda. Major and Margaret's marriage connected the families of Claiborne and Keziah and the widowed Letty. By 1865, Letty also had twelve grandchildren. Slave naming practices indicated that Bill, Claiborne, and Sam each had a son named for him, and Eliza's first daughter was named for her dead paternal grandmother, Patience.

In the three decades preceding the Civil War, plantation com-

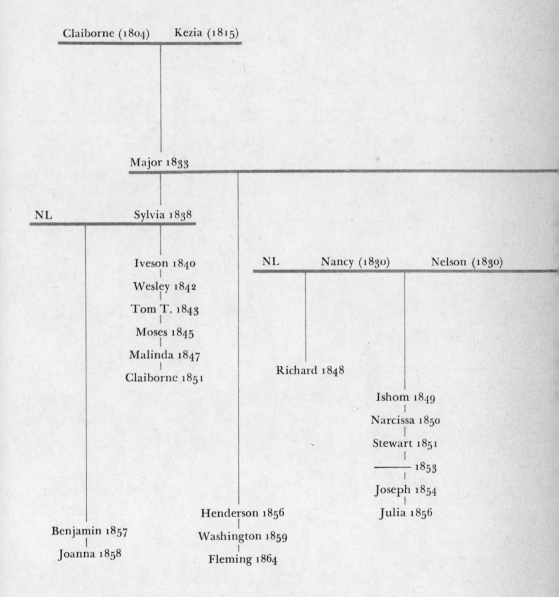

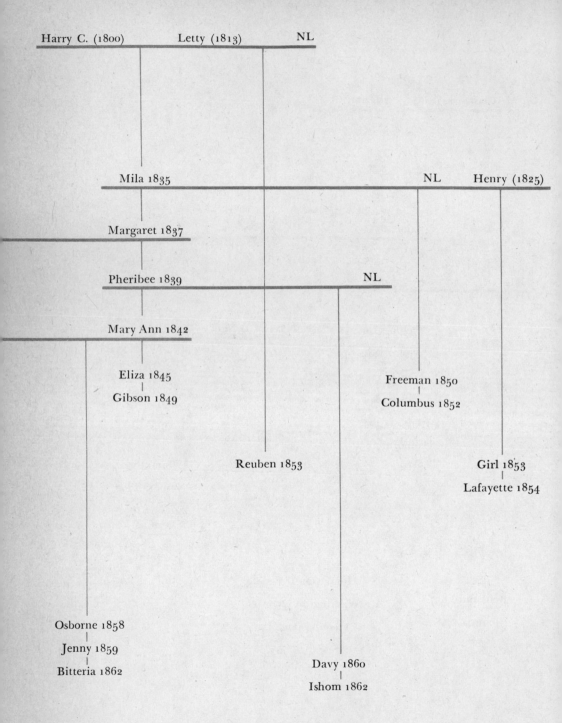

Harry C. (1800)   Letty (1813)   NL

Mila 1835   NL   Henry (1825)

Margaret 1837

Pheribee 1839   NL

Mary Ann 1842

Eliza 1845   Freeman 1850
Gibson 1849   Columbus 1852

Reuben 1853   Girl 1853
                                               Lafayette 1854

Osborne 1858
Jenny 1859
Bitteria 1862   Davy 1860
                             Ishom 1862

Robin (1822)   Betsey (1824)   Sally Ann (1830)   Bill (1797)

Jerry (1841)   Martha (1846)

Jim Henry (1843)

Stillborn (1846)

Stillborn (1848)

Susan (1850)

Girl (1853)

Twins (1855)

Boy (1856)

Aaron (1848)

Ebenezer (1851)

Alexine (1852)

Josephine (1852)

Eldorado (1854)

Wiley (1855)

Joshua (1858)

Hannibal (1860)

—— (1862)

Gracy (1864)

Girl (1863)   Shadrach (1863)

Robert (1865)

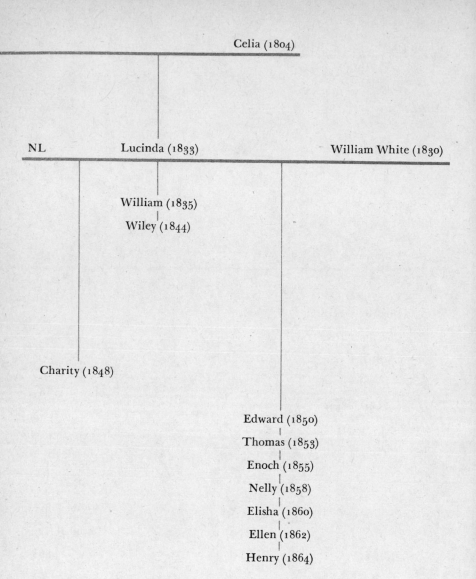

Celia (1804)

NL   Lucinda (1833)   William White (1830)

William (1835)

Wiley (1844)

Charity (1848)

Edward (1850)

Thomas (1853)

Enoch (1855)

Nelly (1858)

Elisha (1860)

Ellen (1862)

Henry (1864)

1	John	—	32	
2	Rachel	—	24	
3	Lewis	—	2½	b. 13 Aug. 1846
4	Caird	—	35	
5	Peggy	—	29	
6	Celhim	—	6	b 1 Sept 1842
7	Daughter	—	4	b 11 Dec 1844
8	Frank	—	3/12	b 11 Dec 1848
9	Cyrus	—	29	
10	Christine	—	28	
11	Shincis	—	29	
12	Erline	—	30	
13	Harry Mch A.	—	35	
14	Violet	—	24	
15	Amanda	—	5	b 26 Dec 1843
16	Henry Wyatt	—	3/12	b 28 Feby 1848
17	Cupira	—	30	
18	Hester	—	22	
19	Robin	—	28	
20	Betsy	—	26	
21	Jerry	—	7	b 4 Nov 1841
22	Little Henry	—	4¾	b 12 May 1844
23	Bill	—	52	
48	Charles	—	21	
49	Sarah	—	28	
50	Lain	—	26	
51	Fanny	—	27	
52	Charlotte	—	9	
53	Letia	—	3½	
54	Tempe	—	5/12	
55	Harry Mc C.	—	48	in Jany 1849
56	Betty	—	36	
57	Usha	—	14	
58	Margaret	—	10½	
59	Phoebe	—	9	b. in Dec 1839
60	Mary Ann	—	6	b. 15 Dec 1842
61	Eliza	—	3½	b 19 Sept. 1845
62	Adaline	—	4	
63	Kesiah	—	34	
64	Major	—	15½	b in June 1833
65	Liburn	—	11	b in Feby 1838
66	Lisson	—	8½	b in June 1840
67	Wesley	—	7	b in Jany 1842
68	Moriea	—	3¾	b 23 Mar 1845
69	Melinda	—	1½	b 6 Feby 1847
70	Pleasant	—	24	

Fragment of Household List of Slaves Belonging to Henry Watson, Alabama, 1840(?)–1865

Fragment of Household List of Slaves Belonging to Henry Watson, Alabama, 1840(?)–1865

munities like those among the Watson and Carlisle slaves emerged over the entire Lower South. They differed in one very important respect from the Good Hope and Stirling slave communities. Those two places contained many old people who could transmit Afro-American norms to the next generation. But in 1843 only Bill and Harry C. among the Watson slaves were at least forty years old. Three women were in their thirties. Letty had just turned thirty, and Celia, who died the next year, and the single woman Ellen were thirty-six. Nineteen of the twenty-five slaves fifteen and older were not yet thirty years old; fifteen were between the ages of sixteen and twenty-four. Henry Watson had purchased a large number of young men and women because a Connecticut tutor wanted to make his fortune in cotton. Over time, a slave community developed whose members replicated all the essential domestic arrangements and mating and sexual patterns found in the Stirling and Good Hope slave communities. Their behavior, once again, indicates how common slave beliefs shaped slave communities. But the values they acted upon had been learned in families from which they had been separated. Detachment from the world they had lived in as children and young adults had not re-made them into "Watson" slaves. The mores they had learned from older slaves accompanied them to distant places. When Solomon Northup lived on a Louisiana plantation with seven former South Carolina slaves, they gave him "a genealogical account" and "often . . . recalled the memories of other days and sighed to retrace the steps to the old home in Carolina." The oldest among them "loved to wander back, in imagination, to the place where he was born." Sale and migration regularly broke up families and shattered kin networks but also spread a uniform Afro-American slave culture over the entire South. Men like the transplanted Yankee Watson set off and shaped this process but did not determine its outcome. Watson's behavior merely showed that Connecticut tutors could become Alabama cotton planters in a single generation. Watson's slaves showed how little time was required for the children and grandchildren of Upper South Afro-American and African slaves to build new slave communities that drew upon the beliefs of their parents and grandparents.[20]

Upon emancipation, the Watson slave community and its constituent families remained together. Emancipation had not required that husbands and wives stay married. That choice was left to the blacks themselves. Four women—Betsey, Mary, Phillis, and Letty—had died during the Civil War, and three wartime marriages had occurred. Except for these few changes, all the men and women listed as husband and wife in the 1861 Watson slave account book chose to remain together. Not a single adult spouse or parent had quit his or her family. A list of the Watson ex-slaves by families drawn up in 1865 shows that, and it was ex-slaves living in these families who disputed their post-emancipation treatment with Watson and his agents. Watson was in Germany in the spring of 1865, having left the management of his properties to his overseer George Hagin and his brother-in-law John Parrish, when his former slaves rejected a contract offered them. Parrish wrote worriedly to Watson in June, "we are at the mercy of the negroes." The ex-slaves had quit work, "rebelled" against Hagin's authority, and "set up claims to the plantation and all on it." A compromise, which promised the blacks part of the crop and said they would be clothed and fed "as usual," also was rejected by the ex-slaves, and Parrish described their complaints as "very ugly." They later turned aside a contract filled with harsh work rules, including one that required them to obey "all orders from the manager . . . promptly and implicitly . . . under all circumstances," another that forbade them to leave the plantation "without written permission from the manager," and a third that charged the support of children too young for field labor against "the parents' interest in the crop and meat." This contract was rejected in "a loud voice and most defiant manner." Not one ex-slave would agree to it. A Freedmen's Bureau officer later worked out a satisfactory arrangement for the rest of 1865. Watson's return in the fall of 1865 did not restore "order." The blacks refused to sign a contract for 1866. Three separate discussions with them proved fruitless. "All my talking, reasoning, and explanations," said Watson, "went for nothing." He turned over the management of his property to Hagin, hoped his old overseer would give his former slaves "the preference" in hiring, and explained to his daughter, "I am clear of the annoyances of next year. . . . They will suffer terribly this winter, but it seems clear that they cannot be awakened to their position and duties till they do suffer." Some time afterward, Hagin sublet individual plots to ex-slaves, a very different arrangement from the rejected 1865 contract, which had sought to impose absolute authority over them.

Adult members of the old Watson slave community kept their families together, successfully repudiated several harsh contracts, and acted in other ways that showed how they interpreted their emancipation. "The women," Watson complained to his daughter late in 1865, "say that they never mean to do any more outdoor work, that white men support their wives, and they mean that their husbands shall support them." The emancipation allowed the slaves to accept or reject practices and values they had been observing among their owners all their lives. In this case, the Watson ex-slaves adopted one practice and stuck to it. Months later Watson again wrote, "The female laborers are almost invariably idle—[they] do not go to the field but desire to play the lady and be supported by their husbands 'like the white folks do.' "[21]

That happened elsewhere, too, among ex-slaves. Frequent complaints of a great labor scarcity by southern white employers in 1865 and 1866 reflected in part the withdrawal of large numbers of women from field labor. In Montgomery County, Virginia, an 1866 Freedmen's Bureau census listed the occupations of 563 ex-slave women at least twenty years old. In this tobacco-producing county where about one third of the 1860 slave population had lived on plantations, about three in five adult women listed occupations, nearly all servants and washerwomen. But married women with children listed occupations far less frequently than single women, married women without children, and women with children but without resident husbands. Slightly less than half the married women with children (47 percent) listed occupations, as compared with about three in four (74 percent) women in all other statuses. Women at least fifty years old in all statuses listed the fewest occupations.[22]

Watson's complaints about the unwillingness of ex-slave women to labor were not unique. A Louisiana planter instructed that rent be charged the nonworking wives of ex-slaves. Theodore Wilson's examination of 1865 and 1866 plantation records convinced him that "the greatest loss to the labor force resulted from the decision of growing numbers of Negro women to devote their time to their homes and children," an action which "had the blessings of their husband[s]" and was more common in 1866 than in 1865. "It was a very general thing," reported the *Southern Presbyterian Review* in 1867, "last year for the freedmen's wives not to be included in the contracts for plantation labor." John deForest, a Freedmen's Bureau officer in Greenville, South Carolina, noticed that "necessity" kept many women at work but thought that families needing Bureau aid had gone "astern simply because the men alone were laboring to support their families." He worried about the "evil of female loaferism."

"Pete," a plantation mistress complained in December 1865, "is still in the notion of remaining but chooses to feed his wife out of his wages rather than to get her fed for her services." On the Louisiana Prudhomme sugar plantation in a seven-month period in 1866 the "average" woman laborer lost twenty-seven days of working time, nearly four times that lost by the "average" man. The Barnwell, Aiken, and Greenville, South Carolina, Freedmen's Bureau Complaint Registers were filled between 1866 and 1868 with complaints from former owners that women refused to work. "Maria," the Aiken white John T. Wise said, "will not work at all," and he added in a later complaint that "some of the women on the place are Lazy and doing nothing but causing disturbance." In Wharton, Texas, a Bureau officer learned from planters that women spent too much time in their cabins. They left their cabins too *"late"* in the morning and quit the field too *"early"* in the afternoon.[23]

The disastrous 1867–1868 cotton crop caused the Boston cotton brokers Francis W. Loring and C. F. Atkinson to inquire systematically of cotton planters as to the industry's condition, and their replies, which filled the pamphlet *Cotton Culture and the South Considered with Reference to Emigration*, also revealed that significant numbers of ex-slave women had quit field labor. Planters in such places as Baldwin, Danbury, Muscogee, and Ogelthorpe counties, Georgia; Forkland County, Alabama; Aiken County, South Carolina; and Panola County, Mississippi made similar observations: "the women have quite retired"; "women seldom now work in the fields"; "all the women are out of the fields, doing nothing." "You will never see three million bales of cotton raised in the South again unless the labor system is improved," predicted a Georgian; "one third of the hands are *women* who *now* do not work at all." "Planters," another explained, "hiring twenty hands, have to support on an average twenty-five to thirty negro women and children in idleness, as the freedmen will not permit their wives and children to work in the fields." "We cannot expect any change," feared an Alabama white, "for it is a matter of pride with the men to allow exemption from labor to their wives which encourages matrimony at a very early age among girls." Such reports depressed the Boston capitalists, who concluded that a "very large proportion of the women have left the fields and stay at home in the cabins." *"This,"* they worried, "in looking to the future, is a serious loss, one over which there is no control."[24]

.   .   .

The study of a sixth slave community allows us once again to shift the comparative focus by enlarging the time span to include substantial numbers of eighteenth-century slave parents. The Carlisle and Watson communities started late in the Afro-American slave experience. Stirling and Cedar Vale slaves born in the late eighteenth century began having children in the early nineteenth century. Too few births occurred among eighteenth-century Good Hope slaves to learn much about them. A developing slave community in which many eighteenth-century births occurred will be examined next. The first birth among them took place in June 1776, and a surviving birth register lists the names of one or both parents of fifty-seven children born before 1800. The entire register recorded the births of 242 children born between 1776 and 1842 and belonging first to the Orange County, North Carolina, merchant and planter Richard Bennehan and later to his descendants and those of the Virginia Scottish cleric John Cameron.[25]

The moment in time that this slave community began is its most salient social characteristic. Most Africans enslaved in mainland North America arrived prior to the War for Independence, nearly half coming between 1740 and 1780. The Bennehan-Cameron slaves who lived so close in time to the forced African emigration may have included some Africans among them. That is unknown. Many were probably the children of Africans. The first generation among them had been born in the 1750s and 1760s, thirty or forty years before the cotton gin was invented and more than half a century before the second great forced migration carried slaves, like those owned in the 1840s and the 1850s by the Alabama planter Henry Watson, from the Upper to the Lower South. In the 1840s, the descendants of some of the early Bennehan-Cameron slaves were shipped by their North Carolina owner to new cotton lands in Alabama. Examination of the adult Bennehan-Cameron slaves living in a developing slave community during the American War for Independence shows the presence of slave sexual and familial norms and of a slave concern for kin beyond the immediate family identical to those we have observed among other slaves in several regions on the eve of the emancipation. It is among these and other eighteenth-century African and Afro-American slaves that the early Afro-American roots of the common familial and social behavior found among slaves nearly a century later are located.

Although the Bennehan-Cameron family ranked among the

South's great slaveholding and plantation families in 1860, their North Carolina slaves had not always been plantation slaves. A visitor in 1848, who said the Cameron holdings covered no less than sixty square miles, believed them "probably the largest landed estate in the Carolinas, perhaps in the Union," and estimated that its proprietors owned at least one thousand slaves. Another contemporary said that the Camerons and Bennehans had as many as "1,900 slaves on absentee owned plantations" in the 1850s. It had not always been that way. Richard Bennehan was the descendant of late-seventeenth-century Irish immigrants to the Virginia Northern Neck. When his father died, Richard was apprenticed to a Virginia merchant. At the age of twenty-five, he moved to the North Carolina Piedmont. Bennehan married well, and in 1803 his daughter Rebecca married Duncan Cameron, then a young and prospering lawyer. The Orange County whites among whom Bennehan settled in the 1760s as an apprentice clerk were mostly new there, too. Many were Pennsylvania migrants, German and Scotch-Irish by birth. Few ever achieved resident planter status. In 1860, 7 percent of Orange County slaveholders owned twenty or more slaves, and half of the county's white landowners did not own a single slave. When Bennehan first settled there, Orange County was the most populous North Carolina county. Its population had grown rapidly in the 1750s and 1760s, and small farmers dominated its economy. In 1755, fewer than one in ten whites owned slaves, and the largest among them held six taxable slaves. Fifty taxable slaves lived in the county. In 1780, only 3 percent of Orange County slaveowners held twenty or more slaves; 95 percent owned fewer than ten. The county had slightly more than two thousand slaves in 1790, but only fourteen whites owned ten or more slaves. Richard Bennehan owned twenty-four slaves in 1790 and was Orange County's largest slaveholder. He had purchased his first slaves fourteen years earlier, and if, as probably happened, they were purchased from local owners, they could not have been plantation slaves.[26]

Like John Cohoon's Cedar Vale slaves, Bennehan's slaves started as small-farm slaves and later became large-plantation slaves. The process began earlier among them than among the Cedar Vale slaves, and it is their behavior before Bennehan became an established planter that is most significant for understanding the later shape of the large Bennehan slave community. The first Bennehan slave woman had a child in July 1776, and by the Battle of Yorktown children had been born to four others. None were yet plantation slaves. All but Dinah lived in conventional slave families (Chart 14). These few slaves were not yet enmeshed in the kin networks common in slave communities three-quarters of a century later. They had belonged to Bennehan for a few years and, at best, had had time to have contact with values identified with the life-style of an apprentice clerk. By 1790, four more Bennehan slave women—Big Esther, Little Esther, Rilley, and Penny—had given birth to children. Sall had left Cato to marry Carolina after Paymore's birth, and she and Carolina had nine children between 1783 and 1805. Cato, in turn, married Betty. They had five children between 1788 and 1801. By 1790, Phebee and Arthur as well as Molly and Daniel had completed their families. So had Dinah, who had children by Jimmy and Isaac and by at least one unnamed man. The Bennehan labor force began expanding rapidly in 1795. Between that year and 1810, a second generation of slave families started among the daughters of Phebee, Dinah, Betty, Molly, Big Esther, Little Esther, and Sall. Bennehan was becoming a planter. The slave families he owned had begun to form enlarged kin networks. He had not forced them into a particular domestic arrangement; they chose their own. A few, like Dinah's daughter Phebee, had all their children by unnamed fathers. Others, like Phebee and Arthur's daughter Isley, first had children by one or more unnamed fathers and then married. Still others had all their children by the same mate.

The behavior of the early generations of Bennehan-Cameron slaves between 1776 and 1842—and especially before 1830—conformed to the behavior of slaves who lived later in time. That common beliefs existed is illustrated in Tables 24 and 25 and Chart 15. Dicey had a first child by an unnamed father in 1824, and after that she had two children by Alfred. Dicey and Alfred were half brother and half sister. Their union was one of two that defied the exogamous beliefs that existed in this and other slave communities.* Bennehan-Cameron slave women had a first child at a much younger age than the other slaves studied. The median age of fifteen women born between 1780 and 1801 at the birth of a first child was 17.7. All but one became mothers for the first time when not yet nineteen years old. In families starting before 1830, slave children grew up among many siblings. Slightly

---

* The Good Hope slaves Fanny and Lewis had the same grandmother but different grandfathers. See page 89.

TABLE 24. BENNEHAN-CAMERON PLANTATION SLAVE FAMILIES AND GENERATIONS, ORANGE COUNTY, NORTH CAROLINA, 1776–1842

Date of birth	Mother	Father	Child	Date of death
First Child Born Between 1776 and 1790				
1. 1776	Phebee	Arthur	Lucy	1814
1778	same	same	Arthur	18??
1781	same	same	Isley	
1784	same	same	Dilsey	1813
1786	same	same	Henry	1812
1789	same	same	Shadrach	
2. 1778	Dinah	Jimmy	Sam	1817
1780	same	not listed	Phebee	181?
1782	same	Isaac	Clarissy	1815
1784	same	same	Tamar	1811
1787	same	same (?)	Jim Frog	1815
1789	same	same (?)	Ishom	1790
3. 1778	Molly	Daniel	Mary	1818
1779	same	same	Sukey	1819
1781	same	same	Aggy	
1783	same	same	George	
1785	same	same	Amey	
1786	same	same	Luke	
1788	same	same	Daniel	
4. 1780	Sall	Cato	Paymore	
1783	same	Carolina	Joe	
1785	same	same	Moses	1810
1787	same	same	Peggy	
1790	same	same	Lucy	1790
1791	same	same	Peter	1794
1793	same	same	Nancy	
1794	same	same	Lewis	
1796	same	same	Ephraim	
1805	same	same	Hedy (?)	
5. 1781	Betty	Jerry	Patty	
1783	same	same	Humphrey	
1786	same	not listed	Charity	
1788	same	Cato	Dycie	1789
1791	same	same	John	1815
1795	same	same	Milley	
1797	same	same	Letty	
1801	same	same	Atsey	
6. 1787	Big Esther	not listed	Nancy	1790
1789	same	not listed	Alfred	1790

T ABLE 24.   *(Continued)*

Date of birth	Mother	Father	Child	Date of death
1791	same	Phil	Virgil	1796
1793	same	same	Mary	1816
1794	same	same	John	1823
1796	same	same	Solomon	1815
1799	same	same	Nathan	1826
1801	same	same	Philip	1825
1801	same	same	Jamima	

	Date of birth	Mother	Father	Child	Date of death
7.*	1788	Penny	Weaver	Polly	
	1791	same	same	Jack	1798
8.*	1788	Rilley	not listed	John	1790
	1790	same	not listed	Peter	1790
	1792	same	not listed	Mariah	
9.	1788	Little Esther	not listed	Anthony	1790
	1791	same	Joe	Grace	
	1796	same	not listed	Rhody	
	1799	same	Lewis	Judith	1825
	1801	same	same	Matthew	

First Child Born Between 1791 and 1810

	Date of birth	Mother	Father	Child	Date of death
1.	1795	Lucy	not listed	Fanny	179?
	1799	same	Jim	Horace	
	1801	same	same	Norvel	
	1806	same	Dick	Joshua	1817
	1808	same	same	Cleon	
	1811	same	same	Sally	1816
	1812	same	same	Moses	1829
	1815	same	same	Peggy	
2.	1796	Phebee	not listed	Lucy	
	1799	same	not listed	Mecklin	
	1803	same	not listed	Isham	
	1806	same	not listed	Daniel	
	1813	same	not listed	William	
3.	1798	Clarissy	not listed	Andrew	
4.	1799	Isley	Francis	Davie	
	1805	same	not listed	Patty	
	1807	same	not listed	Henderson	

* Not included in Chart 15.

TABLE 24. (*Continued*)

Date of birth	Mother	Father	Child	Date of death
1809	same	not listed	Hiram	
1812	same	Dempsey	Zachariah	
1814	same	same	Doshy	
1816	same	same	Phebe	
1819	same	same	John	
1822	same	same	Elias	
1824	same	same	Dilsey	
1827	same	same	Artella	
5. 1803	Tamar	not listed	Olive	
1807	same	Dempsey	Sam	
1809	same	same	Isaac	
1811	same	same	Dinah	
6. 1803	Charity	Arthur	Alfred	
1808	same	not listed	Dicey	
1810	same	Henry	Jesse	1811
1812	same	same	Betsey	
1814	same	same	Jordan	
1815	same	same	Martha	
1819	same	same	Willis	1822
1822	same	same	Henry	
1827	same	Sam	Atsey	
1828	same	same	Mehaley	
7. 1806	Amey	Humphrey	Daniel	
8. 1808	Grace	not listed	Silvey	
9. 1809	Mary	not listed	Virgil	
1812	same	not listed	Albert	
1815	same	not listed	Solomon	
10. 1810	Nancy	not listed	Peter	
1815	same	Philip	Nelson	
1817	same	same	Chaney	
1822	same	same	Polley	
11. 1810	Rhody	Paymore	Milley	
1812	same	same	Cato	
1813	same	John Stradwick	John	
1814	same	Paymore	Davie	181?
1816	same	Charles	Anna	
1819	same	same	Henry	
1822	same	same	Easther	
1824	same	same	Charles	
1829	same	same	Matthew	

TABLE 24.   *(Continued)*

Date of birth	Mother	Father	Child	Date of death
		First Child Born Between 1811 and 1829		
1. 1811	Dilsey	Jerry	Elisha	1816
2. 1814	Milley	Shadrach	Henry	
1816	same	same	Bathena	
1819	same	same	Lucy	
1822	same	same	Shadrach	dead, n.d.
1824	same	same	Letty	
1827	same	same	Tom	
1830	same	same	Betsey	
1833	same	same	Wirt	
3. 1815	Fanny	Anderson	Harrison	
1824	same	Scipio	Alsey	1824
1826	same	same	Peter	
1829	same	same	Charles	
1830	same	same	Peggy	
1833	same	same	John	
4. 1815	Lucy	Lamarque	Jim Frog	
1818	same	same	Sam	
1822	same	same	Phoebe	
1824	same	not listed	George	
1827	same	not listed	Clarissy	
1829	same	not listed	Stephen	
1832	same	not listed	Humphrey	
1833	same	Ben	Ishom	
5. 1818	Judy	Abner	Ellen	
6. 1818	Atsey	Solomon	Solomon	
1819	same	same	John Walker	
1822	same	same	McKenzie (female)	
1824	same	same	Charity	
7. 1819	Jamima	not listed	Mary	
1823	same	not listed	John	1833
1826	same	not listed	Anna	
1829	same	not listed	Mariah	
1833	same	not listed	Rebecca	
1839	same	Henry	Jane	
1841	same	same	Margaret	
8.* 1821	Amy	Yarborough	Abner	
9.* 1822	?	Joe	William	

* Not included in Chart 15.

TABLE 24.   (Continued)

	Date of birth	Mother	Father	Child	Date of death
10.	1823	Margarite†	not listed	Frank	1824
	1826	same	Horace	Cornelia	
	1828	same	Shadrach	Lessey	
	1830	same	Horace	Jim	
	1833	same	same	Dicey	
	1836	same	same	Archie	
	1836	same	same	Phoeby	
	1839	same	same	Frankey	
	1841	same	same	Daniel	
11.	1824	Dicey	not listed	Lenenes	dead, n.d.
	1828	same	Alfred	Henry	
	1831	same	same	Winney	
12.	1824	Silvey	not listed	Frederick	
	1826	same	not listed	Judy	
	1828	same	not listed	Adner	
	1834	same	not listed	Filis	
	1836	same	not listed	Frank	
	1839	same	not listed	Connor	
13.*	1824	Fanny	York	Stoughton	
	1826	same	same	Mary	
	1828	same	same	Zachias	
	1829	same	same	Sidney	
	1834	same	same	Warren	
14.	1826	Molly	Matthew	Lewis	
	1828	same	same	Malinda	
	1830	same	same	Milley	
	1834	same	same	Daniel	
	1836	same	same	Harry (Henry?)	
15.*	1827	Betty (?)	not listed	Crucy	
16.*	1827	Easther	not listed	Hannah	
	1830	same	not listed	Sarah	
	1832	same	not listed	Moses	
	1834	same	Jack Stradwick	Lucy	
	1836	same	same	Ellen	
	1838	same	same	Rachel	
	1841	same	same	John	
	1842	same	not listed	Burrell	
17.	1828	Patty-Ann	not listed	Silas	

* Not included in Chart 15.
† Purchased or born in 1808.

Tᴀʙʟᴇ 24.   *(Continued)*

Date of birth	Mother	Father	Child	Date of death
		First Child Born Between 1830 and 1842		
1. 1830	Judy	Mitchell	Willis	
2.* 1830	Patsey‡	not listed	Eliza	
1833	same	Matthew	Noah	
1834	same	Dandridge	Polly	
1835	same	same	Cinthia	
1838	same	same	Annet	
3. 1831	Betsey	Joe	Richardson	
1833	same	same	Sarah	
1834	same	same	Christopher	
1836	same	same	Solomon	
4. 1831	Cinthia	Daniel	Umstead	
1834	same	same	Wilson	
1837	same	same	Alexander	
5.* 1831	Violet	not listed	Caroline	
6.* 1831	Nelly	Davie	Susan	
7.* 1832	Amy Umstead	not listed	Harriet	
8. 1832	Peggy	not listed	Arthur	dead, n.d.
1834	same	Cato	Paymore	
1835	same	same	Lucy	
1838	same	same	Anderson	
1840	same	same	Rhody	
9.* 1832	Patience	not listed	Jean	
10.* 1832	Gilley	not listed	Nimmy	
11.* 1832	Mary	Ben	Henderson	
1839	same	same	Duncan	
1841	same	same	Zelphia	
12. 1833	Martha	Nat	Miranda	
1835	same	same	Davis	
1837	same	same	William	
1841	same	same	Dicey	
13.* 1834	Mary Cain	Ben	Jesse	
1841	same	same	Ben	
14.* 1834	Mary	Ben Umstead	Morgan	

* Not included in Chart 15.
‡ Purchased or born in 1817.

TABLE 24.   (Continued)

Date of birth	Mother	Father	Child	Date of death
	1836	same	not listed	John	
	1838	same	Ben Lewis (?)	Nelly	
	1840	same	same	Hilliars (?)	
15.	1834	Anna	not listed	Jamima	
	1835	same	not listed	Frances	
	1838	same	William	Freeland	
	1841	same	same	Charles	
16.	1835	Ellen	Ovid	Judy	
	1836	same	same	Violet	
	1838	same	same	Edney	
	1841	same	same	William	dead, n.d.
17.*	1837	Amy	Solomon	Davis	
	1840	same	same	Phoebe	
	1841	same	same	Mariah	
18.*	1839	Sena	Henry	Thomas	
	1841	same	same	Jerry	
19.	1841	Malinsis	Albert	Virgil	
20.*	1841	Dicey	Solomon	Preston	
	1842	same	same	Adeline	

* Not included in Chart 15.

TABLE 25.   NAMING PRACTICES AMONG THE BENNEHAN-CAMERON
PLANTATION SLAVES, ORANGE COUNTY, NORTH
CAROLINA, 1778–1842

Date of birth	Name of newborn child	Name(s) of parents	Relation of newborn child to person with same name
1778	Arthur	Phebee–Arthur	Father
1788	Daniel	Molly–Daniel	Father
1801	Philip	Esther–Phil	Father
1803	Ishom	Phebe	Mother's half brother
1806	Daniel	Amy–Humphrey	Mother's father
1807	Sam	Tamar–Dempsey	Mother's half brother
1809	Isaac	Tamar–Dempsey	Mother's father
1809	Virgil	Mary	Mother's brother
1810	Peter	Nancy	Mother's brother
1811	Dinah	Tamar–Dempsey	Mother's mother

TABLE 25.   (*Continued*)

Date of birth	Name of newborn child	Name(s) of parents	Relation of newborn child to person with same name
1812	Cato	Rhody–Paymore	Father's father
1813	John	Rhody–John S.	Father
1814	Henry	Milly–Shadrach	Father's brother
1815	Solomon	Atsey–Solomon	Father
1815	Jim Frog	Lucy–Lamarque	Mother's half brother
1815	Solomon	Mary	Mother's brother
1816	Phebe	Isley–Dempsey	Mother's mother
1817	Lucy	Milly–Shadrach	Father's sister
1818	Sam	Lucy–Lamarque	Mother's half brother
1819	Mary	Jamima	Mother's sister
1819	John	Atsey–Solomon	Mother's brother
1822	Shadrach	Milly–Shadrach	Father
1822	Phebe	Lucy–Lamarque	Mother's mother
1822	Henry	Charity–Henry	Father
1822	Easther	Rhody–Charles	Mother's mother
1824	Charity	Atsey–Solomon	Mother's half sister
1824	Letty	Milly–Shadrach	Mother's sister
1824	Dilsey	Isley–Dempsey	Mother's sister
1824	Charles	Rhody–Charles	Father
1826	Lewis	Molly–Matthew	Father's father
1826	Judy	Sylvy	Mother's mother's half sister
1827	Clarissy	Lucy	Mother's half sister
1827	Atsey	Charity–Sam	Mother's half sister
1828	Henry	Dicey–Alfred	Mother's stepfather
1829	Matthew	Rhody–Charles	Mother's mother's half brother
1830	Milly	Molly–Matthew	Father's half sister's daughter
1830	Betsey	Milly–Shadrach	Mother's mother
1830	Peggy	Fanny–Scipio	Mother's mother's half brother's daughter
1832	Arthur	Peggy	Mother's mother's brother
1833	Ishom	Lucy–Ben	Mother's half brother
1833	John	Fanny–Scipio	Mother's mother's sister's son
1834	Paymore	Peggy–Cato	Father's father
1835	Lucy	Peggy–Cato	Mother's mother
1835	Judy	Ellen–Ovid	Mother's mother
1835	Solomon	Betsey–Joe	Mother's mother's sister's husband

TABLE 25. (*Continued*)

Date of birth	Name of newborn child	Name(s) of parents	Relation of newborn child to person with same name
1836	Phebe	Margarite–Horace	Father's mother's mother
1838	Anderson	Peggy–Cato	Mother's sister's son
1839	Frankey	Margarite–Horace	Half brother (dead)
1840	Rhody	Peggy–Cato	Father's mother
1841	Ben	Mary C.–Ben	Father
1841	Charles	Anna–William	Mother's father; mother's brother
1842	Dicey	Martha–Nat	Mother's half sister
1842	Virgil	Malinsis–Albert	Father's mother's brother

more than four in five had mothers who gave birth to four or more children, and slightly more than half had mothers who had eight or more children. Some women in each generation—eight among these starting families prior to 1830—had all their children by unnamed fathers. Four had a single child. Phebee and Sylvy, however, had five and six children respectively. But most children born to mothers who had a first child prior to 1830 lived in households that either started and ended as conventional two-parent households or became conventional two-parent households over the full family cycle.

Slaves living in the Bennehan-Cameron community early revealed ties to immediate families and to their families of origin. In nearly half of the families that started before 1820 and in which a father had three or more children, a son carried his father's name. Many children also were named after blood relatives outside the immediate family. Two in five of the one hundred three slave children born between 1803 and 1830 had the name of either a father or another blood relative. One or more children carried a consanguinal relative's name in nearly four of the five families that started between 1790 and 1830 and had in them three or more children. One or more children had the name of either an aunt or an uncle in ten of these fifteen families and the name of a grandparent in eight of these same families. Children in two families had the name of either a great-uncle or a great-aunt, and in another family a child had a great-grandparent's name.

CHART 14. SLAVE BIRTHS IN FAMILIES OWNED BY RICHARD BENNEHAN, ORANGE COUNTY, NORTH CAROLINA, 1776–1781

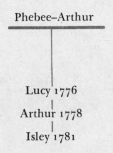

Phebee–Arthur

Lucy 1776
Arthur 1778
Isley 1781

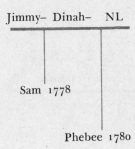

Jimmy– Dinah– NL

Sam 1778

Phebee 1780

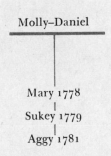

Molly–Daniel

Mary 1778
Sukey 1779
Aggy 1781

Sall–Cato

Paymore 1780

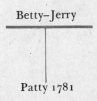

Betty–Jerry

Patty 1781

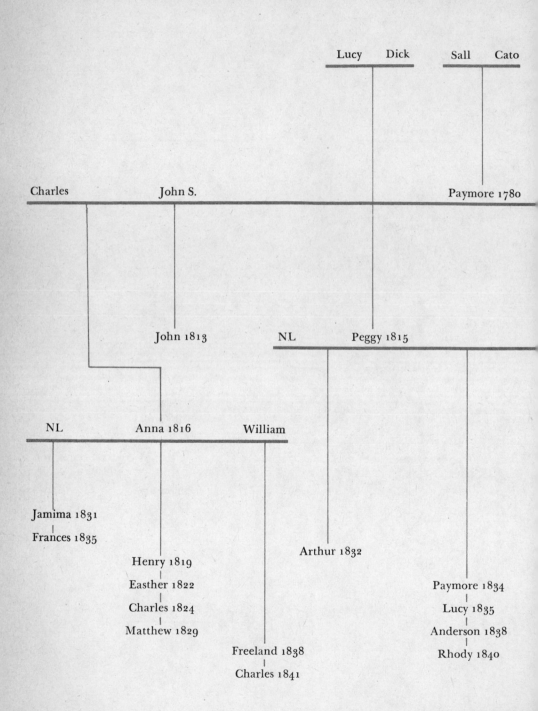

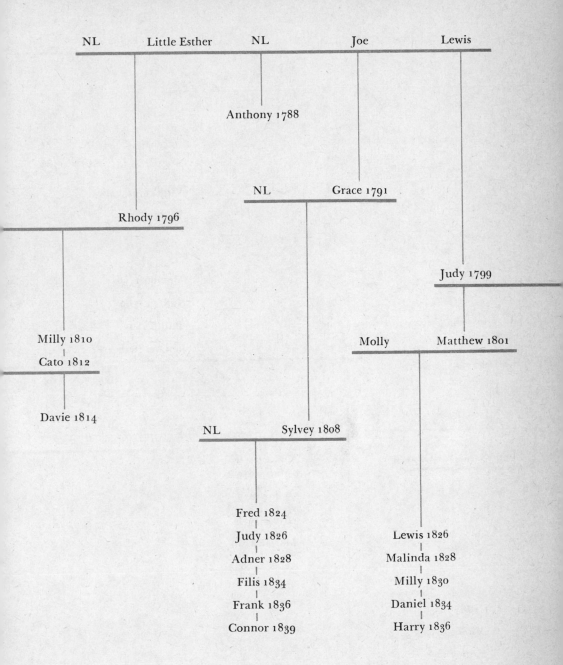

NL   Little Esther   NL   Joe   Lewis

Anthony 1788

NL   Grace 1791

Rhody 1796

Judy 1799

Milly 1810

Molly   Matthew 1801

Cato 1812

Davie 1814

NL   Sylvey 1808

Fred 1824

Judy 1826   Lewis 1826

Adner 1828   Malinda 1828

Filis 1834   Milly 1830

Frank 1836   Daniel 1834

Connor 1839   Harry 1836

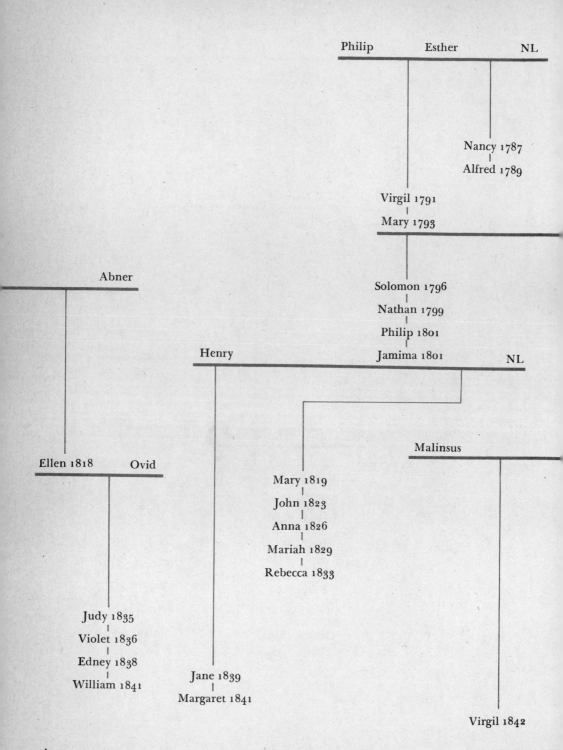

Philip   Esther   NL

Nancy 1787
Alfred 1789

Virgil 1791
Mary 1793

Abner

Solomon 1796
Nathan 1799
Philip 1801
Henry   Jamima 1801   NL

Malinsus

Ellen 1818   Ovid

Mary 1819
John 1823
Anna 1826
Mariah 1829
Rebecca 1833

Judy 1835
Violet 1836
Edney 1838
William 1841

Jane 1839
Margaret 1841

Virgil 1842

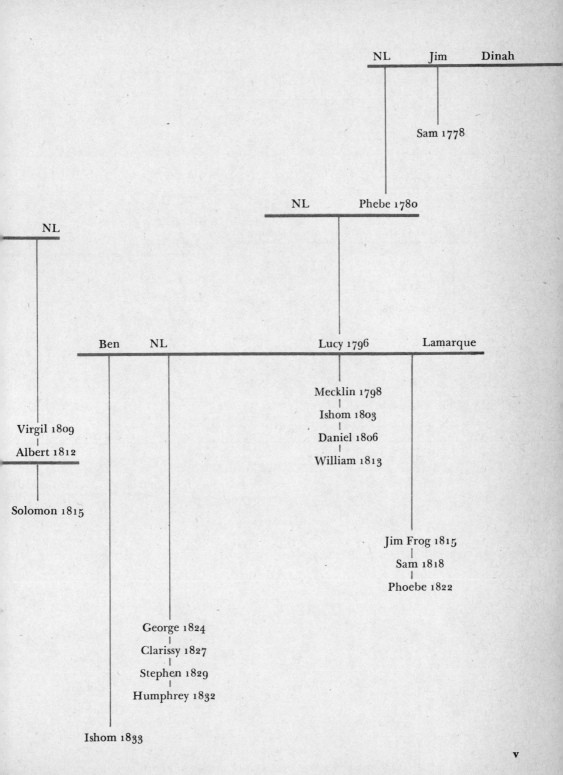

NL   Jim   Dinah

Sam 1778

NL   Phebe 1780

NL

Ben   NL   Lucy 1796   Lamarque

Mecklin 1798
Ishom 1803
Daniel 1806
William 1813

Virgil 1809
Albert 1812

Solomon 1815

Jim Frog 1815
Sam 1818
Phoebe 1822

George 1824
Clarissy 1827
Stephen 1829
Humphrey 1832

Ishom 1833

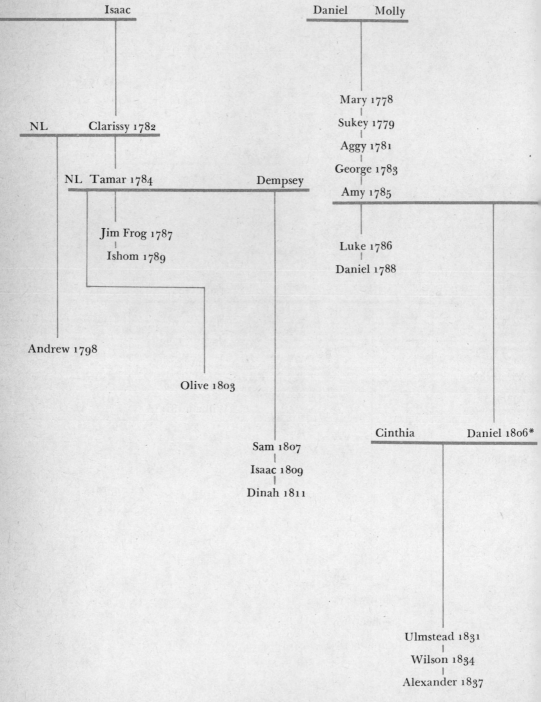

Isaac

Daniel   Molly

Mary 1778
Sukey 1779
Aggy 1781
George 1783
Amy 1785

NL   Clarissy 1782

NL   Tamar 1784   Dempsey

Jim Frog 1787
Ishom 1789

Luke 1786
Daniel 1788

Andrew 1798

Olive 1803

Cinthia   Daniel 1806*

Sam 1807
Isaac 1809
Dinah 1811

Ulmstead 1831
Wilson 1834
Alexander 1837

Cinthia's spouse may have been Daniel, the son of Phebe.

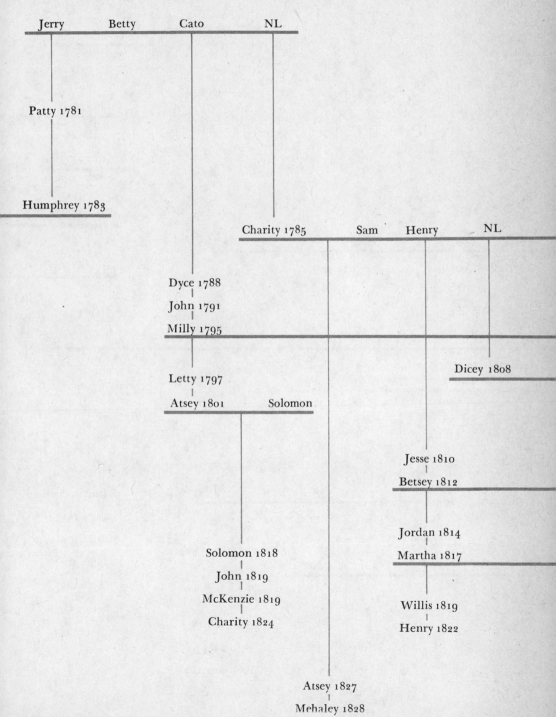

Jerry   Betty   Cato   NL

Patty 1781

Humphrey 1783

Charity 1785   Sam   Henry   NL

Dyce 1788

John 1791

Milly 1795

Dicey 1808

Letty 1797

Atsey 1801   Solomon

Jesse 1810

Betsey 1812

Jordan 1814

Martha 1817

Solomon 1818

John 1819

McKenzie 1819

Charity 1824

Willis 1819

Henry 1822

Atsey 1827

Mehaley 1828

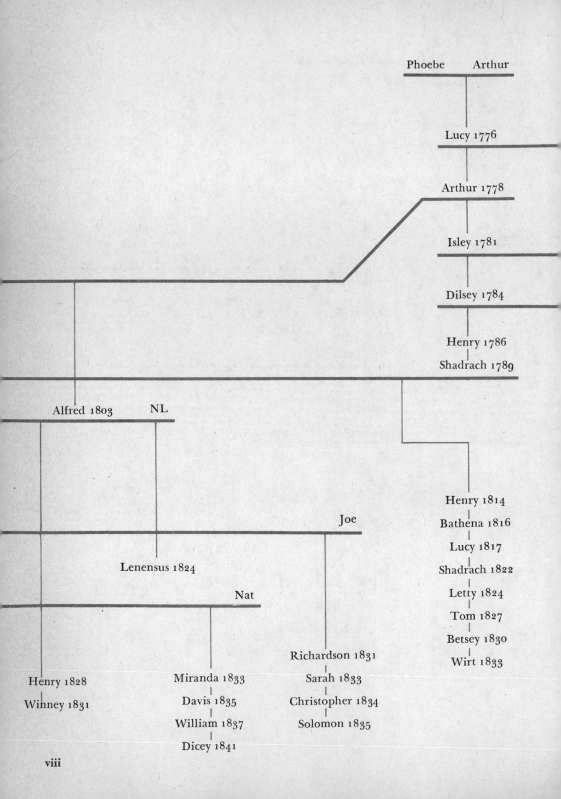

Phoebe   Arthur

Lucy 1776

Arthur 1778

Isley 1781

Dilsey 1784

Henry 1786
Shadrach 1789

Alfred 1803   NL

Joe

Henry 1814
Bathena 1816
Lucy 1817
Shadrach 1822
Letty 1824
Tom 1827
Betsey 1830
Wirt 1833

Lenensus 1824

Nat

Richardson 1831
Sarah 1833
Christopher 1834
Solomon 1835

Henry 1828
Winney 1831

Miranda 1833
Davis 1835
William 1837
Dicey 1841

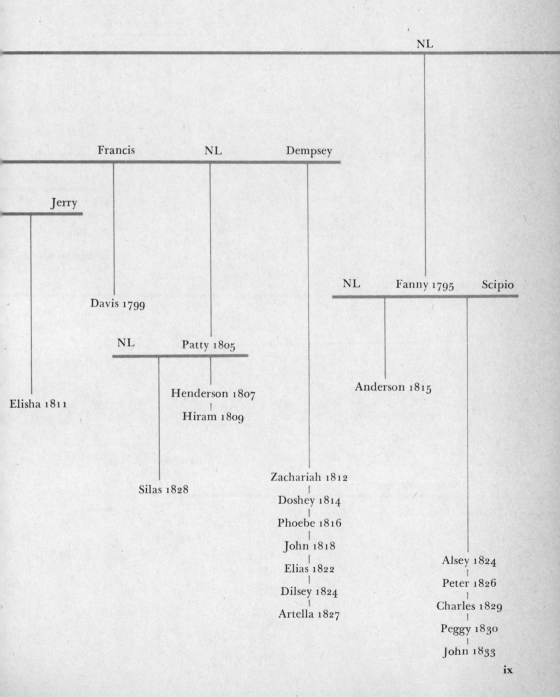

NL

Francis   NL   Dempsey

Jerry

Davis 1799

NL   Fanny 1795   Scipio

NL   Patty 1805

Henderson 1807
Hiram 1809

Anderson 1815

Elisha 1811

Silas 1828

Zachariah 1812
Doshey 1814
Phoebe 1816
John 1818
Elias 1822
Dilsey 1824
Artella 1827

Alsey 1824
Peter 1826
Charles 1829
Peggy 1830
John 1833

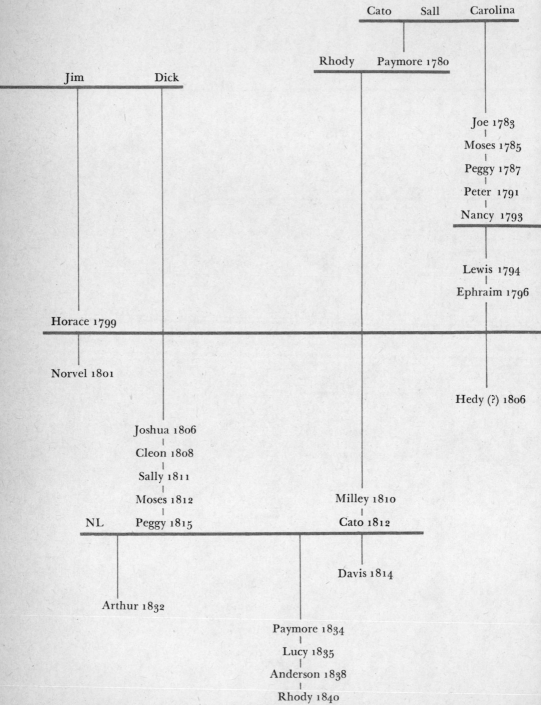

Cato   Sall   Carolina

Rhody   Paymore 1780

Jim   Dick

Joe 1783
Moses 1785
Peggy 1787
Peter 1791
Nancy 1793

Lewis 1794
Ephraim 1796

Horace 1799

Norvel 1801

Hedy (?) 1806

Joshua 1806
Cleon 1808
Sally 1811
Moses 1812
NL   Peggy 1815

Milley 1810
Cato 1812

Davis 1814

Arthur 1832

Paymore 1834
Lucy 1835
Anderson 1838
Rhody 1840

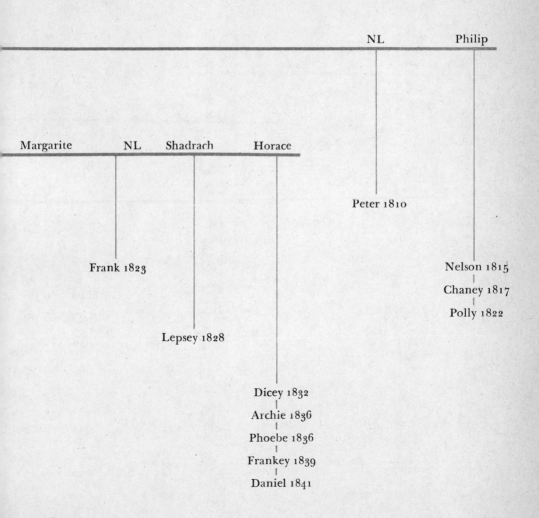

NL   Philip

Margarite   NL   Shadrach   Horace

                                    Peter 1810

Frank 1823

                                              Nelson 1815
                                              Chaney 1817
                                              Polly 1822

          Lepsey 1828

                    Dicey 1832
                    Archie 1836
                    Phoebe 1836
                    Frankey 1839
                    Daniel 1841

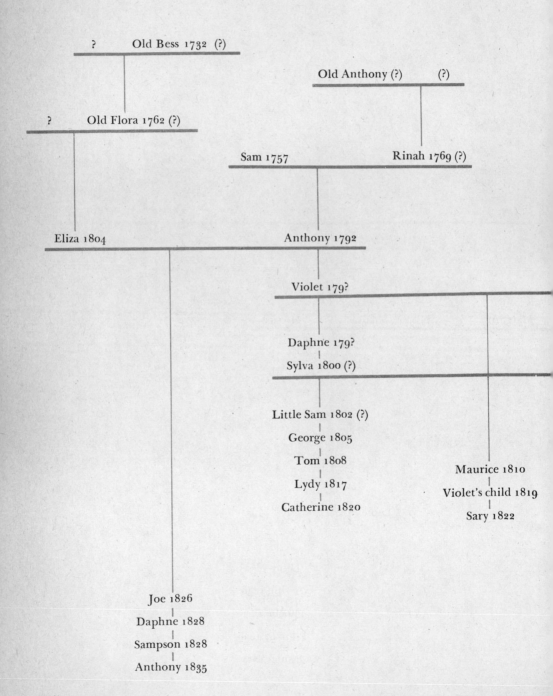

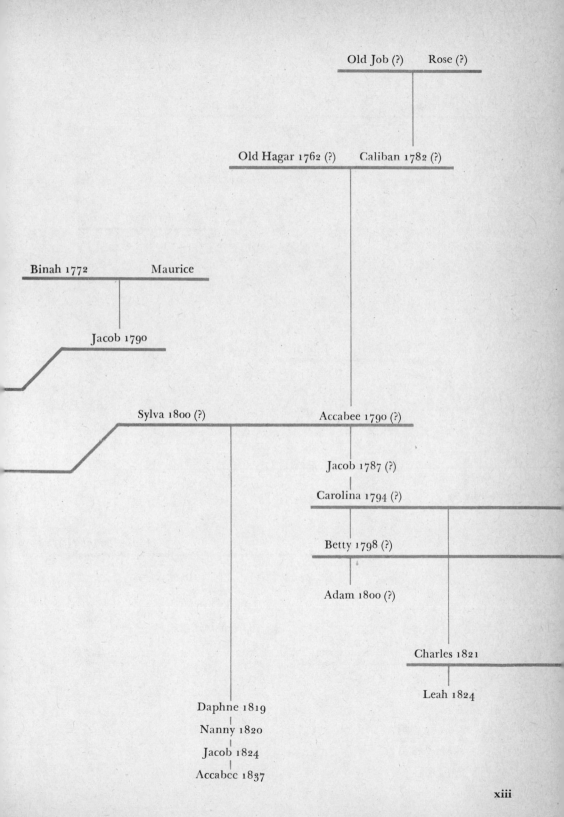

Old Job (?)   Rose (?)

Old Hagar 1762 (?)   Caliban 1782 (?)

Binah 1772   Maurice

Jacob 1790

Sylva 1800 (?)   Accabee 1790 (?)

Jacob 1787 (?)

Carolina 1794 (?)

Betty 1798 (?)

Adam 1800 (?)

Charles 1821

Leah 1824

Daphne 1819

Nanny 1820

Jacob 1824

Accabee 1837

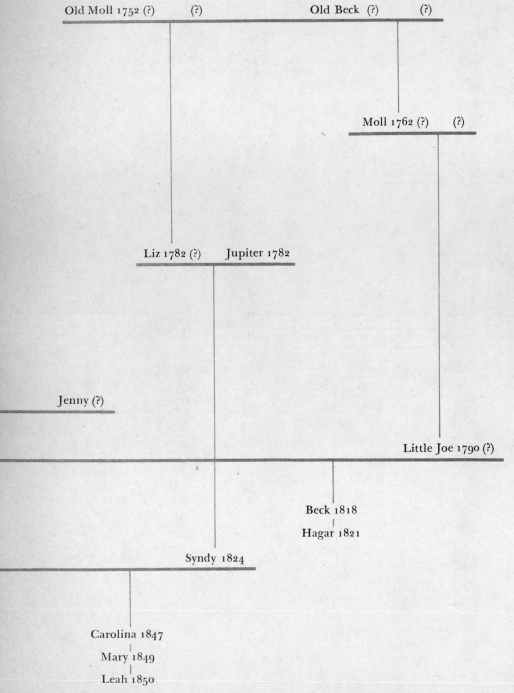

Old Moll 1752 (?)   (?)   Old Beck (?)   (?)

Moll 1762 (?)   (?)

Liz 1782 (?)   Jupiter 1782

Jenny (?)

Little Joe 1790 (?)

Beck 1818
|
Hagar 1821

Syndy 1824

Carolina 1847
|
Mary 1849
|
Leah 1850

That early Bennehan-Cameron slave naming practices were not idiosyncratic is indicated by the reconstruction of some of the kin networks among eighteenth- and early-nineteenth-century slaves owned by the family of Charles C. Pinckney.* A listing of his family's early slaves by Pinckney in 1812 indicates cultural similarities between these South Carolina lowland rice-plantation slaves and those owned by the North Carolina Bennehan-Camerons.[27] Chart 16 shows newborn slave children born after 1790 named for slave fathers, grandfathers, and great-grandfathers as well as aunts and uncles. Similar naming practices occurred among other Pinckney slaves. Betty first had a son Moses by "Mrs. T's Man" in 1822. Five years later, she and African Ned, hired from a white nearby, had the first of five children, a daughter named for Betty's mother Fatima, who was born in 1760. Their second child had his African father's name. Ned was not the only African among these slaves. Old Job, who lived until 1818 and married Rose (whom Pinckney listed as a "free woman"), had been born in Africa, too. Most of the Pinckney slaves listed in Chart 16 were field hands, but Old Flora, who lived from the 1760s to 1841, was a midwife, Maurice was a driver, Old Anthony's son Sam and grandson Anthony were carpenters, and Old Anthony's second grandson Little Sam was a house servant.

A comparison between the Bennehan-Cameron tobacco plantation slaves and those owned by the Louisiana sugar planter Lewis Stirling deepens the cultural significance of this brief comparison to the South Carolina rice planter Pinckney's slaves. Half of the children born in the Stirling slave community between 1850 and 1865 were named for kin, and their parents, mostly born after 1830, belonged to the last generation of Afro-American slaves. Similar intensive naming practices occurred much earlier in time in the developing Bennehan-Cameron community. The Stirling blacks, a late adult slave generation, demonstrated that powerful familial beliefs and kin networks accompanied Afro-Americans into legal freedom. Living in the immediate aftermath of the mid-eighteenth-century forced emigration of Africans, the early generations of Bennehan-Cameron slaves reveal in their behavior how an adaptative culture developed among eighteenth-century Africans and Afro-Americans. The linkage betweent the two provides the vital clue for understanding the essential core of developing slave

---

* A full study of the eighteenth-century Pinckney slaves as well as the families and kin networks among other eighteenth-century slaves, including those belonging to Thomas Jefferson, has been co-authored by this writer, Ira Berlin, and Mary Beth Norton and will be published separately from this work.

communities and for seeing how it was possible for common slave beliefs and behavior to exist on the eve of the general emancipation.

Mid-nineteenth-century descendants of these eighteenth-century Bennehan slaves behaved predictably. The Bennehan-Camerons were supporters of the American Colonization Society, and when Richard Bennehan's son Thomas died in 1847, his will ordered that Virgil and a few other "faithful servants" be freed and "removed to some of our free states or to Africa." Virgil also received five hundred dollars. The next year, Bennehan's nephew Paul Cameron arranged with the American Colonization Society for Virgil to go to Liberia and accompanied him to the ship. Virgil wrote Cameron from Monrovia, "a very fine country," that he was unsure whether he would stay or "return to America." He asked to be remembered "to all my colored friends my Brothers and ant and Ther children . . . Daniel Watson and his family . . . and ucle _____ and the Black Family. . . . All so remembered me to charity . . . old Patty York and grace and her family. . . ." The thirty-nine-year-old Virgil had deep roots in the Bennehan-Cameron slave community. His mother Mary had been born in 1793, the fourth of seven children born to Big Esther. All but one of Big Esther's children were dead by 1830. Virgil's mother Mary died in 1816. She left three young sons. Virgil was then aged seven and the oldest. His mother had each of her three sons by one or more unnamed fathers. Virgil's brother Solomon was born in 1815, the same year that his mother's nineteen-year-old brother, Solomon, had died. Virgil had been named for another uncle, Mary's older brother, who had died in 1796. When her brother had died, Mary was three years old, and when Virgil left for Africa, yet another Bennehan-Cameron slave had his name—the seven-year-old son of Virgil's younger brother Albert and his wife Malinsis.

Another Bennehan-Cameron slave, at a time and in ways as yet obscure, made it to Philadelphia. But Mary Walker's departure did not detach her from her enslaved kin in North Carolina. A letter to Paul Cameron's sister Mildred from J. P. Lesley, a University of Pennsylvania Professor of Mining, in 1859 makes that clear.

I have been lately touched to the heart with a case of heart breaking distress which you have it entirely in your power I find to cure. And I know by my own mother my sister and my wife that there can be no sure confidence placed in anything on earth than that which a man instinctively places upon the delight with which women find they can alleviate or remove distress.

I have come to know one Mary Walker formerly in your family, and I have seen how sick at heart she is about her mother and especially her two children . . . who are still with you, Agnes and Briant. She has been herself in miserable health for some years and sometimes ready to die; but is now in her usual health, able to go about and do her daily work, but very frail and very often suffering. She is a lovely person. . . . She is a sincere and elevated Christian, bears everything without complaint, with a sweet smile and a pleasant word for everybody; and her winning ladylike and conscientious carriage has made her a large circle of friends.

But with all this her heart is slowly breaking. She thinks of nothing but her children, and speaks of nothing else when she speaks of herself at all, which is very seldom. Her mother-heart yearns unspeakably after them and her eyes fall with looking towards the South, over the dreary interval which separates them from her. She has saved a considerable sum of money to buy them, can command more from friends, and will sacrifice anything to see them once again and have their young lives renew the freshness of her own weary spirit. It is in this behalf that I address you,—to realize this hope of hers. She says you were always kind and good. I can imagine that *her* children must be valuable, in fact *invaluable*; that any value named for them must be merely nominal. Therefore I must trust in your goodness of heart and in the remembrance of any sufferings you may have had, and in your own hopes of future happiness, to suggest the various arguments which I could urge for letting this mother bring her children back to her own bosom.

I am a father—and not a mother—yet I can well imagine the heartbreaking longings of this woman after the fruit of her womb, the joys of her youth, the staff and stay of her declining age. She has suffered and still must the exquisite pain of fearing night and day some terrible calamity befalling either or both of her children and especially her daughter; whose blooming womanhood exposes her more terribly than the worst adventures happening to a young man. She feels as if she must die of anxiety and grief and longing love, unless she can get her children with her soon. Not that I think she will die. It would perhaps be better if she could. But she is so well situated, in all merely worldly particulars, that she may perhaps live ten or twenty years; but if she must live so—these years will all be years of lingering heartbreak.

There is no record in the Cameron family correspondence that Mildred Cameron replied.[28]

Virgil and Mary Walker had grown up in a slave community that had its beginnings during the War for Independence. The letter written in behalf of Mary Walker was dated 1859. Many years earlier, the Virginia slave Gooley sent an anxious letter to her former owner, a woman who had moved to Kentucky taking some of Gooley's children and other blood kin with her:

> I have . . . heard you have lost some of your Small Negroes by death. do when you write inform me which of them are dead. I have to inform you that I have had one child since I last Saw you. his Name is Joshua. you will please to tell my Sister Clary not to Let my poor children Suffer & tell her she must allso write & inform me how she & my children are. . . . Remember me to Sucky & Humphrey & there family. . . . Mr. Miller is now on the brink of death, & is about to sell 40 of his Negroes and it is likely Joshua may be one.

The Joshua referred to was Gooley's husband, not her baby. "I wish to Stay with Him as long as possible as you must know its very bad to part man & wife," said Gooley. She went on:

> I should be glad to no what sort of a life Clary leads. . . . be pleased to inform me how my little daughter Judith is & if she is now injoying health. I have no more at present only my best wishes to all my friends & relations and Except my warmest Love & friendship for your Self. . . .
>   P.S. Fanny just as you left her & old Granny Judy goes about & that is all. She has life & that is all. Tell Hannah her Sister is married to Mr. Thornleys Tom. remember me to Jenny Maria & Matildy. Tell all of them to write me.

Half a century separated the letter written for Mary Walker from Gooley's letter, which carried the date November 30, 1807 and was written a year prior to the abolition of the overseas slave trade. Gooley was probably born in the mid-1780s, about the same time that the Bennehan-Cameron slave community was first taking shape, and she was probably the child or grandchild of an African.[29]

5

Aunts and Uncles and Swap-Dog Kin

My dear Sister . . . This is the third letter i have wrote to you since i heard that I had a sister in the land of of [sic] the living.

JOHN RONE (1867)

We had two servants living with us. One was a boy and the other a girl. The boy who was younger always called the girl Aunt.

LUCY CHASE (1863)

Uncle Aleck said, Should each man regard only his own children, and forget all the others?

LAURA M. TOWNE (1868)

We cannot Labor for the Land owners . . . [while] our Infirm and children are not provided for. . . . We are A Working Class of People. . . .

PETITION OF LIBERTY COUNTY, GEORGIA, BLACKS (1865)

Slave naming practices are examined next. They supply evidence about what slaves believed, how Africans and their descendants adapted to enslavement, and especially how enlarged slave kin networks became the social basis for developing slave communities. We shall see that slave naming practices and other evidence indicate how kin obligation was transformed into enlarged slave social obligation.

Naming practices, the anthropologist Meyer Fortes points out, are invaluable historical evidence, often "epitomizing personal experiences, historical happenings, attitudes to life, and cultural ideas and values." That is so in all cultures, including the adaptive culture that developed among Afro-American slaves. "A concern with names and naming," says Ralph Ellison, "was very much part of the special area of American culture from which I come." By studying naming practices, we shall see why, after spending the wartime years among the South Carolina Sea Island ex-slaves, the Yankee William C. Gannett concluded that "to the negro the plantation is his country and the 'family' his state." The rural descendants of slaves put it well. "If you knock de nose," according to a black South Carolina proverb, "de eye cry." That meant, "if you hurt one of the family, you hurt them all."[1]

Most mid-nineteenth-century slaves had common Anglo-American given names, but not too much should be made of that fact. Except for pioneering studies by Lorenzo Dow Turner, Newbell Niles Puckett, and Peter H. Wood, nothing much has yet been written about Afro-American naming systems. Public lists of given names, as the anthropologists Sally and Richard Price point out, reveal little about naming systems and name use within a culture. Records of public given names among enslaved Afro-Americans nevertheless deserve our brief notice. At the general emancipation, the prevalence of common *Anglo-American* names among the ex-slaves is made clear in three quite different sets of documents listing former slaves: an 1864–1865 Davis Bend, Mississippi, marriage register, an 1866 Freedmen's Bureau register of adult blacks living in the Hazelhurst district of Copiah County, Mississippi, and the lists of Newberry and Columbia, South Carolina, and Macon, Georgia, applicants seeking passage to Africa from the American Colonization Society in 1866.[2] In all, 3211 names—nearly evenly divided between males and females—appeared in these three lists. The separate lists revealed common patterns. About one in four men and women had such names as William, George, John, and Henry, and Elizabeth, Mary, Sarah, and Ann. The fifteen most common names everywhere were conventional Anglo-American names (Table 26). A small number had unusual given names.[3] Very few had West African day names, and less than one percent carried Greek and Roman names. If, as has been often suggested, owners frequently bestowed classical names upon slaves, their near absence at the emancipation would mean that significant numbers of blacks rejected such public designations either as slaves or just after their emancipation.[4] A few observant northern white schoolteachers noticed that the former slaves sometimes had more than one given name.[5] Not too much, however, should be made of public name lists. To dwell exclusively upon them obscures the fact that a slave child with a quite common Anglo-American name often carried it for reasons rooted in the developing Afro-American culture.

Naming practices among the Good Hope, Stirling, Cedar Vale, and Bennehan-Cameron slaves—late-eighteenth- and nineteenth-

TABLE 26. RANK ORDER OF GIVEN MALE AND FEMALE AFRO-AMERICAN NAMES IN MISSISSIPPI, SOUTH CAROLINA, AND GEORGIA, 1864–1866

Males

Rank order	Davis Bend, Mississippi, Marriage Register, 1864–1865	Hazelhurst District, Copiah County, Miss., Freedmen's Bureau Register, 1866	American Colonization Society Applicants: Newberry and Columbia, S.C., and Macon, Ga., 1866
1–5	John (27), William, James, Charles, Henry	Henry (41), William, George, James, John	William (28), John, George, Robert, Edward
6–10	Joseph, Thomas, Robert, George, Samuel	Thomas, Richard, Daniel, Charles, Samuel	Isaac, David, Daniel, Samuel, Thomas
11–15	Daniel, Albert, Austin, Benjamin, Isaac (6)	Joseph, Jack, Robert, Benjamin, Alfred (Lewis, Abraham [13])	Alexander, Andrew, Henry, James, Moses (5)
NUMBER	360	847	323
1–5	26%	20%	26%
1–10	40	31	35
1–15	49	40	42

Females

Rank order	Davis Bend, Mississippi, Marriage Register, 1864–1865	Hazelhurst District, Copiah County, Miss., Freedmen's Bureau Register, 1866	American Colonization Society Applicants: Newberry and Columbia, S.C., and Macon, Ga., 1866
1–5	Elizabeth (29), Mary, Sarah, Lucy [Lucinda], Ann [Anna, Anne]	Mary (64), Elizabeth, Ann [Anna, Anne], Jane, Sarah	Mary (27), Elizabeth, Sarah, Ann [Anna, Anne], Maria
6–10	Susan, Frances [Fanny], Harriet, Julia [Julie], Charlotte	Nancy, Frances [Fanny], Harriet, Margaret, Lucy [Lucinda]	Jane, Harriet, Susan, Louisa, Nancy
11–15	Louisa, Jane, Caroline, Emma [Emily], Catherine (Maria) (8)	Emma [Emily], Martha, Caroline, Louisa, Ellen (Milly) (20)	Emma [Emily], Julia [Julie], Martha, Charlotte, Caroline (Ellen, Laura) (5)
NUMBER	360	1002	321
1–5	25%	20%	29%
1–10	38	34	41
1–15	49	44	51

NOTE: Names in brackets are variant spellings. Names in parentheses indicate a tie in ranking. Among the Davis Bend women, for example, eight women each were named Catherine and Maria.

century men and women who lived in Virginia, North and South Carolina, and Louisiana—are evidence of their conceptions of the ties between an immediate family and an enlarged kin grouping. Table 27 summarizes such practices, and the practice of naming children for immediate family members is examined first. A son

TABLE 27. NAMING PATTERNS FOR SLAVE CHILDREN, 1776–1865

Stirling Plantation, West Feliciana Parish, Louisiana, 1807–1865

Child named for	Conventional two-parent slave family				Father-absent slave family	
	PATERNAL LINE		MATERNAL LINE		MATERNAL LINE	
Parent	Fa	14	Mo	0	Mo	0
Grandmother	FaMo	3	MoMo	5	MoMo	3
Grandfather	FaFa	3	MoFa	2	MoFa	4
Great-grandparent	FaMoFa	0	MoMoFa	1	MoMoFa	1
	FaFaFa	0	MoFaFa	1	MoFaFa	0
	FaMoMo	0	MoMoMo	1	MoMoMo	0
Aunt	FaSis	5	MoSis	6	MoSis	7
Uncle	FaBro	4	MoBro	6	MoBro	5
Great-aunt–great-uncle	—		MoFaBro	0	MoFaBro	1
Niece	FaSisDa	1	MoSisDa	0	MoSisDa	3
Nephew	FaSisSon	2	MoSisSon	0	MoSisSon	2
TOTAL		32		22		26
Dead sibling		7				
Affinal kin		9				

Good Hope Plantation, Orangeburg, South Carolina, 1793–1857

Child named for	Conventional two-parent slave family			
	PATERNAL LINE		MATERNAL LINE	
Parent	Fa	5	Mo	0
Grandmother	FaMo	4	MoMo	8
Grandfather	FaFa	3	MoFa	2
Great-grandparent	FaFaFa	1	MoFaMo	1
Aunt	FaSis	2	MoSis	0
Uncle	FaBro	0	MoBro	0
Niece	FaSisDa	1	MoSisDa	1
Nephew	FaSisSon	1	MoSisSon	0
TOTAL		17		12
Dead sibling		0		
Affinal kin		0		

TABLE 27. *(Continued)*

Cedar Vale Plantation, Nansemond County, Virginia, 1811–1863

Child named for	Conventional two-parent slave family				Father-absent slave family	
	PATERNAL KIN		MATERNAL KIN		MATERNAL KIN	
Parent	Fa	4	Mo	1	Mo	0
Grandmother	FaMo	1	MoMo	2	MoMo	0
Grandfather	FaFa	1	MoFa	1	MoFa	1
Aunt	FaSis	3	MoSis	2	MoSis	1
Uncle	FaBro	0	MoBro	4	MoBro	2
Nephew–grand-nephew					MoBroSon	1
					MoMoSisSon	1
TOTAL		9		10		6
Affinal kin		0		0		0

Bennehan-Cameron Plantation, Orange County, North Carolina, 1776–1842

Child named for	Conventional two-parent slave family				Father-absent slave family	
	PATERNAL KIN		MATERNAL KIN		MATERNAL KIN	
Parent	Fa	9	Mo	0	Mo	0
Grandfather	FaFa	3	MoFa*	4	MoFa	0
Grandmother	FaMo	1	MoMo	7	MoMo	0
Great-grandparent	FaMoMo	1				
Aunt	FaSis	1	MoSis	5	MoSis	1
Uncle	FaBro	1	MoBro	5	MoBro	5
Great-aunt–great-uncle	FaMoBro	1	MoMoBro‡	1	MoMoBroSis	2
			MoSisSon	1		
Nephew–niece	FaSisDa†	1				
Grandniece			MoMoBroDa	1		
Grandnephew			MoMoSisSon	1		
TOTAL		18		25		8
Dead sibling		1				
Affinal kin		1				

* Includes mother's stepfather.
† Sister was half sister.
‡ Brother was half brother.

often had his father's name, but it nearly never happened that a daughter had her mother's name. In the four registers, a daughter was given her mother's name once, the Cedar Vale Margaret born in 1857.[6] Naming sons for their slave fathers, however, began early, occurring in families closest in time to initial enslavement. In the seven Bennehan-Cameron families that started between 1776 and 1788, sons had their father's names in three, and in three others a grandson had either a paternal or maternal grandfather's name. Seventeen Stirling men were listed as fathers in families that started between 1807 and 1819, and seven had sons named for them. Three of the seven also had grandsons named for them, along with six of the remaining ten. It is also possible that Josephine had been named for her father, Yellow Joe. The absence of infant girls named for their mothers appears to have been a distinctive slave practice. Nineteenth-century whites, slaveowners among them, regularly named daughters for their mothers. And if the South Carolina free blacks living in Charleston's sixth, seventh, and eighth wards in 1860 were typical of antebellum southern free blacks, so did free blacks.[7]

The reasons for this distinctive slave naming practice remain unknown. A slave child's legal status followed its mother's legal status, and slaveowners rarely recorded the slave fathers' names in plantation birth registers. But the slaves rarely named daughters for their mothers and regularly named sons for their fathers. A slave taboo of unknown origins and meaning may account for this pattern. But it also is possible that children were named for fathers because fathers were more likely to be separated from their children than mothers. Naming a child for its father therefore confirmed that dyadic tie and gave it an assured historical continuity that complemented the close contact that bound the child to its mother. An examination of this naming practice among Mississippi and South Carolina blacks listed in the 1880 manuscript federal census, moreover, reveals its persistence, suggesting that the absence of daughters named for their mothers on these few plantations was not an idiosyncratic social phenomenon. Fewer than one in thirty 1880 households included a child named for her mother, and in just over one in four households a son had his father's name.[8]

The naming of children for their fathers was a particular slave naming practice sufficiently powerful to affect behavior in the immediate post-emancipation decades. It strongly disputes frequent assertions that assign a negligible role to slave fathers and insist that "patriarchal" status came only after black men "acquired property" or assimilated "American attitudes and patterns of behavior" following emancipation and the "breaking down of social isolation." Slaves had their fathers' names on places other than the plantations studied. The Tallahassee free black carpenter

George Antonio and his slave wife, Nancy, even named two of
their children Georgianna and George. "I have a little son
named for myself," boasted the slave overseer Harford to his
Alabama owners. Elizabeth Keckley, a Virginia slave, named her
only son for his grandfather. He belonged to a different owner
than the girl and her mother, and before being sold visited them
twice a year. The fourteen-year-old Elizabeth was separated from
her mother to labor as a house servant, and four years later was
taken to North Carolina, where she had a son by a white. Under
these circumstances, she gave him his grandfather George's name.
When slave fathers were present, however, sons more often carried
their names. In slightly more than half of the plantation families
studied in which a son had a father's name, he was the first-born
son. It rarely happened that he was neither the first- nor the
second-born son. Parents who named sons for their fathers but not
daughters for their mothers contradicted in their behavior the
practice of owners who only recognized "uterine" descent among
them. By so dramatically affirming the important cultural role of
the slave father, the slaves, once more, showed how their beliefs
and practices differed from those of their owners. The slaves Harry
and William Tighman illustrate the affective ties between fathers
and their children. A few months after the Civil War ended,
Tighman, a Somerset County, Maryland, black, wrote to the
Freedmen's Bureau head, O. O. Howard, protesting the indenture
of his son:

> Majer Generall
> Howard My Dear Friend would you be so kind to me & my
> son as to ade us out of dence trubble. there is a certen Mr.
> Edward Howard of this Somerset County M.D. that taken my
> son John Edward during my absence from the county & had
> him unlawfully bound to him by the seceash cort. I have bin
> instructed to call on you & you had the power & disposition
> to Due me & him both justice. I had Just got my son so that
> he was able to be of some help to me & then & not till then
> did the seceash take him away. My dear General be on the
> side of us poor darkes & I pray God to be on your side. Please
> du me the favour to answer this as soon as it may suit your
> conveanance and tell me what you believe of my case. I con-
> clude by saying
>
> I remain your
>
> Obediance Servant
> WM. TIGHMAN

A generation earlier, the blacksmith Harry, who belonged to the family of James K. Polk and was shipped to their new Mississippi plantation and then hired out, reported to his Tennessee owner: "I have Eleven children   I have been faithful over the anvill Block Evr cen 1811   and is still old Harry   my children names 1 Daniel 2 morcel 3 ben 4 Elis 5 Carrell 6 Charles 7 Elushers 8 David 9 Moonrey 10 Carline 11 Opheeler." "Harry," an employer had written during negotiations for his services, "seems to be a good boy."[9]

Newborn children were also named for other immediate family members. Seven Stirling children born between 1844 and 1865 had necronymic names; they were named for dead siblings. (Eight others born in these same years had the names of dead Stirling cousins.[10]) Necronymic naming occurred far less frequently on the other plantations, but the Bennehan-Cameron slave Frankey had a half brother's name, as did Wiley, a boy born on Henry Watson's Alabama plantation. Among the Stirling slaves, Long George and Linder's daughter Roseale was born in 1842 and died in 1847; another daughter born in 1855 had her name. Rosabella, named for her mother's older sister, died as an infant, and her parents named a daughter born four years later Rosabella. Yellow Mary's son Anthony died in his first year, the same year that Yellow Mary's sister named her first child Antoinette. Two years later, Yellow Mary named a newborn son Anthony. Antoinette and Primus lost their first son Duncan but named their second son for him. Serella's first son Wesley, named for his great-uncle, lived from 1858 to 1861, and a son born to her in 1862 was named Wesley. Affy and Jack White were the parents of Evans (1859–1861) and Hannah (1861–1863). Twins born to them in 1864 were named Evans and Hannah.

Scant evidence suggests the origin and meaning of these necronymic naming practices, but Daniel Scott Smith's study of Hingham, Massachusetts, white naming practices between 1640 and 1880 shows that necronymic naming occurred frequently prior to 1800, entirely disappearing afterward. Parents thereby "replaced" a dead child. Nothing is yet known about eighteenth- and early-nineteenth-century southern white naming practices, but if these whites shared the Hingham necronymic naming practice, the eighteenth-century ancestors of the Stirling slaves might have learned it from them. (That is highly improbable, because Hingham whites also often named a first daughter for her mother, a choice rarely made by slaves.) If the Hingham whites typified

eighteenth-century Anglo-Americans and the slaves learned necronymic naming from southern whites, it is then noticed that
this practice lasted much longer among the slaves than among
those from whom they borrowed it.

Other evidence, some of it also from New England, suggests
that slave necronymic naming practices had a quite different
origin. In the *Memoir of Mrs. Chloe Spear, a Native of Africa . . .
Died in 1815 Aged 65 by a Lady of Boston,* Spear described "a
superstitious tradition of her ancestors, who supposed that the
first infant born in a family after the decease of a member was the
same individual come back, just as they saw a young moon after
the old one was gone." This same belief may have been hinted at
by Virginia ex-slaves in 1866. "They said," reported a northern
white, "that . . . 'when your child dies you know where it is,
but when he is sold away, you never know what may happen to
him.' " Early in the twentieth century, a Mississippi ex-slave told
Newbell Puckett that "a child will die if you name him before he
is a month old—seeming to indicate the fact that the spirit should
have a chance to familiarize itself with . . . [the] locality before it
is pegged down." Sarah, who was living on Edisto Island in 1865
but had earlier labored as a Richmond and Charleston house
servant, had a child that year but delayed naming it, according to
the Yankee teacher Mary Ames, "as it is considered bad luck to
give a name to a child before it is a month old." Such evidence
matches what the Cedar Vale plantation records reported: newborn children who died were often listed as "unnamed," "no
name," and "baby." One lived seven months and six days without
being named. If Chloe Spear explained both the origin and
meaning of the necronymic naming practice among the Stirling
slaves, that practice shows that slaves whose domestic arrangements conformed in important if adaptive ways to those common
in the dominant Anglo-American culture acted upon religious
and cultural beliefs of West African origin as late as the Civil
War. Children named for dead siblings had conventional Anglo-
American names, such as Albert, Duncan, Evans, Hannah, and
Wesley, but had been given these names for reasons rooted in
distinctive Afro-American beliefs. The parents who named
them were the children of slaves who had lived on a Louisiana
sugar plantation since before the War of 1812 so they had been
separated from direct contact with West Africa at least half a
century and probably much longer.[11]

Before we examine naming practices for blood kin outside

the immediate family, it should be emphasized that the choice of
particular slave names—and especially the names of fathers, dead
siblings, and other blood kin—rested mostly with the slaves themselves. It defies common sense and is an exercise in misplaced
historical logic even to suggest that Christian owners refused
to name children for their slave mothers but named them for
dead slave siblings thereby sanctioning otherwise often scorned
slave "superstitions." Not all children were given names by their
slave parents, but not all had to for slaves to act upon cosmo-
graphic and cultural beliefs. Only one of several in a family had
to be named for a father, a dead brother or sister, an uncle or
aunt, or a grandparent. "Names," Julia Harn said in recollecting
Ogeechee River, Georgia, rice-plantation life, were "often . . .
left to the wit and ingenuity of the white people unless some
negro parent desired to bestow upon his offspring a certain name."
Duncan Clinch Hayward pointed out that some of his family's
South Carolina rice-plantation slaves asked owners and other
whites to name their children, but that "many" slaves did so
"themselves." The letters written by the overseer John A. Mairs
from a Yalobusha County, Mississippi, plantation contained frequent references to slaves who named their own children between
1850 and 1856:

> "evy increased hir family . . . had two children she cauld
> them by the name of urvin and Mary An"; "sally has increased
> her family and calds her child Burrel"; "Barbra has increased
> hir family . . . has a daughter calds it by the name of Vilete";
> "Mariner has increased hir family . . . Calds him by the name
> of Edwin"; "Daphy has increased her family . . . calls hir
> child by the name of Pol"; "Evy has increased his [sic] family
> . . . Calds his name Annanias"; "evy increased hir family . . .
> calds her child Henry Polk"; "Jane has increased hir family
> has a son and calds his name Manuel"

The names given to most children make it improbable that
owners busied themselves naming newborn slave children and
also casts doubt on the status some historians assign to the
plantation owner as either a "significant other" or a "symbolic
father." Among the more than three hundred children born to
Stirling slaves between 1807 and 1865, one was named Lewis and
another Stirling. Stirling was born in 1855 and was Rosabella and
Alford's third son. The importance attached to his name should
not be exaggerated. His two older brothers, Harry and Joe, had

the names of Alford's and Rosabella's fathers respectively. The older Harry and Yellow Joe were the sons of eighteenth-century Americans, and it is possible that Yellow Joe had a white parent so that Rosabella and Alford's sons were descended from others than slaves. If one of Yellow Joe's and Alford's grandsons lived into the twentieth century, he, like the other plantation slaves born after 1840, had the given name of an eighteenth-century grandfather. Rather than explore further how owners affected slave naming practices, historians would do much better to examine the role played by slave grandparents and other elderly kin. Some evidence hints that they played that role, and it is a well-known fact that grandparents did so in many West African societies. Naming some children for blood cousins suggests that grandparents may have helped pick names. Hagar Brown, born a rice-plantation slave in 1860, assigned precisely that role to her South Carolina mother. "I had Samuel, I had Elias, I had Arthur, I had Beck. . . . I had Sally! I had Sally again. I didn't want to give that name 'Sally' again. Say 'First Sally come carry girl!' Ma say 'Gin 'em name Sally!' . . . Had to do what Ma say. Had to please 'em. Ma name Sally."[12]

Hagar Brown's mother named her grandchild years after the emancipation, but well before that time naming practices showed important connections between parents in immediate families and their families of origin. Children were named for blood kin everywhere, evidence that they did not belong to what Margaret Mead describes as "present bound" generations. Bilateral naming was common. A significant bias toward the maternal line is found among the names of children born in the two-parent Cedar Vale and especially Bennehan-Cameron slave families, but children were named to the maternal and the paternal lines in nearly equal numbers in two-parent Good Hope and Stirling families. How children were named to either line or to both lines can be briefly illustrated. The Stirling slave Phelby had four children, two by Leven and two more by Joe T. The twins Julius and Bartlett were named for maternal and paternal grandfathers, and a son and daughter later were named for Phelby's brother and mother. Ben and Sam were the sons of the Stirling slaves Ben and Delia. Ben named a son for his father. Sam married Harriet, who earlier had had a daughter by an unknown father, a girl named for Harriet's mother. Four of the children born to Sam and Harriet had kin names. Hannah was called for a maternal aunt, and the other three had the names of Sam's father, brother, and sister. Two sons, Lewis and William, were born to the Good Hope couple Bridget and Gabriel. Lewis married Rose and Adnor's daughter Fanny, who had her grandmother's name, and Fanny and Lewis named three children for Lewis's father's father, his father's mother, and his mother's half sister's dead son. William's son carried his father's name and his great-grandfather's name. Five children born to the Cedar Vale couple Huldah, Jr., and Little Bob also were given kin names: a daughter for a maternal grandmother, two other daughters for paternal aunts, and two sons for maternal uncles. The Bennehan-Cameron couple Milly and Shadrach named a son for his father, and four other children for blood kin: one son for a paternal uncle, and three daughters for a maternal aunt, a paternal aunt, and a maternal grandmother.

Such evidence combined with the fact that slave children were named for blood relatives regularly in the decades between 1790 and the emancipation suggests the adaptation of West African kinship beliefs. That does not mean, however, that a straight line can be drawn between eighteenth-century West African kin networks and those existing among Afro-American slaves a century later. In 1909, W. E. B. Du Bois observed that early-twentieth-century Afro-Americans could not "trace an unbroken social history from Africa" but insisted that "a distinct nexus existed between Africa and America" and urged the study of historical evidence that might uncover "the broken thread of African and American social history." The ways in which kinship served Afro-American slaves may help to knot the thread that so concerned Du Bois. The anthropologists Sidney W. Mintz and Richard Price have written cogently about the transmission and transformation of West African beliefs and behavior in New World slave settings:

> What, if anything, might have constituted a set of broadly shared ideas brought from Africa in the realm of kinship? Tentatively and provisionally, we would suggest that there may have been certain widespread fundamental ideas and assumptions about kinship in West Africa. Among these, we might single out the sheer importance of kinship in structuring interpersonal relations and in defining an individual's place in his society; the emphasis on unilineal descent, and the importance to each individual of the resulting lines of kinsmen, living or dead, stretching backward and forward through time; or, on a more abstract level, the use of land as a means

of defining both time and descent, with ancestors venerated *locally*, and with history and genealogy both being particularized in specific pieces of ground.

Enslavement made it impossible for Africans from different cultures to re-create fully the different corporate social organizations common to such societies. Land use in the ways suggested by Mintz and Price was impossible. Furthermore, the naming practices noticed among the plantation slaves studied do not indicate "unilineal descent" but rather hint at ties to the families of both parents.

Nevertheless, naming practices (together with the prevalent exogamous beliefs) show an awareness among the slaves of the "sheer importance of kinship." Mintz and Price go on:

> The aggregate of newly-arrived slaves, though they had been torn from their own local kinship networks, would have continued to view kinship as the normal idiom of social relations. Faced with the absence of real kinsmen, they nevertheless modeled their new social ties upon those of kinship, often borrowing kin terms acquired from their masters to label their relationships with their contemporaries and with those older than themselves—"bro," "uncle," "auntie," "gran" . . .

The adaptive kin networks that developed among the slaves were not "copies" of earlier West African networks but had their roots in antecedent beliefs that kinship was "the normal idiom of social relations." Mintz and Price speculate about the early origins of Afro-American kin networks:

> For such early attempts by slaves to invest social relationships with the symbolism of kinship to be transformed into kinship networks grounded in consanguinity, the first and essential requirement was group stability in time and place, or at least sufficient stability to permit the socialization of offspring within that same group.

Naming practices among the slaves examined do not reveal how symbolic kin ties were converted into kin networks "grounded in consanguinity," but they do reveal that despite the "inescapable constraints" associated with ownership, self-conscious Afro-American slave kin networks developed.[13]

Naming children for blood kin outside immediate families suggests that slaves incorporated elements of the traditional lineal orientation of their West African forebears into their new belief systems. That is hinted at by the order in which children were named for grandparents and occasionally even for great-grandparents as well as by the frequent recurrence of a parent's name in one or more of the families started by his or her sons and daughters. Corporate lineage connections, Paul Bohannon writes of diverse West African cultures, are "central to religious ritual and to cosmography," serving as the "one way in which the small world of the family can be tied to the greater world and ultimately to the supernatural. . . . Only on the birth of a child is a man assured of the 'immortality' of a position in the genealogy of his lineage, or even the security of esteem among the important people of his community. Only on the birth of a grandchild is a man in a position to be truly sure that his name and spirit will live in the history and genealogy of his people." In discussing certain African societies, A. R. Radcliffe-Brown puts it somewhat differently:

> In the passage of persons through the social structure which they enter by birth and leave by death, and in which they occupy successive positions, it is not, properly speaking, children who replace their parents, but those of the grandparents' generation are replaced by those of the grandchildren's generation. As those of the younger generation are moving into their position of social maturity those of the older generation are passing out of the most active social life.

Slave social beliefs caused them to transfer quickly the names of grandparents to grandchildren. Of fifteen Bennehan-Cameron children named for grandparents or great-grandparents, eight were first-born children and eleven either first- or second-born children. Ten of seventeen similarly named Good Hope children were the first-born, and fourteen of seventeen either the first- or second-born. Fifteen of twenty-three named for grandparents and great-grandparents were the first-born in a Stirling slave family, and twenty-one either the first- or second-born. The importance of carrying a grandparents' name forward in time is seen by the fact that one or both grandparents in three-fourths of the early Bennehan-Cameron (1776–1800), Good Hope (1789–1819), and Stirling (1807–1819) families had a grandchild named for him or her.

Such evidence means much more than that children often knew their grandparents, suggesting that elderly slaves played prominent roles in families formed by their children and especially in socializing and enculturating the young. Contemporaries noticed the fierce and often quite harsh discipline used by parents toward their children. That, too, was known among their African forebears. The parent-child relationship, according to Radcliffe-Brown, was usually "one of superordination and subordination," "a relation of social inequality between proximate generations":

> An essential of an orderly social life is some considerable measure of conformity to established usage, and conformity can only be maintained if the rules have some sort and measure of authority behind them. The continuity of the social order depends upon the passing on of tradition, of knowledge and skill, of manners and morals, religion and taste, from one generation to the next.

"Established usage" and the "passing on of tradition" had a place in the world of the slaves, as it did in the world of their African forebears. In West Africa, authority over children was vested in parents but checked by grandparents, who maintained "a relation of friendly familiarity and almost of social equality" with grandchildren. A child could appeal to a grandparent when unfairly treated by a parent. "This may sometimes result," continues Radcliffe-Brown, "in what may be called the merging of alternate generations," adding that "between two proximate generations the relation is normally one of essential inequality, authority, and protective care on the one side, respect and dependence on the other. But between the two generations of grandparents and grandchildren the relation is a contrasting one of friendly familiarity and near equality."[14]

Affective ties bound slave grandparents and their grandchildren. In 1825, when she wrote to the wealthy North Carolina planter John Haywood seeking help in finding a trade for her slave grandson Virgin, Nancy Venture Woods was no longer a slave. The elderly and rheumatic woman explained:

> I have at this time seven in family six grand children and one great grand child and I am now a great grand mother Virgin is the eldest Nancy the next who has now become a mother William Brutus Venter Jone & George is the names of the children that I have taken care of Virgin is desires to be put to a trade and I think it would be the best for him a tailor or shoemaker would suit him best. . . .

After being hired out to a Maryland doctor to satisfy his owner's debts and then being beaten by this man's wife, Isaac Mason returned first to his parents' home but hid at his maternal grandfather's place. The son of his mother's owner, Moses Roper was sold from her when still young. He escaped a South Carolina owner and later returned to visit his North Carolina mother and sister. He remembered that his grandmother, when he was captured and put in a local jail, "used to come to me nearly every day and bring me something to eat, besides the regular gaol allowance." Before being returned to South Carolina, Roper received two or three presents from her. After his mother grew old and lived "in a little hut in the woods after the usual manner of old, worn-out slaves," Moses Grandy said, her children "or other near relations" took it "by turns to go at night" with food for her. A domestic servant to Thomas Jefferson, Alethia Tanner purchased her freedom in 1810 and then saved sufficient money so that in 1828 she bought her sister, ten children, and five grandchildren. Nine years later, she purchased four more grandchildren. These examples merely illustrate the affective ties between children and their grandparents, and much additional study is needed of the relationship between West African generational ties and the later relationships between slave grandparents, their children, and their children's children. But even without such study, naming practices among plantation slaves reveal concern for symbolic ties to older blood kin.[15]

A significant percentage of slaves everywhere also carried the names of aunts and uncles (sometimes even great-aunts and great-uncles). That occurred in two-parent slave families and in families where a woman had all her children by unnamed men. This common naming practice reinforces yet other evidence showing that the forming of a new slave family (either by a marriage or by the birth of a child) did not sever ties to a family of origin and to other immediate families formed partly from that family of origin. Once again, possible adaptations of West African kinship beliefs where particular adult siblings ("mother's brother" and "father's sister") retained important social functions in families headed by brothers and sisters may have existed. Few Good Hope children had the names of uncles and aunts, but nearly half of Stirling, Cedar Vale, and Bennehan-Cameron children named for adult blood relatives were given such names. Although this naming practice may reveal that slaves adapted the obligations between adult siblings that had important functions in all West African societies, too little is yet known to do more than pose questions about the meaning of such behavior. Did naming a child for the adult sibling of a parent mean that extensive reciprocal obligations existed between slave brothers and sisters, which, in turn, shaped relationships within immediate families? If such obligations existed, and their origins lie in earlier West African practices and beliefs, how did these practices change over time? (It remains important here to point out, with M. G. Smith, that the "actual form may be African, yet in order to survive be forced to adapt itself functionally to conditions of existence that often differ substantially from those it originally enjoyed.") Enslavement destroyed traditional corporate lineages, but did it deepen obligations between adult siblings cut off at first for a short time from traditional African groupings? There are yet other questions. How did enlarged kin networks deal with children whose parents had died or had been sold? Did particular adult siblings have special obligations to care for a widowed brother or sister and for orphaned nephews and nieces? If traditional adult sibling obligations linked together generations of separate immediate families, that development may have served as one very important adaptive device allowing slaves in separate immediate families to share responsibilities for the innumerable burdens imposed by Anglo-American enslavement.[16]

Much evidence reveals the presence of obligations and affective ties between slave and former slave adult siblings and between slave aunts and uncles and their nieces and nephews. In 1776, the Virginia planter Landon Carter punished some runaways and "locked . . . Postillion and Tom up," but he could not extract information from "Mrs. Carter's wench Betty, wife to Sawney, brother to Tom." When the runaway Simon returned, Carter believed he had hidden with "his Aunt and Sister in law." Ownership separated the North Carolina sisters Sarah Boon and Lucy Smith by about fifty miles, but letters passed between them. Lucy learned from her sister in 1842 that their mother, who lived with Sarah, had died, and her response described the attachments between adult siblings separated by ownership:

> Your Brother sends his love to you he received your letter but has neglected to answer it his son garner is married to Jacob Harrises Daughter and has got a son. . . . your Brother sends his love to you and all your family give our love to Sister Brother your Mother['s] husband and all your family. accept a portion for your self prey for us your Affactionate Sister

Ex-slaves, like Francis Frederick and Henry Bruce, told how aunts and uncles had affected their lives. After Frederick wrestled with and badly hurt a fellow, his grandmother promised a "flogging when my uncle returned." The young Missouri slave Bruce wanted to marry one of Allen Farmer's slaves, and Farmer tried to keep him from his place. But Bruce visited the woman nearly every week because "the girl's aunt was our mutual friend and made all the arrangements for our meetings." Separated as a child from her Tennessee parents and badly fed by her owners, an ex-slave had an aunt who would "slip meat skins through the crack to us children till the hole would get right greasy." Another Tennessee ex-slave said that his aunt Mary ("my mother's sister") "never married or had any children" and lived with her married sister. Robert Anderson, his brother, and his three sisters (Silva, Agga, and Emma, a three-year-old) were separated from their mother by her sale, and the oldest, the fourteen-year-old Silva, became "a mother to the rest of us children." Isaac Mason's maternal grandfather hid the runaway youth at his uncle's place. After Moses Grandy's daughter purchased her freedom, she searched out her sister and helped the field woman to buy her freedom, too. When Noah Davis decided to apprentice as a shoemaker, he left his Virginia home for Fredericksburg, where his older brother lived. The Kentuckian Andrew Jackson ended up in Wisconsin for the same reason. The free black farmer and barber John C. Stanley, who lived in New Bern, North Carolina, purchased his slave wife and two children in 1805 and two years later his sister-in-law. Pierre Toussaint, who worked as a New York City hairdresser, bought his wife and sister. James Redpath met a Richmond confectioner who after purchasing his own freedom bought his wife, his brother, his sister-in-law and her husband, and that couple's two young children. When the Eastern Shore Maryland free black Amelia Coppin wanted her young son to learn to read and write, she sent him to live with a Baltimore aunt.[17]

The pull between ties to an immediate family and to an enlarged kin network sometimes strained husbands and wives. That was made clear in Amanda Smith's autobiography (1893). She was born in 1857 of Maryland parents with different owners. Her father purchased his freedom, and on her deathbed, her owner freed Amanda, her brothers and sisters, and her mother. "My mother's people," Smith said, "were all in Maryland. She hated to leave her mother, my dear old grandmother, and so never would consent to go North." But her father left Maryland to visit his brother in Pennsylvania, spent more than ten days in a free state, and could not return to his family. After that, Amanda Smith's mother joined him. Sam Berry, who fled the South, lived with his mother, but "an old female slave . . . called Aunt Comfort" raised him. Two sisters and a brother as well as a cousin were sold south from Maryland, and Berry (who later changed his name to James Watkins) headed for an uncle in Hartford, Connecticut:

> The first day . . . I had the great pleasure of meeting with an uncle, who had made his escape about fourteen years before from the very same plantation I had bid adieu to—Mr. Ensor's. Mr. Ensor had informed us that my uncle had been re-taken, and sent to Georgia to pick cotton, for running away. . . . My uncle took me with him to his own house, where I found him comfortably settled, having married. He provided me employment as a farm laborer with Mr. Horace Williams of East Hartford.

Watkins later returned to "try and see my poor old mother."[18]

Dramatic and often poignant incidents exposed the kin ties between other adult siblings. In 1830, a Frenchman purchased Milton Clarke's sister Delia, freed and married her, and took her to New Orleans. Years later, Clarke hired out as a steamboat worker and searched several times in New Orleans before finding her. She then returned to Kentucky to visit her family and planned to raise money to purchase her two brothers. Jane Davis, six of whose children had been sold from her, made it to the District of Columbia with six other of her children in 1857 and sought help to get her family to a Buffalo, New York, brother. "The whole of our family," a runaway to Canada explained in 1863, "bought ourselves," and he described how kin obligations had reached far beyond the immediate family:

> I came from the South in September, 1853, and my family followed in December. My wife had to get a voucher for her freedom before she could come on. . . . I was in slavery until I was about eighteen years old. There were four uncles, myself and mother, and another sister of my uncles. My uncles paid fifteen hundred dollars apiece for themselves. They bought themselves three times. They got cheated out of their freedom in the first instance, and were put in jail at one time, and were going to be sold down South, right away; but parties who were well acquainted with us, and knew we had made desperate

struggles for our freedom, came forward and advanced the money, and took us out of jail, and put us on a footing so that we could go ahead and earn money to pay the debt. We had an uncle in Pittsburgh, who had accumulated a good deal of property since he obtained his freedom. My uncles bought me and my mother, as well as themselves. . . . I never suffered any particular hardship myself. I had a grandfather who had long been free, and when the boys grew up, he would take them and learn them a trade, and keep them out of the hands of the traders; and when they became men and women, having had his industry instilled into them, they would be able and willing to work.

About the time of this interview, a Virginia house servant, separated from her family by sale for four years and later taken by the Union Army to Roanoke Island, met a man who had seen her brother in Norfolk. She quickly had a teacher write him a letter for her because "the man would return that night, and this was her only opportunity." "A woman has this moment gone from me," the teacher Lucy Chase wrote from a Virginia contraband camp in 1863, "who wishes me to write to her sister that another sister died in the tent yesterday, 'half an hour of the sun.' " A letter had arrived asking that the dead sister visit her female sibling. Lucy Chase answered that letter.[19]

Kin obligations beyond the immediate slave family did not disintegrate following the emancipation. Considered in detail elsewhere, they are hinted at here by illustrations of how such obligations reunited broken slave families, protected young children against abusive apprenticeship, and shaped the definition of land use and labor.

A father reconstituted most involuntarily broken slave families, but kin outside the immediate family and grown siblings within it also played that role. Tom Mills and his mother were sold to Texas and separated from their Alabama husband and father. After the war, young Mills's uncle came for them. Sally Wroe's Texas father went to Mexico during the war, and afterward a cousin gathered her family on his rented farm "till pappy comes back." Amy Perry's "auntie" took her from Orangeburg to Charleston. Separated from his Oklahoma parents during the Civil War and bound out to a Texas Cherokee woman, Morris Shepherd stayed with her until "one of my uncles named Wash Shepherd come and tried to get me to go live with him." Cornelius Holmes's father died during the war, and his mother took

the ten-year-old to another South Carolina county and "give me to
my grandpap, Washington Holmes." After Amos Lincoln's
Louisiana father was murdered, his mother took the youth and
her other children to "Shady Bayou to grandpa," a native African.
John Franklin's South Carolina father, a Union Army soldier, did
not return after the war, so his mother moved the family "down
to her daddy's place." Rebecca Jane Grant spent her early years
on the South Carolina Stark plantation near the Georgia border.
Her father had a different owner than his wife, who, while pregnant, was sold with her children to a Beaufort County white.
"All de time," Rebecca Grant remembered, "she'd be a prayin' to
de Lord."

> One night she say she been down on her knees a prayin' and
> dat when she got up, she looked out de door and dere she saw
> comin' down de elements a man, pure and white and shining.
> He got right before her door, and come and stand right to her
> feet, and say, "Sarah, Sarah, Sarah!" "Yes, Sir." "What is you
> frettin' bout so?" "Sir, I'm a stranger here, parted from my
> husband, with five little chillun and not a morsel of bread."
> "You say you're parted from your husband? You're not parted
> from your husband. You're just over a little slash of water.
> Suppose you had to undergo what I had to do. I was nailed to
> the cross of Mount Calvary. And here I am today. Who do you
> put your trust in?" My mother say after dat, everything just
> flow along, just as easy.

After the war, a father, an uncle, and a grandfather reunited her
family.

> First my mother and de young chillun, den I got back. My
> uncle, Jose Jenkins come to Beaufort and stole me by night
> from my Missus. He took me wid him to his home in Savannah.
> We had done been freed; but he stole me from de house.
> When my father heard that I wasn't wid de others, he sent my
> grandfather, Isaac, to hunt me. When he finds me at my
> uncle's house, he took me back.

Rebecca Grant and her grandfather walked sixty-four miles. "I
was foundered," she remembered. "We were all reunited." But
she was not only describing an immediate family. An extended kin
group had come together.[20]

Older siblings played similar roles as these aunts and uncles
and grandparents. Separated from her sister as a young child,
Mattie Gilmore "never seed her no more till after freedom,"
but "after freedom . . . heard she's sick and brung her home, but

she was too far gone." Katie Darling's mother died, and her father, a Union Army soldier, did not return. Her brother took her from an old owner. "One Saturday some niggers come and tell me my brudder Peter am comin'; to [take] me away from old missey Sunday night. . . . Peter was waitin' for me at the lot on the Ware place." After Albert Todd fled his Texas mistress, he took "to the road and sit down and then my sisters come 'long and finds me and takes me to a place where they was livin' on the ranch of a man named Widman." Dora Franks's Mississippi brother took her away and found her a place to work. Two Cape Fear, North Carolina, plantation slaves, David Blount and his younger brother Johnnie, "never knowed who our folks was." "I tried to make a livin' for me and Johnnie," David said, "but it was bad goin'. Den I come to Raleigh and I gets along better. After I gets settled, I brings Johnnie, and we done purty good." Boston Blackwell rejoined a sister. Sold with his mother from Georgia to Arkansas, he left a plantation to join the Union Army. "After peace," he said, "I got with my sister. She's the onliest of all my people I ever seed again." A brother put Mary Lindsay, who lived near the Red River below Fort Washita in the Oklahoma Territory, in contact with her family:

> . . . Some niggers tells me a nigger named Bruner Love living down west of Greenville, and I know that my brother Franklin, 'cause we call him Bruner. I don't remember how all I gets down to Greenville, but I knows I walk most the way, and I finds Bruner. Him and his wife working on a farm, and they say my sister Hetty and my sister Rena what was little is living with my mammy way back up on the Red River. My pappy done died in the time of the War and I didn't know it. Bruner take me in a wagon and we went to my mammy, and I lived with her until she died and Hetty was married.

The Georgian Wylie Neal had similar affective sibling obligations. His parents died during the Civil War. Mustered out of the Union Army, he stayed for a time with his sister, and then he quit Georgia to farm in Arkansas. "We wanted to stay together," said Neal, "is why we all went—my brothers, my two brothers, and a nephew."

Elderly ex-slaves remembered affective adult sibling ties just after the war, and contemporary evidence reveals that, too. Julia Johnson, a thirty-six-year-old, sought transportation funds from the Virginia Freedmen's Bureau for herself and her children, the eleven-year-old William and the two-year-old Kate. Her husband had left her, and she needed money to get from Richmond to her Prince George's County, Maryland, family of origin. With ten dollars of her own and thirty dollars sent by her brother John Rone, she had traveled from Columbia, South Carolina, to Richmond. A letter from her brother accompanied the official transportation request:

My dear Sister

I take my pen in hand to write a few lines to inform you i received your letter and was so glad to hear from you. This is the third letter i have wrote to you since i heard that i had a sister in the land of of [sic] the living; and i don't know wheather you got my letters or not. i am living in Maryland at *Miss Nancy Cores* with my relatives. your Father is living and well. all your cousins send love to you. i am sory that your husband has left you in distress. you must write to me and tell me the news, how all is getting on out where you are and what you are doing, and when i get a letter from you i will try [to] help you to get here with me. and tell me who you are living with. i have been sole too to virginia and to North Caryline for Eighteen years. i have been Back three years to Maryland. i am well at this time. i shall close by saying write as soon as you can and believe me

your loving Brother
JOHN RONE

write to John Rone piscataway Maryland

Rone later wrote the Bureau that she was with her family of origin. He had sent her $10.50 more to get to Alexandria and met her there. "I found her in a very bad condition," said Rone; "I found her with nothing on her head nor the boys."[21]

Upon emancipation, grandparents, aunts and uncles, and even brothers and sisters, not only mothers and fathers, over the entire South protested to the Freedmen's Bureau about the abusive apprenticeship of black children. George P. Douglass wanted the Alexandria Bureau to help his nephew Tim, who had been apprenticed to a distant white before the war and had returned to his family after 1865. The white "prohibited any person from employing the boy." Another black sought a twelve-year-old nephew "stolen" by a white and taken to Fredericksburg. Sally Hunter desired the release of two orphaned nieces allegedly bound out illegally and then abused. The woman Lucy William wanted her grandchildren Ellen and Moses Gilbert freed from an indenture and returned to their parents. The New Orleans Freedmen's Court heard from Sally Loyd that a Point Coupee white "has her niece"; Rose Clayton wanted her granddaughter released from an indenture; another woman made a similar request about her godchild; George Washington's sister had been taken forcibly to Jefferson Parish. The Grenada, Mississippi, black Charles Smith charged that John Sandburn had illegally apprenticed his dead uncle's son and wanted the boy turned over to him. Between January and May 1866, separate complaints about the apprenticeship of Georgia children came to the Macon Bureau from a grandmother and a grandfather. Blood kin other than parents also went to the Selma and Tuscaloosa, Alabama, Bureau. John Spratt protested the abuse of his grandchildren by the Dallas County white Pinckney McIlvaine; Spratt wanted to and could support them. McIlvaine had purchased them before the war, and "they came away with the rest of the family." When their mother became sick, Spratt went "out into the country to notify her relations." She died, and McIlvaine then "carried off the children." Simon Durham pleaded before the Selma Bureau for his younger brother and sister. Legally apprenticed to the Cahaba physician and planter Weeden, they labored at his place when arrested and handcuffed by "three men . . . and started for Benj. Hitts' (their late owner) plantation." The three "had orders to keep them until they become of age." Although the Hitts plantation was about six miles from Weeden's place and Matilda, Durham's sister, was "pregnant and *very* near her delivery," she "was compelled to walk while the men rode." (Matilda and her brother Willis had left Hitts in late 1865 or early 1866. Before that, their father tried to get them but failed. Hitts had threatened to shoot him.) Malinda Sanders worried about her six grandchildren because the white they labored for was moving to Mississippi. She wanted them to remain behind, explaining that "the great [sic] grandmother of these children is amply able to take care of them." Moses Cochran also worried that an employer was going to move away with his brother George, and Jack Prince claimed that a woman had bound his maternal niece illegally. He could care for her. After her father died, another black Alabama child, who lived with her family near the Mississippi border, was indentured. "There was to much hurry to get her," complained her grandmother Lucy Abney. "Her father was hardly cold." "General," the elderly woman appealed, "I don't know the way to apply to you in because I don't know your rules. I have got a white friend to write this for me." Local Bureau officers rejected her claim.[22]

Ties between immediate slave families and larger kin networks affected other important behavior among the ex-slaves. Kin groups had powerfully influenced nearly all aspects of traditional West African community life, including agricultural and other economic activities, but New World enslavement prevented the replication of such organic relationships. Plantation work patterns, the common gang system and the less frequent task system, apparently failed to take into account enlarged slave kin groups, and further study may show that a central tension between slaves and their owners had its origins in the separation of work and kinship obligations. Evidence suggesting such tension is found over the entire South just after emancipation. The historians Joel T. Williamson and William S. McFeely find a close connection between post-emancipation land use and familial and kin beliefs. Williamson says the South Carolina ex-slaves "evinced a strong desire to get away from their former owners" but "also showed a desire to remain on or near their home plantation." Williamson's research left him with "the distinct impression that even as most freedmen left the slave villages they spent their lives on farms carved out of plantations within a few miles of the place of their previous servitude." Such behavior follows from their slave experiences. If ex-slaves had deep ties only to immediate family members and wanted to quit former owners, only their poverty would have kept them close to the "home plantation." The cost of moving fifty miles in 1865–1866 was not that much greater than moving "a few miles." But the extended kin networks among the plantation blacks were sufficient reason to remain in a local familial and social setting. Moving a few miles allowed an immediate family to cut loose from the symbol of its servitude and yet remain attached to the kin networks that had developed among them as slaves. McFeely emphasizes a different point than Williamson:

> Much of the impetus for the establishment of the tenant farmer and sharecropper systems came from the former slaves themselves. Work in a field gang had been one of the most hated aspects of slavery. . . . In exchange for agreeing to care for the dependents—old people and children—for whom the planter had been responsible . . . the freedman farmer obtained from the planter a plot of land he would work on his own.

That was precisely the meaning of an appeal to the Freedmen's Bureau made by rural Georgia blacks in late November 1865. An unknown number gathered in a Liberty County church, picked five "Delegates" to plead their case, and petitioned the Bureau emphasizing mutual obligation and responsibility toward children and older kin:

> We the People of Liberty County . . . appeal to you asking aid and counsel in this our *distressed condition*. We learned from the Address of *general Howard* that We Were to *Return* to the *Plantations* and *Work for our Former owners* at a *Reasonable contract as Freemen*, and find, a *Home* and *Labor, Provided We can Agree. But these* owners of Plantations . . . Says they only will hire or [illegible] the *Prime Hands* and our *old and infirm Mothers* and *Fathers* and our *children Will not be Provided for* and this Will See Sir Put us in *confusion. . . . We cannot Labor for the Land owners* . . . [while] *our Infirm and children are not provided for, and are not allowed to educate or learn. . . . We are Destitute of Religious Worship, having no Home or Place to Live When We Leave the Plantation, Returned to our Former owners; We are A Working Class of People* and We are *Willing* and *anxious* to worke for a *Fair Compensation*; But to *return to work upon the Terms that are at Present offered to us, Would Be We Think going Backe into the state of slavery that We have Just to some extent Been Delivered from.*
>
> We *Appeal* to *you Sir and through you* to the *Rulers* of the *Country* in our *Distressed state* and [illegible] *that We feel, unsettled as Sheep Without a Shephard, and beg your advice* and *Assistance, and Believe that this is an Earnest Appeal from a Poor But Loyal Earnest People.*

Freshly emancipated and descended from three or more generations of slaves, the Georgia blacks condemned their old owners for not providing for "our *old and infirm Mothers* and *Fathers* and our *children*," revealing that their obligations moved backward and forward in social time from their families of origin to the families they then headed as rural laborers. That pull in two directions revealed, once again, how extended kin ties had bound the slaves to one another. About the time they filed this petition, other Georgia ex-slaves and wartime refugees returned home from the South Carolina Sea Islands. "Ay!" the northern missionary W. T. Richardson said of them, "to them, that is holy ground; for it has been watered by their tears and blood. Strange as it may seem to us, the freedmen exhibit strong desires to go back to their former homes, if possible, and enjoy the blessings of freedom, with their families. I know of no other class of persons who manifest stronger local ties."[23]

Few contemporaries and later students of Afro-American behavior realized that these strong "local ties" primarily rested on slave kin networks that bound together immediate families. The Yankee William Gannett, who spent the wartime years among the Sea Islanders, was an exception. "On many estates," he wrote in 1865, "the whole population consists of but two or three distinct families. Everyone is aunt or uncle or cousin to everyone else. The latter titles are so common that abbreviations are necessary: At 'Cl' 'Arkles' Uncle Hercules will turn his head; and even in a quarrel with 'Co' Randy,' the cousinship is not denied." What Gannett noticed among the Sea Island blacks and what was so expressively revealed in the naming practices of Virginia, North and South Carolina, and Louisiana slaves casts fresh light on Melville J. Herskovits's pioneering *The Myth of the Negro Past* (1941). Ten years before its publication, he and two associates studied 639 Monroe County, Mississippi, blacks, and in the later work Herskovits said that these people "represented 171 families . . . the word 'family' in this context signifying those standard primary biological relationships—parents, children, and grandchildren, but not collateral relatives. One group of related immediate families . . . comprised 141 individuals." Such evidence suggested possible continuities with earlier West African cultural practices: "The mere fact that a feeling of kinship as widespread as this exists among a group whose ancestors were carriers of a tradition wherein the larger relationship units are as important as in Africa gives this case importance as a lead for future investigation." Critics, E. Franklin Frazier the most vocal among them, scorned this and similar suggestions. Frazier's own studies had convinced him that "as regards the Negro family, there is no reliable evidence that African culture had any influence on its development," and that "probably never before in history has a people been so completely stripped of its social heritage as the Negroes who were brought to America," because "American slavery destroyed household gods and dissolved the bonds of sympathy and affection between men of the same blood and household."

The Good Hope, Stirling, Cedar Vale, and Bennehan-Cameron slaves deserve a place in this significant controversy. It was over them—and their ancestors and their descendants—that Herskovits and Frazier disputed. Too little is yet known about *eighteenth-century* West African familial and kin life and about the domestic arrangements and kin networks that developed among first- and second-generation eighteenth-century North American slaves to suggest direct continuities between kinship networks that existed among Afro-American plantation slaves in the 1850s and the 1860s and their West African forebears. But enough is now known about such networks in the 1850s and in the 1860s to suggest continuities between slaves in that time and the rural Mississippi blacks Herskovits studied in the third decade of the twentieth century. Herskovits, who knew a great deal about twentieth-century West African and Afro-American communities, did as much to correct distorted views of these peoples as any scholar of his generation, but his failure to study the changing history of enslaved Afro-Americans led him to emphasize direct continuities between discontinuous historical experiences. Yet, a great debt is owed Herskovits for bringing attention to the "extensive relationship groupings" that existed among early-twentieth-century rural southern blacks. That presence convinced him that "African tradition . . . must . . . be held as prominent among those forces which made for the existence of a sense of kinship among Negroes that is active over a far wider range of relationships than among whites." Herskovits's emphasis on a direct continuity with "African tradition" is not essential in weighing the larger implications of such a comparison.[24]

Much, of course, remains to be learned about the changing relationships between class, race, and kinship in American society over the past two centuries, but it will be surprising if further research shows that Lewis Stirling and his family as well as the family of John Foster Dulles's forebears knew anything like the complex kin networks in so closely constructed a physical and social space as the enslaved men, women, and children they owned. Such study probably will reveal that the extended kin networks among plantation slaves were later reinforced by their common quasi-free "peasant" status. Such study promises to confirm the anthropologist Raymond T. Smith's incisive theoretical arguments explaining why the study of the "nuclear family" in isolation from external kin networks distorts all comprehension of the Afro-American lower-class "family." Such study, furthermore, will probably show that enlarged kin networks and the obligations flowing from them were comparatively much more important to Afro-Americans than to lower-class native white and immigrant

Americans, the result of their distinctive low economic status, a condition that denied them the advantages of an extensive associational life beyond the kin group and the advantages and disadvantages resulting from mobility opportunities. Disparate and uneven studies already indicate important extended familial ties among late-nineteenth- and early-twentieth-century southern blacks. W. E. B. Du Bois found "many small communities composed of Negroes which form clans of blood relatives" among rural Georgia blacks. A study of rural blacks near Natchez, Mississippi, by Allison Davis and B. B. and M. R. Gardner uncovered extended families in which "kinship by blood and by affinity was recognized as far as 'third cousins' and 'daughter-in-law's aunt.' "

Studies of kin networks among contemporary whites of different social classes indicating that upward social mobility and contact between related families is inversely related and that "downward social mobility may have the effect of increasing rather than decreasing family cohesion" reinforce such speculations, as do studies of more contemporary Afro-American communities. Virginia Young's study of "Georgiatown" finds that southern black children born out of wedlock or orphaned are cared for in households of "male kinsmen—a paternal grandfather, a paternal uncle, a great-uncle, and a maternal great-uncle." "Family ties," she observes, "through men and emotional ties of men to their kinsmen are socially important in this town, as well as mother-daughter ties." An unpublished study by Demitri Shimkin, Gloria J. Louie, and Dennis Frate of contemporary Holmes County, Mississippi, blacks and migrants from that place to Chicago confirms the importance of the late-twentieth-century rural black extended family. So does a less intensive study by Eva Mueller and William Ladd, which finds that although one-third of blacks studied still lived in their county of birth, three of five in the total population had "all or most of their relatives living near them now in the same community." A far lower percentage of blacks than whites had no relatives where they resided. In addition, Carol B. Stack has shown that during migration from the rural South and in the process of adaptation to late-twentieth-century urban life "clusters of kin align together for various domestic purposes."[25]

There is unusual irony in these findings. The excessive attention given to what has been called "pathological" in the Afro-American historical experience has obscured the adaptive capacities revealed in the extended kinship networks that developed first among the slaves and then among their free children and grandchildren.

No recent historical or sociological study about Afro-Americans more clearly shows how obligations flowed from extended kin ties than Theodore Rosengarten's *All God's Dangers: The Life of Nate Shaw*. A rural Alabama cotton farmer born in 1885 and the son of ex-slaves, Shaw was illiterate when interviewed in his eighty-fifth year by Rosengarten. "I was at home anywhere I went amongst my mother's and daddy's folks," he told him. Dozens of incidents in his long life unpeeled the kin networks that entwined the lives of the children, grandchildren, and great-grandchildren of these Alabama slaves. A single event is selected to show how the world of Nate Shaw had its origins on plantations like Stirling and Good Hope—the death of Nate Shaw's sister Sadie. Shaw explained why he raised one of her children:

> I raised Davey—that was my sister's son, twelve years old when she died and I took the boy. My sister Sadie, my own dear blood sister. My mother was the mother of both we children. When Sadie died she left three boy children—Davey, Tommy, and Henry. She had them chaps by her first husband. And when he died, the father of them children, she married a fellow up there at Litabixee and he was noted, more people noted than one, he was a drag-behind fellow, slow, messin with whiskey through his days. And he got her in a family way and he half treated her. So she gave birth to a baby and it left her in bad shape. And he didn't take care of her. And the baby died. And in a few days after the baby died, she died.

He told what happened after learning of her death:

> . . . [M]y brother Peter come over to my house one day and told me, "Brother, the only sister we is got is dead. Sadie's dead. I was notified about it and I come to let you know." . . . And when we drove into Litabixee that evenin it was little after sundown. And this husband of her'n weren't there, he weren't at home. There was a old lady stayin there with my dead sister—he didn't carry her to no undertaker or nothin like that.
>
> We drive in there—and two of my big uncles . . . they got on their buggies, them and their wives, Uncle Grant Culver and his wife got on their buggy, Uncle Jim Culver and his wife got on their buggy, and all went up to Litabixee with me

and my brother Peter. My sister's own dear uncles just like they was my and Peter's uncles.

Shaw's brother-in-law Ernest Hines returned that night.

> She just died for attention. I said to him when he come in—had a fire out in the yard that night, me and my uncles, our uncles, my and my brother's uncles, and my dead sister's uncles.

Shaw and these others arranged to bury Sadie in the cemetery "where her dear mother is buried, our dear mother," and then Shaw decided to take the boys from Hines. He remembered telling him:

> Well, Brother Ernest, I got a little talk in regards to these little boys my sister died and left. I want to get your consent about it. I'm goin to treat you right. . . . Your wife is dead and gone. These little boys here was the other husband's children. But I'm goin to consult with you as you is the stepfather and they aint big enough and old enough to help themselves. I'll tell you what's on my mind. You ain't the father of these little boys. And you got three or four here yourself, and your children and her children is mixed here by you and her bein married. And I don't think that you are calculated to take care of your children and her children too. And they all on you. You got no wife and it's just you and these children in the house here, you've got em all. You're overloaded and she's gone. . . . These children are not a drop of kin to you. That's one reason I want to take em home with me.

Hines resisted and said his dead wife had asked that he keep them, and "hard words" followed. Shaw threatened him and finally invoked his kin obligations:

> Sadie's request ain't no good in this case. She's dead and gone and she's left two brothers here, which is these boys' uncles. And there's *my* uncles, two big men of em here, all of us connected to these children. They are these little boys' great-uncles. Me and my brother here are their own dear uncles.

Shaw returned with the three boys, told his father what had happened, and said:

> Papa, you is the granddaddy for these little boys and I is their uncle. I'm going to leave it up to you how we'll divide em, if you want em; if you don't want nary one of em or can't keep em, I'll keep all three of 'em.

Shaw's father replied:

> Well, son, I'm perfectly willin to take some of em. I'll tell you
> what I'll do. Bein that you got a houseful of children and
> nobody to wait on them children but their mother, and none
> of em aint big enough to help her with the rest of em—I got
> three or four large girls in my house can wait on em. And
> bein' as it's thataway, I'll take the two least ones, Tommy and
> Henry, and let you keep the oldest one, Davey? He's twelve
> years old and maybe he might be a little help to you. And
> that would keep a crowd off of your wife—if you ain't got no
> children big enough to help her.

The son answered:

> That suits me, Papa, but remember one thing: these little boys
> ain't got no mother and father. I'm only their uncle; me and
> my brother Peter over here is uncles for these three little
> boys . . . and you is their granddaddy. Let's handle em like
> this: don't get the two little boys, the youngest ones, off at
> your house and the oldest one be at my house and we hold
> these little boys apart and won't bring em to see one another.
> I'll bring the little boy that I keep, the oldest one, around to
> your home amongst the other two. And you forward the others
> to my house and let em grow up knowin that they are brothers.
> Don't keep em separated in a way that they'll forget about
> one another. Don't do that, Papa.

That Nate Shaw, his brother, his uncles, and his father were the
children of the adaptive culture developed by their slave forebears is revealed by their concern for Sadie's sons and even more
by the regular appeal to kin obligation Shaw used in explaining
his behavior about half a century after the event.[26]

Obligations rooted in kin ties also affected relations between
slaves unconnected to one another by either blood or marital
ties. That is learned by giving further attention to the slave "aunt"
and "uncle." It is well known that calling adult slaves by such
collateral titles occurred commonly among southern whites
and blacks, but why such terms of address were used and
their social meaning have been little studied. When whites
regularly began addressing elderly blacks by the titles "aunt"
and "uncle" is unknown, but such terms of address were common
in the decades prior to the emancipation. No evidence has yet

been found indicating that whites did so before 1800, and it is
probable that such titles became common in the early nineteenth
century. Slaves—and I mean *Africans, not Afro-Americans*—did
so before that time. Mintz and Price suggest that African slaves
cut off from very different West African social settings "continued
to view kinship as the normal idiom of social relations," and on
slave ships, according to Orlando Patterson, "it was customary
for children to call their parents' shipmates 'uncle' and 'aunt' "
and even for adults to "look upon each other's children mutually
as their own." ("So strong were the bonds between shipmates,"
writes Patterson, "that sexual intercourse between them, in the
view of one observer, was considered incestuous.")

Nineteenth-century whites used kin terms of address toward
slaves for different reasons. They had two purposes: to show
their personal attachment and even respect toward adult slaves
(usually house servants) and to use a nonreciprocal term of address
that defined an essential status difference between a slave and
his or her owners. "Uncle" and "Mister" lived in related but very
different worlds. The slaves had different reasons for using similar
terms of address. The first is simple. On plantations like the
Stirling and Good Hope places, children had uncles and aunts
nearby, older kin related to them by blood or marriage. *Uncle*
Tom was not the product of Harriet Beecher Stowe's imagination:
every Good Hope child born after 1830, for example, had at least
one real aunt and uncle living there, and the terms of address
used by these children reflected nothing more than the realities of
actual kin connections. But parents and other adult blacks also
taught slave children to use such titles when addressing *older
slaves unrelated to them by either blood or marriage.*[27]

Scant but nevertheless suggestive evidence hints that making
children address all adult blacks as either "aunt" or "uncle"
socialized them into the enlarged slave community and also invested non-kin *slave* relationships with symbolic kin meanings
and functions. Only a few antebellum southern blacks remembered the process clearly. The former Eastern Shore, Maryland,
free black Levi Coppin, who was born in 1848, said merely that
"the white people did not permit us to say 'Mr.' and 'Mrs.' to
each other, so, the children, for 'manner's sake,' were taught to
call the older people, 'aunt' and 'uncle.' " ("The slave," Coppin
also observed, "was not allowed to say 'sister and brother' in the
presence of the master. I came near getting a flogging once because
I said to the country storekeeper that I came for a package which

'my sister left there.' 'Your sister!' he shouted. 'Do you mean Mary?' And yet that same man would not hesitate to say that the colt he offered for sale was sister to the one hitched at the post.") A woman who was born a Tennessee slave in 1844 remembered that her master owned four slave families, "Aunt Caroline's family, Uncle Tom's family, Uncle Dave's family, and the family of which I was a member." "None of these others," she said, "were related by blood to us." Her father "had several brothers who lived on other places."

Frederick Douglass and the Yankee schoolteacher Lucy Chase offered explicit reasons why young slaves addressed elderly non-kin by collateral kin titles. Douglass said:

> "Uncle" Toby was the blacksmith, "Uncle" Harry the cart-wright, and "Uncle" Abel the shoemaker, and these had assistants in their several departments. These mechanics were called "Uncles" by all the younger slaves, not because they really sustained that relationship to any, but according to plantation etiquette as a mark of respect, due from the younger to the older slaves. Strange and even ridiculous as it may seem, among a people so uncultivated and with so many stern trials to look in the face, there is not to be found among any people a more rigid enforcement of the law of respect to elders than is maintained among them.

The young had to "approach the company of an older slave with hat in hand. . . . So uniformly are good manners enforced *among the slaves*, that I can easily detect a 'bogus' fugitive by his manners." Lucy Chase made a similar point in 1863: "They show great respect for age as is manifest from one custom of theirs; they always call an older person Aunt or Uncle." The illustration Chase used strengthened her general observation: "We had two servants living with us. One was a boy and the other a girl. The boy who was younger always called the girl Aunt." A kin term of address was even used toward an older youth.[28]

Kin terms of address taught young slaves to respect older ones, kin and non-kin alike, a respect essential to the socialization and enculturation processes in slave communities where older slaves played crucial roles. "It is from the grandparents of both sexes," Meyer Fortes writes of the West African Ashanti, "that children learn of family history, folklore, proverbs, and other traditional lore. The grandparents are felt to be living links with the past." Elderly slaves—fictive aunts and uncles among them—played that role among Afro-American slaves, a role given status within the slave community by investing such persons with symbolic, or fictive, kin titles. A white met an elderly man on a Mississippi plantation and learned from his owner that "Uncle Jacob was a regulator on the plantation; . . . a *word* or a *look* from him, addressed to younger slaves, had more efficiency than a *blow* from the overseer."

Wartime and early postwar northern observers met elderly men like Uncle Jacob over the entire South. Laura Towne said that Sea Island women called a male church elder "their spiritual father" and that such a man had "the most absolute power over them. These fathers are addressed with fear and awe as 'Pa Marcus,' 'Pa Demas,' etc." H. C. Bruce, first a Virginia and then Missouri slave, knew "a great many old men . . . that might be called sages, men who knew the number of days in each month, in each year . . . by means of straight marks and notches, made on a long stick with a knife." Elderly men had important roles in other slave communities. While a Freedmen's Bureau officer in Greenville, South Carolina, John deForest met Uncle Peter, also called Kangaboona, who had a "conceit" based upon his African birth, and Uncle March, then more than eighty years old, who was "the scarer of children," white and black, and whom white adults paid as much as half a dollar to deal with "cases of special depravity." When the teacher William Harmount went to Ascension Parish in 1864 to set up a school, he met Thompson Frazier, formerly a Virginia slave and "the old patriarch of the place and the leader of the people at their meetings."[29]

Slaves apparently often addressed all capable leaders as quasi kin, but children learned to address all older slave men and women (not just leaders) by kin titles, a practice that perhaps bound them to fictive kinsmen and kinswomen, preparing them in the event that sale or death separated them from parents and blood relatives. Socializing children to respect all elderly blacks also may have taught them to hide slave feelings and beliefs from nonslaves. Asked about the attitudes of children toward their parents, Laura Towne said, "I never saw it equaled anywhere— their love and obedience." That was so even though parents "were exceedingly severe." She remembered only one instance of "anything like indulgence toward children." "I think they . . . will bear pain to any extent," said Towne. "If a boy cries too early because he is suffering they will deride him. He must be stoical under trouble and his parents will not suffer complainings.

Children undergo a regular discipline." In return, adult kin and non-kin did their best to protect children. In the summer of 1865, the teacher Mary Ames lived among the Edisto Island, South Carolina, blacks and "asked the children if some of their fathers could not come and fix the stove. They began, 'I haven't any father'—'I live with Aunty.' "[30]

　Further study of the fictive aunt and uncle promises to enlarge understanding of how slave children became slave adults—that is, how the son, brother, and nephew became husband, father, and uncle and how the daughter, sister, and niece became wife, mother, and aunt. But such study needs first to locate fairly precisely in time when kin terms of address toward non-kin adults began to be used regularly by slaves. We shall probably learn that slaveowners called some elderly black men and women "uncle" and "aunt" because as children they had learned that this was the conventional way in which slave children had been taught to address fictive as well as real black adult kin.

Fictive, or quasi, kin played yet other roles in developing slave communities, *binding unrelated adults to one another* and thereby infusing enlarged slave communities with conceptions of obligation that had flowed initially from kin obligations rooted in blood and marriage. The obligations to a brother or a niece were transformed into the obligations toward a fellow slave or a fellow slave's child, and behavior first determined by familial and kin obligation became enlarged social obligation. Just as the fictive aunts and uncles may have bound children to quasi kin, so, too, the ties between a child and its fictive adult kin may have bound childrens' parents to their fictive aunts and uncles.

That much is suggested by Sidney Mintz and Eric Wolf's study of "ritual co-parenthood" and Esther Goody's study of "proparenthood," neither of which deals with slaves but both of which contain insights about the possible ways in which extended kin networks served as the social basis for developing slave communities. In modern Western societies, Goody writes, "all parental roles are concentrated within the nuclear family," but such roles "are potentially available for sharing among kin or even with unrelated neighbors or friends":

To do so is one way of spreading the task of caring for deprived children. But it is also an effective way of forging links between adults—parent and pro-parent—and between genera-

tions—child/parent and child/pro-parent. Where the sharing
of parental roles is institutionalized as in the giving of foster
children and ritual sponsorship, such links are systematically
created. To understand these as simply ways of coping with
crisis situations or of arranging to cope with them should they
occur, is to fail to recognize the way in which many societies
make use of the bonds between parent and child.

Goody suggests that "the particular characteristics of parenthood
. . . [were] adapted to forge new links between people and to reinforce existing ones." Mintz and Wolf examine such relationships
in diverse premodern societies, including late medieval and early
modern Europe, to show how ritual coparentage (*compadre* in
Spain, *compare-commare* in Italy and *godparent* in England)
created quasi-kin ties between a child's parents and that child's
ceremonial sponsors, ties that imposed upon parents and coparents
"reciprocal relations" that made "the immediate social environment more stable" and "the participants more independent and
secure." Coparentage often involved "the conversion of non-kin
relationships into quasi-kin ties complete with constraints on
marriage and sexual relations, the prohibition of quarrels, and
the mutual obligation to provide economic assistance." Who a
parent sought such quasi-kin ties with depended, in part, on the
type of society in which the parent lived. A relatively uniform
social and class structure meant that coparenthood was "prevail-
ingly horizontal (intra-class) in character," but the presence of
"several interacting classes" meant that coparentage might also
be structured "vertically (inter-class) ." Quasi-kin obligations binding parents and coparents of the same social class reinforced
"cohesion within the group," and social solidarities beyond the
immediate family and the enlarged kin networks emerged.[31]

Slaves were not a self-contained class, a social fact affecting how
individual slaves sought protection for themselves and especially
for their children. Some, usually privileged slaves and especially
those belonging to a family over more than one generation, found
protection in a modified "reciprocal coparental relationship" with
an owner and thereby reinforced whatever "paternalist" impulses
existed among some owners. But not all slaves could (or wanted
to) have the protection resulting from cross-class social linkages.
Many slaveowners, moreover, had no such obligation to the slaves
they owned. (The death of a slave gardener in 1844 caused the
South Carolina planter James H. Hammond to mourn the loss
of "a faithful friend," "one of our best men." But when two other

slaves died that year, Hammond scribbled, "Neither a serious loss. One valuable mule also died.") The slaves furthermore developed alternative, if fragile, means for protecting themselves and their children, and fictive kinsmen (the slave "aunt" and "uncle") probably served as very important instrumentalities in furthering slave group solidarity and in ordering a community regularly disordered by the choices owners made.

Eighteenth-century Africans had lived in societies that shared kinship beliefs that bound an immediate family to its family of origin and assigned significant roles to adult brothers and sisters (aunts and uncles), and that is why the African children calling their parents' shipmates "aunt" and "uncle" are so important. It is very improbable that these adults were real kin; initial enslavement shattered consanguinal ties for all but a few African slaves. The conversion of kin relationships into symbolic (or quasi-) kin ties on slave ships is evidence of active adaptive behavior, not just evidence that the middle passage had failed to obliterate social memory. Let us shift from the slave ship to the slave plantation, from the enslaved African to the Afro-American slave. Teaching Afro-American children to call all adult slaves (not just blood kin) "aunt" and "uncle" converted plantation non-kin relationships into quasi-kin relationships binding together slave adults (fictive aunts and uncles) in networks of mutual obligation that extended beyond formal kin obligations dictated by blood and marriage. (Sam Aleckson remembered vividly that the usual morning greeting among South Carolina slaves was "Mornin, brudder Lon'on." "Mornin mi brudder.") Community ties based on quasi-kin connections emerged, flowing upward and outward from the adaptive domestic arrangements and kin networks that had developed over time among the slaves themselves. A teen-ager sold from the Upper to the Lower South after 1815 was cut off from his or her immediate Upper South family but found many fictive aunts and uncles in the Lower South. So did orphan children, as shown by Allen Allensworth's biographer:

> Aunt Phyllis showed him tender sympathy and remarked to aunt Betty that it was a pity " 'ter-tek' dat po' child fum his sick mamma, and brung him on dis place whah he won't meet nobody but a pas'le o' low-down, good-for-nuthin' strangers." This remark attached the boy to aunt Phyllis and he loved her ever afterward. He loved her, too, because she had the same name as his mother. Aunt Phyllis was a big-hearted old soul, and she looked with commiseration on all who suffered affliction or distress.[32]

Obligations rooted in beliefs about ties between adult brothers and sisters and other kin served as "models" for affective obligations binding together larger groups of slaves, a development that involved a special tension unique to slave society and one that changed over time and varied at any moment depending upon particular circumstances. The choice between forming a reciprocal relationship with an owner ("massa" or "missus") or with a fellow slave ("uncle" or "aunt") caused this tension, a tension that had its roots in the conflict between duties based upon ownership and obligations based upon kinship and quasi-kin ties. General class beliefs and behavior among slaves—which resulted, in part, from the transformation of kin obligations into non-kin social obligations—had their roots in the cumulative adaptive beliefs and behavior of several slave generations. It is possible to suggest the broad outline of how this process occurred over time. It involved four interrelated but nevertheless distinct "stages":

1. Family and kinship patterns of belief and behavior associated with traditional West African tribal societies.

2. The destruction of traditional kinship and family patterns following the slave trade and initial enslavement (first in Africa and then in the New World) but accompanied by the slaves investing non-kin relations with *symbolic* kin functions.

3. The emergence of settled Afro-American slave family and kin groups following the initial disruption associated with enslavement and the early creation of symbolic kin networks.

4. The development of inter- and intra-generational linkages between slave families accompanied by the transformation of conceptions of family and kin obligation rooted in blood and marriage into conceptions of quasi-kin and non-kin social obligation.

The process suggested here should not be misinterpreted. Fictive kin are not distinctive to slave cultures; they are found in diverse settings. But because slave society so constricted the associational life of slaves, it is probable that fictive kin were much more important devices for enlarging social relationships among slaves than among dependent classes with wider social choices. Obligation toward fellow slaves, moreover, should not be confused with "class consciousness." Further study may show, as Eric Wolf suggests in his examination of peasant belief and behavior, that kin and enlarged quasi-kin obligation often inhibited the development of such "consciousness." Protecting children involved far more than choosing between duties to an owner and obligations to a slave. Sometimes it meant choosing between obligations to real kin as opposed to obligations to quasi-kin. In certain settings, slave family obligations may have strengthened ties to an owner as contrasted with ties to fellow slaves.[33]

Social obligation—a concern among slaves for non-kin—revealed itself often among the slaves and the ex-slaves. The Maryland free black Levi Coppin's father felt his mother "recklessly generous." "Every old woman in the neighborhood formed a habit of visiting our home frequently, especially about hog-killing time," remembered Coppin. "These dear old women would call mother 'Cousin Jane.' Father would speak derisively of such relationships . . . as 'swap-dog' kin. . . . [S]he believed in sharing with others, especially the unfortunate and needy." Men and women like Coppin's mother existed over the entire South during and just after the Civil War. In the summer of 1863, when "small-pox, chicken-pox, [and] fever" ravaged Parris Island, South Carolina, residents, Sea Island laborers contributed some vegetables and garden produce to a Beaufort army hospital. After this was learned by the Parris Island blacks, they "quietly laid their plan"; a few days later "a fair wagon-load of sweet potatoes, pumpkins, tomatoes, chickens, eggs, ochre, green corn, and melons was sent up on a rowboat" to the Beaufort hospital. The Georgia Freedmen's Bureau head Davis Tillison said that "colored men . . . work . . . hard all day and into the night and . . . give one third of all they earn to support the poor of their own race," behavior learned by Tillison "not from their own lips, but from those of white neighbors." Partly in response to pressure from civilian town officials, the Union Army closed its Vicksburg hospital in October 1865. The Indiana Quakers Elkanah Beard and his wife nursed the most seriously ill; some others went to an army hospital nearby; "over one hundred" were "placed" among Vicksburg's blacks and other blacks nearby; fifty more needed shelter. Mostly ex-slaves had taken them in, people "hardly able to care for themselves." The Greenville, South Carolina, ex-slave Aunt Judy was such a person. While a Bureau agent there, John deForest dealt with her because she had been remiss in paying a white woman several months of rent. Aunt Judy, a mother of two or three small children, was a washerwoman, and deForest learned she had "benevolently taken in and was nursing a sick woman of her own race." The Yankee novelist called it "thoughtless charity," explaining:

> The thoughtless charity of this penniless Negress in receiving another poverty-stricken creature under her roof was characteristic of the freedmen. However selfish, and even dishonest, they might be, they were extravagant in giving. The man who at the end of autumn had a hundred or two bushels of corn on hand would suffer a horde of lazy relatives and friends to settle upon him and devour him before the end of the winter, leaving him in the spring at the mercy of such planters as chose to drive a hard bargain.

"The industrious," deForest worried, "were too much given to supporting the thriftless."[34]

Obligation toward non-kin by ex-slaves revealed itself elsewhere, too. "All indigent or helpless people are being supported by relatives, parents, or friends," said a Lumberton, North Carolina, white clergyman of the ex-slaves in October 1865. Ex-slaves in Atlanta, Georgia, organized to help refugees left outside their town in makeshift "camps" by William Sherman's marching army. The refugees were themselves ex-slaves who had followed the Union soldiers. Smallpox ravaged them in the 1864–1865 winter months, and "a frightful work of death" resulted. Atlanta blacks, hardly any antebellum free blacks among them because Atlanta had fewer than eight such adult male residents in 1860, formed a relief association, picked a committee of five to raise two hundred dollars a month, and used the money to "hire nurses for these colored strangers suffering outside the city." A white missionary described the association's leaders:

> I saw the committee as they were coming from a monthly meeting, a few days since. A barber, a drayman, a day laborer, and two preachers, also day laborers. I asked if they had raised the $200 for March. "We had only $160." "What did you do for the balance?" "We gave notes for thirty days." And that remember from men with families whom they were barely supporting from day to day. The man who gave the answer could not sell all his clothes from his hat to his boots, for a dollar and a half.

The ex-slaves who raised these funds knew each other well. "Brethren," an observer heard one say at a church meeting, "rather than such a thing should happen again, I would give away all my living." "The leaders," this same witness noticed, "seemed to know who would be likely to have a little money, and when they could not pass the hat for the crowd, they called individuals by name. 'Tom, if you've got any money come and give—put it in.' 'Jim, you come right along and put in what you've got. That ain't enough; hain't you got any more?' 'Go to Alice, she can give something,' and so on, till of their poverty they got over twenty dollars." By early 1866, the Atlanta ex-slaves had raised additional monies to "furnish a hospital for colored strangers, so that no more should die naked, starving, and friendless in the streets." The refugee ex-slaves who remained in Atlanta were just as generous. "It is surprising," said a sympathetic northern missionary, "to see . . . how ready they are to help out one another to the last dollar." Similar behavior over the entire South by ex-slaves is one important reason why over its full lifetime the Freedmen's Bureau materially assisted no more than 0.5 percent of the four million ex-slaves.[35]

Obligation toward nonslave kin was most powerfully expressed during and just after the Civil War in the attention ex-slaves gave to black children orphaned by the sale and death of their parents, by parental desertion, and by wartime dislocation. The exact number of orphans can never be known. Some were absorbed into extended kin groups, and others found places with non-kin. Blacks called them "motherless children," and ex-slaves remembered them long after the emancipation. Laura Clark's North Carolina father had been sold away when she was a child. Her sale as a young girl to Alabama cut her off from her mother, too. In the 1930s, she sang:

> A motherless chile see a hard time
> Oh, Lord, he'p her on de road.
> Er sister will do bes' she kin
> Dis is a hard world, Lord, fer a motherless chile.

Care for such children in the wartime and early postwar years came from very poor blacks over the entire South. White relief workers in a Louisiana refugee camp in 1864 noticed a woman (her husband "sick") "taking care of six motherless ones." That same year, in and around Vicksburg "many" black orphans had been "scattered among the colored people," who were "generally very benevolent to such children often setting an example of disinterested kindness." A year later, "hundreds of these little ones . . . [were] being cared for by poor [Vicksburg] freedmen and freedwomen . . . barely able to take care of their own children." That happened in Nashville, too, where ex-slaves shared "a beautiful charity to these poor orphan children, even though starvation may be staring them in the face." "They care for their families," said William Mitchell, a Philadelphia relief worker among them. "Ought we look for this, when we consider the antecedents of the family relation, among the African race? Not only so, but instances are very frequent where the orphan finds shelter and protection beneath the humble roof of a friend or neighbor. There is something touching," concluded Mitchell, "in the phrase 'fellow servant' which is common among the freed people here." Black orphan children found similar refuge in other southern places. Sherman's army deposited slaves in several coastal Atlantic cities early in 1865. "Crowds of young orphan children" were among the refugees left in Wilmington, North Carolina. Some became "street children"; others lived with "freedmen's families . . . who cannot feed them." South Carolina Sea Island blacks called them "Sherman's 'mudderless,' " and in 1868 Laura Towne noticed that "all" such children had been "adopted into" and lived with "families who feed and keep them with superstitious care but cannot afford to clothe the little ones." Similar reports came from New Bern, North Carolina ("children orphaned in the sick season, sheltered by some needy neighbors") ; Atlanta, Georgia (orphaned children "taken in and sheltered by the colored people who have little more than they"); and Norfolk, Virginia ("a slender mother . . . supporting herself, one child of her own, and two orphans," and a sixty-year-old woman caring for her dead brother's five orphaned children and two other children, one its mother "sent long ago in *slave* days to Texas").[36]

Labor and money from ex-slaves and other antebellum blacks also contributed significantly to scattered black orphanages started prior to 1866. "The colored people themselves," said O. O. Howard, started one in New Orleans, and many of its early residents ended up in homes with "parents or friends." When northern relief officials took over another New Orleans orphanage, the New Orleans "poor"—"destitute themselves and troubled by . . . high prices"—contributed fifteen hundred dollars to sustain it. The first Mississippi Valley wartime orphanage, "credited" by John Eaton "to 'Aunt Maria,' a colored woman," started on President's Island near Memphis. The Medina, Ohio, relief worker Martha Canfield opened a Memphis orphanage in late 1864 with the help of the black Baptist clergyman Morris Henderson and several black women. "Uncle Morris Henderson," Canfield wrote in her diary, ". . . brought several colored women who offered their services to assist in sewing," and when Canfield and several black coworkers took ill, "Uncle Morris came [again], bringing several women, who, with willing hands, soon helped us out of the difficulty." Two northern white women started a Fernandina, Florida, orphanage but left for the 1864 summer months to protect their health, putting "two colored women, 'Aunts Adeline and Margaret' . . . in charge." Just after the war ended, blacks either helped start or entirely sustained Beaufort, Charleston, and Mobile orphanages. Sometime in the summer or fall of 1865, Mobile blacks held a fair and raised twelve hundred dollars to build an orphanage. The Beaufort orphanage was "properly officered by the colored citizens." In March 1865, James Redpath, then supervising the newly started Charleston schools, received a letter "in characters uncouth and spelled amiss" from a black woman who wanted an "orphanage" so she and others could leave their children and work the land in their interior. She later pressed him in person, and Redpath got two deserted and filthy buildings from the federal army. They lacked furnishings. "I need twelve women to clean out the Orphan House," Redpath told members of a Charleston black church, "to wash, scrub, and carry out dirt." Twelve volunteered, and others lent "a few cooking utensils." The former house servant to a South Carolina governor worked at the orphanage, and a "society of colored ladies" sewed clothes for its children.

Institutional care matched the voluntary individual and familial attention given to orphaned black children, but the latter was far more important. "It was thought," said Thomas Conway, the head of the Department of the Gulf's Bureau of Free Labor, "that five or ten thousand orphans of freedmen would be thrown upon our hands at the close of the war, but strange to say our numbers have hardly increased." Conway had learned why: "I find the colored people themselves taking into their families the orphaned children of their former friends and neighbors thus saving us the necessity of bearing large expenses in caring for them." Conway's experiences were repeated in the Upper South. "I have on my list," said a Yorktown, Virginia, Quaker relief official in 1867, "forty-one families of widows and infirm, most of whom have children, either of their own or of some relative or friend to provide for. It is remarkable to witness how much these poor people do for orphan children. We often find them with one, two, and three helpless children, not their own, but a deceased brother's, sister's, daughter's, son's, cousin's, and not unfrequently a deceased friend's child."[37]

Kin obligation among Afro-Americans survived enslavement, and enlarged social obligation emerged out of kin obligation. In 1868, blacks memorialized the death of a favored northern white teacher in a St. Helena's Island church. Sympathetic whites, including Laura M. Towne, paid him tribute. So did the "prominent freedman" Hastings Garret. He was then thirty-seven years old, his wife Celia twenty-eight. The couple had two school-age children: the ten-year-old Scipio and the twelve-year-old Nancy. Their third child, born in 1865, was William Sherman Garret, and a daughter born in 1868 was named Ellen Murray Garret. A British woman, Murray, lived with Towne and helped that extraordinary woman run her school. (A son born to the Garrets in 1875 would be named for his father.) After the service ended, Garret "spoke of the necessity for education" and urged that "rich and poor . . . come forward at once and assist in support of the schools, each putting in according to his means." Towne and another white teacher advised that the blacks rely less on outside financial aid and more on their own resources. The "elders and principal men" promised to raise money and "contribute [money] themselves as soon as they could." But cash was short then, so Garret advised that they "set aside a piece of land, work it fruitfully, and devote all its produce to schools." Others spoke, too:

> Uncle Liah, who had previously spoken . . . said that they were all poor, and each could do but little, but this was a work for many. It may be as it was at Indian Hill, where the great burial-ground was raised by each Indian throwing just one handful of earth upon it every time he passed. Uncle Aleck said, Should each man regard only his own children, and forget all the others? Should they leave that poor neighbor widow with her whole gang of children, and give them no chance for a free schooling?

Suggestions such as "each putting in according to his means," setting aside a piece of land for a communal purpose and all working it, and considering free schooling for the "poor neighbor widow's children" had nothing to do with the paternalist beliefs of their former owners or of the Yankee missionaries and school-teachers.[38] What these South Carolina ex-slaves suggested showed how adaptive kin obligations had been transformed by the slaves themselves into larger social and communal obligations. These were the beliefs of men who addressed each other as "Uncle," not "Mister."

6

Somebody Knew My Name

Daniel Payne . . . ordinary fellow . . . formerly slave to Genl. Washington, left him four years ago.
BRITISH NAVAL SHIP REGISTER (1783)

I notice that the negroes seldom or never take the names of the present owners in adopting their "entitles" as they call their own surnames, but always that of some former master, and they go back as far as possible.
ELIZA FRANCES ANDREWS (1865)

It greatly surprised the Mississippi plantation girl Susan Dabney that her family's slaves had surnames. A servant took her to see the older woman's brother marry. "I heard her address him as Mr. Ferguson," she remembered years later, "and at once asked, 'Mammy, what makes you call Henry Mr. Ferguson?' 'Do you think 'cause we are black that cyarn't have no names?' was Mammy's indignant reply." Susan Dabney learned a social fact that remained hidden from most nineteenth-century slaveowners and other whites. Many slaves had surnames; and they often differed from the surnames of those who owned them, a fact unknown to most whites before and after the emancipation. That slaves had surnames is a fact that discloses much more than the interesting finding that they had "two names." Analysis of the surnames slaves retained shows that such decisions served to shape a social identity independent of slave ownership. How and why slaves fixed upon particular surnames reinforced how and why slaves fixed upon particular given names.

A bitter debate a generation after the emancipation caused two ex-slaveowners to admit that slaves had surnames and even to suggest what had shaped the selection of particular surnames. It happened at the First Lake Mohonk Conference on the Negro Question in 1890, and the novelist and former North Carolina Radical Republican Albion W. Tourgee provoked the revelation. A convention delegate scorned the moral obtuseness of southern

blacks by pointing to the alleged "frequent absence of the surname" among them. Tourgee replied, talked briefly about *Bricks
Without Straw* (his 1880 novel in which the ex-slave Nimbus
struggled over picking a surname), and said that the ex-slaves had
been "a little lax in the matter of names" because slave *law* had
denied them surnames. "He was always *nullius filus*," said Tourgee. "His master changed his name as often as he chose." The
blacks therefore made some "experiments in nomenclature," not
as a "racial peculiarity" but as an "eternal testament against injustice." Tourgee's remarks angered two native Virginians from
slaveholding families. A District of Columbia clergyman, A. W.
Pitzer, who had grown up in Salem, said his family's Bible had
the "names of Abraham Watkins and of Harriet, his wife, both of
them negroes and slaves," written in it, and this also happened "in
scores and hundreds of other southern households" where slaves
had "two names." Tourgee dismissed Pitzer. Bible entries "had no
more the quality of a family record . . . than the pedigree of a
thoroughbred horse." Tourgee fell back on legalisms: "A name is
no name unless the bearer has a legal right to it. No slave *could*
have a surname because he could not have a *legal* sire." Then
C. C. Gaines—a Hudson River Valley college president who believed the slaves were but "a few generations removed from
absolute savagery" and said fresh Africans had turned aside the
"good rations . . . provided them" to "devour . . . raw . . . snakes,
lizards, frogs, [and] toads"—admitted that most "plantation
negroes never had but one name," and "if they had a surname at
all this was supposed to be that of master." But Gaines also remembered that slaves had other surnames, sometimes revealing a
"mark peculiar to the person or incident to his history." Sold
slaves "often were known by the surname of an original master
who might then be dead." "You will find many negroes to-day,"
Gaines explained, "who do not retain the surname of their last
owner, but are known by that of a remoter ancestor who years
ago came out of another estate." The ex-slaves "chose such names
as they pleased, and many of them observed such reasonable rules
as to ancestry as naturally applied." Tourgee, who knew much
better than his southern adversaries that black men and women
made coherent choices upon emancipation but knew little about
the slave culture that shaped those choices, did not respond.[1]
   Slave surnames are finally receiving deserved attention, and
evidence shows that slaves over the entire South in the century
and a half preceding the general emancipation had surnames dif-

ferent from their owners'.[2] Conventional historical arguments that
the slaves did not have surnames draw uncritically upon two important historical records. Court records and other legal documents nearly always listed a slave by his or her given name (e.g.,
State v. John, a slave), and plantation business records rarely recorded a slave surname. A typical plantation record illustrating
a conventional practice, such as the list of "Clothing givin [*sic*]
out to Children" in November 1840 on John Ball's South Carolina
Comingtree plantation, gave the names of dependent children by
family but nothing more.[3] A few examples illustrate such evidence:

John's Venus	*Benjamin's Jenny*	*Pompey's Maria*	*Stephen's Amy*	*Cuffee's Daphne*
John	Sue	Toolar	Sambo	Patty
Sukey	Binah	Nippie	Martha	Isaac
Charity	Benjamin	Sylvia	Molley	Nancy
		Alick	Dolly	Rachel

Plantation birth registers examined in Chapters 2, 3, and 4 rarely
listed a slave surname, and such evidence has convinced historians
that the slaves were without family names. Such evidence, however, actually reveals much more about the beliefs and usages of
slaveowners than about the beliefs and behavior of slaves, who
fixed upon particular surnames for the same reasons they had
often fixed upon particular given names. A surname often symbolized the close tie between an immediate slave family and its
family of origin and a social identity separate from that of an
owner. Slaves often retained surnames identified with early owners,
and they and their descendants carried them from the eighteenth
into the nineteenth century, from one owner to another, and from
the Upper South to the Lower South.

Vast but uneven quantities of evidence stretching from 1720
to the emancipation and covering the entire South show that
slaves often had surnames different from their owners', and
evidence about wartime and early postwar blacks is examined first.
Lists wartime planters and Union Army and Freedmen's Bureau
officials kept (1864–1866) indicate that most ex-slaves had surnames and that when the surname was known, relatively few had
the surname of their final owners. In registers recording three
hundred sixty marriages at Davis Bend, Mississippi, in 1864–1865
all the men and women had surnames, and few had those of

prominent Davis Bend planters such as the Quitmans and Jefferson and Joseph Davis. The number living there prior to 1861 is unknown, but not one registrant was a Quitman and only three men and two women were Davises. A work record of the Concordia Parish, Louisiana, Good Hope cotton plantation field laborers for September and October 1864, listed one hundred eight adults. The plantation had been owned by A. V. Davis and its wartime lessee was J. D. Waters. All but eight of the blacks had family names, none a Davis or a Waters. In July 1865, black Mississippi family heads moved during the war to Texas with their families by owner John H. Randolph signed a contract to remain at work that year. The mark "X" accompanied the names of fifty-eight family heads, a significant number of whom were women. The fifty-eight had forty-one different surnames, not one a Randolph. A fourth document listed ex-slaves sent away without the wages promised them by St. Simon's Island, Georgia, planters between April and October 1865. Seven whites drove off nineteen people, all of whom had surnames. Not one had the surname of the person who had sent him away. Thomas Goodbread, for example, drove off Charlotte Smith, Katie Smith, and Mary A. Parish, and Mallory King sent away Clara Wade, Sarah Morgan, George Lock and his wife, and Young Chailler and his two daughters.[4]

Similar surname patterns are found in undated (probably 1866) Mississippi Freedmen's Bureau labor registers for two densely black Mississippi counties: the Yazoo County Silver Creek district and the Copiah County Hazelhurst district. Half of Copiah and four of five Yazoo slaves had lived on plantations in 1860. Nearly all the Yazoo ex-slave men and women labored as field hands. About one in seven Copiah women were house servants. The rest were field laborers. All but six of more than one thousand Copiah males were field hands and laborers. Unlike most contemporary documents, these registers listed former owners' names, and three in four of Silver Creek's 166 adult men had different surnames from their owners'. One in four of 1372 Hazelhurst blacks did not have a surname recorded but two-thirds of the others had a different surname from an ex-owner. The surnames on three plantations, listed in Table 28, show how few family heads or single persons had a former owner's name. The blacks Benjamin Roach employed on his Yazoo Duck Pond plantation did not differ from these others, and Roach, who hired more blacks than any Yazoo or Copiah planter, employed eighty

TABLE 28. SURNAMES OF FORMER MISSISSIPPI SLAVES COMPARED
WITH SURNAMES OF LAST OWNER, 1866

Former Slave Surnames

Walnut Grove Plantation   *Family heads*
  Owner: R. H. Talifero   Adams, Alexander, Chinoy, Cochrane,
      (Hazelhurst)   Gould, Miles, Morris, Rockingham,
                               Stewart, Washington, Wells, Wilker,
                               Winston.

                                             Single persons
                               Birge, Brown, Carter, Giler, Hagan,
                               Hawthorne, Jackson, Rayford, Roach.

Anchorage Plantation   *Family heads*
  Owner: Rebecca McBee   Carter, Crawley, Grimes, Harris, Helms,
     (Silver Creek)   Johns, Ultzion, Vaughn, Witherley.

                                             Single persons
                               Alexander, Davis, Glover, Grundy,
                               Harrison, Jenkins, McBee, McGrew,
                               Oats, Pierce, Rattnew, Taylor.

Mitchell Plantation   *Family heads*
  Owner: Nancy Mitchell   Battice, Burd, Cragg, Dennings, Gordon,
      (Hazelhurst)   Mitchell, Washington.

                                             Single persons
                               Dodd, Easter, Easton, H[a]man, Johnson,
                               Mamma, Scott, Stone, Tucker, White,
                               Williams.

men and women twenty years and older in 1866. All but nine
lived in eighteen immediate families. The families all had surnames, not one a Roach.[5]

Such documents reveal that ex-slaves had different surnames
from their final owners', but it is possible that most (even all) had
picked them upon emancipation. Three other lists are far less
ambiguous. One wartime list included about a thousand persons,
mostly dependent blacks (superannuated men and women, members of fatherless households, invalids, and orphans) who had belonged to different Mississippi and Louisiana owners. All but two
were "black" in color and all but a handful (a shoemaker and
twelve house servants) were field hands. Every person listed had a
surname. Among the four hundred adult women, six in seven
(mostly single women or women heading male-absent families)
had different surnames from their last owner's. Age did not matter.

A second list, an 1866 Princess Anne County, Virginia, military census, included twenty-nine children not yet fourteen years old who lived with families other than their families of origin. Six had a former owner's name. The rest had different names from their owners at the moment of emancipation. It is highly improbable that any of these children had "taken" surnames in the brief period following their emancipation.

The third list, which shifts attention from the ex-slave child to the elderly ex-slave, recorded the name, age, sex, and former owner of nearly every applicant for Freedmen's Bureau relief at Donaldsville in Ascension Parish, Louisiana, between October 1866 and July 1868. By October 1866, harsh Bureau regulations had greatly narrowed the categories of persons eligible for aid. The list included mostly aged, crippled, and ill blacks, and a few women with small children. Among the elderly applicants were men and women who had been owned by prominent local sugar-plantation families, such as the Barrows, the Landrys, the Brands, and the Mannings. Notations sometimes indicated the reasons for aid and included "sick," "old age," "one hand lost in grinding," "lame," "blind," "crippled," "old and broken down," and "old and helpless." Two-thirds of the 241 persons listed were men, and the ages of all the women and all but ten men were listed. Twelve men and six women were not yet fifty years old, and of the rest eighty-seven men and forty-three women were at least seventy years old. A few men had passed their ninetieth year, and Monday Hampton was 103. All the women and all but three men had surnames. The former owners of a few men with surnames were not listed, but 221 men and women gave surnames and named former owners. Nine in ten men and four in five women had different names from their owners'. Some had names of French origin, but most had Anglo-American names. The typical elderly relief applicant had been born in the 1790s and was the son or daughter of slaves born during or before the War of Independence. None could care for themselves. Many probably had been cut off from close kin. If most slaves chose surnames after emancipation and if choosing a surname different from an owner's symbolized independence, such persons were among the least likely to do so. Their age and condition should have attached them closely to a former owner. And yet only one in eight had a former owner's name. Rather than select surnames for the first time or change old ones, it is much more probable that they had used these names as slaves.[6]

Neither their owners nor their Yankee liberators usually realized that many slaves carried surnames into freedom. Partly, that was because the slaves hesitated using surnames with whites, thereby reinforcing the belief that slaves had no surnames. The record wartime Yankees left, not surprisingly, revealed mostly their own confusion. The usually perceptive Elizabeth Botume found it "hopeless to try to understand their titles." Hardly any noticed that blacks rejected former owners' surnames. An army officer remembered the unwillingness of soldiers to take such names, and Whitelaw Reid learned from a Deep South overseer that "precious few of 'em . . . ever took that of the old master." These were unusual observations.[7]

Northerners more commonly said either that ex-slaves paraded their surnames or hid them. A relief worker heard a Sea Island man tell his wife, "Don't call me 'Joe' again; my name is Mr. Jenkins." The same person said "all have surnames . . . a wife taking her husband's." But in Virginia Lucy Chase had to ask "repeatedly for their surnames. . . . They are Judith and John and no more." American Freedmen's Inquiry Commission member James MacKaye believed that lower Mississippi Valley blacks had not been "so rigorously forbidden . . . family names" as South Carolinians. But Rufus Saxton was the Commission's only South Carolina witness who made that point. "We have introduced the practice of giving them all two names," boasted Saxton. Laura Towne, E. W. Hooper, and Robert Smalls disagreed. Slaves did not consider their surnames "family" names, said Hooper, and Smalls, who had a different name from his white father, said that "very few use their father's names—they choose a name for themselves." But Smalls and Hooper did not deny that slaves had surnames. "Their masters never allowed them to use titles and would whip them if they used a second name. Each had a title as near as I can learn," said Hooper.

Smalls put it somewhat differently. Asked if slaves were "permitted to have two names," he replied: "I do not know that there is any law about it; they are accustomed to have two names—a Christian name and sometimes the name of their owner." Owners, Smalls continued, "cared little" about surnames; some wanted "their negroes called after them." The questioning went on:

QUESTION: If you ask a colored man his name, he will always give his Christian name, and if you ask him his other name he always hesitates about giving it. What is the cause of that?

ANSWER: Well, they are apt to go by the one name and when the white folks speak of them they say, "John, that belongs to Mr. So and So," and they hardly ever use their titles.

"Before their masters," Smalls said, "they do not speak of their titles at all." Towne agreed: "They are usually silent about titles; still they have a family name and will tell if asked. . . . The children of a family hold the same title." "I only know of one woman," she went on, "who has not given her name. When asked for it, she invariably replies that her title is in heaven. An old man says when he is asked for his title that he is too old for one now." The unwillingness of slaves to reveal their surnames to owners and other whites calls attention to the danger of studying slave values simply by examining slave behavior as manifested in the interaction between slaves and their owners. A record indicating that slaves infrequently used surnames in dealing with owners is not proof that surnames were uncommon among slaves. It explains why owners rarely knew that slaves had surnames. But it does not show that slaves believed the surname inappropriate to persons of their status. Such a record reveals how the constraints imposed upon slaves affected their behavior toward owners. It tells nothing of their beliefs about the value of the slave surname.[8]

Despite the reticence of slaves in displaying their surnames before whites, some white owners and their descendants knew that slaves had surnames. Slaves, of course, did, too. When Nathaniel Heyward died in 1851, the Combahee, South Carolina, rice planter owned more than one thousand slaves. In a 1937 study of his family's slaves, Duncan Clinch Heyward observed that after emancipation their owners listed the former slaves without surnames, even though "a few of the most prominent Negroes on the plantation, such as the old blacksmith Caesar, were known [to whites] by both given and surnames." Other Heyward slaves also had surnames: "It is well known that among themselves the slaves all had surnames, and immediately after they were freed these names came to light." Ex-slaves had similar recollections. Jacob Stroyer grew up near Columbia, South Carolina, and later insisted that his father, a native African, had discreetly kept a surname different from that of his owner:

I did not learn what name my father went by before he was brought to this country. I know only that Col. Dick Singleton gave him the name of William, by which name he was known to the day of his death. He also had a surname Stroyer, but

he could not use it in public as the surname would be against
the law; he was known only by the name of William Singleton,
so the title Stroyer was forbidden him and could be used by
his children only after the emancipation of the slaves.

A pension claim filed by a Mississippi black soldier's widow made
the same point: "My maiden name was Rebecca Upshur but I
went by the name of my owner [Nathaniel B. Lanier] and was
called Rebecca Lanier."[9]
    A few unusual plantation documents and scattered other
evidence also show that nineteenth-century slaves had different
surnames from their owners'. Nat Turner belonged in 1831 to
Joseph Travis. Born Benjamin Turner's slave, he was later sold
to Putnam Moore. Moore's widow married Travis, but the slave
remained Nat Turner, not Nat Moore and not Nat Travis. James
Redpath learned from a South Carolinian that his "fader belonged to a widow woman named Lucy Roberts. . . . Dat's how I
came to be called Roberts . . . [H]e took her name. After I left
Roberts I belonged to Richardson. I was a present from Roberts
to him. . . . Den I was sold to dis ole man, my boss now." The
runaway Henry Bibb and his mother had a Kentucky owner
named David White. "My mother," said Bibb, "was known by the
name of Milldred [sic] Jackson." (Bibb never knew his father, but
after his mother told him he was James Bibb he took that surname.) Eight slaves tried after the 1822 Vesey "conspiracy" had
surnames, five of them different from their owners'. Robert Smalls
married the Charleston slave Hannah Jones, who belonged to
Samuel Kingman, and in his plea to get to Liberia the Virginian
John Scott complained about his owner John Enders. Sale by his
Georgia owner Charles C. Jones led the slave Abream Scriven to
pen a letter to his wife.
    Runaway slave advertisements rarely noted slaves' surnames.
But P. C. Smith advertised for Edward Winslow, and Anderson
Bowles sought Edmund Kenney. An owner named McAllister
said a young twenty-three-year-old runaway "generally calls herself
Mary Ann Paine." A. M. Willis advertised for "Daniel" who "calls
himself Daniel Turner," and William Cobb sought "Ben (commonly known by the name of Ben Fox)." Gilford Horn sought
Harry, who called "himself Henry Barnes (or Burns), and will be
likely to continue the same name, or assume that of Copage or
Farmer." William Still's invaluable *Underground Railroad* contained brief sketches of slaves assisted to freedom by Still and

others. Of the first 210 successful runaways listed (nearly all from Virginia and Maryland and about one in four a woman), 3 did not have surnames, the evidence for 23 is inconclusive, 8 others had their owners' names, and 176 had different names from the persons they had fled. The pattern was the same for men and women. Although plantation business records rarely listed surnames, one that did showed that slaves did not have their owners' names. William J. Minor's birth and death register (1846–1865) of slaves on one of his absentee-owned Louisiana plantations listed about ninety fathers. All but a handful had surnames, not one a Minor.[10]

Even more impressive evidence demonstrating that slaves and their owners had different surnames are the slave trader and planter Isaac Franklin's records.[11] Born in 1799, Franklin together with his partner, John Armfield, shipped many Upper South slaves to Mississippi and Louisiana in the 1820s and the 1830s. In the mid-1830s, Franklin began buying heavily in West Feliciana plantation lands and in slaves to work these Louisiana properties. At his death in 1846, Franklin owned more than ten thousand acres of land and about seven hundred slaves. Franklin's business records were dotted with slave surnames. A few documents on the slave trade indicate that.[12] But documents describing Franklin's Tennessee and Louisiana plantation slaves between 1835 and 1847 are much more decisive. Purchase into Francis Routh's Louisiana plantation brought Franklin part ownership of 198 slaves (not counting unnamed young children), three in five of whom had surnames. One Routh slave was called Routh. An 1838 inventory of Franklin and Routh's holdings included slaves formerly owned by Ira Smith, Kenyon Kendrick, and William Justice. Two-thirds of the 140 men and women valued at four hundred or more dollars had surnames, not one Franklin, Smith, Kendrick, Justice, or Routh. Inventories after Franklin's death listed 565 slaves on five plantations.[13] One, a small place, had thirty-six slaves, but the others had from ninety-eight to one hundred eighteen slaves. Demographic differences distinguished these plantations.[14] The inventory listed slaves either by families ("his wife" and "her child") or as individuals. Four in five men, women, and children belonged to one or another of 129 immediate families, and there were another 114 "single" people at least fifteen years old, mostly men. Six in seven adults living in families and the same proportion of "single" people had surnames. Not all families shared a common surname. In about 6 percent a wife but not a husband had a surname, and in another 30 percent husbands and wives had different surnames. Different surnames were much more common in families without children than in families with children. Wives sometimes had different surnames from their husbands', an important fact, hinting either at ties to families of origin or the retention of earlier owners' names. But the reason remains unclear.[15] In families where one or both spouses had a surname, the dominant pattern was for both husband and wife to share a surname. That was so in nearly two in three families. This inventory also shows that Franklin's estate managers had not affixed surnames upon their slaves. If they had, the diversity in surname patterns would be inexplicable. Not too much should be made of the surname as a necessary clue to the ties within immediate families. Two Franklin boys, Austin and Bradley, had their fathers' given names, and their fathers did not have surnames. Austin was married to Rachel Hill, and Bradley's wife was Martha Winchester.

Isaac Franklin's slaves were freed less than twenty years after their owner died and were the last adult slave generation. Most had surnames different from their owners' in the 1840s. Scattered evidence also reveals different surnames among some slaves prior to 1815. The British banker Samuel Grist owned many Virginia slaves, and his fifty-eight-page 1808 will arranged for their emancipation at his death and their settlement elsewhere. Grist died in 1815, and the slaves went to rural Ohio in 1818. Fourteen male names are known (mostly family heads), and one had the benefactor's surname. An 1802 petition supporting the slave blacksmith "Jack Neale, alias Jack Warren," convicted of murdering his *third* owner, revealed he first had belonged to Jeremiah Neale and then was sold to "Mr. Lyles," to whom he paid about two hundred dollars toward his freedom. Despite his protests, Lyles then sold him to a man leaving the area. Neale killed the new owner. "The idea," explained the petitioner, "of being torn thus from his wife and children and from his native country drove the poor fellow to despair." "My man George Jones," the Virginian John Peck explained in 1788, "has a wife at Coleport," and about that time the Virginian Sarah Greene petitioned the legislature for her freedom. After her owner, Charles Greene, died, his widow married William Savage. Later, a white named Rice moved Sarah and her children to "Carolina"; her petition carried the surname Greene. Much earlier slaves also had different surnames from their owners'. In 1735 the Goose Creek planter Alexander Dussen advertised for a runaway South Carolinian, a "famous Pushing and Dancing Master," named Thomas Butler. An advertisement in the *Philadelphia American Weekly Mercury* described yet another runaway:

> Runaway in April last from Richard Tilghman, of Queen Anne county, in Maryland, a Mulatto slave, Named Richard Molson, of middle stature . . . about 40 years old and has had the small pox, he is in company with a white woman named Mary, who it is supposed now goes for his wife; and a white man named Garrett Choise, and Jane, his wife, which said white people are servants to some neighbours of Richard Tilghman.

The newspaper was dated August 11, *1720*. George Jones, Sarah Greene, Thomas Butler, and Richard Molson were not unusual eighteenth-century slaves. [16]

Late-eighteenth-century slaves who quit the new nation about a decade before Eli Whitney invented the cotton gin nearly all had surnames, many different from their last owners'. Records containing information about the nearly three thousand black and mulatto men, women, and children, mostly former slaves, who quit New York City when the British Army evacuated that port late in 1783 show this fact.[17] A naval inspection roll for each ship gave for most emigres their names, ages, and status before fleeing to or being captured by the British (slave, freeborn, or indentured servant), the date they departed or were captured, their residence then, and, if slaves, their owners' names.

Family relationships were not indicated, but it is possible that at least 450 family groupings, at least three-fourths with children in them, quit New York. The ship lists failed to include all the children. But the combined lists contain information about 2867 slave and free emigres. Nearly one in four were not yet fifteen years old. Among those at least fifteen years old were sixty West Indians, 123 freeborn mainland men, and 140 freeborn mainland women. Six in seven of those at least fifteen years old (1142 men and 734 women) had been mainland slaves, a few among them manumitted later in life. Interest here focuses only on the slaves. Slightly more than half were men and women aged fifteen to twenty-nine. The rest had been born prior to the French and Indian War. A handful were seventeenth-century blacks but most

were born during the great forced slave emigration to the mainland colonies. By far the largest number had resided in the southern colonies (Maryland, North and South Carolina, Georgia, and
especially Virginia). Counting those with designated residences
shows that nearly three in four had been southern slaves (Table
29).[18] Hardly any had taken advantage of the Earl of Dunmore's
1775 Virginia proclamation, which offered men their freedom if
they left owners to bear arms for the British.[19] All but a few of
the emigre blacks had common Anglo-American given names.
These few men, such as Juba, Mimbo, Mango, Mingo, Quash,
Quaco, Quomo, and Vigo, and women, such as Cutto, Tenah,
Mima, and Cudja, had African names. A small number—mostly
men—had tribal facial markings, including a New Jersey slave
with three long scars in each cheek, a Maryland free black
(married to a New Jersey slave) with a scar on his forehead, and a
thirty-three-year-old woman with three scars in each cheek. Very
few men and women had such markings, but some ship captains
may not have recorded such information. A few emigres were
native Africans, but here, too, the record may have been incomplete. Not all the ship lists recorded places of birth.

Not much is learned from these bare lists about how the slaves
left their owners. But common departure dates indicate that some
families had fled together. Joseph Fowler and his six-year-old
daughter left a Savannah owner in 1780, and George and Betsey
Black and their son fled a Petersburg owner. Charles and Dolly

TABLE 29. AGE AND RESIDENCE OF SLAVES AND FORMER SLAVES,
NEW YORK CITY, 1783

Ages of slaves and former slaves 15 and older, New York City, 1783			*Last residence of slaves and former slaves, 15 and older, prior to settlement behind the British lines, New York City, 1783*		
AGE	MALE	FEMALE	PRIOR RESIDENCE	MALES	FEMALES
15–19	12%	10%	Southern Colonies	65%	63%
20–29	43	50	Middle Colonies	19	18
30–39	24	22	New England		
40–49	13	11	Colonies	6	4
50+	8	7	Not given	10	15
NUMBER	1134	733	NUMBER	1142	734
UNKNOWN	8	1			

Dixon headed one of the largest families that went off in a group. Four children (Myles, Luke, Dick, and Sophia) accompanied them. A fifth (Sally) was born after they quit Willis Wilkinson. Kate Godfrey left her Norfolk owner with two children; a third was born afterward. A Norfolk woman accompanied her daughter, son-in-law, and grandson. Some slaves married after quitting different owners. Jack Sollberry had lived in Roanoke, North Carolina, and his wife Sillo in Beaufort, South Carolina. The elderly Cecil County, Maryland, couple Cato and Sukey Ramsey had different owners. The seventy-five-year-old freeborn Jane Thompson had a five-year-old Norfolk grandson with her. Yet older blacks boarded the British ships. Adam Way had belonged to an Albany, New York, military officer named Broadstreet, was eighty years old, and had written by his name "worn out." The freeborn Peter French, ninety-three years old, was described as "remarkable . . . for his age." Very elderly blacks were unusual ship passengers, and so were slaves with freeborn black or mulatto spouses. The freeborn New Yorker Ishaboo had a wife born a slave but later freed. The Virginian George Lacy was accompanied by his daughter and his wife, who claimed to be freeborn because her mother had been white. Dinah Browne had a New Jersey slave husband with her but claimed to be freeborn because her mother had been a New York Indian. Browne and these others came in families; the twenty-one-year-old Isaac had come alone from Willamsburg, Virginia. Five years before, his parents had purchased Isaac's freedom.

A few leaving the country had prestigious owners. A twenty-one-year-old had belonged to Lord Baltimore, and a fifty-year-old had the same surname as his owner Robert Livingston. Pompey and Flora Rutledge had come from Charleston, quitting South Carolina's governor. Three slaves boarding British ships belonged to the Virginia planter George Washington: the twenty-year-old Deborah Squash (accompanied by her twenty-two-year-old husband Harry Squash), the forty-three-year-old Harry Washington, and the twenty-two-year-old Daniel Payne, who had written by his name, "ordinary fellow . . . formerly slave to Genl Washington, Va., left him four years ago."

Daniel Payne deserves notice for a special reason. It is not his owner that makes him a figure of historical importance but the fact that Daniel Payne had a different surname from George Washington. Payne was not unusual among the slaves boarding the British ships. Five in six of the men fifteen years and older had surnames, and half had different surnames from their owners'. Three in five with surnames had different ones from their owners'. A man's age and place of residence affected whether or not he had a surname: southern slaves and older slaves more frequently had surnames (Table 30). Such variations deserve further study but are not the central fact revealed in these ship registers.[20] Most slaves had surnames, and most with surnames in 1783 had surnames different from their last owners'.

Enslaved Afro-Americans (and some Africans, too), many no more than one or two generations removed from direct contact with West African tribal cultures, had made important cultural decisions. West Africans did not have immediate family names. Nearly all in 1783 had Anglo-American given names and surnames, evidence of the rapid acculturation induced by enslavement and of the slaves' acceptance of a common *Anglo-American* cultural practice. But that so many so early had surnames different from their owners' also shows a powerful *eighteenth-century Afro-American* desire to define immediate slave families in ways that symbolically separated them from their owners. That is why George Washington's runaway Daniel Payne is so important. So was William Lee, who served as Washington's body servant during the War for Independence and retained close ties to the nation's first president. Lee was freed after Washington's death. Five persons appear in Edward Savage's portrait *The Washington Family* (one of the last painted of the national leader): George Washington, Martha Washington, George Washington Parke Custis, Eleanor Parke Custis, and William Lee. When emancipated, Lee was described as a "mulatto man, William, who calls himself William Lee."[21]

TABLE 30. SURNAME PATTERNS OF ALL MALE SLAVES AND FORMER SLAVES FIFTEEN AND OLDER, LISTED IN THE BRITISH SHIP INSPECTION ROLLS, NEW YORK CITY, 1783

		Place of residence		Age	
	All males	SOUTH	OTHER	UNDER 30	30+
No surname listed	16%	13%	21%	19%	13%
Same as owner	34	36	32	32	38
Different from owner	50	51	47	49	49
NUMBER	1142	746	396	615	527

. . .

A century separated slave children freed by the general emancipation from the young expatriate Daniel Payne, born in about
1761. Men and women freed in 1865 selected, retained, or changed
surnames; some of them were among the nearly six hundred
South Carolina and Texas ex-slaves interviewed in the mid-1930s.
When emancipated, most had been young children and teen-age
youths. They nearly all described decisions their parents or other
adults had made. Few discussed slave surname practices. Nevertheless the interviews reveal some of the underlying social and
cultural processes affecting slave surname selection and retention.
The most important fact they reported was that they or their
parents had often either retained or chosen surnames *different* from
their *last owners'*. Two in three Texas blacks and nearly three in
four South Carolina blacks who gave such information had different surnames from their last owners' (Table 31).

Although these men and women gave many reasons for having particular surnames, their description of the relationship between surnames, *immediate* slave families, and slave families of
origin is most important. A few said they had no slave surname.
"Us colored folks didn't git names 'til after de war," said the
South Carolinian Andy Marion. Just as few had parents with two
surnames. "Pa real name was Adam Collin," said Susan Hamilton,
"but he took his master's name."[22] Other parents took owners'

TABLE 31. SURNAMES OF SLAVES AND THEIR LAST OWNERS AFTER
EMANCIPATION AS REPORTED BY SOUTH CAROLINA
AND TEXAS BLACKS INTERVIEWED IN 1937

Surname pattern	All blacks interviewed		Only blacks for whom evidence is available	
	SOUTH CAROLINA	TEXAS	SOUTH CAROLINA	TEXAS
Same surname as last owner	17%	23%	27%	34%
Different surname from last owner	46	47	73	66
Evidence unclear*	37	30		
Total interviews	289	309	181	217

* Among those interviewed, a significant number—and especially women who
married years after emancipation and therefore had a husband's surname when
interviewed—gave inadequate information about their family names upon emancipation.

names. John Bates's parents shortened Mock Bateman's name. Some made no such changes. "My maw and paw lived in Mississippi, and belonged to Marse Greer," said Emma Taylor; "dat's dere name, too." The South Carolinian James Johnson was just as direct: "My daddy took his old master's name." Still others, including some separated as young children from immediate families, also took owners' surnames.[23] Many with surnames different from owners' failed to indicate why. Salomon Oliver merely said his owner had been the Mississippi planter and banker John Miller. Susan Calder had belonged to the Charleston planter and banker Edward Fuller. Sam Mitchell's Sea Island parents, Tyra and Moses Mitchell, belonged to John Chaplin, and the Sea Islander Lucretia Haywood said, "Muh pa name Tony McKnight and he b'long to Mr. Stephen Elliot. My ma name Venus McKnight and she b'long to Mr. Joe Eddings."[24] Others said that their different surnames had nothing to do with slave kin ties. Former owners gave surnames to the Mobile, Alabama, woman Cull Taylor, and the Winnsboro, South Carolina, men Ned Walker and Aleck Woodward, were given surnames by former owners. A few, such as Eliza Hasty's father and the black youth Tom Roseboro, consciously took the names of prominent local whites. Yet others picked the names of black friends or fictive black kin. "I married Frederick Adams," said his wife. "He used to b'long to Miss Tenny Graddick but after he was freed he had to take another name. Mr. Jesse Adams, a good fiddler dat my husband like to hang 'round, told him he could take his name if he wanted to and dat's how he got de name Adams." Separated as a child from his South Carolina parents, Mingo White grew up in Georgia. "The only caren' that I had or ever knowed anything 'bout was give to me by a friend of my pappy. His name was John White. My pappy tol' him to take care of me for him. John was a fiddler. . . . John took me an' kep' me in de cabin wid him." The two had been sold together, and the boy took the surname of his surrogate slave father.[25]

Many ex-slaves remembered choosing surnames that revealed strong attachments to immediate slave families and to fathers and husbands. Among the nearly six hundred interviewed, two picked a mother's surname and two others consciously rejected a father's surname. Thomas Cole and his mother belonged to the Alabamian Robert Cole, and John Gerrand owned his father: "I was sposed to take my father's name but he was sech a bad, onery, no-count sech a man, I jes' take my old massa's name."[26] Cole was unusual among the ex-slaves: most took a father's name. A few took a white father's name. "I never carried his name till after freedom," said the Louisianian Valmar Cormier. Charity Grigsby and her mother belonged to the Alabamian Jim Moore. "My pappy," she said, "was Dan'l Grigsby."[27] Some with slave fathers' names hardly had known them. The Louisiana infant James Cornelius, his mother, and his brother were sold to the Mississippi white Samuel Sandell, and Cornelius said, "I never remembered seeing pappy again; doan know why I am not called Jim Sandell, but mammy said my pappy was Henry Cornelius an' reckon I was given my pappy's name." A. C. Pruitt never knew his father but his mother, Rachel Smith, "say he name Bruford Pruitt." The Texan Yack Stringfellow said: "My daddy come from de Old Africa and was tall and straight as an arrow. He was sold to a man who tooked him to California in de gold rush of 1849 and me and mammy stayed with Massa Hubert. Dat how come my name ain't de same as massa now." George Kye's Arkansas mother impressed his father's surname upon him: "Joe Kye was my pappy's name what he was born under back in Garrison County, Virginia, and I took that name when I was freed, but I don't know whether he took it or not because he was sold off by old Master Stover when I was a child. I never have seen him since. I think he wouldn't mind, good, leastways that what my mammy say."[28]

Other blacks whose slave mothers remarried before or soon after emancipation kept a biological father's name. The Alabamian William Henry Towns said: "Me an' Nellie was Townses, the rest Charlie, Kate, Lula, Bob, and Betty was Joneses. . . . Endurin' slavery my father was sold to anudder slave owner. After de war my mother married Frank Jones; den dese yuther chillun was born." And the Texan John Crawford had a similar experience:

> Pap's name was Tom Townes, 'cause he 'longed to de Townes place. He was my step-pap and when I's growed I tooken my own pap's name, what was Crawford. I never seed him, though, and didn't know nothin' much 'bout him. He's sold away 'fore I's born. . . . Pap Townes would make most everythin'. . . . He was purty good to me, 'siderin' he wasn't my own pap.

Sena Moore and her brothers also kept their father's name. They had lived apart from him with their mother, Phillis Gladney, but their father, George Stitt, visited them regularly until sold from

South Carolina to Arkansas. Phillis Gladney then married "a no count nigger name Bill James," but her children were called Stitt. "My full brothers," said Moore, "was Luther Stitt, Bill Stitt, and Levi Stitt."[29]

Another surname practice common upon emancipation also shows strong ties to a father and husband. It has been seen that family members—especially on farms and small plantations—often had different owners, and that ownership usually separated a man from his wife and children. As slaves, wives and children sometimes had different surnames from husbands' and fathers'. Nearly always, ex-slaves who had lived in such settings remembered taking the father's or husband's surname. A former Virginia slave lived with his mother; the McMurry's owned his father. His old owners wanted the youth "to take the name of Harper." He refused: "My father was named Robinson so I kept his name after I got free." Ben Smith and his mother belonged to John Lever; his father belonged to a Smith. "His name Bob Smith after freedom," said the son. "Dat's how come I be dis day Ben Smith." Two or three plantations separated Lucinda Alexander and her mother from the girl's father. She also took her father's name. So did Jesse Davis, owned by the South Carolina physician Ira Smith. His father Mingo belonged to "de big bugs, de Davis family," and after emancipation "him and all us take de secon' name, Davis." That had also happened prior to emancipation. Lorenza Ezell and her mother were owned by Ned Lipscomb, but her mother "call me after my daddy's Massa, Ezell." That happened elsewhere, too. "[M]ammy," the Tennessean Mary Douglass said, "gave us our pappy's name."[30]

Mary Douglass took her father's surname. But it was not the name of her father's owner, the Tennessee white Isaac Garrett. Like many other adult blacks in 1865, Mary Douglass's father had a different surname from his owner's. Moreover, other ex-slaves put aside a final owner's surname and replaced it with either the surname of an earlier owner or the surname of a parent's or a grandparent's owner. Eliza Smith kept her father's owner's name:

> Both my mammy and my pappy was brought from Africa on a slave boat and sold on de Richmond slave market. What year dey come I don't know. My mammy was Jane Mason, belonging to Frank Mason; pappy was Frank Smith, belonging to a master wid de same name. I mean, my pappy took his master's name, and den after my folks married mammy took de name of Smith, but she stayed on wid de Masons and never did

belong to my pap's master. Den after Frank Mason took all his slaves out of de Virginia County [*sic*], mammy met up wid another man Ben Humphries, and married him.

Eliza Smith had not belonged to Frank Smith, but retained the surname of her father's first owner. Isaac Adams's Louisiana mother was sold to Sarah McGee by Addison Hilliard just before his birth. He called himself Adams: "When my pappy was born, his parents belonged to a Mr. Adams so he took Adams for his last name, and I did too, because I was his son. I don't know where Mr. Adams lived, but I don't think my pappy was born in Louisiana. Alabama maybe. I think his parents come off the boat because he was very black—even blacker than I am." Gill Ruffin grew up on a Texas plantation and lived separately from his father: "My papa was name Reuben Ruffin, and mamma's name was Isabella. We were sold several times, but allus kep' the name of Ruffin." Steve Williams's Louisiana owner Williams sold him to a Texan named Bennett. "Dat's how come," he said, "I's named Williams and my marster named Bennett." Florida whites sold Simp Campbell's father to Texas, too, but he "allus kep' the Campbell name." The Alabamians Berry Smith and William Moore also had surnames belonging to owners from whom their fathers had been sold years before the emancipation. "I was born a slave to Old Marse Jim Harper," said Smith; "Marse Jim brought my pa an' ma from a man by de name o' Smith, an' Pa kep' de name." William Moore belonged to the Selma Waller family in 1865: "My mammy done told me the reason for her and my paw's name am Moore was 'cause afore dey 'longed to Marse Tom Waller they 'longed to Marse Moore, but he done sold them off." Elderly South Carolina blacks reported similarly. Mary Scott's parents belonged to Darby Fulton but called themselves Tina and John Davis because her father had once belonged to a Davis. The Rhett family purchased Lavinia Heywood's mother and maternal grandmother from the Bryants; they remained Bryants. Harry Davis and his mother belonged to the physician W. K. Turner. "My mother," said the ex-slave, "was named Mary and took de name Davis, 'cause befo' freedom come, her was bought by my master, from Dr. Davis, near Monticello." Willis Gillison's father picked an old surname, too: "My daddy was Aleck Trowell. After freedom he was call his own name, Aleck Gillison. . . . My father was sold from a Gillison, first off." That also happened to Frank Adamson's father, who ended up the slave of the planter

Kershaw Peay. "My pappy was bought from de Adamson people; they say they got him off de ship from Africa." Miemy Johnson and her parents were slaves of the planter John Mobley, but after the war her father called himself Johnson because "pappy's pappy b'long to de Johnsons." Jim Henry's father learned from his last owner that he had "come from 'stinguished stock," having been purchased from "de Patrick Henry family in Virginia." "Dat's de reason," said his son, "my pappy and us took dat name in freedom."[31]

Important continuities in slave belief and behavior during the century preceding the emancipation are suggested by those ex-slaves who picked surnames belonging to "owners" other than their last owner, continuities linking together the surname patterns in the 1783 British ship registers, the 1847 Isaac Franklin slave inventories, and post-emancipation name lists such as the Ascension Parish record of aged and dependent blacks. Retention of a slave's first owner's surname related to the sale of a slave and his or her descendants. The earliest useful large record of slave surnames, the 1783 British ship registers, shows that most slaves had surnames and that about three in five with surnames had different ones from those of the men who had owned them. These slaves had all quit their owners. That a small number had no surnames and a larger number had owners' surnames means that having a separate surname was not a condition for fleeing an owner. But why did some—and not all—slaves in 1783 have surnames different from their owners'? When most eighteenth-century slaves first took surnames, they probably took those of their owners. (Some, however, also may have taken a parent's given name: Mahala Moses or Mahala Rose. Ishmael Titus, a Virginia slave who fought well in the French and Indian War, may have taken his father's given name as a surname.) The change from "Harry, the slave of George Washington" to Harry Washington is not a difficult one. But what of Daniel Payne, "ordinary fellow . . . formerly slave to Genl Washington"? He could have picked the surname Payne after quitting his owner, but more probably an owner named Payne had first owned Daniel and his parents, and Payne later sold Daniel to Washington. After the sale, Daniel still considered himself "a Payne," retaining through his old owner's surname a symbolic tie to his slave family of origin. His father (or mother) was Payne's (not Washington's) slave.

Slaves listed in the 1783 ship registers and with owners' surnames therefore probably had never been sold. It follows that slaves sold prior to 1783 who did not flee to the British often retained the family names of earlier owners and carried them forward in time. Let us assume that Daniel Payne had not fled Washington but remained on his plantation, married, and had a son Sam born in 1790 and sold to the Lower South in 1815. If Payne's son ended up on Isaac Franklin's West Feliciana, Louisiana, plantation, the 1847 Franklin inventory would have listed him as Sam Payne—not Sam Washington and not Sam Franklin.

Sale, or separation for other reasons, from a slave family of origin encouraged slaves to retain different surnames from their new owners'. Examining the Florida El Destino and Chemonie plantation records, U. B. Phillips noticed some slaves with the surname of "a preceding owner" and concluded that owners made such distinctions among slaves with similar given names. That hardly was the case. Phillips had so little understanding of the slaves that he could not realize he had uncovered a fact of much greater social importance. The Georgia rice planter Louis Manigault had no such difficulties. "One of our Prime Hands ('Charles Lucas') absconded from the plantation," Manigault wrote in his Civil War diary. "This so named 'Charles Lucas' (from once having belonged to a Mr. Lucas) is the Second Negro thus far who has left the place; the first being a very notorious character, a Carpenter known as 'Jack Savage' (his former Master being a Mr. Savage of Bryan County)." Manigault resented these two slaves who had retained "old" surnames.

Such choices by slaves illuminate the findings of historians who have described the surnames commonly found among freed men and women. Duncan Clinch Heyward noted that "scarcely ever did the Negro choose the name of his or her owner, but often that of some other slaveholding family of which he knew." Joel Williamson noticed among the South Carolina ex-slaves the "striking absence or dearth of [sur]names of some large slave-holders (such as Aiken and Calhoun)." After examining the surnames of 2922 Georgetown County, South Carolina, black men registering to vote in 1867, George C. Rogers, Jr., concluded that they "overwhelmingly" had names similar to those of "their former owners." They often had surnames associated with slaveholding families of "an earlier period," some of which had left George-town County. "There may have been last names in use among the slaves prior to the [Civil] War," inferred Rogers; slaves sold from one owner to another may have "kept some designation among themselves of their former ownership." Rogers observed how the consolidation of Georgetown County slaveholdings in the half century preceding the Civil War affected slave surname patterns. Small slaveholders sold their slaves to more enterprising neighbors and moved on. These slaves retained the surnames of their old owners. That process caused local slave surname patterns to differ from local slave ownership patterns. If slaves sold from one local owner to another retained an initial owner's surname, moreover, slaves sold into the interregional market should have behaved similarly. That is why Isaac Franklin's Deep South plantation slaves were not named Franklin.[32]

In fixing upon a surname belonging to an earlier owner, slaves made two statements about themselves. They rejected close identity with a new owner by keeping an older surname. More important, the retention of a former "owner's name" paralleled in function the naming of children for slave grandparents and aunts and uncles by relating an immediate slave family (or an individual) to a slave family of origin. As time passed, an original owner's name became a slave's name. Sam Aleckson said it well. Aleckson was born a slave in 1852. His father and grandfather had been native Charlestonians, but his great-grandfather had been an African. Aleckson said in 1929:

> I do not know the name my great grandfather bore in Africa, but when he arrived in this country he was given the name Clement, and when he found he needed a surname—something he was not accustomed to in his native land—he borrowed that of the man who brought him. It was a very good name, and as we have held the same for more than one hundred and fifty years, without change or alteration, I think, therefore, we are legally entitled to it.

Aleckson had a point.[33]

Attention has been focused on the relationship between a slave surname and subsequent sale or separation, but what about slaves who had just one owner and whose family of origin had belonged to that owner (or that owner's family of origin) for one or more generations? That slave probably retained the same surname as his last owner if that owner also carried his or her own white forebear's surname forward in time. But *whose* surname had this slave chosen or retained in 1865? That of the last owner? That of the last owner's forebear who had owned this

slave's parents, grandparents, or great-grandparents? Or the surname of a slave forebear *appropriated from an owner earlier in time*
and which then became a slave surname? Examples One and Two
in Chart 17 suggest answers. In both instances, the fictitious whites
Allen and Susan Smith owned the slave couple John and Mary in
1800. John and Mary called themselves Smith. Other whites referred to them as "Smith's slaves" or "the slaves of Smith." John
and Mary remained the property of Allen and Susan Smith's
descendants. So did the children and grandchildren of this slave
husband and wife. Tom, John and Mary's slave grandson, and his
wife Amanda belonged to Susan and Allen Smith's married
grandson Philip Smith (Example One) and to Susan and Allen
Smith's married granddaughter Lydia Adams (Example Two).
If Tom and Amanda belonged to Philip Smith in 1865, whites
would still have called them "Smith's slaves." And if Lydia Adams,
Philip's first cousin owned them, Tom and Amanda would have
been known to whites as "Adams's slaves." But in each instance
Tom and Amanda would have called themselves Smith in 1865. It
did not matter (Example Two) that their last owner—the granddaughter of their slave family's first owner—had the surname
Adams. That much is clear. But what of the example involving
the final owner Philip Smith? *Whose* surname had Tom and
Amanda fixed upon by calling themselves Smith? Their *last owner
Philip Smith? Philip Smith's grandfather*, the white *Allan* Smith?
Or *Tom's slave grandmother and grandfather* and *his slave mother
and father*?

Upon emancipation, former slaves who had been sold "took"
or made public the surnames of their initial owners or the owners
of their families of origin. If John and Mary had appropriated the
surname Smith from an owner in 1800 and if their grandson Tom
called himself Smith in 1865, Tom Smith carried the surname of
his slave grandparents. A by-product of that social process was the
fact that the freed black Tom Smith shared a surname in 1865
with his final owner, the white Philip Smith. That is an important
fact, the accidental result of continued ownership over time. It
does not mean that Tom Smith had "taken" his "owner's name."
This becomes clear, however, only after Tom Smith has been
rooted in his familial past in much the same way that slave
children with the given names of parents, aunts and uncles, and
grandparents on the Good Hope, Stirling, Cedar Vale, and other
plantations became better-known because they, too, had been
rooted in their familial pasts. By 1865, *Smith* had been a *slave*

surname in a particular family *for more than half a century, for three generations.* Tom Smith neither took nor rejected his final owner's surname. He did not face that choice. He carried the surname of a slave grandparent into freedom.

Former slaves who "took" their surname actually worried and even disgusted some old owners. A decent Okolona, Mississippi, planter ordered them not to "adopt the master's name." And a white South Carolinian from a distinguished plantation family complained after the war, "I used to be proud of my name, but now I have ceased to be so, as the two meanest negroes on the place have appropriated it. The old coachman is now Nat Ashby Ravenel, & another man is Sempie Bennett Ravenel." It probably never occurred to Ravenel that his former slaves might have fixed on surnames belonging to their slave forebears.[34]

Not all owning whites were so blinded by their beliefs as to misunderstand or misinterpret the beliefs and behavior of their emancipated slaves. Eliza Frances Andrews was a fine case in point, as revealed in her illuminating wartime diary. She lived on her father's large Washington County, Georgia, plantation about fifty miles from Augusta, and her family had owned about two hundred slaves. The northern evangelical clergyman Mansfield French accompanied the Union Army to Washington County and offered its blacks legal marriages in the summer of 1865. A deeply partisan Confederate, the young Andrews woman greatly detested the pious French and believed conventional plantation marriage sufficient for her family's slaves. French's style offended local whites. A notice in a local newspaper announcing his plans was "issued in the most sensational style, like the news column of the "New York Herald.'" Two white clergymen read it in their churches but one refused. Three others, Andrews' father among them, denied French their private groves to marry the blacks. The Yankee used a black cemetery.

The first day, the Andrews house servant Charity took a new husband. She had been "lawfully married in the Methodist Church" six years earlier to "Mr. Waddy's Peter." "I remembered," Andrews wrote, "how father joked with Peter, when he came to ask for Charity, about having him for a 'nigger-in-law,' but now Charity has taken to herself Hamp, one of father's plantation hands—a big, thick-lipped fellow, not half as respectable looking as Peter but there is no accounting for taste." When others also shed old mates, Andrews felt that French deserved to be

CHART 17. SLAVE AND SLAVEOWNER SURNAME RETENTION PATTERNS OVER TIME

Example One

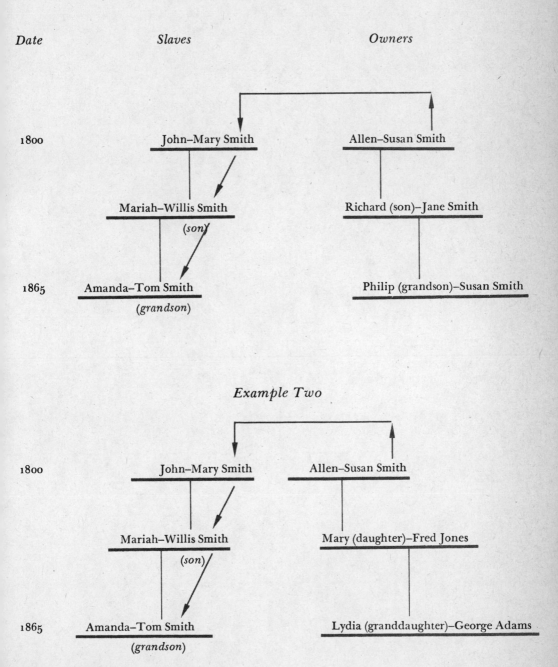

Date	Slaves	Owners
1800	John–Mary Smith	Allen–Susan Smith
	Mariah–Willis Smith *(son)*	Richard (son)–Jane Smith
1865	Amanda–Tom Smith *(grandson)*	Philip (grandson)–Susan Smith

Example Two

1800	John–Mary Smith	Allen–Susan Smith
	Mariah–Willis Smith *(son)*	Mary (daughter)–Fred Jones
1865	Amanda–Tom Smith *(grandson)*	Lydia (granddaughter)–George Adams

prosecuted under the "laws of bigamy." French charged a fee, and she called him a "hypocritical Puritan and a whang-nosed fanatic . . . one of the sleek, unctuous kind that tries to cover his rascality under a cloak of religion." Andrews called the marriages a "harmless farce" but worried because the "negro sisters adore" French. "The poor dupes say they believe he is Jesus Christ— 'anyhow he has done more for them than Jesus Christ ever did.' " Some even called him "their 'white Jesus.' "

Despite her passionate hatreds and intense biases, keen insights followed upon Andrews's learning that her family's slaves had taken surnames. The day Charity married she told Andrews that "she now has two names, like the white folks." "Tatom," the house servant explained, "I'se Tatom now, and Hamp is Mr. Sam Ampey Tatom." Asked how her husband got that name, the black woman responded, "His grandfather used to belong to a Mr. Tatom so he took his name for his entitles." That response greatly impressed the young white woman. The Andrews family, like some other slaveholders, prided themselves on their intimate ties to slave house servants, an intimacy that helped sustain beliefs upholding enslavement. Such "intimacy," however, rested upon dependence and had at its core the belief that house servants often identified more closely with an owner's family than with their own families. One way owning whites could believe that most black servants accepted and even benefited from such dependent "intimacy" was to think that they had no lasting family connections of their own. The choice of surnames rooted within the slave experience itself symbolized for Eliza Andrews the collapse of an entire social and moral order. "All these changes are very sad to me . . . ," Andrews noted.

> There will soon be no more old mammies and daddies, no more uncles and aunties. Instead of "Maum Judy" and "Uncle Jacob," we shall have our "Mrs. Ampey Tatoms" and our "Mr. Lewis Williamses." The sweet ties that bound our old family servants to us will be broken and replaced with envy and ill-will.

Ex-slaves who took surnames or revealed old surnames that had connections to a distant forebear, not a former owner, made choices that cut deeply into the belief system of sensitive owners like Eliza Andrews. Charity's new husband Sam had picked a name belonging to his grandfather's owner. (Sam's grandfather had been born in the eighteenth century.) Eliza Andrews did not find

Sam's an unusual choice, and in noticing that fact she pierced the veil that so frequently distorted the perceptions of even the most well-educated and sensitive slaveowners:

> I notice that the negroes seldom or never take the names of the present owners in adopting their "entitles" as they call their own surnames, but always that of some former master, and they go back as far as possible. It was the name of the actual owner that distinguished them in slavery, and I suppose they wish to throw off that badge of servility.

"Then, too," Andrews added in a flash of penetrating insight, "they have their notions of family pride."[35]

Not even her abiding hatred for the Yankees and her deep and passionate attachments to a disintegrating social order could hide this fact from Eliza Frances Andrews. Her insight, once again, makes the vital connection between the world of Sam Tatom and the world of Daniel Payne, not the world of George Washington.

7

To See His Grand
Son Samuel Die

*Historians begin by looking backward. They often end by
thinking backward.*

FRIEDRICH NIETZSCHE

*I am not ashamed of my grandparents for having been
slaves. I am only ashamed for having at one time been
ashamed.*

RALPH ELLISON

None of the evidence describing the Good Hope and these other
slave communities sustains what the historian Kenneth M. Stampp
aptly dismissed as the "legend . . . of a good time long ago when
Negroes and whites abided happily together in mutual understanding." Nor does it imply that slaves learned little from their
owners and other nonslaves. Instead, it underlines the insight by
Frederick Douglass that the slave was "pegged down to a single
spot" and must "take root there or nowhere."[1] What nourished
that root has been examined in these pages: a cumulative if often
disrupted slave experience which relates slave beliefs in the 1840s
and 1850s first to the beliefs of their parents and grandparents.
It also suggests how a particular social class was formed and why
slaves in the 1840s and 1850s, with very different experiences,
lived in communities whose members shared important social and
cultural beliefs.

Few former slaves revealed the lingering import of that
cumulative experience more strikingly than Henry Highland
Garnet. Born a Chestertown, Maryland, slave, he escaped in the
1820s to begin a long career as an antislavery critic. Garnet
traveled widely, lived in England, worked six years as a missionary
in Jamaica, and headed the African Civilization Society from its
founding just before the Civil War. After the war, he visited
Chestertown for the first time in thirty-nine years and found there
"a fine village" of about two thousand persons living in "the land

of corn, watermelons, and peaches." He dined with William Perkins—to Garnet "a splendid type of an old fashioned Southern black gentleman." Then he visited the Episcopal graveyard to find the burial place of his former owner. "To us," Garnet wrote, "it meant a moment of gratitude to God, with a little triumph mingled in. We were not born to wear the yoke. . . . The old oppressors are all dead, but we live, and have lifted our free hands above their tombs." Four decades had passed, but Garnet was drawn to his birthplace.

> It is beyond our power to describe our feelings [Garnet said of his visit]. Through tears we gazed upon the loved scene. We remembered the stream called the Branch, because we fell into it once and were nearly drowned. The Spencer plantation is cut up into ten farms. Everything had changed greatly. The old trees were foiled, the old mansion gone, everybody whom we once knew was dead. "Our fathers—where are they?" We diligently inquired, and found but two persons, a colored gentleman and lady, who knew us in our childhood. Our friend Mr. Doman, son of our father's friend, "Uncle Joseph Doman," gave us a basket of fruit; and taking a branch of cedar and other memorials, we left New Market and perhaps forever.

Garnet's attachments to the places and people of his youth did not temper his hatred of slavery, any more than a historian's recognition of slave family and kinship mores and feelings implies approval of the institutional setting within which they developed.[2]

The recovery of viable slave families and common patterns of slave behavior in diverse slave settings over so long a period of time allows us to examine several related aspects of the larger Afro-American experience: slave class formation and how that neglected development relates to slave treatment and slave behavior; particular aspects of slave behavior as different as flight and marriage ritual; the perception of the slave family and kin group by owners and other whites; and the explanatory "models" of slave behavior in the influential historical writings of E. Franklin Frazier, Kenneth M. Stampp, Stanley M. Elkins, and Eugene D. Genovese.[3]

A probing essay by the historians George Fredrickson and Christopher Lasch (1967) analyzed some of the limitations in writings about the Afro-American slave. Far too much attention had been given to slave "treatment" in examining the social and psychological effects of slavery on Afro-Americans. Frederickson and Lasch showed that the historian U. B. Phillips had defined that as the central "issue" and that his most severe critics had failed to redefine it:

> By compiling instances of the kindness and benevolence of masters, [U. B.] Phillips proved to his satisfaction that slavery was a mild and permissive institution, the primary function of which was not so much to produce a marketable surplus as to ease the accommodation of the lower race into the culture of the higher. The critics of Phillips have tried to meet him on his own ground. Where he compiled lists of indulgences and benefactions, they have assembled lists of atrocities. Both methods suffer from the same defect: they attempt to solve a conceptual problem—what did slavery do to the slave?—by accumulating quantitative evidence. Both methods assert that plantations conformed to one of two patterns, terror or indulgence, and then seek to prove these assertions by accumulating evidence from plantation diaries, manuals of discipline, letters, and other traditional sources for the study of slavery. But for every instance of physical cruelty on the one side an enterprising historian can find an instance of indulgence on the other. The only conclusion that one can legitimately draw from this debate is that great variations in treatment existed from plantation to plantation. . . .[4]

The slaves studied in the present work—those whose behavior has been reconstructed from diverse plantation records—allow us to redefine some of the important questions that deserve study by students of slave and ex-slave belief and behavior. Despite variations in their treatment, these slaves acted on common beliefs. It did not matter whether they had resident or absentee owners, whether they lived on plantations their entire lives or lived on farms that became plantations, or whether they lived near or had been separated from their families of origin. Such behavior therefore means that the question posed by Fredrickson and Lasch—*what did slavery do to the slave?*—requires first knowing *who the slave was.* How owners treated their slaves affected how individual slaves behaved. But how slaves behaved depended upon far more than their "treatment." Slave naming practices and marital rules (as well as the length of slave marriages in settings where slaves could remarry) are unmistakable evidence of the importance of interior slave beliefs and experiences in shaping their behavior.

But these beliefs and the developing culture that sustained them could not have regularly revealed themselves over time if they were no more than free-floating slave beliefs. That would be expecting the impossible from the slaves.

Institutional arrangements—especially among slaves—had to exist for such beliefs to be acted upon over time, and that is why the inter- and intragenerational linkages between slave families are so important. The significance of this evidence, however, should not be misinterpreted. The immediate family and the enlarged kin group were among the central binding institutions within developing slave communities. In themselves, however, these familial linkages do not explain either the full range of slave beliefs and behavior or their origins. Instead, the presence of these linkages makes it possible to re-examine the development of and changes in slave beliefs and behavior over time.

A cluster of slave beliefs—many of which await study— was sustained by these linkages and defined individual slaves with whom owners dealt. In other words, the *context* which shaped slave behavior was far more subtle than the setting emphasized by those whose primary concern remains the treatment of slaves. Talcott Parsons describes "institutions" as "normative patterns which define what are felt to be . . . proper, legitimate, or expected modes of action or of social relationship." Such norms pervade all areas of social life, and individual behavior usually reflects the presence of some accepted standards of behavior learned from others and shared with others. It is inconceivable that the beliefs and behavior of slaves living on such different places as the Good Hope, Cedar Vale, and Stirling plantations could have existed in the absence of what Stanley M. Elkins describes as "alternative social bases." Their presence, however fragile their structure, is the reason why "treatment" is an inadequate explanation of slave behavior and why the mimetic theories of Afro-American culture that dominated much of the mid-twentieth-century conceptualization of the Afro-American historical experience (and which shaped the influential writings of such able scholars as E. Franklin Frazier and Gunnar Myrdal) are erroneous. The "force of circumstance," Frazier believed, caused the slaves to "take over, however imperfectly, the folkways of the American environment," finding "within the patterns of the white man's culture a purpose in life." Myrdal made a similar point, insisting that "American Negro culture is not something independent of general American culture. It is a distorted development, or a pathological condition, of the general American culture."[5]

Slaves always were affected by the decisions of their owners, and the developing Afro-American culture included beliefs and practices derived from "the folkways of the American environment." But the slave behavior revealed in this study shows the inadequacy of such a conceptual framework and is strong evidence supporting the appropriateness of a bicultural model for studying all aspects of slave and ex-slave belief and behavior over time. That "model," as the anthropologist Charles A. Valentine points out, makes it possible to put aside the "deficit model" that shaped the works of Frazier and Myrdal as well as the oversimplified "difference model," with its "implicit assumption that different culture systems are necessarily competitive alternatives, that distinct culture systems can enter human experience only as mutually exclusive alternatives, never as intertwined and simultaneously available repertoires." Biculturation "helps explain how people learn and practice both mainstream culture and ethnic culture at the same time. Much intragroup socialization is conditioned by ethnically distinct experience . . . but at the same time members of all subgroups are thoroughly enculturated in the dominant culture patterns by mainstream institutions." What Valentine describes as "ethnic cultural socialization" occurs mostly "within family units and primary groups, with much mainstream enculturation coming from wider sources." Viewed in this perspective, the slave bicultural experience was never a static one. It differed in 1740 from what it became in 1790, 1820, and 1860. But it was shaped over time by the development of expanded slave kin and quasi-kin networks and by the presence of intra- and intergenerational slave family linkages.[6]

What a slave child learned always depended upon how that child was taught and who taught that child. A bicultural analysis of slave socialization together with an awareness of the relationship between the slave family and the enlarged slave kin group allows us to view the slave family as far more than an owner-sponsored device to reproduce the labor force and to maintain "social control," a view emphasized in the writings of John Blassingame, Robert Fogel and Stanley Engerman, and Eugene D. Genovese.[7] That emphasis focuses primarily on its utility in disciplining the slave husband and father, a far too narrow perspective. If owners encouraged family formation for that reason (and many did), such decisions had profound, if unanticipated, social and cultural consequences among the slaves and their children. Intergenerational family linkages developed. Passageways for a developing slave culture shaped the interior fabric of developing slave communities, and also served to socialize the slave child. "If a master wished to keep his plantation going," Genovese observes, "he had to learn the limits of his slaves' endurance."[8] How slaves defined those limits resulted primarily from what they had learned as children and young adults from parents, other kin, and older non-kin. Slave-rearing—essential to the economic welfare of most slaveowners—therefore posed a contradiction for all slaveowners. The plantation pyramid developed at its base significant slave familial and kin networks that shaped slave behavior over more than one generation. If most plantation owners found it cheaper to rear than to purchase slaves and more efficient and orderly to permit such rearing to occur in settled slave families, such decisions reinforced the essential slave bicultural experience and became the social basis for developing alternative and sometimes even oppositional forces within slave society.[9]

Two examples illustrate the interplay between family, kinship, and slave belief and behavior. Patience was purchased as a four-year-old in 1828 by the North Carolina Pettigrews and thereby separated from her family of origin. By that time, slaves on the two Pettigrew plantations had developed families and kin networks similar to those on the other plantations studied.[10] The young girl joined a slave community increasingly bound together by expanding affinal and consanguinal ties. She matured within that community, absorbing beliefs about correct behavior from long-time Pettigrew slaves. When a seventeen-year-old, Patience had a child by Dick Buck. She married him two years later, and they lived in a conventional slave family, becoming the parents, in all, of seven children. Dick Buck's sixty-four-year-old father, William, died in 1844, and Patience and Dick named their first son for him. (Dick Buck's brother Glasgow married Amy, and they named a daughter for Dick Buck and Glasgow's mother Abagail. Amy's husband, Demps, had been named for his father.) Theirs was conventional slave behavior. But that is no reason to assume that such familial and kin behavior integrated Patience and Dick Buck efficiently into their owner's code of proper plantation behavior. In 1857, Patience (and quite possibly her twelve-year-old son William) was one of five slaves who made false keys, robbed their owner of $160 in gold and silver, and ran away. Captured, they were flogged and locked up for a time. The next year, Dick Buck was caught carrying flour at night, beaten by a slave patrol, later whipped by the black overseer Moses, and finally put into the Pettigrew "penitentiary." The same year that Patience and the others robbed their owner, the planter David Gavin complained bitterly after the slave Team returned: "[H]e is a mean fellow. I bought him to keep him with his wife and this is the 2d or 3d time he has run away, and lost nearly a years work, I cannot afford to keep him at this rate, he will spoil the rest of my people by his bad example, besides the loss I sustain."[11]

Unproductive slave "habits" rooted in generational family ties also revealed themselves in other ways. The cost efficiencies that came from rearing a labor force in families made for later costly inefficiencies. That was learned by the Louisiana cotton planter Bennet H. Barrow. "What is essentially necessary for his happiness," Barrow said of the slave, "you must provide for him Yourself and by that means create in him a habit of perfect dependence on you—Allow it ounce to be understood by a negro that he is to provide for himself, and you that moment give him an undeniable claim on you for a portion of his time to make for this provision." "Get your negroes ounce disciplined and planting is a pleasure," he wrote in his diary. "A H[ell] without it." A serious obstacle to that discipline, Barrow's records reveal, was what younger slaves learned from older slaves. "Social control" on his and other plantations meant much more than manipulating or satisfying the familial sensibilities of adult male slaves. It also concerned the relations between slave parents and their children, between slave generations. The median age of cotton pickers whipped by Barrow in 1840–1841 was about twenty-three. Most were whipped for inefficient labor. Their age indicates that these men and women had grandparents born in the 1760s and great-grandparents who may have been Africans. Barrow also complained in his diary: ". . . there never was a more rascally set of old negroes about any lot than this. Big Lucy Anica Center & cook Jane, the better you treat them the worse they are, Big Lucy the leader, corrupts every young negro in her power. . . ." The older slaves embittered Barrow, and he regularly whipped the younger slaves. Slaves born in the late eighteenth or early nineteenth century had "improperly" socialized slaves born a generation or two later. Far too many young slaves listened to Big Lucy, and her message was not one that Barrow wanted them to hear. Rearing slaves had some advantages for owners but also resulted in important costs. Big Lucy was not a slave driver. She was a slave "aunt" and grandmother.[12]

Frederick Olmsted shared many of the biases of so many mid-nineteenth-century northern and southern white observers of the slaves. Nevertheless his were among the most astute comments of that time. "I begin to suspect," Olmsted concluded, "that the great trouble and anxiety of Southern gentlemen is—How, without quite destroying the capabilities of the negro for any work at all, to prevent him from learning to take care of himself." On the eve of their emancipation, most slaves learned how to "take care" of themselves from kin and quasi-kin.[13]

Flight from their owners, for example, was vastly more complicated than the mere individual decision to quit slavery. The choice often meant weighing freedom against familial and kin obligation. Runaway notices and advertisements often show that flight within the South followed the sale of either a spouse, a parent, or a child or the decision by an owner to move slaves a great distance. "His wife belongs to Mr. Henry Bridges, formerly of this county, who started with her . . . to South Carolina, Georgia, or Tennessee. It is supposed he will attempt to follow her," wrote a North Carolina owner. Richard, another North Carolina owner believed, "has with him, in all probability, his wife Eliza, *who ran away from Col. Thompson*, now a resident of Alabama, about the time he commenced his journey to that State." Jim, a father in his fifties, was thought by his Barnwell, South Carolina, owner to have headed for Savannah, where his children lived. The twenty-year-old Frederick was believed by his Georgia owner to be near the Mississippi Corprew plantation because "his wife belongs to that gentleman, and he followed her from my residence." Alabama owners predicted that certain runaways would "return to Buckingham or Prince Edward Counties, Virginia, where they were raised," go to Columbia, Tennessee, where "their father and mother live," or be found "lurking about" a wife's residence. Their Georgia owner said that Abram had "a wife at Colonel Stewart's in Liberty County, and a sister in Savannah at Capt. Grovenstine's," and that Frank had "a wife at Mr. LeConte's in Liberty County; a mother at Thunderbolt; and a sister in Savannah." An Essex County, Virginia, white thought Fanny was "where several of her children are living." Prominent Richmond slave traders, who advertised for the pregnant Angeline, said she "had six children, and was raised in Greenbrier, Augusta County . . . [and would] endeavor to go back to Augusta where she was raised. . . ." Jerry was thought to be returning to Kentucky kin from Arkansas. Peter and his wife left an Arkansas owner to return to their old home, were captured, and ran off again. Jesse quit one Arkansas owner to join a brother who had left another Arkansas owner. Another Peter fled his Little Rock owner and apparently headed for Dallas County, where his mother lived. One Arkansas owner was unsure where his Henry was headed because the fugitive had "a wife near Summerville, Tennessee, and also a wife and children in St. Louis." Dick, who quit a Kentucky owner in 1858, was thought to be headed for the Lower South. "He has often been heard to say," reported his owner, "that he was determined to go to New Orleans" and "see his wife in that city." Two years later, the sixteen-year-old "yellow boy" Sam fled his North Carolina owner who had purchased him five years earlier and thought that Sam might be "lurking" at "General Williams's who owns his mother and others of his family." Sam had been sold from them as an eleven-year-old, but his owner believed that the separation had not cut the youth off from affective ties to his family of origin.[14]

The typical runaway slave in the decades prior to the Civil War, however, was not a person seeking kin. Most runaways—perhaps as many as 80 percent—were men between the ages of sixteen and thirty-five. Their marital status remains unknown, but their age might be explained by the unwillingness of many older slaves to quit their families. That is hinted at in the few surviving letters written by slaves who fled to the North. Their choice required unusual courage, but those who made it paid a price, often cutting themselves off from immediate families and larger kin groups. Surviving letters to kin (usually sent through intermediaries) reveal their loneliness and even guilt. Although William Still and his associates, who helped Upper South slaves escape, strongly discouraged fugitives from writing letters to slave relations, Still's classic *Underground Railroad* (1872) is filled with letters showing the psychological costs of flight. Loneliness expressed itself in many ways. Richard Edons told Still that his North Carolina wife "will send a daugretipe to your care whitch you will pleas to send on to me." About twenty-three years old, Isaac Forman, who had hired out as a Norfolk steamship steward and had had permission to visit his Richmond wife once or twice a year, asked Still if he knew "any way" to "get my wife away." A second letter warned, "I must see my wife . . . if not I will die. . . . You have never suffered from being absent from a wife as I have. . . . I consider that to be nearly superior to death." He offered to pay for her, explaining, "I am determined to see her, if I die the next moment. I can say I was once happy, but never will be again, until I see her; because what is freedom to me, when I know that my wife is in slavery." Letters also revealed attachments to parents, older siblings, and kin by marriage. Forman sent regards to his brother, sister-in-law, mother, "and all the family." Another fugitive asked Still to "tell my Mother and Brother and all enquiring friends that I am now safe in a free state." John B. Woods, who contemplated "an adventure after my family," said of his brother-in-law, "I should be as glad to see him as well as any of my own brothers, his wife and my wife's mother is sisters." Nat Ambey, who escaped from Maryland with his wife and whose sisters and brothers had been sold to Georgia, asked Still to write to the Baltimore woman Affy White:

> . . . say to her . . . that I wish to know from her the Last
> Letar that Joseph Ambie and Henry Ambie two Brothers and
> Ann Warfield a couisin of them two boys. . . . I would like to
> hear from my mother sichy Ambie you will Please to write
> to my mother and tell her that I am well. . . . my wife is well
> and doing well and my nephew is doing well   Please tell affey
> White when she writes to me to Let me know where Joseph
> and Henry Ambie is. . . .

Still dealt only with Upper South slaves, and most fugitives came from that region, but after the Mississippi fireman William Thompson fled to Canada an early letter asked his old supervisor "if you got anny word from my mother since i lift there."

Three letters—two sent to Still and a third whose destination is unknown—also illustrate the loneliness that accompanied flight from the South and indicate why the decision to become a fugitive involved far more than a desire to be free. Samuel Washington Johnson, who had hired his time and labored as a Richmond *Daily Dispatch* carrier, asked Still to forward this letter to his wife owned by a Richmond white other than Johnson's old owner:

> . . . I hope you will remember me now just as same as you did
> when I was there with you because my mind are with you night
> and day   the Love that I bear for you in my breast is greater
> than I thought it was   if I had thought I had so much Love
> for you I dont think I ever Left   being I have escape and has
> fled into a land of freedom I can but stop and look over my
> past Life and say what a fool I was for staying in bondage as
> Long   My dear wife I dont want you to get married before
> you send me some letters because I never shall get married

until I see you again   My mind dont deceive and it appears
to me as if I shall see you again

Then destitute, Johnson promised to write again after finding
work. After receiving an answer to an earlier letter, Thomas
Rightso replied:

> . . . I wish to tell All that wantes to know how I made my
> ascape that I made it in the knight when the Moon was gon
> away and thar was no eyes To see but god and it was threw
> him that I am know gitting along and ples to say to my Farther
> and to my fartherinlaw that I feel happy in my ascape untill I
> thinkes about my Wife and I hope that you bouth will talk to
> her and tell Her to be not dischomfiered for I thinks that I
> shall see you agin. Tell him to tell her if she is not sole at
> Chrismous she mus let me know how she and the childrens
> are agatting along and dear farther ples to see her and see If
> thar is anney way for me to Send a man to by her. . . . all
> I wantes is En opportunity to send a man to by her. . . .

Sheridan Ford, whose wife and two children were in a Norfolk
jail, wrote a third letter, pleading with Still:

> . . . i can not but ask not in my name but in the name of the
> Lord and humanity to do something for my Poor Wife and
> children. . . . i Would open myself to that frank and hones
> manner Which should convince you of my cencerity of Pur-
> poest don't shut your ears to the cry's of the Widow and the
> orphant & i can but ask in the name of humanity and God
> for he knows the heart of all men. . . . i cant do any thing
> . . . as i am for i have to lay low. . . . i love my freedom and
> if it would do her and her two children any good i mean to
> change with her but cant be done for she is in Jail in the
> South are not like yours for any thing is good enough for
> negroes the Slave hunters Say & may God interpose in behalf
> of the demonstrative Race of Africa whom I claim descendant.
> . . . Please answer this and Pardon me. . . .

If money could free them, Ford hoped he might get some from his
brother-in-law.[15]

After the Civil War started, it became clear that family obligation had earlier often impeded flight. Escape in family groups
became much more feasible as the Union Army probed the South
and successfully established itself there. The decisions slaves made
in this changed circumstance, one which increased the probability

of successful *family* flight, splendidly illustrate the relationship between manifest slave behavior and latent slave beliefs. They also show why the frequency of individual flight prior to the Civil War is, in itself, an inadequate measure of slave dissatisfaction. Mostly runaways filled Camp Barker near Alexandria, Virginia, between late June 1862 and October 1863. A military register indicates the name, age, sex, and marital (or family) status of each black entering the camp. More than half (61 percent) of those who made it to Camp Barker in the first week entered in family groups. The first day's entries were:

Name	Condition in Life
Andrew Jackson	Father
Wesley Jackson	Boy
James Jackson	Son
Mason Steward	Married
———— Steward	Married
Daniel Steward	Married
Joanna Steward	Wife
Ann Eli Buckner	Single
Julianna Johnson	Single

The next day, entrants included Scipio Johnson and his wife, Sarah, and on the third day Cuffee Dunahoe and his son James arrived. A few days later, the Jusets, the Greens, and the Wilsons arrived. Nine children accompanied these three couples. Five, ranging in age from one and a half to eight years, came with Mary and Allen Green. Some left immediate family members behind, as revealed by some entrants who arrived in November 1862:

Name	Age	Children with parent	Status of spouse or children
America Lankford	35	4	husband behind
Purmy Ballad	40	1	husband behind
Rena Rose	30	3	husband behind
Henry Richards	39	0	wife at Fredericksburg
Vena Edwards	40	0	husband behind
William Field	40	0	four children at Yorktown
Daniel Williams	50	0	wife behind
Mark Edney	59	0	wife behind
George Albright	24	0	wife behind
Anthony Jones	59	0	wife at Hampton
Peter Anderson	57	0	wife at Newport News
Washington Luray	57	0	wife at North Carolina
McKenzie Young	38	0	wife and children behind

The register failed to disclose the reasons these men and women had entered without spouses or without children.

Most entrants, however, arrived in immediate family groups. Table 32, based upon an examination of the familial status of entrants between June 1862 and October 1863, shows that nearly twenty-five hundred men, women, and children entered in these months, about three in four in immediate families. Most persons listed as "single" fit the classic description of antebellum slave runaways. They were young adults between the ages of fifteen and twenty-nine. But the typical wartime runaway arrived in a family group. In January 1863, for example, the thirty-four-year-old widow Harriet Robinson came with four children, the youngest Sarah Jane, a four-year-old. The fifty-year-old George Washington arrived without his wife but with six children (Daniel, Henry, George, Fanny, Ellen, and Payton), ranging in age from six to fifteen. Others came with larger families: Molly Ann and John Taylor with nine children and Margaret and Bob Green with eight children. Kate and George Smith were unaccompanied by children. She was seventy and her husband was eighty-seven years old. Anthony Hungerford, who arrived alone, was nearly as old as George Smith. He had been born a slave in 1776.[16]

A comparison of slave flight in different settings allows us to distinguish between manifest and latent slave values. What was latent belief prior to the disorders associated with the Civil War (the desire by families to flee slavery together) became manifest behavior during that conflict. Examination of slave marriage rituals allows us to study yet another aspect of slave belief and

TABLE 32.   FAMILIAL CONNECTIONS OF EX-SLAVES ENTERING
CAMP BARKER, ALEXANDRIA, VIRGINIA, 1862–1863

Familial status on entry

Adult member of immediate family (husband, wife, father, or mother)	27%
Child with one or both parents	45
Single adult listed as married or widowed	10
Single person with no clear kin connection	18
Number	2399
Unclear	55

NOTE: *Table 32 includes all entrants in the following periods: June 17 to July 31, 1862, August 26 to 31, 1862, and all of January, July, September, and October 1863.*

behavior. Most slaves were not denied the right to marry, but most slave marriages were unaccompanied by civil ritual. That did not mean that slave marriages lacked ritual. Substitute marriage rituals developed among the slaves. In all cultures, marriage, which as Sidney Mintz points out signalizes "the social acceptance of rights and duties concerning such matters as sexual access, co-residence, and economic obligation," is accompanied by public ceremony or ritual. The anthropologist Claude Lévi-Strauss observes:

> The most striking fact is that everywhere a distinction exists between marriage, i.e., a legal group-sanctioned bond between a man and a woman, and the type of permanent or temporary union resulting from violence or consent alone. This group intervention may be a notable or a slight one, it does not matter. The important thing is that every society has some way to operate a distinction between free unions and legitimate ones. Whatever the way in which the collectivity expresses its interest in the marriage of its members, whether through the authority vested in strong consanguinal groups, or more directly through the intervention of the State, it remains true that marriage is not, is never, and cannot be a private business.

Southern civil law did not distinguish between "free" and "legitimate" slave unions. Some slaves everywhere lived in "free" unions, sometimes forced upon them directly or indirectly by owners. But nonlegal ritual and ceremony accompanied most slave marriages. The runaway William Wells Brown knew these as common happenings. "There is no such thing as slaves being lawfully married," Brown said, but "it is common for slaves to be married, or at least to have the marriage ceremony performed." Asked by Frederick Olmsted whether Mississippi clergymen married slaves, a Yazoo owner responded, "Yes, generally one of their own preachers." The white described a variety of marriage ceremonies: "Sometimes they hev a white minister, and sometimes a black one, and if there aren't neither handy, they get some of the pious ones to marry 'em. But then very often they only just come and ask our consent and then go ahead, without any ceremony. They just call themselves married. But most niggers like a ceremony, you know, and they generally make out to hev one somehow."[17]

Most adult slaves on the plantations studied were married, and that was so for adult slaves elsewhere, too. A study of Schedule C in the 1850 and 1860 manuscript federal censuses even suggests that a larger percentage of adult slaves as compared to southern adult free whites were (or had been) married at the time of death.[18] But scant contemporary evidence exists describing the ceremonies and rituals accompanying such marriages. What Brown and the Yazoo owner reported, moreover, was contradicted by other contemporaries, men as different as William Grayson and E. W. Hooper. "It is well-known," the southerner Grayson wrote, "that forms of marriage vary greatly in various places. They are very simple with negroes; as simple as they have been in Scotland, where the mere consent of the parties was held to be enough. Negro marriages are not the less enduring from their lack of form. They usually last for life." The Yankee officer Hooper reported from the Sea Islands in 1862 that "although slavery made them in great measure regardless of the *ceremony* of marriage, it did not take away their birthright of modesty, or the idea of fidelity between man and wife."[19]

An incomplete but nevertheless very important record—a marriage register that recorded 883 slave marriages in the District of Columbia between November 1866 and July 1867—allows us to reconcile the contradictory observations surrounding the ritual and ceremony associated with slave marriage.[20] Registrants gave their names, the length of their marriages, the number of children born in these marriages, and, most important, where and how they had been married. A few—one couple in twenty-five—had first married in the District of Columbia; the rest had migrated there after marriage. A single couple did not give its earlier residence; one marriage had occurred in Atlanta; another in the West Indies. The rest (96 percent) had moved to the District from either Virginia or Maryland. The District register, incidentally, disclosed that whole families—representing a variety of slave experiences—had migrated to a city and retained conjugal connections.[21] A higher percentage—seven in ten—had lived in slave marriages that lasted at least ten years than were listed in either the Virginia or North Carolina 1866 registers. About one in eight couples had been married at least thirty years (Table 33). These registrants were asked who had married them. Some did not know. Others could not remember. Still more named a minister or, if from Maryland, a priest. A yet larger number credited their old owners: "joined by permission of master" or "ceremony read by their master." (There is a difference, of course, between asking an owner for permission to marry and having an owner read a ceremony.) But 421 couples—48 percent—responded, "No mar-

Table 33. Length of Ex-slave Marriages Renewed in Washington, D.C., 1866–1867, Compared with Length of Marriages Registered in Virginia and North Carolina, 1866

District of Columbia

YEARS MARRIED	
Under 5	3%
5–9	28
10–19	39
20–29	18
30–39	8
40–49	3
50+	1
Number	875
Unknown	8

Years married by percent

YEARS MARRIED	DISTRICT OF COLUMBIA	NELSON COUNTY, VIRGINIA	ROCKBRIDGE COUNTY, VIRGINIA	SIXTEEN N.C. COUNTIES
Under 10	31%	45%	49%	51%
10–19	39	23	18	27
20+	30	32	33	22

riage ceremony." Although nearly half of the couples had gone without any marriage ritual sponsored by a white, seven in ten District registrants had lived together for at least a decade. Family solidarity did not need the social cement associated with the prescribed civil and religious norms of the national (or even the regional) culture. These marriages derived their strength from norms within the slave culture itself.

The register, however, should not be read as evidence upholding the views of either Grayson or Hooper. Nearly half the couples reported "no marriage ceremony," but the officiating black clergyman had not asked about irregular marriage ceremonies and rituals. He apparently defined "ceremony" as the conventional Christian ritual. That did not mean that most slaves viewed marriages lacking that ritual as "free unions." Irregular slave rituals—the most important among them "jumping the broomstick"—converted many slave marriages into *legitimate* unions, telling neighbors and kin that the status of a man and woman had changed and impressing new duties and obligations upon husband and wife.

The recollections of elderly ex-slaves and other historical evidence disclose a variety of ways in which slave marriages were publicly announced and legitimized. Some ex-slaves, of course, described marriages without any formal or public ceremony. Preeley Coleman's South Carolina mother married John Solman on the way to Texas, "no cer'mony, you knows, but with her master's consent." Born in Tennessee and moved first to Arkansas and then to Texas, Mary Overton said the slaves "told dey marsters dey wanted to be husban' and wife and if dey agreed, dat was all dere was to it, dey was said to be married." She and her husband had married that way. Sam Polite, who had grown up a Sea Islander, said, "My fadder and mudder ain't marry; slaves do't marry—dey just lib togedder.' "[22] Small numbers of slaves everywhere, and especially favored house servants, however, benefited from marriages carefully supervised by their owners, and the attention some owning families gave to such ceremonies is revealed in detail in Eugene D. Genovese's *Roll, Jordan, Roll*. Elderly ex-slaves also recollected owner-sponsored ceremonies. A Mississippi woman told the historian Charles Sydnor that her owner married her in the fields while she and her husband stood "between the handles of a plow." Other owners brought in a clergyman or a local justice of the peace. John White learned from his Georgia mother that her owner read from an almanac, and Lucinda Elder's mother told her that her owner "give 'em a big supper in de big house and read out of de Bible 'bout obeyin' and workin' and den dey married." Charles Grandy vividly remembered his Virginia owner's role:

> . . . He would lead you an' de woman over to one of de cabins and stan' you on de porch. He wouldn't go in. No, sir, He'd stan' right dere at de do' an open de Bible to de first thing he come to an' read some pin real fast out of it. Den he close up de Bible an' finish wid dis verse:
>
> > Dat yo' wife
> > Dat yo' husband
> > I'se you' marsa
> > She you' missus
> > You married.

Other ex-slaves remembered ceremonies in an owner's house, in "massa's yard," and at the "front gate." Some owners supplied special foods and dress and allowed dances. On Henry Brown's South Carolina plantation, the slaves prepared "everything eatable" at the "master's expense" and then the newlyweds went home "without any readin' of matrimony, man and wife." There was "always . . . a kind of supper and big dance," said a Tennessee ex-slave; "they wouldn't marry 'less you could have a dance."[23]

Slave religious leaders everywhere—sometimes but not always with the approval of owners—cemented slave marriages. Olmsted noticed such preachers on the South Carolina and Georgia rice plantations. When two house servants on Thomas Chaplin's Sea Island plantation married, " 'Robert,' the spiritual leader of the plantation," conducted the service. Wartime Yankee missionaries met the seventy-year-old Sea Island preacher Smart Campbell, who had "married a great many couples with his master's consent." The "eminent patriarch Uncle Abel" married Virginia slaves living on Mary Pryor's family's tobacco plantation. Black priests married some Louisiana slaves, and, according to the Tennessee and Kentucky courts, "colored preachers" were common in those states, too. The Kentucky ex-slave Francis Frederick said that on his plantation "January's Tom" and "Morton's Gilbert" had been "authorized to marry the slaves." "Uncle Peter," another Kentucky slave, went from place to place "marrying members of his own race," and a white told the historian John Coleman that "almost every neighborhood had its negro preacher, whose credentials, if his own assertion was to be taken, came di-

rectly from the Lord." Elderly ex-slaves remembered black clergymen officiating at weddings. Adeline Cunningham said a slave
preacher read the marriage ceremony from "a book" he "keep
hid." "Sometimes," said a Tennessee ex-slave, "Uncle Square Wallace would go through some sort of ceremony. But he didn't know
a letter in the book." "Old man Preacher Tony would marry you
for nothing," Gus Feaster recollected, and Isabella Dorroh's
South Carolina slave parents were married by "an old man, Ned
Pearson, a nigger who could read and write" and who "married
lots of niggers." South Carolina ex-slaves called such men "jack-
legged" preachers. One "pronounced a few words"; the other
made the couple jump "backwards and forwards over a broom."[24]

Jumping over a broomstick served as the most common irregular slave marriage ritual. Sometimes sanctioned and even par-
ticipated in by owners, it transformed a "free" slave union into
a legitimate slave marriage. Other uncommon rituals also accompanied slave marriages. Elderly Kentucky and Tennessee ex-slaves
remembered that some had married "with a lamp, or by carrying
a glass of water on their head." "I was married by the blanket,"
a Georgia slave told John Ball. "We comes together in the same
cabin; and she brings her blanket and lay it down beside mine;
and we gets married that a-way." A. D. Smith, who labored among
the wartime Sea Island blacks as a federal tax officer, said that the
common responses to the question "Who married you?" were
"Parson Blanket married us" and "We married ourselves." These
answers came "seven times out of ten." Disturbed Yankee missionaries even imposed "severe strictures" against Sea Islanders
"marrying in blankets."[25]

"Marrying in blankets" was a far less common irregular
slave marriage ritual than "jumping the broomstick." Varieties of
the broomstick ritual were described by elderly ex-slaves who had
lived over the entire South. The Alabama ex-slave Penny Anderson said a wedding did not include a "preacher or cer'mony." The
slaves prepared a dinner, sang religious songs, and "after supper
dey puts de broom on de floor and de couple takes de hands and
steps over de broom, den dey am out to bed." Sometimes, the
ceremony involved owners and even accompanied a more conventional Christian ritual. The Georgia ex-slave Carrie Davis said
slaves went "up to de white folks' house and jumped de broom."
A Louisiana justice of the peace married Donaville Broussard's
aunt and made her "and the man hold hands and jump over the
broom handle." William Davis, who had been a Tennessee slave,

said: "Dey go in de parlor and each carry de broom. Dey lays de broom on de floor and de woman puts her broom front de man and he puts de broom front de woman. Dey face one 'nother and step 'cross de brooms at de same time to each other and takes hold of their hands and dat marrys dem. Dat's de way dey done, sho', 'cause I seed my own sister marry dat way." Virginia slaves, according to Georgianna Gibbs, jumped "a broom three times"; it was "de license." Men and women "jumps high," remembered the Alabama ex-slave Jeff Calhoun. To "stump you toe on de broom meant you got trouble comin' 'tween you." A Kentucky black said that "the man used to jump the broom and the woman would stand still." Caroline Johnson Harris was married by the elderly Virginia slave Aunt Sue, who mixed Christian and non-Christian religious belief and ritual:

> Didn't have to ask Marsa or nothin'. Just go to Aunt Sue an' tell her you want to git mated. She tells us to think 'bout it hard fo' two days, 'cause marryin' was sacred in the eyes of Jesus. Arter two days Mose an' me went back an' says we done thought 'bout it and still want to git married. Den she called all de slaves arter tasks to pray for de union dat God was gonna make. Pray we stay together an' have lots of chillun an' none of 'em git sol' away from de parents. Den she lay a broomstick 'cross de sill of de house we gonna live in an jine our hands together. Fo' we step over it she ast us once mo' if we was sho' we wanted to git married. 'Course we say yes. Den she say, "In de eyes of Jesus step in to de Holy land of mat-de-money." When we step 'cross de broomstick, we was married. Was bad luck to tech de broomstick. Fo'ks always stepped high 'cause dey didn't want to have a spell cast on 'em —Aunt Sue used to say whichever one teched de stick was gonna die fust.

"It was considered a big wedding to jump over a broomstick," said a Kentucky ex-slave, "but when you just asked them and go to bed after getting permission, then that was a little wedding."[26]

Much remains to be learned about the origins and functions of the broomstick ritual that accompanied so many slave marriages. Historians have mentioned it to describe it as either "quaint" or "curious." The earliest published description so far uncovered is in the ex-slave Willam Wells Brown's *My Southern Home* (1880).[27] Brown revealed nothing of its origins. Study of West Indian and Brazilian slave marriage rituals is needed before

it will be known whether the broomstick ritual was an adaptation
of a West African practice, a ritual learned from whites, a ritual
indigenous to American slaves, or a fusion of diverse cultural
origins. "The "irregular" marriage rituals of eighteenth- and
early-nineteenth-century rural and village white Americans, moreover, have been little studied.[28] Two sources, however (the recollections of the ninety-two-year-old North Carolina ex-slave
Willis Cozart and a charge to a Cheraw County, North Carolina,
jury by a judge in an 1853 bigamy case involving whites), indicate
that some southern whites also used broomsticks in marriage
ceremonies. "De poor white folks done de same thing," said
Cozart. A broomstick ritual followed by "housekeeping" was
accepted as a white common-law marriage by the judge. Too much
should not be made from such fragile evidence. It is possible that
these North Carolina whites learned the ritual from slaves. But
whites who had no contact with Afro-American slaves also jumped
broomsticks. The marriage records of a New England village
parson reported in the *Lowell Offering* included the entry,
"Jumped Johnny S. and his sweetheart Molly over a broomstick,
for a peck of grey beans." The same practice also existed among
nineteenth-century British railroad construction workers. More
than a thousand such men camped in shanty huts near Wood-
land in 1845 "had their own marriage ceremony which consisted
in a couple jumping over a broomstick, in the presence of a room-
ful of men, assembled to drink for the occasion, and the couple
were put to bed at once in the same room." Early-twentieth-century
British folklorists, furthermore, found similar practices common
among British (but not continental) gypsies and also recorded
survivals of the *suvel, besom,* or broomstick wedding ritual among
the Welsh. These scholars disputed its meaning. The practice
among the gypsies was usually viewed as "a survival of jumping
over the branch of a sacred tree" and related to fertility rituals.
But the broomstick also was identified as "the insignia of a witch,"
and jumping over it meant that "evil and witchcraft were powerless when defied by wedded love and wedded loyalty." None of
these students of gypsy culture knew that the practice had been
common among Afro-American slaves, and students of Afro-
American slaves have hardly begun to analyze slave magical beliefs.[29]

Enough is known about the importance of slave witchcraft
beliefs and practices to suggest that the broomstick ritual (whatever its origins) was related closely to Afro-American magical and

religious beliefs. (Such beliefs, of course, were not unique to the slaves. An 1855 Charleston newspaper, for example, complained that southern poor whites "nearly all believed implicitly in witchcraft.") Among the slaves, a long record of such beliefs survives. Olaudah Equiano said that in the 1760s some African shipmates on the way to Georgia believed "we had witches and wizards amongst the poor helpless slaves." A most convincing memoir by the late-eighteenth-century Virginia runaway slave William Grimes testifies in vivid detail to his belief in witches. In 1826, the South Carolina slave Jim was accused of murdering the elderly slave Rachel because Jim and other slaves thought her a witch. Sold from Maryland to South Carolina, Charles Ball met plantation slaves, Africans among them, who "uniformly believed in witchcraft, conjuration, and the agency of evil spirits in the affairs of human life." Henry Bibb lived among Kentucky slaves who often appealed to magic and witchcraft to "prevent their masters from exercising their will over the slaves." He used roots and powders suggested by a conjurer to ward off floggings and to change his owner's "sentiments of anger to those of love towards me." Henry Bruce knew an old slave woman who, together with other Virginia slaves, had hired "a great conjurer" to prevent their sale to Alabama. Whites as well as blacks noticed such slave beliefs. In his celebrated defense of slavery, *Black Diamonds Gathered in the Darkey Homes of the South* (1859), Edward A. Pollard mentioned Pompey, " a very old 'Guinea negro' " who would "talk Guinea 'gibberish' when he got greatly excited" and used "curious spells and superstitious appliances" so that "most of the negroes esteemed him as a great 'conjurer.' " Pollard credited his own "intensely superstitious" beliefs ("founded on the mystery of nature, transcendental, tender, and altogether lovely") to his family's slaves. They saw his dead sister's "spirit among the lonely trees at night." The "intensity" of Aunt Judy's "religious sentiment" especially impressed Pollard. He had heard "her loud and ostentacious prayers among the elder bushes and briars of the brook":

How well do I remember the wonderful stories, with which she used to fill our youthful minds with awe, superstition, and an especial dread of being alone in dark rooms. We were told by her of every variety of ghosts, of witches that would enter through the key-hole and give us somnambulate rides through the thickets and bogs, and worst of all, of awful and terrible visions that had been afforded her of the country of the dead. She had a superstitious interpretation for everything in nature. . . .

Laura M. Towne, perhaps the most acute observer among the northerners who worked among the Sea Island blacks, learned in 1868 that a "poor old woman" had been severely beaten by a man who believed "she 'hagged' or bewitched him," and that a black clergyman, ill with a lingering disease, was "universally" believed to have been "put . . . under a spell" by "a neighbor of his, a good unsuspecting man."[30]

Although the functions of slave magical and other super-natural beliefs remain as yet obscure and little studied, students of contemporary African and early modern British magical and supernatural beliefs and practices, including witchcraft, suggest that such beliefs are most appropriate to "small-scale" societies, often serving as sanctions "against anti-social behavior by support-ing the social virtues." Jacob Stroyer, who grew up in the 1850s on a large South Carolina plantation near Columbia, described just that function in disclosing how the slaves he knew in his youth had dealt with crimes committed among the slaves them-selves:

> The slaves had three ways of detecting thieves, one with a Bible, one with a sieve, and another with graveyard dust. The first was this: —four men were selected, one of which had a bible with a string attached to it, and each man had his own part to perform. Of course this was done at night, as it was the only time they could attend to such matters which concerned them. These four would commence at the first cabin with every man of the family, and the one who held the string attached to the bible would say John or Tom, whatever the person's name was, you are accused of stealing a chicken or a dress from Sam at such a time, then [one] of the other two would say, "John stole the chicken," and another would say, "John did not steal the chicken." They would continue their assertions for at least five minutes, then the men would put a stick in the loop of the string that was attached to the bible, and hold it as still as they could, one would say, "Bible, in the name of the Father and the Son and of the Holy Ghost, if John stole that chicken, turn," that is if the man had stolen what he was accused of, the bible was to turn around on the string, and that would be a proof that he did steal it. That was re-peated three times before they left that cabin, and it would

take those men a month sometimes when the plantation was very large, that is, if they did not find the right person before they got through the whole place.

The second way they had of detecting thieves was very much like the first, only they used a sieve instead of a bible, they stuck a pair of scissors in the sieve with a string hitched to it and a stick put through the loop of the string and the same words were used as for the bible. Sometimes the bible and the sieve would turn upon names of persons whose characters were beyond suspicion; when this was the case they would either charge the mistake to the man who fixed the bible and the sieve, or else the man who was accused by the turning of the bible and the sieve, would say that he passed near the coop from which the fowl was stolen, then they would say, "Bro John we see dis how dat ting work, you pass by de chicken coop de same night de hen went away." But when the bible or the sieve turned on the name of one they knew often stole, and he did not acknowledge that he stole the chicken of which he was accused, he would have to acknowledge his previously stolen goods or that he thought of stealing at the time when the chicken or dress was stolen. Then this examining committee would justify the turning of the bible or sieve on the above statement of the accused person.

The third way of detecting thieves was taught by the fathers and mothers of the slaves. They said no matter how untrue a man might have been during his life, when he came to die he had to tell the truth and had to own [up to] everything that he ever did and whatever dealing those alive had with anything pertaining to the dead, must be true, or they would immediately die and go to hell to burn in fire and brimstone, so in consequence of this the graveyard dust was the truest of three ways in detecting thieves. The dust would be taken from the grave of a person who died last and put in a bottle and water was put into it, then two of the men who were among the examining committee would use the same words as in the case of the bible and the sieve, that is, one would say, "John stole that chicken," another would say, "John did not steal that chicken," after this had gone on for about five minutes, then one of the other two who attended to the bible and the sieve would say, "John, you are accused of stealing that chicken that was taken from Sam's chicken coop at such a time," and he would say, "In the name of the Father and the Son and the Holy Ghost, if you have taken Sam's chicken don't drink this water, for if you do you will die and go to hell and be burned in fire and brimstone, but if you have not you may take it and it will not hurt you." So if John had taken the chicken he would own up to it rather than take the water.

Sometimes those whose characters were beyond suspicion
would be proven thieves when they tried the graveyard dust
and water. When the right person was detected if he had any
chickens he had to give four for one, and if he had none he
made it good by promising that he would do so no more; if all
the men on the plantation passed through the examination
and no one was found guilty, the stolen goods would be
charged to strangers.

"Of course," Stroyer concluded, "these customs were among the
negroes for their own benefit, for they did not consider it stealing when they took anything from their master."[31]

Stroyer's description of this quasi-judicial trial procedure
bears directly on slave magical beliefs and indirectly on slave marriage broomstick ritual. The use of graveyard dirt, according to
the anthropologist William Bascom, had its origins in West African magical beliefs and practices. It is found elsewhere among
New World slaves than in South Carolina, including Mexico.
When the Louisiana ex-slave Marion Johnson used a "voodoo in-
strument" in the 1930s, it was "a small glass bottle . . . suspended
from a dirty twine about six inches long." Johnson twisted the
cords before asking questions of it. Elderly Georgia ex-slaves in
the 1930s still believed in the magical powers of graveyard dust.
Roger Bastide's description of funeral practices among mid-
twentieth-century Dutch and French Guinea Bush Negroes,
moreover, includes an interrogatory process similar to the one
detailed by Stroyer. After the grave was dug, chanting and dancing
followed, "culminating in the so-called 'interrogation of the
corpse.' "

Here we have yet another instance of Fanti-Ashanti practice.
Since every death is regarded as being supernatural in origin,
it is necessary to find out if the deceased has been the victim
of divine retribution (for having violated some taboo) or, alter-
natively, of black magic. The grave-diggers, in tranced or semi-
tranced state, hoist the coffin to their shoulders, and then
move hither and thither as the corpse directs them, while questions are fired at it: "Who killed you? Was it so-and-so?" The
ceremony lasts a long time, and the grave-diggers are kept
moving here, there, and everywhere. Only after the corpse has
been carried back to the house do the elders assemble to interpret the dead man's message.

Far too little is yet known to explain why these interrogatory practices persisted among slaves and their descendants living in such

different cultures, but the functions of the process Stroyer described, not the reasons for its "survival," give it its importance.
The South Carolina quasi-judicial procedure depended for its
success upon widely shared supernatural beliefs within a particular slave community and required that the examining committee
have intimate knowledge about the personal and social character
of each adult questioned. That *strangers* were blamed if the guilty
parties could not be detected strongly hints that the entire procedure served a far larger social purpose than finding a thief. It
subdued conflict *within* the slave community. The procedure
repressed *intraslave* antisocial behavior and thereby related closely
to those witchcraft beliefs and practices, which sanction, in part,
according to Max Gluckman, "the general code of morality, by
putting pressure on individuals to control their feelings—or at
least to avoid showing vicious feeling openly. For if you show
anger, or hatred, or jealousy, against a man, and he then suffers
a misfortune, you may be accused of bewitching him. Correspond-
ingly, it behooves you to act well to your fellows, lest you provoke
them to bewitch you."[32]

So, too, with the slave broomstick ritual. The ex-slaves everywhere who reported its practice rarely defined its function, and its
meaning remains obscure. When owners, for example, partici-
pated in the ritual, did that mean to "hag" them and perhaps
limit their power to break up slave marriages, as suggested by
the aged Virginia slave midwife? Or, more probably, did the
ritual impose supernatural and magical restraints upon a slave
couple and thereby minimize the possibility of overt marital conflict that might disturb the stability of the larger slave community?
The Georgia ex-slave Sheldrick Walthour remembered that after
the "cullud preacher come and say de blessin' on us" but "befo'
de feastin' begin" he and his wife jumped a broomstick. "Dat
show we's gwine stay married," explained Walthour. Josephine
Anderson, who grew up as a Florida slave, described the broomstick ritual as one which "seals de marriage, an at de same time
brings . . . good luck. Brooms keeps hants away. When mean folks
dies, de old debbil sometimes doan want em down der in de bad
place, so he makes witches out of em, an sends em back. One
thing bout witches, dey gotta count everything fore dey could
git acrosst it. You put a broom acrosst your door at night an
old witches gotta count every straw in dat broom fore she can
come in." The Louisiana black Rebecca Fletcher made a similar
point:

I never seen a witch but my Grandma knew lots of 'em, and she done tol' me plenty times what they look like. My Grandma told me about a witch what went into a good woman's house when that woman was in bed. The woman knowed she was a witch, so she told her to go into the other room. Ole witch went out and lef' her skin layin' on the floor, and the woman jumped out of bed and sprinkled it wit' salt and pepper. Ole witch come back and put on her skin. She start hollerin' and jumpin' up and down like she was crazy. She yelled and yelled. She yelled, "I can't stand it! I can't stand it! Something's bitin' me!" Ole witch hollered, "Skin, don't you know me?" She said this three times, but the salt and pepper kept bitin'. The woman took a broomstick and shooed that ole witch right out, and she disappeared in the air.

The survival of slave magical marriage rituals such as jumping the broomstick may have served other functions than repressing intraslave conflict. In describing Tudor and Stuart witchcraft practices, the historian A. D. J. MacFarlane suggests that such magical beliefs "acted in areas where people were anxious, in situations where ideal and practice came into conflict." Slaves married like their owners, other whites, and free blacks, but the culture at large celebrated marriage and protected it in the law for all except the slaves. Owners had the power to break up slave marriages and families for reasons unrelated to slave behavior and feelings. Few experienced the tension between "ideal and practice" more deeply than the Afro-American slave, and that recurrent tension—a tension inherent in ownership—perhaps explains the importance of the slave broomstick marriage ritual.[33]

Slaves and ex-slaves knew the difference between a marriage sanctioned by law and a marriage upheld by ritual. Asked just after the emancipation by the Yankee Baptist missionary Isaac W. Brinckerhoff if she was married, a Georgia ex-slave replied, "I am not married, but I have a husband." Brinckerhoff believed she lived in "sin" and "concubinage." But her answer had a different meaning. She had explained to him that slaves like herself had honored norms which sustained the slave family and slave marriage outside of the inhibiting framework fixed by the law in the slave states. In January 1865, Ohio blacks met in convention at Xenia to form the Ohio Equal Rights League and to advise "our newly emancipated brothers and sisters who have lived together as husbands and wives, according to slave-holding usages, while slaves, as soon as practicable to be married according to law, and thus legalize their marriages and legitimate their children." Many ex-slaves did that, as will be seen in Chapter 9, but that did not mean that they had viewed their earlier slave marriages as lacking legitimacy. A Virginia ex-slave interviewed in the 1930s explained, "You see, it's dis way; God made marriage, but de white man made de law."[34]

A vast scholarly literature, as Fredrickson and Lasch point out, discloses that variations existed in the behavior of owners toward their slaves. Nothing in this study contradicts that finding. It was seen in Chapter 3, for example, how the Virginia slave-owner John Cohoon's behavior toward his slaves and their families changed over time as his needs were redefined, and in Chapter 4 evidence showing the relatively frequent breakup of slave marriages by force and sale was analyzed.

Yet other evidence indicates genuine concern by owners for slave families. When urban slaves were hired, it was difficult to keep family members apart. "In many instances," writes Richard C. Wade, "the man stayed with his wife, even though the couple had different masters. In fact, this became so common that local ordinances increasingly sanctioned the practice." Skilled and unskilled semirural iron workers either owned or hired by the Virginian William Weaver (and so well studied by Charles Dew) left with his permission after Saturday work to remain with their families until Monday morning. (That arrangement did not satisfy all Weaver's slaves. The woodchopper Booker once "lost two weeks going to see his wife," and another time was docked fifty cents because, as the time book noted, the day was "lost going to see wife." Par worked irregularly but "laid up very seldom when he could get a chance to run to his wife.") Other slaves laboring on a river improvement project had been away from their families for six weeks, asked for and were denied permission to visit them, and asked again without success. But after six men left to visit with their families, the overseer allowed the others "a couple of days" with their families. Owners elsewhere had similar troubles. A slave who mined gold fled to Savannah. "Jacob," his owner explained, "has been at me the past month to let him go . . . and see his wife." George Sally quit a Louisiana sugar plantation without out a pass because he could not get permission to visit his wife. An owner had him arrested and then worried about how to deal with him:

I am very much bothered what to do with him—his conduct merits very severe measures—he says he prefers being sold to returning to the Island & even now speaks in a very independent manner, says being in jail is no punishment for him, & that he is very well satisfied there. I had decided to take him to the city [and sell him?], but I am reluctant to do so for many reasons. His father & mother are both excellent creatures & so are his whole family—his being sold would of course give them great trouble. . . .

The white reluctantly gave George Sally "another trial." Other whites allowed such visits regularly. The hirings that the Richmond whites Lewis and Robert Hill negotiated often permitted slaves to "visit their families." One "aristocratic Virginia lady" hired out seven slaves with instructions that they "be allowed to visit their wives twice a year as well as at Christmas time."[35]

Purchase and sale by owners sometimes revealed a genuine concern for slave familial needs and feelings. The Virginia iron manufacturer David Ross, who was also a tobacco planter and merchant and one of the South's largest early-nineteenth-century slaveowners, bought the carpenter James Noble's wife and two small children from an adjoining plantation, explaining that "the woman and children would be of no consequence was it not [for] James Noble's comfort." When Ross moved his Botetourt plantation slaves to his Oxford Iron Works, the elderly Solomon fled the ironworks to be with his wife. Ross hired and then sold him to a Botetourt white to allow Solomon to remain near his wife. Thirty years later, Joseph Anderson hired Henry at the Richmond Tredegar Iron Works and agreed to a request by Henry's owner that he take the man's family: "It will be a great burden to me to take Henry's family and as there are five children I don't think the services of the mother will pay the expenses of keeping them by 30 dollars. Yet if you are not willing to make this allowance, I suppose, to gratify Henry I must take Polly and the children." The Georgia planter David C. Barrow paid sixteen hundred dollars for Tom's wife and child because "Matilda . . . wished to go to her husband," and, after purchasing Eliza and her two children and Lucy, the Alabama planter Hugh Davis complained their owner had driven "a hard bargain . . . made necessary by . . . the women being the wives of my men." Another time, Davis hired out Malinda and Mahala for $125 each, explaining to the renter that "as you have the father of one & the brother of the other, &

as they wish to be with them, I am willing to lose something to accommodate them." (Davis's concern should not be exaggerated. Hester and Harrison fled him in 1859 to get married, causing Davis to write, "I wish them a pleasant bridal tour & a Speedy & Safe return to their friends who will no doubt give them a warm reception." A patrol captured the couple, and the two were jailed. Davis paid twenty dollars in costs and probably had them whipped.) When a dead relative's estate was up for sale, John W. Cotten asked an intimate to buy "a little girl." "I own her parents & her brothers & sisters all," he said, "and I wish you to give $100 more than her value than not get her. Her parents are anxious that I would buy her . . . and it is my earnest desire to gratify them." The Alabama Tait plantation slaves Nathan and King (who left his wife) disputed over the woman Edy. She and Nathan married, and, after their owner purchased three "girls," the Tait overseer worried that they were not "grown," explaining to his owner that he had told King "I would in dever to get you to bey him a nother woman sow he might have a wife at home." In Tennessee, James Guthrie acceded to James Cooper's desire to buy his wife from him. After estimating her replacement cost at between six and seven hundred dollars and telling Cooper that "the price of Black people is Enormously High in this Country," Guthrie fixed the price at $550 and explained, "The Ties of Humanity compells me to part with her under these Serious Circumstances of Restoreing to a Disconsolate Husband a Beloved Wife." Sarah Cooper herself wrote her husband, "I was glad to Hear from you when your Letter come and that you was well and Had not forgot me my dear Husband Try to Redeem me and I will assist you in Reimbursing the Money so that we may git together once More and Live together the Ballance of Our days."[36]

Other owners facilitated slave marriages and encouraged local churches to impose marital discipline upon their slaves. The Florida overseer John Evans agreed to "Let Ansler take L[ittle] Peggy to El Destino with him to marry her," and later reported to his absentee employer that "Jim asked me to let him have Martha for a wife. So I give them Leaf to Marry. both of them is very smart and I think are well matched." The Louisiana planter James Monette's records included such entries as "George and Becky were married last night," and "last night Isaac and Jane were married." Occasional evidence indicates that purchases were encouraged to ease marriages. "I have a girl Amanda," explained a Georgian, "that has your servant Phil for a husband. I should be very glad if you would purchase her." L. V. Hargus helped Ben get a wife who lived on a North Carolina place nearby. Ben first told her owner of his wishes, and then Hargus wrote, "As it appears the boy wants a wife I make no objection. . . ." White churches sometimes enforced monogamy among slaves belonging to church members. (The historian Bobby Jones has also found "instances of expulsion for marrying against a master's will.") An Oglethorpe, Georgia, church expelled a slave for adultery. In September 1864, and on the same day that it dropped forty-one blacks who had "gone off to the enemy," the Upper King and Queen Baptist Church expelled the Virginia slave Marta for "fornication." Whites elsewhere worried about remarriage that followed the sale of a slave spouse. Dispute over this issue among Georgia members of the Millstone Baptist Church caused a regional church body to recommend that married slaves "separated by force" be allowed to "stay in the Church if they . . . take another companion." The Savannah River Baptist Association debated the same issue and finally decided that separation by sale was the civil equivalent of death and "would be so viewed . . . in the sight of God." A generation after the Civil War ended, a southern white remembered that the sale of a spouse beyond a distance of thirty miles "was considered by the clergy equivalent to a divorce because the husband could not walk to his wife and back again between Saturday at sundown and Monday at sunrise."[37]

The separation of slave family members by sale or for other reasons led some sensitive owners to encourage contact between them. After a few of her family's slaves ended up with a niece, the Louisiana woman Rachel O'Connor asked her "how old Sam and John are. Patience wishes to hear from her son very much since his poor father died, & Sam's children keep asking about their father more than usual since they lost their brother Leven. He was everything to them." The Abington planter David Campbell, Virginia's governor between 1837 and 1841, took the elderly butler Michael Valentine, Valentine's sons Richard and David, and Valentine's daughter Eliza Dixon to Richmond, but left behind Valentine's wife Hannah and Eliza's young daughter Mary and her other children. Campbell allowed these slave servants to keep in touch by mail. A white penned letters for Hannah, and in one she told her daughter that her children "talk some Little about you but do not appear to miss you a great deal." She went on:

tell my Dear son Richard that I will have a few Lines written to Him to day his Wife and Friends are all well. His Wife has not yet Received his Letter but I will try and send it to Her between this ——— and Sunday. Give My best Love to Michel & David tell Michel that I am very Happy to Hear that he Has seen all his Relations. . . . tell him he can form no Idea how much I have thought of him since he Left this place and how much I have missed him—

Tell Richard that Aunt Lucinda sais she has Dreamed about him several times since he Left Here—

[In the margin] Give My Love to all Michels Brothers & Sisters & Tell them all to write to Me—tell Richard that Mary sais he must write to Her!

When her husband failed to answer another letter, Hannah complained that he "treated" her "badly," adding "I begin to feel so anxious to hear from you and my children, and indeed from all the family . . . I am afraid my patience will be quite worn out if you do not come back soon. You must write. . . . Tell Richard I have not heard from his wife since she left here." Her daughter-in-law had been "settled" in Mississippi. "Please tell Eliza," a letter sent to Campbell's wife asked, "that her children look very well. I have not found mary eating any dirt since she got her mothers letter. . . . Tell Michael I sent him a letter."[38]

Overt expressions of slave familial feelings deeply affected some owners and other whites who came into contact with these slaves. Whites intervened sometimes to prevent the sale of slaves. After a hired Virginia slave was sold and separated from his family because he had not earned enough, whites who attended church with the man raised sufficient cash to buy him from a trader. Their slave grandmother persuaded a Kentucky clergyman to bid for two teen-aged sisters threatened with distant sale, but a trader outbid him. The purchase of Mima and her child by an Alexandria slave-trading firm led the hard-pressed Virginian Richard H. Carter, who owned Mima's husband, to try to buy them "because of the distress . . . on account of the separation." Carter made a low offer, the best he could, realizing, he told the traders, that "such cannot be your usual way of doing business" but hoping that they would "proceed from a motive of humanity."' Affective slave familial expression enlarged the sensibilities of yet other whites. In 1804, while St. George Tucker's son Henry and the young Virginia slave Bob were away from their families, the white wrote his father:

I enclose a short note from Bob to his mother. Poor little fellow! I was much affected at an incident last night. I was waked from a very sound sleep by a most piteous lamentation. I found it was Bob. "I was dreaming about my mammy Sir"!!! cried he in a melancoly & still distressed tone. "Gracious God!" thought I, "how ought not I to feel who regarded this child as insensible when compared to those of our complexion." In truth our thoughts have been starting the same way. How finely woven, how delicately sensible must be those bonds of natural affection which equally adorn the civilized and the savage. The American and the African—nay the man and the Brute! I declare I know not a situation in which I have been lately placed that touched me so nearly as that incident I have just related.

A few weeks later, Henry and Bob came together after being separated for a time, and the young slave said to Henry Tucker, "I am mighty glad to see you, Sir. . . . I couldn't have been gladder to see anybody but my mammy and my sister." Other whites could not repress the painful feelings associated with sale and the breakup of families. A Charleston widow, forced in 1803 to sell her husband's properties, including some slaves, to satisfy his debts, desperately admitted that their sale distressed her beyond

> any thing I ever did in my life. . . . Poor souls I have nothing to allege against them. I shall *not* sell David nor Ned; let old Betty if you please know that if I should sell her son Tom that I will send her son Sam to her—oh my god what have I done that such severe Trials should have befallen me I must lay down my pen my tears flow too fast to write.

Forty years later, when Thomas B. Chaplin's elegant life-style caused the sale of ten Sea Island slaves, he felt it "mortifying and grieving" to "select out some . . . negroes to be sold—you know not to whom, or how they will be treated by their new owners, and negroes that you find no fault with—to separate families, Mothers & Daughters, Brothers & Sisters—all to pay for your own extravagance."* An Arkansas judge had no difficulty understanding

---

* The full diary extract is printed in Willie Lee Rose, ed., *A Documentary History of Slavery in North America* (1976), 376–77. After the sale, Chaplin noticed that "the negroes at home are quite disconsolate—but this will soon blow over. They may see their children again in time." Four years later, Paul, one of those sold, fled his new owner. After being "out some months," he visited Chaplin. "He sais," Chaplin noted in his diary, "he came to see me knowing that I would not take him, & wants me to buy him. That is next to an impossibility."

the slave mother Sophia. Pyeatt claimed that Spencer had deceived him in selling Sophia (who was separated from her children by the sale) when she was "unsound, unhealthy, and mentally deranged." The angry Pyeatt had stripped the woman, staked her to the ground, whipped her with a fifteen-inch plaited buckskin lash, and salted her wounded back. Her "madness" had made her disobedient. Formerly a well-ordered house servant, she had once fled to "go to her children" and was "obstinate and disagreeable because she wanted to go to her children." When allowed time, she would "make clothes and knit for them." The judge heard this evidence and rejected Pyeatt's claim, convinced that "whatever wildness and aberration of mind might be perceived in the slave . . . was caused by grief, and the excessive cruelty of her owner."[39]

Such behavior reflects creditably on the Arkansas judge and these other whites and shows that ownership, prevailing racial ideology, and the social fiction that marriage rested upon civil statute and high culture did not prevent many owners from recognizing strong slave family feelings. It reveals the ways in which humane owners and other whites acted to benefit some slaves, keeping together and bringing together immediate slave families. But such evidence should be read with great care. It tells very little about what sustained the sexual, familial, and social beliefs among slaves living in such places as the Good Hope, Stirling, and Cohoon slave communities. The quantity of such evidence, moreover, is relatively rare, a point learned by John Spencer Bassett in his study of the Mississippi overseers employed on the absentee Polk plantations:

> There is not a reference to the marriage of slaves in all the 275 letters that have come into my hands. Within this long period (ca. 1833–ca. 1858) many such unions must have occurred on the plantation, but no overseer thought it worth his while to mention one. Also, there may have been divorces or separations of husband and wife. The letters contain no suggestion of such occurrences.

"The overseer," Bassett inferred, "wrote about the things that he thought the owner ought to know. He doubtless assumed that Polk had no concern with a negro marriage or a negro divorce." The quantity of such evidence is far less important than what most owners saw, how they interpreted what they saw, and especially what they did not see. "To Eldistino," a Florida overseer wrote an absentee employer in explaining why an elderly slave went from one to another of his plantations, "to see his Grand son Samuel die." That white was unusual in his perception. Observant owners and other whites dealing with slaves often saw and recorded strong ties within their immediate families, between husbands and wives, and between parents and children. But very few noticed affective kin ties beyond the immediate family. "All except the most dehumanized slaveholders," writes Eugene D. Genovese, "knew of the attachments that the slaves had to their more extended families . . ." No primary evidence, however, shows that owners, so deeply enmeshed in kin networks of their own, realized that slaves did not marry blood cousins and that slave children were often named for uncles and aunts and grandparents. Even the most humane owners, including those whom sale distressed and those who found ownership itself disturbing, were unfamiliar with these cultural beliefs and practices that shaped everyday familial behavior in slave communities.[40]

The absence of such evidence measures much more than the social distance separating slaves and their owners. Privileged social status, even for slaveowners, did not rest upon prescriptive right, and among slaveowners, as in other elite classes, was regularly explained by a "superior" morality. Paternalist beliefs, which often fostered owner responsibility toward slaves, and racial ideology allowed slaveowners to transfer to themselves the adult capacities revealed to them in day-to-day slave behavior. The belief that the adult slave was either a "repressed savage" or a "man-child" legitimized ownership and the exercise of authority as "civilizing" functions. The historian Bertram Wyatt-Brown points out that owners referred to slaves as children "with growing regularity throughout the pre-Civil War era" and that "the idea that slaves were as children was so acute and pervasive that it became a normal assumption." ("So long as slaves were perceived as childlike in their dependency," Wyatt-Brown also notes, "their humanity was tragically denied them.") The genuine self-satisfaction that resulted from the interaction between particular acts of slave behavior and what owners thought of slaves was splendidly revealed by the owner James Petigru:

> The only thing to flatter my vanity as a proprietor is the evident and striking improvement in the moral and physical condition of the negroes since they have come under my administration. When I took them, they were naked and destitute,

now, there is hardly one that has not a pig at least, and with few exceptions, they can kill their own poultry whenever they please.

On other and more important aspects of slave behavior such as their day-to-day familial and kin practices, paternalist and racial ideology also allowed owners to credit such behavior to their own example and effective domination. They could not recognize that the norms sustaining such behavior could have origins outside the immediate master-slave relationship, for that would have cast doubt on the legitimacy of the relationship itself. That is why it is inaccurate to suggest, as does Eugene D. Genovese, that slave-owners, unlike their abolitionist critics, had "no need to deny" that the slave had "a culture, a tradition, and a personality of his own." This observation confuses what slaveowners believed with what they saw. Owners were often attached to favored slaves, nearly always house servants and slaves who had belonged to an owning family over more than one generation, and realized that such men and women had distinctive personalities. But such sensibilities did not rest upon any understanding of slave "tradition," much less of slave culture. Awareness of that culture did not exist and for good sociological reason. Adult slave behavior and the ownership of adult slaves had to be reconciled, and that may explain why many owners, even those who noticed affective slave family ties and were generous in their treatment of favored slaves, believed with George Fitzhugh that slaves, like wild horses, had to be "caught, tamed, and civilized," with Chancellor Harper that among the slaves' "distinguishing characteristics" was an "insensibility to the ties of kindred," and with George S. Sawyer that the "options of parental and kindred attachment" did not "grow in the negro's bosom." Gertrude Clanton Thomas, the wife and daughter of prominent Georgia planters, knew that. Right after emancipation, a former house servant left her ex-slave husband to marry a field hand. The white woman believed a formal divorce necessary and urged that upon her old servant. The servant made other arrangements, and Gertrude Thomas then asked her husband to intervene. He refused; he did not want to "lose a good field hand." Plantation whites, his wife said, had failed in their duty toward the slaves and ex-slaves; they expected no more from them "than from . . . horses and cows."[41]

Sawyer, a Louisiana slaveowner, published his remarks in *An Inquiry into the Origins and Early Prevalence of Slavery and* *the Slave Trade* in 1858, the same year that Nanette, Jane, Serella, and Cecele, residents in the Stirling slave community, had children named respectively for a mother's brother, a mother's dead sister, a mother's half uncle, and a mother's dead niece. A generation earlier, the itinerant merchant William Reynolds witnessed the auction of twenty-three Memphis slaves, a "yellow woman" and her two children among them. "She begged and implored her new master on her knees to buy her children also," Reynolds wrote in his journal, "but it had no effect, he would not do it. She then begged him to buy her little girl (about five years old) but all to no purpose, it was truly heart rending to hear her cries when they were taking her away." That same year, Ben, Clarice, and Liddy were born to Stirling slaves. Ben was named for a paternal grandfather and the girls each for a maternal aunt. Whites profited greatly from owning slave labor but lost much because of beliefs that misconstrued slave behavior. That happened even to the most sensitive and humane among them. Like so many others, they paid a cost that could not be measured in the account books that so regularly balanced profits and losses.[42]*

Abolitionist and other critics of slavery made much of the involuntary breakup of slave families, and with good reason. That does not mean that they understood what kept slave families together. The black abolitionist Martin R. Delany did not exaggerate in 1852 when he complained that "the colored people are not yet known even to their most professed friends among the white Americans." Far more than racial beliefs, however, distorted the perceptions of slave behavior among such persons.[43]

Neither the Civil War nor the Thirteenth Amendment emancipated northern whites from ideological currents that assigned inferior status to nineteenth-century blacks, women, and working-class men. Two early postwar *Nation* editorials about the family illustrate how elite Yankee ideology (the views of those whom the historian John Sproat calls "The Best Men") distorted perception. The editorials mentioned neither slaves nor Afro-Americans but

* See also Bertram Wyatt-Brown, "The Ideal Typology and Ante-bellum Southern History . . . ," *Societas*, V (Winter, 1975), 28, in which he argues that one of the functions of paternalist ideology "was the maintenance of the proper means to distinguish the familiar from the alien, the high from the low, and above all, the marriageable from the outcast. What we call race prejudice was for ante-bellum southerners *the divinely ordained means of separating, demarcating, and defining those who could belong and those who could not, under any circumstances, enter the holy inner circle of blood ties and communal fellowship.*"

fretted over the "Future of the Family," railed against critics of
the dominant "patriarchal" family ideal, and insisted that "real
permanence and strength" in marriage could "never be looked for
amongst average men and women in the absence of a high moral
and religious culture, unless it has a 'home' as a basis." The "great
mass . . . in all countries" had "only been slenderly influenced
by moral and religious ideas." Only "habit and custom" sustained
marriage among them: "the custom of living with one wife"; "the
female custom of submission"; "the male custom of enforcing
obedience by blows and abuse." The great migrations which had
accompanied the transition to modern society dangerously unsettled such traditional restraints and "unquestionably" led to the
decline of "the sacredness of the marriage tie" among the "great
mass." That was the warning in one editorial; a second censured
advocates of more liberal divorce laws and revealed similar
worries about the "lower classes." Such legislation either ignored
the "sexual passion" or treated it "simply as 'lust'—that is, a
depraved appetite, only found among vile men" and no different
from the "love of alcoholic drinks or cockfighting":

> The sexual passion—the animal, brute passion, through which
> God, apparently in ignorance of the laws of "moral progress,"
> had provided for the perpetuation of the human species—is
> the most untamable of all passions. . . . Its regulation . . .
> was the very first step in civilization. The founding of the
> family was the first attempt to regulate it. The first object of
> marriage is still to regulate it.

Civil marriage and the patriarchal family tamed male sexual
"passions" but at some cost. It allowed some men to hold "ex-
travagant notions" of their authority, causing frequently just
complaint but not justifying liberal divorce laws. The reason was
simple. Codified sexual repression (the repression of "instincts"
through the civil law) had removed from man "the mark of the
beast" and encouraged him to gratify "certain propensities which
he is sure to gratify somehow . . . like a human being." But that
repression had a differential effect depending upon social class.
Among the "poor," moreover, the *Nation* found the "tendency
among men to cut all connections with their families and let
wife and children go to the devil . . . far stronger and far more
mischievous than the tendency to rule them with the patriarchal

rod of iron." The *Nation* identified sexual restraint, civil marriage, and family "stability" with "civilization" itself.[44]

Such mid-nineteenth-century class and sexual beliefs reinforced racial beliefs about Afro-Americans. As slaves, after all, their marriages had not been sanctioned by the civil law and therefore "the sexual passion" went unrestrained. Most emancipated blacks, moreover, were very poor and therefore entirely without "high moral and religious culture." In different ways and for different reasons, anti- and proslavery ideologues fed such beliefs and made it nearly impossible for the slaves and ex-slaves to be seen as they were in real life. Many white abolitionists denied the slaves a family life or even, often, a family consciousness because for them the family had its origins in and had to be upheld by the civil law. Few expressed this more clearly than Charles K. Whipple in his pamphlet *The Family Relation as Affected by Slavery* (1858), published by the American Reform Tract and Book Society and awarded a two-hundred-dollar prize as a "premium tract." Because the law denied them civil marriage, it "necessarily annihilated, to the slave, that beautiful, blessed relation, which *we* understand by the 'family' . . . ," said Whipple, William Lloyd Garrison's editorial assistant on *The Liberator*. Slave consciousness reflected the law: "It is obvious that the slave knows nothing of the [marriage] relations which the Bible . . . recognizes, defines, and enjoins." Such laws, sanctioned by a compliant clergy, made the slave, his family life, and his sexual being "clay in the hands of the potter." The slave law also failed to repress "licentiousness":

> Think what is the too well known extent of licentiousness at
> the North—in city and country, among old and young; think
> of the difficulties encountered, and the expense lavished, the
> risks run, the laws violated, and the disgrace hazarded in the
> pursuit of illicit indulgence there; then think what it *must be*
> in the South, where *all* these obstacles are removed; where the
> temptation is always at hand—the legal authority absolute—
> the actual power complete. . . .

"The very *laws* of the South," Whipple believed, "are temptations, instead of obstructions, to sin."[45]

Proslavery apologists denied blacks a family life and sexual norms for a different reason. Although Charles Colcock Jones, the Georgia cleric and slaveholder, agreed that "the divine institution of marriage depends . . . largely upon the protection given it by the law of the land," he nevertheless insisted that "the degraded moral character of the negroes" rested first on the fact that "they are *negroes*." "Vice," Jones wrote in *The Religious Instruction of the Negroes in the United States* (1842), "seems to lose its hideousness in proportion as it shades itself in *black*." Together, the beliefs of bitter adversaries like Jones and Whipple "idealized," as Ralph Ellison has written in another connection, the Afro-American "into a symbol of sensation, of unhampered social and sexual relationships." The myth of unrestrained black sexuality made a ghastly mockery of the family life and behavior, much less the moral and social beliefs, of the slaves and the exslaves.[46]

Beliefs about common lower-class behavior strengthened beliefs about particular Afro-American behavior. Blacks and slaves were not the only mid-nineteenth-century Americans lacking "restraint" and without the benefits of "high culture." The sociologist Lewis Copeland writes:

> It is obvious that these beliefs about Negroes are simply another form of those fictions almost universally applied to the lower classes of society. Wherever one social class looks down upon another as inferior, members of the latter are regarded as brutish in nature and vulgar. They are characterized superior in such animal qualities as strength and endurance, sexual potency, and the lack of sensitivity to pain. They are thick-skulled, dull, and unintelligent, primitive and childlike. Invariably these inferior classes who are regarded thus are also characterized as dirty and immoral, and contact with them is repugnant.

The British historian J. H. Plumb points out that eighteenth- and early-nineteenth-century England had its class stereotypes to match the mythic American slave: "Even the Sambo mentality can be found in the deliberately stupid country yokel or in the cockney clown of later centuries. So, too, the belief, as with Negroes, that they were abandoned sexually, given to both promiscuity and over-indulgence." Slaves and free workers, of course, differed greatly in their status, but both were "the objects of exploitation. Hence we should not be surprised to find similar attitudes." Frederick Douglass made a similar point in 1859 in the *Liberator:* "Men who live by robbing their fellow men of their labor and liberty have forfeited their right to know anything of the thoughts, feelings, and purpose of those whom they rob or plunder."[47]

A dispute in the fall of 1865 between the racist Democratic New York *World* and the antislavery Republican New York *Tribune* about granting the suffrage to the ex-slaves showed how such racial and class beliefs converged. Entitled "Negro Suffrage and Polygamy," the *World* editorial predicted that black suffrage would cause "the wide diffusion of polygamy and its general toleration by the laws." Blacks would be easy converts to "the Mormon faith" and "swarms of Mormon missionaries" would overrun the South and win them over because of "the ungovernable propensity of the negroes to miscellaneous sexual indulgence, and the powerful instinct of their race toward unreasoning superstition." This was "the weakest side of the negro character" and rested on "the innate tendency of the African people." Selected extracts from Malte-Brun's *Geographic-Universalle* and even from Buffon (both reprinted in the original French), David Livingstone's African travel accounts, and John Draper's *Thoughts on the Future Civil Policy of the United States* (1865), a work which argued that cultural traits "descend with the blood," served as supporting evidence. This miscellany of experts convinced the *World* that southern blacks would "listen with greedy ears to a gospel which panders to their strongest propensities," and that masses of black voters would give "polygamists" the "balance of power in our politics" and perhaps cause another Civil War.

"The *World* has an absurdly malignant attack on the blacks as universally unchaste," started the first of two indignant New York *Tribune* responses. The *Tribune* disputed the *World*'s particular worry: before the Civil War, a Mormon missionary had spent three years among Jamaican blacks and converted just two persons (both white women), and two other Mormon missionaries had been chased out of Kingston by angry residents. That the antislavery Republican newspaper put forth its own countermyth to answer the *World* is far more significant than these amusing details. "Female virtue," said the *Tribune,* "needs the protection of law, intelligence, and a consciousness that social position is based on character; with all of which Slavery is incompatible." The *Tribune* did not dispute the *World*'s charges concerning slave "licentiousness" but quarreled over the source of that alleged moral depravity. The *World* attributed such behavior to "race"; the *Tribune* found the cause in "class." "The simple truth," said Horace Greeley's newspaper, "is that enslaved, degraded, hopeless races or classes are always lewd."[48]

It follows, of course, that elite observers found evidence of "moral depravity" among other subordinate groups and classes than Afro-American slaves. Their perceptions of southern "poor whites" and northern Irish immigrants hardly differed from those of the slaves and former slaves. "Slavery," the Massachusetts abolitionist Charles Stearns insisted after managing a postwar Georgia plantation, "had destroyed the moral perceptions of the slaves, leaving them nothing but instinct to guide them." Stearns felt the ex-slave "a living skeleton, a walking frame of bones and ligaments . . . a mass of inorganic matter, loosely thrown together into one heterogeneous compound resembling a human being." An officer who accompanied William Sherman used similar language to describe southern poor whites. They were "so provokingly lazy . . . that they appear more corpses recalled to a momentary existence than live human beings" and were inferior to the "semi-barbarous" Russian serf, the "uneducated" French peasant, and even "a large proportion of the working class in England." (English workers, he said, "are debased but work.") Some Yankee evangels had nearly identical reactions to their encounters with the South Carolina ex-slaves. William C. Gannett saw slavery as "a nursery for perpetuating infancy," and Reuben Tomlinson described the "great mass" of ex-slaves as "to all intents and purposes children, except that they are children with fixed habits, the growth of years, & are therefore even more difficult to manage than children." "We must have nurses for him as with children," insisted Henry Ward Beecher in justifying schooling for the ex-slave. Such observations also did not differ from the characterization of white Kentucky war refugees (the families of Confederate soldiers) by a United States Sanitary Commission officer. They, too, were "as dependent and troublesome as children, and still more unmanageable." Their close family ties and "unwillingness to separate from each other and to go among strangers" showed them an "ignorant and helpless people" with "little self-reliance and no enterprise," people who "herded together like sheep or savages," even more "wretched" than the ex-slaves. "Overgrown children," their "moral character" remained "in a very undeveloped state." "As human beings," they were "almost imbecile." The same point was made in "The Iron Furnace, or Slavery and Secession," a story by John H. Aughey, who had been a Mississippi Presbyterian clergyman, reprinted in the *Anti-Slavery Standard* in 1863. Aughey called poor southern whites "semi-savages" who exchanged wives to facilitate migration to Arkansas and Texas.[49]

Not surprisingly, their earliest contact with the ex-slaves provoked among sympathetic northern observers immediate comparisons with the urban northern poor, nearly always the immigrant Irish. Such comparisons did not await the emancipation. Fanny Kemble, for example, talked with a planter who found the slaves "like the Irish and instanced their subserviency, their flattering, their lying, and their pilfering as traits common to the characters of both peoples." Wartime enemies made similar points about the immigrant poor. The Richmond *Examiner* said that recent immigrants differed from "our ancestors" (who fled "religious and political persecution") because they migrated "merely as animals in search of a richer and fresher pasture" and to "gratify physical want." They lacked "moral, intellectual, or religious wants" and would "practice" for "ages to come" a "pure (or rather impure) materialism." "The mass of them," said the Virginia newspaper, "are sensual, groveling, low-minded agrarians." He is "a creature with all the brutal passions and instincts of man in the first savage state, with some vague intelligence of the material strength of civilization and power to use it, but without any of the higher intellectual and moral qualities which belong to the age." So fumed the New York *Independent* in July 1863. But the object of its scorn was not the slave; the abolitionist religious weekly said this of the New York City Irish.[50]

Northern whites regularly compared the ex-slaves to the northern Irish and other "degraded . . . races or classes." (The comparison moved in both directions.) The early records of the Sea Island, South Carolina, missionaries and schoolteachers were dotted with such contrasts. Laura Towne's first diary entry, dated April 1862, described the Beaufort streets as "full of the oddest negro children, dirty and ragged, about the same as so many Irish in intelligence." That same year, Edward S. Philbrick, who saw the Sea Island blacks as "a herd of suspicious savages," celebrated Saint Patrick's Day by commenting that he had been "agreeably disappointed." "Think," he said, "of their having reorganized and gone deliberately to work here some weeks ago, without a white man near them, preparing hundreds of acres of new crops! The Irish wouldn't have done as much in the same position." He boasted two months later that "the course we have been obliged to pursue would not have got an acre planted by Irish laborers." Other northern whites made similar comparisons. "Dirty and ragged they all were, but certainly no more so than the poor Irish, and it seems to me not so dirty," said one. "They

are much better mannered than the Irish, and I have no trouble
as yet." "I find the nigs rather more agreeable on the whole than
I expected," glowed a third northerner. "They are much to be
preferred to the Irish. . . . Their blackness is soon forgotten. . . .
They are about as offensively servile as I expected." Thomas
Wentworth Higginson made the same comparison: "They often
show the Irish facility in hitting the nail upon the head in what
they say." The complaint by some field hands about their material
condition caused a northern superintendent to note: "A dollar a
day goes as far with them as two dollars with an Irishman in
Massachusetts at the present time." Whites in other places than
the Sea Islands made similar comparisons to the Irish. An Arkansas missionary called the language of the ex-slaves "a peculiar
brogue," and a Maryland schoolteacher felt it easier to teach
blacks than the "Irish servants in our own family" whose "patience
would give out by the time they had learned to spell dog and
cat." Whitelaw Reid found "the masses of resident negroes" in
southern cities "quite as orderly, respectable, and intelligent as
many of the voters in New York that help to elect mayors like
Fernando Wood." Such comparisons often had explicit political
implications. The high-toned Brahmin *Christian Examiner* compared the freedmen to the Irish—"poor, degraded, and sensual"—
and explained the need to make "men of them." A contributor
favored the vote for educated blacks but opposed universal suffrage for either "the ignorant negro of Carolina and Georgia" or
"the ignorant Irishman of Boston." "We, democrats," he insisted,
"do not claim that democracy is good for all people, Esquimaux
and Hottentots as well as Anglo-Saxons." Other lower-class groups
also came to the minds of northern and European observers of the
ex-slaves. A Norfolk schoolteacher found "colored children . . .
altogether superior to the children of the agricultural districts of
England," and Charles Nordhoff called the "habit or proneness
to lie" among former slaves (they "most adroitly tell you precisely
what you want to hear"), a quality they shared with the Irish
and "the common Hindoo" (the absence of "faith in the efficacy
or value of truth is bred in servility and is the fruit of tyranny").
Ten years later, however, Nordhoff shifted ground and compared
the consumption habits of the southern black to those of "a
sailor or a miner, or any other improvident white man."[51]

Upper-class southern whites also made such comparisons, but
it remained for a foreign traveler, a member of the British
Parliament, to make the nearly classic contrast. "Sambo," Robert

Somers wrote, "is a natural-born cockney."* British travelers to the
United States had a special talent for this sort of comparison.
Years later, the Oxford historian Edward A. Freeman advised
an American audience: "The best remedy for whatever is amiss
in America would be if every Irishman should kill a negro and
be hanged for it." Beliefs of this sort prepare us for the *New York
Times*'s greeting to the emancipated Afro-American in May 1865:
"The negro misunderstands the motives which made the most
laborious, hard-working people on the face of the earth clamor
for his emancipation. You are free, Sambo, but you must work!
Be virtuous, too, oh, Dinah! 'Whew! Gor Almighty! Bress my
soul!' "[52]

Not all who witnessed the transition from slavery to legal
freedom misperceived the adaptive capacities of its beneficiaries.
During his first visit to the South Carolina Sea Islands in 1863,
Charles Nordhoff looked into rural slave cabins and said they had
"a cheerless look to a Northern man":

> The cabins are small, and contain two rooms—one called
> by the people the *hall*, wherein is the great open fireplace; the
> other a dark hole, in which the older people sleep, and in

---

* Southern blacks, too, apparently had their fictive "Sambo"—at least according to some of the folk tales collected by the *Southern Workman* in the 1890s. "The
Irishman stories," said the collector, "form as widespread a part of the American
negro folk-lore as do the animal stories." The stories reported emphasized a single
theme: the gullibility, simple-mindedness, and stupidity alleged to be "Irish" traits.
A single such "folk-tale" illustrates this characteristic common to all five reported
in the *Southern Workman* (May 1899) and reprinted in the *Journal of American
Folk-lore*, XLVI (September 1899), 224–28:

> Two Irishmen were walking along one day, and they came across a wagon-
> load of watermelons. Neither one had ever seen a watermelon before, and
> they inquired of some negroes, who were working near by, what they were,
> and what they were good for. The negroes answered their questions very
> politely, and then, as it was their dinner hour, sat down in the shade to
> eat. The Irishmen concluded to buy a melon and see how they liked it.
> They went a little distance and cut the melon, but, taking pity on the
> poor negroes, decided to share it with them. "Faith!" they said, "guts is
> good enough for naygurs." So they cut the heart out of the melon and gave
> it away, and ate the rind themselves.

The "Irish tale" was noticed among Sea Island blacks as late as the 1920s by T. J.
Woofter, who reported the story of "a stuttering slave being beaten up by a
stuttering Irish patrol, because . . . [an] Irishman thought the Negro was mocking
him." (T. J. Woofter, *Black Yeomanry, Life on St. Helena Island*, 76.) The Irish
figured in southern black beliefs in yet other ways. The former Louisiana slave
J. Vance Lewis remembered an Irish overseer named Jimmie Welch and said of
him: "He had many peculiar characteristics, and the Negroes, who have a saying
that 'An Irishman is only a Negro turned inside out,' disliked him almost to the
extent of hatred." The blacks, however, grew more fond of Welch. Once, after they
finished their Saturday labors, Welch delivered to them "an Irish oration on freedom." (J. Vance Lewis, *Out of the Ditch: A True Story of An Ex-Slave* [1910], 16.)

which, too, I believe their valuables are kept. Above is a loft,
a general receptacle for those innumerable odds and ends
which the slaves cherished as "property." The younger people
of the house sleep on the rugs before the fire. . . . The cabins
are, for the most part, whitewashed outside; inside they are
smoke-stained, and on rainy days dark—for there are no glass
windows . . . the fireplace acting as an excellent ventilator. . . .

He noticed a hand-net for fishing in nearly every cabin and
"pictures from the illustrated journals" on some cabin walls.
Nordhoff was at first repelled by what he had seen:

To us, who have been long accustomed to a certain air of comfort and tidiness, it seems extraordinary that these people
should live contentedly in the way they do, one moment
longer than is absolutely necessary. In our minds this squalor
is linked with drunkenness and vicious improvidence; and we
unconsciously dislike those who live in this condition. These
were my emotions, I confess, when I first entered the cabins of
the people here. Those astounding agglomorations of rags, this
which seemed to me the most dreary discomfort . . . all this
made my heart sink, at first, and I said to myself: "oh! dear!
oh! dear! what can be done with all this."

"But I found," he significantly added, "the rags were clean . . .
[and] that the whole affair is not nearly so bad as it looks." Nordhoff was an unusual Victorian American. He was not an apologist
for slavery but rather an able observer of social detail who understood the differences between poverty and pauperism and between
self-respect and moral "depravity."[53]

Lucy Chase learned to make similar distinctions. She and
her schoolteacher sister had grown up in respectable upper-
middle-class Worcester, Massachusetts, comfort, the daughters of
a successful insurance agent, bank official, and newspaper publisher. Her first letter from Virginia in early 1863 described deep
shock. She "saw a painful exhibition of their barbarism" in their
religion. It was "purely emotional; void of principle, and of no
practical utility. They must know what is right! in order to wor-
ship the God of right." Further experiences caused a change in
attitude and in perception. After nearly half a year among the
Virginia slave refugees, she said: "I notice as much individuality
in the faces of [the] Negroes as I do in those of the whites. Their
features are so much lost in the single shadow with which Nature

has veiled their faces, that I once fancied that they would be hard to find and recognize. Black Sue looks herself as well as white Sue." In Norfolk, she watched as runaway and refugee slaves reaffirmed and renewed familial and kin ties and noticed "the delicacy and tenderness with which the Negroes express affection for each other." "They know how to love and how to remember," said the Yankee teacher. The swirl about her caused Lucy Chase to identify closely with those whom she tendered: "I can truly say, white-man though I am, that I have with the negro 'a feeling sense' of this state of transition. . . . Every hour of my life is strange: it is not past, it is not future."[54]

Mid-nineteenth-century Afro-American slaves, southern "poor whites," and Irish immigrants differed very much from one another. They behaved differently. They were treated differently. The range of social and individual choices available to them varied greatly. Each group had a distinctive American experience. But common patterns of behavior within each group depended upon far more than their "treatment." These patterns of behavior were also affected by the existence of particular group feelings, beliefs, and institutions—in short, distinctive historically developed cultures or subcultures. That a distinctive slave culture developed is now clear from this examination of the slave family and enlarged kin group. The persistence of such institutional arrangements among Afro-American slaves, of course, does not define the full range and depth of that developing and changing culture. But their persistence does mean that Afro-American slaves —like these other groups but in a much harsher and more damaging setting—had a coherent social and cultural repertoire (a "past") to draw upon. We need no longer isolate the mid-nineteenth-century Afro-American slave from the full American slave social setting that shaped his or her behavior and that was always present to affect either how slaves responded to treatment or how owners treated slaves. The persistence of distinctive slave institutional arrangements and recurrent slave social and cultural practices associated with the family and the enlarged kin group, furthermore, allows us to examine the appropriateness and utility of the important and influential "models" meant to explain common slave beliefs and behavior in the writings of such able scholars as E. Franklin Frazier, Kenneth M. Stampp, Stanley M. Elkins, and Eugene D. Genovese. Too much attention is given in their works to slave "treatment"; too little attention to slave culture and to the development of distinctive slave feelings, beliefs, and especially institutions.

Neither Frazier nor Stampp, who decisively rejected the racial treatment of the slave family that had characterized so much historical writing prior to 1930, explored the important relationship between the slave family and kin group and the developing slave community and culture. Frazier believed that settled marriage and stable family life existed primarily among slave artisans and house servants and among slaves of "mixed blood." They were the "favored few." The "natural" bonds between mother and child sufficed for the rest. Upon emancipation, "family traditions did not exist among a large section of the population," and the slave family, "at best an accommodation to the slave order," went to "pieces in the general break-up of the plantation system." Frazier posed appropriate questions, asking, "What authority was there to take the place of the master's in regulating sex relations and maintaining the permanency of marital ties? . . . To what extent during slavery had the members of slave families developed common interests and common purpose capable of supporting the more or less loose ties of sympathy between those of the same blood or household?" Slave men and women living in places like the Good Hope, Watson, Cedar Vale, and Stirling communities on the eve of the emancipation answer these questions by showing why and how family traditions and "authority" had come to exist among ordinary slaves.[55]

In *The Peculiar Institution* (1956), Stampp confuses the initial and especially difficult adaptive experiences associated with direct enslavement with slave behavior and beliefs a century later. Although slaveowners "usually more or less encouraged" slaves to "live as families and to accept white standards of morality," Stampp writes that the slave's distinctive condition "inevitably made much of the white caste's family pattern meaningless and unintelligible—and in some ways impossible—for the average bondsman." Slave marriages therefore "lacked most of the centripetal forces that gave the white family its cohesiveness." That may have been so, but it did not follow that the slave family, lacking "both outer pressures and inner pulls" common among nonslave families, was "highly unstable," that the adult male's "only crucial function within the family was that of siring offspring," that "many" slaves revealed a "casual attitude . . . toward marriage," that "most fathers and even some mothers regarded their children" with "indifference," and that "sexual promiscuity" among both men and women was "widespread." Such an analysis rests upon a narrow conception of slave culture. The slaves, according to Stampp, "lost their native culture" and were denied "a workable substitute." They "lived in a kind of cultural chaos" because they had "lost the bulk of their African heritage [and] were prevented from sharing in much of the best of southern culture." The slave "existed in a kind of cultural void . . . a twilight zone between two ways of life, and was unable to obtain from either many of the attributes which distinguish man from beast." He lived "between two cultures." The common patterns of behavior among slaves so different in their experiences as the Good Hope, Cedar Vale, and Stirling slaves are convincing evidence that such men and women did not live in "a kind of cultural void."[56]

That same behavior is reason to dispute the assumptions and the analysis in Stanley M. Elkins's study of slave socialization, *Slavery: A Problem in American Institutional and Intellectual Life* (1959). Elkins poses unusually important questions having to do with slave personality formation and the social determinants of slave behavior, but his answers are marred, in part, by an inadequate understanding of the developing slave family and enlarged kin group. His conception of American slave society derives from a large assumption (a subtle and powerful extension of Frederick Jackson Turner's influential frontier thesis) about the distinctive character of the "premodern" American social structure. "American society, capitalism," he writes, "developed unimpeded by prior arrangements and institutions." "Boundless opportunity" meant that restraints upon individuals functioned ineffectively, and "traditional guarantees of order" became "superfluous." The "dynamics of unopposed capitalism" affected the entire developing social system, including the relations between slaves and their owners, so that the slave, paradoxically, emerged as the most "individualized" of Americans. The law granted absolute power to the slaveowner, a power reinforced by the harsh initial enslavement process. Elkins writes of the first-generation slave:

> Much of his past had been annihilated; nearly every prior connection had been severed. Not that he had really "forgotten" all these things—his family and kinship arrangements, his language, the tribal religion, the taboos, the names he had once borne, and so on—but none of it carried much meaning. The old values, the sanctions, the standards, already unreal, could no longer furnish guides for conduct, for adjusting to the expectations of a completely new life.

The first-generation slave had a single "choice." "Where then," Elkins asks, "was he to look for new standards, new cues—who would furnish them? He could look to none but his master, the one man to whom the system had committed his entire being." A dependency relationship set in early and was the start of a long, repetitive, and self-fulfilling historical process. "The detachment was so complete," Elkins observes, "that little trace of prior (and thus alternative) cultural sanctions for behavior and personality remained for the descendants of the first generation." Several slave generations underwent socialization in a most oppressive circumstance. The "sanctions of the system," Elkins argues in his most essential point, rested entirely with slaveowners. "All lines of authority," he writes, "descended from the master, and alternative social bases that might have supported alternative standards were systematically suppressed." The reality of "Sambo" as "the typical plantation slave" flows easily from this conception of slave society.

Elkins does not deny the slaves marriage and a family life but says that the slave family was not "a meaningful unit" because owner-sanctioned families deepened dependency ties between slaves and their owners, a dependency reinforced by the "daily etiquette and usages of plantation life" which required that "all the true attributes of manhood" be "systematically isolated and placed well beyond the reach" of adult slave men. Marriage allowed them "rights as husband and father unrecognized in law," but "plantation custom" denied the slave husband and father "real authority over his wife and children." He "could be 'boy' or 'uncle,' but never 'father'; *that* role, from the viewpoint of the system and its well-being, was not only superfluous but disruptive." What Elkins calls "the isolating function of this situation" means that "a meaningful relationship between fathers and sons was simply not possible; the only real father on the plantation was the master." The "logic" of the system did not make it so necessary to deny "womanhood" to slave women "in quite the same way that manhood was denied the male slave" so that "whatever real authority existed within the slave community tended to be exercised by women rather than men."

Law and "custom" prevented slave men from breaking "the ring of helplessness and dependence." Even house servants and artisans (those whom owners might allow "a degree of personal autonomy not available to the ordinary field hand") could not escape the system's cruel logic. The absence of sustained slave familial experiences made their advantages personal and momentary, not cumulative and historical:

> . . . This was not something that could be built upon over more than one generation. In the absence of a meaningful family unit, neither the skills, the status, the standards, nor the psychological leeway could very easily be transmitted to his sons. In this sense there was very little that was cumulative in the life of a slave.

"The key to all this, as with everything else," says Elkins, "lay in the hand of the master." Much follows from the argument that "barriers of isolation" were "erected about" the adult male slave, and that the absence of "meaningful" slave family experiences over time made "very little . . . cumulative in the life of a slave." Elkins, for example, found in these social arrangements reasons why "initiative and self-reliance—the prime values of nineteenth-century American society—were so rarely found within the antebellum Negro community, slave or free," and why upon emancipation "a lack of preparation made an initial state of demoralization inevitable as Negroes wandered about the countryside."

Slave behavior rooted in adaptive and protective responses to enslavement has no place in this model of how slaves learned. But if "a meaningful relationship between fathers and sons was simply not possible" and "plantation etiquette" decreed that the male slave be called " 'boy' or 'uncle' but never father," why did so many slave sons carry the names of slave fathers? And if "status" could not be "built upon over more than one generation," why were slave children so often named for slave grandparents? Slave naming practices are reasons to discount Elkins's insistence that the slave family was not "a meaningful unit," that "all lines of authority descended from the master," and that "very little . . . in the life of a slave" was "cumulative." In explaining why "Sambo" was not a mere figment of the white imagination and how the structure of slave society made such character types possible, Elkins differentiates between American slaves and other dependent and exploited classes. "The principle of how the powerless can manipulate the powerful through aggressive stupidity, literal-mindedness, servile fawning, and irresponsibility," he writes, was "deeply embedded in European traditions," serving the dependent individual as "a technique" that allowed him "in a real sense [to] exploit his powerful superiors, feel contempt for them, and suffer in the process no great damage to his own pride."

"All this," Elkins explains, "required the existence of some sort of alternative force of moral and psychological orientation." But, according to Elkins, "the problem of the Negro in slavery times involved the virtual absence of such forces." Slavery posed many problems for American blacks, but, at least for slaves living in such places as the Good Hope, Stirling, and Cedar Vale communities, the absence of "some sort of alternative force of moral and psychological orientation" was not one of them. A cumulative slave experience transmitted through closely related families of different generations was the social basis of this alternative belief system. These same slaves show that what Elkins calls "alternative social bases that might have supported alternative standards" existed among ordinary plantation slaves. The absence of such "alternative social bases"—the critical assumption in Elkins's "model"—is not what made the Afro-American slave experience distinctive. That is learned by studying the interior slave experience on places like the Stirling plantation. A real Sambo, for example, lived there. The son of Miuscuita and Chaney, he later married Frocene and became the father of six or seven children. One of his sons was named Sam.[57]

If the behavior and beliefs revealed in the diverse slave birth registers disclose a fact of single importance about plantation slaves like the Stirling husband and father Sambo, it is that little of genuine importance is learned by examining the slave as a "case study" in "social isolation." The Carolina planter David Gavin mourned the death of "old man Friday" in 1856. "He seemed," Gavin confided in his diary, "like a connecting link between me and grand-father and grand-mother . . . for he could tell me of the actings and doings of them and others of olden times." Slave grandchildren, grandnieces, and grandnephews knew men like Friday over the entire South, slaves capable of transmitting *cumulative* slave experiences and beliefs. That is what Elkins implies in responding to some critics: "The slave family . . . truncated as it was, represented a truly subversive element, a crucial factor in the underlife of the plantation." Lewis Stirling's West Feliciana neighbor, the cotton planter Bennet H. Barrow, would have agreed. He complained in his diary: "I have never been so provoked as I have been for the Last month by my House servants—my cook Hetty has not been seen since morning [—] no one has said a word to her. nothing but pure impidence [*sic*] I thought her the best negro I owned—'till she took Big Lucys son Lewis for a husband."[58]

Most slaves did not live in "social isolation." Neither did they live in the "elaborate web of paternalistic relations" that Eugene D. Genovese says allowed plantation owners to establish their "hegemony over the slaves." Genovese's several works divide into two related phases: the very detailed *Roll, Jordan, Roll: The World the Slaves Made* (1974) and the several more theoretical works that precede it. The theoretical model that informs *Roll, Jordan, Roll*, for example, is carefully outlined in *The World the Slaveholders Made*, where Genovese associates the rise of a "patriarchal and paternalistic ethos" among planters with the existence of a resident planter class and the relatively early suppression of the African slave trade. The slave trade had "necessarily militated against paternalism."

> The foundation of a patriarchal and paternalistic ethos ultimately proved to be . . . the plantation regime itself. The confrontation of master and slave, white and black, on a plantation presided over by a resident planter for whom the plantation was a home and the entire population part of his extended family generated that ethos. . . .
>
> The slave trade closed at precisely the time during which the slaveholders were undergoing a profound metamorphosis. Two tendencies had existed under the slaveholding regime and were to continue throughout its history: the patriarchalism of the plantation community, and the commercial exploitation of the world market.

The closing of the African slave trade (1808), "at the very beginning of the cotton boom and at a critical juncture in the history of American slavery," placed a premium on reproducing a native-born slave labor force, and "the raising of a creole slave force required adequate standards of humane treatment." The high rate at which the resident slave population grew convinces Genovese to write:

> Nothing so clearly demonstrates the relatively good treatment (in the strictly material sense of the word) of the slaves and the paternalistic quality of the masters. The initial motivation to provide the slaves with adequate food, shelter, clothing, and leisure was of course economic, and the economic pressures for good treatment grew stronger over time. . . . Once extended over a generation or two, the appropriate standards of behavior became internalized and part of the accepted standard of decency for the ruling class. The growth of a creole slave population narrowed the cultural gap between

the classes and races and prepared the way for those feelings
of affection and intimacy which had to exist if paternalism was
to have substance.

This analysis is repeated in *Roll, Jordan, Roll*: "The slaveholders'
vision of themselves as authoritarian fathers, who presided over
an extended and subservient family, white and black, grew up
naturally in the process of founding plantations."[59]
    Paternalist beliefs were widespread among plantation owners
on the eve of the Civil War and affected the behavior of many
planters. But no one, including Genovese, has studied how such
beliefs and the practices developed. It therefore remains unclear when in time large numbers of planters internalized such
beliefs. In examining the interaction between slaves and their
owners, it is very important to know whether common owner
beliefs and practices either changed or remained constant between
1790 and 1860. Other aspects of the consequences of paternalist
practices for slaves, however, are far less ambiguous. The suggestion, for example, that the high rate of slave reproduction is
evidence of "the paternalistic quality of the masters" is erroneous.
A high reproduction rate does not depend upon "good treatment."
A detailed scholarly literature shows that diverse populations with
very low living standards increase rapidly. No necessary connection, furthermore, exists between paternalist ideology and either
a high slave birth rate or "stable" slave marriages. High slave
reproduction rates existed decades before the closing of the African
slave trade. The study by Harry R. Merrens of Anson, Bertie,
Chowan, Orange, and New Hanover counties, North Carolina,
between 1755 and 1767, for example, indicates a rapid natural
increase in the slave population in settings where plantations did
not exist and where it was far too early in time for a paternalistic
ethos to thrive.[60] To move forward a full century and to briefly
recollect the 1866 North Carolina ex-slave marriage registers
(Chapter 1, Table 3) is to be reminded that the length of slave
marriages had no connection to the social setting in which slaves
lived. Ex-slaves in farm counties reported marriages lasting twenty
or more years in the same proportion as ex-slaves in plantation
counties. Enduring slave marriages, therefore, did not require the
presence of either a large plantation or a "paternalistic ethos."
    Planter beliefs always affected how plantation whites treated
their slaves, and Genovese's suggestion that most planters internalized the "paternalistic ethos" in the "generation or two" following
the suppression of the African slave trade is an important clue in

studying the beliefs and behavior of slaves and their owners in the
decades prior to the Civil War. His suggestion would fix that
significant moment no earlier than about 1830. The increasing
importance of paternalist ideology about that time, however, means
that the formative development of the slave family, kin group,
and enlarged community occurred before the rapid spread and
internalization of paternalist ideology in the developing plantation class. Mid-nineteenth-century slaveowners—paternalists and
nonpaternalists alike—therefore interacted with slaves who were
the product of these earlier social and cultural developments
among the slaves. These developments, not the beliefs of particular
owners, best explain the uniformities in the behavior of plantation
slaves in the 1840s and 1850s studied in this work. We have seen
the similarities in behavior among slaves living on South Carolina,
North Carolina, Virginia, Alabama, and Louisiana plantations.
But the Good Hope slaves had an owner who lived in
Philadelphia. And the Carlisle slaves were owned by a northern-
born planter who lived in Natchez. The Watson slaves belonged
to a migrant Yankee who started buying them in the 1830s. And
the Cohoon slaves were owned by a farmer who became a planter
after 1830. Only the owners of the Stirling and Bennehan-Cameron
slaves apparently were resident planters who had lived among the
blacks over a long period of time. Their presence affected the
slaves they owned in diverse ways, but the Stirling and Bennehan-
Cameron slaves shared cultural beliefs with these other plantation slaves who had very little, if any, direct contact with owners
over a long period of time. Moreover, the Bennehan-Cameron
slaves, whose owners became model paternalists, fixed upon
domestic arrangements and named children for fathers and blood
kin outside the immediate family between 1776 and 1800 when
their owner was not yet an established planter but a successful
apprentice clerk who had purchased a small parcel of slaves. It is
the behavior of these and other slaves that casts doubt on analyses
that exaggerate the role resident planters played in shaping the
slave family and the full range of social and cultural behavior
associated with it.

Failure to study the development of an adaptive Afro-
American slave culture prior to the spread of paternalist
ideology impairs the detailed description and explanation of slave
belief and behavior in *Roll, Jordan, Roll*. Slave belief and behavior are examined largely as the consequence of a static interaction between slaves and their owners. Convinced that enslavement bound the slaves to their owners "in an organic relationship

so complex and ambivalent that neither could express the simplest human feelings without reference to the other," Genovese suggests that paternalist ideology, which "defended the involuntary labor of slaves as a legitimate return to their master for protection and direction," was internalized by the slaves but transformed in its meaning. The slaves added to the "idea of reciprocal duties . . . their own doctrine of reciprocal rights." That transformation by the slaves "signalled acceptance of an imposed white domination within which they drew their own lines, asserted rights, and preserved their self-respect." A redefined paternalism became "a doctrine of self-protection," and "almost all" slaves shared in these beliefs.* It matters very much in such an explanation of the beliefs and behavior of slaves and their owners just *when* and *how* so significant a transformation occurred. That analysis is not found in *Roll, Jordan, Roll*. It is, however, suggested that "the house

---

* Evidence in *Roll, Jordan, Roll* that the typical slave viewed himself or herself as bound in an "organic" relationship with an owner—the study's essential argument—is scant. The illustrations which serve to show "the recurring idea of mutual obligations in an organic relationship," moreover, are often strained. Instances of kindness and sympathy by some ex-slaves toward their old owners, for example, are described as having "fitted within long-established paternalistic patterns" and as revealing older "organic" ties in a new setting. Genovese writes:

> The attitudes of the slaves grew out of the adjustment they had made to a paternalistic relationship, within which they had defined a role in their own way. When Uncle Osborne, a carpenter in Georgia, remained to work for wages, so that, in a variety of ways, he could take care of the distressed white family, he did not thereby display servility or reject freedom. We know as much because as soon as the worst had passed for the whites, he courteously took himself off to work for himself. . . . The freedmen of the Sea Islands, disappointed and disgruntled as they were by the dashing of their hopes for land, did not enjoy seeing old masters suffer, whether because they were old masters or because they were human beings in trouble. They offered help and even, when they could, gave them money. . . .

The particular acts of sympathy revealed by these two illustrations are not disputed. What matters is their relationship to inward slave values. We examine first the Sea Island freedmen. The evidence used comes primarily from the journalist John Dennett's account of a November 1865 visit there. Dennett met a former planter and physician, who had returned from the mainland after the war. His plantation had been sold from him; he was without funds; he hoped to start a small medical practice, but if that failed, "he supposed his son and himself could put up a cabin somewhere in the vicinity, and get fish and oysters enough to live on." Dennett learned that he planned to return to the mainland for his family, adding, "The gentleman, it is currently reported, has made several visits to the plantation which he formerly owned, and the Negroes living there have collected for his use nearly one hundred dollars." A significant amount of money, the cash had been collected for Dr. Clarence Fripp, a very unusual planter. Two years earlier, a northerner among the Sea Islanders reported that "all" the ex-slaves "speak with great affection of Fripp." The ex-slave Pompey explained one reason why. He had learned from mainland slaves that "two or three of the old proprietors here [the Sea Islands] . . . are now in jail for trying to escape, among them Dr. Clarence Fripp." Fripp had wanted to remain on the islands when the

servants, mechanics, free Negroes, even to a lesser extent the drivers, paced the black community's absorption of Euro-American culture, for they lived intimately with the whites at the same time as they remained attached to their own people." They "led the transformation of Africans" into Afro-Americans. When the "doctrine of self-protection" emerged among "almost all" slaves remains unstudied. But it could not have taken place before the plantation class itself had internalized paternalist ideology. Since that apparently happened "a generation or two" after the closing of the overseas slave trade, it would mean that the slaves transformed paternalist ideology no earlier than the years between the Mexican War and the Civil War. It would have happened when the interregional slave trade was at its height, when old resident owners were scrutinizing day-to-day slave behavior more closely than ever before, when absentee slave ownership was increasing,

---

Union Army invaded them. "He never wanted to go," the northerner learned, "but was carried off by his brothers." Fripp was hardly typical of Sea Island planters, and the behavior of his ex-slaves toward him is testimony of that fact, nothing more.

Dennett reported two other instances in which ex-slaves bestowed small favors upon ex-owners. The owners themselves first asked for such help. Neither instance revealed the generosity shown by Fripp's old slaves. Dennett did not interpret such behavior as revealing deep ("organic") attachments by the former slaves to their old owners:

> Most of the Negroes, I should say, are surprisingly free from a vulgar contempt for these men merely because of their sudden poverty and the shifts and strains to which they see them reduced, and some appear to feel genuine commiseration for them in their distress. But their kindly feeling toward them extends no further than this, and it is, perhaps, remarkable that it should extend so far, for evidently they fear and dislike the slaveholders, both as a class and individually. The probable return of the former owners to the island, the possibility that they may sometimes be compelled to work for them and be governed by them, seem to excite the liveliest apprehensions and very strong expressions of hostility.

The moment these ex-slaves revealed such kindness caused the Yankee schoolteacher Laura Towne to share Dennett's assessment and to attribute it to fear: "The people receive the rebels better than we expected, but the reason is that they believe that [President Andrew] Johnson is going to put them in their old masters' hands again, and they feel they must conciliate or be crushed."

The ex-slave carpenter Uncle Osborne poses different analytic problems than Clarence Fripp's former slaves. One of about two hundred slaves who belonged to the Georgia plantation family of Eliza Francis Andrews, he quit his owner sometime in June 1865. (By mid-August, all but five Andrews slaves had left their old owner.) Before then and at a moment when the Andrews family briefly suffered for essential necessities, Osborne, according to Eliza Andrews, "takes his wages in whatever provisions we need most, and hands them to father when he comes home at night. . . . Father says that except [for] Big Henry and Long Dick and old Uncle Jacob, he is the most valued negro he ever owned." When Osborne departed, the young woman wrote: "He, too, has taken freedom now, but he is not to blame for that. He stood by us when we most needed him, and now he has a right to look out for himself." The same diary entry also detailed the departure of "old Uncle Lewis":

> He is an old gray-haired darkey who has done nothing for years but live

and when antislavery agitation increased and helped divide the nation's political parties. Some slaves everywhere and at all times sought protection by identifying their interests with those of their owners, but the larger economic, social, and political processes that followed the Mexican War were not conducive to the widespread internalization and transformation of paternalist ideology.[61]

Roll, Jordan, Roll does not detail how and when large numbers ("almost all") of Afro-American slaves internalized and transformed paternalist ideology, but its author offers a very forceful ahistorical explanation of *why* that happened. "Accepting a paternalistic ethos and legitimizing class rule" was the necessary price slaves paid for their survival. No alternative existed.

> Unable to challenge the system as such—unable to resist frontally except on desperate occasions and then with little hope of success—they accepted what could not be avoided. In its positive aspect, this accommodation represented a commitment, shared by most peoples, however oppressed, to the belief that a harsh and unjust social order is preferable to the insecurities of no order at all.

And elsewhere:

> Only those who romanticize—and therefore do not respect—the laboring classes would fail to understand their deep com-

---

at his ease, petted and coddled and believed in by the whole family. The children called him, not "Uncle Lewis," but simply "Uncle," as if he had really been kin to them. Uncle Alex had such faith in him that during his last illness he would send for the old darkey to talk and pray with him. . . . A special place was always reserved for him at family prayer, which Uncle Alex was very particular that all the servants should attend, and "brother Lewis" was often called on to lead the devotions. I . . . was brought up with as firm a belief in him as in the Bible itself. He was an honored institution of the town. . . . But now see the debasing effects of the new *régime* in destroying all that was most good and beautiful in these simple-hearted folk. Uncle Lewis, the pious, the honored, the venerated, gets his poor old head turned with false notions of freedom and independence, runs off to the Yankees with a pack of lies against his mistress, and sets up a claim to part of her land!

Lewis and Osborne are not contrasted to suggest either that one was more common than the other or that slaves and ex-slaves indicated great variability in their behavior. Instead, Lewis's behavior before and after the emancipation tells us why it is so difficult to infer inward *slave* beliefs from isolated instances of outward slave and ex-slave behavior toward owners and ex-owners. That does not mean that Eliza Andrews had misinterpreted Osborne's kindness toward her family. But in itself Osborne's behavior is not evidence of "the recurring idea of mutual obligations in an organic relationship." Lewis, incidentally, was Osborne's father. (Genovese, *Roll, Jordan, Roll*, 132–33; John Dennett, *The South As It Is, 1865–1866* [1965], 198–200; E. W. Pearson, ed., *Letters from Port Royal* [1906], 207; Rose, *Rehearsal for Reconstruction* [1964], 346–49; Eliza Francis Andrews, *War-Time Journal of a Georgia Girl* [1908], 286–87, 318–23.)

mitment to "law and order." Life is difficult enough, without added uncertainty and "confusion." Even an oppressive and unjust order is better than none.*

* This assertion rests on admissible evidence, a letter written by a Yankee woman in 1863. Convinced that "a genuinely aristocratic ethos . . . emerged among the slaves," Genovese writes: "Implicit in this demand [by the slaves] for doing things properly lay an insistence upon order. The freedmen, wrote Harriet Ware, a northern abolitionist from the Sea Islands in 1863, 'hate all change and confusion.'" Ware's observation is accurately reported, but it had no relationship at all to "an insistence upon order" by the slaves. She was dealing with the confusion among Sea Islanders that resulted from changed federal policies concerning land use and landownership. The date of the letter (November 15, 1863) is very important in judging its meaning, and the full text is printed below:

> The people are quite disturbed about General Saxton's new order, which Mr. French and Judge Smith have been trying to explain to them at church; in vain, apparently,—for some of the most ignorant of our people thought they should be obliged to buy land, and came to C. in distress at leaving the plantation. Others we hear are selecting their lots, but now comes General Gillmore's order to stop all sales; I am afraid these poor people, who hate all change and "confusion," will have their brains hopelessly confused.

Some confiscated land had been put aside in March 1863 and, prior to Gillmore's intervention, was to be disposed of by auction sales in lots of 320 acres. This and other provisions convinced many Sea Island blacks that landownership would be denied them. Other evidence describing Sea Island black behavior before and after November 1863 allows us to assess the accuracy of Ware's *judgment*. In the winter and spring of 1862, for example, Sea Island blacks had refused to grow cotton, broken cotton gins, hidden the iron pieces essential to repairing the gins, agreed to grow cotton but planted corn between the cotton rows, and then refused to pay the military rent on the land where corn grew. A dispute over paying rent in kind (the "corn-tax") for their private patches continued into the fall of 1863 and led some Yankee supervisors to advise that force be used to collect the corn. Such behavior does not conform to "an insistence upon order" or a fear of "change." The ex-slaves, however, had good reason to fear certain changes imposed by the federal authorities. In April of that same year, for example, Yankee soldiers had forcibly drafted Sea Islanders into the Union Army. Some reluctant "recruits" were killed. "Hamlet's wife Betsey," Harriet Ware then wrote, "came to buy salt, said her husband was carried off the other night and she left with ten children and a 'heart most broke, shan't live long, no way, oh, my Jesus!'" That change was hated; other changes were received with enthusiasm. In late December 1863, the Washington authorities ordered a survey of 60,000 acres of land into 20- and 40-acre tracts to be sold to Sea Island family heads for no less than $1.25 an acre. "Everybody is astir," remarked a Yankee observer, "trying to stake out claims and get their claims considered by the Commissioners." According to the historian Willie Lee Rose, the commissioners were "literally swamped" with pre-emption claims from all over the Islands. The December edict was later reversed. Some Sea Island blacks, finally, behaved in ways meant to provoke changes. On February 9, 1864, for example, Harriet Ware worriedly wrote:

> The women came up in a body to complain to Mr. Philbrick about their pay,—a thing that has never happened before and shows the influence of very injudicious outside talk, which has poisoned their minds against their truest friends. The best people were among them, and old Grace chief spokeswoman.

"I don't see what is to be the end of it all," the Yankee woman feared, "but at this rate they will soon be spoiled for any habit of industry." (Genovese, *Roll, Jordan, Roll*, 114–15; Laura Towne, *Letters and Diaries, 1862–1884*, ed. Holland [1910], 16–17, 20–21; E. W. Pearson, ed., *Letters from Port Royal, 1862–1868* [1906], 184–87, 222–23, 230, 236–37, 248, 250; Jane and William Pease, *Black Utopias* [1963], 134, 143, 149–50; Willie Lee Rose, *Rehearsal for Reconstruction* [1964], 272–96.)

These assertions, and especially the insistence that the alternative to accepting paternalist ideology was either disorder or "no order at all," follow from a failure to examine the long and painful process by which Africans became Afro-Americans, a process that included the development of slave standards and rules of conduct. Enslavement severely narrowed the range of choices available to Africans and early generations of Afro-American slaves, but the imposition of such severe constraints was not synonymous with "disorder."[62]*

An adaptive culture does not develop among the slaves in *Roll, Jordan, Roll.* Instead, "slave culture" itself is made dependent upon the "paternalistic compromise." Rather than shaping the relationship between slaves and their owners, the "culture" is "caused" by the relationship:

> [T]he "happiness" of the slaves could never have arisen from an acceptance of slavery. At best, it had to arise as a function of the living space created by the paternalistic compromise forced on them. That living space meant the possibility of an autonomous spiritual life. . . . Master and slave had both "agreed" on the paternalistic basis of their relationship, the one from reasons of self-aggrandizement and the other from a lack of an alternative.

But the "living space" within which slaves—individually and collectively—asserted their identity and acted upon their beliefs existed before any "paternalistic compromise" could have occurred.† Adaptive cultures do not originate as the consequence of bargains, and autonomous slave naming-practices and marital rules did not depend upon any such compromise. Much in the behavior of slaves was affected and even determined by their regular interaction with owners and other whites, but these and other choices had their origins within the slave experience. Robert

* These formulations are difficult to reconcile with Genovese's penetrating discussion of slave religion. Although I remain unconvinced by his description of slave conceptions of "sin," and doubt that slave Christianity lacked an important millennial strain, his is the most able discussion of this subject to date. "The religion of the slaves," he writes, "manifested many African 'traits' and exhibited greater continuity with African ideas than has generally been appreciated" (*Roll, Jordan, Roll*, 162). Much evidence sustains this argument, but for "continuity" to exist an explanatory "model" is needed that takes into account the passage of time and that allows for the development of slave institutions to sustain such beliefs and pass them along from generation to generation.

† In his review of *Time on the Cross*, Genovese says that although this study "hardly discusses black culture and initiative at all . . . it does make the useful contribution of showing how the living space for such a culture and initiative was created." See Gutman, *Slavery and the Numbers Game*, 165–71.

L. Dabney, a member of a prominent Virginia plantation family and deeply paternalist in his beliefs, explained that slavery "is not an ownership of the servant's moral personality, soul, religious destinies, or conscience; but a property in his involuntary labor. And this right to his labor implies just as much control over his person as enables his master to possess his labor." Developing intra- and intergenerational kin networks and the quasi-kin communal ties that flowed from them helped fill the "space" that Dabney said was left to the slaves. That does not mean that slaves were unaffected by the beliefs and practices of their owners. But it does mean that the alternative to a "paternalistic compromise" was neither disorder nor "no order."[63]

The emphasis on the "paternalistic compromise" as the essential clue to understanding slave belief and behavior also impairs the usefulness of the many details on the slave family that fill many pages of *Roll, Jordan, Roll*. Much is made—and with good reason—of the fact that slaves often distinguished between "good" and "bad" masters (or "treatment"):

> Conditions and experiences varied enormously, but the important question concerns the standards the slaves applied: What did they expect? or, What did they feel they had to settle for? . . . The slaves disagreed about what constituted a good master but did agree on a minimum. . . . A master who used his whip too often or with too much vigor risked their hatred. Masters who failed to respect family sensibilities or who separated husbands from wives could be sure of it. The slaves grieved over the sale of their children but accepted it as a fact of life; however much they suffered, they did not necessarily hate their individual masters for it. But a husband and wife who cared for each other could never accept being parted. . . .
>
> These varied responses reveal both an act of judgment, which in itself carries significance, and an acceptance of the state of things, not as a preference but as a realistic adjustment to a given world. From this very act of qualified acquiescence, the slaves moved to create as much living space as possible. Their acceptance of paternalism allowed them, even in so unjust a relationship, to perceive that they had rights, which the whites could trample upon only by committing a specific act of injustice. The practical question facing the slaves was not whether slavery itself was an improper relation but how to survive it with the greatest degree of self-determination.

Slaves everywhere developed standards by which they judged the behavior of individual owners.[64]

Roll, Jordan, Roll contains convincing evidence that slaves knew the difference between "good" and "bad" owners. Three (not one) distinct but related questions are involved in assessing the significance of such slave distinctions. The first and most important concerns the origins of those standards by which slaves judged the behavior of their owners. The second relates to the treatment of slaves by their owners, and the third to the ways in which slaves perceived and judged such treatment. (A fourth question involves explaining how slaves behaved, but that answer also requires study of the constraints shaping slave behavior. In itself, behavior is not evidence of perception and judgment.) We focus only on the slave family. Genovese's insistence that "many slaveowners went to impressive lengths to keep slave families together," that "the more paternalistic masters betrayed evidence of considerable emotional strain" when faced with sale, and that "an impressive number of slaveowners took losses they could ill afford to keep families together" is not disputed. Such owners existed. But neither their presence nor the assertions that "planters did everything possible to encourage the slaves to live together in stable units" and that "the impressive econometric work by Robert Fogel and Stanley Engerman suggests that separations occurred less frequently than has generally been believed" are substitutes for sustained analysis of how local and interregional sale, involuntary migration with an owner, gift-transfer, and estate division affected the immediate slave family and enlarged slave kin group. Such an analysis is not found in Roll, Jordan, Roll and is its most severe empirical shortcoming. It is not a marginal deficiency. It is as if the impact of the British industrial revolution on the working-class family were studied without reference to child labor in the mines and factories. Analysis of the frequency and character of involuntary slave family dissolution (especially in the years between 1830 and the Civil War) is the essential underpinning for studying how slaves perceived their owners. The best available evidence—that reported by Mississippi and northern Louisiana ex-slaves and discussed in Chapters 1 and 4—discloses that about one in six (or seven) slave marriages were ended by force or sale, a proportion sufficiently high to show that the "paternalistic compromise" was violated frequently enough by slaveowners to corrode any such "compromise" at its core.[65]

No evidence in Roll, Jordan, Roll—or anywhere else for that

matter—discloses that slave parents accepted the sale of their children, whatever their age, as "a fact of life." That statement may reconcile the "organic" relationship between slaves and owners to the fact of frequent sale, but it does so by confusing the realistic expectations of slave parents about owner behavior with slave moral and social beliefs. Most slave sales apart from estate divisions and bankruptcies involved teen-agers and young adults. That was known to most slaves. Sale nearly always, but especially after 1815 and as a consequence of the interregional movement of slaves from the Upper to the Lower South, separated such persons from immediate families and enlarged kin groups. But if the social system sanctioned such sale as essential to the transfer of labor from the Upper to the Lower South and from the inefficient to the efficient owner, it does not follow that the slaves accepted that "norm" as "a fact of life." It is inconceivable that the sale of a slave child or teen-ager named for its grand-parent or another close relation caused its parents and other kin to "grieve" the loss but to accept it as "a fact of life" and not "hate" the owner who had made such decisions. It is far more likely that slave parents and older kin accommodated their behavior, not their beliefs, to the expectation that a child might be sold. That expectation might cause a slave parent to work harder or to in-gratiate himself or herself with an owner or an overseer. The same expectation probably served as reason to socialize one's children to prepare for possible sale, a damaging and unenviable task for any parent. Whether sale occurred later in life is beside the point. Parents and other kin forced into such difficult relationships with slave children had very good reason to "hate" those who had imposed that circumstance upon them. "Good" masters hesitated making such sales; "bad" masters did not; all masters poisoned the relationship between slave parents and their children.

"The strongest," Jean-Jacques Rousseau observed, "is never strong enough to be always the master, unless he transforms strength into right, and obedience into duty." Slaves often com-promised with their owners. Compromise was a necessary and realistic strategy for survival. But the frequent compromises slaves had to make are not in themselves evidence that the slaves viewed themselves as bound in an "organic" relationship with their owners. Nor are they evidence that the slaves had internalized their rulers' "hegemony." "Organic" relationships do not exist; at best, they develop over time. So does the transformation of power into authority. But the core slave experience was not rooted in a "traditional" society; it lasted four, or perhaps five, generations for most groups of slaves. Slave naming-practices over that time—naming children for members of a family of origin and retaining old slave surnames—did not weaken the power of slaveowners. Such practices, indeed, went unobserved among them. "Cultural forms," however, as Sidney W. Mintz writes, "confirm, reinforce, maintain, change, or deny particular arrangements of status, power, and identity." Such slave naming-practices are authentic evidence that slaveowners did not, as Genovese suggests, "command" the slave "culture." They are one way in which slave cultural beliefs denied status arrangements associated with ownership and confirmed concepts of authority rooted within the slave experience.[66]

Whether slaveowners successfully transformed obedience into duty among slaves is an empirical question answered by studying slave behavior. Naming practices among slaves are one important part of such study. So is the behavior revealed by slaves and ex-slaves during and just after the Civil War. Genovese splendidly characterizes that time as "a terrible moment of truth" for slaveowners:

> The masters had expected more than obedience from their slaves; they had expected faithfulness—obedience internalized as duty, respect, and love. They had little choice, for anything else would have meant a self-image as exploitative brutes. This insistence on the slaves' constituting part of the family and these expressions of belief in their loyalty lay at the heart of the masters' world-view.

That time was also a "moment of truth" for the slaves, testing their contrasting loyalties to owners and kin. Few groups of slaves offer a fuller and fairer "test" than those who belonged to the family of Charles Colcock Jones in Liberty County, Georgia. Jones sold some slaves,* but in the main, as Genovese writes, his family "had always concerned itself, according to its own understanding, with the material and spiritual welfare of the slaves" and "fought desperately to preserve its sense of Christian love and obligation."[67]

The letters that passed between members of the Jones family during and just after the Civil War decisively show that even the most benevolent among plantation families had not converted slave duty into slave obligation. Kin obligation proved far more

---

* Letters written by slaves sold by the Jones family appear on pages 36, 103.

powerful.* The Joneses owned 129 slaves in 1860, and they labored on three rice plantations (the Maybank, Montevideo, and Arcadia) along the Georgia coast south of Savannah. Charles Jones died in 1863, but his wife, Mary Jones, and their adult children struggled to maintain as much as they could of their antebellum social world. Their failure resulted partly from the decisions made by their slaves. "With their emancipation must come their extermination," Mary Jones predicted a few weeks after the Union Army captured the Georgia coast; "all history, from their very first existence, proves them incapable of self-government." Slaves whose fidelity had been unquestioned began drifting away in January 1865. The nurse Susan went off to the Union Army, informing the Yankees that her child's father was Mary Jones's soldier son. Susan's husband Mac accompanied her. Porter and his wife Patience quit then, too. Two weeks later, the servant Kate left, "influenced, as we believe, by her father." When Mary Jones quit her plantation in April 1865, twelve servants went with her. She returned that summer, but then only Sue, Flora, and Milton composed her household. Porter and Patience returned but decided to "provide for themselves." Flora quit, telling Mary Jones she "wished to leave for Savannah . . . to meet Joe." Flora promised to return, got some money from the white woman, and never came back. "My heart is pained and sickened by their vileness and falsehood in every way," said Mary Jones; "I am going to be delivered from

---

* If the letters written by members of the Jones family are typical, the behavior of the Jones slaves after the emancipation cannot be attributed to the presence of the Union Army. In July 1865, John Jones reported to his sister that after "insubordination" began to "crop up" among Liberty County blacks, Yankee soldiers intervened and "whipped every negro man reported to them, and in some cases unmercifully." A few were punished by "suspending [them] by the thumbs."

> The effect has been a remarkable quietude and order in all the region. The negroes are astounded at the idea of being whipped by Yankees. (But keep all this a secret, lest we should be deprived of their services. I have not called on them yet, but may have to do so.)

A month later, federal soldiers again used "the strap and sometimes a leather trace" to restore order "generally" among Liberty County ex-slaves. John Jones then described "an evident restiveness generally throughout this region." Two of his ex-slaves "openly rebelled in the field" against their overseer. Several others quit his place and filed a complaint with the Union Army against a foreman who "somewhat bruised" a sixteen-year-old black girl with a strap. She "had been corrected for being out most of Saturday night previously." The Yankee soldiers sent them back to their former owner. The following spring, John Jones's sister disputed with her former slaves over a contract. Blacks who complained to a local Freedmen's Bureau officer were advised to return to work. They were given two other alternatives: to be put "into irons" or to work the Savannah streets "with a ball-and-chain." (*The Children of Pride*, ed. R. M. Myers [1972], 1281–83, 1291–93, 1340–42.)

the race. . . . They are perfectly deluded—will not contract or enter into any engagement for another year, and will not work now except as it pleases them." Before the year ended, the house servant Sue also left. A few years earlier, it had been Sue who said when Charles Jones died that "our dear master has not left any of us poor; he has given us all property to live off until the Blessed Saviour calls us home." When the Union Army occupied the Jones plantation, Sue had described her dead owner's "goodness to his people" to the Yankees. She had hidden potatoes from the troops to feed the white plantation children. Her husband Sam came from Savannah for her in 1865 to take her to a farm. Mary Jones reminded Sue of Sam's past "want of fidelity to her," but she "decided to go." The pained mistress reported their conversation:

> I told her if so, I preferred she go at once; whereupon she withdrew Elizabeth [her child?] in the midst of the last rice-cutting. . . . I told Sue if she was ever in want or ill-treated, she must return to me. She replied: "No ma'am, I'll never come back, for you told me to go," thus in a saucy way perverting my remarks. . . . Although Sue has been disrespectful to me and shown a very perverse spirit, I do remember all her former fidelity; and I am truly sorry for her, for I believe she will feel the loss of her comfortable home.

Months later, Mary Jones complained that "no one has done more to keep the servants away than Sue."

Not much improved for Mary Jones in 1866. Elsie waited on her "until her mother influenced her to leave." Three house servants (Kate, Milton, and Gilbert) were with her on January first. Later that year, Tenah and Niger returned to remain for many years. But in the spring, Mary Jones's son could not convince most of the family's former slaves to labor for the widowed woman:

> I called up [on] all the negroes at Indianola, and the only ones who expressed a willingness to go to Montevideo were: Clarissa and her children (May, Chloe, John, and Jane), Sam and his wife, Big Miley and her girls, Phillis and Lucy, and Silvia and her husband (Billy). All the rest say they are going they do not know where exactly, but nearly all decide upon a return to Liberty. The women are the controlling spirits. Stephney and Pharaoh are very desirous of going to Arcadia, there to work upon any terms imposed. . . . Little John has been . . .

working on his own account upon the adjoining plantations. He says he is going with his father to Liberty, and his father expects to return to White Oaks with Martha and the rest of the children, William, Kate, and family expect to go to Liberty, but not to Montevideo or to Arcadia. Abram proposes the same thing. Robert and family, Niger and family, Pharaoh and family, and Hannah expect to do the same thing. Maria is going to hunt for Dick. Rose says she is going with Cato. Little Miley goes with her husband. Mary goes with her husband. Elsie and family go to Syphax. Hannah goes with Pharaoh. Peggy wishes to go with Sue. Dick and Anthony have already left the plantations. You thus have all their expectations.

William and Kate were among those who did not plan to return. In 1859, Mary Jones had arranged their Sunday morning wedding in the plantation house. The couple had different owners, and a few years later Charles Jones, Jr., had arranged for the purchase of Kate and her children to bring the family together. "William begged me very earnestly," he wrote his father, "to try and purchase his wife and children, for whom he appears to cherish a strong affection." In 1866, an embittered Charles Jones, Jr., explained to his mother about the emancipated slave: "He has always been a child in intellect—improvident, incapable of appreciating the obligations of a contract, ignorant of the operation of any law other than the will of his master, careless of the future, and without the most distant conception of the duties of life and labor now devolved upon him. . . ."

The few slaves who remained loyal to Mary Jones also asserted their independence and protected their families. The carriage driver Gilbert could not be faulted in his fidelity toward the white woman. He received gifts from her son, and Mary Jones reported, "Says he means to 'hang to you to the last.' He desires me to give you a 'tousand tanks.' " When Gilbert and the others who remained negotiated 1867 contracts with their old owner, they shaped the settlements. "Gilbert," said Mary Jones, "will stay on his own terms, but withdraws Fanny and puts Harry and Little Abram in her place and puts his son Gilbert out to a trade. Cook Kate wants to be relieved of the heavy burden of cooking for two and waiting on her husband. Lucy sighs and groans. But I presume these old damsels will remain with me for the present. I have no young ones about even to pick [cedar and live oak] chips." She also contracted with field laborers that year and said, "They dispute even the carrying out and spreading of manure, and wanted a plowman extra furnished. . . . Gilbert is very faithful and so is Charles. They are the exceptions. . . ." A proud and principled woman, Mary Jones quit her Georgia plantation in late 1867. "It is true my child," she sadly wrote her daughter, "this country is in ruins. The people are becoming poorer and poorer. I know not what is to become of them." Mary Jones had not learned what had come quickly to Mary Chesnut. "In their curious, emotional way," she said of her family's slaves in early June of 1865, "they swore devotion to us to their dying day. All the same, the moment they see an opening to better themselves, they will move on."[68]

Even the best-treated slaves (and the slaves belonging to Charles and Mary Jones were among them) had not confused duty and obligation. The behavior of the Jones ex-slaves between 1865 and 1867 shows that the controlling images that gave philosophical meaning to the facts of their ordinary lives differed in origin from the paternalistic ethos so fully acted upon by their owners. That is why a distinction between power and authority is essential in any assessment of the over-all slave system and how it functioned. That slaveowners failed to transform power into authority among the slaves did not make "revolutionaries" of the slaves. But power that is not legitimized in a social order—slave or otherwise—always tends to be either manipulative or coercive. We have returned to the "treatment question" that has dominated the writing of Afro-American slave history. If the slaveholding class successfully legitimized its power among the slaves so that slaves did little more than distinguish between "good" and "bad" masters, it follows that slavery as a social system was far less coercive than its critics maintained. But if that power had not been legitimized among the slaves, coercion and manipulation remained far more important in the day-to-day decisions that kept the system functioning.

Evidence that slaves lived in families and were enmeshed in affective enlarged kin groups is not evidence that slaves were either "badly" or "well" treated. It instead redefines the context which shaped slave belief and behavior. Whether slaves were badly or well treated depended upon the standards of treatment that existed among their owners. But their treatment also depended upon how the slaves behaved. Slave behavior, in turn, depended upon what slaves believed. A record of extensive mistreatment in the decades preceding the general emancipation would not be "proof" that there were more "bad" than "good" owners. It would instead serve as evidence that the slaves had not legitimized the power of their owners and transformed "obedience" into "duty." Owners had many reasons to encourage that transformation, and symbolic expressions of their paternalistic authority are regularly revealed in their behavior. But did nothing exist in either the developing slave culture or the everyday experience of slaves to discourage it? And did slave parents and other older kin have reason to encourage it? No evidence yet exists to show that "almost all" slave parents taught their children that "strength" was "right," and that "obedience" and "duty" were synonyms. Nor does evidence exist that slave conceptions of legitimacy and authority in the 1840s and 1850s were the outcome of a corrupt bargain "forced" upon them by their circumstance. A slave child named for its aunt or uncle or grandparent may also have been taught to obey his or her owner, but that child's duties and obligations flowed in a different direction. A slave child named for an older blood relative, moreover, is striking evidence of what E. P. Thompson characterizes in another setting as a "contest for symbolic authority." That the contestants in this particular historical setting were grossly unequal does not lessen the meaning of the contest. Their inequality, in fact, gives it far greater significance. Slave parents and other older kin and fictive kin had little reason to legitimize the power owners exercised over them and their children, and many reasons to teach their children and other young slaves how to bargain with that power. The recovery of viable slave families and enlarged kin networks in very different plantation settings casts fresh light on slave "treatment" because it casts fresh light on the slaves themselves and the institutional arrangements within their own communities that shaped their belief and behavior. Further study may yet show that the presence of kin and quasi-kin networks within slave communities over the entire South in the 1840s and the 1850s is an important reason why the slave system remained harsh and coercive.

Slaveowners varied in the treatment of their slaves. Some were paternalists. But the developing slave culture was not the mere consequence of slave treatment. That was so for many reasons. "The theory of dependence and protection," John Stuart Mill observed, "is an idealization, grounded on the character and conduct of here and there an individual." That is one reason. Mill offered another: "Long before the superior classes could be sufficiently improved to govern in the tutelary manner supposed,

the inferior classes would be too much improved to be governed."
That, in part, is what Ralph Ellison means by asking, "Can a
people . . . live and develop over 300 years by simply *reacting*?
Are American Negroes simply the creation of white men, or have
they at least helped create themselves out of what they found
around them? Men have made a way of life in caves and upon
cliffs, why can not Negroes have made a way of life upon the horns
of the white man's dilemma?"[69]

8

Taken From Us
by Force

I also remember that I once, among my several runs along the coast, happened to have aboard a whole family, man, wife, three young boys, and a girl, bought here one after another at several places; and cannot but observe here what mighty satisfaction those poor creatures expressed to be so come together again, though in bondage. For several days successively they could not forbear shedding tears of joy, and continually embracing and caressing one another; which moving me to compassion I ordered they should be better treated aboard then commonly we can afford to do it. . . .

JOHN BARBOT (1682)

Most slave communities had their start in the eighteenth century, but no aspect of Afro-American history has received so little attention as the eighteenth-century social and cultural processes by which enslaved Africans became Afro-American slaves. Except for the North Carolina Bennehan-Cameron slaves and those slaves who left with the British in 1783, systematic data on the eighteenth-century Afro-American slave have not been considered in this study. But most African slaves came to the North American mainland in the half century preceding the War for Independence, decades in which the formative development of an Afro-American culture occurred and in which slave communities assumed a distinctive character. The process that began before the English Industrial Revolution, before the closing of African slave trade, before the invention of the cotton gin, and before the forced migration of hundreds of thousands of Afro-American slaves into the Lower South shaped the behavior of slaves on the eve of the emancipation living on such diverse places as the Good Hope, the Stirling, the Cedar Vale, the Carlisle, the Watson, and the Bennehan-Cameron plantations. Slaves carried far more into the nineteenth century and into the frontier Lower South than a capacity to pick cotton and tend other crops, to labor

as domestic servants and artisans, and to reproduce the labor
force. They were the children and grandchildren of Africans
enslaved in the mainland North American colonies and forced
to adapt to the harsh realities associated with initial enslavement.
The social class they belonged to in 1860 had its origins in a social
class whose formation began before 1760. Historians have begun
to recover important aspects of that process, and none more ably
than Edmund S. Morgan in *American Slavery—American Freedom: The Ordeal of Colonial Virginia* (1975).* But it remains
largely uncharted. It is best in these pages to identify critical
elements in that process.[1]

The transformation of Africans into Afro-American slaves
occurred over more than a century preceding the War of Independence, but some moments in that long process are much more
important than others. Statistics on eighteenth-century slave imports locate one of the two most critical moments. In 1700, about
twenty-six thousand Africans and their descendants lived in the
North American colonies, seven in ten in Virginia and Maryland.
We shall return to the pioneer slave population shortly to
examine how historical demographers have begun to reinterpret
its behavior and focus first on the slave trade. Excluding imports
into Louisiana, Philip D. Curtin estimates the total trade to the
mainland North American colonies from 1700 to 1861 at about
four hundred thousand Africans. He also shows that slightly more
than half of all slaves arrived in the forty-year period between
1740 and 1780, and that three in five who came prior to 1808
were brought in those four decades. By 1740, the earlier flow of
"seasoned" Africans to the southern colonies from the West Indies
had become far less important, and afterward most came directly
from Africa. About 210,000 slaves came in these four decades.
Three times as many Africans entered the colonies between 1740
and 1780 as there were slaves living in the colonies in 1730. More
than eight times as many arrived in these same decades as had
lived in the colonies in 1700. Maryland's black population more
than doubled between 1748 and 1782, and Virginia's increased
from about 42,000 in 1743 to 259,000 in 1782.
These comparative statistics serve to locate that moment when

---

* This study was completed before the publication of Morgan's magnificent
work, one which studies servitude and slavery in ways which make all of United
States colonial history look different.

the greatest number of Africans underwent what Richard Hofstadter called a "reluctant adaptation." "To make life possible,"
the anthropologist Roger Bastide writes of New World African
slaves, "they hammered out a new cultural pattern of their own,
shaping it in response to the demands of their new environment."
That happened everywhere and meant developing standards for
perceiving, believing, evaluating, and acting—in short, ordering
new experiences that drew upon but could not replicate old
cultures. Adaptation for freshly enslaved Africans involved a
violent detachment from older cultures, and the emergence of a
new culture. Three important and related aspects of that over-all
process, among others, which affected its outcome are examined in
these pages. The first has to do with the African slaves themselves.
"The slave," C. L. R. James writes, "brought himself; he brought
with him the content of his mind, his memory. He thought in the
logic and language of his people. He recognized as socially
significant that which he had been taught to see and comprehend.
. . . He valued that which his previous life had taught him to
value; he feared that which he feared in Africa." Nevertheless,
James goes on, that same slave "was denied the right to act out the
contents of his mind and memory—and yet he had to do this.
How was this contradiction resolved? What were the new forms
created in the context of slavery?" The anthropologists Sidney W.
Mintz and Richard Price similarly suggest that "deep-level cultural
principles, assumptions, and understandings . . . shared by the
Africans in any New World colony" probably served as "a limited
but crucial resource" in the early adaptation of African slaves
and were "a catalyst in the processes by which individuals from
diverse [African] societies forged new institutions."[2]

Initial enslavement often mixed together men and women
from diverse African societies but did not blot out their consciousness of the social and cultural practices and beliefs associated with
these cultures. Awareness among African slaves of immediate
families and larger kin groups, for example, is indicated in a
document associated with the 1839 Amistad mutiny. Slaves took
over a Spanish schooner and ended in the United States. John
Barber's brief 1840 pamphlet, *A History of the Amistad Captives*,
included brief sketches of the Amistad Africans, who had been
interviewed by the former Mendi slave James Covey (*Kawweli*),
then a young British sailor in New York. All but two described
familial connections. A few, as Barber briefly summarized them,
are indicated below:

Singgbe   His mother is dead, and he lived with his father. He has a wife and three children, one son and two daughters. His son's name is *Ge-war*.

Gilabaru   He is married but has no children. . . . His uncle bought two slaves in Bandi, and gave them in payment for a debt; one of them ran away, and he was taken for him.

Burna   Has a wife and one child, a father, three sisters and brother living.

Sessi   He has three brothers, two sisters, a wife, and three children. He is a blacksmith, having learnt that trade of his brothers.

Ndamma   His father is dead, and he lived with his mother; has a brother and sister.

Kinna   His parents and grandparents were living; has four brothers and one sister.

Ngahoni   He has a wife and one child; he gave twenty clothes and one shawl for his wife.

Fakinna   His father, *Baw-nge* is chief or king. He has a wife and two children.

Burna   His father is dead, and he lived with his mother; has four sisters and two brothers. When his father died his brother married; all lived in the same house.

Kagne   [A] young girl. . . . She says her parents are living, and has four brothers and four sisters; she was put in pawn for a debt by her father which not being paid, she was sold into slavery.

There is no reason to think that the Amistad Mendi and the African slaves who peopled the British southern colonies in such large numbers between 1740 and 1780 differed in retentive capacities. "Like all rude nations," said Alex Hewitt in *An Historical Account of the Rise and Progress of the Colonies of South Carolina and Georgia*, eighteenth-century African slaves retained "a strong attachment to their native country, and to those friends and relations with whom they spent the early years of life."[3]

Hewitt made his observation in 1779, a half century after the start of a little-studied social and cultural interaction between nearly a quarter of a million African slaves and the several varieties of Anglo-American enslavement. It is in these decades of culture contact and culture change that the often bitter dispute among anthropologists and sociologists about "African survivals" belongs, but such study means examining the beliefs and behavior of African slaves and their early progeny, not collecting "survivals" (or a "heritage") among them. Scattered evidence shows that West African beliefs and practices were not entirely discarded during the harsh middle passage, at the various ports of entry, and during the initial phases of mainland enslavement. Those experiences narrowed choice but did not quickly transform diverse African social and cultural beliefs.

• Some Africans and first-generation Afro-Americans sought to establish modified West African polygamous domestic arrangements and even possibly sexual practices. In baptizing early eighteenth-century South Carolina slaves, the Anglican missionary Francis LeJau had to warn them that "The Christian Religion does not allow plurality of Wives," and in the 1740s the traveler Edward Kimber thought he detected such practices among Eastern Maryland's slaves. The demographer Russell Menard furthermore suggests that the low fertility observed among New World African women may indicate that older "attitudes toward child rearing and sexual intercourse" survived initial enslavement.

> In particular, [he writes] West African women usually nursed their children for two or three years and abstained from sexual intercourse until the infant was weaned. Such practice produces an interval between live births of three to four years, much longer than that usually found among European women in the colonies. If widely followed, this practice would severely depress the birth-rate among African-born women.[4]

• Some early eighteenth-century runaways re-created African "villages" in the North American wilderness. In 1728 and 1729 a severe caterpillar plague ruined much of the Caroline County, Virginia, crop and forage, causing deer to descend on the produce needed by settlers. They killed so many deer that hungry wolves attacked their livestock and even the settlers themselves, causing the House of Burgesses to offer a tobacco bounty for dead wolves. During that crisis, some Upper James River slaves fled to the wilderness, and, according to the historian T. E. Campbell, "formed a settlement of their own in the Valley of Virginia near the site of Lexington."

> [T]hey built a town of boughs and grass houses in the manner of the homes of their native land, and set up a tribal government under a chief, who had been a prince among his own people before slave traders brought him across the Atlantic. The fugitives had with them many farming implements which they stole from their masters. These they knew how to use, and since the region in which they settled was outside the area affected by the caterpillars their crops grew, but not for long. The whites located them and the next year military men mustered from all sections of the colony moved on their settlement, killed the chief, and returned his followers to their masters.

"Numerous" slaves were sentenced to death, and to restore "morale" among the slaves the Virginia governor freed one who had "concocted a medicine" said to "cure venereal disease." "News of this liberation," writes Campbell, "spread like wild fire among the slaves," and slaves over all of Virginia "attempted to make medicines to cure all [the] ailments known to man."[5]

• West African religious beliefs and practices also surfaced among African slaves. "Some destroy themselves through despair," said Hewitt of the South Carolina and Georgia slaves, "and from a persuasion they fondly entertain, that, after death, they will return to their beloved friends and native country." After her initial New World enslavement, the New England slave Chloe Spear "wished for *death*; supposing that when she died, she would return to her country and friends." Charles Ball, the late-eighteenth-century Maryland slave who later lived among plantation slaves further south, said that the Africans among them believed "universally" that "after death they shall return to their own country, and rejoin companions and friends," a belief "founded on their religion."[6]

Certain late-eighteenth- and early-nineteenth-century *Afro-American—not African*—social and cultural practices, moreover, indicate the fusion by Africans and their early Afro-American descendants of Anglo-American beliefs, behavior, and institutions with West African beliefs and behavior.

• The election of "governors" (or "kings") by slaves and free blacks in many New England towns and cities after about 1740 suggests such a fusion. The historian Lorenzo J. Greene found that "these 'governors' apparently did exercise considerable control over the blacks. The Negro 'government' had its 'judges,' 'sheriffs,' and 'magistrates,' and its courts probably tried trivial cases between Negroes as well as petty cases brought by masters against

their slaves. . . . The mock Negro government was in direct imitation of the master class, for Election Day with its 'lection cake'
and 'lection beer' provided the biggest holiday in colonial New
England." To Greene this practice reflected "the gradual adoption
of the masters' culture by the Negroes [and] was a subtle form
of slave control." But similar elections existed among African
slaves and their immediate descendants in places so different from
New England as Martinique, St. Lucia, Columbia, Peru, Uruguay,
and Argentina, places where the slaves could not easily "imitate"
common electoral practices. What occurred in the New England
towns, therefore, may have been the adaptation of elective practices
common in West African societies, one that assumed its particular
Yankee character because these slaves lived in New England.[7]

• A similar fusion affected the celebration of Pinkster Day (the
Christian Whitsuntide holy day drawn from the Hebrew Pente-
costal feast fifty days after the Passover) by late-eighteenth-century
blacks in New York and other Middle Atlantic colonies and states.
Albany blacks celebrated on Capitol Hill, soon renamed Pinkster
Hill, and a white remembered:

> Pinkster was a great day, or rather week, for they used to keep
> it up for a week among the darkies. The dances were the
> original Congo dances as danced in their native Africa. They
> had a chief, old King Charley. The old settlers said Charley
> was a prince in his old country. . . . Charley was dressed in
> a strange and fantastical costume; he was nearly barelegged,
> [and] wore a pompon struck on one side. . . . As a general
> thing, the music consisted of a sort of a drum, or instrument
> constructed out of a box with sheepskin heads, upon which
> old Charley did most of the beating, accompanied by singing
> some queer African air. . . .

Adam Blake, a "Guinea Man" and body servant to the "old
patroon Van Rensselaer," played a similar role, dressed in the
"costume of a British general," and had the "power of an auto-
crat." Eel-pots covered with dressed sheepskin served as musical
instruments among the Albany blacks, who sang "an African
refrain, 'Hi-a-bomba-bomba-bomba' " and danced what some called
"the Toto dance." The Albany Common Council prohibited such
"bacchanalian revels" in 1811. Similar celebrations occurred
among New York City, Brooklyn, and Long Island blacks, and in
Pennsylvania and Maryland. "Many can still remember," the
Philadelphian John Watson wrote in 1857, "when the slaves
were allowed the last days of the fairs for their jubilee, which they

employed . . . in dancing the whole afternoon in the present Washington Square, then a general burying ground. . . . In that field could be seen . . . more than one thousand of both sexes, divided into numerous little squads, dancing and singing, 'each in their own tongue,' after the customs of their several nations in Africa."

An important scene in James Fenimore Cooper's novel *Satanstoe*, set in New York City's City Hall Park during a Pinkster "frolic," involved blacks who came as far as forty miles to join resident Afro-Americans "beating banjos, singing African songs, drinking, and worst of all, laughing in a way that seemed to set their very hearts rattling within their ribs." A careful observer of social detail, Cooper explained:

> The features that distinguish a Pinkster frolic from the usual scenes at fairs, and other merry-makings . . . were of African origin. It is true that there are not now, nor were there then, many blacks among us of African birth; but the traditions and usages of their original country were so far preserved as to produce a marked difference between this festival, and one of European origin. Among other things, some were making music, by beating on skins drawn over the ends of hollow logs, while others were dancing to it, in a manner to show that they felt infinite delight. This, in particular, was said to be a usage of their African progenitors.[8]

Such evidence begins to uncover a large social process by which African slaves became Afro-Americans and by which eighteenth-century American slave communities emerged, each the product of distinctive economic, social, and demographic variables. Eighteenth-century South Carolina lowland African slaves, as Peter Wood has brilliantly shown, became Afro-Americans in a quite different setting than eighteenth-century Chesapeake Virginia and Maryland African slaves, but the anthropologists Sidney W. Mintz and Richard Price outline a process that affected all slaves:

> Once effective slave institutions became operative among a miscellaneous aggregate of slaves that aggregate, in turn, would begin to become a community. Thereupon the more diverse or disruptive aspects of life could begin to work themselves out against an existing structure of behavior patterns, as happens in any social system.

These developing Afro-American behavior patterns were reinforced by the development of Afro-American slave institutions
that "took on their characteristic shape *within* the parameters of
the master's monopoly of power, but *separate* from the master's
institutions," and the emergence of such communities defined the
moment when Africans can be described as Afro-Americans. It is
in such developing slave communities that we find the *Afro-
American* sources of the beliefs and behavior revealed much later
by the slaves living on such plantations as Good Hope, Bennehan-
Cameron, Cedar Vale, and Stirling.[9]

The social and cultural settings within which the initially
enslaved and their immediate descendants lived also shaped their
beliefs and behavior. We shift, then, to a second aspect of the
large social process by which African slaves became Afro-American
slaves. Ralph Ellison explains why the study of Afro-American
culture cannot ignore "the intricate network of connections which
binds Negroes to the larger society": "To do so is to attempt
delicate brain surgery with a switch-blade." A "viable theory of
Negro American culture obligates us to fashion a more adequate
theory of American culture as a whole. The heel bone is, after
all, connected, through its various linkages to the head bone."
"Neither social context nor cultural traditions alone," the anthropologists Mintz and Price correctly insist, "can explain an
Afro-American institutional form." A misreading of "social context" leads to as much error as does the neglect of "cultural
traditions." Few errors have done as much damage to understanding the development of Afro-American culture than the frequent
"reading back" of white plantation beliefs and behavior after
1830 into the earlier period of intensive enslavement prior to
1770, because the early development of Afro-American culture
involved far more than the adaptation of African beliefs and
behavior to enslavement. The African slave learned much about
New World cultures from those who first owned him, and the
significant culture change that occurred between 1740 and 1780
has been obscured because so much of that interaction has been
encased in snug and static ahistorical opposites such as "slave" and
"planter" or "black" and "white."[10]

Between 1740 and 1780, a relatively brief period of time,
vast numbers of African slaves entered into a developing Anglo-
American colonial slave society. The slave social class took its formative shape in those decades when so many African men and women

encountered the mainstream cultural beliefs and practices of their owners and other whites. Far too much attention has centered on the interaction between such new slaves and tiny successfully established colonial plantation elites, and altogether too little on the daily contact and cultural interaction between African slaves and owners who either did not become planters or who became planters over time. The historian Aubrey C. Land splendidly characterizes the Virginia and Maryland social order that was the place of initial settlement and culture contact for so many freshly imported Africans. Land advises that the "usual stereotypes of gracious gentlemen, cultured ladies, Negro family retainers, great houses, lavish hospitality, and the like" be put aside:

> Families like these do appear in the planting colonies. But they are hardly typical of the whole social order. Possibly they constituted as many as one twentieth of the families in the tidewater by the decade before the War for American Independence. Statistics plainly tell the story of a population composed mainly of smaller producers, thousands upon thousands who over the decades of our colonial dependence lived their allotted spans and disappeared from the scene leaving hardly a trace: no monumental houses, no archives of family letters upon which historians of later years could draw for illustrations, no proud descendants who revered the memory of great-grandfather so-and-so. . . .
>
> These small fry, then, are the typical planters of the southern colonies. . . . By any standards their lives were drab. Their houses more nearly resembled shacks than the mansions of tradition, and almost all of them disappeared. Their stocks of worldly goods comprised the bare essentials of daily living. . . . Most were literate, without being lettered. The produce of their small plantations included meat, grain, and vegetables for subsistence and tobacco, rice or other staples that could be sold for cash. Even their plantations hardly extended beyond the dimensions of a small farm. Probably the portion of the population falling into this lowest category could be set at one half to two thirds. The total assets of families in this bracket amounted to less than £100.
>
> Above them were other planting families, somewhat better off in worldly goods, education, and manner. The most obvious distinction of these families was their property, which ranged from estates of £100 up to £1,000. Neither poor nor rich, they were families of substance. . . .
>
> Finally, at the top of the scale, the grandees of legend pos-

sessed the great estates in slaves, land, houses, and luxuries. Some of them, a very few, counted their worth in tens of thousands of pounds.

The "head bone" was not as distant from the "heel bone" in 1760 as it was to become by 1860.[11]

That is also made clear by examining white immigration into the southern colonies prior to 1770. On the eve of the War for Independence and at the height of the direct African slave trade, nearly half of the white population south of New England had non-English origins. Large numbers of eighteenth-century white immigrants, moreover, had come as either voluntary or involuntary bound servants. The historian Richard B. Morris suggests that the common estimate that "nearly half of the total white immigration to the thirteen colonies came as bound servants" must be "considered very conservative." Africans fresh to North American enslavement had contact with such people and, more important, were enslaved by them and their immediate descendants as well as by men of more established wealth. The African slave who interacted with such people encountered a New World culture which differed from that of the established colonial elites, and how such Africans became Afro-Americans requires study of the New World transformation of what the anthropologist Conrad Arensberg calls "the culture and sub-culture of the North European pre-industrial and post-medieval class systems and village and family customs." Nearly as much, in fact, needs to be learned about those whites who enslaved Africans between 1740 and 1780 as about the African slaves themselves.[12]

Hardly anything is yet known about the early interactions between native Africans and their first owners. Evidence is available from just a single county. In Caroline County (the Virginia county with the largest slave population), Gerald Mullin finds that the wealthiest families failed to register a single newly acquired African with the county court after 1732. Mostly small slaveholders purchased Africans:

The only wealthy families that purchased Africans were those who had numerous sons and many new homesteads. Thus, in addition to small planters, the chief registrants of young and taxable Africans were tavernkeepers, sailors, horse traders, small-time speculators, and such minor officeholders as constables and road supervisors.

What an African learned about slavery and *about New World culture* differed greatly if that African first had prolonged contact with a wealthy Caroline plantation family like the Beverleys, a small planter, a sailor, or a horse trader. Teasingly suggestive, so scant a record is hardly sufficient to indicate the culture contacts involving the two hundred thousand Africans who became enslaved North American blacks between 1740 and 1780.[13] Although the changing patterns of slave ownership during these decades remain unstudied, the 1790 federal census suggests that in earlier decades Africans in significant numbers had been owned by whites of small means. All but about forty thousand of six hundred thousand slaves lived in the southern states. Most South Carolina slaves (about two in three) were owned in units of twenty or more slaves, but most slaves in 1790 did not live in South Carolina. Four in five lived either in Virginia, Maryland, or North Carolina, and in those states one in three was owned in units of less than ten and another three in ten in units ranging in size from ten to nineteen. It is hardly possible that greater percentages of slaves were owned in large units between 1740 and 1780 than in 1790. Scattered lists of tithable slaves (taxable slaves aged sixteen and older) for some Virginia counties in the 1740s and the 1750s suggest some earlier ownership patterns. About seven in ten Amelia County owners held eight or fewer slaves in the late 1740s. Nearly half of Lancaster County (1745) and two-thirds of Norfolk County (1751) tithable slaves were owned in units of five or less. (Two-thirds of Lancaster and more than four-fifths of Norfolk tithable slaves belonged to owners who held fewer than eleven tithable slaves.) How typical these ownership patterns were remains unknown, but their apparent frequency makes it very appropriate to examine the cultural exchanges and borrowings between African slaves and owners who held fewer than five or even ten slaves. No historian has yet studied the domestic arrangements and other social practices and beliefs among such owners to reveal if they were similar to or differed from those of the tiny plantation elites.

That different class practices existed is suggested in the complaint by established residents to the South Carolina authorities about the absence of adequate governing institutions in that colony's backcountry settlements. "Irregular" marriages among *whites* greatly worried them. The "Common People," complained the petitioners, "hardly know the first Principles of Religion; And so Corrupt are their Morals that a reformation of Manners among them in *our* Time is more to be wish'd for than expected":

Thro' want of Churches & Ministers, many Persons go into the
North Province, there to be Married by Magistrates. . . .
And this, without any previous publication of Banns or any
Sett Form, but each after his own Fancy, which occasions much
Confusion, as they ask no Questions, but couple persons of all
Ages, & ev'ry Complexion, to the Ruin, & Grief of many
families. . . .

From these irregular Practices, the sacred Bond of Marriage
is so greatly slighted, as to be productive of many Great and
innumerable Evils. For many loose Wretches are fond of such
Marriages; On Supposition that they are only *Temporary*, or
Durante Placito: Dissoluble, whenever their Interests or Passions incite them to Separate. Thus they live *Ad Libitum*:
quitting each other at Pleasure, Inter-Marrying Year after
Year with others; Changing from Hand to Hand as they remove from Place to Place, & swapping away their Wives and
Children, as they would Horses or Cattle. Great Scandal arises
herefrom to the Back Country, & Loss to the Community; For
the Issue of such are too often expos'd deserted & disowned:
Beggers are hereby multiplied—Concubinage established (as
it were) *by Law*: The most sacred Obligations are hereby
trampled on, and Bastardy, Adultery, & other heinous Vices
become so Common, so openly practic'd & avow'd as to lose
the Stigma annex'd to their Commission: These are some of
the Main Roots from whence the reigning Gangs of Horse
Thieves have sprung from.

"Whoredom & Adultery overspreads our land," emphasized the
same petitioners.[14] So harsh an indictment need not be accepted
as an accurate description of lower-class rural South Carolinian
white culture to learn that the African slave came into contact with
whites who had very diverse cultural beliefs. The African slave
was not the only new South Carolina settler without a "conventional" marriage ritual.

We may yet learn that between 1740 and 1780 significant
numbers of Africans adapted to their new circumstances and
learned about "conventional" New World social practices and
beliefs from owning (and other) whites whose immediate social
origins had their roots in nonelite northern European and southern white lower- and middle-class cultures. Beliefs and practices
common among mid-nineteenth-century slaves may have involved
a process of initial social class formation more than a century
earlier that included cultural exchanges between Africans and
southern white immigrants who had been (or were the immediate

descendants of) North European passengers on ships captained by "white Guineamen."[15]

A third group—neither the African slaves nor the slave-owners—played an important role in the transformation of the African into the Afro-American between 1740 and 1780. These were the Afro-Americans already settled in the colonies by 1740.

Few more significant differences distinguished eighteenth-century mainland North American slave behavior from that of slaves in other New World settings than the early natural increase in the *native* North American slave population. Between 1700 and 1780, the mainland North American slave population increased from about twenty-six thousand to slightly more than half a million persons. African slave imports partly explained that growth, but the resident slave population itself increased over the century, its decennial rates of increase ranging from 16 to 18 percent. Describing the characteristic pattern in the British sugar islands with their "intense exploitation of the land, high ratios of African-born to total slave population, and high ratios of men to women," Philip Curtin writes:

> These conditions, which were common to all regions of sugar cultivation, tended to produce an excess of deaths over births among the slave population. This net natural decrease . . . was normally balanced by continuous slave imports from Africa. This in turn caused the situation to persist, since the African-born suffered from higher rates of morbidity and mortality than the creoles did, and the imported slaves had a sex ratio unfavorable to a high gross birth rate. As a general tendency, the higher the proportion of African-born in any slave population, the lower its rate of natural increase—or, as was more often the case, the higher its rate of natural decrease.
>
> The phenomenon of a naturally decreasing population was nearly universal in northeast Brazil and the Caribbean sugar colonies, but it was not universal in the Americas as a whole. In other physical and social environments, slave populations could grow by natural increase. The most striking contrast existed between the British mainland colonies and the British Caribbean.

The reasons for this difference and its relationship to family formation and culture change among eighteenth-century North American slaves are as yet unclear, but there is no doubt that "rather than sustaining the regular excess of deaths over births typical of tropical America, the North American colonies developed a pattern of natural growth among the slaves."[16]

Two recent studies (one as yet unpublished), which begin a very much needed demographic and social analysis essential to understanding the distinctive pattern of population growth among eighteenth-century North American slaves, allow us to assign a prominent place to the resident slave population in the social process that made Afro-Americans of Africans. An analysis of the slave population from probate inventories in four Maryland counties (Calvert, Charles, Prince George's, and St. Mary's) between 1658 and 1730 by Russell Menard directs attention to a second critical moment in the eighteenth-century North American slave experience, the transition from an initial slave population that hardly reproduced itself to one that did. At least half of Maryland's slave population lived in these four places. Prior to 1710, "like blacks elsewhere in the Americas," Menard writes, these slaves "apparently failed to reproduce themselves fully." Most slaves were adult native Africans. The inventories listed less than one slave under the age of sixteen for every two adult slaves between the ages of sixteen and fifty, evidence suggesting that the labor force grew by immigration, not by natural reproduction. Menard's examination of similar records in Prince George's and Charles County in the 1720s shows that the ratio of slave children to slave adults nearly doubled despite the continuing flow of Africans to these places. In 1750, more slave children than adults lived in these same four counties.

Such evidence suggests that the 1720s "marked a watershed for the slave population of Maryland's lower Western Shore." Menard explains:

The immigrant slave population possessed several characteristics that tended to depress the rate of natural increase. African-born slaves suffered from high rates of mortality and morbidity, an unbalanced sex ratio, and perhaps an extreme alienation expressed in part as an unwillingness to have children. Most important, immigrant women were well-advanced in their childbearing years when they arrived in the colony. As a result, the initial immigrant population failed to reproduce itself. They did have some children, however, and these children transformed the demographic character of slavery in Maryland. The native-born lived longer and were less sickly than their immigrant forebears, they were more thoroughly assimilated, and there was among them a relatively equal ratio of men to women. Most important, native women began their reproductive careers at a much younger age than their immigrant mothers. Creole women had enough children to improve the natural growth rate in the slave population despite a continuing heavy black immigration, a still unbalanced sex ratio, and the apparent failure of their masters to appreciate fully the benefits of a self-perpetuating labor force.

Although Menard's invaluable study does not examine how these changing patterns of behavior among African and "creole" (or Afro-American) women related to slave family formation, it nevertheless locates that *moment in time* when a very significant demographic shift occurred among Maryland slaves.[17]

Allen Kulikoff's detailed examination of the Prince George's County slaves between 1720 and 1780 complements the Menard study and adds to our scant knowledge of the eighteenth-century slave family. By the 1730s, Kulikoff finds, Afro-American slave kin networks, not just immediate families, were taking shape among the "creole" Prince George's slaves. Over time, sale—especially the sale of children—broke up families, but short-distance sale and estate division spread kin groups over the county. Evidence of such networks is found among the Addison family slaves. When Thomas Addison died in 1727, he was one of the county's largest slaveowners, owning seventy-one slaves, many adult Africans among them. At his grandson's death in 1775, one hundred nine Addison slaves lived on three separate plantations. Two were adjacent to each other, and the third a few miles away. The forty-year-old Ned and his forty-six-year-old wife Joan lived on the main plantation with their four youngest children. Joan's older son Sam lived a few miles away. The sixty-four-year-old Jack Bruce and his fifty-six-year-old wife Sarah lived adjacent to the Addison's Oxon Hill place. Three sons, ranging in age from fifteen to twenty-six, lived at Oxon Hill as did another son, a twelve-year-old, who lived with his older sister and her child. Kulikoff also writes of Peter Harbard, another Prince George's slave:

> Harbard grew up on the plantation of Henry Darnall at the Woodyard; in 1737, he was sold to George Gordon, who lived across the road from Darnall. Peter lived with his grandmother, his father, and several uncles and aunts. . . . He was also friendly with several cousins, children of his Aunt Susan Harbard, who lived on several nearby plantations. Several other relatives lived with Darnall kinfolk in Annapolis.

Kulikoff's study is the first that fits the North Carolina Bennehan-Cameron and South Carolina Good Hope slaves into a meaningful historical setting.[18]

These two studies contain important evidence about the developing Afro-American social setting that shaped the responses of *African* slaves entering the mainland southern colonies in great numbers between 1740 and 1780, and especially those who first lived among settled "Creole" slaves on eighteenth-century farms and especially plantations. The transition to a self-perpetuating slave labor force—a change that led to the emergence of inter- and intragenerational linkages between immediate Afro-American slave families and was essential to the formation of a new social class—occurred in these Maryland counties in the 1720s, and the over-all rate of increase of the native slave population indicates that it happened elsewhere, too. In 1724, Hugh Jones observed that Virginia slaves "are very prolifick among themselves," and thirty-five years later Andrew Burnaby's trip through Virginia and Maryland convinced him that Afro-Americans "propagate and increase even faster" than the whites. The transition to a self-perpetuating slave labor force in other Chesapeake places and especially in South Carolina needs to be studied in careful detail,[19] but if other Virginia and Maryland slaves underwent a similar transition *in about the same time period* as those studied by Menard and Kulikoff, it means that family formation and the early emergence of expanded kin networks among *Afro-American* slaves descended from late-seventeenth- and early-eighteenth-century Africans took shape at the very moment when the greatest number of African slaves began pouring into the mainland colonies. Adaptation to New World enslavement for many among them therefore involved a significant interaction with these and other developing Afro-American institutional forms. The "models" accessible to these Africans were not only those of their owners and other whites nearby. And the new slaves themselves fed into this process a renewed but regular and fresh eighteenth-century African "input."

The slave adaptation to the violent social and cultural processes which transformed the African into an Afro-American saw the emergence of affective familial and kin arrangements. But much of the evidence so far uncovered describes the outcome of these processes, not the processes themselves.

Eighteenth-century newspaper advertisements for runaways,

for example, contain evidence of ties to immediate families and
to families of origin. Gerald Mullin finds in Virginia advertisements "a depth to slave family life—and to the white's tacit recognition of that life." About one in three runaways mentioned in
589 Virginia advertisements left an owner to visit immediate
family members and other kin living at some distance. The percentage of Southern Maryland runaways after 1745, according to
Kulikoff's study, was even higher. Advertisements revealed ties
to a spouse but also to a parent. "His parents are free and live in
Port-Royal," said a Virginia notice. Another told that a runaway's
"parents now belong to Francis Nelson." "He is about Mr. Samuel
Thomae's [sic] in Warwick County," said a third, "where he has
a father and a grandmother." A fourth said a runaway might be
"harboured by Colonel John Snelson's Negroes . . . among whom
he has a wife, or by his Brother John Kenny, a Mulatto Slave belonging to Mr. Thomas Johnson of Louisa." A runaway "girl"
was thought to be either with "a negro fellow (possibly her husband)" or "her Relations in Middlesex." Similar evidence appeared in early Charleston advertisements. The runaway Sue was
described as "being this Country born & having many Relations."
Another owner called attention to "Pompey . . . & Barbary his
Wife a Yellow Wench big with Child." Will ("lame in one of his
legs") and "Hannah his wife" quit the same man. The Angola
blacks Pompey and Menda and their two small children fled a
North Edisto place, and the James Island mulatto Lucy left with
her six- and ten-year-old children. Other owners also offered as
clues ties to an immediate family and to a family of origin. One
man had a mother on a Georgia plantation and a wife who
labored in a Charleston distillery. Another had a wife and father,
each with different owners. Topshom was thought to be with his
mother and father; they had fled another owner. Another was
thought to be with his mother, who had fled a Baltimore owner.
"The Molattoe slave," said another advertisement for a runaway,
"pretends to have an uncle who escaped from his owner . . . and
is said to keep a coffee house near London." Northern colonial
newspapers contained similar information. A Philadelphia slave
was thought to be in New Jersey with his "free mulatto wife . . .
and two children." Westchester County, New York, owners advertised for husbands and fathers thought to be near wives and
children, and in 1755 a slave couple quit an owner, the woman
"in an advanced state of pregnancy."[20]

An owner's death, an estate division, and the sale of slaves involved property transfers which detailed slave familial ties. When William Fitzhugh, the late-seventeenth-century Virginia planter, died in 1701, he owned fifty-one slaves, who were divided nearly equally between his wife and four sons. They had lived in families. Will, Black Peggy, and their son went to Fitzhugh's widow. Another of Will and Black Peggy's sons went to John Fitzhugh and a third to Henry Fitzhugh. Mulatto Sarah and a daughter went to George Fitzhugh, and the planter willed two of Mulatto Sarah's sons to John Fitzhugh. John Fitzhugh also got three of Hannah's children, but Hannah and a daughter went to Fitzhugh's widow. South Carolina wills and inventories prior to 1750 sometimes listed slave families: "one negro man, his wife and five children"; "one negro man and his old wife"; "one old negro man and his wife and child"; "Old Mingo, Jude his wife, and Young Mingo"; and "Old London, Betty, [and] Young London." Faced with economic crisis in 1769, the Virginia planter Bernard Moore devised a lottery scheme to raise cash. His slave assets included the twenty-two-year-old forgeman Billy and "his wife Lucy, a young wench, who works exceedingly well in the house and field"; the thirty-year-old blacksmith Caesar, Nanny his wife, and their children Tab and Jane; Moses, his wife Phebe, and Phebe's daughter Nell; the sawyer Robin, his wife Bella, and their young daughters (the seven-year-old Betty and the twelve-year-old Sukey); the mulatto house servant and mantuamaker Sarah and her child; Eve ("used both to the house and plough") and her child; and the "gang leader" York, his wife, and their child. "I have a Congoer," announced a North Carolinian, "who wants to be sold along with his wife and two children. I do not wish to sell him though I would not refuse to do so, if I find he will not stay here." The Charleston merchant Robert Pringle's decision in 1740 to put the slave Esther on a ship bound for Lisbon revealed ties that bound her to her parents. She could "doe any House Work," spoke "good English being this Province Born," and "was not given to any Vice." "The only Reason" Pringle was "sending her off the Province is that she has a practice of goeing frequently to her Father and Mother, who Live at a Plantation I am concern'd in, about Twenty Miles from Town."[21]

Evidence of early intergenerational familial linkages is clearly revealed in a 1761 list of fifty-five slaves owned by the New Hanover County North Carolinian "Mrs. Allen." (At that time about four in five New Hanover residents were black.) Eight Allen slaves were "single"; the rest, including twenty-eight chil-

dren and twelve grandchildren, lived in six families. Most of the
children and grandchildren had been born to Jack and Sarah,
Peter and Juno, and Phebe (who was dead by 1761), the oldest
being Phebe's thirty-six-year-old son Tom and Jack and Sarah's
thirty-five-year-old daughter Sapho. Jack and Sarah had eight
other living children, and six other of the dead Phebe's children
were still alive. The youngest grandchild listed was the one-year-old
March, the twenty-year-old Betty's son and Daff and Phillis's
grandson. Sapho and Tom were old enough in 1761 to indicate
that their parents had been born in the early eighteenth century,
if not in the late seventeenth century. Three Allen slaves born
between 1745 and 1748—Jack, Peter, and Dublin—were named
for their slave fathers, and Sabrina's second child, born in 1759,
was named for her slave maternal grandmother, Juno.[22]

Other mid-eighteenth-century slaves also were named for their
slave fathers. In 1757, Landon Carter recovered some "lost" slaves,
among them "Carpenter Ralph's son Ralph, George's boy George,
and Nassau's son Nassau." This evidence comes from the correspondence and diaries of the Carters, the well-known eighteenth-
century Virginia plantation family (seven of whose members at
one time owned 170,000 acres and twenty-three hundred slaves
spread over seven counties), records dotted with illustrations of
slave familial ties. "It was supposed that some misfortune might
have been the Consequence if the man had been separated from
his wife," explained John Carter after paying forty pounds to
purchase a woman and her children separated in a will from their
husband and father. After the carpenter Sam fled and stayed away
for a week, he bargained with Robert Carter, who advised an
overseer, "Sam thinks it a hard case to be separated from his wife."
Another Carter worried about Dennis and his wife Frankey because they lived apart from one another, hoped they were "Constant to each other," and wanted them to live together. He also
wanted the seventy-one-year-old Payne to live with "his grand
Children." After Robert Carter, who believed in "moderate cor-
rection in every case," listened to a slave mother's complaint that
an overseer had whipped her son, he felt that "in the present case"
the overseer should have made "allowances for the feelings of a
Mother."[23]

Kept irregularly between 1752 and 1778, Landon Carter's
diaries contain scattered but significant entries about his slaves
and their families. Ties between immediate families as well as
between spouses and their children were detailed. The slave fore-

man Jack Lubbar died in 1774. Grandchildren and great-grandchildren survived him. Carter recorded many different ways in which his slaves revealed their familial concerns. After the pregnant Winney's six-year-old daughter Sarah died of fever, she was "affected with the death of her child." An aunt and a grown sister apparently once hid a runaway. The disappearance of wheat from a storage house caused Carter to write of Talbot: "He may have made away with the grain or the people may have got in when he went out at night with his wife." Nassau, who drank excessively, failed once to wait on Carter, pretending that "his wife was taken dangerous bad." Tom was blamed for the death of two lambs, kept in irons a night, whipped, and then made to hoe. But Tom denied responsibility and worked poorly in the garden. "I thought," said Carter, "he might only be unwilling that his wife's father should be turned out, and obliged to take the garden. I fear, I have now paid for it." The carpenter Guy, who had gone to Currie's to "see his wife as usual on Monday night last," died in the snow. Carter thought he was drunk and wished Guy "had not a wife abroad." Carter also made careful distinctions among some slaves. Nelly was "a very fine woman but Sallatious and ill tempered withall that no husband will keep her too long." He knew some well enough to figure out how family obligation might affect their behavior and even to exploit slave family feelings. Carter believed that Sarah feigned illness and would not let her "lie up." She ran away, and it took nearly a week to find her. Carter had her "locked up; but somebody broke open the door for her. It could be none but her father Manuel, and he I had whipped." Another time, Carter dealt with Jimmy, "a splay footed rascal," whose "lameness" prevented him from working, walking, and even standing. "I found a way this day to make him . . . work pretty heartily," boasted Carter; "I have forbid him coming home to his wife at night and shall have him watched for they that cannot work for me cannot without great deceit walk two or three miles in the night."[24]

Eighteenth-century slaves celebrated their marriages, announcing thereby a change in adult status. Christian marriages were recorded among New England slaves as early as the 1650s, but not much is known about that ritual among slaves in other colonies. Peter Wood finds that the Anglican Society for the Propagation of the Gospel made little progress among early-eighteenth-century South Carolina slaves. Later in that century, however, the Westchester, New York, Anglican cleric John Bartow worried because his literate slave "has got the trick of marrying slaves with the office in Common Prayer Book" and "forbade him because it was a desecration of the Holy rite." Non-Christian marriage rituals existed among eighteenth-century slaves, too. The Quaker John Woolman noticed that Maryland and Virginia "negroes marry after their own way." A generation earlier, Thomas Brickell, who spent two or three years in Edenton, North Carolina, and met owners who "baptised and instructed" slaves to repress their "barbarous and disobedient proceedings" and to instill among them "an abhorrence of the temper and practice of those . . . brought from Guinea," described a marriage ritual that appeared to be a variant of the common West African practice of bride-right:

> Their *Marriages* are generally performed amongst themselves, there being very little ceremony used upon that Head; for the Man makes the Woman a Present, such as a *Brass Ring* or some other Toy, which she accepts of, becomes his wife; but if ever they part from each other, which frequently happens, upon any little Disgust, she returns his Present. These kinds of Contracts no longer binding them, than the Woman keeps the Pledge given her. . . . And though they have no other Cere-mony in their *Marriages* than what I have represented, yet they seem to be Jealously inclined, and fight most desperately amongst themselves when they rival each other, which they commonly do.

Much later in time, early-nineteenth-century Georgia slaves prac-ticed another distinctive ceremony: "The man would go to the cabin of the woman he desired, would roast peanuts in the ashes, place them on a stool between her and himself, and while eating propose marriage." If the woman agreed, "the couple repaired to his cabin immediately, and they were regarded as man and wife."[25]

Affective ties binding together married slaves were noticed everywhere by colonial whites. In the 1715 Yamassee War, the Virginia colony offered to send men to help suppress the Indians, demanded a money payment, and asked that "a Negro Woman . . . to be sent to Virginia in lieu of each Man sent to Carolina to Work till their Returne." South Carolinian whites rejected the offer, finding it "impracticable to send Negroe Women . . . by reason of the Discontent such Usage would have given their hus-bands to have their Wives taken from them which might have occasioned a Revolt also of the Slaves." A few years later, Brickell noticed that the North Carolina slaves, "allowed to plant a sufficient quantity of tobacco for their own use," sold some and purchased "Linnen, Bracelets, Ribbons, and several other toys for their wives and mistresses." Other slaves sought to keep families together or to reunite families separated by ownership. "Dick," a Virginian said in 1788, "is likely to be troublesome. I have wrote down to Mrs. Burwell for his wife, even at the enormous expense of £6." Settled largely by German shopkeepers, artisans, and laborers, Lancaster, Pennsylvania, had twenty-eight slaves in 1775. The town recorder Edward Shippen owned the slave Hannah, and her behavior convinced him that "blacks have natural affections as well as we have." Hannah's husband lived with an owner about seventy miles from Lancaster and visited her periodically. On his departure in 1769, Shippen noticed Hannah's "Grief in parting with him, not knowing whether she will ever see him again." A few years later, Hannah's husband lived with her. Joseph Simon, Lancaster's most prominent merchant, planned to send his "black Wench" to Fort Pitt where he kept a second store. Her husband lived in Lancaster, and she was four months' pregnant. Threatened with separation, according to Simon, she "went on in Such a Manner and would not Stir from Here, sayd she'd sooner kill herself." Two such suicides were recorded in 1746 in the Boston *Evening-Post*. "A very surprizing Tragedy," the suicides involved "a Negro Fellow at the North End and a Negro Woman belonging to a Gentleman at the South End of the Town," who had "contracted an intimate and strict Friendship together." The woman learned of her imminent sale "into the Country," and, according to the *Evening-Post*, "they resolved to put an End to their lives, rather than be parted; and accordingly, at seven o'clock (the Wench being at the House of her countryman), they went up Stairs into the Garret, where the Fellow, as is supposed, cut out the Wench's Throat with a Razor, and then shot himself with a Gun prepared for the Purpose. They were both found lying upon the Bed, she with her Head cut almost off, and he with his Head shot all to Pieces." Theirs was not the last such act of ultimate personal defiance by a slave husband and wife threatened with separation. In the 1930s, the North Carolina woman Annie Tate remembered hearing from her mother that her grandmother had "killed herself 'cause dey sold her husband."[26]

Slave petitions also showed the retention and development of familial and kin ties. An unknown number of Massachusetts slaves (perhaps aided by free blacks) petitioned the British royal governor General Thomas Gage and the Massachusetts General Court for their freedom in 1774. The petitioners revealed an awareness of the political debates then sweeping Massachusetts. "We have in common with all other men a naturel right to our freedoms without Being depriv'd of them by our fellow men as we are a freeborn Pepel and have never forfeited his Blessing by aney compact or agreement whatever," their petition began. But it went on to stress how slavery had damaged the family:

> But we were unjustly dragged by the cruel hand of power from our dearest frinds and sum of us stolen from the bosoms of our tender Parents and from a Populous Pleasant and plentiful country and Brought hither to be made slaves for life in a Christian land. Thus we are deprived of every thing that hath a tendency to make life more tolerable, the endearing ties of husband and wife we are strangers to for we are no longer man and wife than our masters or mistresses thinkes proper married or onmarried. Our children are also taken from us by force and sent maney miles from us wear we seldom or ever see them again there to be made slaves of for Life which sumtimes is vere short by Reson of Being dragged from their mothers Breest Thus our Lives are imbittered to us on these account by our deplorable situation we are rendered incapable of shewing our obedience to Almighty God how can a slave perform the duties of a husband to a wife or parent to his child How can a husband leave master to work and cleave to his wife How can the wife submit themselves to their husbands in all things How can the child obey thear husbands in all things. how can the master and the slave be said to fulfil that command Live in Love Let Brotherly Love contuner and abound Beare yea onenothers Bordenes How can the master be said to Beare my Bordon when he Beares me down whith the Have chanes of slavery and operson against my will and how can we fulfill our parte of duty to him whilst in this condition and as we cannot searve our God as we ought whilst in this situation. Nither can we reap an equal benefet from the laws of the Land which doth not justifi but condemns Slavery or if there had bin aney Law to hold us in Bondage we are Humbely of the Opinion ther never was aney to inslave our children for life when Born in a free Countrey. . . .

That petition was dated 1774, the same year that the South Carolina slave Patty, who became the mother, grandmother, and great-grandmother of so many Good Hope slaves, was born. Her later owner, the Charleston Loyalist Joseph Dulles, did not arrive in the embattled mainland North American colonies until 1777. The 1774 Massachusetts petition was neither the first nor the last such petition. Massachusetts blacks petitioned again a few years later but only to the General Court, reminding it that "Every Principle from which America has Acted in the Cours of their unhappy dificultes with Great Briton Pleads Stronger than A thousand arguments in favours of your petitioners. . . ." The second petition was dated 1777, a year after the first slave child had been born to Thomas Bennehan's North Carolina slaves. She was Phebee and Arthur's daughter Lucy. Her son Horace named his daughter, who was born in 1836 and may have lived through the emancipation, for the child's maternal great-grandmother Phebee. A year after the second Massachusetts petition, Phebee and Arthur had a second child and named the boy for his father. The next year, a slave owned by George Washington left his owner. He was Daniel Payne.[27]

The first petition filed by North American slaves did not await the controversy that led to national independence. It was drawn up much earlier in time and also had to do with the slave family. New Netherlands was settled in 1626. Eleven slave men, among the earliest settlers, built roads and forts and labored as domestics and farm hands. Company records list four of their names: Paul d'Angola, Simon (or Senion) Congo, Anthony Portuguese, and John Fransisco. The Company later imported three women, described as "Angola slaves, thievish, lazy, and useless trash." Anthony van Angola and Lucie d'Angola married in a Dutch church in 1641, and in 1644 some of these African slaves petitioned for their freedom. The response to their petition survives:

> Having considered the petition of the Negroes named: Paul D'Angola, Senion Congo (etal) ; who have served the company eighteen to nineteen years to be liberated, especially as they have been many years in the service of the Honorable West India Company here and have long since been promised their freedom; also that they are burdened with many children so that it is impossible for them to support their wives and children as they be accustomed to do, if they continue in the Company's service, Therefore we do release them and their wives from slavery . . . where they shall be able to earn their livelihood by Agriculture, in the land shown and granted to them. . . .

A swampy area that later became Greenwich Village and Washington Square was given to them. Unless they paid an annual "tribute" to their old owners ("thirty skepels of Maize, or Wheat, Peas, or Beans, and one Fat Hog, valued at 20 Guilders"), they would be returned "to the company's service." The company, moreover, refused to free their children. (Some years later, Lysbet Antonius, one of these children now grown up, was accused of burning her owner's house.) In the early 1660s, the free New Netherlands blacks Emanuel Pierterson and his wife Dorothy d'Angola petitioned the City Court for the freedom of "a lad named Anthony Angola, whom they adopted when an infant and have since reared and educated." They paid the Company three hundred guilders for him. Such was the behavior of Africans enslaved in the 1620s, the same decade that John Winthrop and others started the Puritan colony in the New World. Like Winthrop but under painfully more constricted circumstances, these Africans carried with them to the unsettled North American wilderness an Old World Culture. The date of their petition—1644—is presumptive evidence that its expressions of family obligation had their roots in Old World African cultures.[28]

So did the behavior of an unnamed African woman John Josselyn met during a trip to the New England colonies in 1638 or 1639. She deeply impressed him: "Mr. [Samuel] Mavericks Negro woman came to my chambers, and in her own Countrey language and tune sang very loud and shrill." The woman, who "had been a Queen in her own Countrey," explained her anguish: "Mr. Maverick was desirous to have a breed of Negroes and therefore seeing she would not yield by perswasions to company with a Negro young man he had in his house; he commanded him, wil'd she nill'd she, to go to bed with her, which was no sooner done, but she kickt him out again." "This," said Josselyn, "she took in high disdain beyond her slavery, and this was the cause of her grief."[29]

"Human nature," the historian Edmund S. Morgan observes in describing the family life of eighteenth-century Virginia slaves, "has an unpredictable resiliency, and slaves did manage to live a life of their own within the limits prescribed for them." "Those limits," Morgan insists, "were close but not so close as to preclude entirely the possibility of a private life." Virginia slaves "never married in any formal ceremony," but "it was quite usual for couples to consider themselves as husband and wife and to remain faithful to one another under the most trying circumstances." That was revealed by slaves then in other places too. In 1804, the slave Morris superintended Pierce Butler's slaves on a small island north of St. Simon's Island in the Georgia Sea Islands. During a great storm, Morris's quick thinking saved many lives and prevented property damage. Butler rewarded him with cash and a silver goblet, but only after Morris had declined Butler's offer of freedom. That would have meant leaving his wife, children, and home.[30]

Far too little is yet known about the eighteenth-century social and cultural processes that shaped such slave behavior. The African slaves and their eighteenth-century descendants had been "required to engineer styles of life that might be preserved in the face of terrible outrage." "The daily demands—to eat, to sleep, to love, to grow, to survive—do not become less imperious," as Sidney Mintz reminds us, "because their satisfaction is persistently thwarted by oppression." The Georgia slave Morris showed that in his decision to reject freedom. So did the North Carolina Bennehan-Cameron slaves who named so many of their children born prior to 1810 for their fathers and for blood relatives. And so did Daniel Payne, who had retained a surname different from that of his owner George Washington.[31]

The behavior of these and other men and women is telling evidence that an adaptive Afro-American slave culture was born before the invention of the cotton gin and before the War for Independence. It was mostly the descendants of these mid- and late-eighteenth-century Afro-Americans who were carried into the Lower South in the first six decades of the nineteenth century, slaves who involuntarily spread the culture of their parents and grandparents over new portions of the still-virgin wilderness and who revealed in yet other ways in the Deep South the adaptive capacities earlier revealed in the Upper South by their African and Afro-American parents and grandparents.

Who slaves were in 1800 depended upon who their parents had been in 1760. And who slaves were in 1860 depended upon who their parents had been in 1800 and their grandparents in 1760. In 1857, two Sea Island slaves died, "poor Sandy and his wife Joan." The woman died first, and her husband passed away the next day. A white who knew them said Sandy had died of "mental depression, operating on a feeble constitution." That same year, an Edisto Island black went nightly to mourn his slave wife's death. He slept at her graveside and even talked of digging up her bones and taking them to his hut or cabin.[32]

Sandy and Joan as well as the Edisto Island widower were

probably Sea Islanders all their lives. But the slaves who had belonged to the well-known late-eighteenth- and early-nineteenth-
century Virginia planter and lawyer St. George Tucker were
moved by his son Beverley from Virginia to Missouri. Beverley
Tucker spent twenty years in Missouri before returning to Virginia to succeed his father as Professor of Law at the College of
William and Mary. Letters from Tucker's Missouri slaves trailed
him back to Virginia. In one of them, James Hope asked Tucker
to contact his sister Frances and inquired about other Virginia
relatives:

> Your Servant James troubles you with this scrap. . . . the
> grand & principal object is to get Master to be so kind as to
> inquire about my Sister Frances and request my Sister to
> inform me her Situation how many children she has where
> she is living with her husband . . . and in fine how she is
> getting a long in the world also wither my father is living or
> dead & if dead how long since his decease and wither Dear
> Hope my cozen she used to work about town at Taylors is still
> living in town and how she is & wither my old god father
> Robin Edmonson is still alive
>   If you should see Anthony my cozen please remember me
> to him and his family. . . .
>   if Master cannot make it convenient to see my sister he
> will oblige his Jim by Inclosing this to my sister and as she
> will see the principal object of this has been to inquire after
> her   I hope she answers my inquiries herself

Usa Payton also sent a letter to her Virginia owner. "You all ways
treated Me well & I shall like you for it," wrote the woman. She
asked Tucker for "a present of Some money if you please for Just
at this time I am in particular knead of Some."

> . . . I am well and doing well   I have 10 children a living
> & 3 dead. . . . My husband is well & doing well. . . . I work
> here   I take in washing get a heep to due & I work very
> Hard   nothing more
>   You will please remember me to all of My Coloured
> friends. . . . Tell Sary Magee her daughters has been living
> next door to me for more than a year   She is Maried   her
> and her husband belongs to Sam Dyer

The women Susan (or Sukey) and Ersey had a different reason
than Usa Payton's for writing to Tucker. Tucker apparently

planned to move them to Texas, and they suggested local Missouri sale as an alternative, giving Tucker the names of four Missouri whites who might purchase them. They urged Tucker to write them and fix a price and explained why they wanted to remain in Missouri:

> We, two of your humble Servants[,] . . . write the very feelings of our hearts. . . . As we had been here a long time and had become much attached to the place (our Husbands being here) and as we hated the idea of going to Texas, Mr. Jones was kind enough to let us remain till March, before which time he expected to hear from you on the subject. Our object in writing dear Master is this: We can't bear to go to Texas with a parcel of strangers—if you were there we should go without saying a word, but to be separated from our husbands forever in this world would make us unhappy for life. We have a great many friends in this place and would rather be sold than go to Texas. . . .
>
> We don't think there will be the least difficulty in getting ourselves sold, together with our children from whom we hope you will not separate us. Ersey has six children, the youngest of which is about six weeks old, a fine little Girl. Susan has two Boys, the eldest nearly three years old, and the youngest eight months.
>
> We hope dear Master and Mistress that you will not let us go to Texas, but grant us our humble petition. We are both well, also our children.

Tucker's response is unknown. A few years later, however, a Missouri associate blocked the sale of Uncle Sam. "The poor fellow," said the white, "cried like a child when I told him he should not be separated from his family."[33]

Uncle Sam, Ersey and Susan, Usa Payton, and James Hope were the children and grandchildren of eighteenth-century Africans and Afro-Americans. So were the slave children born after 1830 on such places as the Good Hope, Cedar Vale, and Bennehan-Cameron plantations. The slave birth registers and other documents studied in these pages, however, hardly begin to unfold the fullness of the developing Afro-American culture. They nevertheless show enough to indicate that it was neither imitative nor a collection of what the anthropologist Roger Bastide describes as "impossible 'survivals.'" Instead, the behavior examined is evidence of what Bastide calls "genuine and original 'cultural creations' produced in response to new conditions of life." Enslavement, Sidney Mintz points out, compelled the slaves "to define themselves and to work out new patterns of life under extremely repressive conditions," and the birth registers indicate how they managed some of that difficult task. Mintz writes of all slave societies:

> The fundamental contradiction of such systems lies in their need to deal with men as non-men—that is, to deny the humanity of the slaves themselves. But the slaves are human, and on one level, at least, both masters and slaves know it. Since men are not machines, since they possess will, they can will to live or die—and no slavery system, no matter how humanitarian or cruel, has ever solved the problem.

That contradiction and others "afforded the slaves their opportunities, however slight, to frustrate the institution whose victims they were," and "it is in examining the operations of such systems in practice that the capacities of the slaves, as reasoning human beings engaged in their own defense, are richly revealed." The slave domestic arrangements and kin networks that developed in the century prior to emancipation were far more than productive and reproductive conveniences encouraged by owners to maximize income, to maintain social order, to gratify slave sexual and social needs, and to satisfy paternalist codes. These arrangements regularly drew upon past slave beliefs and practices, which served as "pools of available symbolic and material resources." Young slaves who married and raised families between 1815 and 1860 were the product of a long and often tragic process by which their forebears had adapted to enslavement and developed fragile communities within which these children were socialized. As adults, they were not "imitating" a family "model" known only to the owning class. By 1815 and probably much earlier in time, young blacks had themselves been nurtured in such families and protected by surrounding kin networks. Not all slaves conformed to that "model." That is an unrealistic and romantic expectation.[34]

But most slaves did. Everyday choices made by slave men and women—such as remaining with the same spouse for many years, naming or not naming the father of a child, taking as a wife a woman who had children by unnamed fathers, giving a newborn child the name of a father, an aunt or an uncle, or a grandparent, and dissolving an incompatible marriage—contradicted in behavior, not in rhetoric, the powerful ideology that viewed the slave as a perpetual "child" or a repressed "savage."

In making these "ordinary" choices, slaves showed that rebellion and flight were not the only ways in which they might assert the "humanity of the slaves themselves." Their domestic arrangements and kin networks together with the enlarged communities that flowed from these primordial ties made it clear to their children and grandchildren, to other blacks, and to perceptive whites that the slaves were not "non-men" and "non-women." That is one important reason why Booker T. Washington and countless others were wrong in viewing the emancipated blacks as a "simple people . . . freed from slavery and with no past."[35]

We began with the South Carolina Good Hope slave community and return to it briefly to examine the larger historical meaning revealed in the slave birth records. Let us assume that the fourteen-year-old Good Hope youth Charles was sold in 1850 to an interregional trader and ended up a Mississippi field hand. Charles was the oldest son of India and Primus, both then in their mid-forties, and had nine brothers and sisters. Two had died in infancy, and the youngest, a girl named Diana, was born in 1850. Witnesses to his sale included members of his immediate family, eight aunts and uncles, fifteen first cousins, and his African grandfather Captain, surely reminded by this sale of his much earlier separation from an immediate West African family and kin group. Charles was cut off from an immediate Afro-American family and kin group. The deep psychic and social pain then experienced by Charles and his near and distant kin need not be detailed. It is written large in the history of slavery, and no historian can describe it more precisely and compellingly than Frederick Douglass did:

> The people of the North, and free people generally, I think, have less attachment to the places where they are born and brought up than had the slaves. Their freedom to come and go, to be here and there, as they list, prevents any extravagant attachment to any one place. On the other hand, the slave was a fixture, he had no choice, no goal but was pegged down to one single spot, and must take root there or die. The idea of removal elsewhere came generally in the shape of a threat, and in punishment for crime. It was therefore attended with fear and dread. The enthusiasm which animates young freemen, when they contemplate a life in the far west, or in some distant country, where they expect to rise to wealth and distinction, could have no place in the thought of the slave; nor

could those from whom they separated know anything of that cheerfulness with which friends and relations yield each other up, when they feel that it is for the good of the departing one that he is removed from his native place. Then, too, there is correspondence and the hope of reunion, but with the slaves, all these mitigating circumstances were wanting. There was no improvement in condition *probable*—no correspondence *possible*—no reunion attainable. His going out into the fields was like a living man going into a tomb, who, with open eyes, sees himself buried out of sight and hearing of wife, children, and friends of kindred tie.

Charles's prior familial and social life intensified the suffering the youth would have undergone in being sold from South Carolina to Mississippi.[36]

But Charles carried those earlier experiences with him to the Deep South. The man Charles became was shaped by them. Cut off abruptly from his family of origin and other close kin, Charles first probably experienced a brief period of social isolation, later established fictive kin ties in his new settlement, and finally, in about 1860, married and soon became a father. Separation from the world he had grown up in had not severed Charles from the culture in which he had been socialized. His children, most of them born free, would have learned from their father about his childhood on a large South Carolina plantation owned by a Philadelphian named Dulles. If Charles lived until 1880, his name would have appeared in the pages of the manuscript federal census. He probably would have been listed as a forty-four-year-old married sharecropper (or farm laborer) with as many as six living children, one or two of them named either Captain, Primus, and India. Somewhere in the South Carolina Santee River region, furthermore, a boy born after the emancipation probably was named Charles and later learned that he had been named for an uncle sold as a youth in 1850 to Mississippi. Some of these facts could be learned from the pages of the 1880 manuscript census, but the information reported there revealed nothing about how these few lives had been shaped over nearly a century by the social capacities of Charles, his parents, and his grandparents and by the ways in which they had adapted to enslavement and passed on over time familial beliefs and cultural values. And that same document would not have told that some of Charles's grandchildren probably migrated to New York City or to Chicago in the first three decades of the twentieth century. Or that if they remained in rural Mississippi that Robert Coles might have met them or their children and grandchildren and become convinced by their beliefs and behavior to write in 1964, "Though in no way do I deny what ... [has been] called 'the mark of oppression,' it remains equally true that alongside suffering I have encountered a resilience and an incredible capacity for survival."[37]

Charles and his parents and grandparents remain buried in an historical wasteheap by a misreading of the Afro-American experience, one that has neglected or misinterpreted the adaptive capacities of the slaves. The view of American slavery which finds "its lasting effects on individuals and their children indescribably worse than any recorded servitude, ancient or modern," has been criticized by C. Vann Woodward. "Such a reading of the slave experience," he writes, "carried with it certain unhappy implications, not only about its white architects and perpetrators of the system, but also about its victims and their descendants. . . . For the 'Children of Oppression' could only be assumed to be permanently scarred by such an unprecedented experience of their forebears and to bear evidence of these scars in deficiencies of personality, responsibility, sexuality, mating and childbearing, and family stability." Charles and his parents and grandparents as well as his children and grandchildren reveal the inadequacy of the historical perspective Woodward so cogently criticizes. It is a perspective that distorts our understanding of Charles's grandchildren as well as his grandparents. "The correlation of historic trauma with sociological data," Woodward observes in commenting on the public debate over the "black family" in the 1960s, "had the charitable impulse of 'explaining' and, in a measure, justifying traits often attributed to inherent racial characteristics and at the same time rationalizing modern paternalistic programs of amelioration." The African-born Captain had overcome what Woodward calls "historic trauma." Charles learned that from his grandfather and from his parents, one reason he would have survived the later "historic trauma" associated with sale from South Carolina to Mississippi.[38]

Another kind of judgment, the judgment usually shied away from by historians and social scientists and best left to poets and novelists, is made possible by the behavior revealed by several generations of Afro-American slaves listed in the plantation birth registers. "Contrary to some," the novelist Ralph Ellison says, "I feel our experience as a people involves a great deal of heroism." Neither a sentimentalist nor a romantic, he does not minimize the nearly incalculable individual and social cost that slavery extracted from Africans and their descendants. And he does not ignore how enslavement crushed and damaged some of its victims. "From one perspective," Ellison says, "slavery was horrible and brutalizing." But it does not follow that the slaves "had very little humanity because slavery destroyed it for them and their descendants." Ellison makes a different point: "Any people who could undergo such dismemberment and resuscitate itself, and endure until it could take the initiative in achieving its own freedom is obviously more than the sum of its brutalization. Seen in this perspective, theirs has been one of the great human experiences and one of the great triumphs of the human spirit in modern times, in fact, in the history of the world."[39] The Good Hope slaves Patty and Captain, the Stirling slaves Eveline and Adam, the Cohoon slaves Fanny and Jacob, and the Bennehan-Cameron slaves Pheebe and Arthur would not have described Ellison as an apologist for slavery or as a romantic idealizing the moral and social condition of his slave forebears. They would instead have found in his observations an unusual capacity for insightful and humane sociological generalization that matched their capacities to sustain and develop an individual and a collective identity under oppressive circumstances shared by no other Americans descended from the forced and free eighteenth-century Old World migrants to the bountiful New World.

Historical evidence has a cruel way of playing tricks on those who record it for nonhistorical purposes. Birth and death records kept by plantation whites to measure the changing value *(profits and losses)* of their most prized assets *(slave men, women, and children)* end up an incontestable evidence of the human capacities of these "factors of production" to create and sustain a viable Afro-American culture, a supreme irony in the balance book of history.

PART
TWO

Deep as the Rivers

—Langston Hughes

What surprises one . . . is that families having no legal bond hang together as well as they do.

CHARLOTTE E. McKAY (1866)

It was commonly thought that the negroes, when freed, would care very little for their children, and would let them die for want of attention, but experience has proved this surmise unfounded. On the contrary, I suppose they take as good care of them as do the same class of people anywhere.

DAVID G. BARROW (1881)

We knowed freedom was on us, but we didn't know what was to come with it. We thought we was going to get rich like the white folks. We thought we was going to be richer than the white folks, 'cause we was stronger and knowed how to work, and the whites didn't, and they didn't have us to work for them any more. But it didn't turn out that way. We soon found out that freedom could make folks proud, but it didn't make 'em rich.

UNIDENTIFIED FORMER SLAVE (1937?)

9

Let Not Man Put Asunder

I Elburt Williams & Marien Williams has bin Livin to-
gether 18 years & We Both do affirm that We do want
each other to Live as man & wife the balanc of Life &
being disable to walk & Marien being in the family way
I will send this to you & you will please make it all
Wright with us.
NORTH CAROLINA MARRIAGE AFFIDAVIT (1866)

Now, what does the negro know about the obligations of
the marriage relation? No more, sir, than the parish bull
or village heifer.
ROBERT TOOMBS, Atlanta *Constitution* (1871)

Much has been written of the slave and something of the
freedman, but thus far no one has been able to weld the
new life to the old.
ALBION W. TOURGEE (1888)

The focus in this study now shifts from the enslaved to the emancipated Afro-American, and it is the behavior of ex-slaves like Sarah Miranda Plummer and her family that now receives attention.

Adam Plummer and his wife Emily had different Maryland owners prior to the emancipation. He lived in Mount Hebron, and his wife had her home at some distance in Hyattsville. Their oldest daughter Sarah labored in the District of Columbia, and in late 1860 (or early the next year) she was sold (or taken) to New Orleans. Before that, letters that had passed among the Plummers had helped overcome the barriers imposed by separate ownership. Emily Plummer could not write, and an unknown person penned her letters to "Dear Plummer." She once wrote:

Please send me word by William how my two children are if you do not come your self. Master has promised to be your protector if you can possibly come. Please find out how mother and all my sisters and brothers are and let me know. . . . Saunders woke up Saturday night and asked if papy had come. . . .

Three letters Plummer sent his wife in 1858 and 1859 survive:

> . . . I got home at Thre oClock p.m. marander is well today and love to you and all her brothers and sisters and she is to go to Mr. Thylman Hillary at Three Sister this year while sorrow Encampass me round, and Endless disTresses i see astonished. i cry can a mortal be found. . . .

> . . . I wrote you a letter on first January and I have not Reseveed any answer yet. . . . And Miss Marandia Plummer is left three sister on the 7 febuary She is now in Georgetown with Mr. Clark the methadiese Priceher. . . .

> . . . a littel boy came running to me at my House with a Letter coldse Dait March 31 and I reseve it with open hands and Joyfull Heart, and it Read thus. I am not well myself and the Childrens have ben sick colds you are mistaken that I do not wish to here from you and the Childrens, for i have some things for you and your Childrens last Chrismus. . . . your son Elias plummer is well about a week for I go to see him Miss Marandia plummer is the same. . . . my brother Henry plummer form Goodwood came up to my house Last sunday and saying that the all is well there they all give thir love to you and your Chilldreans. . . .

A letter from Sarah Miranda to her father, which was written on December 2, 1859, also survives. She complained that he had not visited her in Georgetown and had hoped to visit him, "but as some of the family were sick i could not get off, so I will wait a while longer." Sarah went on:

> I went out in the city Sunday to try to hear from you, Grandmother told me that she saw you at market on Saturday. Aunt Rachel has not answered my letter yet. Have you heard from them lately. Please inquire for my brother and let me know how he is. Mother say'es the children are crazy to see me. . . .

A letter from his wife a year later asked if he "heard of merandys trubles."

"Merandys trubles" are revealed in a letter she sent her mother in May 1861 from New Orleans:

> . . . I have been a long time from gorgetown. . . . I write with much grief to say that I was in Alexandria two months, and could not hear from any of you; Jackson . . . saw my grandmother and of course she knew where I was, I hope you

will not think hard of my scolding for that's not half I laid up for you.

I do not blame you because you could not come to see me, I think it very hard that father did not come to see me as he was nearer than you were, though I may hear from you, yet I may never expect to see you again; you will please write to Grandma give my love to her, and tell her I am sorry I didnot come to see her when I went to show my aunt where she lived. . . .

I hope that you will not forget that I am still alive; I send my love to you and to all my inquiring friends, Remember me to my brother, And tell him I hope he has not forgotten to write to me as he promised to do. I write you much grief and my heart is full of sorrow, and I can do no better and I hope you will not Grieve after me, but in the good Providence of God I hope we will meet to part no more; though you will be sorry to hear I am so far yet you will be glad to hear that I met with my aunt Sarah and she was very glad to see me yet she did not know me until I made myself known unto her. . . . I suppose you will answer my letter as soon as you can because I want to hear from you as bad as you do from me.

No other correspondence remains. But pasted into the Plummer family Bible was a sheet with the following notation: "In the year of our Lord, 1866, October 11, Adam F. Plummer, gives his son Henry V. Plummer, permission to go to New Orleans, La., on Napoleon Avenue between Fchoupitoulas and Jesey, for his eldest sister, Sarah Miranda Plummer, Mrs. Sarah Miranda Howard."[1]

The general emancipation removed the restraints that had prevented Henry Plummer from being sent by his Maryland father to Louisiana to get his married sister. Slaves could not make that choice. It cost a good deal in 1866 to travel that distance, a restraint of some importance for many ex-slaves. But the physical and social immobility associated with chattel slavery no longer existed. The Plummer Bible entry was made at a critical moment in the Afro-American experience, a brief time punctuated by the start of the Civil War and the start of Radical Reconstruction. The ex-slaves were not fully "free" in these years. The Union Army and later the Freedmen's Bureau constrained them in severe ways, as did southern state legislatures in the laws commonly called "Black Codes." The ex-slaves, moreover, could neither vote nor give testimony against whites in civil courts. They had few of the general rights and privileges associated with full citizenship. But the war and the emancipation fundamentally changed the context that had limited their behavior. How slaves and ex-slaves commonly behaved at that moment in time (1861–1867)—not fifty years earlier and not fifty years later—is therefore unusually relevant evidence in any assessment of the long-term impact of slavery on slave culture and personality and of the subtle interplay between slave beliefs (or values) and slave behavior. If, for example, the *typical* ex-slave had internalized the "Sambo" mentality or had believed himself or herself bound "organically" to an old owner, ex-slave behavior in these few years should have revealed widespread social and cultural disorganization. Owners themselves often predicted such disintegration and breakdown. Individual ex-slaves everywhere could not manage the transition to legal freedom, and instances of devotion and loyalty to former owners dot the record. There also is much evidence of severe material suffering incident to the wartime devastation and the emancipation. But evidence of widespread social and cultural demoralization among the ex-slaves is uncommon. Its relative absence casts important light upon the slaves as well as the ex-slaves. The behavior of ex-slaves between 1861 and 1867 allows us to examine the relationship between latent slave *beliefs* and manifest slave *behavior*. The ex-slave could do and say what often could not be done and said in "slavery times." It had been nearly impossible then for many—perhaps all but a small minority—to get through the business of daily life without seeming to assent to the dominant value system. How ex-slaves behaved just after the general emancipation therefore allows us to see whether whole ranges of their behavior earlier in time were accurate indicators of their inward beliefs.

A forthcoming study by this author examines in close detail the social beliefs and behavior of the slaves and ex-slaves in the few years between the start of the Civil War and the start of Radical Reconstruction. That vast and little-studied subject is sampled in this chapter to show how beliefs nourished but often barely articulated prior to the Civil War found expression during and just after that conflict. We return to the several themes explored in Chapter 1: the slave and ex-slave soldier as father and husband in Kentucky, slave and ex-slave sexual attitudes and behavior during and just after the Civil War, the attitudes of Maryland ex-slave parents toward the abusive apprenticeship of their children between 1864 and 1867, the concern by Virginia and especially North Carolina ex-slaves with legal marriages in 1866, the ways in which ex-slaves dealt with "plural" marriages resulting from the remarriages that often occurred after a spouse was sold, and, finally, a comparison of marriage registration rates between white and black North Carolina and Mississippi residents in the decades following the emancipation.

Kentucky slaves and ex-slaves who joined (or were impressed into) the Union Army in 1864 and 1865 and their families illustrate the depth of slave family ties and show how these ties shaped the behavior of ex-slaves. About a quarter of a million slaves lived in Kentucky in 1860. Kentucky, however, remained a loyal but deeply divided state during the Civil War. The behavior of its slaves—not the deep political divisions that so bitterly divided Kentucky whites—is what concerns us. Kentucky blacks, mostly ex-slaves, served in the Union Army in large numbers. An unpublished study of Union Army Company and Regimental Descriptive Rolls by Leslie Rowland discloses who among the Kentucky slaves joined the Union Army. Military recruiters and officers listed the occupations of all but 329 of 20,905 black soldiers (Table 34). Nearly all—97.4 percent—were either farmers or laborers.[2] Very few slaves with elite occupations joined the Union Army. They may have been few in number among Kentucky slaves. That is the subject for another study. What matters here is that the typical Kentucky slave who joined the Union Army had the same occupation as the typical Virginia and North Carolina ex-slave who registered a marriage in 1866. Their behavior therefore is further evidence of beliefs held by ordinary slaves upon their emancipation. Kentucky slaves, furthermore, joined (or were impressed into) the Union Army in far greater numbers than slaves in any other southern state. It is probable that the number serving in the Union Army between April 1864 and April 1865

TABLE 34. OCCUPATIONAL DISTRIBUTION OF KENTUCKY UNION ARMY BLACK SOLDIERS, 1864–1865

Occupation

Farmer and laborer	97.44%
Artisan	1.60
Servant	.50
Drayman, wagoner, teamster	.40
High status*	.05
Number	20,576
Unknown	329

* Includes five clergymen and three clerks.

equaled slightly more than half of all Kentucky slave men aged fifteen to forty-four in 1860.

Kentucky blacks were recruited into the Union Army starting in March 1864, a decision that further divided the state's white residents. Before then, Union Army blacks serving in Kentucky had suffered harassment and even worse. So did runaways from the slave states nearby. A Tennessee free black who married a slave widow and took her and her children north through Kentucky in 1863, for example, was convicted of slave-stealing. Until military recruitment began in Kentucky, that state's slaves and free blacks went to Ohio, Indiana, and Illinois to join the Union Army. Some were illegally impressed before 1864 in Kentucky itself. The daughter in a prominent Bourbon County plantation family wrote her mother in March 1863:

> . . . For three or four days the Federals have been taking off the negroes from this county, to work or fight at Lexington, sometimes the cars pass loaded, and yesterday they took nine negro men from Ben Rogers, and one from John Caldwell, gentlemen of my acquaintance, and upon the strength of the fright one of ours has left. He has been gone two days, and we have not heard from him—but I think he will come back, as we have his wife and four children.

Such departures would leave field work undone and upset the minds of the "poor simple minded negroes." The exact number who quit owners like her before March 1864 remains unknown. Some contemporaries put it as several thousand.[3]

Slave options changed in March 1864. Loyal owners received a three-hundred dollar bounty for slaves they let serve in the Union Army. Some whites favored the new policy; it helped fill draft quotas. The Louisville *Press* said the state could not "better afford to spare whites than blacks." After March, slaves were impressed into the Union Army. The Louisville City Council appropriated funds to buy and sell black substitutes, and the municipal prison, along with the town's slave pens, were used to coerce hesitant blacks. A black fair later that year occasioned a police action: the Louisville authorities "captured all the males," imprisoned them, and "forced" the "sound ones" to "enlist." Union Army troops, blacks among them, did that, too, impressing Paducah slave steamboat hands. Compulsion did not force all Kentucky blacks into the Union Army. A second military order dated April 18, 1864, allowed county provost marshals and their deputies to recruit slave soldiers. Two months later, the Union Army welcomed slaves belonging to disloyal owners into military camps. These slaves did not need permission from their owners.

Thousands of Kentucky slaves quit their owners—loyal as well as disloyal owners—in the spring and summer of 1864 to join the Union Army. Herndon, Henderson, Union, and Davies county slaves left in "scores," and the Louisville *Journal* protested that the military policies "entirely demoralized" the slaves, making it difficult for them to be "controlled by their masters." "Negroes," said the *Covington American*, "are coming to this city from the interior in swarms for the purpose of enlisting in the United States Army." About two hundred had arrived in three days. Black volunteers filled the Jessamine County draft quota. "The roads," according to another observer, "are swarming with able-bodied black men, hastening to the various rendezvous to be mustered into the service." About six hundred came to one such place; one hundred ten slaves volunteered in two June days at Lexington; a Lancaster white predicted "they will all go in." Hostile Lebanon whites lashed back violently at the departing slaves. In late May, about two hundred fifty Boyle County runaways made it to Camp Nelson but only after whites, including students, had stoned and even shot at them. A few months later, Elijah Marrs led twenty-seven slaves armed with "twenty-six war clubs and one old rusty pistol" to Louisville. "Great weeping and mourning" accompanied their departure, a "demonstration of sorrow" that Marrs believed unmatched "before or since."

Elderly Kentucky ex-slaves remembered 1864 well. Mary Cross and George Washington Buckner were not yet fifteen years old, and George Conrad, Jr., was an infant. Conrad lived with his parents, and his Henderson County father distilled whiskey. He told an interviewer:

> There were fourteen colored men working for Old Master Joe and seven women. I think it was on the thirteenth of May, all fourteen of these colored men, and my father, went to the Army. When old Master Joe come to wake 'em up the next morning—I remember he called real loud, Miles, Esau, George, Frank, Arch, on down the line and my mother told him they'd all gone to the army. Old Master went to Cynthia, Kentucky, where they had gone to enlist and begged the officer in charge to let him see all of his boys, but the officer said "No." Some way or 'nother he got a chance to see Arch, and Arch came back with him to help raise the crops.

Only Conrad's father returned after the war's end. Buckner lived with a stepfather, an invalid mother, and three brothers and sisters. His mother awakened him to bid farewell to his four maternal uncles. They were leaving together to join the Union Army. Mary Cross's father left his owner, too. Some years before, he had belonged to a debt-ridden farmer who planned to sell him. Mary Cross's grandfather intervened, convinced his owner to buy him, and contributed twenty-five dollars of his own to assure the sale. "I remember," Mary Cross said, "that my father and most all of the younger slaves left the farms to join the Union Army. We had hard times for awhile and had lots of work to do."

Slaveowners had good reason to worry. Potential soldiers were not the only slaves leaving them. "Whole families are running off," said one observer. Some owners offered their slaves wages to keep them from leaving. Seventeen slaves owned by the prominent Union Republican Robert Breckenridge—nine men and "boys," five women, and three children—fled to Camp Nelson. Their flight and that of others like them convinced the Louisville *Journal* that Kentucky slavery was doomed; it urged compensated emancipation. "No family knows when they rise in the morning whether they have a servant to prepare breakfast or not," said the *Journal*. Farmers had lost needed laborers.

> The institution of slavery [the *Journal* feared] will remove itself, and we shall lose nearly all our labor. . . . The question now is, not how shall we save slavery, but how shall we raise our bread, and bake it after we have raised it. . . . The slaves are already turned loose. We have the old and the blind, the lame and the halt, the mother and her brood to feed and to clothe, without anyone to work to maintain them.

Concerned whites focused on Camp Nelson. Within a few months, more than fifteen hundred slave men had gathered there. Later that year, about five thousand black soldiers, men who filled the 114th and 116th United States Colored Infantry, trained there. By the war's end, according to one estimate, between nine and ten thousand slaves—about two in every five Kentucky black soldiers—passed through Camp Nelson. Displeased owners journeyed to the place and, according to Thomas Butler, who managed the camp's United States Sanitary Commission station, pressured their slaves to return "by all kinds of promises and threats." Some owners allegedly kidnapped their slaves; one black recruit was murdered, and whites cropped the ears of two other men. Less

violent whites used a milder tactic to persuade their slaves to
return. They brought the "wives of wouldbe soldiers" to Camp
Nelson, parading them before their slave husbands. The response
by the Camp Nelson blacks to such enticement remains unknown.

But Camp Nelson slaves disclosed strong family attachments
in other very direct ways. Elijah Marrs, the son of a free black
father and slave mother, wrote letters for illiterate recruits. (Before his enlistment, Marrs, who had been taught to read by some
friendly white youths and by attending a night school run by an
elderly slave, had received and answered letters for slaves who had
already enlisted. The men addressed these letters to "their wives,
sons, and daughters.") Sanitary Commission officers also wrote
letters for Camp Nelson slave fathers and husbands, letters that
often sought "redress" for "troubles at home," especially "wrongs
committed on their wives, children, and aged parents." The Camp
Nelson Sanitary Commission superintendent estimated that by
the war's end—in less than a full year—his staff had written "at
least 5,000 letters" for black soldiers.

Slave wives and mothers, often accompanied by children, in
unknown numbers either visited Camp Nelson or fled their owners
to the military station. Their presence upset unsympathetic
military officers, and Camp Nelson's commander Speed Smith Fry,
confronted by what he called the "Nigger Woman Question,"
predicted "obscene and brutal practices." Sometime in early
May, he ordered that a "slave girl" be returned to her owner. She
had worked for several months as a hospital cook, and sympathetic
patients took her from her military guards, dressed her in boy's
clothing, and spirited her away. On May 23, Fry banned runaway
women from Camp Nelson. But three women expelled from the
place returned. Fry had them arrested, tied up, given a "few
lashes," and sent off again. Another camp edict read: "Any negro
woman here without authority will be arrested and sent beyond
the lines and informed that, if they return, the lash awaits them."
Fry's efforts failed. Hardly a day passed in the summer months,
according to Butler, "without bringing . . . wives, children, and
relatives into the camp, either on visits or in pursuit of new
homes." Recruits "frequently sent for their family." Some came,
said John Fee, then working among the Camp Nelson blacks
and himself a Kentucky-born abolitionist driven from that state
in 1859, because of "affection to the husband or father." Others
had been driven off by owners or beaten "unmercifully" by "enraged masters." Butler, Fee, a few other whites, and Fee's black

assistant Gabriel Burdett (whom Butler described as "a noble and extraordinary man") labored to help the families of these soldiers. It became possible for "visitors" to stay one night. But Fry and other officers shared none of these humane instincts. Butler, who later condemned their "incompetence" and called their behavior "sad," and Fee, who filled the columns of the *American Missionary* with evidence of how the slaves had been abused, were no match for Fry and his men.

Lorenzo Thomas, to whom Fry and other camp superintendents reported, supported Fry against his critics. A military order put military necessity, agricultural production, and the morale of loyal Kentucky slaveowners above the familial concerns of these slave soldiers and their wives and children. Thomas ordered women and children along with other blacks unfit for military service from the camps, urged such persons to "remain at their respective homes where, under the State laws, their masters are bound to take care of them," expressed fear that the women would spread venereal diseases among the soldiers, said their presence would "only become an expense to the Government," and insisted that "all this class of people are required to assist in securing the crops, now suffering in many cases for want of labor." In mid-August, Fry again expelled the Camp Nelson women and children. "All officers having negro women in their employment," ordered Fry, "will deliver them up to the patrol to be brought to these headquarters. Any one attempting to evade this order will be arrested and punished." The evicted women and children returned, and Fry chased them—time and again. "They would return," said the angry Fee, "—no place of shelter, and often their husbands gone they were much exposed to temptation." Controversy raged until the Secretary of War ordered the women and children settled in a protected camp, away from the soldiers. "Many . . . by their own efforts had little huts erected with small amounts of provisions." An aged widow among them washed and sewed to pay her way. Her sons—perhaps as many as five of them —served in the Union Army.

The arrangement failed to satisfy Fry, and in late November Fry issued "a very summary notice" driving about four hundred women and children from their settlement "without time or opportunity to get away their little effects." They were "dumped" from wagons and carts "in the streets or by the wayside in extreme cold weather." Intense suffering followed. An observer saw women and children "lying in barns and mule sheds, wandering through the woods, languishing on the highway." Another said some "actually froze to death." The Lincoln County slave soldier Joseph Miller, who had come to Camp Nelson with his wife and four children in mid-October, detailed their abuse and the death of a son in an affidavit:

> . . . [M]y wife and children came with me, because my master said that if I enlisted he would not maintain them, and I knew they would be abused by him when I left. I had then four children, aged respectively ten, nine, seven, and four years. On my presenting myself as a recruit, I was told by the lieutenant in command to take my family into a tent within the limits of the camp. My wife and family occupied this tent by the express permission of the aforementioned officer, and never received any notice to leave until Tuesday, November 22, when a mounted guard gave my wife notice that she and her children must leave camp before early morning. This was about six o'clock at night. My little boy, about seven years of age, had been very sick, and was then slowly recovering. My wife had no place to go. I told him that I was a soldier of the United States. He told me that it did not make any difference; he had orders to take all out of camp. He told my wife and family if they did not get up in the wagon he had, he would shoot the last one of them. On being thus threatened, my wife and children went into the wagon. My wife carried the sick child in her arms. When they left the tent, the wind was blowing hard and cold, and having had to leave much of our clothing when we left our master, my wife, with her little ones, was poorly clad. I followed them as far as the lines. I had had no knowledge where they were taking them. They were in an old meeting-house, belonging to the colored people. The building was very cold, having only one fire. My wife and children could not get near the fire, because of the numbers of colored people huddling together by the soldiers. I found my wife and family shivering with cold and famished with hunger; they had not received a morsel of food during the whole day. *My boy was dead.* He died directly after getting down from the wagon. I know he was killed by exposure to the inclement weather. I had to return to camp that night; so I left my family in the meeting-house, and walked back. I had walked there. I travelled in all twelve miles.

A literate white or black had helped Miller prepare this well-written affidavit. No one helped him bury his son. Miller walked to Nicholsville the next morning. "I dug a grave myself," said the slave soldier, "and buried my own child. I left my family in the meeting-house where they still remain."

Fry's November expulsion of the Camp Nelson women and children strengthened Fee and his other critics and soon caused a reversal of official policy. Congressional supporters helped Fee convince the Secretary of War to open a "refuge" at the embattled Union Army camp. So did the continued flow of slave women and children into Camp Nelson. Their number, Lorenzo Thomas explained to the secretary at the year's end, was "constantly increasing" and "on Christmas Day, a large number arrived, stating they were driven from their homes and in some instances . . . their masters had their cabins pulled down over their heads." Thomas now believed himself "bound to . . . afford them food and shelter." They might even be "profitably employed at Camp Nelson." The women and children stayed at Camp Nelson, but their material circumstance hardly improved. Two hundred and fifty of the four hundred sent away in November returned; one hundred two of them died afterward. "Many," an observer noticed, "had not shoes or stockings. Others had not a change of undergarments, nor enough to keep them warm." Fee himself restricted admission to "the families of colored soldiers, or those dependent upon them for support." In early January, according to him, women and children were "coming by the dozens at a time." Camp Nelson became a refuge for three thousand sixty slaves, mostly women and children.

Material conditions improved in 1865. A Louisville white woman who worked in the camp hospital reported in February that "the wards were full of human wretchedness." She found "a poor woman dying, amidst filth and suffering, for the simplest food, within twenty steps of the superintendent's office." But federal rations made living better. So did a seven-room schoolhouse, four large wards, a dining hall, ninety-seven two-room "cottages," sixty government tents, and fifty cabins "erected by the colored people." Disputes over the status of Camp Nelson refugees between Fee and their owners, however, continued. "We had a case yesterday," Fee reported in late February, "that was a sort of test case. A slaveholder a 'good union man' with a New York woman called to get a slave girl." Fee added:

Capt. Hall said "yes"—"I know Mr. Barnes" "she will be better off there than here." Brother Williams said *no!* The Capt. gave me a private chat. I said *"no!"*—not for one moment!!

Her *father* is here a soldier—natural guardian. We must do
more for her morally what Mr. Barnes as a *chattel* owner will
not do—this is more than "hog and hominy."

Hall "winced and retired." His response remains unknown. Other
Kentucky slave soldiers had trouble that winter over their families.
A few stationed in Nashville received regular furloughs to visit
their Kentucky kin. One learned that his wife's owner "had been
treating her very cruelly, and to some extent on account of her
husband being in the army." A white officer dispatched Elijah
Marrs and ten other black soldiers to help this man "bring the
woman into camp" and, according to Marrs, shoot her owner if
necessary. Marrs and his men could not find her. Another twenty
soldiers were sent. They learned she had "fled to parts unknown."

The Civil War ended in the spring of 1865, but a struggle
over the slave and ex-slave family continued until the final ratification of the Thirteenth Amendment in December of that year.
Federal and state authorities clashed bitterly over the status of the
families of Kentucky's black Union Army soldiers still owned by
their antebellum masters and still subject to the state's old slave
laws. Unlike Maryland and Missouri, Kentucky had not abolished
slavery before the war's end. Not all Kentucky slaves therefore
were free in April 1865. Freedom had come early to slaves (about
sixty-five thousand) owned by disloyal whites, and in March 1865,
after prolonged debate, the Congress freed the wives and children
of slave soldiers. The March 1865 law created intense conflict in
Kentucky, conflict caused by the fact that 28,818 Kentucky blacks
had either joined or been impressed into the Union Army between
April 1864 and July 1865. A military estimate figured that the
March 1865 law freed about seventy-five thousand Kentucky slave
wives and children so that another sixty-five thousand men,
women, and children still remained slaves.[4]

Bitter resentment over the March 1865 congressional law
followed by the Kentucky legislature's rejection of the Thirteenth
Amendment shaped a conflict unique to Kentucky, one that
disclosed the fierce attachment of many ex-slaves, soldiers most
prominent among them, to their families. The military policies
of John M. Palmer and his chief subordinate James S. Brisbin fed
the dispute. Palmer took over military command of Kentucky in
February 1865, and martial law existed in that state until the
following October. His father, a critic of slavery, had left Kentucky
for Illinois, and Palmer later shifted from the Democratic to the

Republican Party over the slavery question. (After the Civil War, Palmer returned to Illinois and became its governor.) "When I came to Kentucky," Palmer explained in a January 1866 speech, "I made up my mind that all that was left of slavery was its mischiefs, and that I would encourage a system of gradual emancipation, a thing that had been desired so long, and which the colored people had pretty well established for themselves." Palmer combatted the antebellum slave laws still in effect in Kentucky after April 1865, and Thomas James, born a New York slave and later a free black minister in the Buffalo and Rochester African Methodist Episcopal Church who had been sent South in 1862 by the American Missionary Association and ended up in Louisville, worked closely with him.*

Enforcement of the March 1865 law by Palmer provoked controversy between the Union Army and resident slaveowners. Kentucky had allowed no legal provision for slave marriage, and the state law recognized no legal tie between slave parent and slave child. Congress, however, had freed the wives and children of slave soldiers. A conflict between state and federal law was inevitable, and Palmer moved decisively in a proclamation concerning the March law. He called it an "act of justice," said it offered black men "an opportunity to earn freedom for themselves and their posterity," and warned that military power would be used to "enforce" the rights of ex-slave soldiers. A military edict, for example, closed the Louisville "slave pens and other private establishments," releasing some blacks held there for "forced enlistment for their master's benefit," for sale to bounty and substitute brokers, and for asking "their indigent masters for wages." "Some 'saucy' wives of negro soldiers" also were freed. James, who supervised this effort on Palmer's orders, found five separate Louisville places ("pens") which kept slaves. Two hundred and sixty, some "in irons," were in the largest place. He released them and sent them to the army-sponsored Home for the Colored

* James was born a slave in Canajoharie, New York, in 1804, separated from his mother, brother, and sister by their sale in 1812, and ran away as a youth to Canada, where he helped build the Welland Canal. He later labored as a woodchopper and warehouse worker in western New York as well as a Buffalo schoolteacher. He married in 1829 and was ordained as a minister in 1833. In 1862, James, then a widower (his wife had died in 1841) was appointed by the American Missionary Association to work among Louisiana and Tennessee blacks. He and his daughter left Rochester but ended up in Louisville. He worked with the Union Army for three years. In about 1870, James remarried. His second wife had been freed by Sherman's army in Atlanta and later sent north with "other colored refugees" (Life of Rev. Thomas James by Himself [1887], 3–21).

Refugees that he ran in the spring and summer of 1865. A black hotel waiter told James that nine black men were locked in the National Hotel. The hotel owners denied the allegation, but another black secretly told James the room they were in, and, after the clergyman found them, James mustered them into the Union Army. That freed them. Although the Louisville Mayor and Common Council protested James's work, Palmer encouraged it. A soldier guarded his residence nightly for eighteen months. No nighttime light was allowed in the refugee camp he managed for "fear of drawing the fire of rebel bushwackers," and camp inhabitants "made their beds on the floor." Sent once to bring a blacksmith suspected of "bushwacking" to Palmer, James was beaten with an iron bar, and his right hand was partially but permanently paralyzed.

James and white officers encouraged slave men to enlist and slave women to marry. "I was ordered by General Palmer," James remembered, "to marry every colored woman that came into camp to a soldier unless she objected to such a proceeding." The ceremony was meant to "secure the freedom of colored refugees," a "ruse" to protect runaway women and children from owners. Army officers, according to the *New York Times*, "tell every able-bodied colored man to enlist, and every single female slave to marry a colored soldier." Two of the Kentucky governor's slaves married black soldiers and claimed their freedom under the March 1865 law. Palmer himself later insisted that some slaves "greatly abused" the law and formed "polygamous alliances" to become free. Black enlistments—between seventy and one hundred a day —continued until early May when ended by a War Department order. "Even old men and boys are found to be fit for duty in invalid regiments and are taken," said Brisbin in a plea to Kentucky's governor that the state abolish slavery. A Kentucky Circuit Court's decision declaring the March 1865 law unconstitutional did not deter Palmer, Brisbin, or the blacks. "Negro enlistment," boasted Brisbin, "has bankrupted slavery in Kentucky."

Conflict over the status of Kentucky slaves continued into the summer and fall of 1865. The Louisville mayor and common council worried that runaways crowded their city to escape rural owners and asked Palmer to help enforce vagrancy laws, protect public health, and prevent these blacks from hiring themselves as free persons. Most were "women and children . . . claiming to be free, and looking to the military authorities for protection and assistance." Palmer at first refused. "Vagrancy," he said, "as a

crime is voluntary idleness and profligacy; the only offense urged
against them is poverty. They fly and none dare employ them, and
because they cannot be employed and live in enforced idleness
they are by many called 'vagrants.' " Palmer freed Jacob Hardin, a
slave imprisoned in Louisville for hiring himself out without his
owner's permission. "Not long since," Palmer told appreciative
Louisville blacks, "a man was arrested. For what do you think?
For stealing some man's watch? No! For stealing some one's pocket-
book? No! For arson? No! For murder? No . . . He wanted to hire
himself out to work to support his wife and children, . . . the lazy,
trifling nigger!" Palmer had not yet finished. Army quartermasters
were ordered to pay wages directly to black employees, not to their
"pretended masters." He and Brisbin also announced that blacks
could sue whites unwilling to pay wages to soldiers' wives and
children. On May 11, Palmer issued Order 32. Meant in part to
ease the flow of unemployed black refugees out of Louisville, it
empowered provost marshals to issue military passes to unemployed blacks and their families. Such passes allowed them to
move "at will in search of employment upon any railroad, steamboat, ferryboat, or other means of travel." They were expected to
pay the "usual fare," and those managing transport facilities who
refused to serve them faced arrest and military trial. The general
encouraged unemployed blacks to leave the state and opened the
Ohio River to them. Order 32 abrogated the old slave code that
still limited the physical movement of slaves and antebellum free
blacks. It opened public transportation to many blacks still considered slaves by their owners.

Palmer enforced Order 32. When Bill Hurd, alleged to have
been a "slave trader," demanded the surrender of a slave woman
he owned but who lived in the refugee camp James managed, the
woman said her husband had enlisted in the Union Army, and that
she had a railroad pass to take her to Cincinnati. Hurd insisted she
had never married and tried to prevent her departure. Palmer
ordered a military hearing, and after it ordered James to "take
her across the river and see her on board the cars." A "file of
guards" accompanied the couple. The woman left for Cincinnati.
Palmer himself estimated in mid-July that as many as five thousand
blacks crossed the Ohio River at Louisville. A *New York Times*
correspondent, who called the migrants "black vomit," noticed
among them "men, women, and children . . . generally upon the
move for some place beyond the reach of their masters." Most
Kentucky slaves and ex-slaves, of course, did not quit that state,

and James, worried that pressure from distressed whites might cause President Andrew Johnson to end martial law there, urged that a delegation of five Kentucky blacks visit the president. A formal address to Johnson stated their concerns. They pleaded for a federal presence to prevent enforcement of the state's slave code and other laws that held down free blacks. Otherwise, Kentucky "jails and workhouses would groan" with black inmates. Federal power was required to "shield" them from long-restrained "brutal instincts." "We have no right of domicile," they said. "We have no right to travel freely. We have no right of self-defense." The president was reminded that "over 30,000" Kentucky blacks, mostly slaves, had "poured out their blood lavishly in the defense of the country" and urged that "this blood . . . be carried to our credit in any political settlement of our native State." To turn the state over to the "control of the civil authorities" meant that these soldiers would suffer "all the grinding oppression of her most inhuman laws if not in their own persons yet in the persons of their women and mothers."

Despite opposition from a leading Louisville black Baptist clergyman, prominent Louisville blacks also planned a public Independence Day celebration. James later claimed credit for convincing Palmer to permit the holiday fete. Palmer's recollection differed. Before that time, Palmer remembered, "an impression [spread] abroad amongst the negroes throughout the State" that they would be declared free that day. "Inflamed by this belief," Palmer told Andrew Johnson, "thousands of them left their masters' houses, and came into our posts at different points in the State. Every nook and hiding-place at such places as Camp Nelson, Lexington . . . &c. was filled with them. They were without work or means."* Owners advertised for some, and whites hesitated to

---

* Camp Nelson remained open until the fall of 1865. In April, the missionary Elnathan Davis, then stationed there, complained that women and children freed a month earlier by Congress were now "being threshed out of their old haunts . . . and compelled to fly." Many went to Camp Nelson. "The husbands and fathers," Davis went on, "are following the flag . . . and the old oppressors, enraged at their loss, strike back at the nation's black defenders through those dearest to them." Elijah Marrs helped guide about 750 women and children from Bowling Green to Camp Nelson and later remembered that "thousands of people were coming in from all directions, seeking their freedom." The "city of refuge" closed in the fall. Federal officials shut it down to "scatter the families." Some months later, a few hundred women and children who remained were described as *the poorest of all creation.* John Fee, who had done much for these and other blacks, quit the place to buy central Kentucky land and resell it to former slaves in small tracts. He also taught in an interracial Kentucky school. "We yet live," Fee boasted in November 1866.

hire "slaves" for fear of prosecution under antebellum law. A committee of Louisville blacks, perhaps including James, met with Palmer to ask when the general would announce the freedom of Kentucky's remaining slaves. Palmer remembered telling them that he lacked such authority. The blacks nevertheless went ahead with the celebration. They picked Johnson's Woods, a grove near the city, and James arranged for resident black soldiers to "protect the colored people in their celebration."

A huge parade through the Louisville streets brought thousands of blacks to Johnson's Woods on July fourth. The superintendent of Louisville's black schools fixed the number parading at twelve thousand, but an *Anglo-African* correspondent figured that ten thousand persons marched and another ten thousand waited at the grove. Eight hundred black soldiers and a military band headed the parade, and another six hundred black soldiers and a second military band closed the line of march. Organized groups of Louisville blacks paraded: children from seven schools; adult members of mutual aid societies such as the Sons of Union, the United Brothers of Friendship, and the Colored Ladies Soldier's and Freedman's Aid Society; one hundred and fifty government employees; and "a car filled with busy workmen, plying the saw, the plane, the hammer, and the mallet." A dinner was fed the soldiers at the grove. Then whites and blacks, including John Mercer Langston, the Virginia ex-slave who had recruited black soldiers and then worked for the Freedmen's Bureau, spoke. Palmer and Brisbin, however, spent much of the day at the Louisville fairgrounds where they heard a well-known actor turned Methodist preacher read the Declaration of Independence. Word reached Palmer that the assembled blacks—"about twenty thousand" in all—would not disperse until they heard from the general. Palmer and Brisbin borrowed a chariot and four piebald horses from a traveling circus at the fairgrounds and made their way to Johnson's Woods. They arrived in the late afternoon.

Just what Palmer told the assembled blacks remains in dispute. Palmer's recollection of the speech differed from the words recorded by the *Anglo-African* correspondent. "My countrymen," he said, "you are substantially free." The general's biographer insists that the blacks "did not hear the word 'substantially,'" shouted and sang as if at "a religious revival," and praised Palmer "as if he was god." "A powerful impulse seized Palmer," writes his biographer, "to set the negroes free," and "he raised his hand and cried, 'My countrymen, *you are free,* and while I command this department the military forces of the United States will defend your rights to freedom!" Years later, Palmer reflected that at that moment "human slavery had ceased to exist." But, according to the *Anglo-African* correspondent, Palmer spoke "substantially as follows":

> You present the strange anomaly of a people who have no home in the land of your birth, no children, no property; you are niggers, slaves, property. . . . But I tell you here to-day, fellow-citizens . . . under . . . the throne of Almighty Ruler of the Universe, under the divine influence of the immortal Declaration of our fathers, that, throughout the length and breadth of our land, *slavery is dead*. . . . There is no slavery in Kentucky, unless you want to be slaves. . . . From now, and henceforth and forever, *you are free*! you, and your children, and your broken families. . . .

Palmer spoke glowingly of the black soldier in the war but returned to the family theme:

> If any one has your children, go and get them. If they will not give them to you, steal them out at night. I do not think you will be committing any crime, nor do I believe the Almighty Ruler of the Universe will think you have committed any. (Applause.) When I want to rob you, I will not steal your babes, nor you, nor the sweat of your brows; but I will come at night when darkness hides the earth beneath its sable mantle, and rob you as you did old massa's hen-roost. (Laughter.)

The general urged the blacks to work only for wages, to quit employers unwilling to pay them, and, in general, to "help yourselves." "You must now work," he added. "You have families to support; your wives will need clothes; your children need books and an education. Freedom confers new obligations. . . ." Military orders meant little. Freedom, the blacks learned from Palmer, depended upon "the resolve that you will be free."

A few weeks after the black Independence Day celebration, Palmer issued Order 49, which expanded Order 32 and greatly facilitated physical mobility among Kentucky's "slaves" and "ex-slaves." It permitted military officers over the state to issue "free passes" to blacks who had piled into their camps. Palmer, who defended his actions to the Secretary of War, said Order 49 was meant to protect soldiers and their families freed by military enlistment. Some, "technically" still the slaves of loyal owners, had taken advantage of Order 49, but Palmer felt obligated to protect the rest from antebellum slave laws. Blacks considered Palmer's "passes" as "their 'free papers' " and rushed to get them. The full range of their response awaits careful study, but the *Western Citizen* described what happened in and near Paris, Kentucky. "Great commotion" among the blacks followed their learning that passes would be issued on July 22. "Numbers" went to town that day, and the military commandant's post "was virtually converted into a general emancipation office." Passes went to all who made application. Then, the news "spread like 'wild fire' throughout the country," and the roads were "literally filled" with blacks "of all ages and sizes, including the lame, the halt, and the blind, in wagons, in buggies, on horseback, and on foot." They created "a perfect jam" near the military office. Guards admitted only women (probably soldiers' wives) that day. But the next day, passes with the endorsement "to go to Cincinnati" were distributed more generously. In November, Palmer estimated that about ten thousand Kentucky blacks had crossed the Ohio River, and a hostile critic said that as many as twenty thousand passes had been issued.

White opposition to Palmer's new edict remained fierce. In late September, a Louisville grand jury indicted Palmer and Brisbin for abducting slaves and otherwise violating the Kentucky slave codes. A Louisville woman advertised her reaction to Order 49:

> WARNING—Any persons hiring my negro women, Charlotte and Flora, both bright mulattoes, about 18 and 17 respectively, I will prosecute for harboring runaways, and sue for hire.
>
> Mrs. Patsey Estelle

On October 12, Andrew Johnson ended martial law in Kentucky but resisted pressures to remove Palmer from his command and refused to repudiate his actions. Hostile whites grew even bolder. The Kentucky Central Railroad ordered its conductors to refuse transportation to "slaves" without written passes from their owners. A Tennessee ex-slave on his way to Cincinnati to gather his family sent there for safety during the war lost the pass given to him by his ex-owner. A Covington railroad official denied the man needed transport. The Louisville and Jeffersonville ferry was closed to blacks, and Palmer had to use force to keep the river open to blacks anxious to leave Kentucky. Palmer's white opponents found the Kentucky courts friendly. Henry P. Reid sued the Kentucky Stage Company for transporting six "slaves" to Lexington without passes from him. The firm said they were soldiers' wives and children and therefore free persons, but a Kentucky judge, later upheld by an appeals court, declared the March 1865 law unconstitutional. Another judge made the same judgment in sending the wife of a black soldier back to her owner. Four civil suits seeking damages up to seventy thousand dollars and the September grand-jury indictment troubled Palmer until a Louisville judge dismissed them in early December 1865 following the ratification of the Thirteenth Amendment. "Thanks be to God who has given us victory," Palmer confided to his wife; "slavery has died in Kentucky, a felon's death, by judicial sentence." Palmer abolished the pass system by announcing that the ratification of the Thirteenth Amendment made it unnecessary. The Kentucky legislature denounced him at the very moment that Louisville blacks "extensively" signed petitions urging that body to define the "rights, duties, and interests of the colored people within the general laws of marriage, divorce, and legitimacy." Kentucky whites blamed Palmer for all their troubles, and in 1866 a Kentucky court found him guilty of a felony for aiding Ellen, the "slave of Womack," in her escape to Indiana. Palmer, the judge said, had incited "a spirit of servile insurrection," encouraged "escape from servitude," and so disrupted the traditional labor system that rural and urban whites, "suddenly left without their accustomed and necessary help," had been "excited almost to revolution." The judge gave far too much credit to Palmer. The process he condemned had started in April 1864, when so large a percentage of Kentucky slave men had quit their owners to join the Union Army and when their wives and children trekked after them.

So severe a social upheaval as occurred in Kentucky between April 1864 and January 1866 tested the strength of slave family ties among soldiers and other slaves. Although the Kentucky Freedmen's Bureau head Clinton Fisk judged that "many persons in the State . . . treat the freedmen justly and generously," he nevertheless said that "fellow-soldiers, yet clad in the uniform of their country's army" had been "the victims of fiendish atrocity from the hands of their former masters." They had returned to their "old homes" for their wives and children and there been "knocked down, whipped, and horribly bruised, and then threatened with *shooting*, should they ever dare to set their feet on the premises of the old master again and intimate that their families were free." "It is dangerous," Fisk reported, "for colored people to go into Logan, Todd, Barren, and the north part of Warren counties after their children." A wife who quit her former owner to live with her husband was followed and shot at. Jordan Finney and his two daughters lived in Walton. Both had soldier husbands. Another daughter belonged to a Boone County white. Finney and an expressman friend went for her, and sixteen armed white men beat them "cruelly with clubs and stones." Returning Confederate soldiers attacked Finney's house three times, "abused the women and children, destroyed all their clothing, bedding, and furniture to the value of $500, and finally drove them from their homes." They did not want "government niggers to live in the county." An old black who took refuge at Camp Nelson told missionaries there he had returned "home" to join his wife "but came near being shot at by her master and his neighbors who were watching for him." Two of their sons served in the Union Army. A cavalry soldier, who met his wife at Camp Nelson, said she had left their children behind because her old owner threatened her with jail or death "if she takes them away." Another soldier showed up at Camp Nelson with his head and face badly cut up. He had "returned to his old home to see his family and was set upon by some white people. . . ." The federal soldiers Elijah Burdette, David Smith, and Henry Bishop had similar troubles. Burdette's old owner had whipped his wife until she was insensible. Bishop's old owner beat the black's two daughters and then kidnaped one away from her employer to hire her to a third white. Marcus Thomas, the son of David Smith's old owner, grew angry with Smith's wife, stripped her naked, knocked her down with a chair, and then bound and whipped her. The soldier Jacob Rile and his family had to leave their former owner's Boone County place after armed whites burned Rile's house and wounded him in the heel. A Lexington physician had three visits in three days from returned Union Army black soldiers. Two had been beaten by their ex-owners, one because he had come for his children. The third caught some white men "ducking his little boy in a pond, and when he attempted to rescue the boy they fell upon him and beat him."[5]

It cannot be argued that the abuse suffered by returning ex-slave Kentucky soldiers and their families resulted from John Palmer's aggressive efforts to enforce the March 1865 law. The families of Kentucky slave soldiers had been abused before Palmer took command. And ex-slave soldiers and their families in other slave states had similar troubles. "The families of slaves enlisted in the army," said a Freedmen's Bureau officer who surveyed the lower Maryland counties in the summer of 1865, ". . . have to endure peculiar hardships from the prejudice existing among the people against those who have been in the army, or who have husbands, fathers, or brothers there." In October 1865, two Alabama ex-slaves stationed in Huntsville were given three-day passes to visit their homes. They camped out along the way and were murdered. Soon after, a Huntsville military chaplain described what happened to an ex-slave infantryman:

> Upon his arrival at his sister's house or cabin in Morgan County, Alabama, his former master finding him to be a soldier turned his Sister's family out of the cabin and informed him that he not stay in that section of the country and fearing from the threats that were made on his life, he was compelled to leave the same day he arrived.[6]

Ex-slave soldiers concerned for their families had difficulties with others than their owners and other southern whites. Men like Speed Smith Fry were more common among the Union Army officers than men like John Palmer. In October 1865, an unidentified ex-slave soldier serving in the 5th U. S. Cavalry and stationed in Lexington, Kentucky, described the abuse of black soldiers:

> . . . when our wives comes to the camp to see us they are not allowed to come in camp and we are not allowed to go out and see them they are drummed off and the officers say go you damn bitches you know that it is to much they are treated so by these officer. . . .
> if you please to allow us the privilege of going home to situate our familys for the winter we are able to situate them by labor if you allow us the privelege.

"We are here," this letter said in another place, "and our wives and children are laying out doers and we have no chance to get a home for them we havent had six days furlough to see our wives and we have been in the army fourteen months." The letter was sent to the Secretary of War.[7]

Neither the coming of the Union Army nor the general emancipation altered the sexual beliefs of southern ex-slaves, southern whites, and northern whites. But the social upheaval associated with the war and the emancipation allowed the ex-slaves to act upon their beliefs in a changed setting and even— for some—to try to reverse sexual and social practices that violated prevalent slave moral and social norms. The task proved difficult.

Union Army soldiers were not all model Victorian gentlemen. The elderly ex-slave Eliza Handy said that those who passed her South Carolina home were "a bad lot dat disgrace Mr. Lincoln" and "insult women both white and black." Tena White lived on a plantation near Charleston, and her mother "shut me up and she gard me" because the Yankee soldiers "do just what dey want" and were "brutish." Three times in less than two weeks, Mary Mallard and her mother Mary Jones recorded how their Georgia rice-plantation slaves resisted the sexual advances of William Sherman's soldiers. Some women hid with their owners. Slave husbands remained "at their homes for the protection of their wives," and "in some instances rescued them from the hands of these infamous creatures." When Sue was being dragged forcibly to her room by a soldier, another soldier intervened. She fled, "dreadfully frightened and thoroughly enraged." The soldier who approached "old Mom Rosetta" was told "he had 'no manners.'" She got away, too. Four soldiers, one of them a black, caused the young black cook to lock herself in the kitchen. They ordered the door opened. "I could scarcely keep from smiling at the metamorphosis," said Mary Mallard. "From being a young girl she had assumed the attitude and appearance of a sick old woman, with a blanket thrown over her head and shoulder, and scarcely able to move." She went unharmed.[8]

Other ex-slave women were far less fortunate. At Haines Bluff, Mississippi, a white Union Army cavalryman raped "a grandmother in the presence of her grandchildren." White soldiers raped two Fortress Monroe, Virginia, women. Two soldiers seized the father and son-in-law of a woman while two others raped her. Another woman was raped "after a desperate struggle" in the "presence of her father and grandfather." A soldier first struck the father after the black "gave vent to his bitter anguish by an irrepressible groan" and then abused a neighboring white woman, who also apparently protested. "The grandfather and the girl came to us," said a sympathetic northern white, "and told us the sad story of their wrongs." New York, New Jersey, and Maine soldiers burned ten slave cabins on the South Carolina Sea Island Jenkins plantation, robbed its residents of food and fowl, furniture, cooking utensils, and even cash. "Some of the troops," a white complained to their commander Rufus Saxton, "have forcibly entered the negro houses, and after driving out the men (in one instance at the point of a bayonet) have attempted to ravish the women." When the men protested and sought to protect "their wives and sisters," they "were cruelly beaten and threatened with instant death." "The morals of the old plantation," Saxton feared, "seem revived in the army of occupation." That happened elsewhere, too. A Natchez black complained to the *Christian Recorder* in June 1865 that husbands and fathers had witnessed the "forcible violation of the virtue of their wives and daughters by white [Union] guards and soldiers." "The emancipation," he bitterly said, "*seems* only to have been a ruse, a base ruse to secure the triumph of *Union* arms." Two months later, Richmond blacks gathered in the Second African Baptist Church to petition the military authorities for redress against Union Army soldiers, who were "gobbling up . . . the most likely looking negro women" and putting them in the New Market jail where some were "robbed and ravished at the will of the guards." They asked for protection or "the privilege of protecting ourselves."[9]

Some southern whites were no less respectful of ex-slave women than these Union Army soldiers. Right after the emancipation, for example, whites raped Nicholas County, Kentucky, black women, and near Hamburg, South Carolina, five masked whites broke into Chandler Garrot's home and raped his wife. The native white Mobile police were no better than either the Natchez or Richmond Union Army soldiers. "The enormities committed by these policemen," said Union Army General Thomas Kilby Smith in September 1865, "were fearful. Within my knowledge, colored girls seized upon had to take their choice between submitting to outrage on the part of the policemen or incarceration in the guard-house." The abuse of a black woman that summer especially enraged the black "Alabama," the Mobile correspondent for the New Orleans *Tribune*. "Hugh McKeever," the Mobile *Advertiser* reported on July 31, "was complained of by a negro wench for knocking her down." Alabama law did not permit blacks to give testimony against whites, and the Mobile mayor dismissed the woman's complaint. The mayor and the *Advertiser* infuriated "Alabama." He asked if the wife of the *Advertiser*'s reporter "is a white wench or a colored lady" and charged that Mobile's mayor lived with a black woman. "How do you feel," he asked of the mayor, "when in the stillness of the night . . .

you return to the bosom of Madame L. and press her to the spot you call your heart. . . . Do you think of those poor [black] women you have out to work upon the public streets, and still have the heart to say you love and respect one of them?" "Alabama" pleaded with the federal authorities to protect the ex-slaves, warned that Mobile's black men might "strike for liberty or death, justice or blood" and repeat "the scenes of San Domingo" without such protection. He concluded, "We have sworn before God to protect inviolate our wives and daughters." The Alabama State Constitutional Convention in September 1865 heard from Mobile's National Lincoln Association, which asked for the franchise, for legal equality, and for laws that would prevent their being "assaulted and insulted in the public streets." "Our wives, our daughters and our sisters," said the petitioners, "are grossly insulted when passing and repassing in their honest vocations." The Constitutional Convention rejected the plea by these men who described themselves as "a part of the family of this great republic, and a part of that family . . . created by the same Almighty Being with whom there is no discrimination on account of cast [sic] or color."[10]

Military occupation and emancipation unsettled the exploitative sexual ties that had bound unknown numbers of slave women to owners and other whites. That issue surfaced early. "We are part of this race, though our skins have a darker hue," said the *Colored Tennessean;* ". . . the best blood of the haughty South runs in the veins of her darker children." "Was it . . . because we were not really human that we have not been recognized as a member of the nation's Family?" Henry Turner asked in an Emancipation Day speech on January 1, 1866, in Augusta, Georgia. "Are there any difference[s] in our women?" Turner went on. *"White men can answer this question better than us."* The black clergyman dismissed the argument that "if you free the negro he will want to marry our daughters and sisters" as a "foolish dream," explaining, "We have as much beauty as they; *all we ask of the white man is to let our ladies alone,* and they need not fear us. The difficulty has heretofore been *our ladies were not always at our disposal."* Slave women had been "insulted or degraded with or without their consent." Sentiment to expel the ex-slaves from the country caused the New Orleans *Tribune* to remind readers of the "powerful attraction, at least from the white race to the black one." "When you speak of separation," advised the *Tribune,* "it is your illegitimates and their unfortunate mothers that you propose to banish from among you. The talk is idle and senseless. The attraction between both races has proved too strong for their ever being severed." When the white Ursin Pellitier and the black Betsey Thomas married in New Orleans, the *Tribune* advised "other Caucasians" to "take a hint and now that the law allows it legitimate their children." It headlined the report of this marriage "THE WORLD MOVES."[11]

Not all sexual ties between slave women and white men were exploitative, and not all interracial contacts between slaves, ex-slaves, and free persons involved black women and white men. The wartime and early postwar records detail isolated but nevertheless significant instances of slave women and white owners deeply attached to one another. In June 1865, when Lurania Clanton appeared before the Augusta, Georgia, Freedmen's Bureau, she was the mother of several children by her former owner Turner Clanton, who had freed the woman and their children on his death. He also had willed them some of his properties. (She filed a complaint against two white men who held her children "as slaves" and also wanted Bureau assistance in securing the property willed to her.)[12] There is also scattered evidence indicating sexual contact and even marital connections between southern white women and slave and ex-slave men. In 1866, the Athens, Alabama, civil authorities arrested a white woman and a black man who lived together and put them in separate cells. The next year, Bill Wyrnosdick, a Crenshaw, Alabama, black, went to jail for thirty days and paid a two-hundred-dollar fine for living with a white female employee. "I proposed to mary hir," Wyrnosdick explained to the Alabama Freedmen's Bureau, "but the judge woodent suffer me. I shall lose my crop if you dont do something for me. . . . I am igonant of the laws of the Country. I will try to do write in the future." About that time, a Fredericksburg, Virginia, court acquitted a black woman charged with assaulting a white woman who had "stolen the affections" of the black woman's husband, causing him to leave her for the white woman. And in New Orleans, the Baton Rouge black Ben Lyon asked the Freedmen's Bureau to help get "two white girls" out of jail. They had dressed in men's clothing and accompanied two "colored men" to New Orleans. They planned to marry them there but were arrested and held in jail. A parish judge would not let them pay their fines.[13]

Exploitative ties between ex-slave women and white men, ex-owners prominent among them, were far more common than these instances of relationships between white women and black men.[14] Ex-slave women everywhere dealt with a legacy that viewed them as dependent sexual objects. Soon after she arrived on the Sea Islands in 1862, Laura M. Towne noticed that black women needing relief "object to going to the young [white] gentlemen . . . for clothing, thinking it will be taken as a kind of advance for notice—such notice as the best of them have probably dreaded but which the worst have sought." Julia Tucker had such an experience. As the widow of Conger Tucker, a Tennessee slave who died a Union Army soldier, she was eligible for his unpaid bounty. She asked a white Memphis lawyer to file her claim but turned him away, explaining, "He used my witness, a young girl named Lucy Reeves, in a very outrageous manner, throwing her down on a sofa, and then thrusting me out of the room." When Edwin, Paul, and Haskins Chaplin returned to the Sea Islands in late 1865 to resume management of their plantation, the armed brothers drove away some whites and blacks, including the ex-slave Jim. They took possession of his house, "lived with his daughter in an improper manner," and threatened to shoot the father "if he came on the place." The old man stayed away for weeks, but black neighbors reported the Chaplins to the Freedmen's Bureau. In Alabama, a returning Confederate soldier shot an ex-slave following a quarrel over the black's wife. Before the war, the white had been "on terms of improper intimacy" with her and had prevented her marriage until he left for the army. The slaves then married. The wounded husband was arrested after the shooting, and an Alabama white lawyer represented him at the request of a returning Confederate general. The ex-slave had been this man's body servant.[15]

Ex-slave women elsewhere severed ties with white men. "My mama and papa split off, and mama get married," recollected Oliver Blanchard. Before the war, his mother had lived on a Louisiana plantation with a white carpenter, Blanchard's father. Born a Virginia slave in 1856, Harriet Ann Davis was her mother's owner's child. He moved his family to Missouri during the Civil War. "He never denied me to anybody," the elderly woman remembered. "My father never married. . . . He loved my mother, and he said if he could not marry Mary he did not want to marry." Her mother, however, "told my father she was tired of living that kind of a life" and "if she could not be his legal wife she wouldn't be anything to him, so she left him." In Nashville, two ex-slaves went to the Freedmen's Bureau in the summer of 1865 to name the white father of their children, reportedly an

"F.F.T.," who, in turn, promised to "support . . . the little freed-men." That same summer, a Hillsborough, North Carolina, county solicitor learned from an ex-slave, away from his wife and children during the war, that his wife had "two light compexioned young-sters added to her first two children." He refused to support them, and his wife wanted to "make oath" as to their paternity. A few months later, the Murfreesboro, Tennessee, Freedmen's Bureau heard complaints from two ex-slaves, the seventy-year-old Unity and the forty-five-year-old Minerva, against their former owner D. Beasley, who had driven them from his place, "a poor one." Beasley, who had left them there because "the Black hearted Yankees were coming" and he wanted to go to "his children," returned after the war. The women said he had told them "they might stay and have everything." Now, they complained, "he drives us into the street." Unity, the Bureau learned, had "suckled Beasley," and Beasley "has cohabited nightly for seventeen years" with Minerva. "They have lain in the same bed that time at night," noted the Bureau officer. Beasley testified, too, and did not deny the allegations. He "drove off the old woman because she could not work & Minerva because she would not submit to his lust." The Murfreesboro Bureau officer fined Beasley nine dollars and ordered that he let the women "stay rent free."[16]

Ex-slave women in South Carolina, North Carolina, Alabama, Georgia, and Texas pressed claims with the Freedmen's Bureau against the white fathers of their children. In June 1865, Emma Hurlbert ("a *very* pretty colored woman nearly white") and Precilla ("black and ugly") each went before the Augusta, Georgia, Bureau. The first wanted James Selkirk, then the Waynesboro Railroad superintendent, to support her child. She said he was its father. The pregnant Precilla claimed that the slave trader O. H. Marshal, who had brought her from North Carolina during the war, was the father of her child and had "turned her out of doors." A Bureau officer convinced Marshal to support her. The next year, Caroline Johnson appeared before the Augusta Bureau to charge that Benjamin Conklin, with whom she had lived "ever since she was old enough" and who was the father of her four children, had driven her off "& refuses to give her clothes or help support the children." About the same time, the Dallas County Bureau heard from the Alabama ex-slave Frances Pollen. William Wade had driven her from his plantation without pay because she "married a colored man on the neighboring plantation, Wade having intended her for his sweetheart." The Bureau ordered that Wade pay her one hundred ten dollars in back wages. The pregnant Clarissa Jones twice dealt with the Greenville, South Carolina, Bureau in 1868. Owned by William Robertson, a Transylvania County, North Carolina, Justice of the Peace, she had been kept on by him after the emancipation. He supplied her with food and clothing for her work. In 1867, Robertson promised her fifty dollars a year to help care for her two-year-old child. The black woman said he was its father as well as the father of her unborn child. "Fearing she would swear both to him," the Bureau record said, Robertson had "brought her into South Carolina & threatened if she returned he would kill her." She asked the Greenville Bureau for help, and it sent her back to North Carolina with a letter urging that "she . . . be justified." But Clarissa Jones could not make it back to North Carolina "before she would be confined," and the Greenville Bureau arranged with the town Commissioners of the Poor to care for her. A sympathetic Austin, Texas, Bureau officer also assisted the ex-slave Emma Hartsfield after she filed a complaint against the Austin white Lary McKenzie, charging that he had "induced her to live with him by a promise . . . [of] a house and a lot." They had lived together more than a year, and she became pregnant. McKenzie, the Bureau report said, "proposed to have her procure an abortion & because she would not do it, is about to sell the house and go away." The Bureau attached his land, and an officer hoped "to try & frighten him into a settlement." The two appeared before the Bureau, and McKenzie "executed a deed to her of Lot No. 8 in Austin with two houses." Emma Hartsfield signed an agreement releasing the father of her unborn child from "all claims." "Pretty dear pay for one year's _____," said a Bureau officer of the settlement.[17]

Settlements of a different kind but also involving black women and white men occurred in Yazoo City, Mississippi. That, at least, was what A. T. Morgan, a Yankee migrant to Mississippi who became a planter and Radical Republican and who married a Virginia-born black schoolteacher recollected in *Yazoo, or on the Picket Line of Freedom in the South* (1884). Morgan learned that prior to the emancipation Yazoo's "colored concubines" had high prestige based upon their ties to prominent Yazoo white men and that for a time afterward they retained "their supremacy . . . in the churches, the schools, and social gatherings." These slave and ex-slave women "ranked according to the rank of their white 'sweethearts,' " Morgan said; "when 'Liz' was the concubine of a wealthy planter she stood at the head of colored 'ciety'; when she became the concubine of a merchant or lawyer she went down one point . . . and thus she continued to descend in the social scale until she became the wife of a 'po no 'count nigger.' " A daughter might sometimes follow her mother's "example" (*often in her very tracks*"), but Morgan also learned that, "as was often the case," a concubine had "too much pride and self-respect to rear daughters for such a purpose—in which case she destroyed herself to prevent it or killed them." Emancipation altered the status of all Yazoo blacks, including these women. "Several" were "turned out of church" for " 'living in adultery' in the sight of man as well as God." That rebuke, according to Morgan, caused some to "inquire whether there was any legal inhibition upon their marriages with 'white sweethearts.' " They also supported the 1868 Radical State Constitution, hoping it would enforce "their rights as heirs in cases where there were none having a prior right." In 1870, the Radical Mississippi legislature repealed the 1865 ban on racial intermarriage. Some Yazoo concubines felt that moment the occasion to demand legal marriage from their "sweethearts." Morgan suggested that they withheld their bodies from these men. They "not only kicked against the pricks, they actually began to wear armor against them." They provoked diverse responses from their lovers: one built "an elegant new resident" for his concubine; another gave her "money"; a third "secretly married" his concubine; a fourth made "promises." Some men "surrendered" all "claims" to "their" women; "the great mass 'bided their time.' " "These last," Morgan remembered, "were harassed nigh unto death by the 'insolence' of the concubines."[18]

Ex-slave women of far less "status" than these Yazoo concubines pressed charges with the Freedmen's Bureau against sexual abuse by white men. Scilia Gedders told the Monck's Corner, South Carolina, Bureau that Warren Carson, the white who managed the farm on which she worked, tried to rape her in the fields, and Jane Harris hired a white Greenville lawyer to press charges against a white who beat her after she resisted his sexual advances. In the summer and fall of 1865, the Murfreesboro, Tennessee, Bureau had three separate complaints from ex-slaves against Andrew B. Payne, "reckoned one of the most respectable among men." A father protested in behalf of his daughter, and so did a mother.* Another woman appeared before the Bureau in her own

---

* Sam Neal told the Bureau that "Payne hires myself and family altogether to work for the season. He has made several base attempts on my daughter; has ordered me off without pay or share of my crop; and because I did not go he got his pistol & threatened to shoot me.—He got Miles Ferguson to beat me & both together beat me badly." The Bureau ordered that Payne and Ferguson each pay Neal twenty-five dollars, and that Neal be allowed to gather the crop and keep his share.

behalf. Tabby Wheatley complained that Payne and Miles Ferguson "took my daughter and beat her badly." When she fled to her mother's cabin, they followed and tried to beat her again. "I would not let them," said the mother. "Payne then jumped on me & Ferguson struck me down a dozen times with a stick. Payne took the girl down [to] the back of the yard & pulled her clothes over her head and beat her holding her head between his knees.* I heard the cries of the girl & ran down. He then let go of the girl and began to beat me again. . . ." A few days before Christmas, Payne made similar advances to Maria Posey, an ex-slave who lived with her five-year-old daughter. When he entered her place, she was in bed:

> I got off the bed and was putting on my shoes when he pushed me back and tried to pull up my clothes. I screamed. He let me alone. I jumped up & ran toward the door.—I then saw a companion of his outside. Payne took up a fire shovel & was going to strike me with it when the man jumped in & took the shovel from him. He then shoved me back on the fire & burned up my dress.

Maria Posey showed the charred dress to the Murfreesboro Bureau officer.[19]

The complaints of the ex-slaves Martha and Eliza Kemp and Manerva Moore to the Amite City, Louisiana, Bureau in September 1865 led to the arrest of the whites Jules Dalyet and D. Clements. According to Martha Kemp, the two men entered her place at three in the morning and awakened the three women. She could not keep them out, and "they went to the girls":

* That Payne pulled up the young girl's clothes and put her head "between his knees" while beating her may have been more than personal idiosyncrasy. A few years later, Almanance and Rockingham County Ku Klux Klan violence against North Carolina blacks and whites included the beating of the daughter of a white woman who ran a rural bordello. She was "forced," writes the historian Allan Trelease, "to expose herself while the Klansmen beat her private parts." An Almanance black died after being whipped and forced by Klansmen to "mutilate his penis with a pocketknife." Other Klansmen made a Rockingham black "go through the motion of sexual intercourse with a Negro girl while they whipped him and forced her father to look on." (A. W. Trelease, *White Terror: The Ku Klux Klan Conspiracy and Southern Reconstruction* [1971], 195, 201–2.) Further study of southern white sexual mores may allow us to understand the seemingly ritualistic character of these sexual punishments. See also the following entry in the Texas Freedmen's Bureau Records, vol. 52, p. 20, called to my attention by Barry Crouch: "Mr. James Haynes reports that ——— Bennett (white boy of 16 years old) had carnal intercourse with one of his Ewes on Sunday 9th June [1867]. The only witness was a colored boy Lee Reid, 13 years old. The State law will not permit him to testify. Mr. H. therefore reports the case here."

I came over to see the officers to see if I could not put a
stop to some of their actions. I then went across to Mr.
Mitchells & tried to wake them up. Mr. Clements came there
and asked me what I was there for. I told him I was after
matches to make a light. Clements said I could not get it at
Mr. Mitchells, he was drunk but wanted me to go & lay with
him until morning. I told him I was a woman of the church &
did not do such things.

Mr. Dalyet came and asked me where I had been. I told
him I was after matches to light my pipe, he said I had been
to the officer's. . . . I told him to go to a white woman & not
to trouble colored women. He said he didn't want me to tell
him about white women any more, he then hit me three times
with his fist twice on the head & once on the collar bone. I ran
and hollowed murder. He said he would shoot me & ran as if
to get a pistol & I ran the other way. He stopped & pulled off
his petticoats, he had been dressed in womens clothes.

Eliza Kemp added further details, telling that Dalyet choked her,
"threw me down — ran his hands under my clothes. I had a child
in my arms, he hit me on the side of the head with his fist &
went out the house." Manerva Moore also was beaten and said
both men "tried to run their hands under my clothes." A black
neighbor, Cicelia, supported the testimony of the three women:

Mr Dalyet & another man came in, I do not know who the
other man was, came in through Mr Charleys window from
their into my room & got into bed, one on one side & the other
on the other & began to jab & punch me. I hollowed for Mrs.
Saul who lives in the next room, I told them not to choke me,
they then started out of the door, the tallest one tried to keep
me from going out of the door. I took a chair & threw [it] at
him. They came back again. I had a candle lit. I told them
it was a shame for them to act so as they were both well known.
They said let's go back. The small one, Mr. D. pulled up his
clothes & went out, he had on women's clothes.

Clements and Dalyet did not deny the charges. They said they
were drunk and did not remember "what they did." Bureau
officers learned they had "always borne a good character." Dalyet,
a young man, owned "no property in his own right" but was "a
strictly up right young man." Clements owned "considerable
property." Convinced that the evidence was "conclusive of insult
to females of color," a Bureau officer fined the men fifteen dollars
each. Their "former standing" explained the light punishment.[20]

Ex-slave husbands and fathers found it difficult to protect their wives and daughters from the conventional sexual insult and even abuse that remained after the emancipation. "The old rule," A. T. Morgan said of Yazoo City whites, "permitted a white man to pinch or put an arm around a colored woman while shopping, or when she was on the street to stare at, make remarks to or about her of an insulting character, or, as was sometimes the case, openly invite an intrigue, and when resented by the lady, press it by some coarse speech or action." "Scores" of Yazoo freedmen, Morgan remembered, demanded "the same courteous treatment in the streets, in the stores, and at their homes for their wives as common decency exacted for other ladies from the public, the merchant and his clerk, or callers at their residences." But many hesitated. "At first," Morgan noticed, aggressive behavior was "met with contempt and often drew out acts of greater license from those white men who had always acted upon the privilege which their color gave them under the old rule." Derision and sometimes violence greeted similar efforts elsewhere. In July 1865, ex-slave men—some of whom had labored on the large Georgia plantation owned by the family of Eliza Frances Andrews—started the Sons of Benevolence. "The negroes," the young white woman wrote in her diary, "are frequently out very late at night, attending the meetings of a society they have formed . . . for the protection of female virtue, and heaven—or rather the other place—only knows what else." Andrews trivialized their effort, but the Georgia blacks filed one complaint with the Union Army that a local white woman had allowed a sick black employee to die of neglect and took another action against "Mrs. Gabe Toombs's Chloe" accused of "keeping company with a Yankee." In Gibson County early in January 1866, Daniel Wood, then about sixty years old, was "taken from his bed at his wife's house in the night by some white men and carried by force to a considerable distance & shot several times." Wood's wife resided at the white Tom Harris's place, and Harris accused Wood of "giving a venereal disease" to his wife as well as "a colored girl" Harris employed. He told Wood "he ought to pay the doctors bills." The elderly ex-slave called Harris "a da-med liar and advanced up to Harris for a fight." The white shot Wood, and later Wood was shot up again by the other whites. Harris admitted he had shot Wood, but the Bureau released him. Wood could not testify because the gunshot wounds had so incapacitated him.[21]

Few former slave husbands suffered a more humiliating public misfortune than that which befell the Virginian Ned Scott for trying to protect his wife from insult in the Richmond streets in June 1865. His wife's affidavit told what happened. The couple walked with two friends along Main Street, and "two Reb boys with grey coats" approached.

> We gave way [said Jennie Scott] so that they could pass, one of them ran against me and struck me in the breast with his fist. . . . [M]y husband told him I was his wife and asked what he had struck me for. He said "I will strike her and you to, you damned nigger." My husband said "no you won't strike her again I will strike you." They called me all kinds of bad names—I was frightened and ran off. They kept cursing me and calling me bad names, and threw rocks at me. I left my husband their and ran home. . . .

Richard Adams, Scott's black friend, said Scott threatened to stab them with a knife if they struck her again. The two whites left the street, passing by several Union Army soldiers. Adams told what then happened:

> One of them, a seargeant without any arms or equipments, came across to Scott and said, "Cant any white man pass the street without being insulted by a damned nigger." Scott said "I didn't insult any one. I only told that man, that was my wife, and I did not want any one to strike her." Then another [Union] soldier ran over and said "Shut up or I will break your damned snout" and struck him in the breast. Another soldier came up and all three jumped on him and knocked him down and beat him. He shook them off from him, and one said, "I'm cut." Another said "I believe I am cut too." They all ran to the Provost Marshals and two got guns, one got a pistol, and one came on horseback. While they were gone Scott ran off.

Scott had stabbed and slightly wounded two New York Union Army soldiers. He was captured the next night, sent to Libby Prison, given a military trial, sentenced to a thirty-day prison term, and made to undergo extraordinary public punishment. According to the New York *Tribune*, the commanding Union Army general had ordered the punishment.

His friend Adams described the punishment:

> The P.[rovost] Marshal then told his men to tie his [Scott's] hands before him. They then tied his hands and "bucked him." They set him on the floor, stretched his hands below his

knees, ran a broom handle through between his knees and
elbows and sawed it off. Two soldiers brought him out on the
sidewalk on Main St., rolled him about quick[ly] two or three
times, then rolled him over on his side, so that he could not
stir. One of the soldiers went across the street, and took a
colored man and made him go across the street and turn Scott
on each side and hit him five licks with a piece of the coffin.
One of the soldiers said if he did not hit him harder, he would
"buck" and gag him. He then hit him five licks harder. They
then let him lie in the hot sun on the walk about two hours.
He begged for water but they would not give it to him. They
then unbucked him, tied his hands behind him, and put a
paper on his back. I don't know what was on it. I can't read.
Then they put two drummers and two fifers before him, and
some soldiers with charged bayonets behind him. They played
the rogue's march, and marched up Main St from 25th St
and back to the Provost Marshals office.

Adams could not read the placard which said, "I have stabbed two
of the Provost Guards." Adams then related what happened after
the march:

They then tied his hands before him and tied his feet, and
put him into a coffin and nailed the top except about a foot
and a fourth. They then set him out doors, and stood up the
coffin.

He stood there till nearly 7 o'clock. They put some meal
on his face and the flies covered it most all over. He could not
get them off. He asked for water but they would not give it to
him. They put him in a wagon in the coffin. Two soldiers
with guns set upon the coffin, one marched behind with a
charged bayonet, and a colored boy named Henry drove the
wagon to Castle Thunder [prison].

The Richmond *Enquirer* and the *Whig* added details that escaped
Adams's notice. Scott, said the *Whig*, "blinked his mealy eyes and
said not a word while in the coffin"; he sweated like "a harvest field
hand." Blacks who surrounded the coffin "seemed very indignant,"
but Union Army soldiers "laughed at the ludicrous figure the
negro cut in the coffin." Headlining its account "NOVEL EX-
HIBITION," the *Enquirer* had "no doubt" Scott had learned "how
to behave himself in the future." Both papers distorted the initial
difficulty. The *Enquirer* said he had "insulted two gentlemen,"
and the *Whig* explained that he had "refused to give the sidewalk
to the soldiers." No one could learn from these newspaper accounts

that Scott's wife had been involved. He had merely been "walking with a negro woman."[22]

Ned Scott had tried to protect his wife from insult. Other ex-slave husbands and fathers responded to even more severe treatment of their kin by white and black men. The Texas black Lucius Halliday complained to the Bureau that Bell Burleson had tried to make his wife go to his room and used "bad and insulting language" toward her. After four Texas whites carried the daughters of Lewis Travis and a black Fanning County neighbor a short distance from their homes and repeatedly raped them, a black, probably Travis himself, asked the Bureau's help. Samuel Baker agreed to work on the Bossier Parish, Louisiana, farm owned by Sally Walker. The white woman later drove him from the place, and the Bureau learned from Baker that "this woman's son about 18 years old was persistent in seducing this Freedman's wife & on his objecting . . . threatened to shoot him & compeled him to leave the place." Ephraim Alexander, a Caddo Parish black, reported even grimmer doings in July 1866:

> . . . John Hudson of Caddo Parish did on the 26th day of July attempt to ravish his wife or the woman he took up with. She escaped from him & on the 27th day of July he attacked this woman Elsa Alexander while she was washing at the creek and unmercifully beat her, bruising & knocking her down, & stamping her with his fist. This same Hudson & his Brothers & Kuff Ruthford about the fourth day of July did beat & otherwise abuse the freedwoman Amanda Mare who is employed by the widow Galt. They had connection with this woman & on her telling it, they beat her. This Freedwoman is [*illegible*].

Some months later, the Amite City black Nathan Sweeney complained to the Bureau that his employer's son had raped one of his daughters. Sweeney and his family then quit the place. John Wright, a Greenville, South Carolina, ex-slave, went to the Bureau in May 1868 to complain against his employer, Robin Craig. Wright had contracted to work Craig's land for half the crop, had started in March, and had been driven off less than two months later without money or crop. He explained why. Craig and his two sons "were after his wife." Wright said "if they did not stop he would retaliate." The whites did not heed his advice; one evening, Wright said, he "did ask the Daughter and Sister of the Parties if she would meet him . . . [at] night." Craig ordered him off the land.[23]

Concubinage—that is, white men living in sustained nonlegal

relationships with black women—did not end with the general emancipation. Its frequency remains in dispute. "Customary rights" are not easily abandoned, and state law after 1865 did little to protect ex-slave women from such relationships. Black delegates to the Mississippi 1868 Constitutional Convention could not convince the white majority to urge the passage of stringent laws punishing concubinage, including imprisonment, fine, and denial of the right to vote and to give testimony. Black delegates such as Matthew Newson and T. W. Stringer, aided by the white Radical A. T. Morgan, urged Convention delegates to order that "the . . . Legislature *shall* provide by law for the punishment of adultery and concubinage." But convention delegates approved the recommendation after changing the obligatory *"shall"* to the conditional *"may."*[24]

Black delegates aided by a few white Radicals pressed the 1868 Arkansas Constitutional Convention just as hard as the Mississippi blacks and with just as little success. Eight black delegates, led by William Grey, then a clergyman and some years before a body servant to the Virginia Governor Henry A. Wise, and James L. White, urged strong legal measures against concubinage as contrasted to racial intermarriage. Grey advocated the death penalty for any white man "found cohabiting with a negro woman" but doubted the wisdom of prohibiting marriages between whites and persons "of African descent," suggesting that the legislature might have to create "a board of scientific physicians, or professors of anatomy, to discover who is a negro." The "purity of the blood has already been somewhat interfered with in this country," said Grey, an "intermixture" that had "taken place illegitimately." White was just as blunt:

> . . . Who is to blame for the present state of affairs? When I look around I see an innumerable company of mulattoes, not one of them the heir of a white woman. This is satisfactory evidence of the virtue of white women. In the late bloody war, these gentlemen left their wives and daughters in the care of colored men for four years, and I defy the gentlemen to cite me a single instance where they have failed to live up to their integrity. Gentlemen, the shoe pinches on the other foot—the white men of the South have been for years indulging in illicit intercourse with colored women, and in the dark days of slavery this intercourse was largely forced upon the innocent victims, and I think the time has come when such a course should end.

He and Gray condemned opponents of intermarriage "in a legitimate form" who refused to prohibit it from "manifesting itself in an illegitimate form." The native white Republican delegate, a Methodist clergyman, Thomas Bradley, wanted to abolish intermarriage but not concubinage. He desired to "build a wall" but to allow some to "scratch under and get to the other race." "I propose that we stop this crawling under fence," responded Grey. "I propose that if persons desire intermarriage with the other race, it should be done honorably and above-board." The northern white Republican James L. Hodges went even further, urging legislation that declared "as man and wife" all men "cohabiting with females without regard to color" and that established paternity "solely on the evidence of the mother." The Arkansas Constitutional Convention delegates evaded the issue: the new constitution did not prohibit racial intermarriage, and delegates condemned "all amalgamation." That "compromise" angered the Little Rock *Gazette.* The new constitution endangered whites by inviting blacks "to marry their daughters and, if necessary, hug their wives." Calling the delegates a "bastard collocation," it said that "any attempt to arouse their consciences is as futile as prodding a rhinoceros with a ribbon pin."[25]

The *Gazette* fired its arrows in the wrong direction. Before and after 1868, southern legislatures frequently prohibited racial intermarriage but did not tamper with the nonlegal ties that bound some black women to white men. In 1870, Malcolm Claiborne, a black Georgia legislator, pressed unsuccessfully for legislation making "putative fathers . . . maintain their bastard children." Six years later, George A. Mebane, a black North Carolina legislator, could not persuade his colleagues to make it illegal for a white man and a black woman "to lewdly and lasciviously associate, bed, or cohabit together." Texas blacks, who asked in 1883 for laws that "punish as rigidly . . . all carnal intercourse between the two races unlawfully carried on as it punishes them for intermarrying," did not get a legislative response. Maryland blacks had great difficulty convincing the legislature to change a law that allowed white but not black women to name the fathers of illegitimate children so that a town or county could force them to support the children. Although the South Carolina legislature banned interracial marriages in 1879, that legislative act also was written into the 1895 state constitution. Robert Smalls, a Beaufort delegate to the 1895 constitutional convention, a longtime leader among the Sea Island blacks, and the mulatto son of a white planter, moved to amend that edict: white men found guilty of cohabiting with black women were to be barred from holding state office, and children born to such "unions" were to bear their fathers' names and share in their inheritances. Smalls must have realized that his proposals would not impress the white majority, which had come together to legitimize disfranchisement. But his thrust delighted another Sea Island delegate, the well-to-do black farmer James Whiggs, who told a white reporter that "the 'coons' had the dog up the tree for a change."[26]

Parents and other ex-slave kin revealed a deep concern over the entire South about the abusive indenture of children that came in the immediate aftermath of emancipation. We focus only on the Maryland ex-slaves and their resistance to the "apprenticeship" that started the day that Maryland's ninety thousand slaves were emancipated, November 1, 1864. So-called "apprenticeship" drew upon Maryland antebellum apprenticeship laws. Local judges had the power to summon the child of any *free* black if after examination the court found it "better for the habits and comfort of the child that it should be bound as an apprentice to some white person." The law provided free black apprentices with none of the nominal protection given to white apprentices. Whites had to be taught a "trade" and "educated"; blacks had to be taught a "trade." A runaway white could not be sold; a runaway black could be sold. To entice away a white meant a twenty-dollar fine; to entice away a black meant imprisonment for at least eighteen months. If a master died, white parents had to consent to the transfer of their children to another master. Black parents had no say in such matters. Not surprisingly, so loose a law— and especially the powers assigned to Justices of the Peace and Orphan Court judges—lent itself to widespread abuse by former slaveowners.[27]

Emancipation occurred on November 1. Old slaveowners and other whites moved quickly to apprentice black children. On November 2, Andrew Stafford, the federal provost marshal in Easton, complained that "many . . . citizens are endeavoring to intimidate colored people and compel them to bind their children to them under the old apprenticeship law." Ex-slave parents had come to him for advice; he had them "file objections." Others, he worried, "will be deterred from doing so by fear." Two days later, Stafford wrote again. Former owners had made "a rush" to the Talbot County Orphan's Court to apprentice ex-slave children.

"Boys of twelve and fourteen," said Stafford, "are taken from their parents under the pretence that they are incapable of supporting them, while the younger children are left to be maintained by the parents." The requirement of parental consent usually was ignored, and, when asked for, judges denied black parents "the choice of homes." The two Talbot judges involved were "so prejudiced against these poor creatures that they do not regard their rights." "In plain terms," Stafford advised a superior, "the Rebels here are showing an evident determination to still hold this people in bondage." Children had been indentured by judges who declared their parents "vagrants before they have enjoy[ed] liberty a single week—in many instances before they have even been permitted to leave their masters. . . . Justice has become a mockery."

Stafford had not exaggerated. Other Maryland whites reported similar behavior by ex-owners over the entire state. John Graham, a Dorchester County resident, saw children "carried from different portions of the County in ox carts, waggons, and carriages" to local courts. R. T. Turner, who lived in Kent County, penned a sad letter to his Baltimore mother and asked her help. He then looked after a mother and her four children, who were threatened with apprenticeship. Old owners, Turner said, "are dragging the little children of Emancipated parents before proslavery magistrates. . . . The Orphan's Court announces publicly that it will give preference to former owners and the poor blacks have not the choice of a master. . . ." Turner believed "the courts, lawyers, judges, [and] . . . juries . . . all in a general sense . . . oppressors," and he advised ex-slaves to either "suffer oppression, or seek homes in other neighborhoods." Other Maryland counties, however, offered no escape. "Since we the people have Parclaimed that Maryland Should be Free," Thomas B. Davis, the keeper of the Sandy Point Lighthouse in Anne Arundel County, wrote to a Baltimore friend, "the Most Bitter Hatred has been Manifested against the poor Devils that Have Just been freed from beneath their Lash." Apprenticeship especially concerned Davis:

> Sam[l] Richardson has taken to Annapolis four children of one of his slaves . . . [over?] the mother's objections in court he has had them bound to him after stating that all they cloth-[ing] they had on were By her. . . . there is a woman down Here by the Name of Jewel. She is also Demanding of the woman she had turned [out] without a stick of winter's clothing, all three children to be bound to her. When she cannot

get Bread for herself. On friday there was upwards of hundred young Negroes on the ferry with their old Masters draged away forseble from there parents for the purpose of Having them Bound. . . . In the Name of Humanity is there no Redress for these poor ignorant downtrodden wreches—Is this is it not Involinterily Slavery? . . .

Davis worried that readers might misinterpret his letter: "Some folks in Baltimore to see this letter would hint that it was [a] fathers interest manifested in young darkies but [it] is not so every one of them are Jet Black and every knot of wool on there Heads Both ends groes in there Schull therefore there is no anglow Saxon in them."[28]

So many ex-slave children were seized and bound without parental consent and so many blacks and whites protested these actions in the week following the emancipation that General Lew Wallace, then Maryland's chief military officer, issued a special military order on November 9 (Order 112) assuring ex-slaves of military protection until the Maryland legislature met the following January. He established a Freedman's Bureau headed by Major William M. Este and instructed provost marshals to hear complaints and to forward evidence to Este. They had the power to make arrests. Wallace abolished the Bureau on January 30, 1865. Papers forwarded to the adjutant general in November reinforced the complaints of whites like Stafford, Turner, and Davis. Jane Kemper wanted help in retrieving her bed clothes and furniture from the Talbot white William Townsend. She had already taken her children from him: "He locked up my children so that I could not find them. I afterwards got my children by stealth and brought them to Baltimore. . . . My master pursued me to the Boat to get possession of my children but I hid them on the boat." Letters from three other black women—Sarah Ann Jackson, Henrietta Clayton, and Barbara Diggs—asked for aid in getting their children from old owners. Whites supported the claims of some ex-slaves. One lived with the West River white N. S. Glover, who said he had "a child at Geo. W. Hides where it was a slave. its Mother being dead he wishes to obtain it and keep it under his care being apprehensive that the said Hide will have the child bound to him." An Anne Arundel white protested that Mrs. Charles R. Stewart was apprenticing ex-slave children and had already bound two "against their father's will."[29]

When Lew Wallace closed the Maryland Freedman's Bureau on January 30, 1865, he forwarded to the Maryland general assembly much of the evidence given to his subordinates in less than ninety days.[30] On November 16, a Harford County provost marshal had the names of twenty-five children apprenticed against their parents' wishes, ten of them not yet ten years old. By the end of that month, the Kent County deputy provost marshal, Bartus Trew, had the names of one hundred thirty indentured black children. Trew could learn nothing about five of them, but of the others two had ill mothers, twenty-one were orphans, and the rest had parents who protested the court actions. Over one hundred more indentures were being readied for action by the Kent County Orphan's Court. A federal officer in Queen Anne's County reported that "hundreds" of children had been improperly apprenticed to former owners, and an Annapolis official said that so many had been apprenticed illegally that it appeared that "every able-bodied negro boy (without regard to age!) would be taken from his parents just at the time when they are becoming able to support themselves."

The complaints of black parents filled the record that Wallace forwarded to the Maryland general assembly. Some had the assistance of whites, and sympathetic whites also filed their own complaints with the federal authorities. A Baltimore and Ohio Railroad ticket agent supported the efforts of an elderly grandmother, and an Ellicott's Creek mother seeking her child had help from her employer and from a lawyer who charged her only five dollars to represent the woman in court. "She is very poor," said the lawyer. The New Town postmaster helped Susan Porter, after a court assigned her three older children to their old owner. Their father then served in the Union Army. Robert Wilson's twelve-year-old daughter and six-year-old son had been bound out against his wishes. The Kent County white Thomas Ringgold said he owed Wilson eighty-four dollars in back wages for 1864 and had promised him a hundred dollars, a house, and a garden for the next year. The Carroll County deputy provost marshal strongly supported a couple whose three sons—aged sixteen, seventeen, and eighteen—had been bound out. Their father owned horses and carriages and had rented land. He needed their labor. "These children," the white said, "are as much slaves as before . . . are forbidden to see their parents . . . doomed to grow up without education, and . . . as perfectly orphaned in the free State of Maryland as if no parents existed." "The colored people here," added a Calvert County white, "can take care of their own children and are willing to do it. . . . But the people here, or a great many of them, don't seem satisfied unless they have negroes." The author of this letter, who said he had written at "the request of the colored people," explained that "the original owners of slaves cannot do without servants, as they have been used to some one and don't want to pay any person for their labor.*

Blacks other than parents, including kin, sought to protect children from illegal indenture. The Toronto-trained surgeon A. T. Augustus, then a Baltimore army doctor and not long afterward the founder of a Savannah hospital for blacks, pressed for the release of Susan Spicer. A livery-stable keeper accompanied Lavinia Brooks, and both were warned they would be shot if they came again for her child. The Baltimore black Samuel Elbert sought the release of a twelve-year-old girl; her mother had been sold South ten years earlier. The child's former owner asked that Elbert come for her, and Elbert reported why:

> I worked for him at the time this child was born and for some time afterwards, and it is on this account that I am interested in the little girl, as she has no one to intercede for her. He said I could not take her unless I could prove that she is my child and that I was married to her mother. That I could not do as it was not so.

Elbert said the former owner threatened him with a gun and a sword, and he therefore asked for help from the military. Grandparents were among those concerned with indentured children. Hester Hall traveled from Baltimore to her former Towsontown home for a grandchild. The child's former owner threatened

---

* Wallace's report included the protests of some Maryland whites who strongly supported the antebellum apprenticeship laws or expressed concern for dependent black children. Benjamin Osborn, for example, had three black children (aged four, eight, and ten) with him. Their father was unknown, and their mother dead. A grandmother wanted to care for them, but Osborn called her "incapable" and wanted for himself that responsibility. He asked Wallace to clarify the status of these children. A Carroll County white had a different problem. He claimed that a thirteen- or fourteen-year-old boy wanted to remain with him, but that the boy's parents opposed such an arrangement. He asked if the boy could be bound out. A third white, the wife of an Episcopal clergyman, claimed the three illegitimate children of a young woman she had purchased years before to prevent her sale to the South. The woman (then married to a "worthless" free black) wanted her children back. In a fourth instance, Sewell Hepburn, a Kent County white, justified the indenture of twelve black children from a single family. He called it "an act of humanity." "These blacks grew up and were the playmates of my children," said a first letter. But a second letter revealed a quite different argument. His older slaves had quit him earlier in the war to join the Union Army. "I am left with no body to black my boots or catch a horse," Hepburn complained. "I am now an old man, and in my younger days labored to raise these blacks. . . ."

to jail the woman. Susan Thomas managed to get two grandchildren from their owner in early November. One went to live
with an aunt. Both were later returned to the white. Lydia Dorsey's
complaint said a Baltimore white had illegally bound her grandchildren to Eastern Shore whites. A Calvert County grandmother
pressed for the release of three grandchildren there. Brothers
worked together.

> I want you to see about my two children and sister Jane's
> [Francis Smallwood wrote his brother from Baltimore]. All
> persons are free now, and Mr. Harrington is not willing to
> let me have my children. . . . My mother and father is very
> much troubled about them. . . . Be careful, that you do not
> go to Mr. Harrington without some white person with you,
> as he is so much opposed to me having my children he might
> do you any injury, therefore take some white friend with you.

Parents themselves, not whites and not other blacks (kin or
non-kin), filed most of the complaints with Wallace's officers,
reporting a variety of difficulties in getting back their children.
The efforts by fathers are examined first. After George Turner's
son was bound out to the Harford white J. S. Richardson, the
father convinced the boy to leave Richardson. The white pressed
legal action against Turner. The Baltimore widower Frisbie
Hinson, who protested the indenture of three children to his dead
wife's old owner, said, "They were arrested by a constable at the
residence of persons where I had placed them." William H. Brown
had other difficulties. He had left his Anne Arundel owner in
about 1860, but two children remained there. He wanted them
back. Solomon Banks wrote of the Baltimore white who held his
daughter Henrietta:

> This girl has been living with Wilson in her slave days, and
> they have got her so that she don't want to leave them, but I
> want to take her from them as they are not giving her any
> wages, and holding her in slavery. I think I ought to take care
> of her as I am her father. I went to Mr. Wilson's for her and
> he drove me from his house, and said I should not have her
> without authority.
>
> Her father,
SOLOMON BANKS
>
> She is not bright and has not sense enough to take care of
> herself.

Perry Riley had similar troubles. A nine- and a seven-year-old son had been indentured to his wife's former Kent County owner, and Riley's protest to the Orphan's Court had been rejected. "I can bring proof," said Riley, "that I am able to support them. I can hire them out, one I can get 20 dollars for, and the other I can get victuals and clothes this year. Please attend to it for me and oblige a poor colored man."

Still other men sought to protect their sons and daughters. The ex-slave John Dennis and his wife had three sons bound out to his old owner, the same man who had sold their mother in 1859. Dennis had tried to join the Union Army in 1863, but his lameness caused his rejection. He went to Boston and returned in 1864 for his sons. "My children," he wrote Wallace, "are naked, and I am able to clothe them as soon as I can get them. Hon. Sir, will you give me some satisfaction if you please?" A Chestertown physician bound the five-year-old son and the seven-year-old daughter of an ex-slave named Berryman, who then served as a Union Army corporal. "I told him," Berryman's wife said of Houston, her former owner, "I did not want them bound out to any one as I was able to support them with the assistance of my father and sister." Houston went ahead. Berryman later took the children from their old owner to his sister-in-law's place. Houston complained to Wallace that Berryman's wife had set his house on fire in the spring of 1864 and then run off. He felt her "lazy and unable to support her children." But her white employer described the ex-slave as "hard working and as far as I can see honest; she is slow but willing to work; she does not appear to have any bad habits."

Mothers also filed formal complaints with Wallace that related their troubles in resisting the indenture of their children. Henrietta Clayton went from Baltimore to the Eastern Shore to try without success to get a son from her old owner. Hester Anthony reported:

> I went to my master after my children and he ordered me away; he told me if I did not go he was going to shoot me; he says before I shall have my children he will blow my brains out; he says I must not step my foot on his farm again. There is three boys with my sister's child; my two boys and my sister's child, Perry, Henry, Tom. Mr. Jimmy Gailes is my master, Eastern Shore Maryland.

A Baltimore woman, Rebecca Sales, described her troubles in detail:

Mrs. Mills and her Son, holds my child in slavery. I went there and they ordered me out of the house to-day, and they locked the door and took the key out of the door, and they tell her not to live with me. I want her to come home and go to school. I feel myself perfectly able to support her, she never was in a church in her life, and don't know the Lord's prayer. I want her brought to 37 Larews alley, between Mulberry and Franklin streets. . . .

Other mothers emphasized that their husbands could support their children. "I am able to provide for them and with the aid of my husband the father of them to protect them," said Mary Ann Ran, whose two children had been indentured. Elizabeth Kennard and her six children had belonged to Mary E. Woodward, who took three of them from Baltimore to be bound out in Anne Arundel County. The black woman's husband was temporarily absent; his wife described him as "a good husband and a kind father." Emily Cuff, who had not seen her son for four years, apparently did not have a husband. Three of those years had been spent in a Maryland prison, and then she labored for a year at Camp William Penn. Friends had written her about her son's mistreatment by his old owner, and she left Pennsylvania for Maryland. "I have heard," she said, "that she tried to sell my child, and I heard too, that he had been very sick by her treatment, please let me know, for my heart is most broke about him, that I may go and get him. . . ." Lucy Lee pressed for a daughter *legally* apprenticed in 1860:

It is hard that I should be deprived of my daughter's aid now in my old days, and that she should be kept a prisoner here in a free land. . . . God help us, our condition is bettered but little; free ourselves, but deprived of our children, almost the only thing that would make us free and happy. It was on their account we desired to be free, for the few years we have to live, what need we care. No good, sir, its for our children. The old bones will sleep as sound in a slave as in a free grave. Give us our children, and don't let them be raised in the ignorance we have; help us, and God will help you at the last day. The last day will bring a fearful reckoning for our old masters, and as he punishes them he will reward you.

The mother was told her daughter would have to serve out the legal indenture.

Some of the women were the wives of Union Army soldiers. Louisa Foster, who traveled from Baltimore to Towsontown to recover three children bound there and whose owner "threatened to chain me down to the floor and whip me if I asked for my children any more," was one. So was Linday Robbins, whose former owner had chased her and three children from his place after her husband joined the federal army. She found work to support them, but they were later taken from her. "My children were forced from me by constables," said the mother, "and I proceeded to the Court House and protested against such an unnatural act but was put out of the court room, and would not even be allowed to speak." Also married to a Union Army soldier, Charlotte Hall pressed the authorities for her son Samuel:

> He is my only child about thirteen years old. I think it hard that my companion should be away from me in his country service and I am at the same time deprived of my only child, contrary to the free laws and institutions for which his father is fighting. . . . I received a letter from my husband a few days since in which he requests you to get the boy at once and hand him over to me.

The Maryland general assembly failed to respond to the evidence General Wallace put before it, and questionable apprenticeship of ex-slave children—critics had reason to call it reenslavement—did not end until 1867, when the United States Supreme Court struck down the antebellum laws that permitted such indentures. An 1867 Freedmen's Bureau survey of two-thirds of Maryland's counties and the city of Baltimore turned up 2281 bound black youths, a count that did not include the heavily black southern Maryland counties. The historian W. A. Low estimates that about ten thousand youths, including those in the southern tier, were apprenticed, a figure that should be measured against the fact that the 1864 emancipation had freed about ninety thousand slaves. Local Bureau officers reported frequent apprenticeships after July 1865: about six hundred "unjust" apprenticeships in Calvert County, nearly that number in Anne Arundel County, and about two thousand complaints to the Annapolis Bureau office. "Not a day passes," said the Annapolis officer, "but my office is visited by some poor woman who has walked perhaps ten or twenty miles to . . . try to procure the release of her children taken forcibly away from her and held to all intents and purposes in slavery." A Prince Frederick County

Bureau officer described "efforts . . . by the freedmen to get the civil authorities to release the children." None had succeeded. A Bureau officer in another place said local magistrates regularly discharged whites accused of illegal apprenticeship or released them on bail "so small as to be simply ridiculous."[31]

Black parents, aided by sympathetic Bureau officers and the Baltimore Association for the Education and Improvement of the Colored Race and its leader the Baltimore Criminal Court Judge Hugh Lennox Bond, protested apprenticeship abuses. Bond insisted that the 1864 Constitution abrogated the prewar law and used his court to protect abused Baltimore children. The general assembly responded by denying the Baltimore criminal court the right to issue writs of *habeas corpus*. The Freedmen's Bureau informally dealt with many instances of alleged illegal apprenticeship but refrained for a time from legal action because of the "inability of complainants to furnish the means required in paying expenses of court and sheriff." Former owners used the courts to their advantage. Julia Handy lived with her five children in Annapolis, and a sympathetic clergyman whose aid she sought said that three could care for themselves and that the mother could find "a comfortable home for the other two." But their former owner had convinced an Annapolis judge to bind all five to him. Julia Handy was arrested twice for trying to get her children and ordered to court after her third effort. Baltimore blacks (three hundred of "the most respectable colored people of Baltimore") tried a different approach and petitioned Andrew Johnson to support the 1866 Civil Rights Act. "Our homes," their petition read in part, "are invaded and our little ones seized at the family fireside, and forcibly bound to masters who are by law expressly released from any obligation to educate them in secular or religious knowledge." Maryland law denied ex-slaves "the safety of our children around the hearth while we are at labor or their support in our old age."

State courts were divided on the legality of apprenticing ex-slave children under old laws affecting only free blacks. In May 1865 Leah Coston petitioned for a *habeas corpus* writ to free her sons Simon and Washington, who had been bound without the permission of their parents. Fourteen months later, the Court of Appeals ordered the boys "delivered to their parents." But the next year, a Maryland circuit court denied a petition for *habeas corpus* in a case supported by the Bureau and argued by the prominent antislavery Baltimore lawyer Henry Stockbridge.

Elizabeth Turner and her mother had belonged to the Talbot County white Philemon T. Hambleton. With "many" Talbot ex-slaves, the eight-year-old girl was indentured to a former owner on November 3, 1864. The children had been "collected under some local authority." Although her mother approved the indenture, Elizabeth's stepfather Charles Henry Minoky brought a complaint against Hambleton. Stockbridge argued that the Thirteenth Amendment forbade such apprenticeships, but the circuit court invoked Dred Scott to assert that the ex-slave children were not "citizens of the United States." The United States Supreme Court ordered Elizabeth's release in 1867, citing the 1866 Civil Rights Act as reason. That decision, according to O. O. Howard, promised "the liberation of hundreds of freed children wrested from parents . . . too poor or too humble to battle successfully with unjust tribunals." Soon after, in one Maryland Freedmen's Bureau subdistrict, 235 apprenticed black youths were freed. But according to a Bureau officer, there still remained "some seven hundred others to go."

It was seen in Chapter 1 that ex-slaves in Mississippi and northern Louisiana registered their slave marriages in 1864–1865 and that a similar registration occurred in 1866 among Virginia and North Carolina ex-slaves. Scattered reports disclose that other slaves who encountered wartime Union Army clergy and other northern missionaries renewed slave marriages. The earliest "contraband" marriage for which a record exists occurred during the first week of September in 1861. "I have been applied to by two contrabands who have lived for years as man and wife . . . ," wrote a northerner from Old Point Comfort, Virginia. The husband and wife had "learned that God's law extends to them," and the white "gladly" married them. This unsigned letter may have been written by Lewis Lockwood, one of the first northern missionaries to travel South. In early September of that year, Lockwood already represented the American Missionary Association at Fortress Monroe. That month, he asked the New York Association office to send him one hundred engraved marriage certificates. "More than half of the married 'contrabands' " Lockwood met had been "married only in slave fashion by taking up together by mutual agreement." Lockwood therefore began marrying contraband men and women. A September 29 letter listed the names of thirty-two couples he married in one week. No other information accompanied that list, as indicated by the following examples:

MARRIED NEAR HAMPTON
SEPT 29/61

Peter Herbert	Merritt Turnor
Judy Herbert	Aurelia Turnor
John Cheeseman	Shadreck Rodgers
Elvy Cheeseman	Caroline Rodgers

Yet another listing of newly married contraband couples was deposited by an unknown clergyman, perhaps Lockwood, at Fortress Monroe late in 1861. Kept on several sheets of paper held together by a thin ribbon, it is a far more informative social document than the earlier list, as indicated by the following examples:

Anthony Cook	32
Lucy Anne Rowe	19
Both Single	

Moses Rowe	46
Nancy Cook	38
Single	
Single	

Gilliom Montegue	50
Catherine Reed	40
Single	
Single	

Geo Taliaferro
Elsie Taliaferro
Both born in county
Acknowledges all his
  Children (4)
Carpenter

Moses Rowe
Nancy Rowe
Both of Gloucester
1 Child
Oysterman

Olmstead Cook
Milly Cook
Both of Gloucester
4 Children
Oysterman

David Reed
Emma Reed
Both of Gloucester
6 Children
Carpenter

Ben Turner
Dolly Turner
Both of Gloucester
4 Children
Farm Hand

Anthony Cook and Lucy Anne Rowe had entered into a new marriage, as did two other couples. The others renewed slave marriages. Lockwood, who found these men and women "peculiar people," married "hundreds" of other contraband couples during the Civil War, and other missionaries and army clergy did the same in Union-held territories over the entire South.[32]

Our interest here is not in these isolated examples of the wartime renewal of slave marriages but in whether the ex-slaves were secure in the nonlegal sanctions that had upheld slave marriages before the emancipation. A reasonable estimate of such sentiment results by comparing the *actual number* of ex-slave marriages registered in different counties by Virginia and North Carolina ex-slaves in 1866 to the maximum number of *possible* 1860 slave marriages. A simple procedure, such a comparison exaggerates the number of actual 1860 slave marriages. Goochland County, Virginia, ex-slaves registered 742 marriages in 1866. In 1860, that county had 1498 adult slave men and 1231 adult slave women. It is assumed that there were 1231 slave couples in 1860, a crude calculation that counts single adults, widowed persons, and persons separated from a spouse by desertion or sale as married. The Freedmen's Bureau registered slave marriages in 1866, and four county registers survive. Examined in Chapter 1, the Rockbridge, Nelson, Goochland, and Louisa county registers disclosed that mostly laborers and field hands registered slave marriages. The percentage of *possible* 1860 slave marriages registered in 1866 was high in all four places: about three in ten among the Rockbridge blacks, nearly half among the Nelson blacks, three in five among the Goochland blacks, and nearly two in three among the Louisa blacks. The two counties with the fewest white residents and the most plantation slaves in 1860 had the highest percentages of *possible* registered slave marriages (Table 35).[33]

A strong desire to legalize slave marriages also was revealed by the North Carolina ex-slaves who registered such marriages with county clerks and justices of the peace in the spring of 1866.[34] Even before the North Carolina legislature ordered the registration of continuing slave marriages, some ex-slaves remarried.[35] The North Carolina statute required the registration of slave marriages by the early fall of 1866 and payment of a twenty-five-cent fee. Failure to do so was a misdemeanor punishable at "the discretion of the court." Some resident northern white missionaries and schoolteachers worried that the ex-slaves needed their guidance, one of them explaining that he had "abundant work" in "urging" them to get "formally married" because of "the licentiousness that undoubtedly prevails" among them. But such persons worried excessively. A black clergyman met an elderly ex-slave in Raleigh who had married "his present wife three times," the third time after the emancipation when "told it was right to have a license." A Raleigh schoolteacher met Wake County ex-slave women who used "their good genius" to raise the twenty-five-cent fee. One "old grey-headed woman," who called at her schoolroom, "had six eggs in her basket; it was all she could spare, as the old hen had a mighty smart chance to set, and toward fall she would bring a chicken." She wanted to "buy a 'ticket'" because "all 'spectable folks is to be married, and we's 'spectable; me and my old man has lived together thirty-five years, and had twelve children." Another woman, who brought a quart of strawberries to buy the "ticket," said, "Me and my old man has lived more than twenty years together; I's proud the children's all had the same father." A third woman carried an empty bag. "Everybody's getting married," she complained, "and my old man can't get the money."[36]

The registration books and copies of the "Negro Cohabitation Certificates" that native white officials used in seventeen North Carolina counties survive and disclose that this old woman had not exaggerated. A high percentage of *possible* slave marriages were registered in all but three counties, and it is among ex-slaves like Elburt and Marien Williams that an explanation is found for that fact. Neither Williams nor his wife could get to a registrar, and a literate friend prepared a statement telling why:

> I Elburt Williams & Marien Williams has ben Livin together 18 years & We Both do affirm that We do want each other to Live as man & wife the balanc of Life & being disable to walk & Marien being in the family way I will send this to you & you will Please make it all Wright with us.

The worry their statement revealed indicates a desire to legalize their slave marriage, and the number of ex-slaves registering marriages shows that the desire was widespread. Overall, a number equal to *at least* 47 percent of possible 1860 slave marriages in these seventeen counties were registered in the 1866 spring and summer months. As with the percentages reported for the four Virginia counties, the 47 percent is *a minimal estimate,* one meant to show the deep concern for legal marriage. Except for the Currituck, Bertie, and Halifax blacks, at least 30 percent of "eligible" couples registered marriages.* In nine counties, including three that had densely black plantation populations (Warren, Franklin, and Edgecombe) and one (New Hanover) that included the city of Wilmington, at least half of "eligible" couples registered marriages (Table 35).

---

* The low Bertie and Halifax returns may reflect nothing more than the failure of county officials to have kept full and accurate records. That is suggested by the fact that Bertie and Halifax blacks performed as well as other North Carolina blacks in registering new marriages after 1872. See page 427.

TABLE 35. MINIMUM PERCENTAGE OF EX-SLAVE MARRIAGES
REGISTERED IN VIRGINIA AND NORTH CAROLINA, 1866

County	Maximum possible number of slave marriages in 1860*	Actual number of ex-slave marriages registered in 1866	Minimum percentage of ex-slave marriages registered in 1866
VIRGINIA			
Rockbridge	796	236	30
Nelson	1304	620	48
Goochland	1231	742	60
Louisa	1944	1234	64
TOTAL	5275	2832	54
NORTH CAROLINA			
PIEDMONT			
Orange	1042	931	89
Lincoln	431	275	64
CAPE FEAR			
New Hanover	1663	1392	84
Robeson	981	583	59
ATLANTIC COAST			
Pasquotank	637	326	51
Washington	553	221	40
Hyde	518	196	38
Beaufort	1248	411	33
Currituck	482	72	15
COASTAL-PLAIN PLANTATIONS			
Warren	2135	1488	70
Johnston	950	560	59
Nash	883	430	49
Edgecombe	1945	966	51
Franklin	1374	800	58
Richmond	1051	310	29
Bertie	1834	297	16
Halifax	2400	163	7
TOTAL	20,127	9452	47

* This column is the smaller number of adult male or female slaves twenty years and older in each county in 1860. It greatly exaggerates the possible number of slave marriages.

Credit for these high registration rates does not belong to southern whites or to northern white missionaries. Unpopular northern whites would have had difficulties dealing with southern white court officers. Significant numbers of northern missionaries and schoolteachers, moreover, lived in only two of the nine counties with the highest registration percentages.[37] No evidence suggests that native whites encouraged conformity to the law. If some did, their influence cannot explain the high registration in the predominantly black counties. It is hard to imagine southern whites managing the registration of nearly ten thousand old slave marriages *in 1866*. It was simply that the ex-slaves themselves—men and women like the Halifax County slaves Defoe Oats and Rosetta Pitts, who had married in 1798—wanted their marriages registered in law. This fact, more than any other, explains the high registration.

How so rural and illiterate a population in such diverse communities, fresh from enslavement, and living in the aftermath of a devastating war that had shattered an established social system learned of the 1866 marriage law and acted to "enforce" it remains one of the many hidden "stories" about the ex-slaves. But even without such information, the registration of such a high percentage of marriages indicates the ex-slaves' widespread approval of legal marriage. A largely illiterate population had knowledge of some of the "rules" governing civil society. Many had learned as slaves what it meant to have a marriage unprotected in the law. When more is known about their behavior in 1865 and 1866, it may show that one of their most important social decisions was the reaffirmation of their marriages and families in the law. The affirmation associated with registration in 1866, however, had its roots in the slave experience, and the large number who voluntarily conformed to the 1866 law so soon after their release from bondage in such diverse communities cannot be attributed to a socialization process whereby owners had impressed their slaves to accept legal marriage after emancipation and to pay a twenty-five-cent fee. A Greensboro judge during Radical Reconstruction, Albion W. Tourgee, emphasized the choices ex-slaves had made in conforming to the 1866 North Carolina marriage law. "Let the marriage bonds be dissolved throughout the State of New York to-day," Tourgee observed in 1890, "and it may be doubted if as large a proportion of her intelligent white citizens would choose again their old partners."[38]

The 1866 North Carolina marriage law was an unusual one.

Most southern states did not require that slave marriages be registered after the emancipation; they merely legalized such marriages. Kentucky and Tennessee had laws similar to the North Carolina law, and study of how ex-slaves responded to those laws promises to enlarge our understanding of the commitment among ex-slaves to legal marriage sanctions. Ex-slaves, however, also re-married in states that had no such laws. Cato Carter remembered that Alabama blacks "had their mar'age put in the book . . . after the breakin' up, plenty after they had growed children." The Virginia house servant Mildred Thomas had a slave broomstick marriage, but after the emancipation she and her husband paid one dollar to have "a real sho' nuff weddin' wid a preacher." The literate slave "old man Pearson" had married Isabella Dorroh's South Carolina parents. They remarried after emancipation, too, " 'cause dey didn't know if de first marriage was good or not." Charlie Davis's parents also remarried after the Civil War. Davis said they "didn't git de time for a weddin' befo'. . . . They called deirselves man and wife a long time befo' they was really married, and dat is de reason I's as old as I is now. I reckon they was right in the fust place, 'cause they never did want nobody else 'cept each other, nohow."[39]

In early February 1865, ex-slaves packed Savannah's Second African Baptist Church to cheer Rufus Saxton's description of William Sherman's military order temporarily distributing land to them. Mansfield French, the New York clergyman who had spent the wartime years among the South Carolina Sea Island blacks, also spoke, urged them to work the land even if they had to "live on roots and wear . . . old clothes," and then admonished them, "You must have but one wife instead of the two or three you used to." "There was a great sensation at this point," re-ported the Boston *Journal* correspondent "Carleton," "laughter and commotion lasting five minutes. . . . They looked upon it as a funny matter." Some slave husbands had more than one wife. Evidence of such ties surfaced right after emancipation. Some Bolivar, Tennessee, ex-slaves worried a Freedmen's Bureau office because they "still attempt to keep from two to three wives." In August 1865, Vina Curtis, a resident of Arkadelphia, Arkansas, complained to the Bureau that her husband, who had cursed and beaten her, had three wives. Fined, he was ordered to marry one of them. A year later, the Bureau fined Hercules Brown, a Monck's Corner, South Carolina, ex-slave for having two wives, and in 1867 the twenty-year-old Lem Hankenson complained to the Barnwell, South Carolina, Bureau that his father America Ashley had two wives and abused his mother and her children. Years after the emancipation, Harry Quarls, born a Missouri slave and moved to Texas, said he had three wives upon emancipation. "Dey wouldn't let me live with but one," said Quarls. ". . . I wants all three." But Quarls married one of them.[40]

Why the Georgia ex-slaves found French's admonition amusing remains obscure, but the difficulties faced by men like Quarls and these few others were uncommon. Far more serious were the moral and marital choices faced by ex-slaves who had remarried after a spouse had been separated from them by sale or for other involuntary reasons. That difficulty had no relationship to either simultaneous polygamy or successive polygyny. Neither the civil law nor the many edicts concerning marriage issued by the Freedmen's Bureau assisted ex-slaves in dealing with the multiple marriages some carried into freedom. An 1865 military ruling affecting North Carolina, Alabama, and Georgia blacks said only that the "common laws governing the domestic relations . . . are in force." The 1865 Mississippi marriage law, typical of the laws passed in other states like Alabama, Florida, Tennessee, and Virginia, announced the legality of ex-slave marriages. In August 1865, Mansfield French drew up for the Freedmen's Bureau rules meant to deal with ex-slaves who had more than one living spouse, but civil marriage laws quickly superseded them.* The Georgia and South Carolina laws evaded the issue. Georgia ex-slaves with "two or more reputed" spouses had "immediately" to select one or face prosecution for adultery and fornication. The South Carolina law allowed ex-slaves three months to make a similar choice. Critics, like O. O. Howard's brother Charles, favored a more "discriminating law," one that required legal marriage but allowed "the old involuntary contracts . . . to be set aside when mutually desired." French found the South Carolina law inad-

---

* An early edict by French required men with more than one wife to choose between them and marry legally. If children were involved, a father "had to select the wife who was the mother of his children." The August 1865 rules affected South Carolina, Georgia, and Florida ex-slaves. A husband could leave his second wife but only if she was childless and consented to his departure and only if the first wife still lived with his underage children and did not have a husband "known to be living." A man living alone but with "two wives restored to him by freedom" had to take the mother of his children as "his lawful wife." Women claimed by two former husbands retained freedom of choice but only if no children were involved. If a woman had children, their father became "her lawful husband." French's meticulous plan did not make provision for women who had children by more than one husband.

equate, causing the South Carolina Bureau to enforce "a very large number" of "bills of separation and reunions with former companions . . . judged . . . more in accordance with the moral interests of the parties." He pressed for legislation permitting "divorce or separation" among men and women who had remarried after being "forcibly separated from their families." Without such a law, French feared the spread of "already painfully evident . . . unhappiness and even demoralization." Other Bureau officers, like Clinton Fisk, urged troubled ex-slaves to go "before some good man, let him hear all the circumstances, and then abide in his decision in good faith and live pure lives in the future." "God," the Kentucky and Tennessee Bureau head warned in *Plain Counsels for Freedmen,* "will not wink at adultery and fornication among you now."[41]

Bureau officers and other whites and blacks helped some ex-slaves to deal with their multiple marriages. The "law" was hardly the issue. The Virginia Bureau had "many cases . . . where a man or woman is claimed by more than one person as husband or wife." Peter Randolph understood the ambiguities in such crises. Randolph, a runaway Virginia slave who settled in Richmond in 1865, said "hundreds . . . returned to their former homes" to find that spouses had remarried. He and several other black clergymen helped them. "The perplexing part," Randolph remembered, "was to determine which were the right ones to marry." James Sinclair, a Presbyterian clergyman and native of Scotland who labored for the Lumberton, North Carolina, Bureau, revealed the confusion that Bureau officers everywhere must have faced. He could not determine whether he dealt with "polygamy" or "concubinage." Sinclair worked out one solution. "Whenever a negro appears before me with two or three wives who have equal claim upon him," Sinclair's superiors learned, "I marry him to the woman who has the greatest number of helpless children who otherwise would become a charge on the Bureau." That normally meant younger women. "Older concubines" had children "able not only to provide for themselves but also for their parent."[42]

No easy solution—legal or otherwise—existed for dealing with ex-slaves bound emotionally to more than a single mate. The Tuscaloosa, Alabama, woman Dilly Hinton had lived with a slave husband for twelve years. He was then sold and later remarried. But his first wife told the Bureau he wanted to live with her. Maudy Rivers and her husband had lived in Vidalia, Louisiana, until he was "taken away" during the Civil War. She was told he had died and remarried. But after the war, he returned to claim her as his wife. Her new husband refused to "give her up." The Beaufort, North Carolina, ex-slaves Ella and Owen Smaw registered their marriage in 1866, but the county clerk revoked the certificate issued to them after John Bryan, another ex-slave "supposed to be dead" and not "heard from for several years," claimed Ella as his wife. His former owner supported Bryan's claim. After the Lumberton, North Carolina, slave James McCullom's wife and two children were sold from him, he waited four years, remarried, and had two children by his new wife. His first wife and children returned after the war. McCullom believed his first marriage "legal" and asked the Bureau's advice. When a District of Columbia clergyman registered slave marriages in 1866–1867, he learned from a registrant that the man had been "separated from his first wife 22 years ago, and having heard from her lately, wishes to leave the present one and live with the first by whom he has several grown children, but none by the last."[43]

Common sense informed by moral and social obligation ironed out many marital tangles in ways that puzzled even sensitive whites. A northern schoolteacher said that these difficulties gave "rise to many a 'naughty' question among the people that would puzzle a lawyer to answer." "We were often sorely perplexed," Elizabeth Botume remembered about such problems among the Sea Island ex-slaves. "All our preconceived ideas of propriety and the fitness of things were set at naught." She recalled four separate instances involving women with two living husbands. Three of the men had been sold from their wives. Charlotte's husband returned after the war to learn his wife had remarried. She had three children: two sons by him and then a daughter by her second husband. "Both men claimed their offspring" and left the woman "in a sore strait." When a carpenter was "away for a long time," his wife remarried. The carpenter returned, rejected his first wife's overtures to have him back, remarried, and then took his daughter from his first wife. Another ex-slave, Kit, was greatly troubled after Sam, Kit's wife's first husband, returned to claim her. No children had been born to either union, and Tina decided that she would choose between her two husbands after spending a few weeks with each. Kit asked Botume to write Tina and plead his case ("fur him want to come here to lib, but him shame"). Tina decided in favor of Kit. The fourth instance involved Jane and Martin Barnwell. After they had a child, he was sold. Jane Barnwell later married Ferguson. Martin Barnwell, however, later returned to claim his wife. When Botume expressed surprise that Jane had remarried and caused these complications, Jane's mother explained, "Never mind, ma'am. Jane b'longs to Martin, an' she'll go back to him. Martin has been a sickly boy, an' de secesh treat him too badly, an' we never 'specs him to lib t'rough all." Botume reconstructed the conversation she had had with Jane and her mother:

> "Martin Barnwell is my husband, ma'am. I am got no husband but he. W'en de secesh sell him off we nebber 'spect to see each odder more. He said, 'Jane take good care of our boy, an' w'en we git to hebben us will lib togedder to nebber part no more.' You see ma'am when I come here I had no one to help me."
>
> "That's so," chimed in the mother. "I tell you, missis, it been a hard fight for we."
>
> "So Ferguson come," continued Jane, "an' axed me to be his wife. I told him I never 'spects Martin *could* come back, but if he did he would be my husband above all others. An' Ferguson said, 'That's right, Jane'; so he cannot say nothing, ma'am."
>
> "But supposing he *does* say something, and is not willing to give you up, Jane?"
>
> "Martin is my husband, ma'am, an' the father of my child; and *Ferguson is a man.*"

Jane Barnwell asked Botume to write to Ferguson, then in the federal army. "I want to treat the poor boy well," she said. But Ferguson still loved his wife. "Martin," he replied, "has not seen you for a long time. He cannot think of you as I do. . . . Come to me, Jane." "Tell him," Jane advised the white teacher, "I say I'm sorry he finds it so hard to do his duty. I shall never write to him no more, but tell him I wish him well." Jane Barnwell refused to sign the last letter Botume wrote to her second husband.[44]

Much more was involved in these decisions then staying with the "right" husband or wife. The presence of children often affected the choice. Mansfield French said men sold to "very remote places," who returned to find "their long lost families," "could not be induced to remain with wives but recently married especially if there were no ties to children to bind them." "It has often occurred," French also observed (perhaps too optimistically) "that the very wives from whom they wished to separate, had a strong, and even similar, reason for gaining former husbands." Elizabeth Botume made the same point: "Sometimes two men claimed the same woman, whilst she coquetted not a little, evidently disposed to take the one that bid the highest. But this rarely happened if there were children." This concern for children born in marriages later disrupted revealed itself in other ways. Among the ex-slave Goochland County, Virginia, husbands who registered slave marriages in 1866, one in four aged forty to forty-nine and three in ten at least fifty years old gave the names of children born to them in earlier marriages. That also happened when the Louisa County, Virginia, ex-slaves registered their marriages. Nearly one in ten of all registrants named children born in earlier marriages, a percentage that increased to about one in seven for registrants forty years and older. Sixty-three Louisa ex-slaves (thirty-four of them men), moreover, registered marriages even though their spouses had died, been sold from them, or quit them for voluntary reasons. Most had lost a spouse through death. Registering such terminated marriages probably was motivated by a desire to legitimize their children in law, a concern that hardly differed from that noticed by French and Botume.[45]

A feeling for all the involved adults sometimes shaped the settlement of these tangled ex-slave marriages. The elderly North Carolina ex-slave Anthony Ransom remembered that the sale of a fellow Hertford County slave's wife was followed by the man's remarriage. "Atter de war," Ransom recollected, "his fust wife comed back an' atter his secon' wife died he married de fust one ober ag'in." Sale separated the Lexington, Kentucky, slave Jerry Sharpe from his wife and two children. He later remarried and had several children by his second wife. A letter from his first wife in 1866 told the bricklayer and gardener that "she desired to come home . . . and end her days with him." Sharpe decided to "support both families," saying it was "the hardest dealins he ever had to do" but calling it "his duty" and announcing he would "stand up to it." A concern for the man his wife married after he was sold from South Carolina to Alabama affected the decision of a middle-aged ex-slave John deForest met. The husband had been gone for about fifteen years and returned to find his wife married to a much older man. He told deForest: "Things is powerfully mixed up. Last week I gets back and finds my wife all right an' powerful glad to see me. But she thought I was dead, an' so she's been married these ten years, an' thar's her old man a-livin' with her now. He's a drefful *ole* man; he can't skasely see. She wants me, and wants him to go away, he won't go." Then working for the Bureau, deForest advised him that he had first claim to her. "An' about the chil'n?" the ex-slave asked. "Why, take your own children, of course," replied deForest. The man answered, "I mean *his* chil'n—the ole woman's chil'n an' *his*."

> She says she won't go ef she can't hev all her chil'n. An' when we offers to take 'um the old man he hollers an' says: "What's to come o' *me?*" He's sich an *ole* man, ye see, he can't so much as see to light his pipe. Arter he's got it filled one of us has to put some fire on it 'fore he can git to smoke. . . .

DeForest turned all of the children over to the first husband. "Tell the old man that," he remembered telling the triumphant first husband. That decision, however, did not cut off the second husband from his wife and children. "The wife," deForest recollected, "clove to the younger husband, while the elder [man] remained in the family as a sort of poor relation."[46]

Solving the marital intricacies that resulted from sale and remarriage revealed that slave affections reached beyond the ties between a separated husband and wife. Sometime before the Civil War, Philip Grey's wife and children were sold from their Richmond, Virginia, owner to Kentucky. She remarried, and before he joined the Union Army she and her second husband had three children of their own. Her second husband died a Union Army soldier. After the war, Grey wrote his wife and asked her to return. She replied:

> I seat myself this morning to write you a few lines to [let] you know that I received your letter the five of this month and was very glad to hear from you and to hear that you was well. this leaves us all well at present. . . . You wish me to come to Virginia. I had much rather that you would come after me but if you cannot make it convenient you have to make arrangements for me and [the] family. I have three little fatherless little girls. My husband went off under Burbridge's command and was killed at Richmond Virginia. If you can pay my passage through there I will come the first of May. I have nothing much to sell as I have had my things all burnt. . . .
> If you love me you will have to love my children and you will have to promise me that you will provide for them as well as if they were your own. I heard that you were coming for Maria but was not coming for me. I know that I have lived with you and loved you then and love you still. Every time I hear from you my love grows stronger. I was very low spirited when I heard that you was not coming for me. . . . You will have to write and give me the directions how to come.

I want when I start to come the quickest way that I can come. . . .

Phebe wishes to know what has become of Lawrence. She heard that he was married but did not know whether it was so. . . . Maria sends her love to you but seems to be low spirited for fear that you will come for her and not for me. John Phebe [?] son says he would like to see his father but does not care about leaving his mother who has taken care of him up to this time. he thinks that she needs help and if he loves her he will give her help. I will now close by requesting you to write as soon as you receive this so no more at present but remain your true (I hope to be with you soon) wife.

WILLIE ANN GREY
To PHILIP GREY

Aunt Lucinda sends her love to you. She has lost her husband and one daughter Betsey. She left two little children. The rest are all well at present. Phebe's Mary was sold away from her. She heard from her the other day. She was well.

Willie Ann Gray worried that her first husband wanted only the children by their marriage. She made it clear that their reunion depended upon his concern for all her children. Philip Grey forwarded her letter to the Virginia Freedmen's Bureau and asked for transportation funds to bring his wife and all of her children back to Richmond.[47]

So far we have dealt only with the behavior of ex-slaves. On one significant social measure—the registration of *new* marriages—it is possible to compare their behavior to that of southern whites. An 1872 North Carolina law required the payment of a one dollar license fee and the registration of all *new* marriages with a county clerk. Some counties, such as the predominantly black Warren County, had required such registration before 1872. Now it had to be done everywhere and at a time when the slave experience had not faded from memory. County officials identified registrants by color. Nonwhite registrants were nearly all the children of slave culture, and their behavior revealed the capacities of their parents to transmit values about marriage and the family from generation to generation. A twenty-year-old registering a marriage in 1872 had been nine years old when the Civil War started, and a similarly aged registrant in 1882 had been three years old in 1865. Those registering marriages between 1872 and 1890 were a particular generation: men and women whose lives bridged the transition from slavery to legal freedom.

Emancipation altered their civil status and enlarged the choices they could make, but too little time had passed by 1872, or even by 1882, to argue that these changes had radically transformed slave culture.

Blacks registering 7638 marriages in seven North Carolina counties did so in exact proportion to their number in the population[48] (Table 36). The counties they lived in differed in important ways. New Hanover included the city of Wilmington, and Bertie, Franklin, Halifax, Nash, and Warren counties produced staples. At least three in five slaves in four counties had been plantation slaves. Only antebellum Halifax had had significant numbers of free black residents. In the seven counties, blacks registered 61.3 percent of all marriages, and blacks made up exactly that percentage of the population. Rural (farm and plantation) and urban blacks observed legal marriage sanctions with the same regularity. Blacks in diverse social settings—and in a state that permitted common-law marriage—placed a high value on legal marriage, at least as high as their urban and rural white neighbors. Except for those few whose parents had been free, none had parents who had been legally married. In registering new marriages and paying one dollar, they disclosed that the denial to their parents of legal marriage had not caused them to accept as normal subsocietal, or nonlegal, marriage sanctions. Most of these blacks owned little, if any, real property; hence their concern with legal marriage could not be due to a worry over inheritance.

Nothing yet is known about the North Carolina whites who also registered marriages, but if sharp class and occupational differences existed between the North Carolina whites and blacks, a lower-class population had registered marriages just as regularly as better-positioned middle- and upper-class whites. Legal marriage, therefore, was highly valued in all social classes, including men and women who had lived for a long time with nonlegal marriage. Their acceptance of legal sanctions indicates that they had a sufficiently powerful set of cultural beliefs to accommodate their needs and transformed expectations to a radically altered social situation, a law passed less than a decade following emancipation. External compulsion did not force registration. That would have been difficult, especially in the densely black counties. No evidence shows that county authorities enforced the law either to uphold a moral code or to collect license fees. Pressure to conform to the 1872 law, therefore, had to have come from within these black communities themselves. That so large a percentage of

TABLE 36. SOCIAL AND ECONOMIC CHARACTERISTICS OF SELECTED NORTH CAROLINA COUNTIES TOGETHER WITH THE REGISTRATION OF BLACK AND WHITE MARRIAGES IN THESE COUNTIES, 1867–1890

County	Percent slaves 1860	Percent slaves Units of 20+ 1860	Percent males, 21+, farm laborer, cash tenant, share tenant, 1910	Total marriages registered	Black marriages as percentage of all marriages	Blacks as percentage of county population 1880
Bertie	57	76	71	1467	59	58
Franklin	58	61	88	1547	59	55
Halifax	53	73	85	1967	72	70
Nash	40	48	92	1080	47	47
New Hanover	46	52	85	1934	61	62
Warren	66	78	82	3079	66	72
Pender	—	—	62	1384	52	56
TOTAL				12,458	61	61

these men and women could neither read nor write is also reason to believe that deeply held norms shaped the decision to marry in law. "We ask them, 'how long have you been married?'" A. D. Smith, the chairman of Board of the United States Direct Tax Commissioners in the South Carolina Sea Islands, had told the American Freedmen's Inquiry Commission in 1863. "They say, 'These are our children.'" The willingness of these same ex-slaves "to take upon themselves the [legal] obligation—even those in advanced age—" of marriage "surprised" Smith.[49] Smith's admiring surprise had far more to do with the beliefs of whites than with those of ex-slaves. The behavior of these North Carolina blacks and whites in the 1870s and the 1880s indicates that legal marriage had as great a moral and social presence in the world of the ex-slaves as in the world of their old owners and other southern whites. Registering a marriage was a conscious decision. Those who did so made a choice, and, living in a cash-short economy, they paid a significant monetary cost.

That also was revealed in the behavior of Mississippi ex-slaves. Many Mississippi whites mocked the desire of the ex-slaves for legal marriage. In November 1865, the Mississippi legislature stamped approval on all slave marriages and declared their offspring "legitimate for all purposes." A Madison County judge dismissed a case involving ex-slaves who disputed the "right to control a child" because the 1865 law had imposed "responsibilities . . . both onerous and unjust" upon them. The judge explained: ". . . [M]any a dusky gallant will, by virtue of the law, be claimed as sire, ancestor, and supporter, [more] than the sons and daughters of Ibsan, a Judge of Israel, who had thirty sons and daughters." Strained historical allusions revealed the judge's belief that blacks could not maintain deep and abiding marital and familial attachments. The 1865 law merely legalized "'livings together' induced by the coercion of masters," and the ex-slaves could not "be held bound by their acts as slaves, when they had no care for the future, no sense of responsibility, no choice. . . ." Similar beliefs prevented other Mississippi whites from perceiving the choices Mississippi blacks made after the emancipation. The Natchez *Courier* was astonished that so many blacks purchased marriage licenses, because that decision bound them to support their children, and the delayed registration of slave marriages proved to others either white radical cupidity or black childlike innocence. Loyal League officials, who urged blacks to legalize slave marriages, were accused of making "large sums of money . . .

frequently extorted from old and ignorant negroes who had children and grandchildren." A hostile white remembered two radical whites who, posing as a minister and as a legal officer, told blacks that children born outside of legal marriage were "bastards" and could not inherit property. Thoughtless blacks paid them four dollars for a marriage license and another fee to assure legitimacy and property transfer. Ex-slaves could only err. If they failed to take legal vows, they lived in "sin." But if they believed plantation "custom" inadequate, white radicals had cajoled them for profit.[50]

The Mississippi ex-slaves were no different in their commitment to legal marriage than the North Carolina ex-slaves. Less complete but nevertheless convincing evidence of black and white Mississippi marriage registration rates makes this clear. In 1870, according to the Republican Mississippi Governor James L. Alcorn, 3427 blacks in thirty-one counties purchased marriage licenses; whites in the same counties bought 2204 licenses. Proportionately more blacks than whites purchased marriage licenses that year. In 1882–1883, controversy raged over an alleged decline in Afro-American "morality" after emancipation, and marriage among Mississippi blacks became one measure of the supposed decline. Charles K. Marshall, the prominent Vicksburg Methodist clergyman, defended the blacks against their critics, citing the marriage licenses issued to whites and blacks in the Hinds County "First District" between January 1879 and January 1883. Of 684 licenses issued, three in four went to blacks. The percentage of licenses issued to blacks (75.3 percent) equaled the percentage of blacks aged fifteen to forty-four (74.5 percent) living in Hinds County in 1880. Like the data from the North Carolina marriage registers, these percentages disclose that blacks purchased marriage licenses in proportion to their number in the population. Upper and Lower South slaves carried diverse experiences into freedom, but they and their children shared a common desire to register new marriages. On this important social measure, Mississippi and North Carolina ex-slaves adapted to legal freedom in a similar way. Alcorn, who worried over "the observance of virtue before and after marriage" and the custom whereby owners had done for slaves "what they were supposed, like children, to be unable to do . . . for themselves," was gratified that "the negroes, when freed from all control . . . entered into marriage of their own accord." The Mississippi marriage license fee had risen from one to three dollars. Alcorn, himself a wealthy prewar planter, described it as "a tax on virtue at the critical moment." "Social history," he said of ex-slaves purchasing marriage licenses, "will probably be searched in vain for any more striking proof that marriage and other laws, when based on nature, duty, and religion command an unfailing homage from the humblest understandings." We need not share Alcorn's Victorian beliefs and rhetoric to realize that he had made a sound historical judgment.[51]

Who the ex-slaves were just after the emancipation and how they defined themselves and their needs depended very much upon who they had been before the emancipation. Their behavior after the emancipation, however, also is significant evidence about latent slave values. Too little time had passed to blur the continuity between slave values in 1860 and ex-slave behavior during and just after the Civil War. Some of the vast but little-studied record of such behavior has been examined in this chapter. Much remains to be studied, but enough is known to enlarge the symbolic meaning of the rhetoric used by ex-Missouri and ex-Georgia slaves. On January 3, 1865, about three thousand blacks, many ex-slaves among them, packed a large St. Louis meeting hall to celebrate their emancipation under a new Missouri law. Handbills and placards decorated the hall's walls. None idealized the recent past. One revealed an important aspect of the consciousness and culture of enslaved Afro-Americans that lay buried for more than a full century in the Freedmen's Bureau manuscript records, in the duplicate copies of the North Carolina "Negro Cohabitation Certificates," and in other little-studied historical documents. It simply read, "Our wives and children are free." A year and a half later, Georgia blacks met at Augusta to protest the many abuses of the ex-slaves that followed upon emancipation. "The dust of our fathers," they reminded Georgia whites, "mingles with yours in the same graveyards; you have transmitted into our veins much of the rich blood which courses through yours. . . . Our mothers nursed you. . . . This is your country, but it is ours, too; you were born here, so were we; your fathers fought for it, but our fathers fed them."[52]

The behavior of ordinary black men and women between 1861 and 1867 casts fresh light on the beliefs and behavior of the slave generation at the time of the general emancipation. That same evidence lays the basis for a re-examination of the family life of thousands of poor rural and urban southern blacks in 1880 and again in 1900, as well as of migrant New York City blacks in 1905 and again in 1925. The slaves had created and sustained very important familial and kin sensibilities and ties. The choices so many made immediately upon their emancipation and before they had substantive rights in the law did not result from new ideas learned in freedom and were not the reflection of beliefs learned from owners. Such behavior had its origins in the ways in which Africans and their Afro-American descendants had adapted to enslavement. Their choices were made possible by the Civil War, by the pronouncement of the Emancipation Proclamation, and by the ratification of the Thirteenth Amendment, actions that freed the slaves. But neither the Civil War, the Emancipation Proclamation, nor the Thirteenth Amendment had made men and women of these Afro-Americans. That had happened long before.

10

Like It Was

*[T]o all wrongdoers custom backs the sense of wrong.
. . . But methinks the great laggard Time must march
up apace and somehow befriend these thralls. It cannot be
that misery is perpetually entailed, though in a land
proscribing primogeniture the first-born and last of Hamo's
tribe must still succeed to all their sires' wrongs. Yes,
Time, all-Healing Time; Time, great philanthropist—
Time must befriend these thralls!*

HERMAN MELVILLE (1849)

*In a long and intimate connection with this folk, I have
never heard a negro refer to his grandfather and any
reference to parents is rare. The negro must be provided
with these motives of the household; he must be made
faithful to the marriage bond, and taught his sense of
ancestry.*

NATHANIEL SHALER (1890)

*Before that nameless prejudice that leaps beyond all this
he stands helpless, dismayed, and well-nigh speechless;
before that personal disrespect and mockery, the ridicule
and systematic humiliation, the distortion of fact, the
wanton license of fancy, the cynical ignoring of the better
and the boisterous welcoming of the worse, the all-pervading desire to inculcate disdain for every black, from
Toussaint to the devil—before them there rises a sickening
despair that disarms and discourages any nation save that
black host to whom "discouragement" is an unwritten
word.*

W. E. B. DU BOIS (1903)

*No one with a mop can expect respect from a banker, or
an attorney, or men who create jobs, and all you have is
a mop. Are you crazy? Whoever heard of integration between a mop and a banker?*

UNIDENTIFIED THIRTY-EIGHT-YEAR-OLD
BLACK MAN (ca. 1965)

Black Americans were almost all poor in the period covered
by this study, whether they lived in the North or the South, in
cities or on farms. But poverty did not entail household disorganization. The adaptive capacities disclosed by Afro-American
slaves in the century and a half preceding the general emancipation also revealed themselves in the nearly three-quarters of a
century that separated the general emancipation from the onset
of the Great Depression. That is made clear from an examination
of state and federal manuscript censuses in 1880, 1900, 1905, and
1925. It permits some inferences about a few pertinent questions:

the composition of the typical *lower-class* Afro-American household, the differences and similarities in households among "privileged" and "ordinary" Afro-Americans, the differences and similarities between urban and rural black and white lower-class households, and the impact of early twentieth-century northern migration on the black household. Such statistical evidence describes the household, not the family, tells nothing about the roles played by adult men and women within such households, and tells nothing about the relationships between persons living in different households. Kin networks, for example, cannot be reconstructed from these census data. Despite these limitations, the data nevertheless disprove conventional beliefs about the lower-class black family. It did not disintegrate following emancipation, and it did not disintegrate as a consequence of the great migration to northern cities prior to 1930.

The pioneer student of the Afro-American family, E. Franklin Frazier, published his first major work in 1932. It was entitled *The Negro Family in Chicago* and contained an introduction by E. W. Burgess, a prominent sociologist. Burgess praised Frazier for describing how "deviant" behavior among Chicago blacks differed according to social class and neighborhood. Frazier deserved that praise. Those differences indicated the grave limitations of prevalent racial "explanations" of Afro-American behavior. Burgess's introduction, not Frazier's work, deserves notice here: it summed up much of the conventional academic view of early-twentieth-century Afro-Americans. The Negro, said Burgess, with "his simple and loose familial and social organization has migrated *en masse*" to the northern cities. "The chief handicap from which the Negro suffers," Burgess explained, "is perhaps not poverty, nor overcrowding, however serious and challenging these problems may be, but the persistence of an unorganized and disorganized family life." Burgess and so many like him were wrong. The typical Afro-American household changed its shape in the half century between 1880 and 1930. But at all times—and in all settings—the typical black household (always a lower-class household) had in it two parents and was not "unorganized and disorganized."[1]

The first large-scale *voluntary* migration by southern Afro-Americans occurred about the time that the 1880 federal census was recorded. Contemporaries called it the "Great Exodus." Migration had been and would remain a central social experience among Afro-Americans. The forced migrations that had accompanied the transatlantic slave trade and the great expansion of the southern plantation system from the Upper to the Lower South come to mind quickly, and so do the voluntary migrants who made it to northern cities in such vast numbers starting just prior to the First World War and continuing for more than another half century. But the 1880 migrants—most of whom left the Lower South for Kansas—were a special group. The adults among them nearly all had been born slaves.

The migrants to Kansas, who quit the South to improve and to protect themselves, often left in family groups. That is suggested by the testimony some gave in 1880 to a United States Senate committee investigating the reasons they left the South. Carleton Tandy, a St. Louis black, collected twenty-one affidavits from black Mississippi and Louisiana migrant men. Most came in family groups; some detailed the familial difficulties of non-migrant kin and neighbors. All but two had been poor "farmers." The forty-two-year-old Louisiana farmer Lewis Woods had been a Madison Parish constable for two years, and Curtis Pollard, a farmer and then sixty-nine years old, had served six years in the Louisiana legislature. Levi Childs, who had lived in Madison Parish, said, "I have no family along with me; I have a wife and two children down south; I brought my parents with me." The cotton farmer Jet Gibbs remembered hiding the black Tom McClennon just after Christmas in 1878: "I had him to board at my house during the biggest snow we had this winter. He was afraid to go back home, and had run off and left his wife and three children, and [his] crop of cotton and corn because of being afraid of being killed. . . ." Daniel Parker also had run off without his wife and two children after organizing Madison Parish tenant farmers to pressure for a rent reduction: "I had to leave without them; if I had tried to start with them there would have been a fuss." George Rogers described the murder of a Madison Parish neighbor's son:

> I went past her house the next morning and saw the son; he was shot all to pieces and was dead; he was a smart boy and read the papers, and the white people there won't allow that; she said there was about twenty-five to thirty people come in there that night, and when they first came in, as this was the only man . . . in there, they made after him first, and she hallared when they made after him and told them he was the only son she had, and do not kill him; they paid no attention to her. . . .

The thirty-year-old Rogers had better luck: "I have a wife and three children with me." Another Madison Parish farmer James Brown told of barely managing as a sharecropper but still bringing kin with him: "I have a wife and three orphan children. . . . I have my mother-in-law with me, and she has five or six children with her; she has no husband." "I was never able to buy anything to eat, for I didn't have any money," said Clarence Winn in explaining why he left with his wife and two children. Lewis Woods had quit Louisiana for a different reason. Arrested by a white physician for allegedly owing him four dollars for medicine, he left Madison Parish after leaving jail: "I was released and moved my family aboard the boat as quickly as I could and staid aboard the boat. . . . I have a wife and four little children with me."

Similar experiences filled the affidavits filed by Mississippi migrants. The sixty-three-year-old farmer Edward Parlor and his wife had lived in Warren County, and Parlor described the hanging of a pregnant Warren County black woman who had planned to leave for Kansas. (The elderly white Laura S. Haviland, who worked among the Kansas migrants, gave a different description of this murder, saying that two white men had first raped and then murdered her. Two black men found her before she died. "They hastened to cut her down," said Haviland, "and as she was breathing her last she whispered, 'Tell my husband.' One watched the corpse, while the other went to inform the husband.") William Jones, his wife, and their two children also came from Warren County. A wife and two children accompanied the twenty-four-year-old Edward Leonard. Some had even more children. A Hinds County farmer had five, and a Washington County farmer had nine children. Wives accompanied both these men. Not all the Mississippi men brought their families. Jacob Stevens, then about twenty-two, had farmed in Hinds County and, with an older brother and sister, rented about forty acres: "We lived and breathed along. Could barely live and that was all." A crowd of about seventy-five white men shot and killed his father and another brother in 1878. "My mother was crying and begging them, so they told her to go away." The two men had been active local Republicans. Another brother died in a dispute over a debt. Stevens quit Mississippi alone: "I think I am too good a man to stay down there and be killed and don't intend to do it. Couldn't carry me back South unless they would chain and carry me back. My people are there, and I would like to see them, but I can't go back. I don't think my people will ever get out of the South. . . ." Other Mississippi men reported violence to their families or friends. A Warren County farmer and blacksmith, J. D. Daniel, whose wife and five children had accompanied him, remembered that "they came in our [Vicksburg political?] club and killed Washington Davenport's son." The dead man's mother later showed Daniel where "they shot him and burned him up." George Weeks also made it to St. Louis from a Warren County farm. He first sneaked onto a boat alone. "I went up to Vicksburg without my wife," said Weeks, "and had to get a colored man, a constable by the name of Andrew Jackson, to bring [my] wife to St. Louis for me."

Other evidence, some of it given by whites, supplemented these few affidavits with additional information about the family among the migrants. An 1877 petition to the National Emigrant Aid Society signed by S. Heath—a clergyman and a "man of hon an Good Morial"—gave the "Reason & why" he and others wanted to migrate to Kansas: "We hav not our rights in law. . . . An near all of the labors hav familys to tak cear. . . ." A Baltimore and Ohio Railroad passenger sold tickets to 763 migrants, among them 235 "half tickets" for children aged five to twelve. "I think half of them were women," he said of the rest. Asked if migrants to Fort Scott were "generally families or men without families," a Kansas lawyer said: "Men and their families; I suppose three-fourths of the entire number, probably, are women and children. Almost all the men are married men, with their women and children." A Kansas relief worker added that some among these men had "put up little cabins for themselves and their families . . . doing any kind of work they can get to do, while their wives take in 'white folks' washing." The old Quaker abolitionist Laura Haviland, who had been a wartime relief worker among the slave contrabands, managed the North Topeka Employment Bureau set up by the Kansas Freedmen's Relief Association. White requests for black labor worried her: "Nineteen out of twenty call for 'a man and his wife without children' or a 'boy' or a 'girl' or 'a single woman.' " She had difficulty honoring such requests: "Few families . . . are without children, and it is not right to let them lie here in the barracks till all the children die, nor can we send the parents and keep the children." Willing to hire children to "Christian people who desire to do them good," she found it "impossible . . . to find boys and girls willing to go among strangers." Haviland explained:

> In the cursed bondage of the past the breaking up of families was the most bitter trial of their hard lot; now they shrink

from anything that looks like separation. Put yourselves in their place. Remember that they cannot read or write; that communication by mail is practically denied them; that they have been robbed all their lives of all those things wherein you are different from them; that family attachments constitute their *worldly all.* . . .

The Quaker woman urged that Great Exodus migrants be hired out but "scattered, family by family."

Black women as well as men wanted to leave the South. J. Henri Burch, employed at the New Orleans Custom House but before that a practicing journalist, disclosed that Mary J. Garrett ("her name is now Mary Jane Nelson—she married this year") had founded a committee of five hundred black New Orleans women in 1878 to support migration and believed it

very natural that they should desire to seek some country where their labor should secure them a home and a heritage. Without homes, there can be no established permanent form of family. The daily laborer is compelled to scatter his family for their sustenance; they are thus subjected to injurious influences, and the parents are left to infirmity without the presence and care of their children.

Southern blacks were "landless and without homes . . . compelled to labor like the peasantry at the will of others." Other reasons than economic and political ones prompted migration. A September 1879 letter from the Grenada, Mississippi, black Joseph Starks asked the Kansas governor for advice about migration:

We want to come out, and have no money hardly. We have to be in secret or be shot, and [are] not allowed to meet. . . . We have about fifty widows in our band that are workmen and farmers also. The white men here take our wives and daughters and do [with] them as they please, and we are shot if we say anything about it. . . . We are sure to have to leave or to be killed.

George Ruby, who had led ten Texas black families to Kansas and who was a northerner by birth and a Louisiana wartime schoolteacher before white violence had driven him to Texas, explained that blacks had to leave the South for "their want of education and of protection for their women." "They say their daughters and mothers and wives are not safe," said Ruby; "that they are liable to be insulted at any time, and if a colored man talks up for his family, he is either shot down or taken out at night, and bushwacked or killed." John G. Lewis, who had left Toronto in 1866 to teach Louisiana blacks and settled in Natchitotches Parish, agreed: "These same parties that are so down on the negro will go into a colored woman's house; will go right in her house and have intercourse with her. I might as well be plain about this. . . ." Carleton Tandy had tried to get similar information from migrant wives, but their husbands would not let them give sworn statements. Tandy nevertheless learned that "a great many" southern black women wanted to "rear their children up—their girls—to lead a virtuous and industrious life," and that "white men" (who had "taken a liking to the negro women down South") "sought the girls." The women migrants "were overawed with fear of those men" but "seemed more determined and spoke more freely than the men," who "seemed more reticent to tell the whole story." They "came right out and stated that these outrages were being perpetrated." According to Tandy, "a great many of these women rose up and said that if their husbands did not leave they would." Rural southern blacks were "not drawn by the attractions of Kansas." "They are driven," Tandy charged, "by the terrors of Mississippi and Louisiana."

Tandy's social observations were reinforced by Laura Haviland, who related two incidents told to her by migrant blacks. Six Mississippi men (three with families) had rented a "plantation." At the year's end, the landlord claimed that their debts far outbalanced the monies owed to them and took seven hundred bushels of wheat, fourteen fat hogs, some corn, and a wagon and a team of animals. After the blacks went to court without success, they told the landlord "just what they thought of this wholesale robbery." A few days later, "masked Regulators" took the men from their beds, hanged them, and lashed their bodies to boards, which were floated down the Mississippi River with a white cloth fastened to each body. Each cloth had written on it, "Any one taking up these bodies to bury them may expect the same fate." The bodies were removed from the river about one hundred miles to the south. "Two of the widows," Haviland disclosed, "sent for the bodies of their husbands, and a number whom I conversed with [in Kansas] attended the funeral and read the notice on the linen, which had not been removed from the bodies." Haviland also talked with Peter Cox, then more than eighty years old. Cox and his aged wife had made it to Topeka from Louisiana. Their youthful deaf and dumb grandson (later killed in Kansas while walking on a railroad track and unable to hear a train whistle) accompanied them. Cox told Haviland:

> Missus I stay'd thar as long as I could, when I seed my brother in de Lo'd hangin' on a tree not more'n a hundred rods from my house, near Baton Rouge. A sistah was hanged five miles off, on de plank road, in West Baton Rouge, in a little woods. Her sistah followed her beggin' for her life, and tole de bull-dosers she couldn't tell whar her husban' was that da's gwine to hang. But da swore she should hang if she didn't tell. . . . O, Missus, I couldn't live thar no longer. I'se so distressed day an' night. De chief captain of dis ban' of murder's was Henry Castle, who wid his ban' of men was supported by Mr. Garret, Mr. Fisher, an' Mr. Washington.

Garret, Fisher, and Washington were Baton Rouge merchants.[2]

Southern rural and urban blacks who did not join the "Great Exodus" often shared beliefs with the men and women who quit the South so soon after the emancipation. A single example—the Arkansas "Howard County riots" in July 1883—illustrates how some nonmigrant rural blacks violently protested the abuse of their familial integrity and then suffered harsh punishment. The Howard County blacks farmed land in a portion of that county, which a white Arkansas militia officer called "a perfect Africa." Two among them, the brothers James and Prince Marshall, disputed with local whites, including Thomas Wyatt, over land titles. Blacks charged that the whites wanted to dislodge them from their small but apparently successful farms. A "common laborer," Wyatt worked as a sharecropper for a more prosperous local white. After the dispute, according to the black "W.C.J.," Wyatt approached James Marshall's daughter while she plowed a field, "questioned . . . [her] virtue," was told by her "to clear out," and then "seized hold of her" and attempted to rape her. She "made such noise that he knocked her down senseless to prevent her from hallowing and made his escape home." "Some of the family" found her "lying on the ground senseless," and the girl's father learned why.

"W.C.J." related what followed:

> [O]ld man James Marshall called in a few colored men of the neighborhood to know what was best to do. They advised him to go to the justice and get a warrant and off he put; when he reached the justice he was told that if he had Wyatt arrested it would get up trouble and to wait until the grand jury met

and let the case go before them. So the old man being defeated in his expectation by going to the justices, made his way to Washington [Arkansas], where he met a lawyer and related his information; the lawyer told him the only thing he could tell him was to go home and if anyone came on his premises interfering with him and his family to go for them; then the old man giving up all hope of anything being done for him he went home, and on his way he determined to have this man Wyatt arrested.

So we called a meeting of colored men at the church Monday night and talked the matter over. So we met about ten o'clock Monday night and discussed what had to be done to our friend . . . and hearing his statement of the matter we agreed to go then and there and arrest this man Wyatt and carry him to Washington before a justice of the peace. Our meeting adjourned at 1 o'clock that night and we began to make preparations to be on time Tuesday morning at Prince Marshall's house. There was but twenty-eight of us who met at the church, but we agreed to get every man we could by next morning; so we set to work about three o'clock, after leaving the church, each man acting as a deputy telling his friend what had occurred and that he must go and assist, and by so doing we secured about thirty more men who went to help arrest Wyatt for [the] attempt of rape on James Marshall's daughter. So we met at Prince's and proceeded to where Wyatt was, and as Joseph Booker was our leader and one of the officers, he was to demand Wyatt to surrender, but when we got thirty or forty yards of Wyatt he broke and ran and hid in the weeds; of course we were looking for him, when he raised up and fired on Joseph Booker and Booker returned the fire and got off his horse and said boys I am shot; in a few minutes he reeled and fell on the ground and then the shooting commenced, seven or eight guns firing. . . .

The blacks disbanded and "went home," but, after learning that "the white men were together hunting for us . . . as many as could got together . . . for our own protection."

Much violence followed Wyatt's death. According to one newspaper dispatch, the blacks had "stabbed their victim in a horrible manner" and "crushed his head to a jelly with the stocks of their guns." More than "two hundred bullets" were found in Wyatt's body. The black Joe Booker also died. A sheriff's posse could not dislodge the blacks who gathered together after the shooting, but the state militia restored "order." In the meantime, according to "W.C.J.," "so-called deputies went into houses and beat colored women, cursed them, and called them all kinds of names, taken [*sic*] the men prisoners, also boys that were only fourteen years old and some old men that are actually seventy-five or eighty, taken out of the bed." Other blacks were killed, and, according to "W.C.J.":

> History never will record a worse murder than the killing of Eli Gamble, Alonzo Flowers, and Johnson [Joe?] Booker's boy. Mr. Booker's son was sitting on the fence, and the mob composed of white men shot him off just as they would a squirrel, and old man Eli Gamble they killed him with his square in hand, making Joe Booker's coffin, who was killed the day before, and Flowers who was waiting to assist in the burial, and not a single one of these white men was arrested. . . .

Some Howard County black men fled to avoid arrest. Forty-three others went to jail, ten of whom were later acquitted. James Marshall and nine others each were sentenced to fifteen years in prison. At least one of Marshall's sons was among these nine. Other Howard County blacks also went to jail, and three—Henry Carr, Charles Wright, and Lige Thompson, accused of heading the group that killed Wyatt—were sentenced to death. An Arkansas Supreme Court decision ordered new trials for Wright and Thompson but upheld Carr's conviction. That happened in early 1884, by which time the wives of the thirty-three imprisoned blacks had sold "all their stock, lands, etc." Charles Wright was executed on April 25, 1884, before a crowd estimated at five thousand. Months earlier, "WC.J.," apparently in hiding, had written to the Arkansas *Weekly Mansion*, a black newspaper: "I want the public to know that if I am solicited to assist in bringing a brutish man to justice for outraging a woman I will do it every time. . . . if . . . we are all caught and hung, I say to the colored men that are left behind to stand firm and if our women are beaten and outraged [to] riddle the perpetrator of it with bullets, let the consequence be as it may."[3]

The migrants to Kansas and similar northern places were typical southern ex-slaves and Afro-Americans. That is learned by examining the occupational (or class) status and the household arrangements of about sixty-five thousand southern Afro-Americans listed in the 1880 manuscript federal census. Nearly all listed in the census that year and aged fifteen and older had been born slaves. These men, women, and children lived in diverse social and economic settings. Entire urban and rural Afro-American communities, not "samples," have been examined. The communities studied include two large cities (Richmond, Virginia, and Mobile, Alabama) and two small towns (Natchez, Mississippi, and Beaufort, South Carolina). Slightly more than two in five Richmond and Mobile residents were blacks. Just over half of Natchez's residents were Afro-Americans, as were three in four Beaufort residents. Natchez, a Deep South river town, serviced the surrounding Mississippi and Louisiana cotton-producing region. Mobile was a port city, and Richmond was the South's premier manufacturing city. Six rural communities—all of them densely Afro-American in population—also have been studied: (1), St. Helena's Island and (2) St. Helena's Township, in Beaufort County, South Carolina; (3) all of rural Adams County, Mississippi; (4) Mount Album and (5) Lane's Schoolhouse in rural Warren County, Mississippi; and (6), the St. Clair, Sandy Ridge, and White Hall "beats" in rural Lowndes County, Alabama. Prior to the emancipation, these rural communities had all specialized in the production of staple crops[4] (Table A-1).*

1880

The Afro-American Rural Male Occupational Structure

Except in the South Carolina Sea Islands, the typical rural southern adult black male worked either as a farm laborer, a sharecropper, or a cash tenant.[5] Significant numbers of Sea Island black men owned small parcels of land. That was not the case among the Mississippi and Alabama rural blacks. The number of rural blacks with artisan skills or more prestigious occupations was tiny everywhere (Table A-2).

The Afro-American Urban Male Occupational Structure

Beaufort, Natchez, Mobile, and Richmond black men had a much more diverse occupational structure than rural blacks, a fact far less important than that rural and urban southern black men shared a common and depressed economic status. City life meant expanded opportunity for northern and southern whites after the Civil War, but that was not the case for most ex-slaves and antebellum free blacks living in these four urban places. Except in the predominantly black Beaufort, most urban blacks shared a uniformly depressed lower-class status. Three in five black Beaufort

* The tables referred to in this chapter appear in Appendix A, pages 477–519 below.

men were either unskilled laborers or service workers, a proportion that rose to seven in ten in Natchez and eight in ten in Mobile and Richmond. Important in all four cities, black artisans held precarious and declining positions in all but a few urban crafts.[6] A tiny and therefore insignificant black middle class existed in these four urban settings (Tables A-3, A-4, and A-5).

Southern Rural and Urban Afro-American Women Workers

Southern census enumerators irregularly or haphazardly recorded the occupations of rural and urban black women. Nevertheless it is clear that large numbers of rural women labored as field hands and very few as house servants or washerwomen. These latter two occupations were most common among urban black women. Examination of urban house servants and washerwomen by age and household status shows that married women with children hardly ever worked as house servants but regularly labored as washerwomen. The typical urban house servant was a young and unmarried black woman whose labor probably contributed income to her family of origin. Little evidence indicates the presence of the loyal "mammy" laboring as a servant for white families. Very few elderly black women had such jobs[7] (Tables A-6 and A-7).

The Southern Urban and Rural Afro-American Household

Examination of the internal composition of 14,345 southern rural and urban Afro-American households and 2050 subfamilies* discloses that nine in ten blacks lived in households that had at their core two or more members of a black nuclear family: a husband and wife, two parents and their children, or a single parent (usually a mother) with one or more children. Single-person households were few and so were irregular households (those in which neither marital nor blood ties connected two or more persons). Black households usually contained between two and seven persons.[8] The typical black household everywhere contained only the members of a core nuclear family. Such households were more common in rural than in urban settings. When a black "nuclear household" expanded to include lodgers who were not kin, such a household became an "augmented household." Most augmented households had a single lodger. Very few had more than two lodgers. Nuclear households expanded in yet another

---

* A subfamily is either a husband and wife, two parents and their children, or a single parent and children living with another nuclear family in the same household.

way by making place for relatives. Such households are called "extended households." Most black subfamilies lived in extended households, but the typical extended black household usually included the core nuclear family and one or two relatives. It was more common for an urban than a rural extended black household to contain a mother or a mother-in-law. But the typical kin living in extended black households were not elderly persons. They were grandchildren, nephews and nieces, and brothers and sisters of the adult family heads. Grandchildren were more common in extended rural households. Brothers and sisters were found most frequently in extended urban households.[9]

By combining all types of households and subfamilies, we find that a husband or father was present in most households and subfamilies. The husband-father household was more common in rural (ranging from 82 to 86 percent) than in urban (ranging from 69 to 74 percent) settings. *Fathers* with unskilled occupations headed families just as regularly as *fathers* with either artisan skills or middle-class occupations. If the slaves had been without a norm that prized the completed immediate family, large numbers of southern blacks in 1880 should have lived in disorganized households. That was not the case. The manuscript pages of the 1880 federal census reveal with unfailing regularity that urban and rural ex-slaves had retained powerful familial connections and that nearly all households had at their core a nuclear family. The typical southern black household, moreover, had at its head a male who was either a farm laborer, a tenant farmer, a sharecropper, an urban service worker, or an urban day laborer (Tables A-8, A-9, A-10, and A-11).

The Father-Absent Afro-American Household and Subfamily

Most rural and urban southern blacks in 1880 lived in husband- or father-present households and subfamilies, but a sufficiently large percentage of households and subfamilies were father-absent to give them special attention. Conventional historians and sociologists, however, have exaggerated their importance and too frequently have described the lower-class black southern family as little more than a "maternal family."[10] Such households and subfamilies were more common in urban than in rural southern settings but were not an "urban" phenomenon.[11] Women at least forty years old headed a large percentage of father-absent households and subfamilies; many of these had been conventional two-parent households in which the husband had died. Nevertheless significant numbers of younger women in rural

as well as urban settings also headed such households and subfamilies. Partly, that is explained by the large surplus of adult
black women of all ages in southern cities and of younger black
women in southern rural areas. In addition, a small but significant
number of rural and urban mothers described themselves to
census enumerators as "single." That so few women over thirty
years of age did so, together with the relatively young age at
which most black women had a first child, strongly indicates that
most young single women with children later married, following
a pattern that had deep roots in black life.[12]

Most southern black women headed neither households nor
subfamilies. Far greater numbers of unmarried black women
under thirty, for example, lived with their parents than headed
households.[13] The "three-generation" male-absent household (a
mother, her daughter, and the daughter's children), considered
the archetypal "matrifocal" family, moreover, hardly existed
among southern rural and urban blacks. Far greater numbers of
elderly black women lived with their husbands or their married
children than in such households. Subfamilies headed by single,
widowed, or abandoned mothers, furthermore, were incorporated
into larger households so that very few young mothers lived alone
with their children.[14] Male-absent households and subfamilies,
finally, had far fewer children than households with a father
present. As a result, between 66 percent and 75 percent of black
children under the age of six everywhere lived with a mother and
a father (Tables A-12, A-13, A-14, A-15, A-16, A-17, and A-18).

A Comparison Between Lower-Class White and Afro-American Rural and Urban Households

Jones County, Mississippi, whites were poor in 1860, and their
material condition had not improved greatly by 1880. Their
households are compared to those of St. Helena's Island and
Township, South Carolina, and rural Adams County, Mississippi,
blacks. "Poor whites," the Jones County whites nevertheless had
a higher economic status than the St. Helena's and Adams County
rural blacks.[15] The nuclear household predominated in all three
places but was most common among the St. Helena's blacks. About
the same percentage of extended households existed in the three
places. Households with lodgers were infrequent among the St.
Helena's blacks, but the proportion of white Jones County and
black Adams County households with lodgers was nearly the same.
Two important differences distinguished the rural black from the
rural white communities. Childless couples were more frequent

among the blacks. Male-absent households and subfamilies headed
by women aged twenty to twenty-nine, moreover, were twice as
common among St. Helena's black women and four times as
common among rural Adams County black women as among
Jones County white women. Nevertheless, the over-all percentage
of male-present households and subfamilies hardly differed in all
three places. It was highest among the St. Helena's Island and
Township blacks (Table A-19).

The Richmond and Mobile black household is next compared
to that in 1880 among native white and Irish residents of Paterson,
New Jersey, an industrial city that thrived on the manufacture
of silk, other textiles, locomotives, and iron. All four communities
had a surplus of adult women, but the adult sex ratio was far more
unbalanced among the Richmond and Mobile blacks than among
the Paterson Irish and native whites. Occupationally, the Paterson
whites lived in a very different world from the southern urban
blacks. Married women with children rarely worked outside their
homes. The native whites and Irish were predominantly working-
class communities, but only one in five native white men and
slightly more than two in five Irish men had unskilled or service
jobs. Four in five Richmond and Mobile black men did such work.
The poorer Richmond and Mobile blacks had proportionately
more subfamilies than the Paterson Irish and native whites. But
the nuclear household was the most common in all four communities. The Paterson Irish had the most nuclear households, the
Paterson native whites the most extended households, and Richmond blacks the most augmented households, but the percentage-
point differences among the groups were small. At least two-
thirds of all Paterson Irish, Mobile black, Paterson native white,
and Richmond black households were nuclear in composition.
The male-absent household and subfamily were more common
among Richmond and Mobile blacks than among the Paterson
native whites and Irish. Occupational differences and especially
the greatly imbalanced black sex ratio predict that fact. Part
of the difference also is explained by the fact that 10 percent
of Richmond and Mobile black women aged twenty to twenty-nine
headed a male-absent household or subfamily as compared with
4.4 percent of similarly aged Paterson Irish and native white
women.* Overall, between 12 and 13 percent of all adult Paterson
Irish and native white women headed households or subfamilies,

---

* Paterson Irish and native white women differed here: 3.5 percent of Irish
women aged twenty to twenty-nine headed male-absent households or subfamilies,
as contrasted with 6.4 percent of native white women similarly aged.

as compared with 17 percent of all adult Mobile and Richmond black women. These are important differences and merit notice and refined study. But once accounted for—a large excess of females, an over-all low male occupational status, the belief among some in motherhood outside of marriage, among other causes— it is the similarities that deserve attention. In 1880, a father or husband was present in four in five Paterson Irish and native white households, as compared with nearly three in four Richmond and Mobile black households[16]* (Tables A-20 and A-21).

1900

The Southern Afro-American Rural and Urban Household in 1900

Important changes in the composition of the urban and rural southern black household occurred between 1880 and 1900. That is made clear in the 1900 federal manuscript census, a historical source that permits examination of the Afro-American household and family on the eve of the great twentieth-century black migration to the North. The occupational and household status of about 12,300 southern black men, women, and children has been studied in three places: (1) portions of St. Helena's Island and Township, South Carolina; (2) portions of Issaquena County, Mississippi; and (3) portions of the Jackson Ward in Richmond, Virginia. The rural places studied were densely Afro-American: forty-six whites lived among 4656 St. Helena's blacks, and 221 whites lived among 4201 Issaquena blacks.[17] The "samples" are smaller than those examined in 1880, and direct comparisons between 1880 and 1900 therefore remain tentative. Nevertheless, in all three places the male occupational structure did not differ significantly

* Very valuable ways of comparing urban black and other predominantly working-class populations are found in Frank Furstenberg, Jr., Theodore Hershberg, and John Modell, "The Origins of the Female-Headed Black Family: The Impact of the Urban Experience," *Journal of Interdisciplinary History*, VI (Autumn 1975), 211–33, an essay which uses mostly quantitative data from the 1880 federal census to compare Philadelphia black households with the households of Philadelphia Irish, German, and native white residents. The essay was published too late to be incorporated in this study. It adds important dimensions to a comparative study of black and nonblack urban households. There is an invaluable analysis of differential mortality rates among Philadelphia whites and blacks that is essential to understanding the reason why male-absent households were more common among Philadelphia blacks than Philadelphia whites. In addition, the authors examine household composition as it relates to real and personal wealth, not simply occupation as in this study. Female-headedness is found to vary inversely with wealth. Moreover, when wealth is examined, the variation between blacks and the diverse white groups is greatly reduced. The authors draw their data on wealth from the 1870 federal manuscript census. Such data are not available in the 1880 federal manuscript census.

in 1900 from that in 1880. Land ownership remained common among the South Carolina blacks but was unknown among the Issaquena blacks. Rural artisans and blacks with higher status were few in number in these two places. Compared to Richmond men in 1880, the Jackson Ward men showed a slight but insignificant improvement, but only one in fifteen was neither a laborer nor a skilled worker. Among women, domestic work declined in importance, and a greater percentage than in 1880 labored as laundresses and washerwomen.[18]

In 1900, the kin-related household still remained the norm, and the size of the household was hardly changed. The percentage of male-absent households and subfamilies increased, but most of them still were headed by elderly women. Far more important changes occurred, especially among the Richmond blacks. The subfamily—that is, a family living with one or more families in the same household—greatly increased. In 1880, Richmond had five subfamilies for every twenty-two households; twenty years later, the Jackson Ward blacks had five subfamilies for every seven households. The simple nuclear household greatly declined in importance. Only two in five Jackson households were nuclear in composition. The number of augmented households increased, but the number of extended households increased even more rapidly. The typical extended household contained the core nuclear family and either nephews and nieces or brothers and sisters of the household heads. The nuclear household retained its commanding importance among rural blacks, but there, too, extended and augmented households increased in number. Why these important changes in the composition of the rural and especially the urban black household occurred between 1880 and 1900 remains a subject for important study. They may have been adaptive strategies to deal with the poverty most blacks knew. And they may have been closely related to the extended kin groups that had developed prior to emancipation. These remain speculations.[19]* Despite

* See the very important study by Crandall A. Shifflett, "The Household Composition of Rural Black Families: Louisa County, Virginia, 1880," *Journal of Interdisciplinary History,* VI (Autumn 1975), 235–60, which appeared too late to be incorporated into the text of this study. By studying the changing composition of rural black and white households over the full family cycle and relating these changes to the economic status of rural blacks and whites, Shifflett shows a close relationship between extended households and low economic status. In this pioneering and very original study, Shifflett finds evidence of the "solidarity of strong black kinship networks" and argues that "the burden of poverty induced black families to rely on kinship networks and to become their brothers' keepers." Similar analysis is needed for other southern rural blacks and also for southern and northern urban blacks.

these important changes in the composition of the household, the typical southern black household in 1900 still had at its head a lower-class husband or father (Tables A-22, A-23, A-24, A-25, and A-26).

Unlike earlier censuses, the 1900 census revealed invaluable information about marriage, family, childbearing, and sexual behavior. It asked women how many children had been born to them and still lived either inside or outside the household, and it asked men and women about the length of their marriages. As in 1880, a small percentage of mothers under forty described themselves as "single." A significant number everywhere but especially in the rural places reported the birth of a child either prior to marriage or during the first year of marriage. Such evidence indicated the prevalence of prenuptial intercourse, childbirth out of wedlock, and bridal pregnancy. But the small number of single women aged thirty and older shows that marriage usually followed either pregnancy or the birth of a child.

Long marriages were common among these rural and urban blacks, and so was the attachment of parent to child. The disorder that accompanied the Reconstruction and Redemption years had not caused casual marriages to occur among women born between 1866 and 1875. Half of the married St. Helena's women in this age group had lived with the same spouse for between ten and nineteen years. Nearly the same percentage of Jackson women had marriages of that length, as did a lesser but still-significant percentage of Issaquena women. Women born between 1846 and 1855 had even longer marriages. Two of three married Issaquena women had lived with the same spouse for at least twenty years, and the percentage was higher among the Jackson Ward women (80 percent) and still higher among the St. Helena's women (85 percent). The length of marriages reported by the St. Helena's and Jackson Ward blacks but not by the Issaquena blacks hardly differed at each age level from the length of marriage reported by Jones County, Mississippi, whites in 1900. In all places studied, furthermore, more than nine in ten children whose mother was not yet thirty years old lived with their parents. If a mother lived alone, the percentage hardly differed. These data, however, are no reason to idealize the condition of the late-nineteenth-century southern black family. The 1900 federal census disclosed how many children were born to women and how many had died by 1900. The median number of children born to rural black women aged forty to forty-nine in 1900 was nearly the same among St.

Helena's and Issaquena women and somewhat lower among the Jackson Ward women. Three in ten children born to these St. Helena's women were dead by 1900, and the number increased to nearly one in two among the Issaquena and Jackson Ward women. The comparable figure among poor white Jones County women was one in five. It cost a great deal to be a parent of a southern rural or urban black child in the decades following emancipation and preceding the great migration to the North (Tables A-27, A-28, A-29, and A-30).

1905

New York City Afro-American Households

Early twentieth-century migration from the rural South to the urban North did not shatter the black family. That is disclosed by a study of the 1905 New York State manuscript census. By 1905, New York City was already attracting black migrants, and the occupational and household status of 14,368 black residents in the San Juan Hill and Tenderloin districts is examined next. Perhaps as many as three-fourths of this population's adults had been born in the South Atlantic states, especially Virginia.[20] About two-thirds were between the ages of fifteen and thirty-nine.[21] Adult women significantly outnumbered adult men, and about one in four women aged fifteen and older was a lodger or lived alone. The occupational status of black men could not have been worse by early-twentieth-century standards. About 5 percent (more than half of these clerks) were not unskilled laborers, service workers, or skilled workmen. Nine percent were skilled workers, and one in four of them either an actor or a musician. Fewer blacks with skills worked in the building trades than as actors and musicians. If these Tenderloin and San Juan Hill men typified the range of occupations held by other 1905 New York City blacks, the scarcity of skilled workers meant that migrant blacks did not threaten the occupational status of skilled white workers. Instead, these men had been bypassed by the industrial advances identified with development of capitalism in nineteenth- and early-twentieth-century America. They either carried few skills with them from the South (a possibility strongly suggested by the deteriorating status of Richmond and Mobile skilled black workers in 1880) or were excluded from many unskilled occupations open to native and immigrant white New Yorkers.

The tiny Tenderloin and San Juan Hill black "middle class" deserves notice mainly because of its insignificant size. Not much differed among these 1905 New York City blacks when compared with the Richmond and Mobile blacks a quarter of a century earlier. Fewer than three hundred men listed occupations that nominally deserve "middle-class" classification. Three in four of the 166 "white-collar" workers were clerks, postal employees, and federal customhouse workers. Ten men called themselves foremen and managers, and another dozen were salesmen and "agents." Half of the thirty-nine professionals were clergymen, physicians, and dentists. Together, the San Juan Hill and Tenderloin districts had as residents three black lawyers and two black schoolteachers. The work of the seventy-seven men engaged in "enterprise" also indicated the over-all depressed status of early-twentieth-century New York City blacks. Twenty-four ran restaurants or were caterers. One manufactured trunks. Very few supervised petty retail enterprises. Eight were proprietors of poolrooms; five were undertakers; a handful dealt in real estate or ran lodging places. Four sold wood; two or three kept saloons; two each were grocers and shoe-store proprietors and one kept a confectionery store. One of seven engaged in "enterprise" called themselves hucksters, dealers, and jobbers. Not all with such non-working-class occupations were "well off." Many boarded nonrelatives in their homes, and their wives and other close kin often labored in unskilled jobs. Three married clergymen, for example, had wives working as domestics or dressmakers. A black listed as a "professor" lived with his wife and his sister. His wife did not work, but his sister labored as a seamstress. So did an architect's wife. A schoolteacher and a druggist each had wives who were janitresses, and a chemist's wife was a cook. The nineteen-year-old son of a widowed lawyer labored as an elevator operator.

Most black males—86 percent—worked as day laborers or in service jobs. And vast numbers of adult black women labored as service workers, washerwomen, and laundresses (Tables A-31, A-32, and A-33).

Largely a young adult population, the economically depressed San Juan Hill and Tenderloin blacks did not live in disorganized households. Less than 10 percent lived alone or in boarding houses. Slightly more than four in five lived in households of between two and seven persons. About 10 percent of households with two or more persons had no residents related by either blood or marriage.[22] Overall, about six in seven New York blacks lived in a household that had at its core two or more persons related by either blood or marriage. Nearly half of these households contained just members of a nuclear family, and two in five were augmented households. Most families took in one or two lodgers; relatively few took in more than three. About one in six households contained kin other than members of the immediate family, a high percentage given the population's migrant character. Except where subfamilies were present, the extended household usually included one relative and rarely more than two. These were most often members of the family of origin: mothers and mothers-in-law, adult siblings, and adult nephews and nieces[23] (Tables A-34 and A-35).

Migration and the changing composition of the Afro-American household (especially the relative decline of the nuclear household) among New York City blacks in 1905 are not evidence that husbands and fathers were less frequently within the family than in the South in 1880 or 1900. A husband or father was present in slightly more than four in five (83 percent) San Juan Hill and Tenderloin households and subfamilies. Nine of ten adult women did not head either households or subfamilies. Among those that did, more than half were elderly women. Women under thirty headed about one in five male-absent households and subfamilies. Most of these (three in four) had one child. One woman under thirty among these nearly fifteen thousand blacks headed a male-absent household that had in it more than two children. Young black women heading households and subfamilies were far less important in New York City in 1905 than in Richmond in 1880. One of every eleven Richmond women aged twenty to twenty-nine headed such a household or subfamily in 1880. In New York City in 1905, the proportion was one of every twenty-five similarly aged women. The typical New York City black household in 1905 had at its head a poor male unskilled laborer or service worker. Six in seven adult New York City black men were either laborers or service workers. And six in seven *fathers* (men living with a wife and children or just their children) were either laborers or service workers. A man's age did not affect the father's place in the family. Eighty-four percent of men aged forty-five and older were either laborers or service workers, and 88 percent of similarly aged *fathers* had similar occupations (Tables A-36, A-37, A-38, and A-39. See Appendix B for a comparison between the 1905 New York City blacks and New York City Jews and Italians in that same year).

1925

Black Manhattan and Its Households in 1925:
Neither Sodom Nor Mecca

Manhattan's black population increased rapidly between 1905 and 1925. By 1930 nearly a quarter of a million blacks lived there. At least seven in ten lived in Harlem. Migration from the South and from the Caribbean region explained this rapid growth. The occupational and household status of 57,853 Manhattan blacks in 1925, about one-third of the island's black residents, are examined. Some still lived in the San Juan Hill district, but seven in eight lived in Central Harlem. Still largely a migrant population, the 1925 blacks shared many demographic and social characteristics with the 1905 group studied. Nearly seven in ten were between the ages of fifteen and forty-four. A large number were lodgers. Nearly three in ten women aged fifteen and older, for example, were lodgers or lived alone. Unlike the 1905 population, this population contained many foreign-born—mostly West Indian—blacks. About one in four black men and women aged fifteen and older was an immigrant. So large a West Indian population in 1925 allows for a comparison of the adaptive behavior of native-born and immigrant blacks. An essential difference distinguished the two groups. The immigrant blacks followed the common European immigration pattern: men outnumbered women in all but one (fifteen to twenty-four) adult age group. Women, however, predominated among the native black migrants. The West Indians and native blacks therefore had quite opposite over-all adult sex ratios: 105 and 85 respectively. Occupationally, the two groups had much more in common than has heretofore been realized. Overall, the occupational status of adult black men improved between 1905 and 1925. The percentage of unskilled laborers and service workers fell significantly between 1905 (86 percent) and 1925 (72 percent). About one in five West Indian men was a skilled worker. A lesser percentage of native black men had skills, but it was higher than in 1905. White-collar work, especially among native blacks, increased over the twenty-year period, too. Neither the West Indians nor the native blacks had gained a significant foothold in either the professions or in businesses of any kind. Less than 4 percent of adult black men were professionals or ran businesses. By these measures, the West Indians and native blacks did not differ. But given the differences in absolute numbers, the tiny central Harlem black middle class

in 1925 was predominantly native-born. Important changes occurred between 1905 and 1925, but in 1925 nearly nine in ten
Manhattan black men were either unskilled laborers, service
workers, or skilled workers (Tables A-40, A-41, and A-42).

Important changes in the composition of the New York City
black households also occurred between 1905 and 1925. The single-
person and irregular household declined slightly in importance
compared with the household with a nuclear core. The shape of
irregular households, however, hardly changed over the two
decades.[24] Households containing just members of an immediate
family declined in importance. In 1925, just one in three West
Indian and two in five native black households were nuclear in
composition. About half of all black households had one or more
lodgers in them, and about one in five households had one or
more relatives other than members of the immediate family. Just
as the household expanded, so, too, did the relative importance
of the subfamily. In 1905, there had been one subfamily for every
eight households. Twenty years later, there was one subfamily for
every three (native blacks) or four (West Indian) households.
The composition of the typical Harlem household in 1925 was
very different from the typical southern rural or urban household
in 1880. Over this half century, the simple nuclear household
declined in importance, and extended and augmented households
as well as subfamilies increased in importance (Table A-43).

The changing composition of the household, a fact of great
importance in describing the adaptive behavior of early-twentieth-
century southern black migrants to New York City, was not
accompanied by any increase in the male-absent household or
subfamily. About five in six 1905 New York City black households
and subfamilies contained either a husband or a father. That was
so in six of seven 1925 households and subfamilies. A father was
present in seven in ten families. That happened more frequently
in West Indian than in native black families. Despite the low
economic status of most males, the adverse over-all sex ratio, the
great number of unattached lodgers, the decline of the nuclear
household, and the increased importance of the augmented
household and the subfamily, the percentage of black women in
all age-specific groups heading male-absent households and subfamilies either remained constant or declined between 1905 and
1925. The male-absent household and subfamily changed in one
important way over these two decades: the subfamily without a
resident father became more important than the household

without a resident father.[25] But the age distribution of the mothers involved remained nearly the same. Slightly more than half of the women heading either households or subfamilies were at least forty years old. Insignificant differences distinguished the native black from the West Indian women. Despite their disadvantaged sex ratio, nearly the same percentage of native black women aged twenty to twenty-nine (4.2 percent) as similarly aged West Indian women (4 percent) headed either households or subfamilies. Overall, the male-absent household and subfamily headed by a young black woman and filled with numerous children was relatively insignificant in 1925. Three percent of all households and subfamilies were male-absent and headed by women under thirty. One percent of all households and subfamilies were male-absent and had in them three or more children. The population studied contained 13,922 households and subfamilies. Just thirty-two— 0.3 percent—were male-absent, headed by a woman not yet thirty, and contained three or more children. Not surprisingly, five in six black children under the age of six lived with both parents. Only 124 children in this community of more than fifty thousand men, women, and children lived with a nonrelative. Fathers, once again, in these and other families were overwhelmingly unskilled laborers and service workers. And fathers with these occupations matched in number the percentage of adult males with these occupations. That was just as true for the native black father as for the West Indian father. Age did not matter. Three in four native black men aged forty-five and older were either laborers or service workers, and 74 percent of native black fathers aged forty-five and older had similar occupations (Tables A-44, A-45, A-46, A-47, A-48, A-49, and A-50).

Central Harlem may not have been Mecca in the middle 1920s. But neither was it Sodom. No evidence whatsoever sustains the assertion in Gilbert Osofsky's *Harlem: The Making of a Ghetto* that "the slave heritage, bulwarked by economic conditions, continued into the twentieth century to make family instability a common factor in Negro life."[26] And that is so because such large numbers of lower-class southern black migrants had adapted familial and kin ties—rooted in their prior historical experiences first as slaves and afterward as free rural southern workers and farmers—to life in the emerging ghetto.

At all moments in time between 1880 and 1925—that is, from an adult generation born in slavery to an adult generation about to be devastated by the Great Depression of the 1930s and the modernization of southern agriculture afterward—the typical Afro-American family was lower-class in status and headed by two parents. That was so in the urban and rural South in 1880 and in 1900 and in New York City in 1905 and 1925. The two-parent household was not limited to better-advantaged Afro-Americans (rural landowners, artisans and skilled workers, and members of the tiny black middle-class elite). It was just as common among farm laborers, sharecroppers, tenants, and northern and southern urban unskilled laborers and service workers. It accompanied the southern blacks in the great migration to the North that has so reshaped the United States in the twentieth century.

Harlem in 1925 differed from rural South Carolina and Mississippi in 1880. So did black residents in both settings. The typical lower-class Afro-American household also changed over that half century. It expanded and grew more complex. That process apparently started in the South between 1880 and 1900 and was greatly accelerated by the migration of vast numbers of poor southern blacks to northern cities prior to 1930. Just how this changing household and the family (or families) within it related to larger Afro-American kinship patterns and just how those kin networks changed between 1880 and 1925 cannot be learned from data drawn from manuscript censuses. Such sources, however, reveal enough about the interior composition of Afro-American households to confound a vast and ill-informed popular and academic mythology that so misrepresented the diverse capacities of the descendants of enslaved Afro-Americans to adapt to changing external circumstances in the century following the general emancipation.

It was such beliefs that Anna Julia Cooper dismissed in the 1890s in discussing Maurice Thompson's "Voodoo Prophecy," a poem published in the *Independent*, perhaps the nation's most widely read religious weekly. The Confederate veteran Thompson celebrated the imaginary abandon and lack of self-restraint that so many whites assumed to be so true about so many blacks. "I am the prophet of the dusky race," Thompson's verses began, "The poet of wild Africa."

> You know the past, hear now, what is to be:
> From the midnight land,
> Over sea and sand,
> From the green jungle, hear my Voodoo-song:

A tropic heat is in my bubbling veins,
Quintessence of all savagery is mine,
The lust of ages ripens in my reins,
    And burns
    And yearns,
Like venom-sap within a noxious vine.

The "heathen" and the "fetich worshipper" had been freed

    To leap and dance,
    To hurl my lance. . . .

You, seed of Abel, proud of your descent,
    And arrogant because your cheeks are fair,
Within my loins an inky curse is pent,
    To flood
    Your blood
And stain your skin and crisp your golden hair.

As you have done by men, so will I do
    By the generations of your race;
Your snowy limbs, your blood's patrician blue
    Shall be tainted by me,
And I will set my seal upon your face!

Yes, I will dash my blackness down your veins,
    And through your nerves my sensuousness I'll fling;
Your lips, your eyes, shall bear the musty stains
    Of Congo kisses,
    While shrieks and hisses
Shall blend into the savage song I sing!

I will absorb your very life in me,
    And mold you to the shape of my desire;
Back through the cycles of all cruelty
    I will swing you,
    And wrong you,
And roast you in my passion's hottest fire.

My serpent fetich lolls its withered lip
    And bears its shining fang at thought of this:
I scarce can hold the monster in my grip.
    So strong is he,
    So eagerly
He leaps to meet my precious prophecies.

Born a Raleigh, North Carolina, slave in 1858 and later a North
Carolina and District of Columbia schoolteacher, Anna Julia
Cooper described Thompson's poem as "merely a revelation of the

white man" and of "no interest as a picture of the black." " 'The
devil is always painted *black*—by white painters,' " she added.
"And what is needed, perhaps to reverse the picture of the lordly
man slaying the lion, is for the lion to turn painter."[27]

Most early-twentieth-century social scientists, many among
them academic "Progressives," shared assumptions about Afro-
Americans with the poet Thompson. The psychologist James M.
Cattell told readers of the *Popular Science Monthly* (1903) that
"a savage brought up in a cultivated society will not only retain
his dark skin, but is likely also to have the incoherent mind of his
race." Three years later, the physical anthropologist Robert Bennett Bean published the results of his measurement of 152 frontal
lobes in black and white brains in the *American Journal of
Anatomy,* findings that reinforced Bean's belief that among blacks
"there is instability of character incident to lack of self-control,
especially in connection with the sexual relation." (Bean, incidentally, also believed that the "Jewish nose" was "a product of
habitual indignation.") Two other early-twentieth-century works
illustrate the prevalence of these and similar beliefs: Howard
Odum's 1910 Columbia University dissertation *Social and Mental
Traits of the Negro* and Arthur W. Calhoun's 1917 classic *A
Social History of the American Family from Colonial Times to
the Present*. Years before Odum won a well-deserved reputation
as a very perceptive student of southern regionalism, his published
dissertation had urged that southern blacks deserved "sympathy"
and "encouragement" to allow "simple success and happiness . . .
for the successfully developed black man." The larger culture,
however, had no "place for a black white man." Odum's work,
which had greatly benefited from the advice and encouragement
given him by such prominent early-twentieth-century social scientists and historians as A. B. Hart, G. Stanley Hall, E. R. A.
Seligman, and Franklin H. Giddings, rested on the belief that "if
the home . . . is bad it needs no logic to see that the total or-
ganism is bad." "Their first and crying need," he said of southern
blacks, "is for home life and training." Odum explained:

> The negro has little home conscience or love of home, no
> local attachments of the better sort. . . . He has no pride of
> ancestry, and he is not influenced by the lives of great men.
> . . . He has little conception of the meaning of virtue, truth,
> honor, manhood, integrity. . . . He does not know the value
> of his word or the meaning of words in general. . . . They
> sneer at the idea of work. . . . Their moral natures are miser-
> ably perverted. Such a statement should not be interpreted as

abusing the negro; for, considering the putrid moral air he breathes . . . there could be no other outcome. . . .

"No people," Odum went on, "can live above their home life." And "in his home life the negro is filthy, careless and indecent. He is as destitute of morals as any of the lower animals. He does not even know the meaning of the word." "Nowhere" in the Afro-American home could one find "restraint." The "utter lack of restraint," he added, "deadens any moral sensibilities that might be present." Blacks had a "powerful sensuous capacity." The absence of restraint caused "the consequent extreme expression of the feelings," "little more than impulses," because the Afro-American "social self has not developed the love of home and family nor the desire to accumulate property." Such social processes rested on Odum's belief that "the negro differs from the whites not only in development but also in kind," and that "a knowledge of this 'kind' . . . is the first essential to a satisfactory discussion of the problem." These differences made the Afro-American "superficial and irresponsible." It had been different decades earlier: "the oversight [*sic*] of the white man in slavery days" had "kept the home of the negro in a more organized state."[28]

Calhoun differed from Odum in explaining early-twentieth-century Afro-American "moral depravity." He did not find their social condition entirely "peculiar to the negro as a race" but said that the "general exploitation of the poor and helpless by the propertied class lays the basis for protean depravity whether the victims be negro or white":

> . . . Primitive traits and the heritage of slavery are slow to be eliminated. . . . Many negroes are still uncontrolled by any serious sense of social responsibility. They give way spontaneously to impulses that civilization seeks to keep under control. . . . At the opening of the twentieth century, the point where the Negro American was furthest behind modern civilization was in his sexual *mores*. Children of ten to twelve knew a hundred vile songs; they were sung in many homes without thought of impropriety. Masturbation was common among children of both sexes and intercourse was begun shortly after or even before puberty. Open cohabitation of the unmarried was very common. Women got standards of decorum from their ideas as to decollete white women, from questionable novels, and from salacious theatricals. Many matings involved no marriage ceremony and paid little attention to legal requirements.

A crude "environmentalist," Calhoun believed that "moral delinquency" was the inevitable result of a "vicious environment."
He admitted, as did Odum, that his generalizations did not apply
to all Afro-Americans but believed that his description of "family
morals" was "applicable in general to a considerable segment of
the negro population even at the present day."29*

Such beliefs caused W. E. B. Du Bois to decry in *The Souls
of Black Folk* (1903) "that personal disrespect and mockery, the
ridicule and systematic humiliation, the distortion of fact, the
wanton license of fancy, the cynical ignoring of the better and
the boisterous welcoming of the worse, the all-pervading desire
to inculcate disdain for every black, from Toussaint to the
devil. . . ." And it was such beliefs that Ralph Ellison addressed
a half century later in his masterful mid-twentieth-century novel:
"I am invisible, understand, simply because people refuse to see
me. Like the bodiless heads you see sometimes in circus sideshows,
it is as though I have been surrounded by mirrors of dark, distorted glass. When they approach me, they see only my surroundings, themselves, or figments of their imagination—indeed,
everything and anything but me. . . ." Du Bois and Ellison were
neither the first nor the last Americans with such perceptions.
Much earlier in time and in a very different America, John Adams
had said that "the poor man . . . is not disapproved, censured, or
reproached; he is only not seen." And Alexander Hamilton had
noticed that "the contempt we have been taught to entertain for
the blacks makes us fancy many things that are founded neither
in reason nor in experience."30

---

* See Appendix C, "A Brief Note on Late-Nineteenth-Century Racial Ideology,
Retrogressionist Beliefs, the Misperception of the Slave Family, and the Conceptualization of Afro-American History," pages 531–544 below.

Afterword

You can make a nigger work, but you cannot make him think.

UNIDENTIFIED SOUTHERN WHITE
to Frederick Olmsted (c. 1855)

Talk him with me, and de Lord will keep you warm under he feathers, he will gather oona to his breast, for he love dem what help de poor.

SMART WASHINGTON (1864)

Only the poor feel for the poor.

JANE SMITH (1866)

She had "no family" which means a great deal to colored people.

ELIZABETH BOTUME (1893)

Taped to the wall of my cell are 47 pictures: 47 black faces: my father, mother, grandmothers (1 dead), grandfathers (both dead), brothers, sisters, uncles, aunts, cousins (1st & 2nd), nieces, and nephews. They stare across the space at me sprawling on my bunk. I know their dark eyes, they know mine. I know their style, they know mine. I am all of them, they are all of me; they are farmers, I am a thief, I am me, they are thee.

* * *

I have the same name as 1 grandfather, 3 cousins, 3 nephews,
and 1 uncle. The uncle disappeared when he was 15, just took
off and caught a freight (they say). He's discussed each year
when the family has a reunion, he causes uneasiness in the clan, he is an empty space. My father's mother, who is 93
and who keeps the Family Bible with everybody's birth dates
(and death dates) in it, always mentions him. There is no
place in her Bible for "whereabouts unknown."

ETHERIDGE KNIGHT, "The Idea of Ancestry"
(Poems from Prison, 1968)

Forty years passed between the recording of the 1925 New York State census (a document showing that family disorganization did not accompany poor southern black migrants to northern cities) and the publication of Daniel Patrick Moynihan's enormously

controversial *The Negro Family: The Case for National Action*
(a document which argued that it did). Although Moynihan emphasized the importance of unemployment as a cause of family
disorganization among lower-class Afro-Americans, he confused
the problems of poor blacks in the second half of the twentieth
century with those of their great-grandparents in the first half of
the nineteenth century. And he misperceived the history of both
groups. "At the heart of the deterioration of the fabric of Negro
society," said the controversial 1965 report, "is the deterioration
of the Negro family," "the fundamental source of the weakness
in the Negro community at the present time." "In its lasting
effects on individuals and their children," American slavery was
"indescribably worse than any recorded servitude, ancient or
modern." Moynihan quoted approvingly from Nathan Glazer's
summary of Stanley Elkins, from Thomas Pettigrew, and from E.
Franklin Frazier to argue that "the slave household often developed a fatherless matrifocal (mother-centered) pattern," and
that severe postemancipation rural and urban poverty meant that
"the Negro family made but little progress toward the middle-
class pattern of the present time." Migration to the North reinforced social and familial disorganization among southern blacks—
a process similar to what had happened in "the wild Irish slums
of the nineteenth century Northeast" where "drunkenness, crime,
corruption, family disorganization, [and] juvenile delinquency"
were "routine." "No one Negro problem" existed, and there was
"no one solution." "Nevertheless," Moynihan said, "at the center
of the tangle of pathology is the weakness of the family structure. . . . It was by destroying the Negro family that white America
broke the will of the Negro people. . . . Three centuries of injustice have brought about deep-seated structural distortions in
the life of the Negro American." Moynihan urged "a national
effort . . . to strengthen the Negro family."[1]

Much criticism greeted the "Moynihan Report." Critics
bitterly debated what came to be called "the slavery-specific
hypothesis." Had slavery bred among Afro-Americans what some
call " a culture of poverty"? "The habit of analyzing data by color
rather than by income levels," the sociologist Hylan Lewis pointed
out in one of the most intelligent critiques, "has tended to support
the slavery-specific hypothesis." Lewis and others convincingly
showed that "Negro-white differences in family structure diminish
when controlled for income and that differences by income are
more striking than differences by color. . . . Since a much larger

proportion of Negroes than of whites are on the lowest income levels, what look like statistically significant differences between Negroes and whites may actually be differences between socio-economic levels" (Table 37). Lewis argued that "since the job is a crucial determinant of where and how the family fits in the society and of the effectiveness of many of the society's rewards, probably the most important single clue to the quality of change in the Negro family and in the community, is . . . the job picture . . . for the male." Lewis later wrote: "The answer to the problem of family disorganization is not one of inculcating marriage and family values in young couples; there is ample evidence that they exist. The critical test is to find ways and means for the young adult male to meet the economic maintenance demands of marriage and family life." Lewis and others like him did not suggest that slavery had been less harsh than Moynihan had argued but denied that the difficulties encountered by poor urban Afro-Americans in the 1960s had their roots in a three-century "cycle of self-perpetuating pathology." "Pseudofacts," the sociologist Robert K. Merton warns, "have a way of inducing pseudoproblems which cannot be solved because matters are not as they purport to be." So does pseudohistory. A vast difference exists in dealing with a problem rooted in "three centuries of exploitation" and one caused by massive structural unemployment.[2]

Few critics of the "Moynihan Report" disputed the accuracy of Moynihan's characterization of the enslaved Afro-American. Instead, they debated its relevance to late-twentieth-century urban America. Most shared his view of the "slave family." The few

TABLE 37. MALE-PRESENT BLACK AND WHITE FAMILIES, 1960

	Black families	*White families*
All families	79%	94%
All rural families	86	96
All urban families	77	93
FAMILIES UNDER $3000		
All families	64	78
All rural families	82	88
All urban families	53	62
FAMILIES $3000+		
All families	93	97
All rural families	95	98
All urban families	92	96

who disputed the conventional history of the "black family" did not glorify slavery but instead emphasized the positive adaptive capacities of the slaves and their immediate descendants and the common misperception of them. Ralph Ellison wrote:

. . . [W]ithin the group, we act out, we make certain assertions, we make certain choices, and we have various social structures, which determine to a great extent how we act and what we desire. This is what we live. When we try to articulate it, all we have is sociology. And the sociology is loaded. The concepts which are brought to it are usually based on those of white, middle-class, Protestant values and life style.

Laura Carper made a similar point. Adult women, she said, had played powerful roles in the families of diverse oppressed groups, not just among Afro-Americans. She caricatured family life in the East European Jewish *shtetl* to make her point:

. . . [The] father was frequently absent, either as a peddler on the road, as an immigrant in America, or as a permanent resident of the house of study who came home only to eat. Newly married couples usually moved into the home of the bride's parents. Among the Hassidic Jews (Hassidism was a movement initiated by the poor), it was common for the father to leave his wife and children without a kopek or a groshen in the house and depart for the Rebbe's court where he would dance and drink and spend all his money. As among the American poor, relations between husband and wife were cold and the roles of each clearly defined. The wife worked and assumed the main burden of supporting the family, and the children became adults before they had ever had an opportunity to be children. The man either struggled desperately to make a living with little success or withdrew entirely into a private male society based on discourse or ecstasy and left the family to shift for itself. What the Jewish man succeeded in doing that the Negro man has failed to do is place a positive value on family desertion and personal withdrawal.

Since the Negro man does not rationalize his role as being a desirable religious achievement, it seems to me he would be easier to integrate into the surrounding culture than the Jew. After all, once integration became a viable possibility, even the Shtetl Jew cast off what no longer served him. And the depth and extent to which oppression and poverty reduced the Jew can be measured by the disintegrative effects of the widespread Messianic movements, two of which emphasized orgiastic sexual practices as a means of insuring the coming of the Messiah.

I have chosen to detail the matriarchal organization of the Jewish family life not because it corresponds to the Negro family but because sociologists look upon Jewish family life as remarkably cohesive. Is the caricature I have drawn of the shtetl family accurate? Of course not. I have applied Mr. Moynihan's method of describing the Negro to a description of the Jew. I lumped a few hundred years of history together and failed to distinguish between people. Pathology is in the eye of the beholder. If one eliminates the positive social function of a cultural constellation, if one ignores the meaning personal relations have to the people involved, if one, in short, uses science to depersonalize, what emerges is always pathology. For health involves spontaneous human feelings of affection and tenderness which the Moynihan Report, like my deliberate caricature of Jewish family life, cannot encompass.

People living under oppression always develop social formations which appear to the surrounding oppressive culture to be excessive or pathological. The form these so-called excesses take varies from culture to culture and person to person within the culture—but no matter how extreme the nature of the adjustment, once the social pressure which created it is removed, a new adjustment develops. A people is not destroyed by its history. What destroys a people is physical annihilation or assimilation, not its family life.[3]

Carper's point bears directly on the "slavery-specific hypothesis." Enslavement was harsh and constricted the enslaved. But it did not destroy their capacity to adapt and sustain the vital familial and kin associations and beliefs that served as the underpinning of a developing Afro-American culture. The capacity of the emancipated slaves to adapt to the general emancipation is evidence of their earlier adaptation to enslavement. And the capacity of early-twentieth-century southern black migrants to adapt to the northern city in 1905 and 1925 is evidence of the adaptive capacities of Afro-Americans living in the rural and urban South between 1880 and 1900. Their household arrangements do not mean that such persons were without "problems." A vast and painful record documents the economic and social—as well as the psychological—costs extracted from poor rural and urban blacks in the decades between the general emancipation and the Great Depression. But that record is not evidence that the black family crumbled or that a "pathological" culture thrived.

Nor is there reason to believe that the poor black family crumbled in the near half century that has passed since the onset of the Great Depression. That remains a little-studied subject, but the broad outlines detailing the vast social and economic processes and pressures affecting the black family in that half century seem clear. They first and most importantly involve a modern Enclosure Movement without parallel in the nation's history. Between 1940 and 1970, more than twenty million Americans—including over four million blacks—left the countryside for the cities. The magnitude of this internal migration is revealed in the fact that almost the same number left Europe for the United States in the entire century between 1820 and 1920. In 1940, half of the nation's blacks lived on the land; by 1965 four-fifths of them were urban. Between 1950 and 1965, "new machines and new methods increased farm output in the United States by 45 percent—and reduced farm employment by 45 percent." In 1945, the South had one tractor per farm, and twenty years later two tractors per farm. One study shows that in 1965 mechanical cotton pickers harvested 81 percent of the Mississippi Delta region's cotton crop. Such machines had harvested 27 percent in 1958. In seventeen Arkansas counties typical of the southern cotton economy, the number of cotton-picking machines increased from 482 to 5061 between 1952 and 1963. Black tenant farmers in these counties declined from 21,862 to 6587 between 1952 and 1959. A fine study of Humphrey County, Mississippi, blacks by Tony Dunbar describes something of the meaning of this mid-twentieth-century transformation and displacement:

> Until a few years ago, every family on a plantation was allowed a small patch of land to grow vegetables for their own use. Many tenants also raised hogs, chickens, and possibly a cow. Today only a few of the planters will allow even their full-time laborers to plant one or two rows of vegetables. For the rest a garden or coops or pens for poultry and livestock are impossible, because rows of cotton or soybeans now push up to the tenant's doorstep. In their drive to get the greatest possible yield from their land, the planters may force the tenants to move their toilets right up to their homes, so that every possible foot of land can be seeded and so that the machines can run straight down the rows without having to detour around the tiny, rickety privies. Even where space does permit the growing of a little truck, most tenants are prohibited from doing so because planters fear that weeds from the garden will spread to the cotton and bean fields, which they like to keep meticulously clean by spraying down poisons from the air.

. . . The planter is out to make money, and, viewed in this way, he is coming of age [by mechanizing]. The last years in the Delta have seen tenants go homeless, truck patches on plantations prohibited or restricted, people dying or being permanently disabled because the planter would not send for a doctor, plantation huts being allowed to fall into complete disrepair, women and children by the thousands left with no way to earn money, women forced to do work for which they are physically unsuited in order to save their families from being told to move out, and countless other shameful events. This has happened, I think, not because the planters have decided to starve the black man out of the Delta, as some have said, but rather because the planters no longer care, except as it affects their own operations, what happens to the tenants on their farms; or, in a larger sense, they do not care whether the black man in the Delta starves or not. . . .

There is nothing predictable now about life on the plantation. No man knows if his home is secure, or if he will be given enough work to support his family. He does not know if he will be placed in a hospital if he is hurt on the job. He has no idea what he will do when he becomes too old to work. If he falls into debt to the planter, he does not know if he will be given enough work to get in the clear. He can no longer expect the planter to give him materials with which to repair his house. If he owes the planter or cannot accumulate any savings, he has no way to leave the plantation. If he can contemplate leaving, he, who has never been 100 miles from Louise, must face a move to Chicago, which he has seen on television but does not really believe in. And what will he do in Chicago? The plantation world is all uncertainty, and the tenant farmer is economically and politically unable to make it any less so.

Urban unemployment and underemployment greeted those driven from the land. The cities had too few jobs. A regular differential in the black-white unemployment rate (two-to-one) made adaptation to northern city life very difficult for migrant blacks, a point made by Daniel P. Moynihan but buried in the dispute over an alleged "tangle of pathology." "The fundamental overwhelming fact is that Negro *unemployment*, with the exception of the few years during World War Two and the Korean War," said Moynihan in 1965, "*has continued at disaster levels for thirty-five years.*" (It was no different in the Bicentennial year.) A year later, the Department of Labor published its first "subemployment index," which included people sporadically unemployed and those working at very low wages. The nonwhite subemployment rate was 21.6 percent, three times the white rate. Subemployment rates in nine slum ghetto areas that same year were staggering—they averaged 33 percent.

These were the pressures operating on the mid-twentieth-century lower-class black family. Not surprisingly, the rate of family breakup (measured by male presence) increased between 1950 and 1970. But that "rate" had little if any connection to "a tangle of pathology" rooted in "deep-seated structural distortions in the life of Negro Americans." The behavior of poor southern black migrants to Central Harlem, among others, in 1925 makes that clear. Poor migrant blacks responded to the devastating pressures of rural enclosure and urban unemployment in diverse but still little-studied ways. Some are revealed in Carol B. Stack's *All Our Kin: Strategies for Survival in a Black Community* (1974), a splendid work that shows how extensive networks of black kin and friends devise ways of dealing with severe deprivation. Elastic household boundaries, not small nuclear families, serve such purposes. So do affective quasi-kin relationships. Whites responded differently. As Frances Fox Piven and Richard A. Cloward have shown in *Regulating the Poor: The Functions of Public Welfare* (1971), the social crisis that accompanied the transformation of rural black unemployment into urban black unemployment was met by a loosening up of "welfare" regulations to contain the severe discontent accompanying that transformation. A new "Poor Law" matched the new Enclosure Movement.[4]

Intense suffering resulted from the interaction between the late-twentieth-century Enclosure Movement and Poor Law, but it has become fashionable, once again, to "blame the victim." Herbert H. Hyman and John Shelton Reed, however, show that little evidence exists "for any socio-psychological pattern of matriarchy peculiarly characteristic of the Negro family on the basis of which social theorizing or social policy could be formulated." And his interviews with black mothers and their children on welfare convince Leonard Goodwin that they want work, not "welfare." "Getting a job" is far more important to these women than to middle-class white women. "Welfare youths from father-less homes," Goodwin's study discloses, "show a strong work ethic, a willingness to take training and an interest in working even if it is not a financial necessity." "Their mothers," Goodwin adds, "favorably influence these positive orientations." But neither the economy nor those who dominate the political decision-making process have as a priority the creation of useful work for those driven in such great numbers from the land. Much has changed in the nation's history in the century following the general emancipation, but wealth and commonwealth still remain polar opposites.[5]

We end with those with whom we began, not the descendants of Afro-American slaves who migrated in the mid-twentieth century to northern urban ghettos but with their great-grandparents, men and women like Mary and Smart Washington and Sarah and Jim and their infant son Ben at the time of the emancipation.

The Yankee schoolteacher Mary Ames, who spent less than a year among the Edisto Island, South Carolina, blacks, came to know the former Richmond and Charleston house servant Sarah and her family well. She kept a brief diary. An early entry, dated mid-May 1865, read:

> Jim and Sarah, with six children, are living in the back part of this house. . . . Sarah is a fine-looking woman, quiet and sensible. She has always been a house-servant, was born and reared in Richmond, and was sold with three children to Dr. Leavitt of Charleston, leaving the father of her children in Richmond. Since that, she has had six children, having had five husbands, or men with whom she was obliged to live, as she was sold from one master to another. Jim was the last one. At the beginning of the war, Sarah and her children were sent with her mistress to Sumterville. When Sherman and his army came along, Sarah was told by her mistress that if she followed the army she must take all her children, not thinking she would go. When the mistress found Jim and Sarah were actually going, she asked one of the Union officers to make Sarah stay behind. He told her he had no power to do that; that the woman was free and could act her own pleasure. Sarah had a mind to stay on, as her mistress had always treated her kindly, but Jim insisted on joining Sherman's train. Just before they left, one Saturday, Campbell, who had been one of Sarah's five husbands, and was the father of her child Anne, came and claimed Sarah. Jim fought and conquered him, thus winning Sarah and her children. They walked nearly a hundred miles, Sarah carrying Margery, a two-year-old child in her arms. She kept the other children in front of her, for many lost their children.

A month later, after the two women knew each other more intimately, Ames made new notations:

> [Sarah] had often seen her children abused—punished severely
> for small faults. She had prayed and prayed that one child—
> her oldest—might die. The girl was not very strong, and had
> the care of a fretful baby, when little more than a baby her-
> self. At last, God heard her prayer, and her child died. No one
> could tell how thankful she was. . . .

Sarah and Jim had a son named for his/father, and the teacher grew
attached to him: "He sleeps on the floor beside my bed. One
night, as he hung over my chair, he was uneasy, and I asked what
troubled him. He whispered, 'Is the reason you don't kiss me
'cause I'm black?' I took him in my lap and held him till he slept."
About that time, Sarah gave birth to a daughter and planned to
name the child *Mary* Emily. But she and her husband became
ill. A neighbor cared for the newborn infant. Jim and Sarah died
in September 1865. "She asked me," Ames said of her last visit
with Sarah, "to take her seven children north to my 'plantation.' "
Neighbors took some of the orphan children; others went to a
Charleston orphan asylum, an institution started and sustained
by Charleston blacks in 1865. Mary Ames's sister came from Springfield, Massachusetts, to take two of Jim and Sarah's daughters
back with her. Two sons ended up laboring in the South Carolina
coastal phosphate mines. "Poor little Ben," Mary Ames later wrote,
"the most affectionate of them all, refused to eat, and died of
home-sickness the next winter."[6]

Less than a month after Sarah died, O. O. Howard, the head
of the Freedmen's Bureau, visited Edisto Island to advise the
ex-slaves that the president, Andrew Johnson, had restored Sea
Island plantation properties to their old owners. "At first," Mary
Ames noticed, "the people could not understand. But they quickly
appointed a committee of three whose members delivered a petition addressed to Johnson."

Dear President Johnson of the United States

> Wee the freedmen of South Carolina . . . prey that god
> may guive you helth & good spirets that when you receive
> theas few notasis that you may receive them as the father did
> the prodical son wee have for the last four years ben studing
> with justis and the best of our ability what step wee should
> take to become a peple. . . .
> after his [Howard's] adres a grate many of the people
> understanding what was said they got aroused & awoke to
> perfect sense to stody for them Selves what part of this law

would rest against us, we said in rafarence to what he said that nothing did apier at that time to bee very opressing upon us but the one thing that is wee freedmen should work for wages for our former oners or eny other man president Johnson of u st I do say man that have stud upon the feal of battle & have shot their master & sons now Going to ask ether one for bread or for shelter or Comfortable for his wife & children sunch a thing the u st should not aught to Expect a man. . . .

The committee explained its needs:

Here is Plenty Whidow & Fatherles that have serve you as slave now losen a home . . . give Each one of them a acres & a 1/2 to a family as you has the labers & the Profet of there Yearly Youth. . . .

It asked "the wise presidon that sets on his seat" to give them "a Chance to Recover out of this trubble."[7]

That was not the first such appeal to an American president by South Carolina ex-slaves. In 1864, Uncle Smart Washington, who had grown up on a St. Helena's Island rice plantation but described himself as a "cooper by trade" and wanted to purchase between ten and twenty acres of land, asked the Yankee teacher Laura M. Towne to intervene with Abraham Lincoln in his behalf. "I been a elder in de church and speretual fader to hep a gals no older [than] oona [you]," a letter to her began. "I know dat womans has feelin' hearts, and dat de men will heard de voice of a gal when dey to hard head for mind dose dat has more wisdom. . . . Do my missus, tell Linkum, dat we wants land—dis bery land dat is rich wid de sweat ob we face and de blood ob we back." Northern speculators among the Sea Island blacks angered Washington:

We born here; we parents' graves here; we donne oder country; dis yere our home. De Nort folks hab home, antee? What a pity dat dey don't love der home like we love we home, for den dey would neber come here to buy all way from we.

"[A]x Linkum for send us *his* word," Washington went on, "and den we satisfy." Sea Island blacks then fought with the Union Army.

Dey wants land *here*, for dere wives to work. Look at de fields! No more but womens and chillens. All de men gone to fight, and while dey gone de land sold from dere families to rich white buckra to scrape, and neber live on.

"Talk him with me," he ended, "and de Lord will keep you warm
under he feathers, he will gather oona [you] to his breast, for he
love dem what help de poor."

It is not known whether or not Washington ever purchased
any land, but he and his wife Mary used their house as "a haven
of rest for all of 'massa's niggers' who need such." They sheltered
persons cut off from kin, including the elderly Old Maria. "She
had 'no family,' " Elizabeth Botume remembered, "which means
a great deal to colored people." Another time, Washington found
his brother ("a poor half-witted fellow") and "brought him 'home
to die.' " In 1868, Washington's "shanty" burned to the ground.
The help he and his wife gave to Old Maria during the fire caused
them to lose everything. The schoolteacher Botume then arranged
with the ladies in "Dr. Clarke's [Boston] church" to make a purse
for him and use this money to build a new cottage. Washington
dictated a letter of thanks to the Boston women. "All the time I
was writing," Botume noticed, "the tears were streaming down his
face":

> My Dear and Honored Friends: According to my distrust
> (distress) and what you have done for me I can say no more
> than "God Almighty forever bless you" for the good kindness
> and what you have all done for me. I aint able to speak; what
> I can do you I lef' it in God's hands (all I can do for you is to
> leave you in God's hands). I was in great *distrust* and I never
> expected to stand on my feet again, but you all put out hands
> and helped me up. . . . My old woman sends precisely a
> thousand and a thousand thanks according as you have lifted
> us out of our *distrust*.
>   Although I had a good house I was burned out, and now
> my house exceeds all the others, by the kindness of my friends
> —o my God!

His new house was twenty-two feet by fifteen feet, a story and a
half high, with two "piazzas" and three rooms. "It is a likely
house, I can tell you," he boasted. "It is the best house on the
island. It has six windows with window-glass, six pair of them."
Washington wanted to send "something . . . to show I ain't forgot
nothing and that the rejoice will never leave my heart. . . ." He
promised to pray for their children and then went on:

> I thank you kindly for the suit of clothes; they fit me well; it
> is my own suit, they fit so. A hundred dollars could not have
> been so much to me. "For I was naked and ye clothed me."
> I think these friends are all working in the laws of God. I

know there be some good Christians in this world, that saves this world. I think for their sakes the kingdom of Heaven will come on Earth. I aint able to say nothing, but I lef' it all in God's hands.

> Your truly friend,
> SMART WASHINGTON

When Elizabeth Botume first met them, Smart and Mary Washington had lived together as husband and wife for more than forty years. One or both may have been born in the eighteenth century. Both were the children of eighteenth-century African or Afro-American slaves. They were among the first St. Helena's Island blacks to accept legal marriage by the northern missionaries. "Him's my wife for sartin, now," Smart Washington explained after the ceremony. "Ef the old hen run away, I shall cotch him sure." ("We thought," Botume confided in her memoir, "there was no danger of good Aunt Mary's running away after so many years of faithful service.") Soon after their house had been rebuilt, Mary Washington died. "I am lonesome to death," her widowed husband told Botume. "Now the old woman is a great missing everywhere; the very dumb animals is all broke up and mourn for him so; an' w'en I hear the creeturs cry, it cuts like a sword through my heart." He married again but without satisfaction and sent his new wife back to her former home. Years before when she had first met and hardly knew Smart Washington, Botume asked if, when a slave, he had been married "more than once." She remembered his brief response: "He hesitated, then said gravely, 'No ma'am, only 'tween we and God.' "[8]

Elizabeth Botume was among those few nonslaves who grasped the essential meaning of the adaptive behavior revealed by ordinary ex-slaves like Sarah, Jim, and Ben and Smart and Mary Washington in their adjustment to legal freedom. It was not that Afro-Americans had been left unscarred by enslavement. Or that they were especially "heroic" and "moral." It was rather that concepts like "right" and "wrong" and familial, kin, and social obligation did not depend for their existence upon "high culture." Harriet Beecher Stowe also learned this lesson. After the Civil War, she visited an east Florida plantation managed by two young Yankee enterprisers. Seven hundred slaves had worked it, but she found only about thirty Georgia, North and South Carolina, and Louisiana black families laboring there, "a fair specimen of the Southern negro as slavery has made and left them." Stowe learned "that, though living all . . . in families, these parties were, many of

them, not legally married." Legal marriages "were few among
them." Nevertheless "they lived faithfully in their respective
family relations." Thomas Wentworth Higginson learned even
more than Stowe. "They seem the world's perpetual children,
docile & gay & lovable," Higginson noted of the Sea Island blacks
in his private journal in December 1862. "I think it partly from
my own notorious love of children that I like these people so
well." More intimate contact with the South Carolina blacks
altered his views. "In reading Kay's 'Condition of the English
Peasantry,' " Higginson wrote in *Army Life in a Black Regiment*,
"I was constantly struck with the unlikeness of my men to those
therein described. I learned to think that we abolitionists had
underrated the suffering produced by slavery among the negroes,
but had overrated the demoralization."[9]

The New Orleans *Tribune*—not the New York *Tribune*—
put it even better than Higginson. "Philanthropists," the black
newspaper worried, "are sometimes a strange class of people; they
love their fellowmen, but . . . these . . . to be worthy of their
assistance, must be of an inferior kind. We were and still are
oppressed, but we are not demoralized criminals." Frederick
Douglass made a similar point: "To *understand* . . . a man must
stand under."[10]

More than a full century separates us from the time when
Thomas Wentworth Higginson, the editors of the New Orleans
Tribune, and Frederick Douglass penned these words. But their
import retains a contemporary meaning, a meaning celebrated
by the poets Dudley Randall and Gwendolyn Brooks and the
novelist Ralph Ellison. "Prefabricated Negroes," says Ellison of
much mid-twentieth-century "social science," "are sketched on
sheets of paper and superimposed upon the Negro community;
then when someone thrusts his head through the pages and yells,
'Watch out there, Jack, there's people living under here,' they are
all shocked and indignant."

Randall writes of the distant past, and Brooks of the present.
In a poem entitled "Ancestors," Randall said:

> Why are our ancestors
> always kings and princes
> And never the common people?
>
> Was the Old Country a democracy
> where every man was a king?

Or did the slave-catchers
steal only aristocrats
and leave the field hands
laborers
street cleaners
garbage collectors
dish washers
cooks
and maids behind?

My own ancestor
(research reveals)
was a swineherd
who tended the pigs
in the Royal Pigstye
and slept in the mud
among the hogs.

Yet I'm as proud of him
as of any king or prince
dreamed up in fantasies
of bygone glory.

Gwendolyn Brooks entitled her poem "What Shall I Give My Children?":

What shall I give my children? who are poor,
Who are adjudged the leastwise of the land,
Who are my sweetest lepers, who demand
No velvet and no velvety velour;
But who have begged me for a brisk contour,
Crying that they are quasi, contraband
Because unfinished, graven by a hand
Less than angelic, admirable or sure.
My hand is stuffed with mode, design, device.
But I lack access to my proper stone.
And plenitude of plan shall not suffice
Nor grief nor love shall be enough alone
To ratify my little halfs who bear
Across an autumn freezing everywhere.[11]

APPENDIX A

Tables for Chapter 10

TABLE A-1. AFRO-AMERICAN POPULATIONS STUDIED, 1880–1925

Urban Population		*Rural Population*	
		1880	
Beaufort, South Carolina	1949	St. Helena's Township, South Carolina	2156
Natchez, Mississippi	3293	St. Helena's Island, South Carolina	4267
Mobile, Alabama	13,827	Rural Adams County, Mississippi	14,554
Richmond, Virginia	19,878	Mount Album, Warren County, Mississippi	2462
		Lane's Schoolhouse, Warren County, Mississippi	1839
		1900	
Jackson Ward, Enumeration District Two, Richmond, Virginia	3436	St. Helena's Districts Nine and Ten, South Carolina	4565
		Issaquena Beats 1, 2, and 3, Mississippi	4114
		1905	
New York City, Tenderloin and San Juan Districts	14,368		
		1925	
New York City, San Juan Hill District and Central Harlem	57,853		

TABLE A-2. RURAL MALE BLACK OCCUPATIONAL STRUCTURE, ALL MALES TWENTY AND OLDER, 1880

St. Helena's Island and Township, South Carolina

OCCUPATION	
Owns land*	49%
Cash tenant	15
Farm laborer	31
Other†	5
TOTAL	1425

Rural Adams County, Mississippi

OCCUPATION	
Farmer	
Owns land‡	6%
Cash tenant or share-cropper	54
Farm laborer	16
Laborer (stated occupation)	22
Artisan§	1
Other**	1
TOTAL	2976

Lane's Schoolhouse, Warren County, Mississippi

OCCUPATION	
Farmer	
Owns land	3%
Sharecropper or cash tenant	14
Farm laborer	18
Laborer	25
Laborer (stated occupation)	28
Artisan††	9
Other‡‡	3
TOTAL	423

* Thirty-two percent owned fewer than ten acres, and another 46 percent between ten and fourteen acres. About 19 percent owned between fifteen and twenty-nine acres. Two percent owned between thirty and thirty-nine acres. Less than one percent owned forty or more acres.

† Carpenter (15), tailor (2), cooper and wheelwright (one each), store clerk (3), grocer, teacher, and clergyman (two each), ferry man, postmaster, customhouse officer, general service, storekeeper, mailman, agent, and student (one each).

‡ This percentage may include some whites who owned land.

§ Carpenter (15), blacksmith (14), brickmason (6), ginwright (2), baker, butcher, harness repair, engineer, sheep shearer, mechanic (one each).

** Clergyman (11), teacher (9), storekeeper, doctor, labor agent, sheriff, constable, coroner (one each).

†† Carpenter (17), blacksmith (4), barber (3), shoemaker, butcher, engineer, (two each), painter, tailor, brickmason, fireman, gunsmith, wheelwright, musician, mechanic (one each).

‡‡ Huckster (4), wood dealer (3), teacher (2), milk dealer, ice-cream dealer, barkeeper, sawmill foreman, justice of the peace (one each).

TABLE A-3. OCCUPATIONAL STATUS OF ADULT BLACK MALES, TWENTY AND OLDER, BEAUFORT (S.C.), NATCHEZ (MISS.), MOBILE (ALA.), AND RICHMOND (VA.), 1880

Occupational status	Beaufort	Natchez	Mobile	Richmond
Laborer	60%	73%	82%	80%
Artisan	27	18	14	15
Other	13	9	4	5
TOTAL	393	690	3032	6056

Major occupations

Beaufort

Laborer (234): Phosphate miner (73), laborer (71), servant, cook, waiter (20), drayman, teamster, coachman (10), sawmill (10), sailor (8), fisherman (6)

Artisan (108): Carpenter (46), brickmason (14), butcher, shoemaker, barber (6 each), tailor, printer, painter (5 each)

Other (51): Farmer (18), clergyman (6), lawyer (4), livery stable (4), public-office holder (13)

Natchez

Laborer (503): Laborer (231), drayman, teamster, coachman (60), servant, cook, waiter (40), porter (25), farm laborer (24), gardener (24), oil mill (22), wood, coal, brick yards (20)

Artisan (125): Carpenter (33), blacksmith, baker (13 each), butcher (10), barber, shoemaker (9 each), bricklayer (8), wood sawyer (7), stationary engineer (5)

Other (62): Farmer (20), clergyman (15), public-office holder (6), teacher (6), barkeeper (5)

Mobile

Laborer (2489): Laborer (1113), drayman, teamster, coachman (264), servant, cook, waiter (240), steamboat hand (190), porter (90), railroad worker (88), cotton pressman (76), gardener (75), sawmill (61), farm laborer (53), shinglemaker (37), turpentine laborer (31)

Artisan (428): Carpenter (135), barber (43), cigarmaker (24), brickmason (23), shoemaker (20), blacksmith (18), baker, wood sawyer (16 each), bricklayer, plasterer, painter (15 each)

Other (115): Huckster, dealer (30), clergyman (15), public-office holder (11), clerk (10), restaurant (10), grocer (7), teacher (6), miller (4), doctor (3)

Richmond

Laborer (4480):   Laborer (1847), tobacco-factory worker (1078), servant, cook, waiter (602), drayman, teamster, coachman (572), porter (198), factory hand (123), iron mill worker (83), dock worker (48), whitewasher (46), railroad worker (40), brickyard (34), boatman (25)

Artisan (928):   Shoemaker (146), carpenter (121), blacksmith (119), barber (108), cooper (89), plasterer (73), bricklayer (49), wood sawyer (46)

Other (295):   Huckster and dealer (120), grocer (45), restaurant (18), public-office holder (17), barkeeper (16), clergyman (15), clerk (10), storekeeper (9), miller (8), teacher (6), undertaker (4), doctor (3)

TABLE A-4.   SOUTHERN BLACK AND WHITE URBAN ARTISANS, TWENTY AND OLDER, 1880

Selected urban crafts with relatively few or no blacks

Mobile			Richmond		
CRAFT	BLACK	WHITE	CRAFT	BLACK	WHITE
Baker	16	42	Stonecutter-mason	15	150
Painter	15	83	Butcher	15	51
Butcher	11	32	Baker	14	70
Tailor	4	34	Painter	8	147
Printer	1	60	Upholsterer-cabinetmaker	8	68
Machinist	0	53	Printer	4	169
			Tailor	3	145
			Cigarmaker	1	139
			Molder	0	108
			Machinist	0	259

Urban crafts with significant numbers of blacks

Natchez

CRAFT	BLACK	WHITE
Carpenter	33	30
Blacksmith	13	5
Baker	13	8
Butcher	10	20
Barber	9	3
Shoemaker	9	9
Bricklayer	8	0
Engineer	5	0

Mobile

CRAFT	BLACK	WHITE
Carpenter	135	228
Barber	43	15
Cigarmaker	24	14
Brickmason	23	26
Shoemaker	20	34
Blacksmith	18	44
Wood sawyer	16	0
Bricklayer	15	0
Plasterer	15	3
Tinsmith	13	20
Cooper	13	13

Richmond

CRAFT	BLACK	WHITE
Shoemaker	146	159
Carpenter	121	488
Blacksmith	119	113
Barber	108	7
Cooper	89	35
Plasterer	73	13
Wood sawyer	46	4

TABLE A-5.   AGE DISTRIBUTION OF BLACK AND WHITE URBAN ARTISANS AND CARPENTERS, 1880

White and Black Artisans Under Thirty, Including Apprentices Aged Fifteen to Nineteen, as a Percentage of All White and Black Artisans, Natchez, Mobile, and Richmond, 1880

	Natchez	Mobile	Richmond
White	38%	41%	46%
Black	28	23	30

Black and White Carpenters by Age, Mobile and Richmond, 1880

City	Total	Under 30	30–39	40–49	50+	Percent under 30	Percent 50+
MOBILE							
White	245	65	45	67	68	27%	24%
Black	139	18	23	40	58	13	42
RICHMOND							
White	501	124	113	124	140	25%	28%
Black	121	10	23	46	42	9	35

TABLE A-6.   OCCUPATIONS OF URBAN BLACK WOMEN, FIFTEEN AND OLDER, 1880

City	Women with listed occupations as percentage of all women fifteen and older	Number with occupations	Servant	Washerwoman	Seamstress	Other
Beaufort	47%	332	31%	29%	10%	30%
Natchez	43	571	60	26	4	10
Mobile Wards 1, 7, 8	46	1574	51	40	5	4
Richmond	53	5581	66	24	2	8

Table A-7. Marital and Household Status of All Black Female House Servants (Including Girls Under Fifteen) and All Black Washerwomen, Fifteen and Older, 1880

Servants

City	Number	HOUSEHOLD STATUS			
		Married, no children	*Married with children*	*Male-absent household with children*	*Single*
Beaufort	117	3%	10%	19%	68%
Natchez	371	4	6	19	71
Mobile	884	10	7	13	70
Richmond	3925	7	5	11	77

Washerwomen

City	Number	*Married, no children*	*Married with children*	*Male-absent household with children*	*Single*
Beaufort	95	7%	28%	35%	30%
Natchez	157	13	26	26	35
Mobile	626	17	25	31	27
Richmond	1303	8	29	28	35

Household Status of Servants and Washerwomen in Absolute Numbers, 1880

City	MARRIED WITH CHILDREN		MARRIED WITHOUT CHILDREN		MALE-ABSENT WITH CHILDREN	
	Servant	*Washerwoman*	*Servant*	*Washerwoman*	*Servant*	*Washerwoman*
Beaufort	12	26	4	7	22	33
Natchez	23	39	16	20	70	43
Mobile	62	158	88	106	118	195
Richmond	187	380	275	104	431	365

TABLE A-8. HOUSEHOLD STATUS OF INDIVIDUAL BLACKS, AND TYPES OF BLACK HOUSEHOLDS, 1880

	In kin-related household	Lives alone	Other	Number of black households two or more persons	Percent including husband and wife or parent-child
Rural					
St. Helena's Island and Township	98%	1%	1%	1332	98%
Rural Adams County	95	3	2	2931	97
Mount Album	97	2	1	522	97
Lane's Schoolhouse	96	1	3	433	95
Urban					
Beaufort	93%	4%	3%	461	91%‡
Natchez	90	2	8*	686	96
Mobile	88	3	9*	2791	97
Richmond	81	1	18†	4612	96
Mobile Ward 7	94	2	4		
Richmond, Jackson and Marshall Wards	95	1	4		

* Five percent were single persons living in white households.
† Eleven percent were single persons living in white households and another 6 percent lived in families but in a white household.
‡ Five percent were kin-related households but did not include a husband-wife or parent-child.

TABLE A-9. SIZE OF RURAL AND URBAN BLACK HOUSEHOLDS WITH TWO OR MORE RESIDENTS, 1880

	Number of people in household				Households with lodgers	
	2–4	5–7	8–10	11+	ONE LODGER	TWO LODGERS
Rural						
St. Helena's Island and Township	53%	34%	12%	1%	80%	13%
Rural Adams County	55	34	10	1	82	14
Mount Album	59	34	6	1	85	10
Lane's Schoolhouse	63	30	6	1	78	20
Urban						
Beaufort	63%	31%	5%	1%	84%	13%
Natchez	60	31	8	1	80	13
Mobile	63	30	6	1	75	20
Richmond	58	32	9	1	65	23
Paterson, New Jersey, white households (Enumeration Districts 164–167)	53	33	11	3		

TABLE A-10. COMPOSITION OF BLACK HOUSEHOLDS AND SUBFAMILIES, 1880

	Black households	Subfamilies in black-white households	Types of households*			Husband- or father-present households and subfamilies	Father-present households and subfamilies
			NUCLEAR	EXTENDED	AUGMENTED		
Rural							
St. Helena's Island and Township	1310	85	83%	15%	2%	87%	83%
Rural Adams County	2831	237	72	18	12	81	76
Mount Album	504	26	84	13	5	86	83
Lane's Schoolhouse	411	38	68	23	14	82	76
Lowndes County	805	29	68	16	19	85	81
Urban							
Beaufort	419	43	71%	22%	11%	70%	64%
Natchez	661	103	58	27	23	69	60
Mobile	2791	429	70	18	14	74	66
Richmond	4612	1059	65	15	23	74	66

* Some households included lodgers and kin. These households are counted as both extended and augmented households. The totals therefore add up to more than 100 percent.

TABLE A-11. OCCUPATIONS OF BLACK FATHERS HEADING HOUSEHOLDS AND SUBFAMILIES WITH CHILDREN COMPARED WITH OCCUPATIONS OF ALL ADULT MALES AGED TWENTY AND OLDER, 1880

	Number of adult males	Number of fathers	*Laborer*		*Artisan*		*Other*	
			ALL MALES	FATHERS	ALL MALES	FATHERS	ALL MALES	FATHERS
Beaufort	393	216	60%	61%	27%	23%	13%	16%
Natchez	690	304	73	72	18	16	9	12
Mobile Wards 7 and 8	3032	869	82	82	14	15	4	3
Richmond	6005	2677	80	78	15	17	5	5
Lane's Schoolhouse	441	239	88*	87*	9	10	3	3

* Includes farmers and farm laborers.

TABLE A-12. FEMALE-HEADED HOUSEHOLDS AND SUBFAMILIES, AND ADULT SEX RATIOS, 1880 (FEMALE = 100)

Place	Percent of females heading households and subfamilies	Percent of households and subfamilies headed by females	Adult sex ratios Female = 100			
			20–29	30–44	45+	ALL 20+
Rural						
St. Helena's Island–Township	10%	13%	82	84	106	91
Mount Album	10	14	78	85	114	94
Lane's Schoolhouse	14	18	65	77	98	86
Rural Adams County	15 est.	19	72	75	107	85
Urban						
Mobile	16%	26%	59	64	88	73
Richmond	14	26	55	64	87	70
Beaufort	20	30	56	70	67	69
Natchez	18	31	58	60	65	61

TABLE A-13. BLACK MALE-ABSENT HOUSEHOLDS AND SUBFAMILIES, 1880

	Headed by women 40 and older	Percent of women heading households in age groups			Male-absent households with only one child under 18*	Single women heading households and subfamilies		Single household and subfamily heads as a percentage of all household and subfamily heads
		15–19	20–29	15+		NUMBER	NUMBER UNDER 30	
Rural								
St. Helena's Island and Township	51%	4%	8%	10%	40%	30	29	2%
Rural Adams County	42	4	16	15	n.a.	165	112	6
Mount Album	37	5	9	10	36	20	13	4
Lane's Schoolhouse	44	8	12	14	44	12	11	3
Urban								
Beaufort	39%	5%	17%	20%	53%	57	31	12%
Natchez	47	5	15	18	55	65	34	8
Mobile	45	3	13	16	51	97	85	3
Richmond	51	1	9	14	49	124	88	2

* This is a percentage of all male-absent households and subfamilies with children under eighteen.

TABLE A-14. MARITAL STATUS OF BLACK WOMEN HEADING MALE-ABSENT HOUSEHOLDS AND SUBFAMILIES, 1880

		Male-absent households and subfamilies				Single female heads as percentage of all females in age-specific groups		
	NUMBER	SINGLE	MARRIED	WIDOW	OTHER OR UNCLEAR	20–29	30–39	40+
Rural								
St. Helena's Island and Township	189	16%	5%	67%	12%*	3%	0%	0%†
Rural Adams County	579	32	12	47	9	8	4	2
Mount Album	77	25	12	63	0	5	4	0†
Lane's Schoolhouse	81	15	1	80	4	4	0†	0
Urban								
Beaufort	137	41%	23%	34%	2%	11%	14%	2%
Natchez	237	27	9	61	3	7	6	3
Mobile	830	11	12	72	5	4	1	3
Richmond	1510	8	23	66	3	2	1	1

* Of these twenty-two women, nineteen said they were divorced. Few black women elsewhere described themselves as divorced.
† One woman each.

TABLE A-15.   AGE OF BLACK WOMEN UNDER THIRTY AT BIRTH
OF FIRST CHILD LIVING WITH THEM, 1880

Age at birth of first child living in household or subfamily

	UNDER 15	15–19	20–24	25–29
Place				
St. Helena's Island and Township	9%	51%	37%	3%
Lane's Schoolhouse	13	54	30	3
Beaufort	11	50	33	6
Natchez	11	55	29	5
Mobile Wards 7 & 8	11	54	32	3
Richmond, Jackson and Marshall Wards	7	40	43	10

	MEAN AGE	MEDIAN AGE
St. Helena's Island and Township	18.6	19.4
Lane's Schoolhouse	18.0	19.3
Beaufort	18.9	19.2
Natchez	18.5	18.9
Mobile Wards 7 & 8	18.2	18.9
Richmond, Jackson, and Marshall Wards	19.7	20.2

Paterson, New Jersey

Irish	21.5	21.9
German	21.4	21.9
British	21.3	21.6
Native white	19.8	20.4

TABLE A-16. HOUSEHOLD STATUS OF BLACK WOMEN AGED FIFTEEN TO NINETEEN, 1880

| | | Single | | | | | | |
| | | | | Boards with nonrelatives | | | Married, with or without | Heads male-absent household or |
Place	Number	Lives with parent(s)	Boards with relatives	BLACK	WHITE	Lives alone	children	subfamily
Mount Album	83	64%	7%	5%	1%	0%	19%	4%
St. Helena's Island and Township	266	72	7	1	0	0	16	4
Natchez	160	60	8	10	10	1	6	5
Mobile	674	56	8	8	12	2	11	3
Richmond	1534	56	4	8	26	1	4	1

TABLE A-17. HOUSEHOLD STATUS OF BLACK WOMEN AGED TWENTY TO TWENTY-NINE, 1880

Place	Number	Married and no children	Married with children	Lives with parent(s)	Heads male-absent household	Other*	Unclear†
Mount Album	193	14%	61%	9%	9%	7%	0%
St. Helena's Island and Township	566	13	60	16	8	3	0
Rural Adams County	1253	12	59	5	16	8	0
Lane's Schoolhouse	187	16	54	7	12	11	0
Beaufort	246	16	37	8	18	20	1
Natchez	368	10	32	16	15	23	4
Mobile	1601	17	33	16	13	19	2
Richmond	3501	13	25	16	9	34	3

* "Other" includes women living alone, boarding with relatives and nonrelatives, and living in white households.
† None of these women were married and had children or headed male-absent households or subfamilies.

TABLE A-18. HOUSEHOLD STATUS OF BLACK WOMEN AGED FIFTY AND OLDER, 1880

Place	Number	Lives with spouse or spouse and children	Lives with married children	Heads household	Other*
St. Helena's Island and Township	374	60%	6%	19%	15%
Rural Adams County	874	50	14	16	20
Mount Album	150	52	8	12	28
Lane's Schoolhouse	121	42	15	16	27
Beaufort	135	31	11	34	24
Natchez	340	33	10	21	36
Mobile	932	31	12	24	33
Richmond	1642	31	9	26	34

THREE-GENERATION HOUSEHOLDS, 1880, HEADED BY BLACK WOMEN AGED FIFTY AND OLDER

Place	Number of households		Percent of all women 50 and older	Percent of all kin-related households
	Grandmother-mother-grandchildren	Grandmother-grandchildren		
St. Helena's Island and Township	11	17	7%	2%
Rural Adams County	31	18	6	2
Mount Album	3	4	5	1
Lane's Schoolhouse	4	3	5	2
Beaufort	5	16	16	5
Natchez	20	9	8	4
Mobile	38	23	7	2
Richmond	68	32	6	2

* Includes women living alone, boarding in black households, living in white households, and living in irregular households.

TABLE A-19.   COMPARISON OF HOUSEHOLD COMPOSITION OF
RURAL BLACKS AND WHITES, 1880

	St. Helena's Island and Township blacks	Rural Adams County blacks	Jones County whites
Total kin-related households and families	1395	3068	662
Nuclear households	83%	72%	70%
Extended households	15	18	19
Augmented households	2	12	13
Ratio of subfamilies to households	1/15	1/12	1/11
Households with just a husband & wife	19%	21%	10%
Percentage of all women 20–29 heading households and subfamilies	8	16	4
Percentage of all women 20+ heading households and subfamilies	11	16	14
Husband- or father-present households and subfamilies	87	81	83
Father-present households and subfamilies with children	83	76	81

Sex ratio: female = 100

20–29	82	73	95
20–44	84	75	85
45+	106	107	98
20+	91	85	88

TABLE A-20.   OCCUPATIONAL STRUCTURE OF PATERSON, N.J.,
IRISH AND NATIVE WHITE MALES AND RICHMOND
AND MOBILE BLACK MALES, 1880

Occupational status	Paterson native whites	Paterson Irish	Richmond blacks	Mobile blacks
Laborer	21%	44%	80%	82%
Artisan	62	45	15	14
Other	17	11	5	4
NUMBER	264	876	6056	3032

TABLE A-21. COMPARISON OF RICHMOND AND MOBILE BLACK
HOUSEHOLD COMPOSITION WITH PATERSON, N.J.,
NATIVE WHITE AND IMMIGRANT HOUSEHOLD
COMPOSITION, 1880

	Paterson		Richmond blacks	Mobile blacks
	NATIVE WHITES	IRISH		
Total kin-related household and subfamilies	1040	2300	5671	3720
Nuclear households	66%	73%	65%	70%
Extended households	19	15	16	19
Augmented households	19	15	23	14
Ratio of subfamilies to households	1/6.7	1/13.6	1/4.4	1/6.5
Households containing just husband and wife	14%	12%	21%	25%
Husband- or father-present households and subfamilies	79	81	73	74
Father-present households and subfamilies with children	75	78	66	66
Percentage of all women 20–29 heading households and subfamilies	6	4	9	13
Percentage of all women 20+ heading households and subfamilies	13	13	17	18
Percentage of all women 50 and older heading three-generation households	4	4	6	7
Women 50 and older heading three-generation households as a percentage of all households	2	1	2	2

Sex ratio: female = 100

20–29	90	75	55	58
20–44	88	80	64	64
45+	79	86	87	88
20+	89	82	70	73

TABLE A-22.   OCCUPATIONS OF ADULT MALES, TWENTY AND OLDER, 1900

St. Helena's, South Carolina

OCCUPATION	
Own land	70%
Rent land	13
Unskilled	14
Skilled	2*
Other	1†
NUMBER	1239

Issaquena, Mississippi

OCCUPATION	
Rent land	81%
Own land	3
Unskilled	15
Skilled	1‡
Other	0§
NUMBER	1781

Jackson Ward, Richmond, 1900

OCCUPATION	
Unskilled and Service	77%
Skilled	16**
White-collar	1††
Enterprise	5‡‡
Professional	1§§
NUMBER	809

* Carpenter (15), fireman (2), butcher, blacksmith, miner, painter, wheelwright, shoemaker (one each).
† Teacher (3), clergy (2), "captain" (2), store clerk (2), postal employee (2), salesman (1), constable (1).
‡ Carpenter (7), blacksmith, fireman, machinist, bricklayer (one each).
§ Clergyman, planter, mail carrier, student (one each).
** Plasterer (33), barber (17), carpenter (17), blacksmith (9), stonemason (9), butcher (8), bricklayer (7), sawyer (7), shoemaker (5), lather (3), cooper (3), painter (3), miscellaneous (17).
†† Clerk (7), mailman (2), book agent, insurance agent (one each).
‡‡ Grocer (9), fish dealer (7), storekeeper (6), junk dealer (3), barkeeper (3), huckster (4), undertaker (3), stove dealer, tobacconist, livery stable, farmer (one each).
§§ Clergyman (2), lawyer, teacher, student (one each).

TABLE A-23. HOUSEHOLD STATUS OF INDIVIDUAL BLACKS, AND TYPES OF BLACK HOUSEHOLDS, 1900

	In kin-related household	Lives alone	Other	Number of black households two or more persons	Percent including husband and wife or parent-child
St. Helena's	96%	1%	3%	1016	96%
Issaquena	93	4	3	1004	93
Jackson Ward	97	1	2	607	97

Number of Persons in Household

	1	2–4	5–7	8–10	11+
St. Helena's	1%	30%	42%	21%	6%
Issaquena	4	41	35	16	4
Jackson Ward	1	22	41	27	9

Table A-24. Composition of Black Households and Subfamilies, 1900

	Number of black households	Number of subfamilies in black-white households*	Types of Households			Husband- or father-present households and subfamilies	Father-present household and subfamilies with children
			NUCLEAR	EXTENDED	AUGMENTED		
St. Helena's	874	56	70%	23%	9%	81%	77%
Issaquena	957	52	71	21	10	84	77
Jackson Ward	456	186	41	31	38	68	62

*Only two black subfamilies—one each in the rural places—lived with a white family.

Table A-25. Black Male-Absent Households and Subfamilies, 1900

	Headed by women 40 and older	Women heading households and subfamilies in age-specific groups			Male-absent households with only one child under 18	Single women heading households and subfamilies		
		15–19	20–29	20+		NUMBER	NUMBER UNDER 30	SINGLE HOUSEHOLD AND SUBFAMILY HEADS AS A PERCENTAGE OF ALL HOUSEHOLD AND SUBFAMILY HEADS
St. Helena's	60%	4%	7%	6%	52%	6	2	0.6%
Issaquena	37	5	12	13	52	29	24	3
Jackson Ward	48	3	13	20	63	29	21	5

TABLE A-26. COMPARISON OF INTERIOR COMPOSITION OF RURAL AND URBAN SOUTHERN BLACK HOUSEHOLDS, 1880 AND 1900

	1880		*1900*	
	ST. HELENA'S ISLAND AND	RURAL ADAMS	ST. HELENA'S	ISSAQUENA
Rural	TOWNSHIP	COUNTY	TOWNSHIP	COUNTY
Nuclear	83%	72%	70%	71%
Extended	15	18	23	21
Augmented	2	12	9	10
Ratio of subfamilies to households	1/15.4	1/11.9	1/14.3	1/17.4
Female-headed households and subfamilies as percent of all households and subfamilies	13%	18%	18%	16%
Females heading households and subfamilies as a percentage of age-specific groups				
20–29	8%	16%	7%	11%
30–39	10	17	16	14
All 15+	10	15	13	13

	1880	*1900* JACKSON WARD (PARTIAL)
Urban	ALL OF RICHMOND	RICHMOND
Nuclear	65%	41%
Extended	15	31
Augmented	23	38
Ratio of subfamilies to households	1/4.4	1/1.45
Female-headed households and subfamilies as percentage of all households and subfamilies	26%	31%
Females heading households and subfamilies as a percentage of age-specific groups		
20–29	9%	13%
30–39	18	20
All 15+	14	17

TABLE A-27.   YEARS MARRIED IN PERCENTAGES BY AGE OF WIFE,
1900

Age of wife	Number	Years married by percent			
		−10	10–19	20–29	30+
		St. Helena's Blacks			
25–34	149	50%	50%	—	—
35–44	141	6	51	41%	2%
45–54	109	7	7	47	39
55+	82	4	—	12	84
		Issaquena Blacks			
25–34	208	61%	36	3%	—
35–44	150	27	32	38	3%
45–54	122	14	19	30	37
55+	61	13	10	13	64
		Jackson-Richmond Blacks			
25–34	180	53%	45%	2%	—
35–44	155	16	47	34	3%
45–54	73	6	12	36	46
55+	22	4	5	—	91
		Jones County, Miss., Whites			
25–34	363	57%	42%	1%	—
35–44	199	10	45	41	4%
45–54	133	1	12	46	41
55+	74	4	1	12	83

TABLE A-28.   AGE OF MARRIAGE OF BLACK WOMEN UNDER THIRTY IN 1900

| | Number | Under 15 | 15–19 | 20–24 | 25–29 | Median age | |
						WOMEN UNDER 30	ALL WOMEN
St. Helena's	509	5%	51%	33%	11%	19.3	20.4
Issaquena	691	9	45	32	14	19.3	21.7
Jackson	453	7	42	39	12	20.6	19.0
Jones County, Miss., Whites	441	7	56	32	5	18.7	not available

MEDIAN NUMBER OF CHILDREN BORN TO MOTHER, BY MOTHER'S AGE, 1900

| Age of mother in 1900 | Blacks | | | Whites |
	ST. HELENA'S	ISSAQUENA	JACKSON	JONES COUNTY, MISS.
15–19	1.2	1.3	1.3	1.4
20–29	3.5	2.9	2.3	2.7
30–39	5.6	4.7	4.6	4.7
40–49	7.5	7.2	5.9	6.1
50+	7.4	6.8	7.1	6.8
Only women with three or more children				
40–49	7.6	8.3	7.2	not available
50+	9.0	8.4	8.9	not available

ALL CHILDREN BORN WHO WERE DEAD BY 1900, BY AGE OF MOTHER

| Age of mother in 1900 | Blacks | | | Whites |
	ST. HELENA'S	ISSAQUENA	JACKSON	JONES COUNTY, MISS.
15–19	13%	13%	0%	21%
20–29	31	27	29	18
30–39	35	39	39	30
40–49	31	48	49	21
50+	40	63	54	27

TABLE A-29. NUMBER OF BLACK FAMILIES WITH LIVING CHILDREN NOT RESIDING IN THEM AND NUMBER OF BLACK CHILDREN LIVING AWAY FROM FAMILY, 1900

Age of wife	Number of families	Families with one or more children not at home	Number of children	Children with family
		Husband, Wife, Children		
		ST. HELENA'S ISLAND		
15–29	181	14%	459	93%
30–44	209	40	1004	84
		ISSAQUENA		
15–29	191	6	441	97
30–44	178	38	752	84
		JACKSON WARD		
15–29	133	7	271	96
30–44	173	20	621	91
		Mother and Children Only		
		ST. HELENA'S ISLAND		
15–29	10	10%	21	95%
30–44	36	31	127	84
		ISSAQUENA		
15–29	52	10	112	93
30–44	30	37	111	82
		JACKSON WARD		
15–29	40	7	70	96
30–44	79	37	236	81

NOTE: *In a number of instances—and especially for mother and children—the number of children still living was not given. This is, therefore, an incomplete table.*

TABLE A-30.   AGE OF OLDEST CHILDREN AND STEPCHILDREN BY LENGTH OF MARRIAGE, 1900

Age of mother	Oldest child born year of marriage	Oldest child older than marriage	Stepchild older than marriage	Oldest child younger than marriage	Total	Percent of mothers with children younger than years of marriage	Percent of mothers with children born year of marriage
			Issaquena				
15–19	9	2	1	15	27	55%	33%
20–29	35	32	21	94	182	52	19
30–39	12	26	16	76	130	58	9
40–49	3	13	7	69	92	75	—
40+	0	4	2	42	48	87	—
			St. Helena's				
15–19	6	2	0	10	18	55%	33%
20–29	21	22	3	110	156	70	13
30–39	14	17	3	93	127	73	11
40–49	7	11	3	79	100	79	—
50+	0	3	0	88	91	96	—
			Jackson Ward, Richmond				
15–19	7	0	0	4	11	36%	64%
20–29	11	13	0	89	113	79	10
30–39	10	9	9	100	128	78	8
40–49	2	7	6	66	81	81	—
50+	1	0	0	25	26	96	—

Jones County, Miss., Whites

15–19	5	0	n.a.*	25	30	84%	16%
20–29	22	9	n.a.	274	315	91	7
30–39	5	18	n.a.	207	230	90	2
40–49	2	8	n.a.	200	210	96	—
50+	2	3	n.a.	170	175	97	—

* Not available.

TABLE A-31.   AGE DISTRIBUTION OF NEW YORK CITY BLACKS,
1900, 1905, and 1910

Age	San Juan Hill and Tenderloin Districts, *1905*		New York City Federal Census, *1910*	
	MALE	FEMALE	MALE	FEMALE
Under 15	17%	18%	16%	16%
15–19	7	7	6	7
20–29	32	34	33	34
30–59	42	38	42	40
60+	2	3	2	3
NUMBER	7004	7364		

SEX RATIOS, NEW YORK CITY BLACKS, 1900, 1905,
1910

Female = 100

Date	Age group	Sex ratio
1900	20+	83
1905	20+	98
1910	20+	87
1900	20–29	74
1905	20–29	90
1910	20–29	79

TABLE A-32. OCCUPATIONS OF ALL BLACK MALES, TWENTY AND
OLDER, TENDERLOIN AND SAN JUAN HILL DISTRICTS,
NEW YORK CITY, 1905

Occupation	
Unskilled laborer and service worker	86%
Skilled worker	9
Nonworker	5
TOTAL	5267

Occupation		*Major categories*
Unskilled laborer and service worker	(4520):	Laborer (1051), building maintenance (857), cook and waiter (887), porter (753), driver (256), servant (171), railroad porter (147), longshoreman (97), building engineer and fireman (62), miscellaneous unskilled (239)
Skilled worker	(462):	Actor and musician (119), building trades (94), barber (75), tailor (47), cigarmaker (41), miscellaneous skilled (86)
Nonworker	(166):	*White-collar:* clerk (96), postal employee (19), salesman and agent (12), U.S. Customs (8), stenographer-bookkeeper (6), manager (6), foreman (4), insurance (4), "banker" (4), broker (3), miscellaneous (7)
	(39):	*Professional:* clergyman (12), physician and dentist (10), lawyer (3), teacher (2), architect (2), law student, music professor, professor, draftsman, designer, chemist, chiropractor, veterinarian, psychologist, "professional" (one each)
	(77):	*Enterprise:* restaurant-caterer (24), dealer-huckster-jobber (11), poolroom proprietor (8), real estate and boarding house (6), undertaker (5), druggist (5), coal and wood (4), grocer (2), saloon (2), shoe store (2), liquor store, tradesman, builder, confectionery store, cigar dealer, trunk manufacturer (one each)

TABLE A-33.   PERCENTAGE OF BLACK AND WHITE WOMEN
WORKING, SIXTEEN AND OLDER, BY AGE AND
MARITAL STATUS, NEW YORK CITY, 1900

	Percentage of total working		
Age	Daughter of immigrant parent(s)	Foreign-born	Black
16–20	57%	71%	66%
21–24	46	48	66
25–34	27	24	57
35–44	19	18	56
45+	15	14	54

OCCUPATIONS OF BLACK WOMEN, NEW YORK CITY,
1900

Occupation	Percent
Servant and waitress	63%
Laundress	20
Seamstress and dressmaker	7
Nurse and midwife	2
Housekeeper and stewardess	2
Janitor and sexton	1
Laborer	1
All other occupations	4
NUMBER	10,546

TABLE A-34.   SIZE OF BLACK HOUSEHOLDS AND NUMBER OF
PERSONS LIVING IN BLACK HOUSEHOLDS BY PERCENT,
SAN JUAN HILL AND TENDERLOIN DISTRICTS,
NEW YORK CITY, 1905

Size of household by number of persons		Percentage of total population
1	7%	2%
2–4	64	48
5–7	23	35
8–10	4	9
11+	2	6
NUMBER	3768	14,366

TABLE A-35.   TYPES OF BLACK HOUSEHOLDS WITH TWO OR
MORE PEOPLE, NEW YORK CITY, 1905

Type	Percent
Irregular households	10%
Kin-related black households without husband-wife or parent-child	4
Kin-related black households including husband-wife or parent-child	86
NUMBER	3490

TABLE A-36.   COMPOSITION OF BLACK HOUSEHOLDS AND
SUBFAMILIES, NEW YORK CITY, 1905

Number of black households	3014
Number of subfamilies in black households	437
Types of households	
Nuclear	49%
Extended	16
Augmented	42
Husband- or father-present households and subfamilies	83
Father-present households and subfamilies with children	67

TABLE A-37.   Occupational Status of All Black Males Aged
              Twenty and Older Compared with
              Occupational Status of Black Fathers Living
              with Wife and Children or Just with Children,
              New York City, 1905

Occupation	All black males 20 and older	All black fathers living with a wife and children or just with children
Laborer–service worker	86%	85%
Skilled worker	9	11
White-collar	3	2
Professional-entrepreneurial	2	2
NUMBER	5267	1139
No occupation listed or unclear		83

Occupation	All black males 45+	All black fathers 45+ living with a wife and children or just with children
Laborer–service worker	84%	89%
Skilled worker	9	5
Other	7	6
NUMBER	796	215
No occupation listed		12

TABLE A-38.   Black Male-Absent Households and
              Subfamilies, New York City, 1905

Number	600
Age of mother known	583
Headed by women 40 and older	52%
Headed by women under 30	19
Women heading households as a percentage of all women in age-specific groups	
15–19	2
20–29	4
Male-absent households and subfamilies with only one child under 18	76

TABLE A-39.   PATTERNS OF SOUTHERN AND NORTHERN RURAL AND URBAN HOUSEHOLDS AND SUBFAMILIES COMPARED, 1880–1905

	St. Helena's 1880	Rich- mond 1880	St. Helena's 1900	Jack- son Ward 1900	New York City 1905
Type of household					
Nuclear	83%	65%	70%	41%	49%
Extended	15	15	23	31	16
Augmented	2	23	9	38	42
Ratio of subfamilies to households	1/15	1/4.4	1/14	1/1.4	1/8
Husband- or father- present households and subfamilies	86%	73%	81%	68%	83%
Father-present house- holds and subfamilies with children	83	66	77	62	67
Women heading house- holds in age-specific groups					
15–19	4	1	4	3	2
20–29	9	9	7	13	4
30–39	10	18	16	19	10

TABLE A-40.   AGE AND SEX DISTRIBUTION OF NEW YORK CITY BLACKS, 1925

Age	West Indian in birth		Native-born		All	
	MALE	FEMALE	MALE	FEMALE	MALE	FEMALE
Under 15	4%	5%	21%	20%	17%	17%
15–24	18	26	15	18	16	19
25–44	68	59	48	48	53	50
45+	10	10	16	14	14	14
NUMBER	6053	5833	21,180	23,442	27,233	29,275
Not given	26	33	52	75	78	108
Born elsewhere*					129	87

* Among these 216 persons of color, 69 were born in Canada (46 of them females), 35 in Africa (31 of them males), 22 in Portugal, 29 in Spain, 24 in England, 7 in France, and 6 in Holland.

They lived on West Ninety-eighth and Ninety-ninth Streets (2157), West 112 Street, (134), West Fifty-second, Fifty-third, Fifty-fourth, Fifty-seventh, Sixtieth, Sixty-first Sixty-second, and Sixty-third streets, and West End Avenue (5329), and in Central Harlem (50,233).

SEX RATIOS, NEW YORK CITY BLACKS (F = 100),
1925

Age group	All	West Indians	Native blacks
15+	93	105	85
15–24	76	77	75
25–44	98	117	92
45+	100	104	99
25+	98	115	94

TABLE A-41.   OCCUPATIONS OF BLACK MALES TWENTY AND
OLDER, TENDERLOIN AND SAN JUAN HILL DISTRICTS,
1905, AND MANHATTAN, 1925

Occupation	1905 Tenderloin and San Juan Hill blacks	1925 native blacks	1925 West Indians
Laborer–service worker	86%	72%	71%
Skilled worker	9	16	21
White-collar	3	8	5
Professional	1	2	2
Entrepreneurial	1	2	1
NUMBER	5148	14,620	5186

TABLE A-42.   MAJOR OCCUPATIONS OF NATIVE BLACKS AND
WEST INDIAN MALES, MANHATTAN, 1925

OCCUPATION	Number	
	NATIVE BLACK	WEST INDIAN
I. Unskilled laborers and service workers		
TOTAL	10,585	3629
Laborer	1887	559
Porter	1784	981
Building maintenance	1346	717
Chauffeur	975	195
Longshoreman	730	142
Waiter	696	169
Railroad porter	636	59
Cook	479	183
Servant	373	101
Driver	266	28
Shipping clerk	185	92
Factory worker	172	155
Messenger	178	23
Building fireman and engineer	354	123
Miscellaneous	498	147

TABLE A-42. (*Continued*)

| | Number | |
| OCCUPATION | NATIVE BLACK | WEST INDIAN |

II. Skilled workers

TOTAL	2265	1085
Painter	174	81
Carpenter	146	195
Bricklayer	72	25
Plasterer	53	15
Plumber	50	14
Other building trades	123	80
Musician	349	50
Actor	130	12
Barber	177	28
Tailor	175	136
Mechanic	143	30
Auto mechanic	94	34
Machinist	90	51
Butcher	52	12
Printer	50	47
Baker	42	13
Cigarmaker	36	63
Shoemaker	15	41
Miscellaneous	199	132

III. White-collar

TOTAL	1234	239
Post-office carrier	478	70
Clerk	226	64
Salesman	110	54
Real estate	123	45
Foreman	32	9
Government clerk	30	4
Other government employees	27	3
Bookkeeper	26	6
Manager	31	0
Miscellaneous	151	36

IV. Professional

TOTAL	279	106
Clergyman	89	26
Physician	49	22
Dentist	34	18
Lawyer	31	9
Teacher	28	14
Chemist	18	2
Chiropractor	14	10
Editor	9	0
Miscellaneous	7	4

Table A-42.   (*Continued*)

	Number	
OCCUPATION	NATIVE BLACK	WEST INDIAN

V. Entrepreneurial

OCCUPATION	NATIVE BLACK	WEST INDIAN
TOTAL	260	64
Retail storekeeper	47	19
Ice and coal dealer	34	2
Restaurateur and caterer	32	1
Undertaker	31	7
Poolroom	31	0
Pharmacist	20	20
Dealer-peddler	16	3
Miscellaneous	49*	12†

* Includes a cabaret owner, three music publishers, a theatrical producer, a broom manufacturer, a newspaper publisher, three bankers, and an insurance-company president.

† Includes a publisher.

Table A-43.   Types of Black Households, New York City, 1905 and 1925

	1905	1925
Type of household	PERCENT	PERCENT
Single person	8	7
Irregular non-kin	9	7
Irregular kin without husband-wife or parent-child	3	3
Kin-related household with core nuclear group	80	83
TOTAL	3768	12,987

TABLE A-44. COMPARISON OF THE HOUSEHOLDS OF MANHATTAN BLACKS, 1905 AND 1925

Type of household	New York City 1905	New York City 1925		
		ALL BLACKS*	NATIVE	WEST INDIAN
Number of households	3014	10,732	7704	2390
Nuclear	49%	39%	40%	34%
Extended	15	21	20	23
Augmented	42	49	48	54
Number of subfamilies	437	3192	2448	563
Ratio of subfamilies to households	1/7.9	1/3.3	1/3.1	1/4.2
Husband- or father-present households and subfamilies	83%	85%	84%	86%
Father-present households and subfamilies	67%	70%	66%	77%

* This column includes 638 additional households and 181 additional subfamilies in which the husband and wife were not both either native blacks or West Indians.

TABLE A-45. FEMALE-HEADED HOUSEHOLDS AND SUBFAMILIES BY AGE AND PLACE OF BIRTH OF MOTHER, NEW YORK CITY, 1925

Age of mother	Number, 1925	Percentage of all female-headed households and subfamilies, 1925	Native Blacks — Percentage of all male-absent households	West Indians — Percentage of all male-absent households
15–19	24	1	1	1
20–29	383	19	18	20
30–39	570	28	27	31
40–49	557	27	27	27
50+	529	26	27	21
TOTAL	2063		1597	466
UNKNOWN	17			

TABLE A-46. NUMBER OF CHILDREN UNDER EIGHTEEN IN FEMALE-HEADED HOUSEHOLDS AND SUBFAMILIES BY AGE OF MOTHER, NEW YORK CITY, 1925

Age of mother	Number of children under 18							TOTAL
	0	1	2	3	4	5	6+	
15–19	0	23	1	0	0	0	0	24
20–29	0	279	72	24	6	2	0	383
30–39	94	302	108	45	15	4	2	570
40–49	268	202	53	19	7	7	1	557
50+	456	61	10	2	0	0	0	529
TOTAL	818	867	244	90	28	13	3	2063
Percent	40%	42%	12%	4%	1%	1%	0%	

TABLE A-47.   PERCENTAGE OF NATIVE BLACK AND WEST INDIAN
WOMEN AGED TWENTY TO TWENTY-NINE HEADING
MALE-ABSENT HOUSEHOLDS AND SUBFAMILIES AS
PERCENTAGE OF ALL WOMEN AGED TWENTY TO
TWENTY-NINE, NEW YORK CITY, 1925

	Number of women	*Percent heading male-absent household or subfamily*
Native black	6369	4.2
West Indian	2227	4.0
Other	40	—
TOTAL	8636	4.1

TABLE A-48.   HOUSEHOLD STATUS OF ALL BLACK FEMALES, NEW
YORK CITY, 1905 AND 1925

1905

	Age Groups			
	UNDER 15	15–24	25–44	45+
Heads of household or subfamily	0%	3%	10%	25%
Wife	0	40	58	26
Daughter	90	26	3	0
Other relative	3	5	3	17
Lodger	6	16	11	13
Lives in irregular household	1	9	12	13
Single	0	1	3	6
NUMBER	1320	1650	3560	800

1925

Heads of household or subfamily	0	3	8	21
Wife	0	35	57	33
Daughter	94	25	4	1
Other relative	3	8	4	13
Lodger	2	22	18	15
Lives in irregular household	1	6	7	12
Single	0	1	2	5
NUMBER	5049	5648	14,636	3942

TABLE A-49.   DISTRIBUTION OF ALL BLACK MALE OCCUPATIONS
COMPARED WITH OCCUPATIONS AND AGES OF NATIVE
BLACK AND WEST INDIAN FATHERS, NEW YORK CITY,
1925

	All native males	*All native fathers*
Laborer	72%	72%
Skilled worker	16	14
Other	12	14
NUMBER	14,620	3129

	All West Indian males	*All West Indian fathers*
Laborer	71%	69%
Skilled worker	21	21
Other	8	9
NUMBER	5186	1658

Native blacks

Occupation	*All native male blacks 45+*	*All native black fathers 45+ living with wives and children or only with children*
Laborer	75%	74%
Skilled worker	11	11
Other	14	15
NUMBER	3850	867
Occupation not given or retired		32

West Indians

Occupation	*All West Indian male blacks 45+*	*All West Indian fathers 45+ living with wives and children or only with children*
Laborer	64%	62%
Skilled worker	22	26
Other	14	12
NUMBER	561	273
Occupation not given or retired		13

TABLE A-50.   HOUSEHOLD STATUS OF BLACK CHILDREN UNDER SIX, NEW YORK CITY, 1925

Household status	
Lodger	3%
Lives with father	1
Lives with mother (kin-related household)	5
Lives with mother (non-kin-related household)	5
Lives with aunt or uncle	1
Lives with grandparents	1
Lives with mother and father	84
NUMBER	4809

APPENDIX B

Black, Jewish, and Italian Households
in New York City in 1905

A useful comparison between the households of New York City San Juan Hill and Tenderloin blacks in 1905 with the household of immigrant Jews and Italians living that same year in New York City is made possible by an examination of the composition of 3711 Lower East Side Jewish households (with a population of 21,460 persons) and 3116 Greenwich Village Italian households (with a population of 14,300 persons).* Meaningful comparisons require that two or more social groups being analyzed share a good deal in common so that similarities and differences between them can be explored. Despite their significant cultural and occupational differences, the immigrant Jews and Italians in these New York City neighborhoods meet that test. But the age and sex distribution of the blacks as well as their occupational status differed very much from both the Jews and the Italians. Blacks inhabited the same island as the Jews and Italians but lived in a different world.

A striking difference between the blacks and the Jews and Italians resulted from the disparity in their age and sex structures. Jews and Italians had a quite similar age structure, but that of the New York City blacks in 1905 differed radically from that of the two immigrant groups and even from the black national population. The 1905 black population was predominantly adult in

---

* All Jewish households recorded in the 1905 New York State manuscript census on the following streets have been analyzed: Rutgers, Cherry, Pelham, Monroe, Water, Pike, Jefferson, Clinton, Madison, Livingston, Henry, Division, Montgomery, Delancey, Rivington, Norfolk, Suffolk, and East Third streets as well as East Broadway and Avenue B. The same source has allowed us to examine all Italian households on the following streets: Hancock, Baxter, Thompson, Mulberry, Bayard, Mott, Canal, Elizabeth, Spring, Prince, Grand, Hester, MacDougal, Sullivan, West Houston, Bleecker, Bedford, Downing, and Carmine streets and the Bowery.

composition: three-fourths of San Juan Hill and Tenderloin blacks were at least twenty years old. The Jews and Italians differed: the percentage that old ranged from 47 to 57 percent. Children not yet fifteen years old were proportionately twice as numerous among the Jews and the Italians as among the blacks. Much more explained these differences than the high infant mortality rate among New York City blacks. The pattern of migration by blacks—itself shaped by the opportunities open to black men and women in northern cities like New York—differed from that of the Jews and the Italians. Family migration and the migration of married men without their families (a form of delayed family migration) characterized the Jewish and Italian migrations to New York City. Few single adult women in either group migrated alone. But single migrants—both men and women—were an important component of the black 1905 New York City population. This is seen by examining the household status of middle-aged black, Jewish, and Italian women that year. Slightly more than one of five black women between the ages of twenty-five and forty-four were lodgers. Another 3 percent lived alone, and about the same percent boarded with relatives. Jewish and Italian women knew the opposite circumstance. Among 2301 Jewish women aged twenty-five to forty-four, only 129 (5 percent) were lodgers. Twenty-eight others lived with relatives, and five lived alone. Data are not available for Italian women in the same age group, but of 1522 Italian women aged thirty to forty-nine, thirty-two were lodgers, sixteen lived with relatives, and three lived alone. Put differently, at the time the census was recorded four times as many black women as Jewish women and nearly nine times as many black women as Italian women lived detached from a family of origin and were then neither married nor living with children in a male-absent household. Different patterns of migration also meant that the black adult sex ratio diverged from that among the Jews and Italians. In 1900 the New York City black adult sex ratio for men and women twenty and older was 82 and for men and women in their twenties 74. Immigrant Jews and Italians had a nearly opposite sex ratio. In the 1905 populations studied, it was 128 for all Jews twenty and older and 133 for similarly aged Italians. The sex ratio among Jewish (130) and Italian (125) men and women in their twenties hardly differed from over-all Jewish and Italian adult sex radio (Table B-1).*

The significant demographic differences paralleled equally

* Tables for this appendix appear on pages 527–530.

important occupational differences between the New York City blacks and the same city's Jews and Italians. In *The Other Bostonians: Poverty and Progress in the American Metropolis, 1880–1970* (1973, pp. 176–219), Stephen Thernstrom has shown that "the 'last-of-the-immigrants' theory" in no way explains the economic and social disadvantages among native and migrant Boston blacks between 1880 and 1940 and that "the problems of black men in a white society were different in kind from those of earlier newcomers." That was also the case in early-twentieth-century New York City. It was more than the fact that larger numbers of married and older black women worked in contrast to white immigrant women; it was also that the Jewish and Italian male occupational structures differed radically from the black male occupational structure. Large numbers of Jewish and Italian men worked in New York City's clothing industry, but it cannot be known from the census pages how many were skilled workmen. The fact that many among them were described as "tailors" and not "operators" suggests the retention of skills by some in a rapidly changing industry. It is assumed that half of the men listed as clothing workers had factory skills. Most Jewish (73 percent) and Italian (86 percent) men studied were blue-collar wage earners in 1905. So were most blacks (95 percent). But this similarity hid very important differences between the black workers and the Jewish and Italian workers, differences similar to those that had distinguished southern urban blacks from white southern urban workers and from the 1880 Paterson native white and Irish workers. Nearly three of five Jewish male *workers* (59 percent) had skills, and nearly one of two (45 percent) Italian male *workers* had skills, but slightly less than one of ten black *workers* (9 percent) had skills. Put another way, three of every ten Jewish men and slightly less than one of every two Italian men were unskilled laborers and service workers, as compared with eighty-six of every one hundred black men. The Jews and the Italians (to a lesser degree) experienced far greater occupational diversity than the blacks. And these were not mere quantitative differences. Nearly 10 percent of *all* Italian and Jewish men, for example, were skilled building-trades workers, as compared with less than 2 percent of *all* black men. Italians and Jews, moreover, had made important inroads into non-blue-collar occupations by 1905. Proportionately twice as many Italian as black men were neither unskilled laborers nor skilled workers, and proportionately five times as many Jewish as black men had white-collar, professional, or entrepreneurial positions. Too much is known to idealize the

material condition of large numbers of 1905 Lower East Side
Jewish and Greenwich Village Italian working-class families. The
high percentage of teen-age boys and girls who labored in the
families of skilled immigrant workers and even in the families of
petty entrepreneurs damages that view. Nevertheless it was much,
much more difficult to be black and lower-class than to be white
and lower-class in New York City in 1905 (Table B-2).

The measures used in this study suggest little family disorganization among these lower East Side Jews and Greenwich Village Italians. Fewer than 6 percent of the residents in each
of these predominantly working-class immigrant communities
lived in single-person or irregular households. The typical Jewish
and Italian household at this peak moment in the "new" immigration—more common among the Italians (60 percent) than among
the Jews (49 percent)—was the simple nuclear household. But
important differences existed between these two groups. The unrelated lodger was much more common in Jewish (43 percent)
than in Italian (19 percent) households, so that slightly more than
two in five Lower East Side Jewish households were augmented
households. But twice as many Italian as Jewish households contained a core nuclear family and one or more close relatives. Why
the enlarged household differed so greatly between immigrant Jews
and Italians remains the subject of further study. So, too, do the
relatively few Jewish (7 percent) and Italian (7 percent) male-
absent households and subfamilies that existed in these two
working-class ghetto communities. The observations of contemporary social workers and the theoretical "models" of social scientists then and later, as well as the judgments of most social
historians, do not prepare the reader for these facts. They argue
with unusual persistence and much success that lower-class white
migration followed by a ghetto experience and economic difficulties severely strained the immigrant working-class family, caused
widespread social "disorganization" and frequently shattered
fragile families. The 1905 manuscript census strains the "theory."
Too little is yet known about the East European Jewish and
Southern Italian household and family prior to early-twentieth-
century mass migration to tell precisely how these New York City
working-class immigrant households indicated an adaptation of
more "traditional" households.* But the 1905 manuscript census

* See Virginia Yans-McLaughlin, "Patterns of Work and Family Organization
Among Buffalo's Italians," *Journal of Interdisciplinary History*, 2 (1971), 299–314,
and Yans-McLaughlin, *Like the Fingers of the Hand: The Family and Community
Life of First-Generation Italian-Americans in Buffalo, New York*, in press (1977)
and a brilliant work.

indicates convincingly that widespread family "breakdown" did not occur among these Jews and Italians (Tables B-3 and B-4).

Because the Tenderloin and San Juan Hill blacks differed so in their age and occupational structures, comparisons between their households and those of immigrant Jews and Italians are difficult to make. At best, such a comparison illustrates how demographic, social, and economic differences shaped diverse patterns of lower-class adaptation to early-twentieth-century urban life. It indicates that immigrant Jews and Italians—as contrasted with migrant blacks—were drawn into the developing urban "sector" and thereby allowed to gain a precarious but nevertheless significant advantage as compared with migrant blacks. Migrant blacks, however, were not just "another immigrant group." Their material and occupational circumstance damages the assertion that migrant blacks arrived in the American city "too late." When contrasted with the experiences of the immigrant Jews and Italians prior to the First World War in places like New York City, it becomes clear that the "timing" of northern black migration is not a reason for its difficult entry.

Direct comparisons of the black migrants with the Jews and the Italians are made with hesitation. The difference in age structure probably explains why blacks had relatively fewer kin-related households with a nuclear core than either the Jews or the Italians. Blacks in the rural and urban South had large families, but unlike the Jews and Italians, black migrants to early-twentieth-century New York had few children and large numbers of households with a nuclear core composed only of a husband and wife. Despite these significant differences, the migrant blacks also revealed some similarities to the Jews and Italians. The nuclear household had been common among rural and urban southern blacks, and it is not surprising that it was just as common among San Juan Hill and Tenderloin blacks (49 percent) as among Jews (49 percent). Blacks and Jews also knew the augmented household in nearly the same proportions. Two in five immigrant Jewish and migrant black households had unrelated boarders in them. If extended households among migrants and immigrants reveal the persistence of important kin ties between two generations of families, the migrant blacks scored well on that measure. More black (16 percent) than Jewish (12 percent) but not nearly as many as Italian (23 percent) households were extended in composition. Given their relative poverty, subfamilies were much more common in the San Juan Hill and Tenderloin districts than on the Lower East Side or in Greenwich Village. Male-absent households and subfamilies as a percent of all kin-related households and subfamilies, finally, were more numerous among the blacks (17 percent) than among the Jews and Italians (7 percent each). But these households all shared important characteristics. About one in three black female household heads lived with children eighteen years and older, a percentage that differed only slightly from the Jewish (29 percent) and Italian household heads (38 percent). Nearly two-thirds of black household heads with children under eighteen had only one child, a far higher percentage than among Jewish (34 percent) and Italian (53 percent) female household heads. Nevertheless nearly half of black female household heads as contrasted to one-quarter of Jewish and Italian household heads were not yet forty years old.

The male-absent household or subfamily headed by a younger woman was more common among the blacks than among the Jews and Italians. But its significance, once again, should not be exaggerated. The occupations available to black men and the distorted sex ratio among young adult blacks are two important reasons that help explain these differences. Would the same differences have existed if the Jewish and Italian sex ratios had been the same as the migrant black sex ratio? It makes a difference if there are 74, as opposed to 125, adult males for every 100 adult females. If age is standardized, a difference remains but shrinks in importance. Four percent of San Juan Hill and Tenderloin black women aged twenty to twenty-nine headed male-absent households and subfamilies, as compared with one percent of similarly aged Jewish women and 1.5 percent of similarly aged Italian women. The percentage point differences decreased among all women under forty, but twice as many black women aged forty and over, as compared with similarly aged Jewish women, headed male-absent households and subfamilies. The difference between Italian and black women aged forty and older was not as great. Between one in four or five black women headed such households and subfamilies, as compared with one of seven Italian women. These were important differences but were not the essential fact revealed in the 1905 New York State manuscript census. Given the striking demographic and socioeconomic disadvantages among migrant New York City blacks, as compared with immigrant Jews and Italians in the first decade of this century, it is surprising that so few households and subfamilies had at their head a black woman not yet forty years old (Table B-4).

TABLE B-1. AGE, SEX, AND SEX RATIOS, BLACKS, JEWS, AND
ITALIANS, NEW YORK CITY, 1905

Age	Blacks		Jews		Italians	
	MALE	FEMALE	MALE	FEMALE	MALE	FEMALE
Under 15	17%	18%	33%	35%	34%	38%
15–19	6	7	12	17	10	12
20–29	32	34	25	22	22	21
30–39	27	23	15	11	16	13
40–49	12	11	9	9	10	9
50+	6	7	6	6	8	7
NUMBER	7004	7364	11,199	10,263	7968	6825

Adults only

20–29	42%	45%	45%	45%	40%	42%
30–39	35	31	28	23	28	26
40–49	15	15	15	18	18	18
50+	8	9	12	14	14	14
NUMBER	5346	5486	6246	4882	4542	3428

Sex ratio

20+	97	128	132
20–29	91	129	125

1900

20+	82
20–29	74

1910

20+	89
20–29	79

TABLE B-2. JEWISH, ITALIAN, AND BLACK MALE OCCUPATIONAL
STRUCTURE, TWENTY AND OLDER, NEW YORK CITY,
1905

Occupation	Jews	Italians	Blacks
Laborer, unskilled	7%	38%	86%
Clothing	45	18	*
Skilled	21	30	9
White-collar	8	4	3
Petty-enterprise	12	9	†

* Fifty-one black tailors are included among the skilled workers.

† Black hucksters and dealers as well as retail storekeepers are included among the "entrepreneurs," but peddlers and storekeepers were sufficiently numerous among the Italians and especially the Jews to be separated out as a special category.

TABLE B-2. *(Continued)*

Occupation	Jews	Italians	Blacks
Professional	4%	1%	1%
Enterprise	3	0.4	1
NUMBER	5990	4469	5267

Composite occupations	Blacks	Jews	Italians
Unskilled labor and service‡	86%	30%	47%
Skilled workers‡	9	43	39
Other	5	27	14
NUMBER	5267	5990	4469

Major Occupations, Jewish Males, New York City, 1905

Labor, unskilled (426): Rags (43), expressman (32), laborer–day laborer (28), driver (26), watchman (25), paper boxes (21), waiter (16), shipping clerk (14), stablehand (13), laundry (13)

Clothing (2706): Tailor (926), operator (826), presser (256), cutter (158), cloaks (99), furrier (50), capmaker (47), shirtmaker (35)

Skilled worker (1252):

Building trades (547): Painter (187), carpenter (171), plumber (57), tinsmith (46), bricklayer (25), contractor (19), plasterer (10)

Other (705): Cigarmaker (94), butcher (57), baker (50), shoemaker (50), printer-lithographer-engraver-compositor (46), jewelry (48), blacksmith (36), bookbinder (26), iron worker (25), furniture-cabinet carver (24), barber (22), glazier (21)

White-collar (469): Salesman (142), real estate (79), bookkeeper (61), clerk (52), agent (25), foreman (20), insurance (17), collector (12), public employees (12)

Petty-enterprise (731): Peddler (271), grocer (63), seltzer dealer (41), saloon (19), coal and ice (16), fruit (18), "stand" (16), druggist (17), shoe store (15), candy store (15), hardware (11), stationery store (9), lunch business (13)

Professions (259): doctor (73), rabbi (61), teacher (60), lawyer (34), dentist (30), author (4)

High-enterprise (147): Manufacturer (65), merchant (60), clothing business (16)

‡ It is not possible to tell from the 1905 manuscript census just how skills were distributed among clothing workers. They have therefore been arbitrarily divided in half among both the Jews and the Italians—50 percent of each being listed as either unskilled or skilled. This "estimate" needs much more careful refinement.

TABLE B-2.   *(Continued)*

Major Occupations, Italian Males, New York City, 1905

Labor, unskilled   (1714):   Laborer (841), candymaker (107), bootblack (103), waiter (98), cook (86), porter (75), expressman and driver (64), flowermaker (55), factory worker (46), street cleaner (39), papermaker (25), servant (21), longshoreman (19), janitor (18), bartender (31), truckman (21)

Clothing   (785):   Tailor (609), presser (73), operator (24), cap–hatmaker (14), ironer (10)

Skilled worker   (1338):
  Building trades   (454):   Carpenter (101), bricklayer (52), painter (48), tile and mosaic (46), stonecutter (43), hod carrier (45), stone polisher (29), plumber (19), mason (16)

  Other   (884):   Barber (185), shoemaker (118), baker (97), butcher (49), musician (45), metal worker (24), machinist (23), cigar-maker (37), blacksmith (32), jeweler (26), cabinet-maker (28), printer (22), artist-sculptor (29), piano (19)

White-collar   (172):   Clerk (71), bookkeeper (43), salesman (26), foreman (8), agent (6)

Petty-enterprise   (105):   Fruit-vegetable vendor (89), grocer (71), fish seller (44), peddler (39), restaurant (33), liquor sales (25), saloon (22), junk (19), coal and ice (15), boarding house (15)

Professional   (37):   Doctor (19), teacher (8), editor (3), music teacher (3), lawyer (2), priest (1)

High-enterprise   (18):   Merchant (11), banker (4), manufacturer (3)

TABLE B-3.   TYPES OF BLACK, JEWISH, AND ITALIAN HOUSEHOLDS, NEW YORK CITY, 1905

Type of household	*Blacks*	*Jews*	*Italians*
Single-person	7%	2%	1%
Irregular	13*	2	4
Kin-related with nuclear core	80	96	95
NUMBER	3768	3711	3116

* 122 of these 476 households contained two or more blood relatives but not persons who were members of the nuclear core.

TABLE B-4. COMPARISON OF KIN-RELATED HOUSEHOLD
              STRUCTURE OF BLACKS, JEWS, AND ITALIANS,
              NEW YORK CITY, 1905

Type of household	Blacks	Jews	Italians
NUMBER	3014	3584	2945
Nuclear	49%	49%	60%
Extended	16	12	23
Augmented	42	43	21
Number of subfamilies	437	159	262
Ratio of subfamilies to households	1/7.9	1/22.9	1/11.2
Husband or father present, households and subfamilies	83%	93%	93%
Households and subfamilies headed only by fathers	3%	3%	3%
Father-present households and subfamilies	67%	92%	91%
Married couples without children under eighteen as a percentage of all married couples by age of wife			
20–29	61%	22%	30%
30–39	60	6	15
40–49	65	9	15
50+	84	52	57
Married couples with three or more children under eighteen as a percentage of all married couples with children			
20–29	17%	27%	32%
30–39	27	75	64
40–49	32	68	61
Percentage of women heading male-absent households and sub-families as a percentage of all women in age-specific groups			
20–29	4%	1%	2%
Under 40	7	2	2.5
40+	22	12	15

APPENDIX C

A Brief Note on Late-Nineteenth-Century
Racial Ideology, Retrogressionist Beliefs,
the Misperception of the Ex Slave Family,
and the Conceptualization
of Afro-American History

> *The negro today is the product of his sad and dismal past. . . . He has no history and never has been a history-maker.*
>
> Speech to the First Mohonk Conference on the Negro Question (1890)

Winthrop Jordan and George Fredrickson, among other historians, have greatly advanced our understanding of changing patterns of American racial ideologies, but more attention needs to focus on how particular strains in postemancipation racial ideology associated with "retrogressionist" beliefs distorted perception of Afro-American family life and sexual behavior and affected the most influential early-twentieth-century conceptualizations of the entire Afro-American historical experience.[1]

The real world inhabited by poor rural and urban southern ex-slaves and their children between 1880 and the start of the vast northward migration after 1900 was invisible to nearly all observers. Partly, that is explained by the increasing popularity in the 1880s and 1890s of the belief that essential "restraining" influences on unchanging "Africans" had ended with the emancipation, causing a moral and social "retrogression" among the ex-slaves. This belief related closely to southern Bourbon political rhetoric that promised to redeem the South and save the nation from political corruption, economic extravagance, and racial and sexual "irregularities" by reimposing dominance over a race and a class that disclosed in the years following the emancipation an incapacity to "restrain" itself and thereby adapt decently to its changed status. "Retrogressionist" arguments often focused on the Afro-American family and sexual belief and behavior. They served, as Fredrickson shows, to "justify a policy of repression and neglect."[2] The twin evils of familial "instability" and sexual "immorality" supported the advocacy of new forms of external control over blacks, including disfranchisement and increasingly rigorous legal separation.

Observers of the Gilded Age Afro-American family and the moral and sexual practices of poor blacks stressed common themes. In the early 1880s, for example, New York *Sun* columnist Frank Wilkeson reported from St. Helena's Island, South Carolina:

> . . . Almost without exception, the women of these islands, who have negro blood in their veins, are prostitutes. It is a hopeless task to endeavor to elevate a people whose women are strumpets. . . . It is absolutely no disgrace for any black girl to have children before she is married. These people are devoid of shame. Their personal habits are so filthy, that I suspected that venereal disease was wide-spread among them. On inquiry of the physicians who practise among them, I found I was correct in my inference. The negroes are saturated with this deadly taint. This being the case, and free love in its vilest sense being practised among them, it can readily be seen how widely diffused this ineradicable poison must necessarily be.

About that time, Annie Porter told readers of the *Independent,* the prestigious national religious weekly, about the "extraordinary relapse" of Louisiana blacks "into barbarism" and said that ex-slave women did not "grasp the idea of physical morality in the slightest sense." Nathaniel Shaler, who had grown up in a family of Kentucky slaveholders, studied with Harvard's distinguished scientist Louis Agassiz, and would later head Harvard's Lawrence Scientific School, made similar points in an 1884 *Atlantic Monthly* article. Whites often overlooked "the peculiarities of nature which belong to the negroes as a race." Familiarity with "the negro folk by long and large experience . . . in youth" convinced Shaler of "the real dangers that this African blood brings to our state." He described "the relatively feeble nature of all ties that bind the family together among these African people":

The peculiar monogamic instinct which in our own race has been slowly, century by century, developing itself in the old tangle of passions has yet to be fixed in this people. In the negro, this motive, more than any other the key to our society, is very weak, if indeed it exists at all as an indigenous impulse.

Social order rested upon stable and settled families:

The modern state is but a roof built to shelter the lesser associations of men. Chief of these is the family, which rests on a certain order of alliance of the sexual instincts with the higher and more human faculties. Next come the various degrees of human cooperation in various forms of business life; and then the power of will, that gives the continuity to effort which is the key to all profitable labor; and, last but not least, the impulse to sexual morality.

"Weak in all these things," blacks were unfit for "an independent place in a civilized state" and were a positive social menace. A peaceful and prosperous state rested upon settled "lesser associations"; otherwise it was "a mere empty shell that must soon fall to pieces. Like other mechanisms, the state has only the strength of its weakest parts." Some ex-slaves had revealed "comparative elevation," but only because of the "external compulsion" imposed by "the will of a dominant race." But most were "falling to the bottom of society," becoming "a proletarian class, separated by blood as well as by estate from the superior classes." Shaler later told *Arena* readers: "In a long and intimate connection with this folk, I have never heard a [Negro] refer to his grandfather and any reference to parents is rare. The negro must be provided with these motives of the household; he must be made faithful to the marriage bond, and taught his sense of ancestry."[3]

"Retrogressionist" ideology had its most effective advocate in the otherwise obscure Jackson, Mississippi, Episcopal rector J. L. Tucker. A northerner by birth, Tucker had fought in the Confederate Army and later settled in the South. During a vigorous debate at the 1882 Richmond, Virginia, Congress of Episcopal Churches, Tucker argued against blacks' controlling their own churches and said that the ex-slaves, "retrograding morally," professed "a form of Christianity without its substance." "What we call morality," Tucker believed, ". . . has no independent lodgment whatever in the native African breast." Enslavement had imposed "outward restraint" upon "absolute barbarians." Only the "fear of punishment taught them what to say; their passions and traditions taught them what to do." "A relapse into many practices of African barbarism" followed the emancipation, a "great descent into evil." Where blacks greatly outnumbered whites, "there we have Africa over again, only partially restrained." "Whole neighborhoods" were without a "single legally married couple." Few married couples remained "faithful to each other beyond a few months . . . often but a few weeks." That was the "true" condition "for millions of the colored people." Printed as a pamphlet with endorsements from white clergy over the entire South, Tucker's charge of social and moral retrogression stirred a brief but important public controversy.[4] Southern whites as well as blacks severely criticized him, the most important among them the white Mississippi Baptist clergyman Charles Marshall and the black clergyman Alexander Crummell.[5] But Tucker, not his critics, became an international expert on the emancipated Afro-American. Published in 1884, the Ninth Edition of the *Encyclopaedia Britannica* cited Tucker as an expert observer on the Afro-American and as witness to the fact that "negroes" were "nonmoral."[6]

The popularity of retrogressionist beliefs also was disclosed in the public reception of Philip A. Bruce's *The Plantation Negro as Freedman* (1889), a study which, as Fredrickson writes, "put the case for a 'black peril' in the South on a firmer foundation" than any other book up to that time. Thirty-three years old when it appeared and not yet the widely known historian of the colonial and the New South, Bruce had grown up in Charlotte County, Virginia, and his life bridged the Old and the New South. His brother-in-law was the popular novelist Thomas Nelson Page; his father had owned a five-thousand-acre tobacco plantation and more than five hundred slaves; his uncle served as the Confederacy's secretary of war. Bruce was not an insular southerner. He had the best formal education available to Gilded Age Americans. He was a University of Virginia graduate, went to Harvard Law School, worked for a time as a Baltimore lawyer, grew tired quickly of the legal profession, and in 1887 joined a brother to manage the Richmond, Virginia, Vulcan Iron Works. An uncle headed one of Birmingham, Alabama's new iron and steel mills, a firm later absorbed by the United States Steel Corporation. Posing as a "traveler," Bruce published a series of articles in the New York *Evening Post* in 1884 that told northern readers that Virginia blacks in their "social, economic, and sanitary ways" were "much superior to . . . the lowest class of those who in our principal [northern] cities work in the unwholesome atmosphere of factories." He turned the articles into a book the following year, which several northern publishers, unhappy with its arguments, rejected. After reworking it, Bruce had the book accepted by the New York publisher G. P. Putnam. It appeared in the popular series "Questions of the Day," surrounded by volumes whose authors included the English social and political theorists Walter Bagehot and Thorold Rogers, the *grande dame* of New York City philanthropists Josephine Shaw Lowell, the skillful advocate of high tariffs F. W. Taussig, the highly regarded political economist David A. Wells, and the aristocratic New York politician and civic reformer Theodore Roosevelt. R. L. Dugdale's influential *The Jukes: A Study in Crime, Pauperism, Disease, and Heredity* also appeared first in this same series. Bruce, whose slim volume served as perhaps the most important connecting link between the "popular" views of Afro-American "decline" common in the 1880s and the detailed "scientific" works published between 1890 and the First World War, warned readers that "the picture drawn will, no doubt, seem gloomy and repelling in its moral aspects." But he had examined southeastern Virginia's blacks "impartially and dispassionately" to learn how they lived when free of "any influence except those that emanate from themselves."[7]

Its first and second chapters ("Parent and Child" and "Husband and Wife") made the volume's central theme clear: blacks could not manage for themselves, and emancipation had caused a severe and increasingly menacing deterioration in their social and moral condition. Unaware of the difference "between a virtue and a vice," slave parents could not instruct "their children in the simplest moral principles." But "the discipline of slavery" was "advantageous in a repressive way to the child, selfish and ruthless as it was too often." Emancipation ended that repression. Whites ceased to exercise traditional authority. Black parental authority could not replace "the discipline . . . enforced by the slave holder," because black parents merely acted "upon all the impulses of their nature." The "average" black parent was "morally obtuse and indifferent, and at times even openly and unreservedly licentious." Their children had "come into the world by the operation of an instinct." Parents did not "foster" chastity among their daughters. "The truth is," Bruce explained, "that the only serious consequence is physical, there being unhappily no stern sentiment even in her immediate family to condemn her." Sexual behavior often required delicate "Victorian" prose but not for Bruce: "the plantation negro is as much a child of nature now, however civilizing the influences that surround him, as if he had just been transported from the shores of his original continent"; the ex-slave saw "no immorality in doing what nature prompts him to do." "Insensibility and want of control" characterized sexual relations "to a very remarkable degree, for the procreative instinct being the most passionate that nature has implanted in his body, it is unscrupulous in proportion." Slavery had not "moderate[d] this instinct." Only settled family life was a "fortification against promiscuous intercourse." Slaves had not known "wholesome" family life: "Marriage under the old regime was very like unlawful cohabitation under the new, only that the master, by the power he had, compelled the nominal husband and wife to live together." Slavery had therefore made "true marriage impossible."

Emancipation loosened "African" impulses. "Lasciviousness," Bruce said, "has done more than all the other vices of the plantation negro united to degrade the character of their social life since' they were invested with citizenship." "The truth is," he went on, "that neither the men nor the women as a mass look upon lasciviousness as impurity. . . . Marriage, however solemnly contracted and however public the religious ceremony sanctioning it, does not hamper the sexual liberties of either of the parties." Bruce especially inveighed against black clergymen (they "offend against the sacredness of their own marriages") and black women who had fewer and fewer contacts with whites and therefore were worse in their ways than the black men. Black women "really mold[ed] the institution of marriages among the plantation negroes; to them its present degradation is chiefly ascribable." The black woman, after all, was "altogether removed . . . from any repressive influence which the whites might exercise over her on close association." (A later chapter dealing with "negro crime" told that the black male found "something strangely alluring and seductive . . . in the appearance of a white woman" because of the "wantonness of the women of his own race." That black women failed to complain of being raped by *black* men counted as "strong proof of the sexual laxness of plantation women as a class.")

These and similar judgments bolstered larger themes than the familial and sexual behavior of plantation blacks. A commentary on all Afro-Americans, Bruce's book argued that "their original spirit as a race has not been modified." The "same weaknesses" were found in "the delegate who sits in the legislature, the teacher who has graduated from college, the preacher who has studied the Bible . . . and the common laborer who toils from morning until night with his hoe and spade." Differences existed in physical stature, not in "natural temperament" or "moral dispositions." Bruce did not believe that American blacks had remained the same over more than two centuries. They had retrogressed after 1865 so that the "character" of the ex-slave's child "approximates . . . more closely to the original African type than the character of their fathers who once were slaves." And "the further development of these traits means the further departure of the negroes from the standards of the Anglo-Saxon." Adult blacks shared with white *children* "a common immaturity of nature." Few "essential differences" distinguished "a colored parent and his children." Blacks of different generations shared "the same dullness of the power of retrospection and [the] same lack of foresight. Age seems to bring the negro no keener sense of the solemn mystery of life. . . . It invests him with little of that dignity which ennobles gray hairs, feeble limbs, and wrinkled faces. . . . As long as life itself lasts, he retains the spirit of childhood." "As a race," said this son of the Old and the New South, "blacks bear the same moral relation to the Caucasian as a child does to an adult." Unobservant and sentimental whites could make no more serious error than to view the Afro-American as "merely a white man in disposition whom the Creator has endowed with a black skin."

Bruce drew logical conclusions. The abolition of slavery cut the black off from "the spirit of white society" and therefore gave "greater vigor" to his "distinctive social habits." That meant "intellectual reversion" and "further moral decadence." Bruce predicted that "with the lapse of years" and further separation from the "tradition of slavery" their "spirit of subservience which they still feel in their association with the ruling class" would decline and that "disorders" would increase. Marriage and family life promised to deteriorate still further, so that "in a few generations formal and legal marriages will be less frequent than . . . now, and the promiscuous intercourse between the sexes will grow more open and unreserved." Such were the consequences of emancipation and the removal of blacks from direct social control by upper-class whites. Bruce advocated harsh remedies. Immediate disfranchisement was essential to prevent "anarchy and barbarism." He even urged that blacks be deported from the United

States, "so suddenly as to wholly blight, for a time, the material
interests of the South." He preferred the South "to be relegated
to its primeval condition" and then "settled again exclusively by
a white population, just as if it were virgin territory."[8]

Public responses to Bruce's book show that many readers—
prominent and well-bred Americans among them—did not view
him as a southern "extremist" voicing an isolated view but rather
as a social analyst articulating a welcome perspective. That is one
reason his book has so much importance to the social historian.
Reactions to it penetrate the "public" mind. The volume did not
sell well, but the quality of its readers more than made up for that
failure. Southern editors praised it with enthusiasm, and so did
northerners who felt it a detached, objective, and informative
work. *Popular Science Monthly* said the book would "dispel any
too ideal view of the black race which the reader may hold." The
Princetonian found it "unprejudiced and impartial," "a book
every American should read." So did the Boston *Daily Advertiser*,
which described Bruce's methods as "impersonal as a scientist's
analysis of some Antediluvian animal." The same newspaper called
Bruce "an intelligent Southerner . . . apparently free of prejudice"
and agreed that "freedom, instead of bettering" the black, had
"perverted him." "Offered freedom," the ex-slave had "accepted
license." "The struggle to free the negro," said the Philadelphia
Evening News, had ended "a failure." And the Hartford *Times*
cheered a volume that accurately portrayed "the shiftless, tumble-
down, animal, good-for-nothing life of most of these people in the
rural parts of the South." Individuals with high reputations
praised Bruce, too. The influential racial Darwinist Frederick L.
Hoffman, who commended Tucker, called Bruce's book "an
admirable little work." Bruce, according to the immigrant statis-
tician, had "exceptional opportunities for observation" and "few"
writing on the blacks "so thoroughly grasped the intricate details
of their subject." Personal letters of congratulations also reached
Bruce. One came from the northern literary lion and "Liberal
Republican" editor George William Curtis. Two others bore the
signature of Jefferson Davis and Grover Cleveland.[9]

A year after Bruce published his influential work, the First
Mohonk Conference on the Negro Question took place. Delegates
to it defined the modern "Negro Problem," rooting it within the
"black family." No more prestigious group of northern and southern whites had come together to discuss the Afro-American condition since the Civil War than those gathered in upstate New

York. The delegate roster included a former United States president, Rutherford B. Hayes; the southern-born secretary of the Board of Missions for Freedom of the Presbyterian Church; the founder of the Hampton Institute, Samuel Armstrong; the editor of the Cleveland *Leader* (a newspaper secretly purchased in the 1870s by John D. Rockefeller); the presidents of Biddle University, Tougaloo College, Eastman College, Swarthmore College, and Cornell University; the editor of the *Christian Union*, Lyman Abbott; the editor of the *Christian Advocate*; Amory D. Mayo, then working for the United States Bureau of Education; and William T. Harris, then the United States Commissioner of Education. Some who had lived and worked among the southern blacks just after their emancipation were there, too: the former South Carolina Yankee schoolteachers Elizabeth Botume and Edna Cheney, the wartime military Superintendent of Freedmen in the Mississippi Valley John Eaton, the former South Carolina slaveholder and Sea Island clergyman (then Rector of the Brooklyn Holy Trinity Church) Charles Hall, and Albion W. Tourgee. Not a single black attended the conference.

These whites pressed for expanded industrial education as well as "persistent self-training in morality" among southern blacks. "The Christian home," said the main conference resolution, "is the civilizer. Ultimately, in the homes of the colored people the problem of the colored race will be settled. . . . The one-room cabin is the social curse of the Negro race, as is the reservation tepee that of the Indian, and the overcrowded tenement-room [that] of our city slums." With rare but important exceptions, speaker after speaker blamed the blacks' difficulties on the blacks themselves. Their lack of restraint and high "culture" doomed even their well-intentioned efforts at self-improvement. Nothing more greatly concerned the delegates than the "moral" condition of the ex-slaves. Their worries rested on articulate racial beliefs and class fears. Some spoke in purely racial terms. "The negro is back in the iron age," said Samuel Armstrong; "the white race is in its golden age." The Presbyterian cleric R. H. Allen pleaded similarly: "We as a race have had two thousand years the start of these people. Give the negro a white man's chance. . . . Remember from whence these people came." "There was not a legal marriage among them for two hundred and sixty years," said Allen, "and of course they had low ideas of marriage and the sacredness of the family relation." The ex-slaves "possessed absolutely nothing" because "slavery had dwarfed their manhood, physically and morally" so that "darkness covered their habitations, and 'gross darkness the people.'" A. D. Mayo disagreed. Slavery had "protected the negro from his lower self." "A pagan savage" had experienced "a brief period of tutelage" because slavery had brought contact with the white "upper strata." Emancipation had ended such ties so that "order, decency, industry . . . [and the] common moralities of every-day life" could no longer be "enforced." Mayo felt it essential for "the Anglo-Saxon to assert his superiority. For lack of this, the vagrant class has been virtually at large, like a plague of frogs and lice all over the land." William T. Harris spoke similarly. Enslavement had taught blacks much "about industry but only a little about the accumulation of property," and that worried the distinguished educator. "All civilized races," he said, "have learned the Roman idea of private property, and blacks had to be taught to make "what are called paying investments." Emancipation, however, had made such education difficult and severed "that community of property and consequently [that] community of interest." A dangerous condition resulted: "There is going on an emancipation in feelings and modes of thinking" which assured "a reversion to the former low state of spiritual life." Schooling might check the process of decay, but the country's leading neo-Hegelian remained worried about the "dangerous classes," hoping that successful schooling would allay "the dangers that threatens us from illiterate white people and especially from illiterate black people." A former Virginia slaveholder then heading a District of Columbia church was much less optimistic. "I believe," he said, "there is such a thing as entailed sin, passing down from father to son by the law of heredity. . . . The negro to-day is the product of his sad and dismal past." His being carried "the same blood" as that of "wild, naked . . . man-eating savages." "He has no history," said the cleric, "and never has been a history-maker."

The novelist Albion W. Tourgee tried but failed to puncture the mythic beliefs that so completely dominated the Mohonk proceedings. Years before, Tourgee had vigorously disputed popular views that had made of the ex-slave "a strange compound of gnome and satyr" and "the great ethnological clown." "We have sought testimony *about* the negro," Tourgee told the Mohonk delegates, "from his avowed friends and confessed enemies, and think we shall obtain the truth by 'splitting the difference between them.'" Tourgee did not idealize the ex-slaves but denied the retrogressionist assumptions held by most of the Mohonk delegates. Afro-American labor had helped build the nation's material foundations, and after emancipation poor ex-slaves had "paid a larger proportion of their income for charitable and religious purposes than any people known to history." The Afro-American was not "a mere *appendage* of the white race" but "an actual and meritorious creditor of American civilization." Andrew White, then the president of Cornell University, silenced Tourgee and urged that the conferees return to "the true line of our deliberations." "How," he asked, "shall the evolution of a better future for the colored race be secured while the peace and prosperity of the white race shall remain unharmed? . . . We know that we have been miserable sinners; let us press forward, and see if the future cannot be made to atone for the past. . . . I believe . . . that there is a great Negro Problem." White had missed Tourgee's essential argument. His final sentence made that clear. And he and most of the other delegates reinforced the popular myth that had made of late-nineteenth-century Afro-Americans nothing more than the bearers of "incurable immorality." The strains in American racial thought they reflected and helped shape were those of comfortable and well-educated Americans, not lower-class northern or southern whites. (Their racial beliefs still await careful study.) These elite experts agreed that the absence of high culture and "restraining" norms among Afro-Americans doomed the Afro-American family, held back Afro-American material development, and explained the "Negro Problem." The poor always reveled in abandon and improvidence. That was what made them poor. It was even worse among the black poor, and most blacks were poor.[10]

Retrogressionist ideology affected far more than the definition of the late-nineteenth- and early-twentieth-century "Negro Problem." It had a lasting influence on the conceptualization of the Afro-American historical experience. Retrogressionist ideology, not merely a free-floating racism, became the underlying model for studying "American Negro Slavery" among more than two generations of academic historians, a much more important fact than the praise Bruce received from the former president of the Confederate States of America and the former president of the United States of America. The "Negro Problem" had a "past" as well as a "present" and a "future."

The racial and social myth of Afro-American "retrogression" coincided in time with the early professionalization of historical writing and became reified in monographic historical writings about black enslavement in premodern America. Ulrich Bonnell Phillips, whose academic writings on slavery and on the South delved deeply into source materials and set the dominant pattern for four decades of early-twentieth-century historical scholarship, was a "retrogressionist." That belief affected his conception of the Afro-American historical experience. "A century or two ago," explained Phillips in 1904, "the negroes were savages in the wilds of Africa. . . . Those who were brought to America, and their descendants, have acquired a certain amount of civilization . . . in very large measure the result of their association with civilized white people." Phillips paraphrased Bruce: "Several keen-sighted students have already detected a tendency of the negroes, where segregated in the black belt, to lapse back toward barbarism. Of course, if its prevention is possible, such retrogression must not be allowed to continue." Early in his career (and in greater detail in his later and more substantial writings) Phillips, living in the Age of Jane Addams, sought to show that slaveowners ("the better element of the white people") "did what we call, in the modern phrase, social settlement work." The "patriarchal feature" of Anglo-American enslavement was not the product of the plantation system but served a racial function made "necessary" because "the average negro has many of the characteristics of a child, and must be guided and governed, and often guarded against himself, by a sympathetic hand." Dominance by well-bred, upper-class whites—not "whites" but "the planter and his wife and children and his neighbors"—was essential "for example and precept among the negroes." Phillips wrote in 1905: "It is mistaken to apply the general philosophy of slavery to the American situation without very serious modification. A slave among the Greeks or Romans was generally a relatively civilized person, whose voluntary labor would have been far more productive than his labor under compulsion. But the negro slave was a negro first, last and always, and a slave incidentally." So began an influential strain in American historical writing that would view enslavement as beneficial to Africans and their Afro-American descendants and that would define "treatment" as the essential question for historical study. The study of slave belief and behavior became the study of their treatment by owners.[11]

Retrogressionist ideology did much more than provide an underpinning for the disfranchisement of American blacks and for their isolation from the mainstream of the national culture. It supplied a way of reinterpreting the entire Afro-American experience so that enslavement became essential to "civilization" and emancipation became evidence of the essential social and moral incapacities of the Afro-American descendants of African slaves. Americans soon would learn about the social and moral collapse of the half-savage/half-infant ex-slave. "A black skin," explained John Burgess in *Reconstruction and the Constitution*, "means membership in a race of men which has never of itself succeeded in subjecting passion to reason, has never, therefore, created any civilization of any kind." Granting the suffrage to the former slaves "simply establish[ed] barbarism in power over civilization." James Ford Rhodes put it differently. Suffrage meant that blacks "simply acted out their nature" and were "not to blame . . . What idea could barbarism thrust into slavery obtain of the rights of property?"[12]

Sentimental white southern chroniclers like Myrta Lockett Avery soon would write, in such books as *Dixie After the War*, that "the negro quarters on the Southern plantation" had been "the social settlements for Africans in America" and that the "strange and curious race-madness of the American Republic" had by emancipation taken "a child-race out of a warm cradle." White dialect writers fed this fantasy, which soon became the dominant version of the Afro-American historical experience. Harry Stillwell Edward's story " 'Ole Miss' and Sweetheart" had as a central character an "old mammy [who] lives out her years in sight of the grave of her mistress, where she may better preserve the memory of happier days." In Thomas Nelson Page's "Marse Chan," the loyal house servant Old Sam told the reader, "Dem was de good ole times, marster—de bes' Sam ever seen." (Page himself told readers of *McClure's Magazine* in 1904 that "the negro has retrograded as a workman.") And the poetess Howard Weeden had an old black say in *Bandanna Ballads*:

> I ought to think 'bout Canaan, but
> It's Ole Times crowds my mind,
> An' maybe when I gits to Heaben
> It's Ole Times dat I'll find.

This from a trusted ex-slave, but then there always remained the "savage" black:

> Original in act and thought,
> Because unlearned and untaught.

So wrote Irwin Russell in a poem appropriately entitled "Christmas Night in the Quarters."[13]

Retrogressionist beliefs saturated the early twentieth-century popular media as well as historical writing and academic social science. "Past" and "present" came together to predict a gloomy twentieth-century "future" for the descendants of enslaved Afro-Americans. Such beliefs disclose why so little about Afro-American familial beliefs and behavior was understood by late-nineteenth-century northern and southern whites and why in the immediate decades preceding the great twentieth-century migration from the South to the North black capacities to adapt to changing external circumstances were frozen in a racial ice that has still to melt fully. Enslavement had not been the setting in which Africans became Afro-Americans. Instead, slaveowners had policed unchanging "Africans." Emancipation followed by Yankee paternalism had been even more futile. The southern black was in a worse social and moral condition in 1900 than in 1860. Hence the modern "Negro problem," more properly defined as the "African problem." And hence the close relationship between American racial beliefs about Afro-Americans and late nineteenth-century European beliefs about colored peoples deserving imperial domination and needing social control. The Charleston *News and Courier* put it well in 1898. "Freed from the control of his owner, and wickedly put on civil equality with him," said this newspaper of the ex-slave, "his natural lawlessness and savagery were asserted. . . . Everybody knows that when freed from the compelling influence of the white man he reverts by a law of nature to the natural barbarism in which he was created in the jungles of Africa."[14]

Notes

PART ONE: *The Birthpangs of a World*

Chapter 1: Send Me Some of the Children's Hair

1. Robert S. Starobin, ed., *Blacks in Bondage: Letters from American Slaves* (1974), 87–92, 105.
2. J. H. Croushore, D. M. Potter, eds., John deForest, *A Union Officer in the Reconstruction* (1948), 343.
3. H. L. Swint, ed., *Dear Ones at Home: Letters from the Contraband Camps* (1966), 123–24, 242–43.
4. Albion W. Tourgee, "The South as a Field for Fiction," *Forum*, VI (December 1888), 408–10.
5. T. B. Bottomore, *Sociology: A Guide to Problems and Literature* (1971), 181.
6. See, for examples, Walter L. Fleming, *Civil War and Reconstruction in Alabama* (1905), 271, 381, 523, 763–64; Arthur W. Calhoun, *Social History of the American Family*, III (1917–9), 58–59; Edward B. Reuter, *The American Race Problem* (1938), 204; Francis Simkins and Robert Woody, *South Carolina During Reconstruction* (1932), 331, 359–60.
7. E. Franklin Frazier, *Negro Family in Chicago* (1932), 33–34; *id., Negro Family in the United States* (1939), 89, 95–98; *id., Negro in the United States* (1949), 313, 627. In his influential 1939 study and in his later works, Frazier shifted significantly from what he had written about the slaves in 1930. "Social interaction," he insisted then, "created a moral order in which the lives of the whites and Negroes were intertwined. At the same time the Negroes lived in a little society of their own which represented some degree of moral autonomy." This emphasis disappeared in Frazier's later works. See E. Franklin Frazier, "The Negro Slave Family," *Journal of Negro History*, XV (April 1930), 198–259.
8. Montgomery County, Virginia, manuscript census, 1866, volume 137; York County, Virginia, manuscript census, 1865, volume 511; Princess Anne County, Virginia, manuscript census, 1866, volume 511; Rockbridge County, Virginia, Marriage Register, volume 271; Nelson County, Virginia, Marriage Register, volume 283; Gooch-

land County, Virginia, Marriage Register, volume 236; Louisa
County, Virginia, Marriage Register, volume 280; Virginia Freedmen's Bureau Mss., Record Group 105, National Archives.

9. Such statistical information has many limitations. The data available, for example, tell very little about many of the customary
relations regulating behavior between household members, including such matters as sexual behavior, child-rearing practices,
sibling relations, the reckoning of descent, and the roles of adult
men and women within families. These materials have yet another limitation. The *form* in which historical evidence is recorded greatly affects how historians later use such information.
The marriage registers and the military population censuses examined here recorded information dealing only with separate
black households. It therefore revealed little about kin connections between households and about other aspects of the community structure. Such sources show the importance of the nuclear
household among the emancipated slaves but in no way indicate
the importance of this domestic arrangement relative to other
arrangements. Without such information, it is misleading to
extrapolate seeming "similarities" (or "differences") between white
and black (or slave and free) households, and it is just as erroneous
to suggest that such different populations attached similar meanings and importance to a particular type of domestic arrangement.

10. York blacks mostly farmed and fished, growing potatoes and corn
and laboring as oyster fishermen. Princess Anne blacks shared the
Dismal Swamp with their North Carolina neighbors, but enough
arable land allowed some to grow corn, potatoes, and oats and to
tend livestock. Montgomery County blacks lived in western Virginia and grew mostly tobacco. The three populations differed
in other ways. In the 1850s, Montgomery's slave population had
increased, while York's slave population declined. Princess Anne's
slave and free population had fallen sharply between 1830 and
1840 but then stabilized. In 1860, nine in ten of the 8354 blacks
in these three counties were slaves. The proportion of blacks to
whites varied; about one in five Montgomery residents was black,
about two in five Princess Anne residents, and just over one in
two York residents. Slaveholding patterns also differed. Princess
Anne County had few plantations. Small units of ownership were
nearly as common among Montgomery slaves, but about one in
three lived on units of twenty or more slaves. In York County,
two in five slaves lived on units of twenty or more slaves.

11. Only the York blacks seem directly involved in the Civil War.
The area fell early to the Union Army and became a haven
for runaways. Just where they came from remains unknown, but

their flow made for other differences between the York and other blacks. York had fewer young people, and adult men and women differed greatly in age.

12. Two elderly Montgomery black farmers doubled as clergymen, but not another Montgomery black had a high-status occupation. Although the York men had more diverse occupations, significant similarities existed between them and the Montgomery men. Many "oyster farmers," the absence of servants, and a relatively large percentage of laborers explained essential differences. There also was a scattering of wartime soldiers and sailors, a few shopkeepers and clerks, a schoolteacher, and a physician.

13. Deficient enumeration procedures prevent us from knowing the exact interior composition of these households, and nothing can be learned about kin connections between immediate households. All-black censuses, moreover, do not reveal how many single people or whole families lived in white households. The enumerators furthermore failed to distinguish between boarders and relatives. In my estimate of "single" persons, I have assumed that all persons not members of an immediate nuclear family are "single" and living alone. That assumption exaggerates the number of "single" persons, including among them adopted children who retained original family names, husbands and wives with different surnames, consanguinal and affinal kin, and unrelated boarders. Still, among the Montgomery blacks less than 13 percent of men and less than 11 percent of women could have been "single." Some of these must have resided with whites. Two-thirds of the seventy-three "single" females aged ten to twenty-nine worked as servants, and many among them probably lived with white families. Using the same method, I estimate that about 10 percent of Princess Anne blacks were "single."

14. Nelson County lay between Charlottesville and Lynchburg, and Rockbridge County was just to its west. Goochland and Louisa counties were between Richmond and Charlottesville. Goochland, Louisa, and Rockbridge had had a "surplus" of adult male slaves, but Nelson slave men and women had nearly balanced each other. Slave ownership patterns differed in these places. Three of four Rockbridge slaves had lived on units of fewer than twenty slaves, but in Nelson County extensive tobacco farming meant that three of five slaves lived on units of twenty or more slaves. That percentage was just as high among the Louisa slaves. It was somewhat lower among the Goochland slaves, but three in ten Goochland slaves had lived with fifty or more slaves. Goochland was one of Virginia's important plantation counties. The four counties differed in other ways. Goochland had more free blacks than the

other three places. Nelson whites and blacks nearly balanced each other in number. Rockbridge blacks were less than one-fourth of that county's population. Goochland and Louisa counties were predominantly black in population. Nearly two-thirds of the 1860 residents were blacks and at least nine in ten of the blacks were slaves.

15. E. Franklin Frazier, *Negro in the United States,* 308–9.

16. The manuscript marriage registers and "Negro cohabitation certificates" for the seventeen North Carolina counties are filed separately by county at the North Carolina Department of Archives and History, Raleigh, North Carolina. I am indebted to C. F. W. Coker and his staff for making these and other materials there available to me. Other statistics used to analyze the 1866 North Carolina marriage registers—unless otherwise noted—are drawn from the 1860 and 1870 federal censuses of population and agriculture.

   Registration procedures and record-keeping varied among the seventeen counties, and what was recorded or retained in some counties appears more complete than for other counties. A Beaufort county clerk used as the register a volume that had served a similar purpose for antebellum white Beaufort marriages, squeezing the names of black men and women onto pages where space remained unfilled with white names. That method does not increase confidence in the exactness or completeness of the Beaufort register. Different problems limit the Bertie, Washington, Halifax, and Edgecombe registers and certificates. These counties did not keep registration books. Bertie and Washington clerks retained scattered lists of names or slips of paper containing the name of a single *couple.* Bertie and Washington justices of the peace apparently forwarded these slips and sheets of paper to the County Clerk, who filed them but did not transcribe them into a registration book. Halifax and Edgecombe officials also used informal lists but combined them with special printed forms that supplemented handwritten "certificates of cohabitation." Hundreds of printed certificates with proper names and dates written in are found in the Edgecombe records.

17. At about the same time as these North Carolina blacks registered marriages, the Rockbridge and Nelson County, Virginia, ex-slaves also reported the length of their marriages to Freedmen's Bureau officers. A significant difference existed in the two methods of registration: the Virginia blacks dealt with northern whites, but the North Carolina blacks registered their unions with local southern whites. If either the Virginia or the North Carolina blacks exaggerated in their reports or the Virginia Bureau and local North Carolina white officials misrepresented information given

them by blacks, serious discrepancies should exist in the two sets of records. They do not. The pattern in the North Carolina registers confirms what the two Virginia registers revealed.

18. Data on these similarities and differences between the counties draw again from the published 1860, 1870, and 1880 federal censuses of population and agriculture. A good summary of the social and economic differences between the three major North Carolina regions is Joseph C. Sitterson, *Secession Movement in North Carolina* (1939), 1–15. But the basic social history of North Carolina—and one of the finest studies in American social history—is Guion G. Johnson, *Ante-bellum North Carolina: A Social History* (1937). On North Carolina free blacks, see the pioneering study by John Hope Franklin, *Free Negro in North Carolina, 1790–1860* (1943). The data on free black property ownership in Table 9, page 43, are drawn from this volume, pp. 230–34.

19. About one in four lived on units of less than ten slaves. In five of the seventeen counties with surviving registers, the number of such ownership units ranged from three in ten to four in ten. Except for the Washington and New Hanover slaves, in all the *nonplantation* counties fewer than half lived on units of twenty or more slaves.

20. See, for examples, Charlotte McKay, "Domestic Relations of the Freedmen," Poplar Springs, Va., 9 April 1866, *National Freedman*, II (May 1866), 143–45; Joseph Warren, Vicksburg, 18 May 1864, to John Eaton, *Extracts from Reports of Superintendents, first series* (1864), 39–40; J. Chandler Gregg, *Life in the Army in the Departments of Virginia and the Gulf, Including Observations in New Orleans* (1868), 204, 220; Peter Kolchin, *First Freedom: The Responses of Alabama Blacks to Emancipation and Reconstruction* (1972), 60.

21. We can tell this by comparing the slave and free-black models available to slaves in the seventeen North Carolina counties. If we assume that all adult free blacks were married, except for the Halifax blacks (and there is reason to suspect the completeness of the Halifax marriage register), their number did not exceed the number of those slave couples who registered marriages at least five years old in 1866. In Edgecombe, Johnston, Lincoln, and Warren counties, at least ten times as many slave couples as free blacks knew one another as husband and wife. Except in Halifax, New Hanover, and Robeson counties, moreover, the free blacks themselves appeared to be in an overwhelmingly disadvantaged material condition (Table 9, page 43).

22. John Eaton, *Grant, Lincoln, and the Freedmen* (1907), 33–36; Miss L. Humphrey, Camp Fiske, Tenn., 20 Aug. 1863, to the editor, *American Missionary*, VIII (October 1863), 235–36.

23. Blacks also registered marriages in Arkansas, northern Louisiana, and western Tennessee. See for examples of such registrations, John Eaton, *Report of the General Superintendent of Freedmen, Department of the Tennessee and State of Arkansas* (1864), 89–94; *New York Evening Post*, n.d., reprinted in *Littell's Living Age*, 84 (March 1865), 568–70; Miss Geist, Vicksburg, 18 Oct. 1864, to the editor, *Freedmen's Bulletin*, I (November 1864), 49; David Todd, Pine Bluff, 3 Dec. 1864, to the editor, *American Missionary*, IX (February 1865), 39–40; Laura Haviland, *A Women's Life-work* (1882), 267; Joseph Warren, "Report on Visit to Natchez," c. August 1864, Dept. of Freedmen, RG 105, NA; report of Thomas Calahan, *Extracts from Reports of Superintendents of Freedmen, first series* (1864), 39–40.

24. Bound Volumes of Marriage Registers, 1864–1865, Davis Bend, Natchez, and Vicksburg, Mississippi, Mississippi Freedmen's Bureau Manuscripts, volumes 43, 44, and 45, Record Group 105, National Archives.

25. Six blacks (two men and four women) married whites.

26. *New York Evening Post*, n.d., reprinted in *Littell's Living Age*, 84 (March 1865), 568–70.

27. Sixty-eight percent of male registrants and 58 percent of female registrants declared both parents black. Age-specific rates for males ranged from 65 percent (men aged thirty to thirty-nine) to 72 percent (men fifty and older) and for females from 56 percent (females aged fifteen to twenty-nine) to 63 percent (females aged forty to forty-nine). The combined registers hide significant differences between the three registers. Natchez men and women recorded the highest percentage listing both parents as black. Vicksburg and Davis Bend women reported the lowest percentages. Nearly two-thirds of Natchez women (64 percent) claimed two black parents, but the percentage was lower among Vicksburg (54 percent) and especially among Davis Bend (49 percent) women. No explanation has been found for these differences.

28. Northern white observers were surprised that so many of the registrants described themselves as "black." A Natchez army officer believed their claim "below the truth," saying that the registrants were unwilling "to own any . . . mixture of blood which is not obvious." "They are already beginning," asserted John Eaton, "to be ashamed of mixture which was formerly a matter of pride." Eaton may have exaggerated the change in attitude. Shipped from Tennessee to Mississippi before the war, an ex-slave remembered an elderly black woman beating her and calling her "a God damned yellow bitch," and Dora Frank, whose mother's owner was her father, said that the other Mississippi slave children "used

to chase me 'round an' holler at me, 'Old Yallow Nigger.' Dey didn't treat me good, neither." Eaton, *Report of General Superintendent . . . 1864*, 89–94; *New York Evening Post*, n.d., reprinted in *Littell's Living Age*, 84 (March 1865), 568–70; *Unwritten History of Slavery (Fisk)*, 133–37; *American Slave, Mississippi Narratives*, VII, 49–55.

29. Although much physical movement occurred among Mississippi slaves during the Civil War, much nevertheless can be learned about the prior status of the men and women registering antebellum marriages in 1864 and 1865. On registering a marriage, the husband and wife each gave a residence separately. We cannot tell whether an 1864–1865 residence differed from that before 1861, but much else was revealed by the residence registrants listed. Only scattered couples gave geographically separate residences, and a small fraction of the total claimed distant residences. That a few did, however, suggests that they considered these faraway places their *permanent* homes. A very small percentage of the civilian male registrants and of all females gave as their residence places a good distance from Adams and Warren counties, including Baltimore, Richmond, and Cairo, Illinois, and even Chicago and New York. Most men and women in this small group claimed the border and coastal South as their homes: New Orleans and Baton Rouge, Virginia, Maryland, North and South Carolina, Tennessee, Kentucky, and Arkansas. In all, two of five male registrants then served in the Union Army and listed a military company or regiment rather than a residence. Most probably had been Mississippi and northern Louisiana slaves, nearly all connected with the newly recruited (or impressed) federal Mississippi military units. More than half of the soldiers listed in the Natchez register, for example, belonged to the Sixth Mississippi Infantry (Colored), and all the Davis Bend soldiers registering marriages served in the Sixty Fourth Colored Infantry. Nearly all civilian men listed a local residence. The civilian Vicksburg and Natchez male registrants revealed striking residential similarities: seven of ten listed the county in which they registered a marriage. One of four Natchez civilian male registrants and one of six Vicksburg civilian male registrants resided in Louisiana places nearby. Female registrants hardly differed from these civilian males; 167 women and 161 men listed distant residences. Nearly half of these women (81) gave as residence either Tennessee, Kentucky, or Arkansas. The next largest groups came from Virginia, Maryland, and North and South Carolina (37), New Orleans and Baton Rouge (23), and Alabama and Georgia (13). A few (4) listed Missouri, and northern states claimed nine. The men reported similar distant residences: Tennessee, Kentucky, and Arkansas (37), Vir-

ginia, Maryland, and the Carolinas (30), New Orleans and Baton Rouge (18), Alabama and Georgia (9), Missouri (2), and the northern states (5).

Registrants from places nearby broke down as follows:

MALES

Vicksburg Registrants, 856: Vicksburg and Warren County (69 percent), Louisiana (16 percent), other Mississippi counties (8 percent), other and illegible (7 percent).

Natchez Registrants, 1598: Natchez and Adams County (69 percent), Louisiana (24 percent), other Mississippi counties (5 percent), other and illegible (2 percent).

FEMALES

Vicksburg Registrants, 2367: Vicksburg and Warren County (61 percent), Louisiana (15 percent), other Mississippi counties (18 percent), other and illegible (6 percent).

Natchez Registrants, 1900: Natchez and Adams County (68 percent), Louisiana (23 percent), other Mississippi counties (6 percent), other and illegible (3 percent).

30. The percentage of slaves owned in units of twenty or more slaves ranged from three in four (Warren County) to nearly nine in ten (Concordia Parish). A high percentage were owned in units of fifty or more slaves: Warren (46 percent), Adams (62 percent), and Concordia (78 percent).

See Vernon Wharton, *The Negro in Mississippi, 1865–1900* (1947), 39–42, and Clement Eaton, *The Growth of Southern Civilization, 1790–1860* (1961), 43.

31. Davis Bend had the fewest registrants and proportionately the oldest in the three groups. Two in five Davis Bend registrants were at least fifty years old. In Vicksburg, 63 percent of women and 44 percent of men were under thirty.

32. Overall, in three of five marriages registered one or both of the registrants had experienced an earlier terminated marriage. The percentages varied as follows: Natchez, 49 percent; Vicksburg, 65 percent; and Davis Bend, 77 percent. These earlier unions include marriages ended by death. One in four registered marriages included an earlier marriage ended by force, and the percentages again varied by place of registration: Natchez, 16 percent; Vicksburg, 39 percent; and Davis Bend, 31.5 percent. All these estimates assume that all registrants were renewing slave marriages. Many were marrying for the first time, but their number cannot be determined from the available data.

33. There were variations in what Davis Bend, Natchez, and Vicksburg registrants aged forty and older reported. Vicksburg and

Davis Bend registrants reported many more earlier marriages broken by force than did Natchez registrants.

34. Thomas Calahan quoted in Joseph Warren, 18 May 1864, to John Eaton, printed in *Extracts from Reports of Superintendents*, first series, ed. J. Warren (1864), 39–40; Eaton, *Report of General Superintendent . . .* (1864), 89–94; Joseph Warren, Memphis, 10 April 1865, to John F. Perry, printed in *Reports Related to Colored Schools in Mississippi, Arkansas, and West Tennessee, April 1865*, ed. J. Warren (1865), 14–15.

35. Thomas W. Knox, *Camp-fire and Cotton-Field* (1865), 433–35; Laura Haviland, *A Woman's Life-work* (1882), 288–89; Elkanah Beard, Vicksburg, 6 Jan. 1865, to J. W. Evans, *Freedmen's Friend*, I (February 1865), 32; A. Eberhart, Vicksburg, 1 Feb. 1864, to C. H. Fowler, State of Mississippi files, American Missionary Association Archives; Samuel Thomas, "Report," April 1864, *Extracts from Reports of Superintendents of Freedmen*, ed. J. Warren, first series (1864), 9; A. L. Mitchell, Vicksburg, 31 May 1864, to John Eaton, *Extracts from Reports of Superintendents*, ed. J. Warren, second series, June 1864, 21–22.

36. S. G. Wright, Natchez, 1, 4, 1–7, April, 23 May 1864, to George Whipple; An Officer of the U.S.A., Natchez, n.d., to ———, SGW and others, Natchez, 1 April 1864, to General Tuttle, manuscript letters in American Missionary Association Archives; unsigned Natchez dispatch, 8 April 1864, *New York Tribune*, 30 April 1864; W. L. Marsh, Vicksburg, 18 Aug. 1864, to C. C. Leigh, and Lydia Daggett, Natchez, n.d., to the editor, *Commonwealth*, n.d., reprinted in *Freedmen's Advocate*, I (October 1864), 33–36; Joseph Warren, Vicksburg, 16 April 1864, to John Eaton, printed in *Extracts from Reports of Superintendents of Freedmen*, ed. J. Warren, first series (1864), 47–49.

37. "Memphis Riots and Massacres," 39 Congress, First Session, *House of Representatives Report 101, 1865–1866* (1866), *passim*.

38. American Freedmen's Inquiry Commission, 1863, Letters Received, Office of the Adjutant General, Main Series, 1861–1870, file 7, pp. 20–33, 82–90, Reel 201, National Archives.

39. On the limitations of this "model," see Robert Fogel and Stanley Engerman, *Time on the Cross: The Economics of American Negro Slavery*, 2 vols. (1974), and Herbert G. Gutman, *Slavery and the Numbers Game: A Critique of Time on the Cross* (1975). How this "model" continues to affect the study of the slave family can be easily illustrated. More than half a century ago, U. B. Phillips insisted that the "group sale" of slaves was common and that family breakup was rare. Such sales kept slave families together and "served doubly in comporting with scruples of conscience and

inducing to the greater contentment of slaves in their new employ." Phillips said that economic necessity and ideology encouraged owners to sustain "stable" slave families. (U. B. Phillips,
American Negro Slavery [1918], 369.) Many decades later, this
emphasis continues to influence how slave history is written. It
fits into diverse explanatory "models" that stress the power of the
slaveholding class to shape and reshape slave belief and behavior.
See, for recent examples, Eugene D. Genovese, *The World the
Slaveholders Made* (1969), 96–99, and *Roll, Jordan, Roll: The
World the Slaves Made* (1974), 70–75, 451–52; John Blassingame,
The Slave Community: Plantation Life in the Antebellum South
(1972), 80; and Fogel and Engerman, *Time on the Cross*, I, 142 and
passim.

40. Sidney W. Mintz, "History and Anthropology: A Brief Reprise,"
in Eugene D. Genovese and Stanley Engerman, eds., *Race and
Slavery in the Western Hemisphere: Quantitative Studies* (1975),
477–94.

41. S. W. Mintz, "Creating Culture in the Americas," *Columbia
Forum*, XIII (Spring 1970), 4–11, and "Toward an Afro-American
History," *Journal of World History*, XIII (1971), 317–32.

42. Philip Curtin, *The Atlantic Slave Trade: A Census* (1969), *passim;*
C. Vann Woodward, "Southern Slaves in the World of Thomas
Malthus," in CVW, *American Counterpoint: Slavery and Racism
in the North-South Dialogue* (1971), 78–106.

43. An interaction between Anglo-American slave society and Afro-
American slave culture shaped slave behavior, and an understanding of the two serves as a starting point in any analysis of slave
belief and behavior. It is important to distinguish between "society" and "culture." The anthropologists Eric Wolf and Sidney
W. Mintz and the sociologist Zygmunt Bauman have written well
on these differences. Wolf describes "culture" as "the historically
developed forms through which the members of a given society
relate to each other" and views "society" as "the element of action,
of human manoeuver within the field provided by cultural forms."
By viewing "cultural forms as defining fields for human manoeuver" and "human manoeuver" as "always pressing against
the inherent limitations of cultural forms . . . we shall have a
more dynamic manner of apprehending the real tensions of life."
Mintz puts it somewhat differently, finding in culture "a kind of
resource" and in society "a kind of arena," the distinction being
"between sets of historically available alternatives or forms on the
one hand and the societal circumstances or settings within which
these forms may be employed on the other." Bauman insists that
for analytic purposes the two—"culture" and "society"—need

discrete study to understand fully human behavior. Such behavior, "whether individual or collective, is invariably the resultant of two factors: the cognitive system as well as the goals and patterns of behavior as defined by culture systems on the one hand, and the system of real contingencies as defined by the social structure on the other." The historical study of diverse social processes requires that "both systems, as well as their interaction . . . [be] taken into consideration." Such an analytic framework makes it possible to put aside crude reductionist models and to study slave belief and behavior as much more than the response to an oppressive social circumstance and as much more than the mere reflection of "rules" imposed from "above." It allows for the study instead of the common choices made by enslaved Afro-Americans, choices shaped by the regular interaction between such "rules" and the accumulating historical experiences of enslaved men and women.

    "Foreword" by S. W. Mintz in *Afro-American Anthropology, Contemporary Perspectives*, eds. Norman E. Whitten, Jr., and John F. Szwed (1970), 1–16; Eric Wolf, quoted in Mintz, "Foreword," 9–10; Zygmunt Bauman, "Marxism and the Contemporary Theory of Culture," *Co-Existence*, V (1968), 171–98.

44. James Hugo Johnston, *Race Relations in Virginia and Miscegenation in the South, 1776–1860* (1970), 45–47; *Journal of Negro History*, XIII (1928), 90–91.

45. "Petition of Lucinda to the Legislature, 27 Nov. 1815," in Phillips, ed., *Plantation and Frontier Documents* (1909), II, 161–62; *Negro in Virginia (WPA)* (1940), 123–24.

46. Maria Perkins to Richard Perkins, n.d., printed in Phillips, *Life and Labor in the Old South* (1929), 212.

47. Abream Scriven to Dinah Jones, 1858, printed in Starobin, ed., *Blacks in Bondage*, 57.

48. R. H. Tawney, *Social History and Literature* (1950), 7–9.

Chapter 2: Because She Was My Cousin

1. In 1834, Mrs. Anne Heatly Lovell willed the Good Hope plantation to her nephew Joseph Dulles. His sister was married then to the South Carolina congressman Langdon Cheves. Their father, Joseph Dulles, had left Ireland in about 1777 and settled in Charleston to become a hardware merchant. He married Sophia Heatly and prospered, owning ten slaves in 1790 and serving later in that decade as the Charleston Commissioner of Streets and Lamps. He moved to Philadelphia in 1810 but maintained business connections with his South Carolina enterprises, and at his death in 1818 lived on Philadelphia's fashionable Walnut Street

and owned two Charleston house lots, other Charleston real estate, and 753 acres in the Colleton district. His wife was descended
from the early-eighteenth-century South Carolina Heatly family,
which had settled in what became Saint Matthew's Parish. The
younger Joseph Dulles inherited the Good Hope plantation from
his mother's sister, an enterprise that specialized in the production
of Santee, or long-staple "black-seed," cotton. I am indebted to
Mrs. Granville T. Prior, the director of the South Carolina Historical Society, for making much of this information available.
See also Samuel G. Stoney, *The Dulles Family in South Carolina*
(1955), 1–14.

2. Good Hope Plantation Birth Register, 1760–1857, mss. copy, South
   Carolina Historical Society, Charleston, S.C. I am indebted to
   Stanley Engerman for bringing this unusually important docu-
   ment to my attention.

3. Peter Laslett, *The World We Have Lost* (1965), 82–83; Pierre
   Goubert, "Legitimate Fecundity and Infant Mortality in France
   during the Eighteenth Century: A Comparison," *Daedelus*, 98
   (Spring 1968), 593–603; Moncure Conway, *Testimonies Concerning
   Slavery*, second edition (1865), 20.

4. *Alvany (a free woman of color) v. Powell*, 1 Jones Esq. 35, December 1853, printed in Helen T. Catterall, *Judicial Cases Concerning American Slavery and the Negro* (1926–37), II, 179–80. See
   M. G. Smith, "Social Structure in the British Caribbean About
   1820," *Social and Economic Studies*, I (1953), 71–72, for an opposite argument. "As property," Smith observes, "slaves were prohibited from forming legal relationships or marriages which would
   interfere with and restrict their owner's property rights." This is a
   correct statement, but it does not follow from it that "slaves lacked
   any generally accepted mode of establishing permanent mating
   relationships outside of legally recognized marriage among themselves" and that the "mating of slaves was typically unstable." An
   opposite but neglected argument is found in Melville J. Herskovits, *The Myth of the Negro Past* (1941), 139. Herskovits does not
   deny that enslavement "gave a certain instability to the marriage
   tie"; no one can deny that fact. But he realizes that "many" slaves
   "who lived out their lives on the same plantation were able to
   establish and maintain families." "It is far from certain," Herskovits added, "that undisturbed matings have not been lost sight of
   in the appeal of the more dramatic separations that did occur in
   large numbers."

5. John W. Blassingame, *The Slave Community: Plantation Life in
   the Antebellum South* (1972), 82; T. R. R. Cobb, *Law of Slavery*
   (1858), ccxix–ccxx; Toombs 1856 speech printed in A. H. Stephens,

A Constitutional View of the Late War I (1868), 641–43; *Pro-Slavery Argument* (1852), 41, 44–45; *Southern Literary Messenger,* I (1844), 329–39, 470–80; *DeBow's Review,* 28 (1860), 52.

6. For other contemporary observations about slave sexual behavior, see *Facts Concerning the Freedmen. Their Capacities, and Their Destinies. Collected and Published by the Emancipation League* (Boston, 1863), 3–12; "Interview with J. R. Roudanez," in James MacKaye, *The Mastership and Its Fruits* (1864), 4–6. See also Charles Lyell, *A Second Visit to the United States of North America* I (1849), 271–73. Lyell's wife came to know an Alabama woman who had raised "a colored girl" to be "modest and well behaved." The young slave woman became the mother of "a mulatto child." "The mistress," Lyell reported, "reproached her very severely for her misconduct, and the girl at first took the rebuke much to heart; but having gone home one day to visit her mother, a native African, she returned, saying that her parent had assured her she had done nothing wrong, and had no reason to be ashamed." Lyell felt this to be evidence of "the loose code of morality which the Africans have inherited from their parents."

7. Testimony before the American Freedmen's Inquiry Commission, 1863, file 2 (pp. 4–5), file 3 (pp. 4–7, 42–43, 63–64, 70, 85, 100–105, 125–26, 160, 223–24), file 8 (p. 28), Letters Received, Office of the Adjutant General, 1861–1870, Main Series, Rccls 200 and 201, National Archives.

8. Charles Nordhoff, "Freedmen of South Carolina," in Frank Moore, ed., *Papers of the Day #1* (1863), 21–24; Mary B. Chesnut, *A Diary from Dixie* (1949), 121–23; F. L. Olmsted, *Journey in the Back Country* (1863), 113–14, 153–55; Harriet Beecher Stowe, *Key to Uncle Tom's Cabin* (1854), 298–301; *American Slave, South Carolina Narratives,* III, iv, 208–9.

9. Peter Gaskell, *Manufacturing Population of England* (1833), quoted Margaret Hewitt, *Wives and Mothers in Victorian England* (1958), 54; Bronislaw Malinowski, "Parenthood—the Basis of Social Structure," in V. F. Calverton and Samuel D. Schmalhausen, eds., *New Generation* (1930), 129–43; *id., Sex and Repression in Savage Society* (1927), 195.

10. *Unwritten History . . . (Fisk),* 1–6, 67–69, 77–79, 123–27, 153–54; *American Slave, Texas Narratives,* IV, i, 62–65, *South Carolina Narratives,* II, ii, 200–203; 1854 diary notation quoted in Bobby Frank Jones, "A Cultural Middle Passage: Slave Marriage and Family in the Antebellum South," unpublished Ph.D. dissertation, University of North Carolina, 1965, 169; Lunsford Lane, *Narrative of Lunsford Lane* (1842), 11; Nordhoff, "Freedmen of the South," in Frank Moore, ed., *Papers of the Day #1,* 23–24.

11. Botume, *First Days Amongst the Contrabands* (1893), 125–27, 162–167; Nordhoff, "Freedmen of the South," 21–24; Austa French, *Slavery in South Carolina* (1863), 180–87, 190–91.

12. *Alvany (a free woman of color) v. Powell*, 1 Jones Esq. 35, December 1853, printed in Catterall, *Judicial Cases Concerning Slavery*, II, 179–80; *State v. Tackett*, 1 Hawks 210–22, December 1820; *State v. Samuel, a slave*, 2 Devereux and Battle's Law, 177–185, December 1836; *State v. John, a slave*, 8 Iredell 330–39, June 1848; *Alfred, a slave v. The State of Mississippi*, 37 Miss. 296–99, October 1859; *Samuel Adams v. William Adams*, 36 Ga. 236–37, June 1867; *Timmons v. Lacy*, 30 Texas 126, April 1867; *American Slave, South Carolina Narratives*, II, i, 13–16, ii, 129–33; testimony of Robert Smalls, A. D. Smith, and E. G. Dudley, American Freedmen's Inquiry Commission, 1863, file 3, Office of the Adjutant General, Letters Received, Main Series, 1861–1870, Reel 200, National Archives; *Letters from Port Royal* (1906), ed. E. W. Pearson, 86–87; Zora Hurston, "Hoodoo in America," *Journal of American Folklore*, 44 (October–December 1931), 391, 400–401; Stowe, *Key to Uncle Tom's Cabin* (1854), 298–301; Chesnut, *Diary from Dixie*, 122. See also *Smith, a slave, v. The State*, 9 Ala. 990–98, June 1846; *William v. The State*, 33 Ga. Supp. 85–94, March 1864; Johnson, *Ante-bellum North Carolina: A Social History*, 538–39; Johnston, *Race Relations in Virginia*, 305–6.

13. Volume 482, Virginia Freedmen's Bureau Mss., Record Group 105, National Archives. For examples of other cases in which husbands charged wives with infidelity, see Complaint Book, Tuscaloosa, Ala., vol. 136, Alabama Freedmen's Bureau Mss.; Barnwell, South Carolina, Complaint Register, 1867, S.C. FB Mss.; Greenville, S.C., Complaint Register, 1868, S.C. FB Mss.; Alexandria, Va., Complaint Register, Va. FB Mss.; Capt. S. C. Schaeffer, Christianburg, Va., 30 Nov. 1867, to O. O. Brown, Box 44, Va. FB Mss. (courtesy of Donald Nieman), Record Group 105, National Archives.

14. Chesnut, *Diary from Dixie*, 148–49; testimony of Henry Judd and Harry McMillan, American Freedmen's Inquiry Commission, 1863, file 3, Letters Received, Office of the Adjutant General, Main Series, Reel 200, National Archives; *Drums and Shadows* (1940), 154.

15. Testimony of Robert Smalls and Laura M. Towne, American Freedmen's Inquiry Commission, 1863, file 3, Letters Received, Office of the Adjutant General, Main Series, Reel 200, National Archives.

    In a little-read essay, E. Franklin Frazier asserted that after emancipation southern blacks "rationalized between the 'natural' impulse to seek sexual satisfaction outside of marriage and the teachings of the Church" with "the quasi-theological doctrine that 'two clean sheets cannot soil each other.' " Premarital and extra-marital sexual intercourse, accordingly, were not "sinful" when involving two Christians. I have found no evidence suggesting such beliefs. See EFF, "Sex Life of the African and American Negro," printed in Albert Ellis and Albert Abarbanel, eds., *Encyclopedia of Sexual Behavior* (1961), and reprinted in Robert Staples, ed., *The Black Family: Essays and Studies* (1971), 109–18. Similarly, no evidence sustains Eugene Genovese's confused contention that the "slaves did not separate marriage or sex itself from love" but instead "held the theory that good Christians did not sin by sleeping together out of wedlock, for they were pure and therefore could not defile each other" (Genovese, *Roll, Jordan, Roll*, 472).

16. Botume, *First Days Amongst the Contrabands*, 125–27, 162–67; Frances Butler Leigh, *Ten Years on a Georgia Plantation Since the War* (1883), 164, 227–28, 246–48.

17. *Southern Workman*, January 1895, reprinted in *Journal of American Folklore*, VII (April–June 1895), 155–56; *American Slave, South Carolina Narratives*, II, ii, 200–203; Kenneth Little, "West African Town," *Diogenes*, 29 (Spring 1960), 27; Hyman Rodman, *Lower-Class Families: The Culture of Poverty in Negro Trinidad* (1971), 234; Theodore Rosengarten, *All God's Dangers: The Life of Nate Shaw* (1974), 3–13, 23–24.

18. T. J. Woofter, *Black Yeomanry* (1930), 77, 205–7; Charles Johnson, *Shadow of the Plantation* (1934), 47–50, 66–71, 80–81.

    Genovese points out that the extent of "fornication, illegitimacy, and adultery" among "lower class" whites "remains problematical" but nevertheless finds "no reason to believe that it was one whit less than among the slaves" (Genovese, *Roll, Jordan, Roll*, 466). Recent studies, however, show a sharp decline in premarital intercourse among nineteenth-century whites in all social classes, and Chapter 10 below indicates significant differences between postbellum blacks and southern and northern lower-class whites.

    For suggestions of possible continuities in antebellum slave premarital sexual behavior after 1865, see Hallowell Pope, "Unwed Mothers and Their Sex Partners," *Journal of Marriage and the Family*, 29 (August 1967), 555–67. Pope interviewed nearly a thousand North Carolina white and black mothers of children born out of wedlock in the 1960s. Among both groups, the investigator found that "the amount of promiscuity—both concurrent and serial—was limited." "Most of the women had 'gone with' their sex partners *exclusively* for at least six months *before* becoming pregnant." Most had intercourse with one man and only a small percentage with four or more men. Far fewer black than white women had intercourse with men whom they knew to be married. The black women expected marriage less frequently than the white women.

19. See, for example, P. E. H. Hair, "Bridal Pregnancies in Rural England in Earlier Centuries," *Population Studies* XX (November 1966), 233–43; D. S. Smith and Michael S. Hindus, "Premarital Pregnancy in America, 1640–1971: An Overview and Interpretation," *Journal of Interdisciplinary History*, V (Spring 1975), 537–570; John Knodel, "Two and a Half Centuries of Demographic History in a Bavarian Village," *Population Studies*, XXIV (November 1970), 353–70; P. E. H. Hair, "Bridal Pregnancy in Earlier Rural England Further Examined," *Population Studies*, XXIV (March 1970), 59–70.

20. Frederic Bancroft, *Slave Trading in the Old South* (1931), 74–75, 79–86; *Proslavery Argument* (1852), 40–44, 368; *American Cotton Planter*, I. n.s., 295, II, 331, III, 76; Olmsted, *Seaboard States* (1857), 280; J. C. Reed, *The Brother's War* (1905), 48–49, 156, 334, 432; J. S. Bassett, *Plantation Overseer* (1925), 21–22, 260–61; Phillips, *American Negro Slavery* (1918), 85–86; Phillips, ed., *Plantation Documents* (1909), I, 179; W. K. Scarborough, *The Overseer: Plantation Management in the Old South* (1966), 68–70, 91–92, 97; W. D. Postell, *The Health of Slaves on Southern Plantations* (1951), 111, 119; Thomas W. Knox, *Camp-Fire and Cotton-Field: Southern Adventures in Time of War* (1865), 355–359; *Southern Cultivator*, V (1847), 142–43, VI (1848), 120, XVI (1858), 273–74, 319; J. W. DuBose, "Recollections . . ." *Alabama History Quarterly*, I (Spring 1930), 65–66; *DeBow's Review*, XVIII (1855), 715 XX (1856), 656, XXII (1857), 44, XXVIII (1860), 52–53.

21. E. M. Pendleton, "On the Susceptibility of the Caucasian and African Races to the Different Classes of Diseases," *Southern Medical and Surgical Journal* (1849), reprinted in *Southern Medical Reports*, II (1849), 338; John H. Morgan, "An Essay on the Production of Abortion Among Our Negro Population," *Nashville Journal of Medicine and Surgery*, XIX (August 1860), 117–123. Evidence of plantation-slave infanticide is found in F. M. Green, ed., *Ferry Plantation Journal, Jan. 4, 1838–Jan. 15, 1839* (1961), 25–26, and R. M. Myers, ed., *The Children of Pride* (1972), 527–28, 532–33, 544. Various southern rural abortifacts are detailed in George Stetson, *The Southern Negro as He Is* (1877), 20; N. N. Puckett, *Folk Beliefs of the Southern Negro* (1926), 331–32;

Hylan Lewis, *Blackways of Kent* (1955), 91; *Frank Brown Collection of North Carolina Folklore*, VI (1961), 6–7. Hinton's and Redpath's testimonies are in American Freedmen's Inquiry Commission, 1863, files 8 and 9, Letters Received, Office of the Adjutant General, Main Series, 1861–1870, Reel 201, National Archives. For a denial of infanticide, see J. W. Alvord, Savannah, 13 Jan. 1870, to O. O. Howard, in JWA, *Letters from the South Relating to the Condition of the Freedmen Addressed to Major General O. O. Howard* (1870), 8.

22. *Odom v. Odom*, 36 Ga. 286–320, June 1867; *American Slave, South Carolina Narratives*, II, ii, 11–26, 166–70, 200–203, III, iii, 17–19; *Texas Narratives*, IV, ii, 35–40, V, iv, 190–94; *Arkansas Narratives*, IX, ix, 9–13; *Unwritten History (Fisk)*, 1–6, 55–58, 67–69, 77–79, 103–8, 141–51; *Negro in Virginia (WPA)*, 89; Jacob Stroyer, *Sketches of My Life in the South* (1879), 8–12, 31–33.

23. Austa French, *Slavery in South Carolina and the Ex-Slaves* (1863), 46, 93–94, 180–87, 190–91; *American Slave, South Carolina Narratives*, II, ii, 43–71, 298–332; *Texas Narratives*, IV, ii, 290–95, V, vi, 174–78; *Mississippi Narratives*, VII, 11–17; *Arkansas Narratives*, IX, iii, 341–42; Swint, ed., *Dear Ones at Home* (1966), 61.

24. Discussion of the social importance of exogamy is found in Claude Lévi-Strauss, "The Family," in H. L. Shapiro, ed., *Man, Culture, and Society* (1956), 142–70.

25. Union, Miss., Baptist Association, *Minutes, 1828* (Natchez, 1828), 6, cited in Kenneth K. Bailey, "Protestantism and Afro-Americans in the Old South: Another Look," *Journal of Southern History*, XLI (November 1975), 457; Allen Parker, *Recollections of Slavery Times* (1885), 66–67; *American Slave, Texas Narratives*, V, iv, 92–94; *Arkansas Narratives*, IX, iii, 318–22, iv, 102–3. See also the interview with Tom Cox in *Negro in Virginia (WPA)*, 85–86. For a marriage that may have violated the primary incest taboo, see Emily Blackman, Okolona, Miss., 1 May 1867, to the editor, *Pennsylvania Freedmen's Bulletin* (June 1867), 7. She knew an ex-slave family from Alabama in which "the present wife is the daughter of the first one, both being here, and often at school together, with the husband on pleasant terms, the latter always making of his first wife as his 'mother-in-law.' "

26. Herskovits, *Myth of the Negro Past*, 64; L. P. Mair, "African Marriage and Social Change," in Arthur Phillips, ed., *Survey of African Marriage and Family Life*, part I (1953), 4; Chalmers Gaston Davidson, *The Last Foray, The South Carolina Planters of 1860: A Sociological Study* (1971), 5–6; I am indebted to Mr. Kulikoff for showing me portions of his fine study, as yet unpublished. He finds that, between 1730 and 1790, 42 percent of white

Prince George's County marriages for which records exist were between persons closely related by blood or marriage. The percentages of cousin marriages increased: from 12.5 percent in 1730–1760 to 21.3 percent in 1760–1790. Some cousin marriages involved second cousins, but most were between first cousins.

A single instance has been found where slaveowners talked of prohibiting marriages between cousins. In 1856, the Virginia planter Thomas Jefferson Massie argued that only slaves "unconnected by blood" should be allowed "to pair off," fearing that kin-related marriages would make the slaves "little better than the monkeys of their native land." (Quoted in Phillips, *Life and Labor in the Old South*, 238–39.) V. Alton Moody suggested that "some" Louisiana sugar planters "strictly prohibited" slave cousin marriages. "Planters themselves," said Moody, "would marry cousins, but their negroes were too valuable to be permitted to degenerate." No evidence accompanied this assertion. (V. Alton Moody, "Slavery on Louisiana Sugar Plantations," *Louisiana Historical Quarterly*, VII [1924].)

27. A. R. Radcliffe-Brown, "Introduction," in A. R. Radcliffe-Brown and Daryll Forde, eds., *African Systems of Kinship and Marriage* (1950), 3, 66–67; Elizabeth Botume, *First Days Amongst the Contrabands*, 48; testimony of Laura Towne and Robert Smalls, 1863, American Freedmen's Inquiry Commission, Office of the Adjutant General, Letters Received, Main Series, 1861–1870, file 3, pp. 65, 105, 108–9, Reel 200, National Archives.

28. Testimony of Smalls and Towne as cited in footnote 27; *Journal of Charlotte Forten*, ed. Ray A. Billington (1953), *passim* and especially 142–46; unnamed superintendent, quoted in J. M. McKim, 24 July 1862, to the editor, *Liberator*, 8 Aug. 1862; Nordhoff, "Freedmen of the South," in Moore, ed., *Papers of the Day #1* (1863), 23–24.

29. Jones, *Religious Instruction of the Negroes in the United States* (1842), 110–11; testimony of Robert Smalls, 1863, American Freedmen's Inquiry Commission, Office of the Adjutant General, Letters Received, Main Series, 1861–1870, file 3, pp. 65, 105, 108–9, Reel 200, National Archives.

30. Incomplete plantation birth registers—those failing to list a father's name—are not used in this study. It is possible, however, to show some of the kin connections linking together slave generations on some such places. One such register exists for the St. Helena's Island, South Carolina, Fripp rice plantation and listed births for more than half a century, ending during the Civil War. Despite the absence of fathers' names, some of the kin connections that developed in immediate families started by Daphney, Rachel,

and Grace (each of whom had a first child before 1810) can be
shown. Ten children, twenty-nine grandchildren, and seven great-
grandchildren were descended from them. Matilda named a
daughter for her mother Rachel and a son for her brother Moses.
Daphney's daughter Jane named her daughter Daphney and she in
turn named her first daughter Jane. Daphney's other daughter
named her daughter Martia; Martia's only daughter had the same
name as her maternal aunt Jane. Two of Grace's daughters named
children for their maternal grandmother, and another had a son
named for his maternal uncle Peter. Marriages surely occurred
among these three women and their daughters, but the partial
register gives no information on them. (Plantation Birth Register,
Fripp Plantation, John Edward Fripp Papers, Southern Historical
Collection, University of North Carolina, courtesy of Stanley
Engerman.) See also "List of Negroes in Families," Reed-Lance
Papers, kindly supplied to me by Peter H. Wood. It recorded birth
dates for children born between 1793 and 1833. The list contains
the name of only one father. Nevertheless it is possible to infer
some of the intra- and intergenerational ties for seventeen of
twenty-one immediate Reed-Lance families. By the 1820s, Reed-
Lance children lived among Afro-American grandparents, aunts,
uncles, and cousins. Caty and Cupid called their first son after his
father, and one of Lydia's granddaughters was named Lydia.
Mary's first son Joe carried the name of his maternal uncle.

31. U. B. Phillips, *Life and Labor in the Old South* (1929), 196;
American Slave, South Carolina Narratives, II, ii, 27–29. See also
John Dixon Long, *Pictures of Slavery in Church and State* (1857),
14–18, 230–31; *Proslavery Argument* (1852), 56–57; William R.
Taylor, *Cavalier and Yankee* (1961), 283–84, for examples of the
belief that slaves lacked a self-conscious historical "past," a culture.
In his *Vindication of Slavery*, Chancellor Harper said of nineteenth-century Africans: "Regardless of the past, as reckless of the
future, the present alone influences their actions. In this respect,
they approach nearer to the nature of brute creation than perhaps
any other people on the face of the globe!" Another example of
these assumptions is in James Kirke Paulding's popular novel
Westward Ho!; some slaves, about to be sold, at first expressed
sorrow, but when a minstrel began plucking his banjo their sad-
ness was "immediately replaced by joy." The slaves, Paulding explained, were "the very prototypes of children in their joys, their
sorrows, their forgetfulness of the past, their indifference to the
future." The Philadelphia antislavery critic John Dixon Long, a
Methodist clergyman and the son of Maryland slaveholders, saw
"no need of French pictures and obscene books to corrupt youth
in the South. The living pictures are the slaves." Dancing, "one

of their favorite amusements," illustrated their lewd debasement: "The banjo is of all instruments the best adapted to the lowest class of slaves. It is the very symbol of their savage degradation. They talk to it, and a skillful performer can excite the most diverse passions among the dancers." Long remembered seeing enslaved men and women "dancing, rapidly whirling around, whooping and yelling with brutal delight, alike unmindful of the past and future."

32. E. P. Thompson, *The Making of the English Working Class* (1963), 11.

33. Almost without exception, historians of the slave family and of slave culture have followed the schema sketched by the pioneering student of the slave family E. Franklin Frazier. In his major works, Frazier virtually ignored the slave family prior to 1840. (That theoretical error rested, in part, upon a factual error. Frazier believed that "it was not until about 1840 that the number of Negro women equalled that of men.") He and others gave scant attention to slave kin ties beyond the immediate family, an error that had more to do with a flawed sociology than with actual slave life. To commence with evidence that cannot reveal kin networks is to guarantee that kin networks will not emerge from even the most detached and serious study. That error flawed Frazier's pioneering studies, allowing him to write that "when one undertakes the study of the Negro, he discovers a great poverty of traditions and patterns of behavior that exercise any real influence on the formation of the Negro's personality and conduct." E. Franklin Frazier, *Negro Family in the United States*, 23–24; E. Franklin Frazier, "Traditions and Patterns of Negro Family Life in the United States," in E. B. Reuter, ed., *Race and Culture Contacts* (1934), 194.

34. *Life and Times of Frederick Douglass* (1962), 99–100; Benjamin Quarles, *Frederick Douglass* (1968), 1–6.

35. John Trowbridge, *Desolate South* (1866), 539–40; B. A. Botkin, ed., *Lay My Burden Down* (1945), 1–2; Jane Smith, Port Royal, S.C., n.d., to the editor, *Freedmen's Record*, II (March 1866), 54–56.

Chapter 3: Take Root There or Nowhere: I

1. Family life and kin contacts among urban slaves need further study. The discussion in Richard C. Wade, *Slavery in the Cities: The South, 1820–1860* (1964), 117–24, is inadequate. The excess of slave women, which he emphasizes, is a fact of central social importance in examining the urban slave family. Wade's volume contains additional useful evidence, but that data hardly warrant

his insistence that "family ties were weak at best" and that "male and female slaves found their pleasure and love wherever they could, knowing that attachments could only be temporary if not casual. Some contrived a more permanent arrangement, but their number was small. Generally relations were neither prolonged nor monogamous. . . . The very looseness of the mating . . . made a meaningful family unit even more difficult." Compelling evidence of the emergence of enlarged urban-slave and free-black kin networks is found in Loren Schweninger, "John H. Rapier, Sr., A Slave and Freedman in the Ante-bellum South," *Civil War History*, 20 (March 1974), 23–24, and "A Slave Family in the Ante Bellum South," *Journal of Negro History*, LX (January 1975), 29–44.

2. Robert Lofton, for example, grew up as a slave in McDonough, Georgia. He and his mother belonged to Asa Brown. The town postmaster owned Lofton's father, and Lofton remembered of his youth:

> There was another woman my master owned. Her husband belonged to another white man. My father also belonged to another white man. Both of them would come and stay with their wives at night and go back to work with their masters during the day. My mother had her kin folks who lived down in the country and my mother used to go out and visit them. I had a grandmother way out in the country. My mother used to take me and go out and stay a day or so. She would arrange with mistress and master and go down Saturday and she would take me along and leave her other children with this other woman.

(*American Slave, Arkansas Narratives*, IX, iv, 267–70.)

3. E. F. Frazier, "Negro Slave Family," *Journal of Negro History*, XV (March 1930), 236.

4. Phoebe and Cash's letter is printed in Robert Starobin, "Privileged Bondsmen and the Process of Accommodation . . . ," *Journal of Social History*, V (Fall 1971), 46–71, and Starobin, ed., *Blacks in Bondage* (1974), 42–57.

5. Stirling Plantation Birth Register, 1805–1865, and 1846 and 1857 Inventories, Stirling Plantation, West Feliciana Parish, Louisiana, mss. copies, LSU Plantation Records, courtesy of Stanley Engerman. I am also indebted to Mrs. Ellen E. Regner of the Department of Archives at the Louisiana State University Library for supplying information about Louis Stirling and his family.

6. The 1860 federal Louisiana agricultural census listed three plantations owned separately by Lewis Stirling, Sarah Sterling (149 slaves), and M. C. Sterling (127 slaves). These other two Sterlings spelled their names differently from Louis Stirling, and it is not known if the three were related.

7. Three separate markings in the register suggest its over-all accuracy but do not tell that all slave births were recorded. Sucky's son Baptiste (b. 1823) and Yellow Louisa's son Joseph (b. 1838) did not have the name of a father recorded in the registers. But the notation "a molato" next to each of the names suggests white fathers. Josiah (b. 1835), the son of Chaney's Liddy, is also listed without a known father, but in one register it was marked, "Wilson is the father." Wilson was then married to Eveline, and the first of their thirteen children had been born. The incompleteness of the early entries (1807–1819) is indicated in the note following "Generation with First Child Born Between 1807 and 1819," Table 14. That table, furthermore, does not include the names of eleven women and their twenty-one children (all born between 1833 and 1842) who belonged to Jonathan Turnbull and were hired by Stirling. Fathers' names were listed for two of these women.

   Seven of the eleven women not included in Chart 3 had their first child between 1807 and 1819. The failure of their names or those of their children to appear in later generations suggests that they had been sold. Of the eleven women not included in Chart 3, only two—Ellen (five children) and Patience (six children)—had more than two children.

8. Wiley, who married Josephine in 1863, was Josephine's older sister Margaret's half sister's son. Phelby, who married Leven in 1856, was her husband's older sister Eveline's husband's sister's daughter. Francoise and Monday also had an affinal connection; he was her mother's brother's wife's half-sister's husband's brother. Little George, who married Kitty, was the son of Long George and Linder, and Kitty was Hannah's daughter; Hannah's sister Margaret married Adam, who was Nelly's half-brother, and Nelly was the wife of Linder's brother Erwin.

9. A number of children born before 1820 and listed as dead by that time are not included. The registers listed their mothers' names but not their dates of birth and the names of their fathers. Big Judy, for example, had given birth to five children who were dead by that time.

10. There were occasional exceptions to this pattern. Julius and Sucky had three children (1810, 1813, and 1816), and then Sucky was listed as the mother of four additional children (1818, 1820, 1823, and 1827) by unnamed men. It is not revealed whether Julius died or was sold, but his name never again appeared in the registers. Yellow Joe, Big Hannah's husband, was dead by 1845, and in that year and in 1848 Big Hannah had children by unnamed fathers.

11. Twelve households with only unnamed fathers started between 1856 and 1865. In five a mother had only one child each and in

five others two children each. Sarah and Cecele had four children each. Some of these women probably settled into permanent unions after emancipation.

Over the entire span of the birth register (1807–1865), twenty-eight women gave birth to sixty-six children by unnamed fathers. One-third of these women were either the daughters of Leven and Big Judy or their granddaughters. Two of five children born to these twenty-eight women were born to these nine women.

12. E. Franklin Frazier, "Traditions and Patterns of Negro Family Life," Reuter, ed., *Race and Culture Contacts* (1934), 198; Kenneth Stampp, *Peculiar Institution*, 344. Two of many other examples are Robert E. Park, "Introduction," in Charles S. Johnson, *Shadow of the Plantation* (1934), xix, and Abram Kardiner and Lionel Ovesey, *The Mark of Oppression* (1951), 45. Exaggeration of the importance of the male-absent slave family was first seriously criticized in Bobby Frank Jones, "A Cultural Middle Passage," unpublished Ph.D. dissertation, University of North Carolina, 1965.

13. The numerical ratio of men to women over time on the Stirling plantation is unknown. The plantation may have had a surplus of women and a rule that forbade slaves from marrying slaves on other farms and plantations. If that was so, it might explain the presence of this type of domestic arrangement. But that is mere speculation. In the text, it assumed that an even balance existed between the sexes and that Stirling women could marry but that some chose not to do so. It is also possible that some considered themselves "co-wives" and had settled ties to a husband who resided with another woman. See William J. Goode, "Illegitimacy in the Caribbean Social Structure," *American Sociological Review*, XXV (February 1960), 21–30, for a discussion of deviation from a common norm.

14. Register of Refugees, Camp Barker, Alexandria, Virginia, June 1862–October 1863, Virginia Freedmen's Bureau Mss., Record Group 105, National Archives.

15. J. C. Cohoon Plantation Ledger, Cedar Vale Plantation, Nansemond County, Virginia, 1811–1863, pp. 112–27, mss. copy, Alderman Library, University of Virginia. See also C. G. Holland, "The Slave Population on the Plantation of John C. Cohoon, Jr.," *Virginia Magazine of History and Biography*, 80 (July 1972), 331–40.

16. The number of children named for blood relatives was probably larger than shown here, for two reasons. Margaret and Tom's sons Tom, Lewis, and Jack and Fanny and Jacob's son Charles probably had wives owned by different masters, and after their sale Amy and Lucy may have settled into marital unions. Some children born on the Cedar Vale plantation probably carried the

names of blood kin born before Cohoon purchased their parents or grandparents or before Cohoon married and gained Mary Everett's slaves. His wife had owned Bristol and Margaret, and one of Margaret's Cedar Vale children was named Bristol. The older Bristol may have been Margaret's father or brother. Nancy, who also had belonged to Mary Everett, had a son named Sam prior to her owner's marriage to Cohoon. Nancy's daughter Betsey had a son named Sam (1843).

17. James Redpath, *The Roving Editor; Or, Talks with Slaves in the Southern States* (1859), 312–24.

18. The names of Edmond, Dick Pitts, Jack Beeman, Isaac Holmes, and Lewis Orton appear in Cohoon's records but *only as fathers* of children born to his slaves. Not one was born on his plantation, not one was listed among the slaves he purchased, and not one had his name recorded in Cohoon's death lists.

19. *DeBow's Review*, XXX (1861), 74; Cobb, *Law of Negro Slavery* (1858), ccxviii. I am indebted to Stanley Engerman for supplying the Massie letter to me.

20. See the tables in U. B. Phillips, "Origin and Growth of the Southern Black Belt," *American Historical Review*, XI (July 1906), 798–816. Phillips used tax and census records to show changing patterns of slave ownership in selected Upper and Lower South counties. The percentage of slaves living on nonplantations declined between 1790 (and 1820) and 1860, even when county populations remained stable or increased. Many slaves born in these counties and slaves brought there by purchase or by in-migration of their owners probably shared the experiences of the Cohoon slaves—first living on small farms and then on plantations. The distinction between "small farm" and "plantation" slaves at a given moment in time remains important but should not blur the fact that small-farm slaves often became plantation slaves and carried that prior experience with them into a new social setting.

21. A fine discussion of slave gift-transfers is found in E. W. Phifer, "Slavery in Microcosm, Burke County, North Carolina," *Journal of Southern History*, XXVIII (1962), 137–60. A similar perspective on the importance of gift-transfer is found in James Redpath's interview with the former Kentucky and Missouri slave Malinda Moll in the 1850s, in *The Roving Editor*, 312–24.

22. J. G. Taylor, *Negro Slavery in Louisiana* (1963), 123–35; Ralph Flanders, *Plantation Slavery in Georgia* (1930), 172–73; Robert Q. Mallard, *Plantation Life Before Emancipation* (1892), 47–53; U. B. Phillips, *Life and Labor in the Old South* (1929), 238–39; Ethan Allen Andrews, *Slavery and the Domestic Slave Trade*

(1836), 102; *American Slave, South Carolina Narratives*, II, i, 38–41, 149–51, 229–33, 299–303, III, iii, 100–102, 139–45, 164–66, 209–12, iv, 35–37, 42–44, 51–54, 170–73.

23. Typed manuscript copy of Torbert plantation records, pp. 97–99 and 230–31, Department of Archives and History, Montgomery, Alabama.

24. Princess Anne County, Virginia, manuscript census, 1866, Virginia Freedmen's Bureau Mss., vol. 511, Record Group 105, National Archives.

25. *Memphis Argus*, 12 July 1865 (courtesy of Armstead Robinson); Hugh L. Bond, Baltimore, 28 Jan. 1865, to the editor, *Pennsylvania Freedmen's Bulletin* (February 1865), 1; speech of Bayley Wyatt, enclosed in undated letter from Jacob Vining, Yorktown, Va., to the editor, *The Friend*, n.d., reprinted *Pennsylvania Freedmen's Bulletin* (March 1867), 15–16.

Chapter 4: Take Root There or Nowhere: II

1. Slave sale invoices nearly always indicate no more than a slave's age and sex. The dangers in using such evidence as clues to slave family structure and how sale affected that structure are indicated in Herbert G. Gutman, *Slavery and the Numbers Game: A Critique of Time on the Cross* (1975), 108–23.

2. See William Calderhead, "How Extensive Was the Border State Slave Trade: A New Look," *Civil War History*, XVIII (March 1972), 42–55. Calderhead's excellent study of slave sales in eight Maryland counties between 1830 and 1840 shows that 1991 slave sales involving the sale of 5073 slaves occurred. The population of these counties in 1830 was 46,840. Just how so high a volume of sales affected the slave family, however, cannot yet be known. We must first study the slave family in these Maryland places. But if the average slave family in 1830 had four members, then there were 17 sales per 100 families and 43 slaves sold per 100 families. See Gutman, *Slavery and the Numbers Game*, 137–38.

3. Bound volumes of Marriage Registers, 1864–1865, Davis Bend, Natchez, and Vicksburg, Mississippi, manuscript copies, Mississippi Freedmen's Bureau Mss., volumes 43–45, Record Group 105, National Archives. Some of this material is used by John Blassingame in *The Slave Community: Plantation Life in the Antebellum South* (1972), 89–92 and especially the table on page 90. Blassingame's analysis is very different from that in this study. The data reported in the table on p. 90 are inaccurate.

4. The registrars elicited only partial information from these men and women. The evidence has three limitations. First, not all those

registering marriages renewed old unions. An unknown number married for the first time. The registrars failed to indicate which marriages were new marriages. Second, the registrar asked each person if he or she had had an earlier marriage. A negative answer elicted no further questions. The registrars did not ask people who had lived together as husband and wife and simply remarried how long such unions had lasted. As a result, the evidence is not directly comparable to that found in the Virginia and North Carolina marriage registers. Third, men and women detailing an earlier terminated slave marriage were not asked *when* that marriage had ended. They told how long it lasted, gave a reason for its termination, and usually indicated how many children it had produced. But that was all. If, for example, a sixty-year-old registrant said he or she had been married earlier for five years, it is not known whether that union ended when the respondent was aged twenty-five, thirty-five, or fifty-five.

5. The high percentage of women as opposed to men aged twenty to twenty-nine reporting the death of a former spouse may be explained by a number of factors including wartime deaths among slave husbands and the relative frequency with which younger women had older males as spouses.

6. *Negro in Virginia (WPA)* (1940), 74; *American Slave, South Carolina Narratives*, II, ii, 233–36; Frederic Bancroft, *Slave Trading in the Old South* (1931), 65.

7. Among those who had experienced an earlier but terminated marriage for any reason, just over half of the males (50 percent) and females (55 percent) had children born in these unions. The percent reporting children depended upon the ages of the respondents. Age-specific percentages by sex follow: *Males*, twenty to twenty-nine, 39 percent; thirty to thirty-nine, 54 percent; forty to forty-nine, 57 percent; fifty and over, 61 percent; *Females*, twenty to twenty-nine, 47 percent; thirty to thirty-nine, 56 percent; forty to forty-nine, 66 percent; fifty and over, 63 percent.

8. Swint, ed., *Dear Ones at Home* (1966), 123–24, 242–43.

9. Women aged twenty to twenty-nine, not surprisingly, reported a much higher percentage of disrupted marriages lasting five to fourteen years (31 percent) than men similarly aged (20.5 percent). The explanation, in part, rests on the fact that slave women took spouses at an earlier age than slave men. This difference, incidentally, suggests the accuracy of the information reported by these illiterate respondents.

10. *American Slave, South Carolina Narratives*, II, ii, 203–206; *Texas Narratives*, IV, i, 62–65. The effects of estate divisions on the slave family and slave kin networks need very much to be studied. In his careful study, Edwin W. Phifer points out: "In a general way,

it may be said that the small slaveholder more commonly made special provisions in his will for his slaves than did the large slaveholder with multiple heirs, whose will was usually more impersonal in order to make it more easily administered." (E. W. Phifer, "Slavery in Microcosm: Burke County, North Carolina," *Journal of Southern History*, XXVIII [May 1962], 137–60.) Phifer's distinction is very important. If it holds up for other southern places, it will mean that slaves on large plantations which rarely sold slaves experienced the danger of family breakup much more regularly on the death of an owner than slaves owned in smaller numbers. Tensions affecting slave family life therefore would have differed on such places: on small units of ownership, slaves had reason to fear breakup while an owner lived; on large units of ownership, that fear was most common when an owner died. See Gutman, *Slavery and the Numbers Game*, 132–37.

11. A marriage register similar to the one used in Mississippi also was used by the military clergy to register 222 Pine Bluff, Arkansas, marriages between March 12, 1864, and July 21, 1865. The Pine Bluff registrants shared common social and demographic characteristics with these other black men and women. The Arkansas males (24 percent) and females (26 percent) of all ages had experienced even more forcible breakups of earlier marriages than the Mississippi males (19 percent) and females (16 percent). More terminated marriages lasting more than five years and about the same percentage lasting fifteen or more years occurred among the Arkansas registrants as compared to the Mississippi registrants. Pine Bluff was in Jefferson County, Arkansas, and the distribution of slaves by units of ownership in 1860 nearly exactly paralleled that in Warren County, Mississippi. More than seven in ten (72 percent) lived on units of twenty or more slaves. (Pine Bluff, Ark., Marriage Register, Arkansas Freedmen's Bureau Mss., Record Group 105, National Archives.)

12. Solomon Northup, *Twelve Years a Slave*, reprinted in Gilbert Osofsky, ed., *Puttin' On Ole Massa* (1969), 365.

13. *American Slave, South Carolina Narratives*, II, pt. ii, 6–10, pt. iii, 33–34. I am indebted to John Strawn for certain of the formulations in this paragraph.

14. Biographical information on Duncan is found in Morton Rothstein, "The Antebellum South as a Dual Economy: A Tentative Hypothesis," *Agricultural History*, XLI (October 1967), 373–82; Paul Gates, *The Farmer's Age* (1960), 148–49, 154, 407; Clement Eaton, *Growth of Southern Civilization* (1961), 43.

15. Carlisle Plantation Lists, 1851, 1856, 1861, Concordia Parish, Louisiana, mss. copies, Louisiana State University Plantation Records, Columbia University microfilm copy. In this brief period, the

Carlisle slaves increased from 141 to 158 men, women, and children, an increase mostly explained by a favorable balance between births and deaths, not purchases. One slave, Alex, was listed as sold in the 1861 register. Not a single one of the seven inhabitants of three 1851 households appeared again in either the 1856 or the 1861 lists, suggesting that some were sold. Adult slaves not listed in 1851 but listed later probably were purchased and included the married couple Jerry and Clarissa and a few women aged fifteen to nineteen (Amanda, Minerva, Malinda, and Malvina, among them). It does not appear that the plantation managers added unattached young men by purchase in this decade.

16. Una Pope-Hennessey, ed., *Aristocratic Journey . . . Letters of Mrs. Basil Hall . . . 1827–1828* (1931), 223; Frederick L. Olmsted, *Cotton Kingdom*, II (1861), 209–10; David Ross, 30 April 1812, to Robert Robertson, quoted in Charles R. Dew, "David Ross and the Oxford Iron Works," *William and Mary Quarterly*, 31 (April 1974), 211–12; Kingsley, *Treatise on the Patriarchal or Cooperative System of Society as It Exists . . . Under the Name of Slavery* (1834), quoted in Phillips, *American Negro Slavery* (1918), 294–295; Julia F. Smith, *Slavery and Plantation Growth in Antebellum Florida, 1821–1860* (1973), 32–33.

17. *DeBow's Review*, X (June 1851), 621–27, and XI (October 1851), 369–72; Charles C. Jones, *The Religious Instruction of the Negroes in the United States* (1842), 132–35. A few plantation owners allowed slave divorce after harsh punishment or some other deprivation. A Louisiana sugar planter permitted divorce after a month's notice and allowed remarriage after the individual received twenty-five lashes. James Hammond's plantation manual allowed slave couples to separate for "sufficient cause" and required that they be given one hundred lashes. They then had to wait three years before remarrying. A slave marrying a second time received half the customary marriage bounty (five dollars' worth of household goods). "Had a trial for Divorce and Adultery cases," Hammond noted in his diary on December 26, 1840; "flogged Joe Goodwyn and ordered him to go back to his wife. Ditto Gabriel and Molly and ordered them to come together again. Separated Moses and Amy finally. And flogged Tom Kollock . . . [for] interfering with Maggy Campbell, Sullivan's wife." This one diary entry is reason enough not to idealize slave married life. But it also shows that slave behavior on the Hammond plantation—where the whip punished owner-defined transgressions—was not defined by external "rules." The Hammond slaves paid a heavy price for acting upon their own conception of an incompatible marriage. They nevertheless made a choice. (Stampp, *Peculiar Institution*, 342–43; "Plantation Manual of J. H. Hammond," n.d., mss. copy, South Carolina Historical Society, cour-

tesy of Stanley Engerman; W. T. Jordan, *Hugh Davis and His Alabama Plantation* [1948], 98; Robert Fogel and Stanley Engerman, *Time on the Cross*, I [1974], I, 128; William Johnson, *Natchez: Ante-Bellum Diary of a Free Negro*, W. R. Hogan and E. A. Davis, eds. [1951], 568–69; *Unwritten History . . . [Fisk]*, 139–42; Phillips, *Life and Labor in the Old South*, 270.)

18. Brief biographical information about Henry Watson appears in Eaton, *The Growth of Southern Civilization, 1790–1860* (1961), 35–36, 114–15.

19. Annual Lists of Slaves by Household and New Births, Henry Watson Plantation, Greene County, Alabama, 1843–1865, mss. copies, courtesy of Stanley Engerman.

20. Solomon Northup, *Twelve Years a Slave*, reprinted in *Puttin' on Ole Massa*, ed. Gilbert Osofsky (1969), 325–27, 347, 356, 365.

21. Peter Kolchin, *First Freedom: The Responses of Alabama Blacks to Emancipation and Reconstruction* (1972), 32–33, 62–63; J. H. Parrish, 19, 25 June 1865, to Henry Watson, J. A. Weymus, 14 July 1865, to HW, contract for the hire of Negroes for the year 1865 dated 26 June 1865, and HW, 16 Dec. 1865, to Julia (Watson), Henry Watson mss., Perkins Library, Duke University, Durham, N.C.

22. Montgomery County, Virginia, population census, 1866, Virginia Freedmen's Bureau Mss., vol. 137, Record Group 105, National Archives.

23. Theodore Wilson, *The Black Codes of the South* (1965), 53–54; *Southern Presbyterian Review* (April 1867), 286; John deForest, *A Union Officer in the Reconstruction* (1948), 94; Aiken, S.C., Complaint Register, May–August 1866, Barnwell, S.C., Complaint Register, May–October 1866, Greenville, S.C., Complaint Register, March–April 1868, South Carolina Freedmen's Bureau Mss., Record Group 105, National Archives; J. W. McConaughy, Wharton, Texas, 9 July 1866, to W. H. Sinclair, volume 122, pp. 80–81, Texas Freedmen's Bureau Mss., RG 105, NA (courtesy of Barry Crouch).

24. Francis W. Loring and C. F. Atkinson, *Cotton Culture and the South Considered with Reference to Emigration* (Boston, 1868), 4, 5, 9, 13–16, 20, 22, 24, 72–75, 103, 109, 137.

25. "Memo of the birth of Negro children Commencing June 1776," Cameron Family Papers, Southern Historical Collection, University of North Carolina, Chapel Hill, N.C.

26. Between 1762 and 1768, Bennehan worked for a Petersburg, Virginia, firm that sold supplies to North Carolina farmers and slaveowners and then became the partner of the Hillsboro, North Carolina, Scot merchant William Johnston, who was the financial

agent for the Transylvania Company, which financed Daniel Boone's early Kentucky and Tennessee explorations. He helped suppress the North Carolina Regulators. Bennehan married into a prominent Halifax family and began purchasing land in May 1776. In 1800, he owned 4065 acres and forty-four slaves. He and his wife and two children lived in a plantation "mansion" built in 1799. In 1803, Bennehan's daughter Rebecca married Duncan Cameron. The next year, Cameron, not yet thirty, built Fairntosh, a plantation house just at the point where the Eno and Flat Rivers join to form the Neuse River. Duncan's father had graduated from King's College, Aberdeen, and then migrated to Virginia in 1770 to serve as a cleric until his death in 1815. Born in 1776, young Cameron read for the law in Virginia and settled in Hillsboro in 1797. A very successful career followed. A prominent Federalist, Cameron served as a Superior Court judge, headed the State Bank of North Carolina for two decades, and was a member of the state Board of Internal Improvements. Cameron died in 1853. He was then one of North Carolina's wealthiest citizens. His son Paul Carrington Cameron married the daughter of Thomas Ruffin, then chief justice of the North Carolina Supreme Court and one of the Old South's most distinguished jurists. On the eve of the Civil War, Paul Cameron, who had served in the state legislature, owned at least thirty thousand acres of land. He was a banker as well as a planter, and actively promoted North Carolina railroad development, was a stockholder in North Carolina's first cotton mill, and also invested in Augusta, Georgia, cotton mills. Cameron led the North Carolina Democratic delegation in the 1876 national convention that nominated Samuel J. Tilden. The Cameron Orange County plantation buildings, including some slave quarters, still stand but are owned by the Liggett-Myers Tobacco Company. A large Raleigh shopping center is called Cameron Village. See Charles Richard Sanders, *The Cameron Plantation in Central North Carolina (1776–1973) and Its Founder Richard Bennehan* (1974), *passim*, and Hugh T. Lefler and Paul Wager, eds., *Orange County, 1752–1952* (1953), 14–16, 24–40, 83–84, 95–106, 323, 325–26.

27. I am indebted to Ira Berlin for making this material from the Pinckney records, deposited in the Library of Congress, available to me.

28. Virgil, Monrovia, 1848, to P. C. Cameron, and J. P. Lesley, Philadelphia, 4 Sept. 1859, to Miss Mildred Cameron, Cameron Family Papers, Southern Historical Collection, Chapel Hill, N.C.

29. Gooley, Port Royal, Va., 30 Nov. 1807, to Dear Mistress, Duke Marion Godbey Papers, University of Kentucky, Special Collections (Film), courtesy of Leslie Rowland.

Chapter 5: Aunts and Uncles and Swap-Dog Kin

1. William C. Gannett, "The Freedmen at Port Royal," *North American Review*, CCVIII (July 1865), 1–28; F. W. Bradley, "South Carolina Proverbs," *Southern Folklore Quarterly*, I (March 1937), 99–101; Ralph Ellison, *Shadow and Act* (1963), 152, 246–47; Meyer Fortes, quoted in Richard and Sally Price, "Sarameka Onomastics: An Afro-American Naming System," *Ethnology*, XI (October 1972), 341–67. I have learned much from the Prices's splendid study.

2. Davis Bend, Mississippi, Marriage Register, 1864–1865, and Yazoo County and Copiah County, Mississippi, Labor Registers, undated (probably 1866), Mississippi Freedmen's Bureau Mss., Record Group 105, National Archives; Newberry and Columbia, South Carolina, and Macon, Georgia, lists of applicants to the American Colonization Society, courtesy of William Cohen. See also Price and Price, "Sarameka Onomastics," *Ethnology*, XI (October 1972), 341–67; Lorenzo Dow Turner, *Africanisms in the Gullah Dialect* (1949), 31–43; Newbell Niles Puckett, "Names of American Negro Slaves," in George Murdock, ed., *Studies in the Science of Society* (1937), 470–94; Peter H. Wood, *Black Majority* (1974), chap. 6.

3. Uncommon male names included LaGrand, Perch, Radick, Ranvil, and Wakalee, and uncommon female names included Abarilla, Crecy, Hasty, Leathy, Pathena, Ordecia, Reate, Ritty, and Sarilla. Further study may show that some of these names had their origin in West African given names. A beginning discussion of the transformation of the West African given name into an Anglo-American given name is found in Wood, *Black Majority*, chap. 6.

   The use of diminutives (Big Sarah and Little Sarah) and color designations ("Yellow" Joe) also deserves additional study. It remains unclear whether the enslaved used such names among themselves or whether they were designations fixed by owners to distinguish slaves with similar names from one another. A way to examine this would be to study the frequency with which such names were used after the general emancipation by the ex-slaves.

4. Only three male American Colonization Society applicants had classical names. Just as few among the Davis Bend males—2 of 360—had classical names. Nine Copiah County males had similar names. An 1866 Yazoo County Freedmen's Bureau register listed 1285 male names. Seventeen had classical names.

   These records differ slightly from a list, studied by George C. Rogers, of given names among 2922 Georgetown, South Carolina, black males who registered to vote in 1867. About 10 percent of these men had either a classical or a West African given name. (G. C. Rogers, *History of Georgetown County, South Carolina* [1970], 438–41.)

On West African day-naming practices among New World slaves, see J. L. Dillard, *Black English: Its History and Usage in the United States* (1972), 123–35, and especially Peter H. Wood, *Black Majority* (1974), chap. 6. The given-name lists used in this study deal with a late moment in the slave experience. Further study may show that West African names and their English variants were much more common earlier in time, as suggested by Wood, and by a listing of eighty-four slaves (three-fifths of them men) given in 1811 by the Georgia Sea Island planter Thomas Spaulding to settle a debt with the merchant George Scott. Most had common Anglo-American names, but about 15 percent had African names, and African names were more common among the women than the men. (E. Merton Coulter, *Thomas Spaulding of Sapalo* [1940], 137. The full list, filed in the Chatham County, Georgia, courthouse, was supplied to me by the court clerk, Ben P. Axson.) On day-naming among the Fanti and Ashanti, see Roger Bastide, *African Civilisations in the New World* (1971), 12, and for the retention of day names among coastal Georgia blacks into the early decades of the twentieth century see *Drums and Shadows* (1972), 48, 148, 198.

5. Evidence that some slaves had more than one given name is found in Elizabeth Botume, *First Days Amongst the Contrabands* (1893), 45–48, 61–62; Elizabeth Kilham, "Sketches in Color," *Putnam's Magazine*, V (January 1870), 32–33; Miss Warren, Pine Bluff, Ark., 4 Jan. 1865, to the editor, *Freedmen's Bulletin*, I (March 1865), 77.

    Botume remembered among the Sea Island slaves "that 'Cornhouse' yesterday was 'Primus' to-day. That 'Quash' was 'Bryan.' The old folks told me these were 'basket names.' 'Nemseys (namesakes) gives different names.' " Blacks themselves sorted out multiple given names. When Smart Washington tried writing all his children's names in a family Bible, he seemed puzzled at first. "So many people give them basket names, I ain't 'zactly know myself which de right one," he admitted to Botume. But he managed.

6. See W. D. Postell, *Health of Slaves on Southern Plantations* (1951), 116, in which the planter Robert Mackay is recorded as noting "Juba . . . died in child birth 22 June 1815, the child is named Juba." Children possibly were named for *dead* mothers, a subject worth further study.

7. 1860 federal manuscript census, Charleston, S.C., wards 6, 7, and 8. In one of six free black households with a mother not yet fifty years old and one or more daughters, a daughter had her mother's name. A far greater percentage of sons in the same wards had their fathers' names. That was so in two of five free black Charleston households.

8. All black households in Beaufort, South Carolina, and Malloy's Store and Lane's Schoolhouse, Warren County, Mississippi, have been examined as well as all St. Helena's Island, South Carolina, households listed on pages 41 to 88 of the 1880 federal census. No difference existed in the three places. In all, naming practices were studied in 1270 households.

9. E. Franklin Frazier, *Negro in the United States* (1949), 3–21; Harford's letter in Starobin, ed., *Blacks in Bondage: Letters of American Slaves* (1974), 36–37; J. F. Smith, *Slavery and Plantation Growth in Antebellum Florida* (1973), 114–18; Elizabeth Keckley, *Behind the Scenes: Thirty Years a Slave and Four Years in the White House* (1868), 17–25, 31–57; Harry's letter printed in John S. Bassett, *Southern Plantation Overseer* (1925), 21–22, 260–61; Tighman's letter printed in W. A. Low, "The Freedman's Bureau and Civil Rights in Maryland," *Journal of Negro History*, XXVII (1952), 221–46.

10. All these Stirling children were named for a mother's or father's sister's child. In 1855, for example, Francoise and Monday named their first son Levi. Twenty-five years earlier, Monday's oldest sister Clarice had given birth to a son named Levi. The boy died in 1835. The Good Hope slave children Elizabeth, Benjamin, and Nathan, born between 1849 and 1854, also had the names of children born earlier to a paternal or maternal aunt.

11. *Memoir of Mrs. Chloe Spear, a Native of Africa . . . Died in 1815 Aged 65, By a Lady of Boston* (1815), 17; Daniel Scott Smith, "Child Naming Patterns and Family Structure Change, Hingham, Massachusetts, 1640–1860," unpublished paper, Clark Conference on the Family and Social Structure, April 27–29, 1972 (courtesy of D. S. Smith); Puckett, quoted in Herskovits, *Myth of the Negro Past* (1941), 190; C. G. Holland, "The Slave Population on the Plantation of John C. Cohoon, Jr., Nansemond County, Va., 1811–1863," *Virginia Magazine of History and Biography*, 80 (July 1972), 340; Mary Ames, *From a New England Woman's Diary in Dixie in 1865* (1906), 90; Charlotte E. McKay, "Domestic Relations of the Freedmen's," *National Freedman*, II (May 1866), 143–45.

12. Meyer Fortes, "Kinship and Marriage Among the Ashanti," in A. R. Radcliffe-Brown and Daryll Forde, eds., *African Systems of Kinship and Marriage* (1950), 276; Julia Harn, ed., "Old Canoochee, Ogeechee Chronicles," *Georgia Historical Quarterly*, XVI (1932), 150; John Spencer Bassett, *The Southern Plantation Overseer as Revealed in His Letters* (1925), 185–215; Duncan Clinch Heyward, *Seed from Madagascar* (1937), 96–98; *American Slave, South Carolina Narratives*, II, ii, 10–16, III, iii, 33–34.

13. W. E. B. Du Bois, *The Negro-American Family* (1909), 9; Sidney

W. Mintz and Richard Price, "An Anthropological Approach to the Study of Afro-American History," unpublished paper, February 1974, 67–68 and *passim*. I am very much indebted to Mintz and Price for letting me read and quote from this extraordinarily important study.

14. Paul Bohannon, *Africa and Africans* (1964), 158–73; Radcliffe-Brown, "Introduction," in Radcliffe-Brown and Forde, eds., *African Systems of Kinship and Marriage*, 27–30.

15. Woods letter in Starobin, ed., *Blacks in Bondage*, 87–92, 105; Isaac Mason, *Life of Isaac Mason as a Slave* (1969), 10–18; Moses Grandy, *Narrative of the Life of Moses Grandy* (1969), 10–38; Moses Roper, *A Narrative of the Adventures and Escape of Moses Roper from American Slavery* (1970), 1–25; Herbert Aptheker, *To Be Free* (1948), 36.

16. M. G. Smith quoted in Roger Bastide, *African Civilisations in the New World* (1971), 30. On the adaptive capacities of contemporary Africans from quite different tribal communities, see Remi Clignet, "Urbanization and Family Structure in the Ivory Coast," *Comparative Studies in Society and History*, VIII (1966), 385–401. See, however, Elaine Cumming and David M. Schneider, "Sibling Solidarity: A Property of American Kinship," *American Anthropologist*, 63 (1961), 498–507, for an argument that in bilateral kinship systems "sibling solidarity" remains important throughout life.

17. *Diary of Colonel Landon Carter of Sabine Hall*, ed. J. P. Greene (1965); Smith letter in Starobin, ed., *Blacks in Bondage*, 87–92, 105; Francis Frederick, *Autobiography of Francis Frederick of Virginia* (1869), 7; H. C. Bruce, *New Man* (1895), 107–9; *Negro in Virginia (WPA)*, 127–28; *Unwritten History (Fisk)*, 139–43; Robert Anderson, *From Slavery to Affluence: Memories of Robert Anderson, Ex-Slave* (1927), 5; Isaac Mason, *Life of Isaac Mason as a Slave* (1969), 10–18; Noah Davis, *A Narrative in the Life of Reverend Noah Davis . . .* (1859), 14; Andrew Jackson, *Narrative and Writings of Andrew Jackson of Kentucky . . .* (1969), 21; Benjamin Quarles, *Black Abolitionists* (1969), 60–62; James Redpath, *Roving Editor . . .* (1859), 11–12; Levi J. Coppin, *Unwritten History* (1919), 17–21; Moses Grandy, *Narrative of the Life of Moses Grandy* (1969), 10–38.

18. Amanda Smith, *An Autobiography* (1893), 18–32; James Watkins, *Narrative of the Life of James Watkins* (1852), 11–34; Elizabeth Keckley, *Behind the Scenes* (1868), 54.

19. *Narratives of the Sufferings of Lewis and Milton Clarke . . .* (1846), 75; E. F. Frazier, *Negro Family in the United States* (1939), 12–13; William Still, *Underground Railroad* (1872), 41, 394–95; S. G. Howe, *The Refugees from Slavery in Canada West* (1864),

73–74; Miss E. James, Roanoke Island, N.C., 13 Aug. 1864, to the editor, *American Missionary*, VIII (October 1864), 236–37; *Dear Ones at Home*, p. 37.

20. *American Slave, South Carolina Narratives*, II, i, 20–25, ii, 39–42, 84–86, 177–86, 294–97; *Texas Narratives*, V, iii, 17–19, 86–106, iv, 36–40, 223–24; *Indiana Narratives*, VI, 160–61; *Oklahoma Narratives*, VII, 236–41; *Unwritten History (Fisk)*, 123–27.

21. *American Slave, Texas Narratives*, IV, i, 278–80, ii, 71–73, V, iii, 236–46, iv, 223–34; *Oklahoma Narratives*, VII, 49–55; *North Carolina Narratives*, XIV, 110–16; Norman R. Yetman, ed., *Views from Slavery* (1970), 27–32, 207–11, 234–36; John Roan, Piscataway, Prince George's County, Md., 5 Aug. 1868, to My Dear Sister, and JR, 5 Nov. 1868, to Dear Sir, Virginia Freedmen's Bureau Mss., RG 105, National Archives, courtesy of John O'Brien.

22. Freedmen's Complaint Register, Alexandria, Va., Virginia Freedmen's Bureau Mss.; New Orleans, La., Freedmen's Bureau Court Register, 1866–1867, vol. 137, Louisiana FB Mss.; Grenada, Miss., Register of Complaints, 1866–1867, Mississippi FB Mss.; Tuscaloosa and Selma, Ala., Complaints of Freedmen, vols. 136 and 180, Alabama FB Mss.; Complaints and Trials, 1866, Macon, Ga., Georgia FB Mss., RG 105, NA; Peter Kolchin, *First Freedom* (1972), 63–67.

23. Joel T. Williamson, "Black Self Assertion Before and After Emancipation," and William McFeely, "Unfinished Business . . . ," in Nathan Huggins, Martin Kilson, and Daniel Fox, eds., *Key Issues in the Afro-American Experience* (1971), I, 227–31, and II, 14–15; Williams and others in Behalf of the People of Liberty County, Ga., 28 November 1865, to Col. Sickles, Commissioner, Georgia Freedmen's Bureau Mss., RG 105, National Archives (courtesy of Edward Magdol); W. T. Richardson, n.d., to the editor, *American Missionary*, IX (November 1865), 244–45. See also Williamson, *After Slavery: The Negro in South Carolina During Reconstruction, 1861–1877* (1965), 311–12, where Williamson writes that "the demands of kinship above the immediate family were deep and wide" and evidenced in "local migratory movements" and "in the lists of settlers located on state lands by the Land Commission." An excellent description of the breakup of the slave-gang labor system is found in D. G. Barrow, "A Georgia Plantation," *Scribner's Magazine*, XXI (1881), 830–36. This article contains sketches of residence patterns before and after the breakup of gang-labor work.

24. William Gannett, "The Freedmen at Port Royal," *North American Review*, CVIII (July 1865), 1–28; Herskovits, *Myth of the Negro Past*, 167–86; Frazier, *Negro Family in the United States*, 258 ff., and *Negro in the United States*, 3–21.

25. Raymond T. Smith, "The Nuclear Family in Afro-American Kinship," *Journal of Comparative Family Studies*, I (1970), 55–70; Du Bois, *Negro American Family* (1909), 56; A. Davis, B. B. Gardner, and M. R. Gardner, *Deep South* (1941), 410–12; Carol B. Stack, "The Kindred of Viola Jackson: Residence and Family Organization of an Urban Black Family," in Whitten and Szwed, eds., *Afro-American Anthropology: Contemporary Perspectives* (1970), 303–12; Demetri B. Shimkin, Gloria T. Louie, and Dennis Frate, with the editorial assistance of Edith M. Shimkin, "The Black Extended Family: A Basic Rural Institution and a Mechanism of Urban Adaptation," unpublished paper presented at the Ninth International Congress of Anthropological and Ethnological Sciences, Chicago, August–September 1973, 171–72, 183, and the summary of this study ("The Black Family: A Proud Reappraisal") by Hamilton Bims in *Ebony*, XXIX (March 1974), 118–27; Eva Muller and William Ladd, "Negro-White Differences in Geographic Mobility," in Charles V. Willie, ed., *The Family Life of Black People* (1970), 102–14; Alfred N. Mirande, "The Isolated Nuclear Family Hypothesis: A Reanalysis," in John Edwards, ed., *Family and Change* (1969), 153–63; Eugene Litwak, "Occupational Mobility and Extended Family Cohesion," *American Sociological Review*, 25 (February and June 1960), 9–21, 388–95; Virginia Young, "Family and Children in a Southern Community," *American Anthropologist*, 72 (April 1970), 269–88.

26. Theodore Rosengarten, *All God's Dangers: The Life of Nate Shaw* (1974), 59, 206–13.

27. Orlando Patterson, *Sociology of Slavery* (1967), 150, 169–70; Mintz and Price, "An Anthropological Approach to the Study of Afro-American History," *passim*; Mitford Matthews, *Dictionary of Americanisms* (1951), 1793. I am indebted to the following people for answering my inquiry concerning the use of kin terms of address among slaves and whites prior to 1800: John Hope Franklin, Winthrop Jordan, Edmund Morgan, Willie Lee Rose, and C. Vann Woodward. See also St. Clair Drake, *The Redemption of Africa and Black Religion* (1970), 12–14.

28. Frederick Douglass, *My Bondage and My Freedom* (1885), 69 ff.; Levi Coppin, *Unwritten History* (1919), 17–21; Frazier, "Negro Family," *Journal of Negro History*, XV (March 1930), 235; testimony of Lucy Chase, American Freedmen's Inquiry Commission, file 2, p. 24, Letters Received, Office of the Adjutant General, Main Series, 1861–1870, Reel 200, National Archives.

29. Unidentified Missouri letter, n.d., to the *Oberlin Evangelist*, n.d., reprinted in Harriet Beecher Stowe, *Key to Uncle Tom's Cabin* (1854), 49–50; Ellen Patrick, Charleston, 7 April 1867, to the editor,

Freedmen's Record, III (July 1867), 118; John deForest, *A Union Officer in the Reconstruction* (1948), 55–58; W. H. Harmount, "Colored People in the Parish of Ascension, La.," *Freedmen's Advocate,* I (November 1864), 40; Laura M. Towne, *Letters and Diary of Laura M. Towne* (1912), 142–48; Fortes, "Kinship and Marriage Among the Ashanti," in Radcliffe-Brown and Forde, eds., *African Systems of Kinship and Marriage,* 267.

30. Testimony of Laura M. Towne, American Freedmen's Inquiry Commission, 1863, file 3, 66–67, Office of the Adjutant General, Letters Received, Main Series, 1861–1870, Reel 200, National Archives; Mary Ames, *From a New England Woman's Diary in 1865* (1906), 111.

31. Sidney W. Mintz and Eric R. Wolf, "An Analysis of Ritual Co-Parenthood (Compadrazgo)," *Southwestern Journal of Anthropology,* VI (Winter 1950), 341–68; E. N. Goody, "Forms of Pro-Parenthood: The Sharing and Substitution of Parental Roles," in Jack Goody, ed., *Kinship, Selected Readings* (1971), 321–45.

32. Sam Aleckson, *Before the War and After the Union* (1929), 105; James Hammond, diary entries 29 April and 22 June 1844, quoted in Kenneth Stampp, *Peculiar Institution,* 325; Charles Alexander, *Battles and Victories of Allen Allensworth* (1914), 27.

33. See Eric R. Wolf, "Specific Aspects of Plantation System in the New World: Community, Sub-Cultures, and Social Classes," in *Plantation Systems of the New World* (1959), 136–46. Plantations, Wolf observes, were often characterized by a "predominance of personal face-to-face relationships," but these were "not the same kind of personal relationships which occur in tribal or peasant communities. . . . They differ from kin and other face-to-face relationships in that they retain the *form* of personal relationships but serve *different functions.*" Wolf explains:

> When a plantation owner returns to the plantation at Christmas to give presents to the children of his workers, or when he lends money to a worker whose wife stands in need of expert medical care, or when in the past he supervised the flogging of a recalcitrant peon at the plantation whipping post, he is using the form of personal relationships, while carrying out functions which maintain the plantation as a system of labor organization.
>
> In these acts he carried out operations of a technical order (to use a phrase of Robert Redfield's) which are still mediated through cultural forms that bear the personal stamp. He involves himself in relationships which carry affect, either positive or negative, in order to underline the dependent position of the laborer in contrast to his own status of dominance. He thus reinforces the managerial relation between the worker and himself. This hybrid wedding of

form and function also characterizes the periodic plantation ceremonies which involve the entire labor force and which serve to
underline the role of the plantation owner as a symbolic "father,"
who distributes food and favors to his symbolic "children." . . .

The worker, in turn, must seek personal relationships with the
plantation owner. He will attempt, whenever possible, to translate
issues of the technical order into personal or moral terms. This he
does not because he is incapable of behaving in non-personal terms,
but because the social system of the old-style plantation forces him
to adopt this manner of behavior. The owner is the source of his
daily bread and of any improvement in his life chances. He is thus
the only one capable of reducing the worker's life risks and materially raising his prospects. The worker therefore addresses his
pleas to him, and the culturally sanctioned way to do this is through
a ritual pantomime of dependence. . . . All of these acts of dependence draw the owner into the worker's personal debt, and surround the technical relationship of master and dependent with the
threads of personalized ritual exchanges. These ritual acts that symbolize dependence and dominance cannot, of course, involve all the
workers on the plantation in equal measure. Many may be called,
but only a few will be chosen; most must remain outside the personalized circle. Nevertheless, this social selection furthers the maintenance of the plantation as a going concern, since it builds up in the
labor force general expectations that personal contact with the
owner will help ease the burdens of life.

As a corollary, these personalized ritual exchanges on the old-
style plantation tend to inhibit the growth of a consciousness of
kind among the labor force. The individual family, rather than the
labor force as a whole, becomes the carrier of the ritualized exchange
with the owner. . . .

Wolf's emphasis on the "hybrid wedding of form and function"
and on the "ritual pantomime of dependence" provides powerful
ways of examining the behavior of both slaves and their owners.
The emphasis on the ways in which owners bargained with "families" may provide a vital clue to the different statuses of house
servants and field hands. It is also possible that the intensive
familial networks that developed among slaves provide some explanation for the relative absence of slave rebellion.

34. Coppin, *Unwritten History*, 17–21; Francis Gage, Parris Island,
S.C., 29 Aug. 1863, to the editor, *New York Tribune*, n.d., reprinted in *Liberator*, 16 Oct. 1863; *Proceedings of Freedmen's
Convention of Georgia Assembled at Augusta, August 1–10, 1866*
(1866), *passim*; Elkanah Beard, Vicksburg, Miss., 20 and 31 Oct.
1865, to the editor, *Friends' Review*, XIX (1865), 184–86, 218–20;
John deForest, *A Union Officer in the Reconstruction*, 97–99.

35. James Sinclair, Lumberton, N.C., 2 Oct. 1865, to C. J. Wickersham, North Carolina Freedmen's Bureau Mss., Record Group

105, National Archives, courtesy of Edward Magdol; E. P. Smith, Atlanta, n.d., to the editor, *American Missionary*, X (May 1866), 97–98; Mrs. E. T. Ayres, Atlanta, n.d., to the editor, *AM*, X (March 1866), 63; John Dennett, *South as It Is* (1965), ed. H. M. Christman, 269–70; "Speech of O. O. Howard," *AM*, X (June 1866), 23–28; "Report of Commissioner O. O. Howard," 41 Cong., Second Session, *Executive Documents 1869–1870*, 487–515 *(Serial 1412)*.

36. *American Slave, South Carolina Narratives*, IV, ii, 259–60; *Alabama Narratives*, VI, 72–73; C. E. Smith, 28 Dec. 1864, to the editor, *National Freedman*, I (Feb. 1865), 13–14; Joseph Warren, 6 July 1864, to John Eaton, *Extracts from Reports of Superintendents of Freedmen, second series, June 1864* (1864), 65; Edward Wilkes, Vicksburg, 20 May 1865, to the editor, *NF*, I (June 1865), 149–56; *American Missionary*, X (April 1866), 73–74; *Pennsylvania Freedmen's Bulletin* (April 1867), 6–7 and (February 1869), 8; Juliet Smith, New Bern, 21 Jan. 1865, to the editor, *Freedmen's Advocate*, I (Feb. 1865, supplement), 1; Miss S. S. Smith, Norfolk, 30 March 1864, to the editor, *AM*, VIII (June 1864), 137–38; H. C. Fisher, Norfolk, 29 Nov. 1865, to W. G. Hawkins, *NF*, I (December 1865), 352; L. E. Williams, Richmond, 30 Dec. 1865, to the editor, *NF*, II (February 1866), 16; O. O. Howard, *Autobiography*, II (1903), 261–62; E. C. P. and W. F. Mitchell, Nashville, n.d., to the editor, *Friends' Review* XVIII (1864–1865), 363, 758–59.

37. *Freedmen's Advocate*, II (January 1865), 2; *Freedmen's Bulletin*, I (November 1864), 48 and II (February 1866), 38; Miss Geist, Natchez, 18 Oct. 1864, to the editor, *FB*, I (November 1864), 49; Martha Canfield, Memphis, 1 March 1865, to John Eaton, and Martha Canfield, "Extracts from Diary," *Extracts from Documents in the Office of the General Superintendent of Refugees and Freedmen. Memphis, March 1865* (1865), 11–24; Howard, *Autobiography*, II, 261–62; Howard White, *Freedmen's Bureau of Louisiana* (1970), 78–83; John Eaton, *Final Report* (1864), 88; M. Burch, Ferandina, Fla., 14 Nov. 1864, to C. C. Leigh, *National Freedman*, I (July 1865), 183–86; James Redpath, Charleston, n.d., to the editor, *NF*, I (April 1865), 211–13; John Dennett, *South as It Is* (1965), 304; John Blassingame, *Black New Orleans, 1860–1880* (1973), 169–70; Thomas Conway, *The Freedmen of Louisiana, Final Report of the Bureau of Free Labor* (1865), 14–15; Yorktown Superintendent, 21 Jan. 1867, to the editor, *Friends' Review*, XX (1867), 380.

38. Laura M. Towne, St. Helena's Island, S.C., n.d., and 29 March 1868, to the editor, *American Freedman*, III (April and June 1868), 396–97, 431–32. The biographical data on the Garrett family is found in the 1880 federal manuscript census.

Chapter 6: Somebody Knew My Name

1. Susan Dabney Smedes, *Memorials of a Southern Planter* (1955), 71; Isabel G. Barrows, ed., *First Mohonk Conference on the Negro Question Held at Lake Mohonk, Ulster County, New York, June 4–6, 1890* (1890), 18, 25–27, 69–70, 107.

2. For an analysis of slave surnames different from the one offered in these pages, see Eugene D. Genovese, *Roll, Jordan, Roll: The World the Slaves Made* (1974), 444–50. Genovese argues that slaves with surnames appeared "in all parts of the South." "The strongest evidence for the appropriation of surnames by the slaves or of their pressure to compel slaveholders to grant them the 'privilege' comes from the Mississippi Valley and the South Carolina and Georgia coast," he says, "for these were the regions with the biggest plantations and the greatest degree of stability. Elsewhere surnames appeared less frequently, but there was a tendency toward their use, which may well have paralleled the growth in community stability." "Masters," Genovese writes, "sometimes gave their slaves surnames; more often, with or without their masters' consent or even knowledge, the slaves took surnames for themselves." No evidence shows either that masters "sometimes gave their slaves surnames" or that slaves "pressured" their owners to force that concession from them. Slave surnames were not more common in "regions with the biggest plantations and the greatest degree of stability." Slaves with surnames different from their owners', as shall be seen, are good evidence of instability.

3. "Clothing Givin out to children Not Working by Families, Nov. 1840," John Ball Comingtree Plantation, Cooper River, S.C., mss. copy, South Carolina Historical Society, courtesy of Stanley Engerman.

4. Davis Bend, Miss., Marriage Register, 1864–1865, Mississippi Freedmen's Bureau Mss., RG 105, National Archives; "Agreement dated 29 July 1865," Washington County, Texas, John Randolph Papers, Louisiana State University Plantation Records, Roll 8, Columbia University microfilm copy; Good Hope Plantation, Concordia Parish, La., 1864–1866 mss. records, L.S.U. Plantation Records, Roll 8, Columbia University microfilm copy; "Supplementary List of Planters Who Have Sent Freedmen Away Without Payment to Nov. 15, 1865, St. Simon's Island, Ga.," Letters Received, Office of the Adjutant General, "Racial Violence in the South (1865–1866)," Main Series, 1861–1870, Roll 505, NA.

5. Hazelhurst (Copiah County) and Silver Creek (Yazoo County) Labor Registries, ca. 1866, Mississippi Freedmen's Bureau Mss., RG 105, National Archives.

6. Undated listing of Davis Bend, Mississippi, Home Colony, residents, Freedmen's Bureau Mss., RG 105, NA (courtesy of Steven Ross); Princess Anne County, Virginia, 1866 ms. census, Va. FB Mss., RG 105, NA; Ascension Parish, Louisiana, Applications for Relief to the Freedmen's Bureau, October 1866–June 1868, La. FB Mss., vol. 260, pp. 132–39, RG 105, NA.

7. If slaves hesitated in using surnames before owners, there was no reason for them to reveal themselves quickly to northern newcomers. That would have confused northerners and reinforced the common belief that slaves did not have surnames, a confusion compounded among schoolteachers who dealt with blacks who would have known the least about secret slaves surnames. See Elizabeth Kilham, "Sketches in Color," *Putnam's Magazine*, V, (January 1870), 32–33; Charlotte McKay, "Domestic Relations of the Freedmen," *National Freedman*, I (May 1866), 143–45; *American Slave, Texas Narratives*, V, iv, 182–86. For evidence of Yankee efforts to impose surnames, see M.R.S., "Our Sea Island Schools," *Pennsylvania Freedmen's Bulletin* (December 1866), 5–6, and Wilmur Walton, Stevenson, Ala., 12 April and 15 May 1865, *PFB* (1865), 30, 46–47.

8. Testimony of Rufus Saxton, Laura M. Towne, Robert Smalls, and E. W. Hooper, 1863, American Freedmen's Inquiry Commission, file 3, pp. 1–4, 66–67, 98–99, Letters Received, Office of the Adjutant General, Main Series, 1861–1870, Reel 200, National Archives; James MacKaye, *Mastership and Its Fruits: The Emancipated Slave Face to Face With His Old Master . . .* (1864), 5; *Letters from Port Royal* (1906), ed. E. W. Pearson, 52; *Dear Ones at Home: Letters from the Contraband Camps* (1966), ed., H. L. Swint, 37; Elizabeth Botume, *First Days Amongst the Contrabands*, 45–48; Whitelaw Reid, *After the War* (1866), 532; Port Royal, S.C., dispatch, 8 March 1863, *New York Tribune*, n.d., reprinted in *Anti-Slavery Standard*, 21 March 1863.

9. Duncan Clinch Heyward, *Seed from Madagascar* (1937), 96–98; Jacob Stroyer, *Sketches of My Life in the South* (1879), 9–10; pension claim of Rebecca Bailey (34850), National Archives, courtesy of Robert Clarke.

Postwar pension records are an invaluable source for studying much about the enslaved Afro-American. A small number filed by the kin of deceased Mississippi Union Army soldiers—all former slaves—have been examined. They show that slaves often had surnames different from their owners'. "My first owner," said the deposition of Clarissa Green, "was Benjamin Blake, [and] my second and last was Benjamin Roach." "My maiden name," added the Yazoo resident, a native Virginian, "was Polly Taylor." Mintie

Wallace applied for a pension due her dead son Washington
Wallace. She had belonged to Thomas Magruder. Her husband
was called Alfred Wallace in 1840, the year of his death. Rocksie
Ann Dines and her husband Virgil Dines belonged to J. B. Greaves
in 1860. Before she married, the slave woman had been called
Roxanna Lyons. Cato Jones and his wife were the slaves of Lewis
Jones. Prior to their marriage, Jones's wife's name had been
Lucinda Mills. Wash Creeley admitted in a pension claim that he
had used two surnames. He had belonged to Benjamin Roach but
never called himself Roach. "My name before the war," he said,
"was the same as it is now but some people call me Reuben.
When I enlisted I gave the name of Reuben Smith. My father
was named Jim Creeley. My mother was named Polly Smith, and
I enlisted in that name. Since I came out of the army I have called
myself Wash Creeley and I go by that name." See the pension
claim records of Clarissa Green (35281), Mintie Wallace (228935),
Rocksie Ann Dines (34230), Lucinda Jones (34316), Emily Creeley
(742623), National Archives, courtesy of Robert Clarke.

10. James Redpath, *Roving Editor* (1859), 56; *Narrative of the Life
and Adventures of Henry Bibb, An American Slave*, reprinted in
Puttin' On Ole Massa, ed. Gilbert Osofsky (1969), 64; *The Trial
Record of Denmark Vesey*, ed. J. O. Killens (1970), 92, 122, 126,
127, 141–44; "Papers of Cynthia Beverley Tucker," n.d., printed
in G. P. Coleman, ed., *Virginia Silhouettes* (1934), 54–55; Okon
Edet Uya, *From Slavery to Public Service, Robert Smalls* (1971),
7; *Blacks in Bondage: Letters of American Slaves*, ed. Robert S.
Starobin (1974), 58, 107–9; newspaper runaway advertisements
printed in Harriet Beecher Stowe, *Key to Uncle Tom's Cabin*
(1854), 159–61, 331, 342, 349–51, 359, 362; William Still, *The
Underground Railroad* (1872), 46–272; William J. Minor Louisiana
Plantation birth register, courtesy of Stanley Engerman.

11. Wendell H. Stephenson, *Isaac Franklin, Slave Trader and Planter
of the Old South* (1938), *passim* but especially 31–32, 104, 126–29,
138–45, 157–61, 165–91.

12. A partial New Orleans customhouse manifest dated January 1833
included the names of thirty-two slaves shipped there from Alexandria, in all eight families. Seven included children. Couples
headed three families. Mothers—three of the women twenty-one
years old or younger—headed the others. All the families had surnames. Another document surviving Franklin's slave-trading enterprise is a list of slaves purchased in 1839 from the Amherst County,
Virginia, white Thomas Hundley. None were older than twenty-
five. Most were young adults nineteen to twenty-two, and the
women had infant children. It is unknown whether Hundley had

first purchased them for resale. All had surnames, not one a Hundley.

13. Franklin's 138 Tennessee slaves are not included among these 565 men, women, and children.

14. Overall, the six plantations had a distorted age structure: 201 of the 565 slaves were not yet fifteen years old, and of the remaining 365 men and women *only seven men and six women* were between the ages of fifteen and nineteen. Unless Franklin had purchased slaves in an unusual way, these age distributions suggest strongly that Franklin was still a slave trader. The plantations also had a large surplus of young unmarried males. Hardly any women fifteen and older were single; nearly half of the men similarly aged were unmarried.

15. It is quite possible that significant numbers of slave women had different surnames from their husbands'. North Carolina blacks registering their marriages in 1866 recorded two names, and significant numbers of couples—two in three—in Johnston County had different surnames. Many husbands and wives had different owners and may have simply reported this fact. The registers did not list the names of old owners. The Johnston blacks also reported the length of slave marriages. Seven of ten couples married less than ten years had different surnames, but only about half of those married twenty or more years did. No explanation for this difference has been found. It is possible that the men and women retained the surnames of owners after marriage, but that would not explain who so many women with long slave marriages dropped the surname of an owner for that of a husband or a husband's owner. Let us assume, however, that wives consciously retained different surnames. In free society, nineteenth-century women took their husbands' surnames on marriage and thereby symbolically transferred a primary loyalty from a family of origin to a conjugal mate. One-third of Johnston County black registrants fitted what nonslave society knew as a commonplace social ritual. The adoption of a common surname for the rest, however, was not a requirement for long marriages or registering such marriages in 1866. The point can be made differently: Johnston County slave couples with different surnames lived in settled unions. ("Negro Cohabitation Certificates," 1866, Johnston County, North Carolina, ms. copy, North Carolina Department of Archives and History, Raleigh, N.C.) Elderly slaves interviewed in the 1930s cast little light on the presence of different surnames among slave husbands and wives. Only a handful recollected that practice. John Bectom grew up in Cumberland County and Jane Anne Privette Upperman in Nash County. Bectom recollected that when

slaves belonging to separate owners married, "the woman did not take the name of her husband" but "kept the name of the family who owned her." "My father," said Jane Upperman, whose parents had different owners, "wus named Carroll Privette an' my mother wus Cherry Brantly, but after she wus free she began to call herself by my father's name. Father belonged to Jimmie Privette across the Tar River whar ma lived." (*American Slave, Alabama Narratives*, VI, 92–93, 189–92; *Oklahoma Narratives*, VII, 227–29; *North Carolina Narratives*, XIV, i, 95–96, and XV, ii, 368–69.)

16. J. H. Johnston, *Race Relations in Virginia* (1970), 188–89, 322–27; John Peck, 8 Sept. 1788, to Robert Carter, printed in Phillips, ed., *Plantation and Frontier Documents*, (1909) II, 44–45; "Eighteenth Century Slaves as Advertised by Their Masters," *Journal of Negro History*, I (April 1916), 302–4; Peter H. Wood, *Black Majority* (1974), 245; *Journal of Negro History*, III (April 1918), 100–102.

17. The British ship registers are found in the Miscellaneous Papers of the Continental Congress, 1774–1785, and are dated 1783, Roll 66, microcopy 247, and Roll 7, microcopy 332, National Archives. I am very much indebted to Robert Clarke for calling this invaluable material to my attention. On the Dunmore Proclamation, see Benjamin Quarles, "Lord Dunmore as Liberator," *William and Mary Quarterly*, XV (October 1958), 494–507, and Thad W. Tate, *Negro in Eighteenth Century Williamsburg* (1965), 215–21.

18. Indication of the prior residences of males fifteen years and older come from the lists for the ships *L'Abundance, Concord,* and *Peggy.* Such residences were listed for 125 of 131 males as follows: *New England*: Boston (6), Fairfield, Conn. (2), Norwalk, Conn., New London, Conn., Newport, R.I., and "New England" (1 each); *Middle Colonies*: "New Jersey" (8), "New York" (6), Tappan, N.J., Morristown, N.J., Hackensack, N.J., Courtland Manor, N.Y., Brooklyn, N.Y., and Chester County, Pa. (1 each); *Maryland*: Cecil County (2) and Somerset County (1); *North Carolina*: Roanoke (1); *Georgia*: Savannah (2), Augusta and "Georgia" (1 each); *South Carolina*: Charleston (12), Santee (4), James River and "South Carolina" (2 each), Ashley River, Goose Creek, Georgetown, and New River (1 each); *Virginia*: Norfolk (20), Portsmouth (6), Nansemond (5), Gloucester, Princess Anne, and Craney Island (4 each), Hampton (3), "Virginia" (2), and Essex, North Landing, Newport, King George, Rappahannock, Stafford, Jamestown, Warwick, James River, Surry, and Kent (1 each).

19. A fine discussion of the proclamation is Benjamin Quarles, "Lord Dunmore as Liberator," *William and Mary Quarterly* XV (October 1958), 494–507.

20. It is not possible to do a similar analysis for the female adult

slaves because all but a small number who had spouses had the
same surname as their husbands. A rough separation of seemingly "single" women fifteen and older suggests a variation from
the male pattern. Of 346 such women, 45 percent lacked surnames,
17 percent had the same surname as their owner, and 38 percent
had different surnames. But the age distribution biases these percentages, because two-thirds of these single women were not yet
aged thirty. Single women thirty and older differed: 36 percent
lacked surnames and 47 percent had different surnames from
owners'. The percentage with the same surname as a last owner did
not change. If only single women with surnames are counted, two-
thirds of those thirty and older had different surnames from
their owners'.

21. *The Negro in Virginia (WPA)*, 23, 24, 37.

22. *American Slave, South Carolina Narratives*, II, ii, 223–36, III, iii,
167–71, iv, 160–62; *Texas Narratives*, IV, i, 289–94; *Alabama Narratives*, VI, 111–12; *Unwritten History (Fisk)*, 19–22, 103–8.

23. *American Slave, South Carolina Narratives*, II, i, 224–26, 326–28,
III, iii, 42–44, iv, 157–59; *Texas Narratives*, IV, i, 51–53, 66–67,
188–89, V, iii, 268–70, iv, 9–14, 73–75; *Alabama Narratives*, VI,
356–57.

24. *American Slave, South Carolina Narratives*, II, i, 51–54, 170–71,
329, ii, 2, 223–36, 279–88, III, iii, 200–204, 271–76; *Texas Narratives*, IV, i, 1–3, ii, 81–86, V, iv, 197–98; *Oklahoma Narratives*, VII,
233–35; *Unwritten History (Fisk)*, 41–47.

25. *American Slave, South Carolina Narratives*, II, i, 10–12, ii, 30–33,
252–57, III, iv, 42–43, 174–80, 253–56; *Texas Narratives*, IV, ii,
106–8, 216–18; *Alabama Narratives*, VI, 363, 413–22.

26. *American Slave, South Carolina Narratives*, II, i, 80–97, ii, 212–14,
III, iii, 23–37; *Texas Narratives*, IV, i, 225–35, V, iv, 114–15. See
also *Oklahoma Narratives*, VII, 275–80.

27. *American Slave, South Carolina Narratives*, III, iv, 31–34, 247–52;
Texas Narratives, IV, i, 54–58, 252–53, ii, 55–59, 187–92; *Alabama
Narratives*, VI, 171.

28. *American Slave, South Carolina Narratives*, II, i, 127–30, 330–35;
Texas Narratives, IV, i, 160–62, ii, 47–49, V, iii, 218–22, iv, 30–32,
67–69, 83–84; *Mississippi Narratives*, VII, 26–33; *Oklahoma Narratives*, VII, 172–75.

29. *American Slave, South Carolina Narratives*, II, iii, 17–19, 209–12;
Texas Narratives, IV, i, 45–46, 137, 257–59, ii, 50–54, 195–97;
Alabama Narratives, VI, 385; *Oklahoma Narratives*, VII, 298–99a;
Mississippi Narratives, VII, 101–3.

Some former slaves took the surnames of their mothers' new

husbands. After his father died, Sam McAllum's Mississippi mother
remarried. The young black took his stepfather's name. Louis
Fowler's Georgia father had been a white, but sometime after his
birth his mother married a slave nearby named Fowler. Isaiah
Jeffries never knew his father. His mother had several children
by different men and later married. "My mother's husband was
named Ned," Jeffries said. "After she married Ned, den he jest
come to be our Pa, dat is he let her give us his name."

30. *American Slave, South Carolina Narratives*, II, i, 65–69, 263–66,
III, iii, 191–93, 221–22, iv, 95–99; *Texas Narratives*, IV, ii, 25–32,
V, iv, 236–239; *Oklahoma Narratives*, VII, 73–75; *Unwritten History (Fisk)*, 121–22.

31. *American Slave, South Carolina Narratives*, II, i, 13–16, 205–9,
260–62, ii, 117–19, 266–70, 276–78, III, iii, 59–61, iv, 81–87; *Texas Narratives*, IV, i, 185–87, 191–92, V, iii, 4–7, 132–37, 262–64, iv,
128–33, 179–88; *Alabama Narratives*, VII, 1–5; *Mississippi Narratives*, VII, 128–29.

A few elderly former slaves remembered that they or their
fathers had surnames that reached into the past but had no apparent connection to an earlier owner. The Bossier Parish white
Robert J. Looney had owned the Louisiana slave child Chris
Franklin. "My pappy's name Solomon Lawson," said Franklin.
"He 'longs to Jedge Lawson, what lives near us. When freedom
come, he done take de name Sol Franklin, what he say am he
pappy name." "My father's name was Nathan Greene," said the
former Aberdeen, Mississippi, slave George Greene. "I reckon he
went by that name I can't swear to it. . . . I don't know whether
my father used his master's name or his father's name. His father's
name was Jerry Greene, and his master's name was Henry Bibb.
I don't know which name he went by, but I call myself Greene
because his father's name was Jerry Greene." At the war's end,
Cynthia and Isaac Thomas belonged to the Texas white I. D.
Thomas. "But after freedom," according to their son Harrison
Beckett, Isaac Thomas went "back to Florida and find he people
and git he real name, and dat am Beckett." Martin Jackson also
picked a name, a modification of his grandfather's given African
name. Born in Texas in 1847, he was raised by his father after his
mother died. "One of my grandfathers in Africa," said Jackson,
"was called 'Jeaceo,' and so I decided to be a Jackson" (*American
Slave, Arkansas Narratives*, IX, iii, 104–5).

32. U. B. Phillips, introduction, in Phillips and J. D. Glunt, eds.,
Florida Plantation Records (1927), 33; A. V. House, ed., "Deterioration of a Georgia Rice Plantation," *Journal of Southern
History*, IX (February 1943), 107–8; Heyward, *Seed from Madagascar*, 96–98; Joel Williamson, *After Slavery: The Negro in South*

Carolina During Reconstruction, 1861–1877 (1965), 309–12; George C. Rogers, Jr., *History of Georgetown County, South Carolina* (1970), 438–39.

33. Sam Aleckson, *Before the War, and After the Union* (1929), 17–18.

34. Emily Blackman, Okolona, Miss., 1 May 1867, to the editor, *Pennsylvania Freedmen's Bulletin*, June 1867, 7; Quarles, *The Negro in the Civil War* (1953), 287–88.

35. Eliza Frances Andrews, *War-Time Journal of a Georgia Girl, 1864–1865* (1908), 3–21, 338–39, 344–48, 357–58.

Chapter 7: To See His Grand Son Samuel Die

1. Kenneth M. Stampp, *The Peculiar Institution* (1956), 322, 333.

2. H. H. Garnet, n.d., to the editor, *Anglo-African*, n.d., reprinted in *Freedman's Journal*, I (October 1865), 38–39.

3. See also my review-essay of *Time on the Cross: The Economics of American Negro Slavery* published first under the title "The World Two Cliometricians Made, A Review-Essay of F+E=T/C," *Journal of Negro History*, 50 (January 1975), 54–227, and then in an edited version entitled *Slavery and the Numbers Game: A Critique of Time on the Cross* (1975). This chapter ignores much contemporary sociological writing on the Afro-American slave family. Such writings rarely contain serious historical analysis and are often filled with generalizations that bear no relationship to real slave experiences. See, for example, Nathan Glazer's insistence that "there was something comic about calling the woman with whom the master permitted him [the adult male slave] to live with a 'wife,' " Daniel P. Moynihan's assertion that "with the emancipation of the slaves the Negro American family began to form on a widespread scale," and Jessie Bernard's judgment that slave marriages were little more than "a matter of external adaptation— not . . . internal conviction—a matter of institutionalization, but not of acculturation." (Nathan Glazer, "Introduction," Stanley Elkins, *Slavery: A Problem in American Institutional and Intellectual Life* [1963], ix–xii; Daniel P. Moynihan, *The Negro Family: The Case for National Action* [1965], 16; Jessie Bernard, *Marriage and Family Among Negroes* [1966], 27–29.)

4. George Fredrickson and Christopher Lasch, "Resistance to Slavery," *Civil War History*, XIII (December 1967), 315–29.

5. Talcott Parsons, *Essays in Sociological Theory Pure and Applied* (1949), 203; E. Franklin Frazier, *Negro Family in the United States* (1939), 15, 367; Gunnar Myrdal, *An American Dilemma* (1944), 928.

6. Charles A. Valentine, "Deficit, Difference, and Bicultural Models of Afro-American Behavior," *Harvard Educational Review*, 41 (May 1971), 137–57.

7. See, for examples, Eugene D. Genovese, *World the Slaveholders Made* (1969), 96–97, *In Red and Black* (1971), 112, and *Roll, Jordan, Roll: The World the Slaves Made* [1974], 451–52; John Blassingame, *Slave Community: Plantation Life in the Antebellum South* (1972), 80; Fogel and Engerman, *Time on the Cross*, I, 5, 127, 142. "[M]ost slaves," Genovese wrote in 1969, "probably did have the possibility of marital stability because their masters provided it. They provided it for two complementary reasons: they could more easily control married slaves with families, and their Christian consciences demanded it." Two years later, he wrote that "planters did everything possible to encourage slaves to live in stable units; they recognized that man was easier to control if he had a wife and children to worry about." And in *Roll, Jordon, Roll*, it is asserted that "the masters understood the strength of the marital ties among their slaves well enough to see in them a powerful means of social control." Blassingame finds that slave-owners who "encouraged monogamous mating arrangements . . . did it to make it easier to discipline their slaves." Fogel and Engerman try to convince readers that "it was to the economic interest of planters to encourage the stability of slave families and most of them did so."

8. Genovese, *In Red and Black* (1971), 111.

9. For a subtle and intelligent discussion of the differences between alternative and oppositional forces and how they develop and alter in meaning over time, see Raymond Williams, "Base and Superstructure in Marxist Cultural Theory," *New Left Review*, 82 (November–December 1973), 3–16.

10. Incomplete birth lists and slave lists for the Pettigrew plantation slaves are found in volumes 13, 22, 25, 29, and 43, Southern Historical Collection, University of North Carolina, Chapel Hill, N.C. Partial but hardly complete families and kin networks can be constructed stretching from 1780 and the Civil War. The behavior revealed nevertheless conforms in all ways to that described on the other plantations studied in this work. Slaves usually settled into long marriages; most children grew up in two-parent households; some women had a first child by one man (sometimes unnamed in the records) and then married.

11. The family history discussed in this paragraph is based upon study of the lists cited in note 10. The materials on slave misbehavior are in Robert S. Starobin's excellent study, "Privileged Bondsmen and the Process of Accommodation: The Role of the House-

servants and Drivers as Seen in Their Own Letters," *Journal of Social History*, 5 (Fall 1971), 59–65 and *Blacks in Bondage* (1974), 14–35. See also Stampp, *Peculiar Institution*, 95–96, 324.

12. Barrow's difficulties with his slaves and their unproductive labor are examined at length in Gutman, *Slavery and the Numbers Game*, 16–48, but see Edwin Adam Davis, ed., *Plantation Life in the Florida Parishes of Louisiana, 1836–1846, as Reflected in the Diary of Bennet H. Barrow* (1943), *passim*.

13. F. L. Olmsted, *A Journey in the Seaboard Slave States in the Years 1853–1854* (1904), I, 64.

14. Good discussion of the circumstances surrounding flight is found in Stampp, *Peculiar Institution*, 109–24, and Genovese, *Roll, Jordan, Roll*, 648–57. Extracts from runaway advertisements suggesting flight to kin appear in Stampp, as cited; Phillips, ed., *Plantation and Frontier Documents, 1643–1863* (1909), II, 85–86; J. B. Sellers, *Slavery in Alabama* (1950), 168–69; W. E. B. Du Bois, *Negro American Family* (1909), 23–25; William Goodell, *The American Slave Code in Theory and Practice* (1853), 119–21; O. W. Taylor, *Negro Slavery in Arkansas* (1958), 216–17; J. W. Coleman, *Slavery Times in Kentucky* (1940), 57–64; Julia Floyd Smith, *Slavery and Plantation Growth in Antebellum Florida* (1973), 77; *Richmond Enquirer*, 5 Aug. 1836, quoted in Robert Bremner, ed., *Childhood and Youth In America: A Documentary History*, (1970), I, 378; Frederic Bancroft, *Slave Trading in the Old South* (1931), 201, 206; Hugh Lefler and Paul Wager, eds., *Orange County, 1752–1952* (1953), 103.

15. William Still, *The Underground Railroad* (1872), 44, 64–65, 103–4, 151–52, 158–59, 299–300, 402. The Walker and Rightso letters are printed in Robert Starobin, ed., *Blacks in Bondage: Letters of American Slaves* (1974), 153–57. See also Carter G. Woodson, ed., *Mind of the Negro* (1926), 559–60 and *passim*.

16. Camp Barker, Alexandria, Virginia, Register of Refugees, Virginia Freedmen's Bureau Mss., Record Group, 105, National Archives.

17. Sidney W. Mintz, "History and Anthropology: A Brief Reprise," in Eugene D. Genovese and Stanley Engerman, eds., *Race and Slavery in the Western Hemisphere* (1975), 477–94; Claude Lévi-Strauss, "The Family," in Harry L. Shapiro, ed., *Man, Culture, and Society* (1956), 142–70; William Wells Brown, *Narrative of William Wells Brown: A Fugitive Slave* (1847), 37–39; F. L. Olmsted, *Journey in the Back Country* (1860), 153–55.

18. Schedule C in the 1850 and 1860 census recorded information about people (black and white as well as slave and free) who had died in the twelve months preceding June 1 of the census year,

giving the date and the cause of death and indicating the person's age, sex, color, occupation, and marital status. Census enumerators, however, often failed to list the marital status of slaves at their death, leaving that census column blank. But a few 1850 and 1860 South Carolina enumerators consistently indicated slave marital status, and their record has been examined for all adult slaves in St. Helena Parish, Beaufort County (1850), Georgetown County (1850), Marion County (1860), the northern district of Spartanburg County (1860), and St. Luke Parish and Prince William Parish, Beaufort County (1860).

These places revealed common slave marital and occupational patterns. Nearly all listed were field hands and common laborers. All but 9 of the 62 Georgetown County slave males who died in 1849–1850 were laborers. Of 316 slaves with listed occupations in 1850 and 1860, five of six were either field hands or laborers.

Together, the 1850 and 1860 death lists indicated the marital status of 177 slave males and 181 slave females. Only 35 were neither married nor widowed. Not one of the 58 St. Helena Parish men and women was single at the time of death. Only 5 of 126 Georgetown County blacks were single. The number of single adult slaves was greater in 1860 than in 1850 but still relatively small. A comparison by age and sex to the adult whites listed in these same schedules shows that among both younger and older whites a higher percentage were single than among similarly aged slaves. The 1850 and 1860 censuses are combined to illustrate this point. Five of eleven white males and five of seven white females aged twenty to twenty-nine were single at death as contrasted to nine of 40 male slaves and two of 23 female slaves of the same age. Five of 32 white males and two of 23 white females fifty and older were single at death as contrasted to 12 of 101 slave males and 4 of 103 slave females fifty and older.

The distinction between married and widowed blacks by age furthermore hints at the very great importance of marriage in the slave community. All 22 of the widowed 1850 St. Helena's Parish blacks were at least sixty years old. The widowed were just as old in 1860: only 1 of 11 widowed men and 3 of 23 widowed women were not yet fifty years old. Hardly any slaves aged twenty to thirty-nine were not widowed at their deaths. Younger adult slaves, of course, regularly lost spouses by death. The 1860 schedules, for example, indicated that 15 men aged twenty to twenty-nine were married at the time they died. But only 1 of the 29 women aged twenty to thirty-nine was listed as a widow at the moment of death. The relative absence of widows among slave men and women not yet forty years old does not mean that young married slaves failed to lose spouses by death. Instead, it suggests that only

old age deterred remarriage among slaves on the death of a spouse.
Powerful pressures—either from within the slave culture or from
slaveowners—clearly encouraged quick remarriage. The reasons
for this pattern remain unclear and deserve careful study. If these
scattered examples are typical, they may explain why so few Good
Hope slave adults in 1857 were either single or widowed and why
nearly all those listed as "single" were aged men and women.
(Schedule C, U.S. Federal Census, 1850 and 1860, South Carolina,
mss. copies.)

19. *DeBow's Review*, XXVIII (1860), 52; *Facts Concerning the Freedmen* (1863), 3–12.

20. District of Columbia Marriage Register, 1866–1867, unnumbered
volume, Freedmen's Bureau Mss., RG 105, NA.

21. The officiating cleric marked a few words after the names of many
couples to indicate the diverse experiences these former slaves had
encountered: "Bland owns House and Lot also Horses and Hack."
"Smith is a Baptist minister and is intelligent and industrious.
Owns house and lot." "Are thought to be very old, but have
seldom received aid." "Boswell is a plasterer. Has steady employment and good wages." "The wife of this man has earned enough
at washing to pay for House and Lot val. at \$1500." "This man
is said to be very abusive of his wife." "Evans is a shoemaker and
owns a shop." "Lewis is a shoemaker working with Evans." "Mrs.
Sanford is the mother of 21 children. Is still a strong woman.
Married in 1815 and has yet 10 children."

22. *American Slave, South Carolina Narratives*, II, i, 330–35, III, iii,
276; *Texas Narratives*, IV, i, 43–44, 240–41, ii, 246–48, V, iii, 128–
131, 162–64; iv, 187–89; *Alabama Narratives*, VI, 71–76, 318–19.
See also *Texas Narratives*, IV, ii, 71–73, 114–47, 163–65, V, iii, 65–
67, iv, 73–74.

23. *American Slave, South Carolina Narratives*, II, ii, 233–36; *Texas
Narratives*, IV, i, 62–65, 75–83, 147–48, 307–8, ii, 55–59, 225–27,
V, iii, 48–61, 148–51, iv, 19–23, 166–69; *Alabama Narratives*, VI,
106–9, 306–7; *Oklahoma Narratives*, VII, 322–29; *Negro in Virginia (WPA)*, 80–84; *Unwritten History of Slavery . . . (Fisk)*, 13–
17, 41–47, 67–69, 111–13, 129–32; Genovese, *Roll, Jordan, Roll:
the World the Slaves Made*, 475–81; Charles Sydnor, *Slavery in
Mississippi* (1933), 62–64. Dances, dinners, and special dress at
owner-sponsored marriages are detailed in *American Slave, South
Carolina Narratives*, III, iii, 184–87; *Texas Narratives*, IV, ii, 17–
20, V, iii, 48–67, 148–51, iv, 6–8, 134–37, 166–69, 184–85.

24. Olmsted, *Journey in the Seaboard Slave States* (1856), 448–49;
American Missionary, VII (April and June 1863), 88–89, 139;

Charles C. Jones, *Religious Instruction of the Negroes in the United States* (1842), 132–34; R. Q. Mallard, *Plantation Life Before Emancipation* (1892), 47–53; R. M. Myers, ed., *The Children of Pride* (1972), 1154; Willie Lee Rose, *Rehearsal for Reconstruction* (1964), 137–38; Ralph Flanders, *Plantation Slavery in Georgia* (1933), 172–73; G. G. Johnson, *Social History of the Sea Islands* (1930), 131–40; T. J. Woofter, *Black Yeomanry* (1930), 210; J. G. Taylor, *Negro Slavery in Louisiana* (1963), 123–25; Sarah Pryor, *Reminiscences of Peace and War* (1904), 148–49; J. T. Coleman, *Slavery Times in Kentucky* (1940), 57–64; *Autobiography of Francis Frederick of Virginia* (1869), 28–31; *Solomon McReynolds v. The State (Tenn.)*, 5 Cauldwell, 18–26, 1867; *Stewart v. Munchandler*, 2 Bush 278–82, Summer 1867 (Ky.); *American Slave, South Carolina Narratives*, II, i, 63–64, 319–29, ii, 43–71, III, iv, 57–58, 247–49; *Texas Narratives*, IV, i, 266–68, ii, 135–36, 193–94, V, iii, 252–53; *Unwritten History (Fisk)*, 109–10. The Young marriage certificate is found among the Lincoln County, N.C., "Negro Cohabitation Certificates," N.C. Dept. of Archives and History, Raleigh, N.C.

25. *Unwritten History (Fisk)*, 103–8; *Suppressed Book About Slavery* (1864), 214–15; testimony of A. D. Smith, AFIC, 1863, file 3, Letters Received, Office of the Adjutant General, Main Series, 1861–1870, Roll 200, National Archives; Rose, *Rehearsal for Reconstruction*, 89.

26. *American Slave, South Carolina Narratives*, II, i, 319–323; *Texas Narratives*, IV, i, 151–53, 156–59, 188–90, 202–11; ii, 21–24, 118–26; V, iii, 62–64, 107–9, 236–46, 270–73, iv, 45–46, 134–37, 289–94; *Alabama Narratives*, VI, 155–56, 255–57, 370–73; *Oklahoma Narratives*, VII, 203; *North Carolina Narratives*, XIV, i, 30–31, 103, 118, 185, XV, ii, 174–76, 193–95, 374, 431–35; *Negro in Virginia (WPA)*, 81–82; *Unwritten History (Fisk)*, 85–87, 89–91, 97–100, 149–51; John B. Cade, "Out of the Mouths of Ex-Slaves," *Journal of Negro History*, XX (July 1935), 302–8; John W. Coleman, *Slavery Times in Kentucky* (1940), 57–64; Joe Grey Taylor, *Negro Slavery in Louisiana* (1963), 123–35; Orville W. Taylor, *Negro Slavery in Arkansas* (1958), 188–202, and "'Jumping the Broomstick': Slave Marriage and Morality," *Arkansas Historical Quarterly*, XVII (1951), 217–31.

27. William Wells Brown, *My Southern Home*, 176–77, quoted in Bell I. Wiley, *Southern Negroes, 1861–1865* (1938), 105.

28. Late-nineteenth-century American folklorists collected enough scattered and isolated examples of what Alice Morse Earle called "ameliorated and semi-civilized survival[s] of the customs of savage people" among colonial *white* settlers to suggest that here is yet

another rich area for comparative study. So did students of more
recent American "folk culture." A visitor to a Southwestern Missouri town in the mid-nineteenth-century recollected that a settler's
daughter said to him: "We-uns can marry ourselves by kissing
over a candle." And an early-twentieth-century folklorist described
a wedding celebration among Hanover Germans in Concordia,
Missouri, during which the bride and groom stood at one end of
a field, the groom with a broom in his hand. Young men raced
toward him from the opposite end of the field, and the winner
received the broom, which "symbolically designated him as the
next groom to be." The following night "occurred the charivari
in its most deafening form." Earle, furthermore, collected data
and lore about what she called "a most despicable, ungallant
bridal custom" among eighteenth-century New Englanders: the
"smock marriage" or the "marriage in a shift." It involved only
widows in their remarriage, and these women wore just a thin
dress or no clothing, allegedly to symbolize that they carried no
debts into their new marriages. In Newfane, Vermont, an army
officer married the widow Hannah Ward in 1789. "The bride," a
report noted, "stood with no clothing on within a closet, and held
out her hand to the major through a diamond-shaped hole in the
door, and the ceremony was thus performed. She then appeared
resplendent in brave wedding attire, which the gallant major had
previously deposited in the closet for her assumption." Another
widow, this one from Westminster, Vermont, wedded "while nude
and hidden in the chimney recess behind a curtain." Noting that
this practice had close relationship to wife-sales, in 1839 the
Philadelphia *World* described how a "country" resident could not
convince two aldermen to marry him to a naked widow whose late
husband had died $150 in debt. The woman stood naked behind
a blanket until the aldermen convinced "the widow Venus" to
"put off the costume of a goddess" and wear clothing "appropriate to a modern wedding among the civilized." (*Journal of
American Folklore*, I [July–September 1888], 169; A. M. Earle,
Old-Time Marriage Customs in New England," *ibid.*, VI [April–
June 1893], 97–102; W. G. Bek, "Survivals of Old Marriage Customs Among the Low Germans of Missouri," *ibid.*, XXI [January–
March 1908], 60–67; Philadelphia *World*, n.d., reprinted in *Niles
National Register* LVII, 31 Aug. 1839, 7–8.) I am in debt to
Michael Gordon for calling the Philadelphia "shift marriage" to
my attention.

29. *American Slave, North Carolina Narratives* XIV, i, 185; *Jersey
City Telegraph*, 22 April 1853 (courtesy of Douglas Shaw); *Lowell
Offering*, n.d. (courtesy of Allis R. Wolfe); Terry Coleman, *Rail-
way Navvies* (1965), 21 (courtesy of Gregory Kealey); W. A. Crooke,

"Lifting of the Bride," *Folk-lore*, 13 (1902), 226–51; T. W. Thompson, "Ceremonial Customs of the British Gypsies," *Folk-lore*, LXXII (1913), 336–38; *Journal of Gypsy Lore Society*, n.s. II (1909), 242–45; M. E. Lyster, "Marriage Over the Broomstick," *JGLS*, n.s., III (1911–1912), 198–200. W. A. Crooke, a British folklorist, related the broomstick ritual to other marriage rites in which the bride was lifted in one or another fashion and saw these all as survivals of "a pagan or pre-Christian rite of marriage to which the actual service in the church was a supplement." W. A. Crooke, "The Lifting of the Bride," *Folk-lore*, XIII (1902), 226–51.

30. *Life of Olaudah Equiano, or Gustavus Vassa, the African, Written by Himself*, reprinted in *Great Slave Narratives*, ed. Arna Bontemps (1969), 121; F. L. Olmsted, *Journey in the Seaboard States*, I (1857), 389; *Slavery in the United States: A Narrative in the Life of Charles Ball, a Black Man* (1837), reprinted as *Fifty Years a Slave* (1970), 164–65; "Life of William Grimes, the Runaway Slave," quoted in Charles H. Nichols, "The Case of William Grimes . . . ," *William and Mary Quarterly*, VIII (October 1951), 552–60; H. C. Bruce, *New Man* (1895), 52–59; Edward A. Pollard, *Black Diamonds Gathered in the Darkey Homes of the South* (1859), 58, 75–76, 115–22; L. M. Towne, St. Helena's Island, S.C., 29 March 1868, to the editor, *American Freedman*, III (June 1868), 431–32; unsigned letter, Beaufort, N.C., 30 April 1867, to the editor, *American Missionary*, XI (June 1867), 126–27. I am indebted to Peter H. Wood for bringing the Welsh Neck, South Carolina, murder to my attention.

31. Jacob Stroyer, *Sketches of My Life in the South* (1879) 9–10, 27, 42–45, 47–50; Max Gluckman, *Custom and Conflict in Africa* (1959), 81–95, and *Politics, Law, and Ritual* (1965), 221–24, 247–51.

32. William Bascom, "Acculturation Among the Gullah Negroes," *American Anthropologist*, XLIII (1941), 43–50; *American Slave, Arkansas Narratives*, IX, iv, 120; Roger Bastide, *African Civilizations in the New World* (1971), 57–58; Gluckman as cited in note 31; *Drums and Shadows* (1972), 32, 39, 79, 87, 94, 117. A brief description of an irregular judicial proceeding among Louisiana sugar-plantation blacks after emancipation is found in J. Vance Lewis, *Out of the Ditch: A True Story of an Ex-Slave* (1910), 18. On the magical powers of graveyard dust among New World slaves, see also Colin A. Palmer, "Religion and Magic in Mexican Slave Society," in S. L. Engerman and E. D. Genovese, eds., *Race and Slavery in the Western Hemisphere: Quantitative Studies* (1975), 322–23.

33. Miles M. Fisher, *The Master's Slave: Elijah John Fisher* (1922), 5; O. K. Armstrong, *Old Massa's People: The Old Slaves Tell*

Their Story (1931), 170; interview with Josephine Anderson, 1937, printed in J. F. Smith, *Slavery and Plantation Growth in Ante-bellum Florida 1821–1860* (1973), 196–97; *Gumbo Ya-Ya* (1945), 250; Gluckman cited in note 31; A. D. J. MacFarlane, *Witchcraft in Tudor and Stuart England* (1970), 247. See also A. J. H. Latham, "Witchcraft Accusation and Economic Tension in Pre-Colonial Calabar," *Journal of African History*, XIII (1972), 249–60; M. G. Marwick, *Witchcraft and Sorcery* (1970) and *Sorcery and Its Social Setting* (1965), *passim*.

34. Isaac W. Brinckerhoff, "Mission Work Among the Freed Ne-groes . . . ," 192, mss. copy Colgate-Rochester Library; *Proceedings of a Convention of Colored Men, Xenia, Ohio, Jan. 10–12, 1865* (1865), reprinted in Herbert Aptheker, ed., *Documentary History*, I (1951), 528–30; *Negro in Virginia (WPA)*, 86.

35. Richard C. Wade, *Slavery in the Cities* (1964), 62–74; Charles B. Dew, "Disciplining Slave Ironworkers in the Antebellum South: Coercion, Conciliation, and Accommodation," *American Historical Review*, 79 (April 1974), 393–418; Robert Starobin, *Industrial Slavery in the Old South* (1970), 77; J. C. Sitterson, *Sugar Country: The Cane Industry in the South, 1735–1860* (1953), 103; Clement Eaton, "Slave-Hiring in the Upper South: A Step Toward Freedom," *Mississippi Valley Historical Review*, XLVI (March 1960), 664–66. Hiring out, of course, did not always work to the advantage of slave familial needs. The relationship between hiring out and the slave family—especially in the decades prior to the Civil War—needs careful study. The magnitude of hiring out is one reason. Another is the development of extended kin ties among slaves so that individual slaves hired out and thereby cut off from an immediate family might have found kin to sustain them while "hired out."

Edward Phifer, the historian who has authored the most careful local study of a rural slave community, suggests that "often hiring . . . created the greater hardship and grief for the slave" than sale. This is a significant finding when it is realized, as Frederic Bancroft pointed out, that "in numerous Virginia villages the hirings on a single day must have outnumbered the sales there during the whole year." The North Carolina planter David Gavin indicated some of the troubles hired slaves had in his diary notation dated 4 January 1856:

> . . . Beck belonging to Mrs. S. E. West came here this week, she is not pleased with living with Capers Griffith, her son Jim, who staid at Jos. H. Howel got burned last saturday night, and has neither clothes nor blanket. She is breeding. I expect I shall have trouble with these negroes of Mrs. West this year for no person seems to want the women who are all breeding. Jim has fits and ought to go with his mother.

When slave children were hired out, they were often separated from one or both parents. "Today, Tom, as we call him, entered our service," Francis Lieber noted in late October 1835. Lieber then lived in Columbia, South Carolina. "He is about fourteen years old, and we pay his master $4.50 a month. The little boy brings with him a blanket, which is all he ever had to sleep upon. He has but one shirt. Slavery is abominable in every respect." The next day, Lieber remarked: "Last night Matilda and Abby (the nurse) made a mattress and pillow for Little Tom." Here was an instance where non-kin had assumed the role of surrogate parents, and that may have happened quite frequently when hiring out involved young children. (Frederic Bancroft, *Slave Trading in the Old South*, 145–61; E. W. Phifer, "Slavery in Microcosm: Burke County, North Carolina," *Journal of Southern History*, 28 [May 1962], 137–60; Gavin diary entry, 4 Jan. 1856, cited in Jones, "A Cultural Middle Passage," 195.)

36. C. B. Dew, "David Ross and the Oxford Iron Works," *William and Mary Quarterly*, 39 (April 1974), 213–14; *Negro in Virginia (WPA)*, 50; Cotton to Willis, 1839, quoted in Bobby Frank Jones, "Cultural Middle Passage," 200; C. L. Mohr, "Slavery in Oglethorpe County, Georgia," *Phylon*, 33 (Spring 1972), 11–12; Weymouth T. Jordan, *Hugh Davis and His Alabama Plantation* (1948), 76–79, 100; U. B. Phillips, *American Negro Slavery*, 513, and *Life and Labor in the Old South*, 277–78; James Guthrie to James Cooper, 1818, printed in Starobin, ed., *Blacks in Bondage: Letters of American Slaves* (1974), 106–107.

37. U. B. Phillips and J. D. Glunt, ed., *Florida Plantation Records* (1927), 34–35, 140, 145; Arthur Tiedemann, "Slavery in Rural Louisiana, 1840–1860," M.A. thesis, Columbia University, 1949, *passim*; Phillips, *American Negro Slavery*, 513, and *Life and Labor in the Old South*, 277–78; Guion Johnson, *Antebellum North Carolina, A Social History*, 535–36; Mohr, "Slavery in Oglethorpe County, Georgia, *Phylon*, XXXIII (Spring 1972), 9–11; Bobby Jones, "Cultural Middle Passage," 156; Frederic Bancroft, *Slave Trading in the Old South*, 206–7; Southern Man to the editor, *New York Sun*, 2 March 1883.

38. J. G. Taylor, *Negro Slavery in Louisiana* (1963), 124–25; Hannah Valentine letters printed in Starobin, "Privileged Slaves and the Process of Accommodation . . . ," *Journal of Social History*, 5 (Fall 1971), 46–71, and *Blacks in Bondage*, 42–57, 64–77.

39. Ethan Allen Andrews, *Slavery and the Domestic Trade* (1836), 113–14; R. H. Carter letter in M. D. Conway, *Testimonies Concerning Slavery* (1864), 24–25; Clement Eaton, *Growth of Southern Civilization* (1961), 51–52; Tucker and McCroskey letters in G. P.

Coleman, ed., *Virginia Silhouettes* (1934), 9–15; *Pyeatt v. Spencer*, 4 Ark. July 1842, 562–70.

40. John Spencer Bassett, *Southern Plantation Overseer* (1925), 21–22, 260–61; Phillips and Glunt, eds., *Florida Plantation Records* (1927), 34–35, 140, 145; Eugene D. Genovese, *Roll, Jordan, Roll* (1974), 455–56.

41. Bertram Wyatt-Brown, "The Ideal Typology and Ante-bellum Southern History . . . ," *Societas*, V (Winter 1975), 1–29; Genovese, *In Red and Black* (1971), 260; *Proslavery Argument* (1852), 56–57, 457; Sawyer quoted in George Fredrickson, *Black Image in White America* (1971), 98; Gertrude Clanton Thomas diary quoted in Mary E. Massey, *Bonnet Brigades* (1966), 19–20, 278. See also the splendid discussion of the tendency in antebellum southern novelists either to portray the black as "child-dependent" or to dehumanize him by "stressing his animality" in William R. Taylor, *Cavalier and Yankee* (1961), 282–85.

42. "Journal of William Reynolds," 1839–1840, quoted in Eaton, *Growth of Southern Civilization*, 50–51.

43. Martin Delany quoted in Earl Thorpe, *The Mind of the Negro* (1961), 76.

44. *Nation*, VII (3 Dec. 1868), 453–54 and X (26 May 1870), 332–33; *Nation* (10 June 1870), 367, quoted in N. G. Hale, *Freud and the Americans* (1971), 34. See also Hale, *Freud and the Americans*, 24–46, and Peter Cominois, "Late Victorian Sexual Responsibility and the Social System," *International Review of Social History*, VIII (1963), 18–48, 216–50.

45. Charles K. Whipple, *Family Relation, as Affected by Slavery* (1858), *passim* but especially 6–9 and 11–14.

46. Charles C. Jones, *Religious Instruction of the Negroes in the United States* (1842), 103–4; Ralph Ellison, *Shadow and Act* (1964), 97.

47. Lewis Copeland, "The Negro as a Contrast Conception," in Edgar T. Thompson, ed., *Race Relations and the Race Problem* (1939), 157; Frederick Douglass, *Liberator*, 11 Nov. 1859, quoted in Earle Thorpe, *Mind of the Negro* (1961), 90; J. H. Plumb, "Slavery, Race, and the Poor," *New York Review of Books*, XII (March 13, 1969), 3–5; Christine Bolt, *Victorian Attitudes to Race* (London, 1971), 41 and *passim*.

48. *New York World*, 12 Oct. 1865; *New York Tribune*, 13, 14 Oct. 1865.

49. Charles Stearns, *Black Man of the South and the Rebels* (1872), 1–35, 121; George Ward Nichols, *Story of the Great March from*

the Diary of a Staff Officer (1865), 193; James McPherson, *Struggle for Equality* (1964), 166, 175–76; J. S. Newberry, *United States Sanitary Commission in the Valley of the Mississippi During the War of the Rebellion, 1861–1866* (1871), 529–36; Mattie Childs, Natchez, Miss., 26 July 1864, to the editor *Freedmen's Advocate* I (September 1864), 30; "Speech of Henry Ward Beecher," Philadelphia *Inquirer,* 12 Oct. 1865; John H. Aughey, "The Iron Furnace, or Slavery and Secession," reprinted in *Anti-Slavery Standard,* 31 March 1863.

50. Fanny Kemble, *Journal, 1838–1839* (1961), 129–30, 332; F. L. Olmsted, *Seaboard Slave States* (1857), 127–28; *Richmond Examiner,* n.d., reprinted in Olmsted, *Journey in the Back Country* (1860), 428; *New York Independent,* XV (23 July 1863), 4.

51. Laura Towne, *Letters and Diaries* (1912), ed. R. S. Holland, 6; *Letters from Port Royal* (1906), ed. E. W. Pearson, 15, 18, 22, 75, 180–81; Stearns, *Black Man of the South,* 369; J. O. Lyman, Ft. Smith, Ark., 25 Feb. 1869, to the editor, *American Missionary,* XIII (June 1869), 128; C. A. Crafts, Muirkirk, Md., 31 May 1866, to the editor, *Freedmen's Record,* II (July 1866), 131; Whitelaw Reid, *After the War,* 301; J. A. Sherman, Norfolk, 29 Nov. 1865, to the editor, *AM,* X (January 1866), 2–3; John Trowbridge, *Desolated States,* 232–33; Charles Nordhoff, "Freedmen of South Carolina," in Frank Moore, ed., *Papers of the Day #1* (1863), 24–25; Charles Nordhoff, *Cotton States in the Spring and Summer of 1875* (1876), 19–21; *Christian Examiner* (May 1864), 344–45, and (June 1865), 230–38; William Allen diary, cited in William H. and Jane H. Pease, *Black Utopia: Negro Communal Experiments in America* (1963), 152–59; testimony of Major Bolles and T. W. Higginson, 1863, American Freedmen's Inquiry Commission, files 2 and 3, Letters Received, Office of the Adjutant General, Main Series, 1861–1870, Reel 200, NA.

52. Robert Somers, *Southern States Since the War* (1871), 14; *New York Times,* 17 May 1865; Edward A. Freeman, quoted in B. N. Schwartz and Robert Disch, eds., *White Racism* (1970), 58.

53. Charles Nordhoff, "Freedmen of South Carolina," in Frank Moore, ed., *Papers of the Day #1* (1863), 18–19.

54. *Dear Ones at Home: Letters from the Contraband Camps* (1966), 21, 58, 95–96, 98, 123–24, 144.

55. E. Franklin Frazier, *Negro Family in the United States,* (1939), 89, 95–98; *Negro Family in Chicago* (1932), 33–34, *On Race Relations* (1968), ed., G. F. Edwards, 191–202. A more detailed examination of Frazier's explicit model is found in H. G. Gutman, "Le phénomène invisible: le composition de la famille et du foyer noir après la Guerre de Sécession," *Annales E.S.C.,* 27 (1972),

1197–218. That essay is reprinted in the *Journal of Interdiscipli-nary History*, VI (Autumn 1975), 181–210. The evidence in Frazier's classic study *The Negro Family in the United States* deserves far less attention than the explicit "model" that shaped Frazier's conception of the slave family and of slave society. Frazier believed that double-headed households were most common among privileged slaves such as artisans and house servants, and that the male-absent household was an appropriate adaptation to enslavement by "non-elite" slaves. Chapters 1 through 5 (pages 1–107) are devoted to the slave family. Careful reading of these chapters shows that they rest on scant historical evidence and that such evidence is used merely to illustrate the larger "model" that infused Frazier's work. The best way to argue that double-headed households were uncommon among slave field hands is to ignore evidence of their presence.

56. Kenneth M. Stampp, *The Peculiar Institution*, 28, 340–46, 363–64. Stampp modifies his earlier view of the Afro-American slave family in "Rebels and Sambos: The Search for the Negro's Personality in Slavery," *Journal of Southern History* (1971), 369–72.

57. Stanley M. Elkins, *Slavery: A Problem in American Institutional and Intellectual Life* (1963), *passim* but especially 32, 37, 49, 50, 61, 81, 88–89, 101–2 (notes 132 and 133), 128–29, and especially "Negro Slavery in North America: A Study in Social Isolation (1961)," printed in the second edition of *Slavery*, 239–45.

58. David Gavin, diary entry, 13 Sept. 1856, printed in Stampp, *Peculiar Institution*, 324; Davis, ed., *Plantation Life in the Florida Parishes*, 173; Elkins, "On Slavery and Ideology," in Ann Lane, ed., *The Debate Over Slavery, Stanley Elkins and His Critics* (1971), 325–78. Twice in 1971 Elkins published brief responses to his critics in which he recognized that his earlier work had given insufficient attention to what he calls "the 'underground culture' of slavery: the music, the folk tales, the techniques of resistance, often highly subtle—a black folk culture, in short, behind which a slave might protect his human integrity, despite the overwhelm-ing power of the master and of the white world that surrounded him." Elkins finds in the research of historians like Sterling Stuckey and Roy Simon Bryce-Laporte "a growing inclination to regard American slavery, for all its repressions, as somehow less debilitating psychologically, less destructive of the slave's essential personality, than was once supposed."

Elkins commends Bryce-Laporte for suggesting that the "prob-lem of *resistance*" be "fully contained . . . within a theoretical framework" that "does not require 'revolutionary' or even 'politi-cal' activity" but "leaves room for a wide range of overt, covert, and even unconscious forms of resistance." In his own work,

Elkins has not allowed a place for the development of such a range of behavior. The point he makes here is important. Historians of slaves and other dependent and exploited social classes too frequently focus their research on the most extreme forms of resistance—what is called "revolutionary" behavior. Such behavior occurs infrequently among all populations, and its absence often causes historians to find "explanations" for nonevents. It makes much more sense to give attention to what Elkins calls the "wide range of overt, covert, and even unconscious forms of resistance" that occur among such people. See Elkins, "The Social Consequences of Slavery," in Nathan Huggins, Martin Kilson, and Daniel Fox, eds., *Key Issues in the Afro-American Experience*, I [1971], 139, and Elkins, "On Slavery and Ideology," in Lane, ed., *Debate Over Slavery*, 355–56.

59. Eugene D. Genovese, *The World the Slaveholders Made* (1969), 96–99; *id., Roll, Jordan, Roll, The World the Slaves Made* (1974), 74.

60. Harry R. Merrens, *Colonial North Carolina in the Eighteenth Century* (1964), 75–81; James Henretta, *Evolution of American Society* (1973), 57–63. See also the very important essay "Southern Slavery in the World of Thomas Malthus" in C. Vann Woodward, *American Counterpoint: Slavery and Racism in the North-South Dialogue* (1971), 78–106.

61. Genovese, *Roll, Jordan, Roll*, 3, 7, 30, 89–91, 114–15, 125, 143, 148, 441, 658.

62. Genovese, *Roll, Jordan, Roll*, 7, 90–91, 115.

63. Genovese, *Roll, Jordan, Roll*, 148; Robert L. Dabney, *A Defence of Virginia and Through Her of the South* (1867), 214.

64. Genovese, *Roll, Jordan, Roll*, 124–25.

65. Genovese, *Roll, Jordan, Roll*, 452–54, 457; Genovese, *In Red and Black* (1971), 112.

66. Genovese, *Roll, Jordan, Roll*, 658; Sidney W. Mintz, "Foreword," in Norman Whitten and John F. Szwed, eds., *Afro-American Anthropology, Contemporary Perspectives* (1970), 1–16; Jean Jacques Rousseau, *Social Contract and the Discourses*, trans. G. D. H. Cole (1950), 6.

67. Genovese, *Roll, Jordan, Roll*, 97–113.

68. *The Children of Pride*, ed. R. M. Myers (1972), 177–78, 184–85, 248, 465–66, 996–98, 1022, 1028, 1224, 1232, 1241–42, 1247–48, 1266–67, 1284–86, 1291, 1293–94, 1296, 1301–13, 1318–19, 1321, 1326–27, 1370–71, 1374, 1376, 1406–07, 1409; Mary B. Chesnut, *Diary from Dixie* (1949), 538.

69. John Stuart Mill, *Principles of Political Economy*, II (1869), 325; Ralph Ellison, *Shadow and Act* (1964), 315.

Chapter 8: Taken From Us by Force

1. The most important studies include Lorenzo J. Greene, *The Negro in Colonial New England* (1942); Edmund S. Morgan, *Virginians at Home: Family Life in the Eighteenth Century* (1952), 67–71; Philip D. Curtin, *The Atlantic Slave Trade: A Census* (1969); Gerald W. Mullin, *Flight and Rebellion: Slave Resistance in Eighteenth Century Virginia* (1972); Peter H. Wood, *Black Majority: Negroes in Colonial South Carolina from 1660 through the Stono Rebellion* (1974); Russell R. Menard, "The Maryland Slave Population, 1658 to 1730: A Demographic Profile of Blacks in Four Counties," *William and Mary Quarterly*, 32 (January 1975), 29–54; Allan Kulikoff, "Tobacco County: Population, Economy, and Society in Eighteenth-Century Prince George's County, Maryland, Slaves and Slave Society," June 1974, unpublished manuscript; and Stanley L. Engerman, "Some Economic and Demographic Comparisons of United States and West Indian Slavery," 1975, unpublished manuscript.

2. Roger Bastide, *African Civilisations in the New World* (1971), 23–24; C. L. R. James, "The Atlantic Slave Trade and Slavery," *Amistad*, I (1970), 132–33; Richard Hofstadter, *America at 1750* (1971), 93; Sidney W. Mintz and Richard Price, "An Anthropological Approach to the Study of Afro-American History," unpublished mss., 1974, *passim*.

3. John W. Barber, *A History of the Amistad Captives* (1840), reprinted in Sidney Kaplan, "Black Mutiny on the Amistad," in Sidney Kaplan and Jules Chametzky, eds., *Black and White in American Culture* (1971), 291–330; Alex Hewitt, *An Historical Account of the Rise and Progress of the Colonies of South Carolina and Georgia* (1779), 347–48, reprinted in B. R. Carroll, ed., *Historical Collections of South Carolina* I (1842).

4. "Eighteenth Century Maryland as Portrayed in the 'Itinerant Observations' of Edward Kimber," *Maryland Historical Magazine*, LI (1956), 327; Wood, *Black Majority*, 140–41. Suggestions of polygamous slave domestic arrangements in other places are found in Frank J. Klingberg, "British Humanitarianism at Codrington," *Journal of Negro History*, 23 (October 1938), 451–86; B. W. Higman, "Household Structure and Fertility on Jamaican Slave Plantations: A Nineteenth Century Example," *Population Studies*, 27 (November 1973), 539. Menard's suggestion is in "The Maryland Slave Population, 1658 to 1730," *William and Mary Quarterly*, 32 (January 1975), 29–54. Evidence of prolonged nursing among nineteenth-century slave mothers is reported in Genovese, *Roll, Jordan, Roll*, 498–99. See also William R. Bascom, "Acculturation Among the Gullah Negroes," *American Anthropologist*, XLIII (1941), 43–50.

5. T. E. Campbell, *Colonial Carolina: A History of Caroline County* (1964), 71–72. Brief mention of these events is found in Herbert Aptheker, *To Be Free* (1948), 12, and *American Negro Slave Revolts* (1943), 179. See also D. J. Mays, *Edmund Pendleton, 1721–1783: A Biography* (1952), I, 8–11.

6. Alex Hewitt, *An Historical Account of the Rise and Progress of the Colonies of South Carolina and Georgia* (1779), 347–48, printed in B. R. Carroll, ed., *Historical Collections of South Carolina* I (1842); *Memoir of Mrs. Chloe Spear, A Native of Africa . . . Died in 1815 aged 65, by a Lady of Boston* (1815), 17; Charles Ball, *Slavery in the United States* (1837), 219–22. A general discussion of the belief that spirits returned to Africa is found in Bastide, *African Civilisations in the New World*, 46. Evidence of this belief among Georgia Sea Island blacks in the 1930s is reported in *Drums and Shadows* (1972), 6, 15, 16, 25, 31, 76, 101. There also is evidence of the retention of other religious beliefs among enslaved Africans. See Ball, *Slavery in the United States*, 15–24, 164–65; E. Merton Coulter, *Thomas Spaulding of Sapelo* (1940), 83, and the stimulating discussion of the religious functions of the "iron pot" in George P. Rawick, *From Sundown to Sunup: The Making of the Black Community* (1972), 39–44.

7. Orville H. Platt, "Negro Governors," *Papers of the New Haven Historical Society*, VI (1900), 315–35; Hubert H. S. Aimes, "African Institutions in America," *Journal of American Folklore*, XVIII (1905), 15–32; and Lorenzo J. Greene, *The Negro in Colonial New England* (1942), 249–55. The only discussion by a contemporary black of these elections I have found is in W. J. Brown, *Life of William J. Brown* (1883), 1–17. Discussion of similar practices in other slave settings is found in Bastide, *African Civilisations in the New World*, 91–98.

8. Alice Morse Earle, *Colonial Days in Old New York* (1962), 195–202; John F. Watson, *Annals of Philadelphia and Pennsylvania*, II (1857), 265 (courtesy of Eric Foner); J. F. Cooper, *Satanstoe* (1937), 49–61. Such usages in northern colonies and states with relatively small black populations direct attention to the need for a careful search of evidence dealing with festivals and celebrations in the southern colonies and states with their more dense slave settlements.

9. Mintz and Price, "An Anthropological Approach to the Study of Afro-American History," unpublished mss., 1974, 37–39.

10. Mintz and Price, "An Anthropological Approach . . . , 65; Ralph Ellison, *Shadow and Act* (1964), 246–47.

11. Aubrey S. Land, ed., *Bases of the Plantation Society* (1969), 1–3.

12. Richard B. Morris, *Government and Labor in Early America* (1946), 314–15; Conrad Arensberg, "Comment," in Vera Rubin, ed., *Caribbean Studies: A Symposium* (1960), 97.

13. Mullin, *Flight and Rebellion*, 15.

14. Printed in Harvey T. Cook, *Rambles in the Pee Dee Basin*, I (1926), 201–6.

15. Lewis Gray, *History of Agriculture in the Southern United States* (1958), 507, 531, 1025.

16. Curtin, *Atlantic Slave Trade: A Census*, 28–30, 73.

17. R. R. Menard, "The Maryland Slave Population, 1658 to 1730 . . . ," *William and Mary Quarterly*, 32 (January 1975), 29–54.

18. Allan Kulikoff, "Tobacco County: Population, Economy, and Society in Eighteenth-Century Prince George's County, Maryland, Slaves and Slave Society," June 1974, unpublished manuscript. I am in debt to Mr. Kulikoff for allowing to cite this material. The age of Prince George's slave mothers at the birth of a first child between 1710 and 1759 ranged from 17.8 to 18.8, an age that approximated the age of slave mothers at the birth of a first child on plantations like Cedar Vale, Good Hope, and Bennehan-Cameron, a seeming continuity that deserves more careful study. The first and most important fact to be learned is the age at first birth of West African women prior to their enslavement. Such evidence will allow us to see whether or not enslavement and early "creolization" encouraged a drop in the age at which women had a first child. It is possible that the relatively high age of African slave mothers after their arrival in the New World was a transitory phenomenon. A very important portion of Kulikoff's study entitled "The Beginnings of the Afro-American Family in Maryland" is published in Aubrey C. Land, Lois Green Carr, and Edward C. Papenfuse, eds., *Law, Society, and Politics in Early Maryland: Essays in Honor of Morris Leon Radoff* (1976).

19. South Carolina especially deserves careful study. Peter H. Wood has begun such study in *Black Majority* (1974), 143–66. Wood finds a high rate of natural increase prior to 1720 and then a decline in the 1720s. His study ends in 1740. The decline is based upon Varnod's 1726 census of St. George Parish. Thirteen hundred slaves then lived in the parish, and Wood compares the children per slave woman (1.17/1) to the children per white woman (2.24/1). Wood associates the low birth rate

> with general worsening of black living conditions associated with the intensification of staple agriculture. . . . But already in the 1720s and 1730s the arbitrary grouping of slaves to create and main-

tain plantations in the wilderness had adverse effects upon Negro family life. Men and women were thrown together in increasingly random proportions on increasingly large holdings as the period progressed. And far from giving such license to any innate promiscuity imagined by white masters, such conditions apparently served more to frustrate desires for enduring intimacy and reduce the likelihood of procreation.

There are, however, difficulties using Varnod's census. According to Wood, 536 slaves lived in St. George Parish in 1720; six years later, the parish had 1300 slaves. The slave population increased two and a half times in these six years, an increase surely accounted for primarily by adult male and female slaves being either purchased or moved into the parish. That increase may explain the low ratio of children to women.

Much remains to be known about when in time the South Carolina slaves made the transition to a self-perpetuating labor force. The transition, as Kulikoff's study suggests, is associated with high fertility, settled domestic arrangement, and expanding kin networks among slaves. South Carolina prohibited the importation of slaves in 1741, a prohibition that lasted until 1750. The resumption of the slave trade after that date greatly increased the flow of Africans into South Carolina. Between 1750 and 1769, nearly three times as many slaves entered South Carolina (36,722) as entered Virginia (12,895). Careful research is needed on family formation among first- and second-generation South Carolina slaves *before 1750*. If such study shows similar patterns to those uncovered by Menard and Kulikoff, those Africans entering into South Carolina after 1750 would, like those entering Maryland in earlier decades, have encountered developing Afro-American institutional forms. (A useful summary of slave-trade statistics is found in Herbert S. Klein, "Slaves and Shipping in Eighteenth Century Virginia," *Journal of Interdisciplinary History*, V [1974], 385–86, 393–94.)

20. Mullin, *Flight and Rebellion*, 108–110; Wood, *Black Majority*, chap. 9; Kulikoff, "Tobacco Country," unpublished ms.; *Virginia Gazette*, 3 Feb. 1774, cited in L. P. Schwartz, "Slave Discipline in Virginia," M.A. thesis, Columbia University, 1947; "Eighteenth Century Slaves as Advertised by Their Masters," *Journal of Negro History*, I (April 1916), 170–84, 216; Edgar McManus, *Black Bondage in the North* (1973), 114–15.

21. *William Fitzhugh and His Chesapeake World, 1676–1701* (1963), 377–79, 382; "Wills, Inventories, and Miscellaneous Records," W.P.A. transcript mss., State Archives, South Carolina, courtesy of Ed Troy; Mullin, *Flight and Rebellion*, 13, 84–85; Wood, *Black Majority*, chap. 9; Arthur Calhoun, *Social History of the American Family*, I (1917–19), 327–28.

22. James M. Robins Papers, vol. I, document dated Feb. 7, 1761, Massachusetts Historical Society. I am indebted to Mary Beth Norton for making this invaluable document available to me.

23. D. D. Wax, "Whither the Comparative History of Slavery," *Virginia Magazine of History and Biography*, 80 (January 1972), 85–93; Mullin, *Flight and Rebellion*, 27–28, 71.

24. *Diary of Colonel Landon Carter of Sabine Hall*, ed. Jack P. Greene (1965), 159, 217–21, 289, 291, 329, 348, 411, 493, 547, 648.

25. Peter H. Wood, *Black Majority* (1974), 136–42; Lorenzo J. Greene, *Negro in Colonial New England*, 195; John Woolman, quoted in Calhoun, *Social History of the American Family*, I, 327; Thomas Brickell, *Natural History of North Carolina* . . . (1737 reprinted in 1968), 271–76; Hopkins, *Massalina's Questions*, 170, quoted in Ralph Flanders, *Plantation Slavery in Georgia* (1933), 172–73. I am indebted to John J. Waters for calling the observation by John Bartow to my attention.

26. Wood, *Black Majority*, 127–28, 134, 141; Brickell cited in Aubrey C. Land, ed., *Bases of Plantation Society* (1969), 227–28, 231–32; Mullin, *Flight and Rebellion*, 27; Jerome H. Woods, "The Negro in Early Pennsylvania: The Lancaster Experience, 1730–1790," in Elinor Miller and Eugene D. Genovese, eds., *Plantation, Town, and County: Essays on the Local History of American Slave Society* (1974), 441–52; *Boston Evening Post*, 8 Dec. 1746, courtesy of Robert Twombly; *American Slave, North Carolina Narratives*, XV, ii, 333.

27. *Collections of the Massachusetts Historical Society*, 5 ser., III (1877), 432–37, reprinted in Herbert Aptheker, ed., *Documentary History*, I (1951), 8–10; Robert Twombly, "Black Resistance to Slavery in Massachusetts," in William O'Neill, ed., *Problems and Issues in American Social History* (1973), 11–56.

28. Roi Ottley and W. J. Weatherby, eds., *Negro in New York* (1967), 1–8; Herman D. Bloch, *Circle of Vicious Discrimination* (1969), 7.

29. John Josselyn, *An Account of Two Voyages to New England Made During the Years 1638, 1663* (1865), 26.

30. Edmund S. Morgan, *Virginians at Home: Family Life in the Eighteenth Century*, 67–71; Caroline Couper Lovell, *Golden Islands of Georgia* (1932), 85–86, courtesy of Wallace Heath.

31. Sidney W. Mintz, *Caribbean Transformations* (1974), 75–77; Mintz and Price, "An Anthropological Approach to the Study of Afro-American History," 1974, 12–13.

32. Guion G. Johnson, *Social History of the Sea Islands* (1930), 134–35.

33. These letters appear in Mrs. George P. Coleman, ed., *Virginia*

Silhouettes: Contemporary Letters Concerning Negro Slavery in the State of Virginia (1934), 35–36, 38–40, 45–46.

34. Bastide, *African Civilisation in the New World*, 27; Mintz, "Toward An Afro-American History," *Journal of World History*, 13 (1971), 317–31.

35. Booker T. Washington, *Future of the American Negro* (1899), 25.

36. Frederick Douglass, *Life and Times of Frederick Douglass* (1962), 97.

37. Robert Coles, *Children of Crisis* (1967), *passim*.

38. C. Vann Woodward, *American Counterpoint, Slavery and Racism in the North-South Dialogue* (1971), 51–52.

39. "A Very Stern Discipline: An Interview with Ralph Ellison," *Harper's Magazine*, May 1967, 84.

PART TWO: Deep as the Rivers

Chapter 9: Let Not Man Put Asunder

1. The Plummer letters are printed in Carter G. Woodson, ed., *Mind of the Negro* (1926), 523–28. The Bible notation is found in Nellie Plummer, *Out of the Depths, or the Triumphs of the Cross* (1927), reprinted in Frazier, *Negro Family in the United States*, 171.

2. I am very much indebted to Leslie Rowland for making this material available to me from her own research, a detailed study of Kentucky blacks during and just after the Civil War. A fuller description of these data is found in Gutman, *Slavery and the Numbers Game*, 72–75.

3. The enlistment of Kentucky slaves ending in the establishment of the Camp Nelson refuge as described in this and the eleven paragraphs that follow is based upon the following sources: War of the Rebellion, *Official Records*, series III, vol. IV, 50, 174–78, 233–34, 429–30, 451, 459–60, 467–68, 474, 501–2, 540–49, 1017–19; dispatches from newspapers such as *New York Times*, Chicago *Tribune*, Cincinnati *Gazette*, Louisville *Journal*, and Louisville *Press*, reprinted in *Anti-Slavery Standard*, 28 Feb., 28 March, 27 June, 11 July, 19 Sept., 31 Oct. 1863 and 19 March, 3, 18, 25 June, 9, 23 July, 10 Sept., 22 Oct., 17 Dec. 1864; *American Slave, Indiana Narratives*, VI, 9–10, 30, 98–99, and *Oklahoma Narratives*, VII, 39–44; letters from John Fee and other Camp Nelson residents in *American Missionary*, VIII (July, September, December 1864), 179–80, 222–23, 294, and IX (February, March, April 1865), 30–31, 56–57, 85; John Fee manuscript letters from Camp Nelson dated 2 Jan. and 21 and 25 Feb., 1865, American Missionary Asso-

ciation Archives; Anna Dicken Troutman, Paris, Ky., 28 March 1863, to her mother, Dicken-Troutman-Balke Mss., Special Collections, University of Kentucky Library (courtesy of Leslie Rowland); May 1864 order printed in *Liberator*, 24 June 1864; Joseph Miller affidavit enclosed in Humanitas to the editor, *Liberator*, 9 Dec. 1864; *Independent*, 24 Dec. 1864; Lewis and Richard Collins, *History of Kentucky* I (1882), 128–49; E. P. Marrs, *Life and History* (1885), 9–23, 55–57; George T. Palmer, *A Conscientious Turncoat: The Story of John M. Palmer* (1941), 174; Stephen Jocelyn, *Mostly Alkali: A Biography* (1953), 34; J. S. Newberry, *The U. S. Sanitary Commission in the Valley of the Mississippi* (1871), 378–86, 519–36; Mary E. Massey, *Bonnet Brigades* (1966), 273; E. Merton Coulter, *Civil War and Readjustment in Kentucky* (1926), 156–214. The events at Camp Nelson apparently were repeated at other military places. Rowland has supplied me with an example drawn from her own research. On September 3, 1864, a Union Army officer at Louisa reported to a superior concerning the troubles "masters who are loyal" had in claiming the wives and children of soldiers:

> On the 31st of Aug. 1864 the Sheriff of this Co. with a civil process arrested a negress, inside the Post Guard line but outside the guard lines of the 109th U. S. C. I., when he was assailed by some Fifteen or Twenty men of the 109th U. S. C. I. as he alleges with guns and the negro woman taken forcibly from him by the aforesaid soldiers.

The commander of the 109th assured the sheriff that the woman would be turned over and the black soldiers arrested. He complained that the sheriff had used "insulting language towards me and my command." "The woman spoken of," he went on, "came into my camp several days ago with her husband, when I directed that she could not remain, as we do not employ women in any capacity and she at once left, and I was not aware that she had returned until I began my investigation. . . . As it is now dark and she has no place to go I have not sent her out side my lines." These items are found in Box 3, M–14, 1864, Letters Received, Entry 2173, Military District of the Ohio, Record Group 393, National Archives.

4. The dispute over the March 1865 law as discussed in this and the following ten paragraphs draws upon the following sources: *New York Times*, 1, 13 March, 26 July, 6, 20 Aug., 28 Oct., 10, 17 Dec. 1865 and 22 Jan. and 5 Nov. 1866; New York *Tribune*, 1 May, 2 June, 15 July, 2 Aug. 1865; Charles A. Roxborough, Richard Johnson, Jere. Merriweather, Henry H. White, and William Butler, n.d., to the President, printed in New Orleans *Tribune*, 29 June 1865; *Western Citizen*, n.d., reprinted in New Orleans *Tribune*, 13 Aug. 1865; Collins and Collins, *History of Kentucky*, I, 157–65; G. T. Palmer, *A Conscientious Turncoat*, 164–90;

Coulter, *Civil War and Readjustment in Kentucky*, 263–68; *Autobiography of James L. Smith* (1881), 128–30; *Life of Rev. Thomas James by Himself* (1887), 3–5, 14–21, 24; John M. Palmer, *Personal Recollections of John M. Palmer: The Story of an Earnest Life* (1901), 226–66; John Mercer Langston, *From the Virginia Plantation to the National Capitol* (1894), 236–40; Louisville correspondent, n.d., *Anglo-African*, n.d., reprinted in *Liberator*, 21 July 1865; John M. Palmer, 27 July 1865, to Andrew Johnson, *Liberator*, 1 Aug. 1865; JMP, Washington, 2 Oct. 1865, to E. M. Stanton, *Liberator*, 3 Nov. 1865; JMP, Louisville, 15 and 16 Oct. 1865 to EMS; EMS, Washington, 20 Oct. 1865, to JMP; E. D. Townsend, Washington, 20 Oct. 1865, to JMP, and Louisville *Union Press*, n.d., printed in *Liberator*, 3 Nov. 1865; *New York Times*, n.d., and Cincinnati *Gazette*, n.d., reprinted in *Anti-Slavery Sandard*, 12 Aug., 9 Sept., 11 Nov. 1865; D. D. Dennehy, Louisville, 5 July 1865, to the editor, *National Freedman*, I (July 1865), 189–90; *Commonwealth v. Palmer*, 2 Bush 570–80, October 1866 (Ky.); *Corbin v. Marsh*, 2 Duvall 193, December 1865, in Catterall, ed., *Judicial Cases Concerning American Slavery and the Negro*, I, 449–54. Conditions at Camp Nelson in this period are described in letters printed in the *American Missionary*, IX (June 1865), 121–22 (August 1865), 186–87 (October 1865), 229–30 (November 1865), 246–47; X (January 1866), 18 (February 1866), 32 (November 1866), 246–47. See also Marrs, *Life and History* (1885), 61–65.

5. E. Davis, Camp Nelson, 20 April 1865, to the editor, *American Missionary*, IX (June 1865), 121–22; *New York Times*, 26 July 1865; House of Representatives, *Executive Document 70*, 39 Cong. 1st Sess., 1866, 203–7, 234, 236–39.

6. "Report of W. Clark," Maryland, printed in *Anti-Slavery Standard*, 26 Sept. 1865; Major General B. H. Grierson, Huntsville, Ala., 10 Jan. 1866, to W. D. Whipple, in Office of the Adjutant General, Letters Received, Main Series, 1861–1870 ("Racial Violence in the South, 1865–1866"), Reel 505, National Archives.

7. Anonymous Black Soldier, Lexington, Ky., 22 Oct. 1865, to E. M. Stanton, in Colored Troops Division, Letters Received, A–420, Box 112, 1865, Record Group 94, National Archives, courtesy of Leslie Rowland.

8. *American Slave, South Carolina Narratives*, II, ii, 252–57, III, iv, 196–98; Mary Jones and Mary Mallard diary entries, 17, 22, 29 Dec. 1864, *The Children of Pride* (1972), ed. Myers, 1230, 1233, 1237.

9. Cincinnati *Gazette*, n.d., and *Free South*, n.d., reprinted in *Anti-Slavery Standard*, 14 March, 18 July 1863; unsigned letter, Fortress Monroe, Va., 8 Aug. 1862, to the editor, *Independent*, n.d., reprinted in *Liberator*, 8 Aug. 1862; W. T. Richardson, Beaufort,

S.C., 24 Aug. 1864, to the editor, *American Missionary*, VIII (November 1864), 261–62; Rufus Saxton, Beaufort, S.C., 30 Dec. 1864, to E. M. Stanton, *War of the Rebellion, Official Records*, series III, iv, 1028–30; F. Houston Murray, Natchez, 14 July 1865, to the editor, *Christian Recorder*, n.d., reprinted in New Orleans *Tribune*, 14 July 1865; Richmond dispatch, New York *Tribune*, 8 Aug. 1865. See also the testimony of Saxton, Dudley, Judd, Hooper, Smith, Dix, and Hinton in American Freedmen's Inquiry Commission, 1863, file 2, p. 3, file 3, pp. 5–7, 42–43, 85, 116, 224–25, file 8, p. 32, in Letters Received, Office of the Adjutant General, Main Series, 1861–1870, Reels 200 and 201, National Archives, for additional evidence concerning sexual contact between Union Army soldiers and black women. Some witnesses viewed such contact as evidence of prostitution. A. D. Smith made significant distinctions. He found no evidence of prostitution among Sea Island women until 1863 and then briefly among the Hilton Head women. None existed among the Beaufort women. Smith attributed the difference to the fact that the Beaufort women had available work. Hooper said most of the prostitutes were Florida refugees. They "are encouraged by the soldiers constantly," said Hooper, "and the officers protect and conceal them." Among the Commission witnesses, only Richard Hinton discussed the sexual contacts between Union Army soldiers and southern white women. "I have seen white women who call themselves ladies," Hinton said, "stand on the street and call Union soldiers as they were passing by 'sons of bitches,' 'God damn them,' and use all such phrases; and I have never been to any locality where the officers and the men, who were so disposed, did not sleep with all the women around." Hinton commanded black troops in Arkansas, Kansas, Missouri, and the Indian Territory. See also the May 1865 letters written by Henry Turner, then serving as an army chaplain with black soldiers in North Carolina, as quoted in Leon Litwack, "Free at Last," in T. K. Harevan, ed., *Anonymous Americans* (1971), 157–58. Before crossing a river near Smithfield, black soldiers stripped naked. "Secesh women," Turner wrote in the *Christian Examiner*, the official publication of the African Methodist Episcopal Church, watched them "with the utmost intensity. I suppose they desired to see whether these audacious [black] Yankees were really men, made like other men. . . . So they thronged the window, porticos, and yards, in the finest attire imaginable. Our brave soldiers would disrobe themselves, hang up their garments upon their bayonets and through the water they would come, walk up the street, and seem to say to the feminine gazers, 'Yes, though naked, we are your masters.'"

10. 39 Congress, First Session, *House of Representatives Executive Document No. 70, 1866–1867*, 207; *Loyal Georgian*, 27 Jan. 1866,

reprinted in *Black Press, 1827–1890,* ed. Martin Dann, 90–91; "Statement of T. K. Smith," New Orleans, 14 Sept. 1865, *Schurz Report,* 57–59; "Alabama," Mobile, 5, 14, 31 July, 2 Aug., 25 Sept. 1865, to the editor, New Orleans *Tribune,* 8, 18, July, 5, 8, 9 Aug., 28 Sept. 1865; "The Black Population of Mobile," n.d., to the Secretary of War, in Letters Received, Office of the Adjutant General ("Racial Violence in the South, 1865–1866"), Main Series, 1861–1870, Reel 505, National Archives.

11. New Orleans *Tribune,* 6 Aug. 1865; New Orleans *Tribune,* n.d., reprinted in *Anti-Slavery Standard,* 9 Sept. 1865; *Colored Tennessean,* 12 Aug. 1865; *Celebration of the First Anniversary of Freedom Held in the Springfield Baptist Church, January 1st 1866, and Containing an Outline of an Oration Delivered on the Occasion by Chaplain Henry M. Turner* (1866), 6–11.

12. Trial Docket, 1865, Augusta, Ga., Freedmen's Bureau, vol. 158, pp. 2–5, Georgia Freedmen's Bureau Mss., Record Group 105, National Archives. For other instances of lasting attachments between ex-slave women and white men, see Isaac Brinckerhoff, "Mission Work Among the Freed Negroes," 30–31, mss. copy, Colgate-Rochester Divinity School Library; *Dear Ones at Home,* 54–55, 60–61, 73; W. G. Hawkins, "Report," n.d., *National Freedman,* I (August 1865), 242–44; Port Royal dispatches, 23 Dec. 1861 and 7 April 1862, *New York Times,* n.d., reprinted in *Anti-Slavery Standard,* 11 Jan. and 3 May 1862.

13. Bill Wyrnosdick, Crenshaw Co., Ala., 22 May 1867, to Wager Swayne, cited in Kolchin, *First Freedom* (1972), 62; James Johnson, Fredericksburg, Va., 31 Jan. 1868, to O. O. Brown, Va. Freedmen's Bureau Mss. (courtesy of Donald Nieman); New Orleans Freedmen's Bureau Court Register, vol. 137, entry dated 14 March 1867, Louisiana Freedmen's Bureau Mss., RG 105, National Archives. See also *American Slave, North Carolina Narratives,* XV, ii, 106–8, 213–14, 260, and James H. Johnston, *Race Relations in Virginia* (1970), 250–58, for other evidence of ties between slave men and white women. The most detailed evidence describing such relations is found in Richard J. Hinton's unpublished testimony before the American Freedmen's Inquiry Commission in December 1863, file 8, AFIC, Letters Received, Office of the Adjutant General, Main Series, 1861–1870, Reel 201, National Archives. The English-born Hinton was an abolitionist who recruited slave soldiers in Kansas and then served as an officer among them. He told the Commission:

> . . . I have never seen it alluded to publicly but my relations with the colored people have led me to believe that there is a large amount of intercourse between white women and colored men. I

have never found a bright looking colored man, whose confidence I have won, who has not told of instances where he has been compelled . . . by his mistress or white women of the same class to have connection with them. I have conversed with an old physician Dr. Macey of Leavenworth on the subject, and he says that he knows from his experience in Virginia and Missouri that a very large number of white women, especially the daughters of the small planter[s], who were brought into direct relations with the negroes, had compelled some of the men to have something to do with them. . . .

Hinton said even more:

I know of a case in Platte County of a planter's daughter who had a black child. She refused to tell who the father was at first, but, finally, under threats, revealed his name. The man, however, made his escape to Kansas. The child was reported to have died but the man believed it was killed. Captain Matthews, a colored man, who has been an agent of the Underground Railroad and helped to recruit a great many colored soldiers says that a colored man told him that a young girl got him in the woods and told him she would declare he attempted to force her, if he didn't have connection with her.

The same observer suggested that such ties were not always involuntary responses by slave males:

I have generally found that, unless the women had treated them kindly and won their confidence, they have to be threatened, or have their passions raised by actual contact, which a woman who goes as far as that would not hesitate to give. A colored man by the name of Patrick H. Miner, a Louisianian by birth, and the son of old Col. Miner, who had a plantation near New Orleans, has told me [of] several cases of the same kind. He is a graduate of Oberlin College, light colored and a fine handsome-looking body, and attractive in that respect. For several years he was steward on one of the Mississippi River boats and he says that the colored men on that river knew that the women of the Ward family of Louisville, Ky., were in the habit of having the stewards, or other fine looking fellows, sleep with them when they were on the boats. He told me of one of the women of that family who was on the boat he was on, who gave him five dollars and told him to come to her house in Louisville on a certain day giving him particular directions as to the door at which he was to knock. He went there and was shown to the room adjoining her bedroom, where he waited till after dark, when, as his presence was needed on the boat, and she did not make her appearance, he left, but he had no doubt that she wanted him to have connection with her. I can't see how it can be otherwise under the circumstances. Take the border counties of Missouri; the majority of the population were poor whites from North Carolina and Tennessee, who came out to the virgin lands of Missouri and got off well. Their sons got a flashy education which they completed in the slave quarters and the bar-rooms; and their daughters were

> sent to such schools as they had at Platte City, where they were
> taught no solid accomplishments. The girls knew that their brothers
> were sleeping with the chambermaids or other servants, and I don't
> see how it could be otherwise than they too should give loose to
> their passions. It was a great deal so far for them to have one of
> these colored fellows than a white man. . . .

Hinton was not a detached observer. Nevertheless his suggestion
that young white women on farms and small plantations had more
"direct relations with negroes" than plantation women is one that
deserves careful study. An inadequate discussion of the sexual and
marital ties between white women and black men is found in John
Blassingame, *Black New Orleans, 1860–1880* (1973), 202–10. Blassingame's inferences from census data are entirely questionable.

14. Recollections of sexual ties between slaves and whites, mostly
    owners, by elderly ex-slaves are found in *American Slave, South
    Carolina Narratives*, II, pt. i, 34–37, 127–40, 149–51, 324–25, pt. ii,
    34–37, 294–97, III, pt. iii, 146–50, 194–96, 209–212, 226–30, pt. iv,
    31–34; *Texas Narratives*, V, pt. i, 12–13, 151–53, 182–84, 202–11,
    222–24, 240–42, 252–53, 307–8, pt. ii, 50–59, 68–70, 87–89, 205–7,
    260–64, VI, pt. iii, 157–61, 190–92, pt. iv, 27–29, 80–82, 106–8,
    187–89; *Oklahoma Narratives*, VII, 165–68, 233–36; *Unwritten
    History* . . . (Fisk, 1968), 1–6, 19–25, 37–39, 85–87; 101–8, 115–
    119.

15. Laura M. Towne, *Letters and Diary of Laura M. Towne* (1912),
    ed. R. S. Holland, 24–25; H. G. Judd, Beaufort, S.C., 14 Dec. 1865,
    to Major H. W. Smith, Letters Received, Office of the Adjutant
    General, Main Series, 1861–1870 (Racial Violence in the South,
    1865–1866), Reel 505, National Archives; Joint Committee on
    Reconstruction, *1866 Report*, III, 59–62; Deposition of Julia
    Tucker, 17 Jan. 1870, Memphis, Tenn., in 41 Congress, Second
    Session, *House of Representatives Executive Document No. 241*,
    104–5.

16. *American Slave, North Carolina Narratives*, XIV, i, 233–35; *Texas
    Narratives*, IV, ii, 90–92; Cincinnati *Gazette*, n.d., reprinted in
    New Orleans Tribune, 24 May 1865; *New York Tribune*, 6 Sept.
    1865; Murfreesboro, Tenn., complaints, enclosed in John Seage,
    Murfreesboro, Jan. 1866, to J. D. Alden, T/42–39–3, Tennessee
    Freedmen's Bureau Mss., Record Group 105, National Archives.

17. Trial Docket, 1865, Augusta, Ga., Freedmen's Bureau, vol. 158, 2–5,
    and Docket of Cases Tried (1866), Augusta, Ga., Freedmen's Bu-
    reau, 16 Oct. 1866, vol. 157, 20–21, Ga. Freedmen's Bureau Mss.;
    Austin, Texas, entry, 4 June 1867, vol. 52, p. 5, Texas Freedmen's
    Bureau Mss. (courtesy of Barry Crouch); Greenville, S.C., Com-
    plaint Register, March 1868, pp. 46–59, South Carolina Freedmen's

Bureau Mss.; Selma, Ala., Register of Complaints, 23 Oct. 1866, vol. 186, Alabama Freedmen's Bureau Mss., Record Group 105, National Archives.

18. A. T. Morgan, *Yazoo, or on the Picket Line of Freedom in the South* (1884), 55–59, 132, 357–59, 361–63, 432–35. See also Arthur Calhoun, *Social History of the American Family*, III, 27–29, in which Calhoun distorts Morgan's account to argue that "the colored women had come out of bondage with grossly perverted standards."

19. Monck's Corner, S.C. Complaint Register, March 1867, pp. 22–23, and Greenville, S.C., Complaint Register, March 1868, pp. 46–59, South Carolina Freedmen's Bureau Mss.; Murfreesboro, Tenn., complaints enclosed in John Seage, January 1866, to J. D. Alden, T/42–39–3, Tennessee Freedmen's Bureau Mss., Record Group 105, National Archives.

20. "Register of Complaints," Amite City, La., 11 Sept. 1865, Louisiana Freedmen's Bureau Mss., Record Group 105, National Archives.

21. Morgan, *Yazoo*, 319–23; Eliza Frances Andrews, *War-time Journal of a Georgia Girl, 1864–1865* (1908), 349–50; John W. Jones, Rev. and Super. (Freedmen's Bureau), Gibson Co., Tenn., 24 Jan. 1866, to C. B. Fisk, T/142–39–5, Tennessee Freedmen's Bureau Mss., Record Group 105, National Archives.

22. Affidavits of Jennie Scott and Richard Adams and clippings from the *Richmond Whig* and *Richmond Enquirer*, 8 June 1865, Virginia Freedmen's Bureau Mss., Record Group 105, National Archives. A summary of the affidavits and some additional details are found in New York *Tribune*, 17 June 1865. Brief mention of Scott's abuse is in Herbert Aptheker, *To Be Free* (1948), 21. See also Bertram W. Doyle, "Race Relations Before and After 1868," *Journal of Negro History*, XVIII (January 1933), 28.

23. *Lucius Halliday v. Ben Burleson*, 4 Oct. 1966, vol. 51, p. 49, and Charles Garretson, 24 Sept. 1867, to Hardin Hart, vol. 5, p. 146, Texas Freedmen's Bureau Mss. (courtesy of Barry Crouch); Record of Complaints, Shreveport, La., 1866, vol. 441, pp. 5, 31, and Register of Complaints, Amite City, La., 1866, vol. 204, p. 161, Louisiana Freedmen's Bureau Mss.; Greenville, S.C., Complaint Register, May 1868, pp. 132–33, South Carolina Freedmen's Bureau Mss., Record Group 105, National Archives.

24. *Journal of the Mississippi Constitutional Convention* (1868), 199–200, 211–12, 333, 542, 739; Morgan, *Yazoo*, 339.

25. Paul C. Palmer, "Miscegenation as an Issue in the Arkansas Constitutional Convention of 1868," *Arkansas Historical Quarterly*, 24 (Summer 1965), 99–119; Joseph St. Hilaire, "The Negro Dele-

gates in the Arkansas Constitutional Convention of 1868, A Group Profile," *Arkansas Historical Quarterly*, 33 (Spring 1974), 43–69; Du Bois, *Black Reconstruction* (1935), 549.

26. Ethel M. Chistler, "Participation of Negroes in the Government of Georgia, 1867–1870," unpublished M.A. thesis, Atlanta University, 1932, p. 57; F. Logan, *Negro in North Carolina, 1877–1890* (1964), 199–200; *Proceedings of the State Convention of Colored Men Held at Austin, July 10–12, 1883* (1883), reprinted in Aptheker, ed., *Documentary History* (1951), 686–91; L. D. Rice, *Negro in Texas, 1874–1900* (1971), 148–50; Jeffrey R. Brackett, "Notes on the Progress of the Colored People of Maryland Since the War," *Johns Hopkins University Studies in Historical and Political Science*, VIII (1890), 66, 72–73, 75–79; George Tindall, *South Carolina Negroes* (1952), 60, 252, 296–99.

27. A fine discussion of the Maryland apprenticeship laws is in "The System of 'Negro Apprenticeship' in Maryland, Judge Bond's Decision," *Freedmen's Record*, I (July 1865), 105–7. But see also Jeffrey R. Brackett, *Negro in Maryland* (1889), 218–24, on antebellum Maryland vagrancy and apprenticeship laws and W. S. Myers, *Self-Reconstruction of Maryland, 1864–1867* (1909), 20–23.

28. The Stafford, Graham, Turner, and Davis letters, all dated between 2 and 15 November 1864, are in Letters Received, Office of the Adjutant General, Main Series, Roll 280, National Archives.

29. A copy of Order 112, dated 9 Nov. 1864, together with the letters mentioned in this paragraph are found in the source cited in note 28.

30. The evidence in this and the following six paragraphs comes from the documents that accompanied Lew Wallace's report to Maryland General Assembly: Document J in the Maryland State Reports for 1865 entitled *Communication from Major General Lew Wallace in Relation to the Freedmen's Bureau to the General Assembly of Maryland* (1865), 95 pp.

31. The evidence in this and the following two paragraphs is from W. A. Low, "The Freedmen's Bureau and Civil Rights in Maryland," *Journal of Negro History*, XXXVII (July 1952), 221–46; *American Freedman*, II (May 1867); *Freedmen's Record*, I (July 1865), 105–7, and II (March 1866), 39–40; *Anti-Slavery Standard*, 21 Sept. 1865; petition printed in *Baltimore American*, 19 March 1866 (courtesy of Janet McGowan); V. M. Olds, "Freedmen's Bureau as a Social Agency," unpublished dissertation, Columbia University, 1966, 185; *Coston v. Coston*, 25 Md. 500–505, April 1866; *In re Turner*, 24 Federal Cases 337 (1 Abbott US 84–88), October 1867; 39 Congress, 2d Session, *Senate Executive Documents No. 6, 1866–1867*, 24, 34, 90; 39 Congress, 1st Session, *House of Representatives Documents No. 30, 1866–1867*, 385; O. O.

Howard, 1 Nov. 1867, to the Secretary of War, 40 Congress, 2nd Session, *Executive Documents, 1867–1868,* 659–60, 691; O. O. Howard, 14 Oct. 1868, to the Secretary of War, 40 Congress, 3rd Session, *Executive Documents, 1868–1869,* 1032.

32. A manuscript copy of this early Virginia contraband marriage list is in the National Archives, Record Group 105, and was supplied to me by Elaine Everly. On Lockwood's early activities, see Benjamin Quarles, *Negro in the Civil War* (1953), 121–22, 288–90; *Negro in Virginia (WPA),* 188–89; *Boston Journal,* n.d., reprinted in *Anti-Slavery Standard,* 28 Sept. 1861. I shall deal with the patterns of wartime marriage among contrabands in another volume, but examples of such marriages are found in Harriet Jacobs, Alexandria, Va., 7 May 1863, to ———, New York Yearly Meeting of Friend's Society, *Special Report on Colored Refugees* (1863), 12–13; William Walton, Stevenson, Ala., 12 April and 15 May 1865, to the editor, *Pennsylvania Freedmen's Bulletin* (1865), 40, 46–47; T. W. Conway, North Carolina, n.d., to the editor, *Anti-Slavery Standard,* 25 Oct. 1862; James Tynes, Norfolk, 1 July 1864, to the editor, *American Missionary,* VIII (August 1864), 189; *Dear Ones at Home,* 33–38, 56–57, 120–22.

33. Rockbridge, Nelson, Goochland, and Louisa County, Virginia, Marriage Registers, vols. 236, 271, 280, 283, Virginia Freedmen's Bureau Mss., Record Group 105, National Archives. How the Freedmen's Bureau managed the registration of former slave marriages is as yet unknown. Most Rockbridge blacks, for example, registered in a twelve-day period, but whether these and other blacks reported to a central location or were visited by a Bureau officer is unclear. That is a matter of some importance in judging the significance of the total number registered. The registers, furthermore, do not tell whether persons reporting slave marriages had lived together as husband and wife or had been owned separately but still nevertheless believed themselves married.

34. The manuscript marriage registers and "Negro cohabitation certificates" for the 17 North Carolina counties are filed separately by county at the North Carolina Department of Archives and History, Raleigh, N.C. I am again indebted to C. F. W. Coker and his staff at this splendid repository for making these and other materials there available to me. Other statistics used to analyze the 1866 North Carolina marriage registers—unless otherwise noted—are drawn from the 1860 and 1870 federal censuses of population and agriculture.

Registration procedures and record-keeping varied among the seventeen counties, and what was recorded or retained in some counties appears more complete than for other counties. See Chapter 1, note 16, p. 548.

35. The aged former Orange and Wake County slaves Mattie Curtis and Rena Baines remembered that their slave parents remarried upon emancipation, and what these two women recollected in the 1930s matched scattered contemporary evidence for the immediate postwar months. A Warren County white Episcopal cleric, for example, married 150 couples in two July 1865 days, blacks spurred by rumors that only married persons would get land later that year and also by a desire to be "married 'by the book.'" The Lumberton Presbyterian cleric James Sinclair, himself an antebellum Scot immigrant, also married former Robeson County slaves in 1865 and early 1866 and as a Bureau officer refused to let a husband and father "contract with the former Master for his children [and] his wife" unless the couple first took legal vows. When he appeared in early 1866 before the Joint Committee on Reconstruction, Sinclair had married more than two hundred former slave couples, putting them "within the pale of legitimacy and under the control of family government." Marriages among the ex-slaves, however, did not impress many white North Carolinians. Most, according to a New York *Tribune* correspondent, found "this eagerness among the darkies to get married" a "good joke." According to Sinclair, they viewed legal marriages among former slaves as "a matter of ridicule." "They do not believe the negroes will respect those relations more than the brutes . . . ," he added; "the whites laugh at the very idea of the thing." Some former slaves mocked legal marriage for different reasons. The same *Tribune* reporter heard a Bureau officer address more than twenty-five hundred Warren County blacks and remind the adult males among them that they were "sacredly bound to regard the mothers of their children as their wives" because the "laws of God and man" commanded them to "live with and support them." A black in the crowd interrupted to ask how this was possible "on three bushels of corn a year." See *American Slave, North Carolina Narratives*, XIV, i, 221, XV, ii, 193–95; New York *Tribune*, 6, 8 Sept. 1865; James Sinclair, Lumberton, N.C., 2 Oct. 1865, to C. J. Wickersham, N.C., Freedmen's Bureau Mss., RG 105 (courtesy of Edward Magdol); Joint Committee on Reconstruction, *1866 Report*, II, 166–70, 190.

36. *American Slave, North Carolina Narratives*, XV, ii, 184–86; 39 Cong., 2 Sess., *Sen. Exec. Dec. 6, 1866–1867*, 198; J. B. Browning, "The North Carolina Black Code," *Journal of Negro History*, XV (October 1930), 464–65; Rev. S. E. Laidler, New Bern, 22 March 1866, to Brother Whipple, American Missionary Association Archives, NC file; Juliet B. Smith, New Bern, n.d., to the editor, *National Freedman*, II (March 1866), 119; George Newcomb, Elizabeth City, N.C., 5 April 1866, to the editor, *National Freedman*, II (April 1866), 142; unsigned letter, Raleigh, 14 June

1866, to the editor, *Freedmen's Record*, II (July 1866), 133; A. W. Wayman, *My Recollections of African Methodist Episcopal Ministers* . . . (1881), 131.

37. For a contrasting view, see John Blassingame, *Black New Orleans, 1860–1880* (1973), 2, 79, 84. Blassingame writes that when rural slaves arrived in New Orleans they "had little understanding of . . . family obligations," insisting that "the crippling effects of slavery, with its tendency toward family disorganization, continued for several years in the Negro community after the war." He adds later that "in spite of slavery's legacy of immorality and instability, Negroes responded enthusiastically to the urgings of white missionaries, Negro ministers, and newspaper editors to adopt new family mores. Denied an opportunity for legal marriage or preserving family unity in slavery, Negroes adopted most of the missionaries' Victorian values regarding the family." The suggestion that "Negro leaders, ministers, and teachers, and Freedmen's Bureau agents and army officers, began a massive campaign to strengthen the black family during and after the War" is supported by scanty evidence. And behavior of these North Carolina blacks is evidence that former slaves did not need external prodding— by whites or other blacks—to legalize their slave unions. Such behavior, moreover, is not evidence of the adoption of "Victorian values."

38. A. W. Tourgee, "The Negro's View of the Race Problem," in Isabel Barrows, ed., *First Mohonk Conference on the Negro Question . . . , 1890* (1890), 113.

39. *American Slave, South Carolina Narratives*, II, i, 250–53, 326–28; *Texas Narratives*, IV, i, 206–7; *Alabama Narratives*, VI, 155–56; *Unwritten History of Slavery (Fisk)*, 41–47; *Negro in Virginia (WPA)*, 82–83.

40. J. O. Upery, Superintendent, Hardeman City, Bolivar, Tenn., 17 Jan. 1866, to C. B. Fisk, T/142–39–2, Tennessee Freedmen's Bureau Mss., Record Group 105, National Archives; Complaint Register, Arkadelphia, Ark., 14 Aug. 1865, vol. 47, p. 21, Arkansas Freedmen's Bureau Mss., RG 105; Monck's Corner, S.C. Complaint Register, 23 Aug. 1866, pp. 10–11, S.C. Freedmen's Bureau Mss., RG 105; Barnwell, S.C., Complaint Register, 5 June 1867, p. 12, S.C. Freedmen's Bureau Mss., RG 105; *American Slave, Texas Narratives*, V, iii, 222–24; Savannah dispatch from Carleton, *Boston Journal*, 17 Feb. 1865.

41. State marriage laws are conveniently reprinted in 39 Cong., 2 Sess., *Senate Executive Documents No. 6, 1866–1867*, 124–25, 170–209; the full text of French's marriage rules is in 39 Cong., 1 Sess., *House of Representatives Executive Documents No. 70, 1865–1866*,

108–111; Joint Committee on Reconstruction, *Report 1866* (1866), III, 36, 45; Mansfield French, 6 Nov. 1866, to Robert Scott, Office of the Commissioner, Annual Reports, Box 4, South Carolina Freedmen's Bureau Mss., RG 105; Rose, *Rehearsal for Reconstruction* (1964), 236; Abbott, *Freedmen's Bureau in South Carolina, 1865–1872* (1967), 105–8; Peter Kolchin, *First Freedom: The Responses of Alabama's Blacks to Emancipation and Reconstruction* (1972), 60; Clinton Fisk, *Plain Counsels for Freedmen* (1866), 31–32.

42. O. O. Brown, Richmond, 19 May 1866, to O. O. Howard, 39 Congress, First Session, *House of Representatives Executive Documents No. 120, 1865–1866*, 45; Peter Randolph, *From the Slave Cabin to the Pulpit* (1893), 89–91; James Sinclair, Lumberton, N.C., 2 Oct. 1865, to C. J. Wickersham, North Carolina Freedmen's Bureau Mss., RG 105, NA (courtesy of Edward Magdol).

43. Tuscaloosa, Ala., Complaint Book, 11 Dec. 1866, vol. 136, p. 114, Alabama Freedmen's Bureau Mss., RG 105; Vidalia, La., Court Record, 26 March 1866, vol. 511, p. 3, Louisiana Freedmen's Bureau Mss., RG 105; "Negro Cohabitation Certificates," Beaufort County, North Carolina, mss. copy, North Carolina Department of Archives and History, Raleigh, N.C.; District of Columbia Marriage Register, 1866–1867, unnumbered volume, Freedmen's Bureau Mss., RG 105, National Archives; William Birnie, 22 Nov. 1867, to Allen Rutherford, cited in W. M. Evans, *Ballots and Fence Rails* (1966–1967), 92.

44. Unsigned letter, Raleigh, N.C., 14 June 1866, to the editor, *Freedmen's Record*, II (July 1866), 133; Elizabeth H. Botume, *First Days Amongst the Contrabands* (1893), 154–56, 160–63.

45. Mansfield French, 6 Nov. 1866, to Robert Scott, Office of the Commissioner, Annual Reports, Box 4, South Carolina FB Mss., RG 105, NA; Botume, *First Days Amongst the Contrabands*, 160; Goochland and Louisa County, Virginia, Marriage Registers, 1866, volumes 236 and 280, Virginia FB Mss., RG 105, NA.

46. *American Slave, North Carolina Narratives*, XV, ii, 197; [Lexington] *Union Standard*, 5 Oct. 1866 (courtesy of Leslie Rowland); John deForest, *A Union Officer in the Reconstruction* (1948), pp. 56–58.

47. Willie Ann Grey, Salvisa, Ky., 7 April 1866, to Philip Grey, Richmond, Letters Received, Assistant Commissioner, Virginia FB Mss., RG 105, NA. Grey's transportation request apparently was denied by Bureau officers.

48. Manuscript copies of these North Carolina marriage registers are deposited at the North Carolina Department of Archives and History, Raleigh, N.C., and I am in debt to C. F. W. Coker, the

Division Administrator of Archives and Records, and his staff for making these materials available to me.

49. Testimony of A. D. Smith, American Freedmen's Inquiry Commission, 1863, file 3, pp. 51–52, Letters Received, Office of the Adjutant General, Main Series, 1861–1870, Roll 200, National Archives.

50. Wharton, *Negro in Mississippi* (1947), 227–28; J. S. McNeily, "From Organization to Overthrow of Mississippi's Provisional Government," Mississippi Historical Society, *Publications Centenary Series*, I (1918), 135–36; 32 Cong., 2 Sess., *Sen. Exec. Doc. 6, 1866–1867*, 193–94; J. T. Wallace, *History of the Negroes of Mississippi, 1865–1890* (1927), 96–98; Rose H. Moore, "Economic and Social Conditions in Mississippi During Reconstruction," Ph.D. dissertation, Duke University, 1937, 359–60; Clifton Ganus, "Freedmen's Bureau in Mississippi," Ph.D. dissertation, Tulane University, 1953, 258–62; *American Freedman*, I (June 1867) and (July 1867), 238–39, 252–54.

51. "Annual Message of Governor James Alcorn to the Mississippi Legislature Session of 1871," quoted in Robert Somers, *Southern States Since the War, 1870–1871* (1871), 250–53; Charles K. Marshall, *The Colored Race Weighed in Balance* (1883), 12–14. Population figures for 1870 and 1800 are drawn from the published federal censuses for these years.

52. St. Louis letter, n.d., *The (Baptist) Examiner*, 23 March 1865; *Proceedings of the Freedmen's Convention of Georgia . . . at Augusta, Georgia, August 1–10, 1866* (1866), *passim*.

Chapter 10: Like It Was

1. E. W. Burgess, "Introduction," in E. Franklin Frazier, *Negro Family in Chicago* (1932), ix–xii.

2. 46 Cong., 2 Sess., Report 693, *Report and Testimony of the Select Committee of the U.S. Senate to Investigate the Causes of the Removal of the Negroes from the Southern States to the Northern States in Three Parts* (Washington, 1880), I, 10, 13, 90, 220–22; II, 211–14, 234–35, 292–93, 302–20, 419, 426, 422; III, 5, 8, 36–37, 43–68, 363–64, 371–72, 397–98, 417; Laura Haviland, *A Woman's Life-work* (Cincinnati, 1881), 482–505. Background on the "Great Exodus" is found in Wharton, *Negro in Mississippi*, 112–16; *Journal of Negro History*, IV (January 1919), 51–92; Arna Bontemps and Jack Conroy, *They Seek a City* (1945), 37–53; John G. Van Deusen, "The Exodus of 1879," *Journal of Negro History*, XXI (April 1936), 111–29.

3. W. C. J., n.d., to the editor, Arkansas *Weekly Mansion*, 1, 8 Sept. 1883; Arkansas *Weekly Mansion*, 11, 25 Aug., 10, 24 Nov., 8, 22 Dec. 1883 and 26 Jan., 2 Feb., 15 March, 19 April 1884; Arkansas *Gazette*, 12, 14, 19 Aug. 1883; Little Rock dispatch, 25 April 1884, Cincinnati *Weekly Press*, 1 May 1884.

4. Most residents in the four rural counties had experienced ante-bellum plantation life and field labor. Seven of ten Warren County slaves lived on units of twenty or more slaves in 1860, and even higher percentages of such units of ownership existed in Adams, Lowndes, and Beaufort counties. Seven of the ten Beaufort County slaves, moreover, lived on units of fifty or more slaves. Post-emancipation staple production and commercial agriculture dominated their economic life. Lowndes County ranked fourth in cotton production among Alabama's sixty-eight counties in 1880. Although Adams and Warren counties ranked much lower among Mississippi cotton-producing counties, ex-slaves there worked cotton farms and former plantations. Just over half of tilled Lowndes County acres were planted in cotton, and the percentage was nearly as high in Adams County. One of five tilled Lowndes acres was planted in corn, but a federal investigator worried that Adams and Warren counties had a "remarkable deficiency in home supplies." Sea Island blacks had a substantial corn crop, and half of Beaufort County's tilled acreage was devoted to growing rice and cotton.

These four rural places were densely black in population, and examining black households there means studying them in relative isolation. The four counties became more densely black between 1860 and 1880, ranging in the latter year from 72 percent (Warren County) to 92 percent (Beaufort County). In 1880, Beaufort County had more blacks relative to whites than any other in the country. Two Alabama counties had a higher percentage of blacks than Lowndes. Most county whites, moreover, lived in towns and villages; county percentages therefore hide the density of rural black settlement. If Natchez blacks and whites are excluded, nine of ten rural Adams County residents were blacks. Just one in ten Mount Album residents was a white; more than four in five Lane's Schoolhouse residents were blacks. Rural Beaufort County had even fewer resident whites. St. Helena's Township included thirty-three whites among its 2819 residents; St. Helena's Island had sixty-five white and 4261 black residents. That so few whites lived in these rural places means that few white "models" existed for blacks to "imitate." The few whites these rural blacks dealt with on a day-to-day basis differed in their class status. A black Sea Islander who encountered a resident white nearly always met a merchant or a store clerk. A Mount Album black probably met a farmer. Because Lane's Schoolhouse included a rural village, blacks there most often had contact with artisans and laborers.

Commenting on the emancipated rural black men, E. Franklin Frazier observed: "The pattern of behavior and ideals which he took over from the white man were acquired through formal imitation of people outside his social world. In their social isolation the majority of [plantation] Negroes were forced to draw upon the meager social heritage which they had acquired during slavery." The rural blacks examined here all experienced the social isolation emphasized by Frazier, but it varied from place to place. If "formal imitation" was as essential as Frazier and others have suggested, the Sea Island black households should have differed significantly from those in rural Mississippi. That was not the case. Neither the presence nor the absence of "white models" affected the types of households in which rural blacks lived. Rural blacks in all places had quite similar households.

5. Sixteen of the 870 Lowndes County, Alabama, men did not work the land. They included two clergymen, a grocer, a miller, two artisans (a carpenter and a blacksmith), and ten laborers, five of them railroad workers. At most, twenty-three men owned land, nearly all between thirty and seventy-five acres. The rest were either cash tenants (21 percent), sharecroppers (33 percent), or farm laborers (41 percent). The population census listed nine of ten of the nearly five hundred Mount Album, Mississippi, men as "farmers." Three owned land. No more than thirty-one were cash tenants, and the rest—more than nine of ten—were farm laborers. About one in ten had other occupations: forty-seven unskilled laborers (including thirty-three servants, nine laborers, two draymen, two railroad workers, and a gardener), and five with artisan skills (two carpenters, a blacksmith, a butcher, and a bricklayer). The Mount Album black community also included a merchant, a constable, and three clergymen.

The land-tenure and credit system in nearly all these rural South Carolina, Mississippi, and Alabama counties bound black agricultural workers to the land, reinforcing their lower-class status and making them dependent upon landowners and merchants. Eugene D. Hilgard, formerly a Professor of Agriculture at the University of Mississippi, showed this in his *Report on Cotton Production in the United States*, a part of the 1880 federal census. A county-by-county survey, Hilgard's study included responses from resident whites concerning the local systems of labor and credit. A common credit system existed everywhere. How blacks farmed and how whites hired black labor differed in the Sea Islands from the other places studied. "A large number own farms," the Beaufort correspondent reported to Hilgard; "a still larger number rent lands for cultivation; and even the laborers are paid most generously by granting the use of a certain number of acres of land for stipulated services." Such arrangements sometimes included a dwelling and fuel. Five to seven acres went to blacks in exchange for two days of their labor each week ("the two-day system") on land whites owned. Black Sea Island farmers used implements of "the simplest and cheapest description," and their "chief reliance" was "upon the hoe." Whether they rented or owned land did not affect how they marketed crops or purchased necessities. They dealt in "a few country stores, where . . . traders, invariably white, . . . collect and dispose of the crop and supply the community with such articles of food and dress as are required." Prices paid by blacks varied "from 20 to 100 percent above the market value of the goods, according to the amount of competition among the storekeepers." Mississippi and Alabama blacks shared an onerous credit system with the Sea Island blacks but labored under different conditions. "The large cotton farms or plantations," said Hilgard's Lowndes County correspondent, "are almost altogether worked on the share system." In return for furnishing all but the laborer's board, a landlord received half the crop. If a black just rented the land, he returned one-fourth of the cotton and one-third of the corn grown. The crop-lien system dominated the Lowndes County credit structure. "Credits are universal," said this same observer, "and regularly consume the entire crop of the laborer." Warren and Adams County, Mississippi, farmers had quite similar economic dealings. Wages paid to men ranged from $100 to $150 a year; "women and boys" received "a lesser amount." Sharecropping arrangements cost blacks from one-fourth to three-fourths of what they grew. Other arrangements meant the return of a lesser share. Among the Mississippi blacks, furthermore, the crop-lien system had become "very general and to the extent of the whole or three-fourths of the growing crop."

6. Far fewer everywhere than the unskilled laborers, the black artisans—ex-slave craftsmen, perhaps, important among them— had a central place in the urban black occupational structure. Compared with southern white urban artisans, black artisans made up a relatively small percentage of the black working class. But the absence of a significant middle class greatly increased their importance within the black community. Twice as many Beaufort and Natchez and three times as many Mobile and Richmond black men were artisans as were middle-class in occupation.

Men with skills played important roles in all nineteenth-century working-class communities. Indigenous community leadership came much more regularly from the artisans than from the less advantaged unskilled laborers, and especially among ethnic and racial minorities artisans shared that role with lawyers and clergymen, and small businessmen and local politicians, themselves often from artisan origins. Except in Beaufort which had so few white workers and in a scattering of nearly all-black crafts elsewhere, the black artisans were much less secure in their economic position than their number suggests.

Over-all occupational percentages hide much. In 1880 most black artisans bunched together in a few urban crafts. Mobile, for example, had one black tailor and Richmond a single black millwright. Black artisans everywhere specialized in—or had been narrowed into—just a few major crafts. Carpenters and brickmasons made up slightly more than half of Beaufort's black artisans, and the same percentage (55 percent) of Natchez artisans worked as carpenters, barbers, cigarmakers, and bricklayers. The manuscript census recorded skills for 921 Richmond artisans: four of five labored as shoemakers, carpenters, blacksmiths, barbers, coopers, plasterers, bricklayers, and wood sawyers. That black artisans crowded together in so few urban crafts cannot be understood without examining their position relative to white artisans. The presence of white Natchez, Mobile, and Richmond artisans in 1880 disputes the widely held belief that ex-slaves dominated the southern urban crafts. Some urban crafts had so few blacks in 1880 to indicate clearly that entry also had been denied to slaves. Even crafts that had relatively large numbers of black artisans were not entirely "black crafts." Natchez, Mobile, and Richmond barbers and wood sawyers nearly all were black, but that happened in very few other crafts. Natchez had only black stationary engineers, wood sawyers, and bricklayers, and its blacksmiths and bakers were predominantly black. Bricklaying and plastering were largely black crafts in Mobile and Richmond, and the Richmond barrel makers were nearly three-fourths black. But most other urban crafts with significant numbers of blacks also had a good share of whites, their number often greater than the black number. No urban craft revealed this relationship more clearly than carpentering. Carpenters made up an important proportion of black artisans everywhere (two of five in Beaufort, one of four in Natchez, three of ten in Mobile, and one of eight in Richmond), but white carpenters nearly equaled the number of black Natchez carpenters, and almost two-thirds of Mobile's and four-fifths of Richmond's carpenters were white men.

In 1880, blacks dominated a handful of urban crafts. The ages of white and black artisans, furthermore, indicate that whites were rapidly displacing them in the others or gaining entry as

young men into occupations denied to young blacks. Mobile and
Richmond carpenters, for example, were much older than white
carpenters there: including young apprentices, one of four white
Mobile and Richmond carpenters had not yet turned thirty, as
contrasted with 13 percent of Mobile and 9 percent of Richmond
black carpenters. Sons were not "inheriting" that skill from their
black fathers, and that was so in most other artisan crafts. Young
white males made up a much larger percentage of the white
artisan class than did young black males of the black artisan class.
Two in five white Mobile artisans were not yet thirty years old; a
far smaller proportion of Mobile black artisans were that young.
The percentage-point difference was nearly that great among
young Richmond artisans, and there one of six was a barber. The
reasons for such differences in the ages of white and black artisans
are not yet known, but their importance is obvious. The southern
urban crafts in the 1870s had attracted far more young white than
young black men, a process indicating that the status of black
artisans was in decline. It is probable that slave artisan skills had
been relatively few in number—or, more than adequate in a relatively closed market, that they could not be sustained in a competitive market. But it is also possible that when written the history
of Reconstruction in southern cities may reveal that white artisans
gained or strengthened their control of important urban crafts
and closed them to ex-slave artisans and their sons. If that happened, this conflict for control of the job market did not involve
just blacks and southern white workers. In 1880, one of twenty
white Richmond workers had a northern father or had himself
been born in the North, and two of five were immigrants or the
children of immigrants. The percentage of "alien" white workers
was even higher in Natchez and Mobile. Fifteen percent of white
Natchez workers were of northern origin, and nearly three of five
were immigrants or the sons of immigrants. Over one in ten white
Mobile workers came from the North or had a northern father,
and no fewer than two of three had immigrant parents or had
been born in Europe. Whatever the causes for their decline, black
artisans—so central in communities with an insignificant middle
class—had a precarious economic position in 1880.

7. Rural black women labored in the South, but deficiencies in the
enumeration of such work make precise study of it difficult. Many
engaged in casual, if not regular, field labor, and much smaller
numbers were hired as domestics or had other jobs. This is known
from extant labor contracts and other contemporary sources. The
deficiencies in enumeration can be easily illustrated. The census
enumerator only assigned occupations to single St. Helena's Township women and to those heading households, but on St. Helena's

Island the enumerator reported that nine of ten women aged twenty and older labored in the fields or at other farm work. Such strikingly divergent data reveal more about faulty enumeration methods than about the labor black women performed and make it difficult to estimate how many women worked and how age and marital status affected their labor. Nevertheless the incomplete returns reveal information about women with *listed* occupations. Despite its sparseness, the St. Helena's Township enumeration reported the presence of an elderly midwife, and the St. Helena's Island enumeration listed seventeen women working at other than farm labor: eleven servants and cooks (three of them married), a widowed seamstress, and five teachers (nearly all young). More is learned from the Mississippi enumerations. Fifty-three Mount Album women (one in ten of those with listed occupations) did not perform regular farm labor: all but six were house servants. Nearly the same pattern existed in Washington and Kingston, the two largest Adams County census districts. Four of five women had occupations listed, and nearly nine of ten worked the land. Few married women labored as house servants: only one of four servants was married; the rest were single or headed male-absent households. A scattering of other Adams County women labored as seamstresses and washerwomen. A dozen women—four married and two the young heads of households—taught school. The village economy affected the pattern of female employment in Lane's Schoolhouse. One of five with known occupations was a servant; mostly single women and heads of male-absent households did such work. Nearly all other laboring women worked as farm laborers (except one who owned twenty acres), laborers, washerwomen, and seamstresses. A few had other occupations: an eighty-year-old midwife, a widowed dyer, a grocer, a peddler, and four married schoolteachers. One teacher was married to a teacher; the others were married to a carpenter and two laborers.

Beaufort, Natchez, Mobile, and Richmond women had a different occupational pattern from these rural and village black women, but it was just as narrow as their men's. Most urban black women who worked labored as house servants and washerwomen. Because the town had so few white residents, Beaufort black women differed somewhat from the others. Nevertheless common patterns existed everywhere, patterns that become very significant when employed young women aged fifteen to nineteen and girls not yet fifteen are included. Census enumerators listed occupations for between 43 percent (Natchez) and 53 percent (Richmond) of all black females fifteen and older in Beaufort, Natchez, Richmond, and Mobile's first, seventh, and eighth wards (two of three black Mobile women lived in these three wards).

Three of five Beaufort women were house servants and washer-women, and between 86 percent and 90 percent of Natchez, Mobile, and Richmond women did similar work. Black women had few other occupations. A scattering everywhere were "laborers" or had unusual jobs. Except in Beaufort, very few managed petty retail enterprises. Just four Natchez women traded in goods (a market woman, two hucksters, and a coffee-stand keeper). Two grocers, a restaurant keeper, and five hucksters lived in the Mobile wards, and sixteen Richmond women worked as grocers, shopkeepers, eating-house proprietors, hucksters, and market women. Their insignificance is seen by the fact that tiny Beaufort had fourteen women doing such work. Not a single Mobile, Natchez, or Beaufort woman had a white-collar job, and the entire Richmond female population included a saleswoman, a young bookkeeper, and a woman working in a photographic gallery. Only schoolteaching allowed small numbers, nearly always young and unmarried women, to escape ordinary jobs. Few in number, women school-teachers nevertheless outnumbered men schoolteachers everywhere.

The age and household status of such women suggests a great deal about black attitudes toward the working mother. Except in Beaufort, house servants greatly outnumbered washerwomen. Natchez had nearly two and a half and Richmond three times as many house servants as washerwomen: 3925 Richmond women worked as servants, cooks, and nurses, compared with the city's 1303 washerwomen. Relatively few unmarried *rural* black women were house servants. That was also so in the towns and cities. We consider first only *adult* house servants and washerwomen: black women at least twenty years old. Between 42 percent (Mobile) and 50 percent (Beaufort) of *all* adult black women lived with a spouse or a spouse and their children. The percentage of married adult washerwomen reflected this over-all distribution and ranged from 35 percent (Beaufort) to 42 percent (the three Mobile wards), but the percentage of married adult house servants was much lower and ranged from 13 percent (Natchez) to 23 percent (Beaufort and the Mobile wards). Part of the explanation for this important difference resulted from the widespread employment of women under twenty years of age as servants. Between two-thirds (Beaufort) and three-fourths (Richmond) of *all* servants were single females, including children under fifteen, older daughters living with one or both parents, unmarried women of all ages but especially those between fifteen and twenty-nine, and elderly women cut off by death or for other reasons from a husband or from children.

An opposite pattern existed among the washerwomen. Between two-thirds (Richmond and Natchez) and nearly three-fourths

(Mobile) were married women with or without children and females heading male-absent households. Because their absolute number differed so greatly, it is essential to disregard these percentages and to examine the absolute numbers. Richmond and Mobile had between two and a half and three times more servants than washerwomen, but in *absolute numbers* twice as many Richmond and three times as many Mobile *married black women with children* worked as washerwomen as labored as house servants. Relatively few married mothers worked as house servants; as a group, they preferred washing and ironing to domestic service. Unless whites entirely dictated such choices, this fact suggests that married mothers wanted to labor in their own homes rather than in white homes. However arduous, such labor allowed them to control their time and gave them fuller access to their children than outside domestic service. The pressure of a father and a husband, moreover, may have worked to keep them at home. The relative insignificance of the married mother as house servant is illustrated in another way. Servants under twenty, including girls under fifteen, greatly outnumbered them everywhere. The choices these married mothers made were significant. Washing clothes was neither remunerative nor pleasant work, but many chose it as their occupation. Such decisions are reason to doubt the belief then (and even later) that black mothers gave more attention to the families of former owners and current employers than to their own families. Too many mothers labored at home over a washtub to sustain that belief.

The ages of washerwomen and especially of servants disclose even more than these facts. Because so many mothers and married women worked as washerwomen, it is not surprising that they were older as a group than the house servants. Between 36 percent (Beaufort) and 44 percent (Natchez) of washerwomen were at least forty years old. Except for Natchez, which had an unusually large number of elderly black women, servants were much younger. Those at least forty years old were only 18 percent of the Beaufort and less than 30 percent of the Richmond (26 percent) and Mobile (29 percent) servant populations. A large percentage everywhere were not yet twenty years old. White preference for younger female servants (a decision that may have had significant sexual implications), black need for a second family income, or a combination of both may explain why so many servants were not yet twenty years old and even under the age of fifteen. Natchez female servants under twenty exceeded those sixty and older. (One in ten Natchez servants was not yet fifteen years old!) Mobile and Richmond servants not yet fifteen years old equaled or greatly outnumbered elderly "mammies." At least one in five (Natchez) and as many as one in three (Beaufort) house servants were not yet twenty years old. This evidence contradicts yet another erroneous but popular belief about ex-slave women: the assertion that the typical house servant was an aged "mammy" who remained in her antebellum place out of loyalty to a white family or because whites had a special concern for such women. Elderly black women worked as domestics for these or other reasons, but visitors to white households much more regularly found there a young woman or a child servant rather than a loyal and aged "mammy." Unless these young women had come in unattached from rural areas or lived entirely cut off from their families of origin, it is probable that many worked as house servants to supplement incomes earned by their mothers and fathers.

8. Everywhere, more than half of the households contained between two and four persons. If the household size reported in 1880 in four Paterson, New Jersey, census enumeration districts typified that common among northern white workers, then the urban and rural southern black household did not differ in size from the white working-class household. Large numbers of immigrant (especially Irish, English, German, and Dutch by birth) and native white workers lived in these four districts. Fewer households with between two and seven residents existed in this predominantly working-class white community (87 percent) than in any of the rural and urban southern black communities studied.

9. Most subfamilies in black households lived with kin in extended households. About half of all Richmond subfamilies had an affinal or a consanguinal tie to the host family, but the percentage was much higher in the other places: Mobile (61 percent), Natchez (75 percent), rural Adams County (75 percent), Mount Album (80 percent), Beaufort (82 percent), Lane's Schoolhouse (89 percent), and St. Helena's Island and Township (98 percent). Although most black subfamilies lived in extended households and not among strangers, most extended black households did not contain related subfamilies. Except for St. Helena's Island and Township, about one in three extended households included a subfamily. The rest usually comprised an immediate family and one or two relatives. Between half and three-fifths of all single relatives in extended rural households were women of all ages, a percentage that increased to between two-thirds and four-fifths in the cities. A mother or mother-in-law was more common in the urban extended households: about one of four Natchez, Mobile, and Richmond single relatives in extended households were elderly mothers. The typical single relatives in extended households, however, were not elderly women but grandchildren, nieces and nephews, and brothers and sisters. This fact hints at significant

continuities between an immediate family and the two families of origin. Grandchildren were more common in extended rural households; brothers and sisters were more common in extended urban households. Together, these three sets of blood kin made up between two-thirds (Beaufort) and three-fourths (St. Helena's Island and Township) of all single relatives in extended households. Apart from pointing to connections between an immediate family and a family of origin, such patterns suggest the rarity of matrifocal authority.

10. "Motherhood outside of institutional control," insisted E. Franklin Frazier of emancipated southern black women, "was accepted by a large group of Negro women with an attitude of resignation as if it were nature's decree." No fewer than five chapters in Frazier's *Negro Family in the United States* argued this point. Such were "the simple folkways . . . of peasant folk." "In the rural areas of the South," Frazier went on, "we find the maternal family functioning in its most primitive form as a natural organization." Three-generation adult male-absent households—a grandmother, her daughter, and the older woman's grandchildren—represented for Frazier the "ideal" matrifocal household. Frazier seriously challenged for the first time the then dominant racist arguments (quite common at the turn of this century and even later) that saw in the male-absent household evidence of widespread moral depravity and sexual looseness among the former slaves. Frazier described the male-absent household as an adaptation first to slavery and then to the depressed lower class of emancipated rural and urban southern blacks. In the post–Civil War decades and for still another generation, Frazier argued that the "matriarchate"— "the House of the Mother"—flourished among southern blacks. A narrow "class" analysis allowed him to insist that property-owning black farmers and small numbers of blacks with skills and middle-class occupations headed households in the South's urban bourgeois enclaves, but these did not count for nearly as much as the "matriarchate." After emancipation, according to Frazier, "the maternal-family organization, a heritage from slavery . . . continued on a fairly large scale." These generalizations about the southern black household rest on very inadequate historical evidence. Seventy pages of text devoted to the "House of the Mother" include six pieces of historical evidence for the critical decades between 1870 and 1900: a letter from the Yankee schoolteacher Elizabeth Botume, an extract from A. T. Morgan's semifictional memoir *Yazoo* (1884), and two quotations each from Philip A. Bruce's *The Plantation Negro as Freedman* (1889) and J. Bradford Laws's Department of Labor study, "The Negroes of Cinclaire Central Factory and Calumet Plantation" (1902). Despite the

absence of evidence, Frazier's arguments gained widespread acceptance, so that in 1966 Nathan Glazer could write that Frazier's
work "remains solid and structures all our thinking on the Negro
family." Without offering additional evidence, Glazer said that
"an extension of the matriarchy" occurred after emancipation.

11. The percentage of male-absent households and subfamilies varied
from place to place and especially between rural and urban areas,
ranging from 13 percent (St. Helena's Island and Township) to
18 percent (rural Adams County) among rural blacks and from
26 percent (Mobile) to 31 percent (Natchez) among urban blacks.
If the male-absent household had its origins as an adaptive device
to enslavement, it should have been at least as common in rural
areas as in towns and cities. Custom and tradition were more
tenacious in rural than in urban places.

12. The 1880 census listed the "civil condition" of all respondents in
three separate categories: "single," "married," and "widowed/
divorced." A small but nevertheless significant number of mothers
everywhere described themselves as "single." Where the imbalance
in the sex ratio was greatest (rural Adams County, Natchez, and
Beaufort), the percentage of male-absent households and subfamilies headed by single women was greatest. Single women
headed two in five Beaufort and three in ten rural Adams County
male-absent households and subfamilies. But in itself the unbalanced sex ratio is not a full explanation for the presence of single
mothers. The willingness of some black mothers everywhere to
describe themselves as single shows that they attached no shame
to motherhood outside of marriage. The age of women under
thirty in 1880 at the time their oldest child then living in the
household was born also shows that childbirth prior to marriage
was often followed by marriage itself. Leaving the Richmond
women aside, we find that the mean age hardly differed in the
other places, ranging from 18.0 (Lane's Schoolhouse) to 18.9 (Beaufort). Nevertheless, relatively few women under thirty headed
male-absent households and subfamilies. The mean age of St.
Helena's Island and Township mothers at the birth of their first
living child, for example, was 18.6, but only 3.5 percent of St.
Helena's women aged twenty to twenty-nine described themselves
as single mothers. If motherhood outside of marriage was widely
sanctioned, the percentage should have been far higher. In addition, about one in ten mothers under thirty in 1880 gave birth
to a first child prior to a fifteenth birthday. Unless marriage followed such births, the percentage of single mothers under thirty
would have been much higher.

The absence of a father resulted from other causes than his
death or the single status of a mother. Except in Lane's School-

house and St. Helena's Island and Township, a significant
percentage of heads of male-absent households and subfamilies
described themselves as married women. That percentage ranged
from about 9 percent (Natchez) to 23 percent (Beaufort and Richmond) of the heads of all male-absent households and subfamilies.
Among Richmond women aged twenty to twenty-nine, the percentage calling themselves married rose to nearly 40 percent. There
is no way to tell from census schedules whether such women had
been permanently abandoned by their husbands or whether the
men were temporarily absent.

13. Women aged twenty to twenty-nine had been born between 1851
and 1860. They grew up as slave children and matured as young
women during the "chaos" and "disorder" of the Reconstruction
era. The percentage of them heading households was larger than
among "comparable" white women. Relatively few urban men
in this age group married, and that also was the case for urban
women. Between seven in ten (at Lane's Schoolhouse) and three
in four (at Mount Album) women aged twenty to twenty-nine
were married, but that percentage fell to 38 percent in Richmond
and 54 percent in Beaufort. Rural married women with or without
children far exceeded the number heading households and subfamilies. Even though rural Adams County had a shortage of
young adult men, four times as many women had husbands as
headed households. Among St. Helena's Island and Township
and Mount Album blacks, more than eight times as many had
husbands as headed households. In the towns and cities where the
sex ratio posed insuperable obstacles, the percentage difference
was smaller. Nevertheless, in Mobile and Richmond four times
as many women had husbands as headed households. Single urban
women living in diverse household arrangements, moreover, exceeded female household heads. Too few older persons lived in
Beaufort to allow single women there to remain with their parents
in large numbers, but in Natchez, Mobile, and Richmond between
one-third (Richmond) and 45 percent (Natchez and Mobile) of all
single women lived with their families of origin. That also was
so for slightly more than four in five single St. Helena's Island
and Township women. Large numbers of women in their twenties worked as cooks, nurses, and servants, but only a small number
(again with the exception of Richmond) lived in white households. A single woman each lived in a Lane's Schoolhouse and
St. Helena's Island and Township white household. Not one lived
in a Mount Album household. Six Beaufort women lived in white
households, and about 8 percent of Mobile and Natchez women
aged twenty to twenty-nine did so. One in five Richmond women
resided in a white household. (The city that had the largest per-

centage of young black women residing in white households also had the lowest percentage of young urban black women heading households and subfamilies.) Except in Beaufort, where one in ten women in this age group lived alone, only a scattered number lived alone in the other cities and the rural areas. The two rural Sea Island communities together had only seven women in this status. One in twenty-six lived alone in Mobile, and that proportion rose to one in thirty-four in Natchez, and one in sixty in Richmond.

The common observation by whites in the 1880s that young black women were promiscuous is not sustained by examining further the status of urban women aged twenty to twenty-nine. By combining the number of married women with children and the number of female heads of households with children, it is found that in Natchez (46 percent), Mobile (46 percent), and Richmond (35 percent) less than half of all women had resident children. The percentage was slightly more than half (55 percent) among Beaufort women. One in ten Natchez women was married without children and one in three was single without children. In Richmond, slightly more were married but childless, and nearly half (47 percent) were single and without children. Apart from showing that urban black women in large numbers married in their mid- or late twenties, these facts suggest much else. Unless further research reveals an unusually high infant-mortality rate or the widespread practice of birth control or infanticide among *these* women, the high percentage of single women without children casts serious doubt on arguments about widespread promiscuity. The number without children together with an urban sex ratio for men and women aged twenty to twenty-nine that ranged from 54.7 (Richmond) to 58.9 (Mobile) suggests that sexual abstinence, not promiscuity, was common for many of these single women. The sex ratio weakened the social position of young black women and was sufficient reason in itself to encourage "illegitimacy" and even prostitution among them. That would have happened in any population with such an imbalanced sex ratio, not just among former slaves. When these unfavorable conditions are taken into account and when it is realized that these women lived in "Redeemed" southern Bourbon cities and that the courts offered them little protection (in 1880, the manuscript census lists one black lawyer in Richmond and none in Mobile), the alleged "matriarchal" power of women fades in importance. We ask ourselves instead why so few young rural and especially urban black women lived in male-absent households.

14. The male-absent household and subfamily differed in composition from households that contained a husband or a father, differences

which suggest how poor blacks coped with the shortage of males. Most important, the simple nuclear male-absent household—just a mother and her children—was much less common among all male-absent households than the simple nuclear male-present household—a husband and wife, two parents and their children, or a father and his children. That was so in both rural and urban areas. The percentage of rural male-present nuclear households as a percentage of all male-present households ranged from 82 percent (Mount Album) to 70 percent (rural Adams County) and for father-absent nuclear households from 64 percent (Mount Album) to 35 percent (Lane's Schoolhouse). Similar differences existed in the towns and cities. The husband-father nuclear household ranged from 67 percent (Beaufort) to 54 percent (Natchez), and the female-headed nuclear household from 57 percent (Beaufort) to 38 percent (Richmond). As a result, the female-headed nuclear household everywhere was a relatively small percentage of *all kin-related households*, ranging from 8 percent (St. Helena's Island and Township) to 10 percent (rural Adams County) and from 10 percent (Richmond and Beaufort) to 13 percent (Mobile). Here is suggestive evidence of two kinds. It hints that these women found it more difficult to manage a household without help than men who headed households.

It also indicates that widowed and even single women with children were not shunned by other kin and non-kin. Either lodgers and kin helped to fill such households, or the women themselves lived in other households as subfamilies. The male-absent augmented household—a woman, her children, and unrelated lodgers—was more important in the urban than in the rural communities. Few of these augmented households, however, had *male* lodgers in them who were ten years or less older than the female head. Hardly any of these augmented households therefore hid common-law marriages or casual sexual alliances. Not one of Beaufort's seven augmented households had such a male, and only six of thirty-six did in Natchez. Nine percent of Richmond's 221 female-headed augmented households included such a male lodger. Excepting Richmond, furthermore, the female-headed extended household was more common everywhere than the augmented household, and more often than not female kin of all ages lived in it. Finally, a high percentage of the subfamilies living in white but especially in black households were just a mother and her children. As a percentage of all subfamilies, the mother-children subfamily ranged from 55 percent (St. Helena's Island and Township) to 80 percent (Mount Album) among rural blacks and from 50 percent (Mobile) to 75 percent (Natchez) among urban blacks.

If young and elderly married couples are not counted, the

importance of the *female-headed subfamily* increases significantly. A large percentage of women heading subfamilies lived with their families of origin. In Richmond, Mobile, Natchez, and Beaufort, between at least two in five and half of all women heading sub-families lived with either a parent (usually a mother) or both parents. An even higher percentage did so in the rural communities. Forty-four of forty-seven heads of St. Helena's Island and Township subfamilies lived with one or both parents. In addition, kin-related households with subfamilies everywhere included a small number of subfamilies headed by a sister, a niece, or a mother related to the household head. A married couple with children, for example, might take in the husband's or wife's mother and some of her unmarried children. Parents apparently believed that young daughters with children but without resident spouses needed protection. That much seems clear from examining the household status of *all* women under thirty heading house-holds or subfamilies. Except in Beaufort, a significant percentage everywhere lived with parents or other kin. Too few elderly blacks lived in Beaufort to allow that so thirty of its forty-eight female-headed subfamilies lived in simple nuclear households. None lived in a white household, seven lived with parent(s), eight boarded with relatives, and three boarded with nonrelatives. Beaufort was unusual. Sixty rural Sea Island women under thirty headed households and subfamilies. One boarded with a nonrela-tive, and fifteen lived alone. The rest—three of four—resided in households headed by their parents (22), a widowed mother (12), and other relatives (10). Natchez, Mobile, and Richmond also differed from Beaufort. Just over half of Natchez women under thirty with children lived with parents or relatives. In a town where large numbers of black women lived in white households, only eight of more than sixty under thirty and with children resided in such households. Richmond and Mobile (Wards 6, 7, and 8) blacks repeated the Natchez pattern, so that about two in five women heading such households lived in households headed by older kin, most usually their parent(s). It has been seen that the female-headed nuclear household was unusual, and such a household headed by a woman under thirty was even less common. As a percentage of all kin-related black households, it had rela-tive importance only in Beaufort (8 percent), but young black women there predominated in the population. It had little im-portance in either Richmond (2 percent), Natchez (2 percent), Mobile's sixth, seventh, and eighth wards (2.5 percent), or St. Helena's Island and Township (1.5 percent).

15. In 1880, 3469 whites and only 359 blacks lived in Jones County. A small number of whites, including a few merchants, clergymen,

and physicians, lived in Ellisville village, but most Jones County whites worked the land as farmers and farm laborers. The Jones County farmers grew mostly corn, oats, potatoes, and some rice. Not well off in 1880, they nevertheless knew a better material circumstance than either the rural Adams County or St. Helena's Island and Township blacks. Nine of ten Jones County farms were owner-operated. Most black Adams County farmers labored as sharecroppers, tenants, and farm laborers. And the Jones County farms were much larger than those owned by Sea Island blacks. Four of five owner-operated Jones County farms were of between 50 and 499 acres. Nevertheless, the Jones County farmers did not prosper. The average value of all farms there, including the land, buildings, and fences, was $385, and production per white resident was $29, as compared with about $400 and $470 per *rural white* Adams County and Beaufort County resident. The Jones County whites, poorer than these rural southern whites, nevertheless had a material advantage over most rural southern blacks.

16. Even these important differences should not be exaggerated, as illustrated by comparing the household status of unmarried Mobile and Richmond black and Paterson native white and Irish women aged twenty to twenty-nine. More than half of single Paterson native women (58 percent) and Irishwomen (63 percent) lived with one or both parents, a much higher percentage than among the single Richmond (26 percent) and Mobile (31 percent) black women. About one in five Richmond (19 percent) and two in five Mobile (38 percent) black women living away from their parents headed either households or subfamilies. But so did one in three Paterson native white women (32 percent) living away from their family of origin. If single women living with one or both parents are included, the percentage heading households and subfamilies drops for all three groups. It remains largest among the Mobile blacks (26 percent) but is nearly equal among the Richmond blacks (14 percent) and the Paterson native whites (13 percent).

17. Most of the St. Helena's blacks had been born in South Carolina, but just over half (54 percent) of Issaquena men and women fifty years and older were not Mississippi natives. The largest number had been born in Virginia (three in ten), Maryland, North and South Carolina, Kentucky, and Tennessee. Some among these, no doubt, had been sold or moved into the Deep South as slave children or young adults.

18. If the occupational status of Jackson ward black men hardly changed between 1880 and 1900, that was not the case for Jackson ward black women. Laundresses and washerwomen, servants, and

seamstresses account for the work of nine in ten Jackson women with listed occupations. But the percentage of these women laboring as servants declined greatly between 1880 and 1900. About three in ten were engaged in domestic work, a sharp percentage drop in twenty years. Still 204 Jackson ward women labored as cooks, nurses, chambermaids, and servants in 1900. Such work remained unappealing to married women with children, and just one in ten with such jobs was a married mother. The rest were single women, childless married women, and mothers heading male-absent households. Among all women listing occupations and aged forty and older, two in five labored as laundresses or washerwomen. But among married mothers that old, four in five did such work.

19. Extended and augmented households increased in importance in both places, but it was the extended household that grew most rapidly. In 1900, about one in four St. Helena's and just over three in ten Jackson ward black households included a relative other than the members of the immediate family. The increase in extended households may have been related to the constricted economic opportunities available to blacks. The type of kin living in these extended households changed in important ways. A large percentage of rural and urban kin in 1880 had been females; the sexes were more evenly distributed in 1900. Grandchildren, by far, and then nephews and nieces were the most important kin in the rural St. Helena's (84 percent) and Issaquena (67 percent) extended households. Brothers and sisters to either a husband or a wife followed in importance. In the extended Jackson ward households, grandchildren were far less important. Brothers and sisters to the husband and wife along with nephews and nieces accounted for seven of ten extended kin living in such households. Except on St. Helena's, where there were nineteen households composed of a grandparent with his (4) or her (15) grandchildren, the most common form of household which did not include a married couple or one or both parents with children was the household containing siblings. But these households were few in number. And so were three-generation "maternal" households. The Jackson ward had seventeen such households, but in eighteen other extended households a young mother without a spouse lived with both of her parents. Far fewer households of this character were found either in St. Helena's or Issaquena, and in both rural places the three-generation "maternal" households were equal in number to the household that had in it a young mother with both of her parents.

20. Because the 1905 census listed only the place of birth for foreign residents, nothing can be learned from it about migration patterns

by native blacks. The published 1900 and 1910 federal censuses revealed such information, as did a 1905 survey of New York City black tenement dwellers conducted by Mary White Ovington and summarized in her classic study, *Half A Man: The Status of the Negro in New York* (1911). The percentage of New York–born blacks fell between 1900 (45 percent) and 1910 (37 percent) as migrants from other northern states, from foreign places and especially from the Caribbean islands, and from the American South and especially from the South Atlantic states made it to the great metropolis. In 1910, 45 percent of the state's black residents had been born in the South, and of this number more than nine of ten came from the South Atlantic states, Maryland, and the District of Columbia. Foreign-born blacks also increased in importance between 1900 (3.6 percent) and 1910 (9.6 percent). All of these percentages included young children born in New York State to southern or foreign-born black parents, so that these over-all figures greatly underestimated the proportion of adult migrants. Demographic and social data has been gathered on all blacks living in the following Tenderloin streets: Twenty-first, Twenty-fourth to Forty-third, Forty-sixth to Forty-eighth, and Fifty-first to Fifty-third streets between Sixth and Eighth avenues. In addition, similar information was collected about San Juan Hill blacks living west of Tenth Avenue on Fifty-ninth to Sixty-third, Sixty-seventh, and Sixty-eighth streets.

21. See W. E. B. Du Bois, "The Negroes of Farmville, Virginia, A Social Study," *Bulletin in the Department of Labor*, XIV (January 1898), 9, in which Du Bois pointed out how the pattern of migration to northern cities largely involved "persons in the twenties and thirties, leaving an excess of children and old people." "The proportion of children under 15," Du Bois explained of these village Prince Edward County, Virginia, blacks, "is also increased by the habit which married couples and widowed persons have of going to cities and leaving their children with grandparents. This also accounts for the small proportion of colored children in a city like Philadelphia."

22. About 10 percent of the total population lived in 476 irregular households. Not all such households contained unrelated residents. One in four had in them two or more persons related to one another. Of these 122 households, ninety-one included brothers and sisters (usually young adults), and another twenty-five had in them an aunt or uncle with that person's nephews or nieces. The typical migrant kin-related irregular household had in it persons related to one another in a family of origin. Neither these irregular kin-related households nor those with only unrelated members were large in size. Two of every five had just two inhabitants,

and another two of five had either three or four residents. Only
6 percent of these irregular households had six or more residents.
Hardly any contained young children: in all, the 476 irregular
households had thirty-four children under the age of fifteen in
them. It seems clear therefore that these irregular households
had very few completed or broken nuclear families. Some probably included men and women living together as husband and
wife in common-law relationships. Such marriages were then legal
in New York State. A common-law marriage, however, was not
possible in two of five of the 476 households because these contained only either men or women. In nearly three of four of
remaining households (6 percent of all households with two or
more residents) men and women were close enough in age to suggest the possibility of either casual sexual ties or common-law
marriages among some of them.

23. The percentage of extended households hardly differed between
1880 and 1905. Urban New York City blacks in 1905 were mostly
migrants. It is striking evidence of the tenacity of kin ties among
these lower-class blacks that extended households were just as
common among New York City blacks in 1905 as among rural
Mississippi and South Carolina blacks in 1880. But the extended
household was less common among New York City blacks in 1905
than among southern rural and urban blacks in 1900. Leaving
aside related subfamilies (most often a woman with her children),
the typical New York City extended black household in 1905
contained either a mother (or mother-in-law) or an adult sibling
(a brother or sister to either parent in the household and usually
aged between fifteen and twenty-nine). Nephews and nieces followed in importance and were also usually between the ages of
fifteen and twenty-nine. Hardly any grandchildren lived in the
extended urban black household in 1905.

Yet another pattern observed in the 1880 black households
appeared among the 1905 New York City black households. The
female-headed nuclear household—that is, a mother and just her
children—was unusual: 6 percent of all kin-related households.
Three in ten male-absent households and subfamilies were simple
nuclear households (31 percent); the rest were extended (14 percent) and augmented (37 percent) households or subfamiles (22
percent). Most black male-absent households and subfamilies were
not isolated family units. Instead, a mother and her children lived
with either boarders or relatives. Men of approximately the same
age as the mother lived in three in ten of the 222 female-headed
augmented households, and if some of these men and women lived
together as husband and wife these were not "male-absent households." Very few boarders were unrelated children. At least half

(52 percent) of the 135 female-headed subfamiles belong to an extended household, related by blood and less frequently by marriage
to a second family in the household. Some were mothers with
young children who lived with a married son or daughter. Others
were widowed, single, or divorced women who lived with their
parents or, occasionally, with another relative. Very few of these
extended households were three-generation female-headed households. About one in twenty female-headed households was a three-
generation household, and only 0.9 percent of all kin-related black
Tenderloin and San Juan Hill households were three-generation
female-headed households. The migration of rural and urban
southern blacks to New York City in the late nineteenth and early
twentieth centuries had not increased the importance of the male-
absent black household or subfamily. Poor New York City blacks
incorporated women cut off from a spouse into larger households.
That was so in 1880, and migration to the North had not given
these poor blacks reason to abandon such women.

24. The composition and size of irregular households hardly changed
between 1905 and 1925. In 1925, 45 percent of such households
contained two persons, as contrasted with 42 percent in 1905. The
number with six or more people increased 0.4 percent. In the 1382
irregular 1925 households, there lived seventy-nine children under ·
the age of fifteen. A larger percentage in 1925 (32 percent) than
in 1905 (26 percent) had related persons in them, and once again
brothers and sisters predominated. Nearly seven in ten kin-related
irregular households had a sibling core. The percentage of irregular households with persons of the same sex also remained constant: 40 percent in 1925, as compared with 41 percent in 1905.
The Manhattan black population had increased at a staggering
rate between 1905 and 1925, but the place of the irregular household in this larger black community had not become more important in these twenty years.

25. Dramatic changes occurred in the types of male-absent units
between 1905 and 1925. As a percentage of all female-headed households and subfamilies, the simple nuclear and augmented household dropped from 67 percent in 1905 to 53 percent in 1925. The
female-headed extended household increased slightly, but the
greatest increase occurred in the percentage of male-absent subfamilies, increasing from 22 percent (1905) to 35 percent (1925).
*For the first time, the typical male-absent domestic arrangement
was the subfamily.* Although the three-generation matrifocal household still remained quite uncommon, its frequency increased
slightly over this twenty-year period from 0.9 percent to 1.1 percent. The percentage of augmented father-absent households with
male lodgers near the same age as the mother increased between

1905 (31 percent) and 1925 (37 percent). Despite these changes and especially the increased importance of the subfamily, the ages of women in male-absent households and subfamilies together with the number of children in such domestic units followed the 1905 pattern.

26. Gilbert Osofsky, *Harlem: The Making of a Ghetto* (1963), 133–34.

27. Maurice Thompson, "A Voodoo Prophecy," *Independent*, n.d., reprinted in Anna Julia Cooper, *A Voice from the South by a Black Woman* (1892), 212–15.

28. Howard Odum, *Social and Mental Traits of the Negro: Research into the Condition of the Negro Race in Southern Towns* (1910), *passim* but especially 36–42, 150–76, 213–37; J. M. Cattell and R. B. Bean cited in George W. Stocking's excellent work *Race, Culture, and Evolution* (1968), 132, 152, 188; Joseph A. Tillinghurst, "The Negro in Africa and America," *Publications of the American Economic Association* (1902), 160.

29. Arthur W. Calhoun, *A Social History of the American Family from Colonial Times to the Present*, III (1917–19), 41–50.

30. W. E. B. Du Bois, *The Souls of Black Folk* (1903), reprinted in *Three Negro Classics* (1965), ed. J. H. Franklin, pp. 218–219. Ralph Ellison, *Invisible Man* (1952), 7–8.

Afterword

1. The "Moynihan Report" and many articles revealing the full controversy surrounding it are found in Lee Rainwater and William L. Yancey, eds., *The Moynihan Report and the Politics of Controversy* (1967). The report itself is reprinted on pages 39 to 124. Moynihan's notion that social disorganization and familial breakup are common among poor classes ("the Wild Irish") moving to cities is widely held. Unpublished studies of the New York City Irish prior to the Civil War by Carole Groneman and of the Buffalo, New York, Italians between 1905 and 1930 by Virginia Yans McLaughlin convincingly show the adaptive capacities of these two poor immigrant groups. Familial disorganization was quite uncommon. See also Appendix B above on the New York City Jews and Italians in 1905.

2. See the essays by Hylan Lewis and Elizabeth Herzog printed in Rainwater and Yancey, eds., *The Moynihan Report and the Politics of Controversy*, 314–53. Table One is adapted from Andrew Billingsley, *Black Families in White America* (1966), 14. See also Lewis, "The Changing Negro Family," in Eli Ginzberg, ed., *The Nation's Children*, I (1960), 136, and Lewis, "Culture, Class, and Family Life Among Low-Income Urban Negroes," in Arthur

M. Ross and Herbert Hill, eds., *Employment, Race, and Poverty* (1967), 158. A survey of male-absent households in 1970 is reported in the *New York Times*, 27 March 1971. The number of male-absent black households increased to 27 percent. The percentage for whites increased from 6 percent to 9 percent between 1960 and 1970. At high income levels the gap narrowed. Among whites with reported family income of $10,000 or more 3 percent were male-absent and among blacks at a similar income level the figure was 6 percent.

3. Ellison's comments appear in *Daedalus* (Winter 1966), 438. The Carper essay first appeared in *Dissent* (March–April 1966) and is reprinted in Rainwater and Yancey, eds., *The Moynihan Report and the Politics of Controversy*, 466–73.

4. Frances Fox Piven and Richard A. Cloward, *Regulating the Poor: The Functions of Public Welfare* (1971), 183–247; Arthur M. Ross, "The Negro in the American Economy," in A. M. Ross and Herbert Hill, eds., *Employment, Race, and Poverty* (1967), 3–49; Tony Dunbar, *Our Land Too* (1971), 6–104; Carol B. Stack, *All Our Kin, Strategies for Survival in a Black Community* (1974), *passim*; *New York Times*, 25 April 1965.

5. Herbert H. Hyman and John Shelton Reed, " 'Black Matriarchy' Reconsidered: Evidence from Secondary Analysis of Sample Surveys," *Public Opinion Quarterly*, XXXIII (Fall 1969), 346–54; Leonard Goodwin, *Do the Poor Want to Work? A Social Psychological Study of Work Orientations* (1972), *passim*.

6. Mary Ames, *From a New England Woman's Diary in Dixie in 1865* (1906), 14–16, 64–65, 88–94.

7. Ames, *From a New England Woman's Diary*, 90 ff.

8. Letter from Uncle Smart, n.d., printed in *Philadelphia Press*, 31 May 1864, reprinted in James McPherson, *Negro's Civil War* (1965), 297–99; Laura M. Towne, *Letters and Diary* (1912), 162, 182–84; Elizabeth Botume, Old Fort Plantation, S.C., 18 March 1868, to the editor, *Freedmen's Record*, IV (July 1868), 112–13; Botume, *First Days Amongst the Contrabands* (1893), 61–62, 157, 241–45.

9. Harriet Beecher Stowe, *Palmetto Leaves* (1873), 291–92; Thomas Wentworth Higginson, *Army Life in a Black Regiment* (1869), 253. The Higginson diary entry is in James McPherson, *Struggle for Equality* (1964), 202.

10. New Orleans *Tribune*, 31 Aug. 1865, quoted in William McFeely, *Yankee Stepfather* (1968), 186; Frederick Douglass, *Life and Times of Frederick Douglass: The Complete Autobiography* (1962), 161.

11. Ralph Ellison, *Shadow and Act* (1964), 130; Dudley Randall, ed., *The Black Poets* (1971), 148, 166–67.

Appendix C

1. Winthrop Jordan, *White Over Black* (1968), and George Fredrickson, *The Black Image in the White Mind* (1971).

2. Fredrickson, *Black Image in the White Mind*, 244–82.

3. Wilkeson dispatches, New York *Sun*, 28 Dec. 1882, 9 Feb. and 28 March 1883; Annie Porter, "A Great Danger" and "A Few Plain Words," *Independent*, 28 Dec. 1883 and 9 Feb. 1884; Nathaniel Shaler, "The Negro Problem," *Atlantic Monthly*, LIV (November 1884), 696–709; Shaler, "The Nature of the Negro" and "The African Element in America," *Arena*, II (November 1890), 664–65 and III (December 1890), 23–35. Criticisms of these and similar writers are found in Charles K. Marshall, *Colored Race Weighed in the Balance* (1883), 61–63; "Southern Man" to the editor, New York *Sun*, 2 March 1883; New Orleans *Times Democrat*, n.d., reprinted in *New York Times*, 13 May 1883; *New York Globe*, 3 Feb. and 5 May 1883 and 2 Feb. and 1 March 1884; Indianapolis *World*, n.d., reprinted in *Arkansas Weekly Mansion*, 8 March 1884; T. Thomas Fortune, *Black and White* (1885), 68–69, 73–74, 77–79.

4. J. L. Tucker, *The Relation of the Church to the Colored People* (1883), 1–87; *New York Times*, 28 Oct. 1882; Frank G. Ruffin, *Negro as a Political and Social Factor* (1888), 14–15; Louis Tucker, *Clerical Errors* (1943), 1–15; New York *Observer*, undated shredded copy, 1883, New York Public Library.

5. Charles K. Marshall, *The Colored Race Weighed in Balance*, second edition (1883), 1–64; Alexander Crummell, *A Defense of the Negro Race in America from the Assaults and Charges of Rev. J. L. Tucker, D.D., of Jackson, Mississippi*, reprinted in Crummell, *Africa and America. Addresses and Discourses* (1891), 83–125. See also W. H. Leonard, Corpus Christi, Texas, n.d., to the editor, New York *Globe*, 28 April 1883; Atlanta *Constitution*, n.d., reprinted in New York *Globe*, 2 June 1883; *Arkansas Weekly Mansion*, 18 Aug. 1883; T. Thomas Fortune, *Black and White: Land, Labor, and Politics in the South* (1885), 73, 183–85; Blanche Bruce, n.d., to C. K. Marshall, *New York Times*, 25 Sept. 1883; "Resolutions passed 25 Jan. 1883, Jackson, Miss.," and I. G. Richmond, n.d., to the editor, Richmond *Whig*, n.d., reprinted in Tucker, *Relation of the Church to the Colored Race*, 85–89; *People's Advisor* (Canton, Miss.), n.d., reprinted in New York *Observer*, 12 April 1883.

6. *Encyclopaedia Britannica*, Ninth Edition (1884), XVII, 316–18. Favorable comments on Tucker appear in H. S. Fulkerson, *The Negro: As He Was; As He Is; As He Will Be* (1887), 55–61; Frank G. Ruffin, *The Negro as a Political and Social Factor* (1888), 14–21, 24–25; W. Laird Clowes, *Black America: A Study of the Ex-Slave and His Late Master* (1891), 110–12; Frederick L. Hoffman, *Race Traits and Tendencies of the American Negro*, in *Publications of the American Economic Association*, XI (August 1896), 207.

7. Philip A. Bruce, *The Plantation Negro as Freedman* (1889), v–ix; Darrett B. Rutman, "Philip Alexander Bruce: A Divided Mind of the South," *Virginia Magazine of History and Biography*, 68 (October 1960), 388–406; L. Moody Simms, "Philip A. Bruce and the Negro Problem," *Vermont Magazine of History and Biography*, 75 (July 1867), 348–62; George Fredrickson, *Black Image in the White Mind*, 244–82.

8. Bruce, *Plantation Negro as Freedman*, 1–28, 83–85, 126–29, 136–41, 242–61.

9. Rutman, "P. A. Bruce: A Divided Mind . . ." 388–406; Frederick L. Hoffman, *Race Traits and Tendencies of the American Negro*, 194, 202, 228, 231–32; S. P. Fullinwinder, *Mood and Mind of Black America* (1969), 49–50.

10. Isabel C. Barrows, ed., *First Mohonk Conference on the Negro Question Held at Lake Mohonk, Ulster County, New York, June 4, 5, 6, 1890* (1890), *passim*. See also Albion W. Tourgee, *An Appeal to Caesar* (1884), 96–103, 220–23.

11. Ulrich B. Phillips, "The Plantation as a Civilizing Factor," *Sewanee Review* (1904), and "The Economic Cost of Slaveholding in the Cotton Belt," *Political Science Quarterly* (1905), reprinted in Phillips, *Slave Economy of the Old South*, ed. Eugene D. Genovese (1968), 83–89, 117–35.

12. James Ford Rhodes, *History of the United States (1893–1906)*, VII, 232, and John Burgess, *Reconstruction and the Constitution* (1905), 133.

13. Myrta Lockett Avery, *Dixie After the War* (1906), 179, 196–97, 373, 392, 401; Thomas Nelson Page, "The Negro: the Southerner's Problem," *McClure's Magazine*, 23 (1904), 100; the dialect story-tellers and poets are quoted in Paul M. Gaston's excellent study *The New South Creed: A Study in Southern Mythmaking* (1970), 180–85.

14. Charleston *News and Courier*, 11 Jan. 1898, quoted in George Tindall, *South Carolina Negroes, 1877–1890* (1952), 260.

Subject Index

An index of personal names and titles appears on pages 658-664.

abolitionists, perceptions of slave families, 293–6

abortion, 80–2 *n*

Adams County, Miss., Afro-American community, 442, 477 *t. See also* rural communities

adaptation, xxiii–xxiv, 3, 7, 34, 36, 90–3, 102, 132–5, 355–7, 465; in eighteenth century, 329–43, 352–3; and endogamous marriages, 90 and *n*; and marriages broken by sales, 154–5; and naming practices, 93; and plantation system, 102, 132–3, 135. *See also* explanatory models; paternalism

address, terms of, 216–20, 222; socialization function, 217–18; white use of, 216–17

adultery, 67–70, 75, 287, 558–6 *n*.15

Africa: emigration to, 169, 182; family, kinship beliefs, 211–12, 222; grandparent-grandchild ties, 198–200; marriage patterns, 91; tribal markings, 242. *See also* slave trade; West Africa

African Civilization Society, 257

African names, 186, 242, 576 *n*.4, 590 *n*.31

African slaves: adaptation of, 329–43, 351–3; celebrations, 333–4; childrearing practices, 331; electoral practices, 332–3; family, kinship awareness, 329–330, 351–2; and owners 335–40; polygamy, 331; religious beliefs, practices, 332; sexual practices, 331; villages, re-creation of, 331–2

Afro-American culture, 3, 33–7, 151–4, 169–71, 260–1; adaptation practices, 355–60; and Anglo-American institutions, 332–40; and "creolization," 34, 340–3; in eighteenth century, 33–4, 169, 170–1; and emancipation, 34–7; mimetic theories, 260–1; and lower-class whites, 338–40; retrogressionist concepts of, 541–4; surnames, 244; transmission, 33–4; 554–5 *n*.43; and Upper to Lower South migration, 151–2, 154, 165

Alabama, xxiv; ex-slave soldiers and families, 385; kin networks, 214–16; remarriages after emancipation, 418; sexual attitudes toward blacks, 387–8; slave ownership units, 16, 44 *t. See also* Watson plantation

Albany, N.Y., Pinkster Day celebration, 333–4

American Colonization Society, 182; names of applicants, 186, 187 *t*, 575 *n*.4

American Missionary Association, 412

Amistad mutiny (1839), 329–30

Anchorage plantation, Miss., 234

Anglican Society for the Propagation of the Gospel, 347

Arkansas: Constitutional Convention (1868), 400–1; marriage registers, 154, 571 *n*.11

artisans: marriage patterns, 13–14; New York City (1905), 450–1, 523–4, 527–9 *t*; urban communities (1880), 443, 479–82 *t*, 626–8 *n*.6; white displacement of, 627–8

basket names, 576 *n*.5

Beaufort, S.C., Afro-American community, 442, 477 *t. See also* urban communities

Bennehan-Cameron plantation, N.C., 169–84, 311, 327; birth register, 169; childbearing, 171; eighteenth-century slaves, 170–1; families, generations, 171, 172–8 *t*, 180; freed slaves, kinship ties, 182–4; kin networks, 171, 181–4; naming practices, 178–80 *t*, 180–2, 189 *t*, 190, 192, 195, 198, 199

bicultural models, 261–2

birth control, 80–2 *n*

birth registers, 46–7, 96–7; and adaptive practices, 356–7, 359; Bennehan-Cameron plantation (N.C.), 169; father's name in, 46, 59 and *n*; Good Hope plantation (S.C.), 46–7, 52–8 *t*, 59–60; Stirling plantation (La.), 104, 105–13 *t*; surnames in, 232; and time factor, 96–7

Black Codes, 365

Index of Names and Titles

A subject index appears on pages 648-657.